Jesus and the Heritage of Israel

LUKE THE INTERPRETER OF ISRAEL

David P. Moessner and David L. Tiede,
General Editors

VOLUME 1

Jesus and the Heritage of Israel
Luke's Narrative Claim upon Israel's Legacy

Jesus and the Heritage of Israel

Luke's Narrative Claim upon Israel's Legacy

Edited by David P. Moessner

TRINITY PRESS INTERNATIONAL
Harrisburg, Pennsylvania

The editor offers special thanks to the Pew Trusts for a grant in 1994, which enabled significant progress in this project, and to John Pinkerman, who prepared the indexes.

Trinity Press International, P.O. Box 1321, Harrisburg, PA 17105
Trinity Press International is a division of the Morehouse Group

Cover art: Saint Paul fleeing Damascus in a basket. Enamel plaque from reliquary or altar in England, 1180–85. Victoria and Albert Museum, London. Erich Lessing / Art Resource, New York

Cover design: Annika Baumgardner

Library of Congress Cataloging-in-Publication Data
Jesus and the heritage of Israel : Luke's narrative claim upon Israel's legacy / edited by David P. Moessner.
    p.   cm. – (Luke the interpreter of Israel series)
    Includes bibliographical references and index.
    ISBN 1-56338-293-8 (pbk. : alk. paper)
    1. Bible. N.T. Luke – Criticism, interpretation, etc. 2. Bible. N.T. Acts – Criticism, interpretation, etc. 3. Israel (Christian theology) – History of doctrines – Early church, ca. 30–600. I. Series. II. Moessner, David P.
BS2589 .J48 2000
226.4′06 21–dc21   99–040251

Printed in the United States of America

00   01   02   03   04   05   06   10   9   8   7   6   5   4   3   2   1

Contents

Part I
CLAIMING THE HERITAGE
THROUGH THE PROLOGUES

Section A
The Formal Functions of the Prologues
in Their Greco-Roman Literary Setting

Section B
The Material Claims of the Prologues
and Ancient Greek Poetics

Part II
REFRAMING THE HERITAGE
THROUGH LUKE'S GOSPEL–ACTS

Section C
Driving to the Crux: Luke's Gospel–Acts and the Story of Israel:
"Inasmuch as many... it seemed good to me also to write
... that you may have a firm grasp of the true significance
of the traditions which you have been taught" (Luke 1:1, 3–4)

Contributors

L. C. A. ALEXANDER
University of Sheffield, U.K.

DAVID L. BALCH
Texas Christian University

CARL R. HOLLADAY
Emory University

WILLIAM S. KURZ
Marquette University

DANIEL MARGUERAT
Université de Lausanne, Switzerland

I. HOWARD MARSHALL
The University of Aberdeen, U.K.

RICHARD PERVO
University of Minnesota

ECKHARD PLÜMACHER
Dr. theol., Berlin, Germany

VERNON K. ROBBINS
Emory University and University of Stellenbosch, South Africa

DARYL D. SCHMIDT
Texas Christian University

GREGORY E. STERLING
Notre Dame University

CHARLES H. TALBERT
Baylor University

ROBERT C. TANNEHILL
Methodist Theological School, Delaware, Ohio

MICHAEL WOLTER
University of Bonn, Germany

Abbreviations

AB	Anchor Bible
ABD	D. N. Freedman, ed., *Anchor Bible Dictionary*
ABRL	Anchor Bible Reference Library
AGJU	Arbeiten zur Geschichte des antiken Judentums und des Urchristentums
AnBib	Analecta biblica
ANRW	*Aufstieg und Niedergang der römischen Welt*
BBB	Bonner biblische Beiträge
BETL	Bibliotheca ephemeridum theologicarum lovaniensium
BTB	*Biblical Theology Bulletin*
BZ	*Biblische Zeitschrift*
BZNW	Beihefte zur ZNW
CBQ	*Catholic Biblical Quarterly*
CBQMS	Catholic Biblical Quarterly Monograph Series
CD	Cairo (Genizah text of the) *Damascus* (*Document*)
CRINT	Compendia rerum iudaicarum ad novum testamentum
CurTM	*Currents in Theology and Mission*
DJD	Discoveries in the Judaean Desert
EKKNT	Evangelisch-katholischer Kommentar zum Neuen Testament
ETL	*Ephemerides theologicae lovanienses*
EvQ	*Evangelical Quarterly*
EvT	*Evangelische Theologie*
ExpTim	*Expository Times*
FFNT	Foundations and Facets: New Testament
FHJA	Fragments from Hellenistic Jewish Authors
FRLANT	Forschungen zur Religion und Literatur des Alten und Neuen Testaments
GCS	Griechischen christlichen Schriftsteller

GWU	*Geschichte in Wissenschaft und Unterricht*
HDR	Harvard Dissertations in Religion
HKAW	Handbuch der klassischen Altertumswissenschaft
HTKNT	Herders theologischer Kommentar zum Neuen Testament
HTR	*Harvard Theological Review*
IBR	Institute for Biblical Research
ICC	International Critical Commentary
IG	*Inscriptiones Graecae* (1873–)
JAC	Jahrbuch für Antike und Christentum
JBL	*Journal of Biblical Literature*
JBTh	Jahrbuch für biblische Theologie
JETS	*Journal of the Evangelical Theological Society*
JJS	*Journal of Jewish Studies*
JQR	*Jewish Quarterly Review*
JSHRZ	Jüdische Schriften aus hellenistisch-römischer Zeit
JSJ	*Journal of the Study of Judaism in the Persian, Hellenistic, and Roman Period*
JSJSupp	JSJ Supplements
JSNT	*Journal for the Study of the New Testament*
JSNTSup	Journal for the Study of the New Testament Supplement Series
JSOT	*Journal for the Study of the Old Testament*
JSOTSup	Journal for the Study of the Old Testament Supplement Series
JTS	*Journal of Theological Studies*
KEK	Kritisch-exegetischer Kommentar über das Neue Testament
LCC	Library of Christian Classics
LCL	Loeb Classical Library
LD	Lectio divina
NICNT	New International Commentary on the New Testament
NIGTC	The New International Greek Testament Commentary
NJBC	R. E. Brown et al., eds., *The New Jerome Biblical Commentary*
NovT	*Novum Testamentum*
NovTSup	Novum Testamentum Supplements

NRT	*La nouvelle revue théologique*
NTD	Das Neue Testament Deutsch
NTS	*New Testament Studies*
OTP	J. H. Charlesworth, ed., *The Old Testament Pseudepigrapha*
PIBA	*Proceedings of the Irish Biblical Association*
PRE	*Paulys Real-Encyclopädie der klassischen Altertumswissenschaft*
PSI	*Papiri Greci e Latini, Pubblicazioni della Società italiana per la ricerca dei papiri greci e latini in Egitto* (1912–)
RB	*Revue biblique*
RHPR	*Revue d'histoire et de philosophie religieuses*
RThPh	*Revue de théologie et de philosophie*
RTR	*Reformed Theological Review*
SBL	Society of Biblical Literature
SBLDS	SBL Dissertation Series
SBLMS	SBL Monograph Series
SBLRBS	SBL Resources for Biblical Study
SBLSBS	SBL Sources for Biblical Study
SBLSP	*SBL Seminar Papers*
SBLSS	SBL Semeia Studies
SBLTT	SBL Texts and Translations
SBS	Stuttgarter Bibelstudien
SC	Sources chrétiennes
SNTS	Society for New Testament Studies
SNTSMS	SNTS Monograph Series
SUNT	Studien zur Umwelt des Neuen Testaments
TDNT	G. Kittel and G. Friedrich, eds., *Theological Dictionary of the New Testament*
THKNT	Theologischer Handkommentar zum Neuen Testament
ThV	*Theologia Viatorum*
ThZ	*Theologische Zeitschrift*
TLZ	*Theologische Literaturzeitung*
TRE	*Theologische Realenzyklopädie*

TRu	*Theologische Rundschau*
TU	Texte und Untersuchungen
TWNT	G. Kittel and G. Friedrich, eds., *Theologisches Wörterbuch zum Neuen Testament*
UPZ	U. Wilcken, *Urkunden der Ptolemäerzeit* 1 (1922–27), 2 (1957)
WMANT	Wissenschaftliche Monographien zum Alten und Neuen Testament
WUNT	Wissenschaftliche Untersuchungen zum Neuen Testament
ZNW	*Zeitschrift für die neutestamentliche Wissenschaft*
ZTK	*Zeitschrift für Theologie und Kirche*

Introduction

Two **Books** but *One* **Story?**

David P. Moessner and David L. Tiede

The Acts of the Apostles is a strange new dish. . . . strange, I say, and not strange.
Not strange, for it belongs to the order of Holy Scripture; and yet strange, because
peradventure your ears are not accustomed to such a subject.

CHRYSOSTOM, *Homiliae in Principium Actorum*, iii, 54

Chrysostom's words ring as true today as they did in the fourth century C.E. The colorful tales and exotic miracles of Acts strike many contemporary readers as strange, as if they were perusing a sensationalist tabloid. Still others entertain the opposite opinion, finding Luke's "second book" remarkably plain, "naked history," to echo the church father Jerome. Whichever sentiment prevails, the rather checkered reputation that Chrysostom attests in his day seems to have continued through much of the history of the church. The Acts of the Apostles, including its relation to its "first book," the Gospel of Luke, remains enigmatic and nondescript — "a strange new dish."

A brief glance over the history of modern interpretation of Luke's two "volumes" again reveals the ambiguous status Acts has achieved. In the pre-Enlightenment era, Acts was the first history of the Christian church. Subsequently certain "critical" stances of the "modern" era such as F. C. Baur's and the Tübingen school's early catholicism began to prevail. But viewed from either angle, Acts was still regarded until World War I as a *tertium quid,* a new "synthesis" of the early church, different in "kind" from its Gospels and epistles. During this period between the wars, scholars were largely preoccupied with the identification of possible "sources" for Luke's volumes. Much of the scholarship of Great Britain intended to demonstrate the "historical accuracy" of Luke and Acts, while continental assessments were seeking to map the theological development of primitive Christianity through *form-critical* research. It was not until the postwar period that Luke's "two-volume project" emerged as a unified, literary whole, however differently this whole, "Luke-Acts," now appeared to its interpreters.

Following his earlier study of the narrative form and purposes of Luke-Acts, H. J. Cadbury saw the two volumes as presenting the history of Jesus and his followers.[1] In H. Conzelmann's view, Luke-Acts was a reconstrual of the church

---

1. His *Making of Luke-Acts* was published in 1927 (New York: Macmillan), republished by Henry J. Cadbury in 1958, and reprinted by SPCK (London) in 1968. But it was not until the 1950s

at the "end of history" in a larger *heilsgeschichtliche* scheme of God.[2] In the flowering of *redaction criticism* of the 1950s and 1960s interpreters attended to Luke's compositional enterprise, including the evaluation of speeches in Acts as characteristic of Hellenistic historiography,[3] with particular interest in the theological agenda of the evangelist as redactor. The students of Rudolf Bultmann sought to demonstrate that Luke had transformed Mark's focus on Jesus' crucifixion into a theology of history and that Luke's depiction of Paul altered or compromised Paul's "gospel."[4] Already at that stage, however, scholars like Paul Minear were objecting that rather than being caught up in Christian schemes of history, Luke was addressing larger religious and cultural concerns: "From the first to the last chapters of the corpus, it is 'the hope of Israel' which is at stake."[5]

Thus if Acts seemed a "strange new dish" to Chrysostom, Luke-Acts has appeared to many contemporary audiences as even more exotic fare. Although in the decades of the 1960s and 1970s Luke-Acts was becoming an exegetical given for much of North American interpretation, in Europe, Australia, and developing countries a much greater reticence in linking the volumes in anything more than common authorship or canonical affiliation continued to dominate the interpretive climate. In fact, it was during this "storm center" (W. C. van Unnik)[6] of controversy that the major construals of this century, those of Cadbury–Lake–Foakes Jackson[7] and Conzelmann, were quickly dissipating, leading in the 1980s and 1990s to exegetical shipwreck and theological gridlock — "not accustomed to such a subject!"

As the new millennium dawns, *Jesus and the Heritage of Israel* gathers an amazing sea change of opinion that the Hellenistic writer Luke remains concerned throughout his two volumes with Israel's history. These studies are illumined by renewed appreciation of the several ways varied groups read Israel's scriptures in the first century C.E., informed by extensive research of Greco-Roman rhetoric and literary art, and attentive to Luke-Acts as a story intended to persuade. A new consensus is emerging that Luke as the interpreter of Israel presents a

---

that Cadbury's insights into Luke's compositional design were joined with the monumental *Beginnings of Christianity* (see n. 7), which made "Luke-Acts" an accepted notion among North American exegetes.

2. *Die Mitte der Zeit* (Tübingen: J. C. B. Mohr [Paul Siebeck], 1953). Translated by Geoffrey Buswell from the German as *The Theology of St. Luke* (London: Faber and Faber, 1961).

3. See Martin Dibelius, "The Speeches in Acts and Ancient Historiography," in *Studies in the Acts of the Apostles* (London: SCM, 1956), 138–85; the German original appeared in 1951.

4. See esp. *Studies in Luke-Acts*, ed. L. E. Keck and J. L. Martyn (Nashville: Abingdon, 1966), e.g., Philipp Vielhauer, "On the 'Paulinism' of Acts," 33–50; Ulrich Wilckens, "Interpreting Luke-Acts in a Period of Existentialist Theology," 60–83; and Hans Conzelmann, "Luke's Place in the Development of Early Christianity," 298–316.

5. "Luke's Use of the Birth Stories," in Keck and Martyn, *Studies in Luke-Acts*, 116.

6. W. C. van Unnik, "Luke-Acts, a Storm Center in Contemporary Scholarship," in Keck and Martyn, *Studies in Luke-Acts*.

7. *The Beginnings of Christianity*, ed. F. J. Foakes Jackson and K. Lake, 5 vols. (New York: Macmillan, 1922–33); republished in paperback edition in 1979 by Baker Book House, Ann Arbor, Michigan.

carefully crafted argument *in two parts* to lay claim to a culmination of Israel's traditions in Jesus of Nazareth, Messiah of Israel.

This volume marks an "environmental alteration" that sees Luke-Acts in a new light. But the reader will quickly discover that the sea of interpretation is hardly becalmed. The sheer range of interests and divergent opinions of this multinational group of scholars of antiquity reveal considerable differences, even in their views of the meaning of "Israel" and the relation of "Christianity" to the Jewish people(s) at the end of Acts. Nonetheless, this collection of essays documents the exciting rediscovery of Luke's "Hellenistic" Gospel as alive to the thoroughly Jewish question of Jesus and Israel. However wide the gulf on significant issues remains, the "sea" itself has changed significantly. Whether or not Luke succeeds in this effort to persuade, this author argues consistently that Jesus of Nazareth is Israel's true heritage and enduring legacy to the world.

Jesus and the Heritage of Israel marks the first time in the history of interpretation that a team of international scholars of Greco-Roman antiquity, early Christianity, and the Lukan writings has devoted attention to two telling issues: (1) *The relation of Acts to the Gospel of Luke in a larger narrative enterprise.* What is at stake if Acts is (not) read as a sequel to Luke as one larger narrative claim? Is there an overarching plot which encompasses both volumes and subsumes individual themes or topics to a comprehensive authorial intention? (2) *The meaning of "Israel."* In early Christian interpretation, who or what is "Israel"? Is the answer the same at the beginning of Luke as at the end of Acts? Who or what is the "church" in relation to "Israel"? And who is Jesus of Nazareth in relation to both?

Part One, "Claiming the Heritage through the Prologues," explores the rhetorical conventions of Greco-Roman *prooemia* in highlighting the strategies and goals that Luke engages in his volumes. What is the relation between formal convention and substantive claims (L. Alexander; D. Schmidt)? Is the Gospel prologue only a convenient "address label," or does it attend as well to the overarching *content* and *purpose* of the two-volume enterprise? What audience expectations are aroused (V. Robbins; D. Moessner)? In short, what standards is Luke invoking to advance his interpretation of the "events/matters brought to fruition" (Luke 1:1)?

Part Two, "Reframing the Heritage through Luke's Gospel–Acts," illumines the relation of Luke's second "volume" to the first by inquiring about the consistency and coherence of Luke's narrative-thematic strategies in retelling the story of Israel's legacy in Jesus of Nazareth. In the past, such interest was devoted to the ways Luke redacted or edited portions of Mark or "Q," and so on, in composing his Gospel; or what sources lay behind the progression of the events in Acts. In the sea change of perspective, attention is now riveted on Luke's larger persuasive project, the diegetic-rhetorical strategies and prototypes by which he construes the traditions and constructs his narrative. Is Acts to be read in tandem with the Gospel of Luke? If so, how does Acts "follow" Luke?

An opening essay probes this relationship head-on: Should Luke and Acts be read as one larger story in two volumes or is Acts more of a sequel, a continuing saga of an emerging people but not intrinsic to the purpose of the Gospel (R. Pervo)? The three following contributions continue this quest by writing about the larger shape of Luke and Acts and their relation to Hellenistic Jewish narratives. Does the Gospel, followed by Acts, look like any Jewish presentations of their past or present? Are there comparable narratives of promise and fulfillment, of "events/matters brought to fruition"? Is Luke intentionally recasting Hellenistic Jewish narrative (W. Kurz; C. Holladay; G. Sterling)?

The next cluster of four essays treats the public, thoroughly Hellenistic agenda of Luke's two volumes for Mediterranean auditors, be they Jew or Greek. How intelligible to Greco-Roman audiences are the *speeches* within the larger narrative presentation? How do they function? Do the speeches of Acts reach back to the "speeches" of Jesus to make Luke's first volume more comprehensible within a larger authorial purpose (D. Balch; E. Plümacher)? How would the lengthy sea voyage of Paul be received by Greco-Roman hearers? Does it make sense within a larger two-volume enterprise (C. H. Talbert and J. H. Hayes)? Finally, does the *end* of Acts effectively close the narrative? How would Paul's parting words be interpreted in light of the two-volume portrayal of Israel? Is there a satisfactory ending to Luke and Acts (D. Marguerat)?

The final group of essays drives to the crux of this volume: the relation of Jesus to the heritage of Israel. Is there an overarching story of Jesus and Israel in the two volumes? What is lost if Acts is not read as a continuation of one larger narrative? What is the meaning of "Israel" by the end(ing) of Acts? How can Jesus of Nazareth define Israel's legacy when so many of the Jewish people(s) do not acknowledge him in this role (M. Wolter; R. Tannehill; I. H. Marshall)?

•

The new and largely uncharted sea of Luke as the interpreter of Israel presents an exhilarating voyage of discovery as well as a challenge to previous "passages." Many of the contributors have been laboring in the galleys of the North American Society of Biblical Literature or in the Luke-Acts Seminar of the Society for New Testament Studies (SNTS) for more than twenty-five years. All know the stars that guided the earlier journeys,[8] all have become experienced navigators among various ports in the Mediterranean basin. Yet much remains to be explored, and this volume represents only a restricted sampling from a much greater pool of topics deserving attention.

As a new millennium dawns, you are invited to set sail with sixteen leading international scholars on this first exploration of the emerging sea consensus of the Lukan writings that *Jesus* is *the Heritage of Israel!*

---

8. In addition to works mentioned above, J. Jervell's writings should be noted, particularly his *Luke and the People of God* (Minneapolis: Augsburg, 1972; see esp., "The Divided People of God," 41–74), as well as E. Haenchen's *Die Apostelgeschichte* (Göttingen: Vandenhoeck & Ruprecht, 1956; Eng. trans., 1971), which became the dominant commentary during the 1960s–'70s.

Part I

Claiming the Heritage through the Prologues

Section A

The Formal Functions of the Prologues in Their Greco-Roman Literary Setting

Chapter 1

Formal Elements and Genre

Which Greco-Roman Prologues
Most Closely Parallel
the Lukan Prologues?

L. C. A. Alexander

"The Lukan Prologues" is a courtesy title for the opening few verses of Luke's Gospel and the Acts of the Apostles. In the case of the Gospel, the formal prologue (or "preface"; I use the words interchangeably) is readily identified by syntax and style, demarcated by a recognizable change of register at 1:5. In the case of Acts, as we shall see, the matter is not quite so clear, precisely because the formal markers of preface style disappear after Acts 1:1 while the syntactical unit is still incomplete. Nevertheless, there is something to be said for starting our investigation with Acts simply because, despite this fuzziness on the formal side, the beginning of Acts does emit certain clear signals to the reader — at least to the reader in tune with ancient literary convention — which provide a useful foundation for the more complex issues raised by the Gospel prologue. Thus by working backward from Acts we can progressively narrow down the options for reading the conventional codes of the prologue to the Gospel — as well as highlighting the continuity between the two volumes.

The Prologue to Acts:
Acts 1:1ff.

Acts begins in a clearly recognizable conventional style demarcated from the rest of the narrative by certain formal markers: the authorial voice (first-person singular verb ἐποιησάμην); the second-person address (vocative form of the name Theophilus); and the reification of the activity of writing itself (τὸν μὲν πρῶτον λόγον). None of these features occurs anywhere else in Acts. Theophilus is never invoked again, either in name or, as was common in dedicated works in antiquity, by the use of the second-person pronoun. And the author never again steps back from the role of narrator to reflect on his own activity as

9

a writer and creator of *logos*, though he does occasionally insert himself into the narrative as a participant in group action — which is a rather different convention.[1]

This opening sentence, then, has a momentary distancing effect, creating a framework around the story's action as if to remind the reader that it is, after all, a literary creation, a *logos* "created" by a particular writer (he does not give his name) and addressed in the first place to a particular reader. Such a reminder can have a disconcerting effect when it occurs in the middle of a narrative, like the sudden pause to change the reel in an old movie theater, which reminds the viewer that we are watching film, not live action, and that what we see is dependent on someone else's technical skills — and by implication on someone else's viewpoint. But the effect is short-lived. Luke, to use this writer's conventional name, slows down the action sufficiently to remind us briefly of his existence, and to warn latecomers that they have missed a substantial part of the story: but he skips the title sequence of the second reel, sweeping us straight back to the Mount of Olives (as we learn in 1:12) to hear Jesus speaking ("live, on camera") to the apostles.

The vividness of this striking opening sequence is achieved by a series of narrative ellipses which defy syntactical analysis. The main clause (τὸν μέν...), which summarizes the contents of the first *logos*, lacks its expected parallel main clause (ἐν δὲ τούτῳ...), which would normally have described the contents of the second volume.[2] Instead, having introduced Jesus as the subject of a subordinate relative clause (περὶ πάντων...ὧν ἤρξατο), which is effectively in an object clause describing the contents of the "former treatise," Luke slips straight into narrative depiction of Jesus' conversations with his disciples via a second relative clause (οἷς καὶ παρέστησεν ἑαυτόν) grammatically dependent on ἀποστόλοις. But then a further slippage in v. 4 from indirect speech (παρήγγειλεν αὐτοῖς) to direct speech (ἣν ἠκούσατέ μου) brings the reader into direct encounter with the resurrected Jesus, speaking not to "them" but to "you" — an anacoluthon which modern translations tend to mask by supplying "he said." The direct narrative mode resumes at v. 6, and once established is never abandoned: there is no return to the authorial framework, even at the end of the book where an ancient reader might possibly (though not necessarily) expect to find it.

There is sufficient conventional language in the opening clause, however, to establish a number of key pointers for the ancient reader of Acts. First, Acts

---

1. On the distinction between author and character in the we-passages, cf. J. Wehnert, *Die Wir-Passagen der Apostelgeschichte: Ein lukanisches Stilmittel aus jüdischer Tradition* (Göttingen: Vandenhoeck & Ruprecht, 1989).

2. "Expected": that is, according to the common patterns of Greek idiom in which a clause or phrase denominated by μέν is normally followed by a parallel denominated by δέ (or an equivalent adversative particle). There are of course parallels to Luke's failure to follow this expected pattern: see D. W. Palmer, "The Literary Background of Acts 1:1–14," *NTS* 33 (1987): 427–38. But this does not alter the fact that these uses are all, in one way or another, unusual.

is "Volume II": readers who begin here have missed a lot of essential information, very little of which will be directly explained for their benefit. Key facts about Jesus are summarized in 1:2–3, but even here there is a flood of unglossed names and religious terminology which would puzzle the uninitiated: Who are the "apostles"? Who was "John"? What is the "holy spirit"? What does "the kingdom of God" mean? What had Jesus "suffered," and why did he have to produce "proofs" that he was alive? No friendly footnotes ever explain these terms. We have to work them out as we go along — or, preferably, go back and read the first volume to find out. For the reader of Acts, in other words, the opening sentence makes it evident that the two volumes have to be read in sequence. This is not of itself sufficient to establish that the author conceived his work from the outset as a two-volume set;[3] but it is quite clear to the reader that the narrative of Acts presupposes the narrative of the Gospel and is a continuation of it.

Second, the opening few words are usefully informative — oddly enough, more informative than the Gospel prologue — about the subject matter of the first volume. It dealt with "what Jesus began both to do and to teach" — that is, with the words and actions of a teacher. There are two generic implications here. A book devoted to the words and deeds of an individual would fall most naturally either into the general category "biography" or into the related genre of historical monograph focused closely around significant episode(s) in the life of an individual (like Arrian's *Anabasis of Alexander*, or the projected volume on Cicero's consulship).[4] But an individual whose activities include "teaching" is likely to be famed for intellectual prowess rather than military or political achievements. That such a person should have followers (also called, as we later discover, "disciples," i.e., "students"), who are instructed after his death to continue to propagate his teaching, would occasion no surprise: the Greco-Roman world was familiar with the idea of teaching passed down from a famous thinker via a succession of pupils, and these "successions" were sometimes recorded by members of the various philosophical schools.[5]

Third, the distinctive authorial voice of the opening sentence plays a crucial role in encouraging the reader to place the text which follows in a particular socio-literary context. Its effect may be compared with that of the classic voices of the BBC newsreaders on a small boy growing up in wartime Ulster:

> Every evening at nine, with the immutable regularity with which we said the family rosary, my father would switch on the wireless. And there would be a different England. The glorious solemnity of Big Ben filled our Irish kitchen: my very first

---

3. On the prefaces to second volumes, see more fully Loveday C. A. Alexander, "The Preface to Acts and the Historians," in *History, Literature, and Society in the Book of Acts*, ed. Ben Witherington III (Cambridge: Cambridge University Press, 1996), 73–103.

4. See D. W. Palmer, "Acts and the Ancient Historical Monograph," in *The Book of Acts in Its Ancient Literary Setting*, ed. Bruce W. Winter and Andrew D. Clarke, vol. 1 of *The Book of Acts in Its First-Century Setting* (Grand Rapids, Mich.: Eerdmans, 1993), 1–29.

5. This view is documented and discussed in L. C. A. Alexander, "Acts and Ancient Intellectual Biography," in Winter and Clarke, *The Book of Acts in its Ancient Literary Setting*, 31–63.

sense of drama came from that moment of complete silence between the ending of the chimes and the first of the nine reverberating gongs. Then: "This is the BBC Home Service, and this is Alvar Liddell with the Nine O'clock News...." The beautifully modulated voices, the rational moderation ("so far, these reports are unconfirmed," was a phrase that ran like a leitmotif through the news bulletins of my childhood), the largeness of the issues, all seemed totally unrelated to the tight bigotries of Northern Ireland's streets. For me, the BBC was quintessentially English — and provided an enormous sense of security.[6]

For the first readers of Acts, this "sense of security" is evoked not by the accents of BBC English but by the carefully chosen dialect of Greek academic prose which Luke adopts for this prologue. The effect is created partly by the potential detachment of author from narrative which is implied by the use of the first person (*das schriftstellerische Ich*). But this is not enough in itself. John's references to "writing" in a "book" (John 20:30–31; 21:25) seem naive by comparison with the polished periphrases of Acts 1:1. Luke's ἐποιησάμην τὸν λόγον echoes Greek prose writers from Herodotus onward.[7] It evokes a world of ordered, rational discourse which, like that of the wartime BBC newsreader, is capable of considering alternative explanations, of detailing reports without necessarily believing them, of sifting truth from falsehood and suspending judgment pending further information. That this tone is swallowed up so soon in the narrative of Acts is, admittedly, disconcerting — but at least it shows a reassuring awareness of that larger world of discourse. In a second volume, particularly, such a brief reminder of the narrative's conceptual parameters is within the bounds of acceptability. It simply presupposes (and refers back to) a framework which has been more emphatically established in the preface to the first volume.

But it would be going too far to claim that the stylistic register of the opening verse of Acts is sufficient to locate the text within a particular genre. "Greek academic prose" is not a genre but a wide field of discourse. Its origins are identified closely with the fifth-century historians, Herodotus and Thucydides, who did much to establish the characteristically detached and rationalistic voice of Greek historiography. But their work has to be seen within the broader context of Ionian *historia*, a word which encompasses scientific and philosophical investigation as much as historical narrative, and which also produced prose treatises on such diverse subjects as medicine, mathematics, and rhetorical theory. Somewhere along the line, the historians acquired literary pretensions, which made the rhetorical presentation of the story as important as the story itself, and began to drive a wedge between historiography and the old broad *historia* tra-

---

6. George J. Watson, "Cultural Imperialism: An Irish View," quoted in *The Rattle of the North: An Anthology of Ulster Prose*, ed. Patricia Craig (Belfast: Blackstaff Press, 1992), 275; first published in *Yale Review* (1986).

7. Full references in Loveday C. A. Alexander, *The Preface to Luke's Gospel: Literary Convention and Social Context in Luke 1.1–4 and Acts 1.1*, SNTSMS 78 (Cambridge: Cambridge University Press, 1993), 144–45 [hereinafter: *Preface*].

dition. By the first century C.E., Greek prose had become a complex and varied phenomenon encompassing a wide range of genres and subgenres.

The prologue to Acts is simply too short to allow us to locate Luke's work more precisely within this larger field. It does however contain some clues which should caution us against identifying Luke-Acts too quickly with Greek historiography. Dedication — addressing a text to a named individual by inserting his or her name in the first sentence — is a convention reasonably widespread in Greek literature: but it is not normally associated with historiography. Similarly, the habit of intervolume recapitulation, which is common across a broad range of genres, is found only occasionally in history. The historians may have felt that it was too utilitarian, too little adapted to the demonstration of rhetorical skill. Whatever the reason, it is a fact that the historians preferred either to have no introductory material between volumes or to have a fresh, rhetorically varied preface for each as if each new volume were a separate monograph. I have dealt with these points more fully elsewhere,[8] and will return to their generic implications more fully below. For the moment, I simply note that although neither of these factors is decisive in itself, they would be sufficient to alert the contemporary reader to look beyond Greek historiography for Luke-Acts' generic affiliations.

The Gospel Prologue: Luke 1:1–4

Formally speaking, the prologue to Luke's Gospel consists of an introductory sentence spanning the first four verses. Unlike the preface to Acts, this formal introduction forms a complete sentence, which is readily detachable from the start of the narrative proper at Luke 1:5. The same formal features as we have observed in the Acts prologue reappear here (authorial first person; second-person address to Theophilus; objective discussion of the project in hand), amplified to deal briefly with the topics of predecessors (v. 1), sources of information (v. 2), the author's qualifications (v. 3), and his purpose in writing (v. 4). The author does not give his name, but since he uses a masculine participle for himself we can at least narrow down the possibilities on his gender. What are the genre options for a preface of this type?

Luke's Prologues and Greek Historiography

Luke's two volumes present a connected, sequential narrative of events in the recent past, and most discussions of their genre begin with the assumption that "history" is the obvious literary category in which to put them.[9] The prologues

---

8. Full discussion in Alexander, "The Preface to Acts and the Historians," 89–92.

9. The position argued here has been set out more fully in Alexander, *Preface*, chap. 3, and in "The Preface to Acts and the Historians."

are frequently cited in support of this identification, as if it were somehow self-evident that any Greek prose narrative which begins with this kind of formal preface must be a "history." What seems to be happening here is a confusion between the broader category "Greek academic prose" and the specific genre "history." To the broader category the Lukan prologues most certainly belong. But the specific genre of the work needs to be established much more carefully, by paying attention as much to the negative parallels as to the positive ones.

In many ways the most striking formal feature of the prologues is their personal nature. As we have seen, this feature catches the eye immediately within the context of biblical narrative, which normally uses the public, impersonal voice of the third-person narrator rather than the confidential tone of a private communication between two individuals. But this tone is equally foreign to Greek and Roman historiography, which throughout its long history retains the fundamentally impersonal narrative stance of ancient epic Thus while the classical historians do use the authorial first person occasionally to create a space to stand back and comment on their material, they are "notably reluctant to break the mould of impersonal narration inherited from their epic predecessors."[10] In Herodotus and Thucydides, the author introduces himself at the outset in the third person, not the first, and both Thucydides and Xenophon use the third person when their own actions are included in the narrative. Similarly, the use of a second-person address (dedication) is extremely rare in both Greek or Roman historiography.[11] Josephus's _Antiquities_, which is often cited in this context, is in fact the earliest extant example of a dedicated historical work, and it may not even have been in existence when Luke put his two volumes together. Moreover, that the work is dedicated to Epaphroditus is not revealed directly in the preface to the _Antiquities_. He is mentioned in passing at I.8 (in the third person, not the second), but the second-person address which is the formal literary marker of dedication does not appear anywhere in the work's twenty volumes until the end of the _Life_ (§430). In other words, we must be careful to distinguish between the social custom of dedicating a book to a patron or friend, and the literary convention of inserting that patron's name into the opening sentence of the book in the vocative case. In social terms, Luke's relationship with Theophilus may have been very similar to that of Josephus with Epaphroditus,[12] but there is nothing to suggest the parallel in the formal structure of the prefaces to the two works. There is a much stronger parallel with Josephus's _Against Apion_, which does insert Epaphroditus's name into the prefaces of both volumes. But _Against Apion_ does not fall into the literary genre "history."

The evidence for other dedicated histories rests on the indirect testimony of later writers since the works in question do not survive. Unfortunately, this means that we cannot easily determine whether a statement that a work was

10. Alexander, "The Preface to Acts and the Historians," 85.
11. Alexander, _Preface_, 27–29; "The Preface to Acts and the Historians," 85–89.
12. The range of options for understanding Theophilus's position is discussed fully in Alexander, _Preface_, chap. 9.

"written for" a particular individual refers to the social custom of dedication to a patron or friend, which could take any one of several literary forms of expression, or to the literary convention of inserting an individual's name in the opening sentence. What is clear is that, even on a maximal reading of the evidence, none of these "dedicated" texts belongs to the mainstream of Greco-Roman historiography. The *Chronica* of Apollodorus (second century B.C.E.) and the *Olympiads* of Phlegon of Tralles (early second century C.E.) fall into the category of learned chronography rather than history. A rather different though equally "fringe" group is represented by the compilers of "barbarian history" like Manetho and Berossus, both of whom are said to have dedicated their works to the Hellenistic kings under whose patronage they worked. Both were non-Greeks trying to win their work a place in the world of Greek literature, and this may provide a particular social context for the dedication. The *Antiquities* of Josephus, who knew and used both works, falls into the same tradition.

The scant evidence for dedication in historiography, then, suggests the tentative conclusion that a history is most likely to be dedicated if either its subject matter or its author (or both) have some kind of "fringe" status. Both chronography and ethnography fall at the fringes of the discipline of history, at a point where it is furthest from rhetorical pretension and closest to the broader tradition of learned *historia*. Such researches might well form the raw material on which a rhetorical historian might work, but they would not themselves count as "history." It has been convincingly argued, indeed, that the whole field of antiquarian research, including the "Antiquities" of non-Greek peoples like those of Dionysius and Josephus, should be distinguished from the rhetorical genre of history and operated with a distinct set of conventions.[13] If Luke's prefaces indicate any kind of generic link with historiography, we should be looking somewhere in the area of ethnography, as argued by Greg Sterling,[14] or perhaps in the area of "the history of culture, religion, and institutions," as argued recently by Hubert Cancik.[15]

Luke's Prologues and Apologetic

Manetho, Berossus, and Josephus all share another kind of "fringe" status: they are all non-Greeks striving to write up their own national histories in a format acceptable to the dominant culture. The case of Josephus is particularly informative here. The same dedicatory formulas — and the same dedication — which appear briefly at the end of the *Antiquities* recur in fuller form in *Against Apion* (I.1; II.1; II.296). This is a polemical work in two volumes, argumentative

---

13. Arnaldo Momigliano, *Studies in Historiography* (London: Weidenfeld & Nicolson, 1966), esp. chaps. 1, 8, and 11.

14. G. E. Sterling, *Historiography and Self-Definition: Josephos, Luke-Acts, and Apologetic Historiography*, NovTSup 64 (Leiden: Brill, 1992).

15. Hubert Cancik, "The History of Culture, Religion, and Institutions in Ancient Historiography: Philological Observations Concerning Luke's History," *JBL* 116/4 (1997): 681–703.

rather than narrative, written to counter certain unfavorable views of Judaism propagated by Apion and others. Epaphroditus, the dedicatee, is addressed directly at the beginning of each volume and at the end of the second, where he is described in rather conventional terms as a "lover of truth" who, like other potential readers, is "desirous of knowing about our race" (II.296). The work belongs to a group of texts — it would be too precise to call it a genre — normally described as "apologetic," and the dedication may be compared with the fictitious address to Philocrates in the earlier *Letter of Aristeas*, which likewise purports to provide an account of things Jewish for a non-Jewish audience. In other words, the common factor which explains the dedication in these works (and in Manetho and Berossus) is not the literary genre of the text but the social situation of the writer, which generated a particular need for a patron with access to the dominant culture. The value of having such a patron is well seen in Josephus's account of the publication of the *Jewish War*, which received (or so he tells us) enthusiastic commendations from Titus and Agrippa (*Life* 361–67).

On the face of it, this could well provide a natural and obvious parallel for the situation in which Luke-Acts first appeared. Many commentators have classified Luke-Acts as an "apologetic" work, presenting the case for the Christian community much as Josephus does for the Jewish community.[16] As Josephus himself makes clear, this kind of enterprise was common to a number of the indigenous cultures of the Greek East, competing with each other to demonstrate the antiquity and philosophical respectability of their native traditions. The full-blown Christian apologetic which appears in the second century clearly owes a great deal to the apologetic literature of Diaspora Judaism, and there is nothing inherently unlikely in the supposition that Luke was aware of that tradition and adapted its agenda, and perhaps also some of its polemical tone, to the purposes of the Christian community.

But it must be stressed that classifying Luke-Acts as "apologetic" does not in itself solve the problem of genre. "Apologetic" is a widely used and little-defined term, and I use it here to describe a stance adopted by a number of writers who employ a wide variety of literary genres to further their apologetic ends. Greg Sterling (see n. 14 above) uses the term "apologetic historiography" to cover a range of texts including Manetho, Berossus, and Josephus's *Antiquities*. But, though the term is a useful one, it is not immediately obvious that it describes a literary genre.[17] It may be simpler to describe these works as belonging to the wider literary genre of antiquarian history/ethnography, and noting that they share a common apologetic stance. If the genre extends further than the stance in one direction (not all ethnographic works are apologetic), then equally, in another direction, the stance extends further than the genre (not all

---

16. Useful surveys of apologetic readings of Acts may be found in Philip F. Esler, *Community and Gospel in Luke-Acts*, SNTSMS 57 (Cambridge: Cambridge University Press, 1987), 205–19, and in Stephen E. Pattison, *A Study of the Apologetic Function of the Summaries of Acts* (Ann Arbor, Mich.: University Microfilms, 1990), 10–35.

17. See Palmer, "Acts and the Ancient Historical Monograph," 15–18 (cited in n. 4 above).

apologetic works fall into the genre of ethnographic historiography). If we are to place Luke-Acts in this category, then, it can only be by virtue of a shared apologetic stance. In terms of literary genre, Luke's work has little in common with either *Antiquities* or *Against Apion,* and even less with Manetho and Berossus.[18]

Moreover, Josephus himself makes it clear that the social situation which calls forth apologetically oriented history or polemic, and which makes the services of a patron in the dominant culture especially desirable, is not in itself sufficient to inspire the literary convention of dedication. Copies of the *Jewish War,* he tells us, were "presented" to various members of the imperial family and "many others," all of whom showed the kind of gratifying support and interest which we would expect of a dedicatee (*Life* 361–67). But there is no clue to this social situation in the text, at least not via the formal courtesy of a dedication. Historiographical convention dictated that the narrative stance in the text should remain strictly impersonal, and Josephus is faithful to this convention even to the extent of relating his own appearances in the *War* in the third person, in contrast with the *Life,* where the same events are related in the first person. In other words, the presumed social context which may call forth a dedication — and it must be stressed that it is a presumption, even where we have a named dedicatee[19] — cannot of itself answer the literary question why this text rather than that should bear a formal dedication. In order to find a literary context for Luke's work, we must try to find a genre in which dedication is at home in a way that it is not in historiography.

Luke's Prologues and Greek Technical Prose

That literary context is most easily supplied, as I have argued at length elsewhere, if we look back to the broader tradition of Greek academic prose and the social contexts in which it was produced. Not that all texts in that tradition were dedicated, by any means. But dedication belongs in that context in a way that it never did in historiography, and the tradition tends to throw up short, personalized prefaces of the Lukan type. Detailed analysis (which cannot be repeated here) allows us to see, I believe, how these personalized prefaces developed within the intellectual matrix of the schools independently of rhetorical theory and in response to particular social situations — of which the need for and dependence on patronage is one, but only one. They are found in texts on a wide range of subjects. Handbooks on medicine, mathematics, engineering, rhetorical theory, letter writing, and astrology all seem at home with a common preface style (often a common preface structure as well), and with a limited range of terminology and ideas for use in prefaces. It is at first sight surprising

---

18. I have tried to explore some of the implications of reading Luke-Acts as apologetic in "The Acts of the Apostles as an Apologetic Text," in *Apologetics in the Roman Empire,* ed. M. Edwards et al. (London: Oxford University Press, 1999), 15–44.

19. The whole subject of dedication and literary patronage needs further investigation. Preliminary thoughts appear in Alexander, *Preface,* chap. 8.

that the list includes some rhetorical treatises, but the reason is clear once we understand how the conventional code governs the choice of literary register in a formal culture like the Greek of the early empire. The rhetorical writers could command a much more elaborate style, and in many cases a much greater literary competence, than many of the scientific writers analyzed, but it was not appropriate to deploy the full resources of literary rhetoric for a teaching manual. I have analyzed this material in detail in *The Preface to Luke's Gospel.*[20] Here a few examples must suffice to show some of the linguistic and structural parallels.

Luke's preface consists of a single periodic sentence using the first person ("I decided," v. 3) and incorporating a direct address to a named second person (dedication). There is no attempt to integrate either the address or the author's prefatory remarks into the main body of the narrative. Both the first-person format and the second-person address are repeated at the beginning of the second volume (Acts 1:1), but nowhere else in the text.

1. Structurally, the preface is centered around a main verb which announces the author's *decision to write:* literally, *"it seemed good to me . . .* to write it all up . . . in an orderly fashion" (v. 3).

2. This decision is brought into direct relation to the dedicatee by the use of *second-person pronouns:* " . . . to write it all up *for you,* most excellent Theophilus . . . so that *you* might realize . . ." (vv. 3–4).

Around this core are clustered four subordinate clauses (one of them participial) which give added information about the author, his subject matter, and his purpose in writing. Between them, these four clauses cover four distinct preface topics:

1. The *reason for writing,* which is the existence of other writers ("Since many have undertaken the task of compiling an account . . . ," v. 1).

2. The *sources of the material* ("just as the tradition was handed down to us by the original eyewitnesses and ministers of the word," v. 2).

3. The *author's qualifications* ("having followed everything carefully and thoroughly," v. 3).

4. The *intended effect of the book* ("so that you may realize the reliability of the things in which you have been instructed," v. 4).

Although many of these features can be paralleled elsewhere in Greek literature — we are not talking about a hermetically sealed field of discourse but a common dialect of pragmatic, rational prose — it is my contention that it is only in the "scientific tradition," that is, in the working handbooks and teaching manuals of a variety of technical subjects, that we regularly find short, detachable first-person prefaces, with or without a second-person address, which parallel Luke's preface both in structure and in vocabulary. Even where these technical

---

20. See n. 7 above. Full references to all the texts cited here will be found in that volume.

prefaces are longer, or where methodological remarks of a "prefatory" nature are scattered through the treatise, it is easy to identify in this tradition close parallels both to the range of topics Luke deals with in his preface and to the distinctive way he deals with them. Thus the key structural features of Luke's preface can all be paralleled in these technical prefaces:[21]

1. *Statement of the author's decision to write* (*Preface*, 70–71). This is almost invariably the grammatical center of the first or major sentence of the preface. Vocabulary varies from the factual ("I have decided," "I think it necessary") to the florid ("I have dared," or "I alone have succeeded"). Luke's ἔδοξε, echoing the formal civic language of decrees, is paralleled in Galen, Hermogenes, and Vettius Valens (*Preface*, 127). Luke also echoes the values embedded in the scientific tradition in his choice of verbs and adverbs to characterize his writing project. A concern for "order" (ἀνατάξασθαι, καθεξῆς) and a concern for "accuracy" (ἀκριβῶς) are both characteristic of these prefaces (*Preface*, 95, 110, 131).

2. *Dedication* (*Preface*, 50–63; 73–75). As I have argued above, the personal tone evoked by dedication is at home in the technical manuals of the various school traditions in a way that it is not in historiography. The "customization" of a treatise to a particular dedicatee is achieved, first, by inserting the dedicatee's name in the opening lines of the book (see Luke 1:3); second, by using the personal pronoun *soi* at appropriate points in the preface and elsewhere ("I have decided to write *for you*"; see Luke 1:3); and, third, by referring at least one of the preface's subordinate clauses to this person. Conventional preface courtesy provides two options. The earlier prefaces of the Hellenistic period frequently place the dedicatee in the opening clause, but later prefaces are more likely to include him or her in a final clause or sentence describing the book's effect on the reader. See paragraph 6 below.

3. *Statement of the reason for writing, which is other writers* (Luke 1:1; *Preface*, 76–77, 106–16). There are many reasons for writing a book, and ancient books very often begin with a "since" clause. Referring to one's predecessors is one of the most common forms of this convention, and there are abundant parallels in the scientific tradition, especially in the imperial period. Some writers use this theme polemically, to distinguish their own work from that of their predecessors, but in many cases "the work of others is mentioned solely to demonstrate that the subject is worth spending time on."[22] This is particularly clear in the prefaces of Luke's contemporary Hero of Alexandria:

> Since the subject has been thought worthy of treatment by others, I too...
> (*Pneumatica* pref.; *De Automatis* pref.)

> Since the subject is useful and others have written on it, I think it necessary...
> (*Dioptra* pref.)

---

21. See Alexander, *Preface*, 69.
22. Alexander, *Preface*, 77.

It is important to note this pattern, since it is too readily assumed that Luke's "Since many have undertaken ... " (v. 3) necessarily implies criticism of his predecessors. In fact, his "it seemed good to me also" (κἀμοί, v. 3) suggests rather the complementary relationship found in Hero and others. It is also worth noting that Luke avoids the more bombastic versions of this topos, like this example from the astrological herbal of Thessalus:

> Since many have attempted in this life, most august Caesar, to hand down to posterity many marvelous things, without any of them being able to bring their promises to fruition because of the darkness of Destiny looming over their minds, I think that I alone of all humanity from the beginning of time have achieved something marvelous.... [23]

4. *Statement of the sources of the material* (Luke 1:2; *Preface*, 116–25). Luke describes his predecessors' subject matter, which is also by implication his own, as "an account of the matters which have come to fruition in our midst, just as the tradition was handed down to us by the original eyewitnesses and minsters of the word" (vv. 1–2). The technical writers tend to claim one or more of three types of authority for their material: written sources, personal experience, and tradition (*Preface*, 78–87). The first is by far the least frequent. The second, using a nexus of key words — *autopsia, peira, empeiria*, "toils" and "travels" — goes back to the common tradition of Ionian *historia* which also underlies the Herodotean tradition of historical investigation. The third is particularly important in the craft traditions, in which the accurate passing-on of authentic tradition is much more important than originality or "research." Luke uses much the same language as the engineers and medical writers who represent these "craft" traditions. Note particularly Vitruvius and Hero, who frequently cite material as "what I have received from my teachers," or as "what has been handed down by the ancients."[24]

> We shall recount to you, then, just as we received the tradition (καθότι καὶ αὐτοὶ παρειλήφαμεν) both in Alexandria, where we were introduced to most of the craftsmen who concern themselves with this subject, and in Rhodes, where we were made known to not a few master carpenters and learned from them ... (Philo of Byzantium, *Belopoeica* pref.)

> Since the subject of Pneumatics was thought worthy of study ... we also deemed it necessary to bring into order (εἰς τάξιν ἀγαγεῖν) the things handed down in tradition by the ancients (τὰ παραδοθέντα ὑπὸ τῶν ἀρχαίων).... (Hero of Alexandria, *Pneum.* I pref.)

Both in his adoption of the standard "tradition" terminology of the schools (καθὼς παρέδοσαν), and in tracing this tradition back to "the beginning" (ἀπ᾽ ἀρχῆς), Luke adopts exactly the conventional language we would expect for an

---

23. Ps.-Thessalus, *De Virtutibus Herbarum* I pref.
24. Vitruvius X.11.2; cf. IX.1.16, X.13.8; Hero, *Pneum.* I pref. (cited above); *Catoptr.* pref., *accepta ab hiis qui ante nos descriptione dignificari*; *Metrica* I pref.; *Dioptra* pref., τά τε ὑπὸ τῶν πρὸ ἐμοῦ παραλειφθέντα ... γραφῆς ἀξιῶσαι.

unpretentious manual which claims to present an orderly account of a particular teaching tradition. But by describing the tradents as αὐτόπται, he is also claiming that the tradition has roots in "personal experience." The term *autopsia* is as much (if not more) at home in the scientific tradition as among the historians. It has a particular link with geographical exploration, and in some contexts seems to mean little more than "well-traveled"; but it is also associated with the empiricist school of medicine, and by the second century c.e., if not before, it gives a general impression of "firsthand experience of the facts."[25]

5. *Statement of the author's qualifications* (Luke 1:3; *Preface*, 125–36). Like so many of these preface writers, Luke uses a participial clause to make significant claims about the status of his material. As I have argued elsewhere (*Preface*, 128–30), παρηκολουθηκότι is not a claim on Luke's part to have witnessed the events of his history, or even to personal research and investigation, but simply to have "followed" — the ambiguity in the English is also there in the Greek — the tradition faithfully. "What we have here is a claim to fidelity and comprehension in transmission rather than to any personal contribution by the author: Luke is proud to have 'received and understood' the message passed on to him by the 'eyewitnesses and ministers of the word'" (*Preface*, 134). Both the syntactical structure and the specific claim to fidelity in transmission, with or without the additional claim to personal experience, can be readily paralleled among technical authors:[26]

- But of these matters there are many which I have observed by myself, others I found written in Greek books... following in whose footsteps (*quorum secutus ingressus*) I have written out in this book what I considered to be sufficient... (Vitruvius VIII.3.27)

- In order that every detail may be thoroughly easy for you to follow (εὐπαρακολού-θητά), I shall set out the text...and methods of operation...some of which I have performed myself, while others I observed as a student of Zopyrus in Alexandria. And Posidonius, who studied with the same doctor, would testify with us that this man performed cures with the highest degree of fidelity to Hippocrates [lit.: following (κατακολουθῶν) Hippocrates]. (Apollonius of Citium I pref.)

- But we exhort you and those who will read these notes to pay attention not to our rhetorical prowess but to our diligence and experience in the facts themselves (τὴν ἐν τοῖς πράγμασιν μετ᾽ ἐμπειρίας ἐπιμέλειαν). For with the highest degree of accuracy (μετὰ γὰρ πλείστης ἀκριβείας), having derived most of our knowledge from investigation at first hand (τὰ μὲν πλεῖστα δι᾽ αὐτοψίας γνόντες), and having accurately understood the rest from secondary authorities... (τὰ δὲ ἐξ ἱστορίας ἀκριβώσαντες), we shall attempt to write up (ἀναγράψασθαι)... (Dioscorides, *De Materia Medica* I pref. 3.4-11; c. 70 c.e.)

---

25. For the detailed arguments for this position, see Alexander, *Preface*, 34–41, 120–23.

26. On the importance of "tradition," see L. C. A. Alexander, "The Living Voice: Scepticism towards the Written Word in Early Christian and in Greco-Roman Texts," in *The Bible in Three Dimensions*, ed. D. J. A. Clines, S. E. Fowl, and S. E. Porter (Sheffield: Sheffield Academic Press, 1990), 221–47.

- And I have diligently composed for you this treatise on antidotes, most noble Piso, having investigated everything carefully (ἀκριβῶς ἐξετάσας ἅπαντα) ... (Galen, *Ther. ad Pis.* pref.; probably second century C.E.)

- I have written up this treatise, not using elegant language but as one who has firsthand experience of the facts (αὐτόπτης γενόμενος τῶν πραγμάτων), having put the matter to the test through much toil and suffering ... (Vettius Valens VI.9; second century C.E.)

6. *Statement of the intended effect of the book* (Luke 1:4; *Preface*, 136–42). A final clause which describes the book's intended effect on the reader is common in technical prefaces. In addressing the dedicatee at this point as the inscribed reader, Luke is following a common form of dedication courtesy (cf. paragraph 2 above):

- And you, if you are persuaded by [or: obey] what I say, will be able to understand (παρακολουθήσεις) their accuracy (ἀκριβείᾳ). (Diocles of Carystus, *Letter to Antigonus* pref.; c. 300 B.C.E.)

- In the first book, King Ptolemy, I have made clear to you ... ; but in this book I shall set out ... so that you may have full knowledge (ἵν᾽ ... ἔχῃς ... ἐπίγνωσιν) of the Hippocratic theory on joints complete in three books. (Apollonius of Citium III pref.)

- And I am sketching out for you as concisely as possible this outline of the prescribed rules of the art ... : for I think that in this way not only will [Euclid's] treatise be easy for you to survey, but also most other treatises of those who have made reference to geometry. (Hero of Alexandria, *Def.* pref.)

But the topos is also common in nondedicated prefaces, with a view to the book's effect on readers in general. Compare the preface of Hero, *Pneum.* I, which ends, "for thus it will come about that those who subsequently wish to become involved in mathematical studies will find assistance"; or the same author's *Belopoeica*, "so that the tradition may be easy to follow (εὐπαρακολούθητος) for all."[27] Cognates of the verb παρακολουθεῖν appear surprisingly often in these "result" clauses (*Preface*, 96, 128), but the ἐπιγινώσκειν group is also common (*Preface*, 137). Many of the technical writers also share Luke's assumption that the reader will already be familiar with the book's contents ("the things in which you have been instructed"; *Preface*, 192–93). But it is also noteworthy that Luke's phraseology here has wider echoes of the businesslike language of the papyri, where ἐπιγνῶναι τὸ ἀσφαλές seems to mean "find out for certain."

---

27. The formulaic nature of the phrase comes across clearly in Vitruvius VI.6.7: "As far as I could, I have explained the distributions ... so that they may not be obscure to builders; now I shall give a summary exposition of the methods ... according to Greek customs, so that these may not be unknown."

What Do the Prologues Tell Us about the Genre of Luke-Acts?

> The use of literary convention necessitates the existence of a shared world of discourse in which writer and readers can assume a certain basic level of understanding as a foundation for communication: the writer may take the reader along unexpected paths, but the journey cannot even begin unless the two have a basic level of mutual understanding.[28]

Prefaces have a particular role to play in guiding readers' expectations at the beginning of a text and giving them clues as to what is to come. But they do not tell the whole story, and the guidance they give may be as much by suggesting a certain tone and register as by providing explicit clues as to subject and genre.

The dominant view has identified "history" as the particular genre to which Luke's two volumes belong. But, as we have seen, the prologues do not provide clear indications in that direction. For the informed ancient reader — and Josephus provides a useful example of such a reader's grasp of the subtle etiquette of literary convention — Luke's prologues contain too many features which are not normally associated with historiography (e.g., dedication), and not enough of the characteristic style and language which would be considered appropriate for the highly literary art of writing history.[29] At most, such a reader might regard Luke's work as potential "raw material" for a real historian to polish and refine, much as Lucian regards the "soldier's diary" produced by an army surgeon in the Parthian War.[30] This judgment, it should be noted, is a purely literary one. To say that Luke does not follow the generic etiquette of Greek historiography is not to say that his narrative may not be well-informed and historically accurate (Lucian's surgeon is a case in point). The judgment is, moreover, strictly limited to the expectations aroused by the preface. The historiographical credentials of Luke's narrative as a whole have to be argued on other grounds.

If Luke is writing history, the preface conventions he chooses would locate his work on the fringes of the genre, precisely where historiography overlaps with the broader enterprises of Ionian *historia* — with ethnography or cultural history, perhaps. But that is tantamount to saying that the prologue itself does not provide any precise indications of genre. Within the general field of academic discourse, it is normally up to the author to indicate the book's subject matter in the opening sentences of the text, and that is something that Luke signally fails to do. The subject matter of the book never emerges clearly from Luke 1:1–4. The narratives of the "many," we are told, concerned "the business which has been brought to fruition in our midst" — but we never find out what that business was, and Luke's language seems deliberately neutral and colorless in comparison with the introductions to the other Gospels, or indeed with the miracle-studded story which he is about to tell. The "business" (τὰ πράγματα) which is Luke's subject

---

28. Alexander, *Preface*, 210.

29. For further detail on this point see Alexander, *Preface*, chap. 3, and idem, "The Preface to Acts" (see n. 3 above).

30. Lucian, *How to Write History* 16.

does not even have the heroic flavor of the πράξεις ("deeds, exploits") which are more often associated with historical narratives. And Luke does not exploit either of the other two points in the preface where we might have expected an explanation of his subject matter. He tells us that he has decided to write, and that Theophilus has received instruction, without ever saying what the writing and the instruction are *about*. It is only in the retrospective preface to Acts that Luke gives his readers a clear indication of genre, with the passing remark that the "former treatise" concerned the words and deeds of a teacher. This will confirm something that readers must by this time already have perceived, that Luke's work has a strongly biographical focus, and that the hero who forms its focus is more like a philosopher than a politician or a warlord. With hindsight readers can pick up the hints of the Gospel preface which already point in this direction. What Luke is presenting is precisely a written version of "instruction" already heard orally[31] — in fact of a teaching tradition.

For any reader familiar with the conventional language of the technical treatises and school manuals, this hint would be sufficient to establish a socio-literary framework for reading Luke's work. "All the reader is told to expect is an account of tradition, carefully (or accurately) 'followed' and then written down 'in an orderly fashion'" by a writer who has access to the authentic and original tradents. It is

> a written confirmation of something the dedicatee (and by implication the reader) has already heard. If these expectations are modest, they are also perfectly fitted to the traditional account which follows and to the Christian narrative world which it creates. For the reader who is an "insider," the reassurance lies precisely here: this is an accurate account *of the tradition*. The text is not set against the tradition but in alignment with it. Luke promises not independent "investigation" but faithful recording of received tradition (v. 2); he does not challenge his predecessors but ranges his own work alongside theirs ("it seemed good to me also"); the "order" that he promises is probably no more than the inevitable concomitant of the move from oral storytelling to written narrative.[32]

But even for the reader who comes to this material as an "outsider" — and Galen and other ancient writers give us vivid sketches of the many ways in which this kind of "school" text could fall into other hands[33] — Luke provides implicit reassurance in the way he uses the formal preface style to plug his work into the larger world of rational academic discourse. Luke's lexical choices give this short section of the Gospel a distinctive feel.[34] There is a reassuring moderation in the allusion to other tellings of the same story (v. 1). The word "attempted"

---

31. On the links between κατήχησις and school contexts, see Alexander, *Preface*, 139.

32. Quotations from Alexander, *Preface*, 201–2.

33. Details in L. C. A. Alexander, "Ancient Book-Production and the Circulation of the Gospels," in *The Gospels for All Christians*, ed. R. J. Bauckham (Grand Rapids, Mich.: Eerdmans, 1997); cf. Alexander, *Preface*, 62–63; 187–212.

34. For detailed analysis of all these lexical items, see Alexander, *Preface*, chap. 6.

(or "undertaken") may suggest the merest hint of critique of these other versions, but their imperfections, if any, are never explained, and Luke implicitly aligns his own project with theirs (v. 3) and uses the same sources of information (v. 2). His own "decision to write" (v. 3) is a comfortingly humanistic affair — inappropriately so, apparently, to a later church tradition which inserted "et spiritui sancto" in mimicry of the apostolic claim to inspiration of Acts 15:28.[35] The qualifications which Luke himself claims for his task are more modest: he has "followed everything closely [or: accurately] from the beginning" (v. 3). All three terms belong to the carefully moderated discourse of academic writing. Accuracy, rather than beauty of style, is a prime value in this discourse. "Following" a source or an argument (something every good student should be able to do) implies both attentiveness to detail and a successful grasp of the issues. Going back to "the beginning" evokes at once the first principles of logical understanding, fidelity to the "original" and oldest sources of tradition, and the author's own long standing in his chosen field — all guarantors of excellence in their different ways, but none of them out of the reach of a diligent student. And the overall purpose of the project is equally modest — no startling new information, nothing strange or shocking, and no bombastic claims to be revealing "the truth." The "sense of security" evoked by the tones of the BBC newsreader (ἀσφαλεία, v. 4) is precisely what Luke's prefaces provide for the reader in tune with ancient preface convention.

Finally, how do these findings about the prefaces tie in with the overall theme of Luke as the interpreter of Israel? At the formal level, the most striking thing about the Gospel preface is precisely its lack of explicit reference to the biblical narrative world which forms such a strong subtext to the infancy narrative, and indeed to the whole of Luke's two-volume work. The theme of Israel — the "hope of Israel," as Paul puts it at Acts 28:20 — is, as I have argued elsewhere, foregrounded in an emphatic manner in the narratives which frame the whole work, that is, in the four-chapter narrative prologue to the Gospel (Luke 1–4) and in the two-chapter narrative epilogue to Acts (chaps. 27–28). This theme comes momentarily to the surface again at the narrative "peak" which forms the center of the two volumes (Acts 1:6).[36] But again, the full significance of the hints provided in this narrative prologue about the Gentile mission and the conflict induced by it (e.g., at Luke 2:32, 34) may only strike the reader in retrospect, on a rereading which takes full account of the whole narrative of Acts up to its ambiguous and disturbing ending. The formal preface (Luke 1:1–4) places itself quite deliberately outside this narrative framework, choosing the neutral, secular vocabulary of academic discourse to an extent which is remarkable even among the comparable prefaces of Hellenistic Jewish texts.[37] But even here a retrospective rereading may find hints of what is to come. The third-order

---

35. Ibid., 127.

36. See further Loveday C. A. Alexander, "Reading Luke-Acts from Back to Front," in *The Unity of Luke-Acts*, ed. J. Verheyden, BETL (Louvain: Peeters, 1999), 3–30.

37. Alexander, *Preface*, chap. 7.

discourse of the preface, focusing on the writer and on his contact with those entrusted with passing on the tradition, may be seen in hindsight as an anticipation of the narrative of Acts, whose heroes are precisely those tradents. And the ambivalent term πεπληροφορημένων (v. 1), which may be read "forwards" simply as a rather pompous indication of completeness,[38] must surely on rereading "backwards" evoke the intertextual complexities with which Luke encourages the reader to locate this story within the grand narrative of Israel's history.

---

38. Ibid., 111–12.

Chapter 2

Rhetorical Influences and Genre

Luke's Preface and the Rhetoric
of Hellenistic Historiography

Daryl D. Schmidt

The opening of Luke's Gospel claims that it is passing along a reliable story about the past. Modern scholars continue to debate the status of this statement. Is Luke in fact making a historiographical claim? We cannot here finally resolve this problem, but we can seek to appreciate better the implications of Luke's preface for reading Luke-Acts. Luke's claim must be assessed more fully in light of the rhetoric of Hellenistic historiography, while at the same time looking closely at what Luke's text itself seems to say. Before we begin such an analysis we note only briefly the current trend in the scholarly discussion.

Luke's preface has been the subject of much scholarly scrutiny.[1] We make no attempt to survey the long history of debate over the intent of the preface. There is currently a renewed focus on this issue due in part to the work of Loveday Alexander.[2] Her assessments have become the foundation for further

---

1. The classic treatment remains that of Henry Cadbury, especially his "Commentary on the Preface of Luke," in vol. 2 of *The Beginnings of Christianity*, ed. F. J. Foakes Jackson and Kirsopp Lake (1920–33; reprint, Grand Rapids, Mich.: Baker Books, 1979). See also the following works by Cadbury: *The Style and Literary Method of Luke* (Cambridge: Harvard University Press, 1920); *The Making of Luke-Acts* (New York: Macmillan, 1927; 2d ed., London: SPCK, 1958); "The Purpose Expressed in Luke's Preface," *The Expositor* (ser. 8) 21 (1921): 431–41; "The Knowledge Claimed in Luke's Preface," *The Expositor* (ser. 8) 24 (1922): 401–20; "'We' and 'I' Passages in Luke-Acts," *NTS* 3 (1956): 128–32. A careful assessment of his contribution and complete bibliography can be found in Mikeal C. Parsons and Joseph B. Tyson, eds., *Cadbury, Knox, and Talbert: American Contributions to the Study of Acts*, SBL Centennial Publications (Atlanta: Scholars Press, 1992).

W. C. van Unnik championed a strong historical purpose in Luke's preface: see "Remarks on the Purpose of Luke's Historical Writing," in *Sparsa Collecta: The Collected Essays of W. C. van Unnik*, pt. 1, NovTSup 29 (Leiden: Brill, 1973), 6–15; "Once More St. Luke's Prologue," *Neotestamentica* 7 (1973): 7–26; "Luke's Second Book and the Rules of Hellenistic Historiography," in *Les Actes des Apôtres: Traditions, rédaction, théologie*, ed. J. Kremer, BETL 47 (Louvain: Louvain University Press, 1977), 37–60.

For an overall annotated bibliography see Joel B. Green and Michael C. McKeever, *Luke-Acts and New Testament Historiography*, IBR Bibliographies 8 (Grand Rapids, Mich.: Baker Books, 1994). For extensive bibliography on the prologue, see recent commentaries, such as John Holland, *Luke 1:9–20*, Word Biblical Commentary 35A (Dallas: Word Books, 1989), 3–4.

2. Loveday Alexander, "Luke's Preface in the Context of Greek Preface-Writing," *NovT* 28

scholarly insights. She has successfully called into question a long-standing premise of much New Testament scholarship that Luke's preface exhibits features of
conventional Greek historiography. The more precisely Luke's preface is defined,
the more difficult it is to find a model for it in the Greek historians.

Alexander's alternative proposal is that the closest formal parallels to Luke's
preface are to be found in writing that has been characterized as *Fachprosa*,
technical prose.[3] This "scientific tradition" of literature is then contrasted with
history, per se, as a rhetorical style of writing. In setting up the contrast this way,
it is clear, as least superficially, that Luke(-Acts) has less in common with the
major multivolume ancient histories than with less pretentious shorter writings
of the Hellenistic era. While this distinction may have some validity, it may also
conceal as much as it reveals about the historiographical influences on Luke.

In the analysis that follows, I do not intend to make assumptions about genre,
other than this: raising the question of genre at the start only gets in the way
of appreciating Luke's preface. Rather, observations about genre more appropriately belong to the task of identifying sources for the rhetorical influences seen
in Luke's preface. Here I am using "rhetoric" in a less formal way than does
Alexander. As applied to features of Luke's preface, I mean simply: What other
Hellenistic writing sounds this way? Then we can ask the question: What other
features do these writings share? And finally, Does this help us read Luke-Acts?

Luke's Preface

We begin with a provisional reading of what the text seems to say.

Ἐπειδήπερ πολλοὶ ἐπεχείρησαν ἀνατάξασθαι διήγησιν περὶ τῶν πεπληροφορημένων ἐν ἡμῖν πραγμάτων, [2]καθὼς παρέδοσαν ἡμῖν οἱ ἀπ᾽ ἀρχῆς αὐτόπται
καὶ ὑπηρέται γενόμενοι τοῦ λόγου, [3]ἔδοξε κἀμοὶ παρηκολουθηκότι ἄνωθεν
πᾶσιν ἀκριβῶς καθεξῆς σοι γράψαι, κράτιστε Θεόφιλε, [4]ἵνα ἐπιγνῷς περὶ ὧν
κατηχήθης λόγων τὴν ἀσφάλειαν.

(1986): 48–74; *The Preface to Luke's Gospel: Literary Convention and Social Context in Luke 1.1–4 and
Acts 1.1*, SNTSMS 78 (Cambridge: Cambridge University Press, 1993), based on her 1978 Oxford
University Ph.D. thesis; "The Preface to Acts and the Historians," in *History, Literature, and Society
in the Book of Acts*, ed. Ben Witherington (Cambridge: Cambridge University Press, 1996), 73–103;
and now her contribution to this volume in the previous chapter.

    3. Lars Rydbeck, *Fachprosa, vermeintliche Volkssprache und Neues Testament: Zur Beurteilung der
sprachlichen Niveauunterschiede im nachklassischen Griechisch* (Uppsala, 1967). One of the concluding
sections (pp. 186–99) of Rydbeck's work has been translated as, "On the Question of Linguistic Levels and the Place of the New Testament in the Contemporary Language Milieu," in *The Language of
the New Testament: Classic Essays*, ed. Stanley E. Porter, JSNTSup 60 (Sheffield: Sheffield Academic
Press, 1991), 191–204. I think it is unfortunate that Alexander initially chose to call this "scientific
writing." The label "scientific" can easily mislead those, such as Colin Hemer, who then take it to
mean "designed primarily for conveying factual information" (*The Book of Acts in the Setting of Hellenistic History*, WUNT 49 [Tübingen: J. C. B. Mohr (Paul Siebeck), 1989], 324), although Alexander
herself does not say this.

Since many others have undertaken to put together a narrative account of the events that have run their course among us, ²as the original eyewitnesses and ministers of the word passed them on to us, ³I too decided, since I had been following closely everything from early on, to write an orderly account for you, most excellent Theophilus, ⁴so that you might realize the reliability of the things in which you have been instructed.

A number of key terms used here have received an abundance of scholarly scrutiny in order to discern their historiographical significance. Among these terms several deserve renewed attention, especially those that depict the author's relationship to the events described.

First of all, the author begins, others have put together διήγησιν περὶ … πραγμάτων, an account of events, which were passed on by οἱ ἀπ᾽ ἀρχῆς αὐτόπται καὶ ὑπηρέται γενόμενοι τοῦ λόγου. These transmitters of the tradition, the "eyewitnesses" and "servants of the word," are described in the same grammatical construction, a participle with a single article, οἱ … γενόμενοι, which suggests at least an overlapping group of persons characterized by these two nouns, αὐτόπται καὶ ὑπηρέται, rather than two distinct — and possibly sequential — groups.

Alexander reminds us that the term αὐτόπται, in both historiographical and "scientific" writing, is not the same as "eyewitness" in English, which tends only to mean someone who happened to be present during an event. The Greek notion is clearly one of "autopsy," to (go) see for oneself. The implications are more of having traveled to the original site of the event, after the fact, than actually having experienced the event firsthand.

The second group, "the servants of the word," is usually given a theological interpretation because of the association with "the word" (λόγος). Even Alexander thinks the combination is most likely "a Christian term."[4] There is nothing about ὑπηρέται, however, that gives it any technical meaning, and Acts 1:1 refers back to the whole of the Gospel of Luke with the term τὸν πρῶτον λόγον. Alexander notes in passing the use of ὑπηρέτης in Acts 26:16. Here the voice at Paul's conversion appoints him to be ὑπηρέτην καὶ μάρτυρα ὧν εἶδες, "a servant and witness of what you have seen." A more generic sense than "servant" is simply one who "attends" to someone. But how does one "attend" to what one has seen? In a historiographical parallel discussed below I note the description of Diodorus Siculus, a historian writing a century before Luke, that historians are "servants of Divine Providence" (ὑπουργοὶ τῆς Θείας προνοίας), which directs the whole of human history. It thus seems unnecessary to label the parallel term in Luke's preface an explicitly "Christian" term.

A second set of equally scrutinized words in Luke's preface relates to the qualifications the author claims for writing about this tradition, of which he him-

---

4. Alexander, *Preface*, 123. Likewise, C. F. Evans labels it "a unique expression, of Christian, possibly Lukan, creation" (*Saint Luke*, TPI New Testament Commentaries [Philadelphia: Trinity Press International, 1990], 127), based on the vocabulary used, not on the semantic content.

self was not "an eyewitness and servant."[5] His relationship to the tradition was that of someone who παρηκολουθηκότι ἄνωθεν πᾶσιν ἀκριβῶς, "investigated everything carefully from the very first" (NRSV). The term translated "investigate" is at times even rendered "research," although its root sense is simply "follow." The more technical connotation seems paralleled in a statement Josephus makes about the historian's task (*Contra Apion* 1.53). In denouncing his critics, he calls attention to his own role as a direct participant in events he writes about. Anyone claiming to present παράδοσιν πράξεων ἀληθινῶν, a factual account, must learn about it ἀκριβῶς, accurately, by παρηκολουθηκότα τοῖς γεγονόσιν, following closely what happened, or παρὰ τῶν εἰδότων πυνθανόμενον, inquiring from those who knew about it. As David Moessner notes, Josephus gives preference here, as elsewhere, to "following closely" the events, rather than investigating them later. The distinction, Moessner argues, is that one "follows" contemporary events as they happen, but one "investigates" past events that had not been "followed" at the time; or in reference to sources, one "follows" the flow of a story in a text that is already familiar, but one "investigates" an unfamiliar text. The more natural claim made in Luke's preface would then be that he either "stayed actively informed" about events "from the beginning" or became an "informed" reader of everything that happened.[6] Alexander makes a similar distinction based on the evidence from "scientific" writers.[7] Cadbury had always insisted that Josephus's distinction as applied to Luke's preface meant the author was claiming some firsthand knowledge, at least for parts of Acts, and had nothing to do with "research."[8]

Finally, the author used this knowledge to write about events καθεξῆς, in an orderly way, so that the events would have ἀσφάλειαν, certainty or credibility, for the informed reader. The combination of καθεξῆς with ἀκριβῶς is often taken to be virtually synonymous with "factual accuracy."[9] It is then suggested that it is functionally equivalent to knowing something assuredly or to having

---

5. Cadbury disputes this gap between the author and the eyewitnesses, based on his contention that in the next clause the author claims contemporary knowledge of the events ("Knowledge Claimed," 409).

6. David Moessner, " 'Eyewitnesses,' 'Informed Contemporaries,' and 'Unknowing Inquirers': Josephus' Criteria for Authentic Historiography and the Meaning of ΠΑΡΑΚΟΛΟΥΘΕΩ," *NovT* 38 (1996): 105–22, esp. 120–22.

7. Alexander, *Preface*, 128, 134.

8. "Commentary," 501f.; "Knowledge Claimed," 403–9; " 'We' and 'I' Passages," 130–31. See n. 1 above for full citations. For a recent defense of "investigation" see Darrell L. Bock, *Luke*, 2 vols., Baker Exegetical Commentaries on the New Testament (Grand Rapids, Mich.: Baker Books, 1994, 1996), 1.59–60.

9. I. Howard Marshall is typical of this approach in simply asserting: "Luke's concern for ἀσφάλεια must imply a concern for accuracy, and the other phrases in the prologue, ἀκριβῶς and καθεξῆς, confirm this" ("Luke and his 'Gospel,' " in *Das Evangelium und die Evangelien*, ed. P. Stuhlmacher [Tübingen: J. C. B. Mohr (Paul Siebeck), 1983], here 305).

Syntactically, ἀκριβῶς most naturally goes with the preceding clause and only καθεξῆς with what follows, despite the attempt to link them together by J. Kürzinger, "Lk 1,3: . . . ἀκριβῶς καθεξῆς σοι γράψαι," *BZ* 18 (1974): 249–55. Colin Hemer is adamant in insisting that the goal expressed in Luke's preface is "to chronicle what really happened . . . to show that the proclamation of divine events is rooted in a matter-of-fact reality which the reader can know to be true" (*Book of Acts*, 85).

assured knowledge.[10] Van Unnik had earlier noted Polybius's use of the term in contrast to hearsay evidence, but van Unnik surely goes too far in insisting that Luke "was concerned with the 'infallibility' of the facts," that "he wants to remove doubt about the exactitude" of the events to give readers "complete certainty."[11] Luke's terms do not carry such clear connotations of infallible exactitude. As noted below, such notions are in fact foreign to the rhetoric of ancient historiographical prefaces.

How does making the account "orderly" (καθεξῆς) contribute to the reader's "certainty?"[12] Luke's use of this term in the narrative of Acts is instructive here. After Peter's encounter with Cornelius in Acts 10, Peter immediately has to explain himself back in Jerusalem. The account he gives is said to be καθεξῆς (11:4), but it is not a verbatim report that repeats what had just happened. The reader recognizes that Peter's καθεξῆς account is not limited to the description given earlier by the narrator. The most noticeable discrepancy is in Peter's version of what Cornelius said to him about the vision that prodded the encounter with Peter (10:30–33). In Peter's version the messenger explains the purpose of sending for Peter by saying that "he will give you a message by which you and your entire household will be saved" (11:14), none of which Cornelius had actually reported in the first version. When Peter recaps this incident before the Jerusalem council, he adds the further interpretation that this was God's way of choosing him to be the means of bringing the good news to the Gentiles, who also will be "saved by grace" (15:7–11). In what sense then is Peter's account of the incident considered καθεξῆς (11:4)? Clearly not for its factual accuracy in reproducing Cornelius's own perspective, nor in establishing a "correct" chronology of the event, but in retelling the incident from a "narratival" perspective, that is, within the larger sequence and purpose of the narrative.[13]

Hemer then imposes this reading on all the terms in the preface, so that ἀκριβῶς is "to know facts" accurately (98).

10. Alexander, *Preface,* 140; van Unnik, "Once More," 18 and n. 75.

11. Van Unnik, "Remarks on the Purpose," 13, 14.

12. For discussions of the term, in addition to works cited earlier, see Günther Klein, "Lukas 1,1–4 als theologisches Program," in *Zeit und Geschichte* [*Festschrift* for R. Bultmann], ed. Erich Dinkler (Tübingen: J. C. B. Mohr [Paul Siebeck], 1964), 193–216; Martin Völkel, "Exegetische Erwägungen zum Verständnis des Begriffs ΚΑΘΕΞΗΣ im lukanischen Prolog," *NTS* 20 (1973–74): 289–99; Franz Mussner, "Καθεξῆς im Lukasprolog," in *Jesus und Paulus* [*Festschrift* for W. G. Kümmel], ed. E. Earle Ellis and Erich Grässer (Göttingen: Vandenhoeck & Ruprecht, 1975), 253–55; Gerhard Schneider, "Zur Bedeutung von καθεξῆς im lukanischen Doppelwerk," *ZNW* 68 (1977): 128–31; Fearghus Ó Fearghail, *The Introduction to Luke-Acts: A Study of the Role of Lk 1,1–4,44 in the Composition of Luke's Two-Volume Work,* AnBib 126 (Rome: Pontifical Biblical Institute, 1991), 102–10; David Moessner, "The Meaning of ΚΑΘΕΞΗΣ in the Lukan Prologue as a Key to the Distinctive Contribution of Luke's Narrative among the 'Many,'" in *The Four Gospels 1992* [*Festschrift* for Frans Neirynck], ed. F. van Segbroeck et al., 3 vols., BETL 100 (Louvain: Louvain University Press, 1992), 2.1513–28.

For an analysis of these terms as they function didactically in prefaces of biographical writings, see Vernon K. Robbins, "Prefaces in Greco-Roman Biography and Luke-Acts," *SBLSP* 14:2 (1978): 193–207, and his contribution in this volume.

13. See especially the careful analysis of this text in Moessner, "The Meaning of ΚΑΘΕΞΗΣ." "Consequential" might better translate this term than "orderly."

Robert Tannehill emphasizes that the common element in these two uses of καθεξῆς is that "both passages refer to narration." Peter's narration is made persuasive for his hearers, who share Peter's experience, because it is "told from Peter's point of view," which means that "Peter in his report is following the order of his own experience." For Tannehill this is a "suggestive parallel to the author's strategy for the whole work, as explained in the prologue." Luke writes καθεξῆς and puts the narrative in order, an order that discloses why these events are seen as having reached their fulfillment (πεπληροφορημένων, 1:1). It is the narrative order given to the events that brings the reader assurance.[14]

Contemporary Influences

Any attempt to assess potential influences on Luke's preface is limited by the definition of the task. Alexander overthrows the conventional scholarly wisdom about Luke's use of Greek historiographical conventions by searching for parallels to the preface's formal features only. There are indeed noticeable formal parallels between Luke's preface and a general category of writings from the "scientific tradition," as Alexander calls *Fachprosa*. The status of the category *Fachprosa* requires further clarification.

At times Alexander's use of "scientific writing" seems to assume near-genre status (an issue she seeks to clarify in this volume). The features Alexander isolates as part of her "objective description" of Luke's preface are primarily grammatical features.[15] She thus finds evidence that further confirms Rydbeck's thesis that these prose writings share "an intermediate grammatical level" of Greek, at once more literate than vernacular, popular usage, but also without the "literary pretensions" of elevated style. Rydbeck identified this linguistic level in a range of writings that included competently written papyri, popular philosophical literature, technical prose, and the New Testament.[16] *Fachprosa* as a level of language use is not genre-specific. It is, to be sure, not the same level of language use as found in the large multivolume works of Polybius and Diodorus. But that was just Rydbeck's point. *Fachprosa* is *Zwischenprosa*, a level of language use that lies between truly vernacular spoken Greek and the style seen in Polybius and Diodorus, which Rydbeck called *schönliterarisch ambitiösen hellenistischen Literatur-*

---

14. Robert C. Tannehill, *The Narrative Unity of Luke-Acts: A Literary Interpretation,* 2 vols. (Philadelphia: Fortress, 1986), 1.11–12. Against earlier attempts to interpret the term *als eines chronologisch strukturierten Begriffs,* Völkel argued rather that καθεξῆς was characteristic of any uninterrupted literary sequence ("Exegetische Erwägungen," 293, 298). See also Robert L. Brawley, *Centering on God: Method and Message in Luke-Acts* (Louisville: Westminster/John Knox, 1990), 39, and Rebecca I. Denova, *The Things Accomplished among Us: Prophetic Tradition in the Structural Pattern of Luke-Acts,* JSNTSup 141 (Sheffield: Sheffield Academic Press, 1997), 105–6. For the sense of hindsight Luke gives the reader see, for example, Rainer Dillmann, "Das Lukasevangelium als Tendenz-schrift: Leserlenkung und Leseintention in Lk, 1,1–4," *BZ* 38 (1994): 86–93.

15. Alexander, "Luke's Preface," 53.

16. Rydbeck, "On the Question of Linguistic Levels," 199.

sprache.[17] However, something written at this level is not necessarily void of all historiographical influences.

The most common convention of ancient writing was that the opening sentence should indicate to the reader the general topic or subject matter. This is as true for prologues that run many pages as it is for the one-sentence prefaces that Alexander studied. This common practice became especially obligatory in historical writing. As Donald Earl noted: "At the very least the opening sentence must make clear that it is with history that the author is concerned."[18] Earl begins with the opening of Herodotus:

Ἡροδότου Ἁλικαρνησσέος ἱστορίης ἀπόδεξις ἥδε, ὡς μήτε τὰ γενόμενα ἐξ ἀνθρώπων τῷ χρόνῳ ἐξίτηλα γένηται, μήτε ἔργα μεγάλα τε καὶ θωμαστά, τὰ μὲν Ἕλλησι τὰ δὲ βαρβάροισι ἀποδεχθέντα, ἀκλεᾶ γένηται, τά τε ἄλλα καὶ δι' ἣν αἰτίην ἐπολέμησαν ἀλλήλοισι.

What Herodotus the Halicarnassian has learned by inquiry is here set forth; so that the memory of the past may not be blotted out from humankind by time, and that great and marvellous deeds done by Greeks and foreigners, and especially the reason they warred against each other may not lack renown. (LCL, adapted)

With this opening sentence Herodotus indicates the subject matter of the entire (multivolume) writing.[19] In a work of literature, this single sentence begins the formal Προοίμιον, which may run for several pages, as Alexander notes.[20] The *prooemium* developed into "the character almost of an independent literary form."[21] The sections following the opening sentence lauded the importance of the topic and gave a rationale for the structure of the volumes in the whole work. In the case of Thucydides the opening discourse runs twenty-three sections before the narrative begins — something of a record. The Hellenistic historian Dionysius began his twenty-book history of Rome with a preface that rivaled Thucydides. Dionysius also displayed the rhetorical style of his day by beginning with an expression of dislike for such prologues, but felt compelled to write one nonetheless. Other Hellenistic historians, such as Polybius, Diodorus, and Appian, followed the precedent of extended prologues somewhat more modestly than Dionysius. If this tradition defines the standard preface for historical writing, then Luke's preface is not in this category.

Not all writers of history, however, attempted to emulate the grand tradition of Thucydides. Alongside the literary pretensions of the great encompassing histories just mentioned, more practical writings with more functional prefaces also existed. Earl cites the opening sentences of Xenophon's shorter writings as good examples. Xenophon's "Memorabilia" begins:

---

17. Rydbeck, *Fachprosa*, 177.

18. Donald Earl, "Prologue-Form in Ancient Historiography," *ANRW* I.2 (1972): 842–56, esp. 843.

19. Aristotle labels this approach old-fashioned and unpleasant because it was not a well-formed period (*Rhet* 3.9.2).

20. Alexander, *Preface*, 30.

21. Earl, "Prologue-Form," 842.

Πολλάκις ἐθαύμασα, τίσι ποτὲ λόγοις Ἀθηναίους ἔπεισαν οἱ γραψάμενοι Σωκράτην, ὡς ἄξιος εἴη θανάτου τῇ πόλει.

I have often wondered by what arguments those who drew up the indictment against Socrates could persuade the Athenians that his life was forfeit to the state. (*Mem.* I.1.1, LCL)

The preface concludes with a statement of the charges against Socrates, which Xenophon then begins to analyze with the simple transition: Πρῶτον μὲν οὖν... "First then..." Xenophon's *Symposium* with Socrates provides a similar example of a brief opening sentence and simple transition:

Ἀλλ' ἐμοὶ δοκεῖ τῶν καλῶν κἀγαθῶν ἀνδρῶν ἔργα οὐ μόνον τὰ μετὰ σπουδῆς πραττόμενα ἀξιομνημόνευτα εἶναι ἀλλὰ καὶ τὰ ἐν ταῖς παιδιαῖς· οἷς δὲ παραγενόμενος ταῦτα γιγνώσκω δηλῶσαι βούλομαι. Ἦν μὲν γάρ...

To my mind it is worth while to relate not only the serious acts of great and good men but also what they do in their lighter moods, such as an experience I had that I would like to narrate. It was on the occasion of... (*Sym.* I.1.1, LCL, adapted)

Xenophon then directly begins his historical reminiscence, which seems in part designed to sketch a more realistic version than the recently published, and destined to become famous, account by Plato.[22]

Other examples can be added from outside the writings of historians. Arrian begins his "Discourses of Epictetus," after the epistolary greeting to Lucius Gellius (χαίρειν), with this sentence:

Οὔτε συνέγραψα ἐγὼ τοὺς Ἐπικτήτου λόγους οὕτως ὅπως ἄν τις συγγράψειε τὰ τοιαῦτα οὔτε ἐξήνεγκα εἰς ἀνθρώπους αὐτός, ὅς γε οὐδὲ συγγράψαι φημί.

I have not composed these Words of Epictetus as one might "compose" books of this kind, nor have I of my own act published them to the world; indeed, I acknowledge that I have not "composed" them at all. (Epict. *Disc.* 1., pref. 1, LCL)

What these prefaces lack, compared to Luke, is a dedication. Although dedications became "commonplace" in the Hellenistic age, especially for "writers of plain prose,"[23] they were not common in prefaces of historical writings.[24] It is primarily on this basis that Alexander has shifted the focus from historians to technical writers. Before considering the examples she has isolated, we can note several prefaces with dedications that others often cite when looking for parallels to Luke-Acts.

Jewish Hellenistic writers are especially pertinent. The most interesting example is that of Josephus's two books, *Against Apion*. The two prefaces begin:

Book I: Ἱκανῶς μὲν ὑπολαμβάνω καὶ διὰ τῆς περὶ τὴν ἀρχαιολογίαν συγγραφῆς, κράτιστε ἀνδρῶν Ἐπαφρόδιτε, τοῖς ἐντευξομένοις αὐτῇ πεποιηκέναι φανερὸν περὶ τοῦ γένους ἡμῶν τῶν Ἰουδαίων, ὅτι καὶ παλαιότατόν ἐστι....

---

22. So O. J. Todd in the LCL introduction (530).

23. Michael S. Silk, "Dedications, Greek," in *Oxford Classical Dictionary*, ed. Simon Hornblower and Anthony Spawforth, 3d ed. (Oxford: Oxford University Press, 1996), 318.

24. Alexander, *Preface*, 27–29; "Preface to Acts," 85–89.

In my history of our *Antiquities*, most excellent Epaphroditus, I have, I think, made sufficiently clear to any who may peruse that work the extreme antiquity of our Jewish race.... (*Con. Ap.* I.1, LCL)

Book II: Διὰ μὲν οὖν τοῦ προτέρου βιβλίου, τιμιώτατέ μοι Ἐπαφρόδιτε, περί τε τῆς ἀρχαιότητος ἡμῶν ἐπέδειξα....

In the first volume of this work, my most esteemed Epaphroditus, I demonstrated the antiquity of our race.... (*Con. Ap.* II.1, LCL)

The preface of Book II immediately brings to mind the opening of Acts:

Τὸν μὲν πρῶτον λόγον ἐποιησάμην περὶ πάντων, ὦ Θεόφιλε, ὧν ἤρξατο ὁ Ἰησοῦς ποιεῖν τε καὶ διδάσκειν....

In the first book, Theophilus, I treated everything Jesus used to do and to teach....

Similar retrospective prefaces occur in a number of Philo's treatises. In *Life of Moses*, Book 2 begins: Ἡ μὲν πρότερα σύνταξίς ἐστι περὶ... ("The former treatise dealt with..."). This work was designed as two books, as was Josephus's *Against Apion*, and Book 1 ends anticipating Book 2.[25] Given the variety of writings with retrospective prefaces, such a preface in Acts, by itself, does not define its literary relationship to Luke.

Our primary focus remains the preface of "the first book," Luke's Gospel. An important comparison often cited is the opening of the so-called *Letter of Aristeas:*

Ἀξιολόγου διηγήσεως, ὦ Φιλόκρατες, περὶ τῆς γενηθείσης ἡμῖν ἐντυχίας πρὸς Ἐλεάζαρον τὸν τῶν Ἰουδαίων ἀρχιερέα συνεσταμένης, διὰ τὸ σὲ περὶ πολλοῦ πεποιῆσθαι, παρ' ἕκαστα ὑπομιμνήσκων, συνακοῦσαι περὶ ὧν ἀπεστάλημεν καὶ διὰ τί, πεπείραμαι σαφῶς ἐκθέσθαι σοι, κατειληφὼς ἣν ἔχεις φιλομαθῆ διάθεσιν, ὅπερ μέγιστόν ἐστιν ἀνθρώπῳ, προσμανθάνειν ἀεί τι καὶ προσλαμβάνειν, ἤτοι κατὰ τὰς ἱστορίας, ἢ καὶ κατ' αὐτὸ τὸ πρᾶγμα πεπειραμένῳ. οὕτω γὰρ...

Since the account of our meeting with Eleazar, the High Priest of the Jews, is worth recording, Philocrates, and since you yourself are particularly concerned, as you keep reminding me, to hear the why and wherefores of our mission, I have tried to set out the matter clearly for you, knowing your scholarly mind; it is indeed a most important human function, as the poet says,

> always to add knowledge, ever to acquire it,

---

25. Darryl W. Palmer describes sequential prefaces as retrospective, prospective, or a combination ("Acts and the Ancient Historical Monograph," in *The Book of Acts in Its First-Century Setting*, vol. 1: *The Book of Acts in Its Ancient Literary Setting*, ed. Bruce W. Winter and Andrew D. Clarke [Grand Rapids, Mich.: Eerdmans, 1993], 1–29, here 22), and gives a varied list of examples. Mikeal C. Parsons and Richard I. Pervo, *Rethinking the Unity of Luke and Acts* (Minneapolis: Fortress, 1993), object to comparing Acts to Book 2 of *Against Apion* and *Life of Moses*, since Book 1 in each case ends with an explicit anticipation of a sequel (62–63).

whether by historical research or through actual experience of events. For in this way... [26]

Here we have not only formal similarities with Luke's preface, including a dedication, but also linguistic ones. This author likewise calls his writing a διήγησις περὶ..., acknowledges the value of both historical research and direct experience of τὸ πρᾶγμα, and writes to someone directly addressed with a note of assurance: σαφῶς ἐκθέσθαι σοι, exactly parallel to Luke's καθεξῆς σοι γράψαι.

To appreciate the similar tone of these prefaces with the preface of Luke, we can contrast the examples that Alexander isolates from the "scientific" traditions. Of the four texts she carefully analyzes, one of the most "comprehensive examples" is a treatise attributed to Demetrius.[27] Although it may share certain syntactical features with Luke's preface, the similarities seem more superficial than the extent of the differences. Merely reading the text in translation (edited to reflect the Greek syntax) will indicate its differences from Luke:

> Since according to the theory that governs epistolary types, Heraclides, [letters] can be composed in a great number of styles, but were written in those which always fit the particular circumstance [to which they were addressed], and while [letters] ought to be written as skillfully as possible, they are in fact composed indifferently by those who undertake such services for men in public office, and since I see that you are eager in your love to learn, I have taken it upon myself, by means of certain styles, to organize and set forth [for you] both the number of distinctions between them and what they are, and have sketched a sample, as it were, of the arrangement of each kind, and have, in addition, individually set forth the rationale for each of them, partly assuming that this pleases you too, since you will know that you are making your splendid life surpass others, not in banquets, but in professional skills, and partly believing that I shall share in the praise that will properly [redound to you].

It does not seem likely that the reader of Luke's preface was reminded of such a treatise, with its opening sentence more than two-and-one-half times as long as Luke's, and lacking Luke's rhetorical motifs. Without its dedication there would be little reason to consider this preface to be more parallel to Luke than other prefaces with historiographical elements.

Does the presence of a dedication in the prefaces of Luke and Acts exclude them completely from the category of historical writing? The most Alexander will allow is a small intersection of historiography with "the broader, non-rhetorical tradition of philosophical and technical prose" that she calls "scientific literature." She thus maintains a divide between the "rhetorical pretension" of

---

26. Greek text from Moses Hadas, ed., *Aristeas to Philocrates* (New York: Harper & Brothers, 1951); trans. adapted from John R. Bartlett, *Jews in the Hellenistic World: Josephus, Aristeas, the Sibylline Oracles, Eupolemus*, Cambridge Commentaries on Writings of the Jewish and Christian World 200 B.C. to A.D. 200 (Cambridge: Cambridge University Press, 1985).

27. Alexander, *Preface*, 69–70, text on 214–15. See also text and translation in Abraham J. Malherbe, *Ancient Epistolary Theorists*, SBLSBS 19 (Atlanta: Scholars Press, 1988), 30–31.

historiography proper and a more "scholarly, scientific" kind of historical tradition, and contends that both Luke and Acts are more "fully at home in the broad
tradition of technical prose, and much less so among the historians."[28]

Other scholars of course continue to disagree. Ó Fearghail acknowledges that
dedications are "not found in the writings of the well-known Greek and Latin
historians," but are "typical rather of works of a strictly didactic nature such as
scientific and rhetorical treatises," as well as some Jewish Hellenistic writings
(as noted above) and "Roman historical writings of minor importance." Thus for
him the presence of a dedication in Luke's preface "does not represent a problem
for the identification of the basic genre of Luke-Acts as history."[29]

The matter seems to rest on whether one places the major weight on formal
features, as Alexander does, or on what Luke's preface actually seems to say. To
better assess the rhetoric of Luke's preface we must first consider more carefully
the rhetoric of Hellenistic historiography.

The Rhetoric of Hellenistic Historiography

We remind ourselves again of the observation of Donald Earl that from Herodotus and Thucydides down to the Latin historians one finds "remarkable . . .
unanimity" that "the opening sentence must make clear that it is with history
that the author is concerned," and that most historians indicate rather explicitly
their subject matter. This same principle was at work in other prose writers on
subjects as diverse as agriculture and medicine, who "all make genre and subject absolutely plain at the beginning of their works." In "the great majority of
surviving works" the same pattern is revealed: "The function of the first sentence is to establish, if not the specific topic to be treated, at least the literary
genre to which the work belongs, history, dialogue, oratory and so on." Earl then
concludes: whether "history, epideictic oratory, philosophical dialogue, political
treatise or whatever, your first sentence had to announce what you were writing." There may well have been a practical reason: "The first sentence and first
paragraph performed much of the function of the title page and list of contents
in a modern codex."[30]

Prefaces for writings identified as historiographical typically included a statement of purpose containing language usually interpreted as a commitment to
factuality. Herodotus's stated purpose was "that the things which have happened may not be blotted out," of which Terrance Callan writes that Herodotus

---

28. Alexander, "Preface to Acts," 101, 103.

29. Ó Fearghail, *Introduction*, 167. Joel B. Green is equally insistent: "Formal, grammatical features cannot mask the significant discontinuity one recognizes when moving from the substance of
the scientific tradition to the narrative of the Third Gospel. Nor do the affinities between Luke and
the scientific tradition simply negate the identification of Luke 1:1–4 and Luke-Acts with the tradition of Greco-Roman historiography" (*The Gospel of Luke*, NICNT [Grand Rapids, Mich.: Eerdmans,
1997], 4).

30. Earl, "Prologue-Form," 843, 846, 849, 856.

aimed "simply to preserve the memory of the past." Fourth-century historians sought other goals. Isocrates introduced an "educational" goal that affected historians until the time of Polybius, who contended there was a "corrective" in "the knowledge of things which have happened before." Callan sees in this "a greater concern for factual accuracy," which by the first century had become a trend "to present a true account of something," for example, in Josephus, and in later writers, such as Tacitus, Arrian, and Dio Cassius.[31] Callan's conventional interpretation of the language about "factual accuracy" is subject to serious critique, as noted below.

Colin Hemer exemplifies recent attempts to continue to treats Acts as straight Hellenistic historiography. He takes the claims about "accuracy" in historical prefaces to be direct claims about historicity.[32] His argument is built on a conventional contrast between rhetorical historians, such as Dionysius, the model for Josephus, and Polybius, who restored the "exacting standards" established by Thucydides.[33] Unlike Josephus, "prone to sensationalize and exaggerate, Luke is restrained," and "never rhetorical." This author rather "shares with some of the best minds of antiquity a concern for what actually happened" — in the words of Polybius, the author of Luke writes an "impartial" history that "seeks the strictly true account."[34] Even if Luke-Acts is read as Hellenistic historiography, assumptions about its factual accuracy cannot be sustained.

In a recent collection of essays on Acts, Ben Witherington reiterates Hemer's themes. Witherington begins with an essay by classical historian W. J. McCoy on the current state of Thucydidean studies, to which Witherington appends his own comments about Thucydides' legacy: "Luke intends to be seen as a serious Hellenistic historian of contemporary events, rather like a Polybius or a Thucydides." Witherington focuses on speeches. Both Thucydides and Polybius include extensive speechmaking in their histories and both make claims about the veracity of the speeches. Witherington endorses the view that Thucydides sought to base his speeches on what was actually spoken, and he assumes Luke's intent was the same, "to write accurately on a serious subject without neglecting certain concerns for style and rhetorical conventions."[35]

There are two assumptions in this approach that must be challenged. The first is that Thucydides and Polybius were normative models for serious Hellenistic

---

31. Terrance Callan, "The Preface of Luke-Acts and Historiography," *NTS* 31 (1985): 576–81, here 578, 579.

32. Hemer's monograph, *The Book of Acts in the Setting of Hellenistic History* (1989), was edited by Conrad Gempf after Hemer's untimely death in 1987. Some of Hemer's arguments may have been left incomplete, but his overall perspective is quite clear.

33. Ibid., chap. 3, esp. 65–67, 77–78.

34. Ibid., 85, 97–98. For Hemer, this author was "an eyewitness and companion of Paul," likely "Luke" himself (408, 413–14).

35. Ben Witherington III, ed., *History, Literature, and Society in the Book of Acts* (Cambridge: Cambridge University Press, 1996). See W. J. McCoy, "In the Shadow of Thucydides" (3–23), with "Editor's Addendum" (23–32), esp. 25, 27.

historians, and the second is that their rhetoric about "accuracy" is an objective statement of purpose. Both of these assumptions prove to be unfounded.

The first assumption implies the feasibility that the author of Luke-Acts would look to Thucydides and/or Polybius as a model for writing history. The emerging consensus today is that "the rules and procedures of Hellenistic historiography derive largely from rhetoric."[36] Polybius's attempt to resurrect Thucydidean historiography must be seen as a reaction, not as the norm. Thucydides and Polybius are "untypical and exceptional" in their own time; Thucydides was mostly "ignored in antiquity" and his text was obscure to Hellenistic readers. Likewise, Polybius was not a popular writer, although he became a model for a few other historians, such as Josephus.[37]

Thucydides had a very limited reception in the ancient world, even among other historians. Thucydides was not an easy author to read, his Homeric rhetorical devices were not fashionable, and his causal explanations of historical events "kept the gods out" of the picture. But the biggest factor was Thucydides' narrow subject matter: "a long and destructive, but actually non-recurrent inter-Greek war," which was not of lasting interest in the Hellenistic world.[38] In criticizing other historians, Polybius appears to adopt Thucydidean principles of historiography, without crediting Thucydides (as Thucydides had not mentioned Herodotus). Polybius, likewise, was not widely imitated, and even acknowledged himself that "there is something forbidding about my work . . . and that it is open to criticism on account of the monotony of its style."[39]

Polybius's critique of his predecessors and contemporaries has often been treated as though Polybius were appealing for "nothing but the facts," and attacking any use of rhetoric. Polybius's complaint is rather that others, by inappropriately embellishing subjects with a grandiose style of rhetoric, have not used the right kind of rhetoric in their speeches. Unlike the more limited scope of earlier histories, only "Polybius' theme — the creation of the Roman world-empire — was sufficiently grand for him to use the grand style on those occasions and for those episodes where it was appropriate." Even when Polybius claims to give a (more) truthful account, it remained the case that "a 'truthful' account

---

36. W. R. Connor, "Historical Writing in the Fourth Century B.C. and in the Hellenistic Period," in *Cambridge History of Classical Literature,* ed. P. E. Easterling and B. M. W. Knox (Cambridge: Cambridge University Press, 1985), 458–71, here 466.

37. Emilio Gabba, "True History and False History in Classical Antiquity," *Journal of Roman Studies* 71 (1981): 50–62, here 50, 52.

38. Simon Hornblower, "The Fourth-Century and Hellenistic Reception of Thucydides," *Journal of Hellenic Studies* 115 (1995): 47–68, here 63–64, 66. Hornblower notes that only a single papyrus fragment of Thucydides survives from the early Hellenistic (B.C.E.) era. For a description of the fragment as "unmistakably" third century B.C.E., and thus the earliest surviving, though "erratic," text of Thucydides, see E. G. Turner, "A Third-Century B.C. Fragment of Thucydides," *Journal of Hellenic Studies* 76 (1956): 96–98.

39. Book IX, preface. F. W. Walbank contends: "The lessons to which he was most attached fell largely on deaf ears" ("Profit or Amusement: Some Thoughts on the Motives of Hellenistic Historians," in *Purposes of History: Studies in Greek Historiography from the 4th to the 2nd Centuries* B.C., ed. H. Verdin, G. Schepens, and E. de Keyser, Studia Hellenistica 30 [Louvain: Louvain University Press, 1990], 253–66, here 266).

has to be written in a style appropriate to the subject matter, τὰ καθήκοντα,"[40] the basic rhetorical principle followed by historians.

A critical assessment of these historians is provided by Dionysius at the end of the first century B.C.E. Dionysius himself wrote history, as well as taught rhetoric, but is more important for his criticism of other writers.[41] Most of the examples Dionysius gives of bad style are from historians. Among these, mostly minor, historians, whose style is "such as no one can bear to read to the final flourish of the pen," Dionysius includes Polybius,[42] who is not surprisingly excluded from those Dionysius recommends: "Herodotus, Thucydides, Xenophon, Philistus, and Theopompus (these being the writers whom I judged to be most suitable for imitation)," primarily in aspects of rhetorical style. Thucydides receives the harshest criticism for failing the historian's most important task of choosing a noble subject matter. He chose "a single war...neither glorious nor fortunate, but which had best never happened at all or, failing that, should have been consigned to silence and oblivion and ignored by later generations."[43] Thucydides is further faulted for where he begins, what events he includes, how he arranges them, and the begrudging attitude he expresses throughout. What is left to admire about Thucydides? The way he portrays emotions and writes with force and intensity. Theopompus, "the most illustrious" student of Isocrates, receives the highest praise for his rhetorical skill, and especially for choosing material that has practical benefit (ὠφέλεια).[44]

The writings of Theopompus are all lost, but his praise by Dionysius indicates his important influence on Hellenistic historiography. By Sacks's estimate, Theopompus is just one of "nearly a thousand [Greek] historians" whose writings were lost and whose legacy must be assessed through fragments preserved in numerous other ancient writers. Sacks describes this diverse lost heritage as defying categorization, increasingly rhetorical, inclined toward the dramatic, entertaining and innovative, giving rise to biography, romance, and universal history.[45]

---

40. Thomas Wiedemann, "Rhetoric in Polybius," in Verdin, Schepens, and de Keyser, *Purposes of History*, 289–300, here 290, 296. See also F. W. Walbank, "Polemic in Polybius," in *Selected Papers: Studies in Greek and Roman History and Historiography* (1962; Cambridge: Cambridge University Press, 1985), 262–79.

41. See Kenneth S. Sacks, "Historiography in the Rhetorical Works of Dionysius of Halicarnassus," *Athenaeum* 61 (1983): 65–87; Clemence Schultze, "Dionysius of Halicarnassus and His Audience," in *Past Perspectives: Studies in Greek and Roman Historical Writing*, ed. I. S. Moxon, J. D. Smart, and A. J. Woodman (Cambridge: Cambridge University Press, 1986), 121–41.

42. Dionysius of Halicarnassus, *On Literary Criticism* 4 (LCL, *Critical Essays* II, 43). W. R. Connor notes that "Polybius was often excluded" from canonical lists of Hellenistic historians ("Historical Writing in the Fourth Century B.C. and in the Hellenistic Period," 458.

43. Dionysius, *Letter to Pompeius* 3. See also Sacks, "Historiography."

44. Dionysius, *Letter to Pompeius* 6.

45. Kenneth S. Sacks, "Historiography, Hellenistic," in *Oxford Classical Dictionary*, 3d ed., 715–16. Klaus Meister calls Theopompus "one of the most widely read and influential Greek historians in Graeco-roman times" ("Theopompus," in *Oxford Classical Dictionary*, 3d ed., 1506). For the fragments see Felix Jacoby, *Die Fragmente der griechischen Historiker*, 2 vols. (1929; reprint, Leiden: Brill, 1962), 2.458–71, translated in Gordon S. Shrimpton, *Theopompus the Historian* (London and Kingston, Ontario: McGill-Queen's University Press, 1991).

A similar assessment is made by Emilio Gabba: the classic historians, Thucydides and Polybius, were not widely read in a culture more interested in popular legends and novels, even paradoxographical and pseudohistorical literature, a trend exemplified in Lucian's satirical "True Stories" (Ἀληθῆ Διηγήματα).[46] T. P. Wiseman reminds us that "in the Greek tradition...the historian's immediate public would *hear* his work, not read it," which encouraged writing for the public ear.[47] It thus should not be surprising that the "historical" literature popular in Hellenistic culture was not that of Thucydides and Polybius, who are quite unlikely to have been the inspiration for the author of Luke-Acts.

Theopompus and Ephorus, rather, were "regarded as the major historians of the Hellenistic period." They established the trend for "universal" or "catholic" history, with its focus on "acts" (πράξεις). The first writing called "Acts" was likely that about Alexander, but the term soon became a common feature of Hellenistic historiography.[48] Theopompus's major writing was *Philippica*, a "history of Philip" of Macedon — in fifty-eight books. It was a universal history of "the deeds of the Greeks and barbarians," as Photius described it.[49] Ephorus survives as the major source of Diodorus Siculus's universal (library of) history, *Bibliotheke*, originally in forty books, imitating Polybius, but now mostly lost.[50]

For a comprehensive view of the narrative literature associated with Hellenistic historiography, see the essays of Arnaldo Momigliano: "Greek Historiography," *History and Theory* 17 (1978): 1–28, with an extensive bibliographical appendix; *Studies in Historiography* (London: Weidenfeld and Nicolson, 1966); *The Development of Greek Biography: Four Lectures* (Cambridge: Harvard University Press, 1971); *Alien Wisdom: The Limits of Hellenization* (Cambridge: Cambridge University Press, 1971); *Essays in Ancient and Modern Historiography* (Middletown, Conn.: Wesleyan University Press, 1977); *On Pagans, Jews, and Christians* (Middletown, Conn.: Wesleyan University Press, 1987); *The Classical Foundations of Modern Historiography* (Berkeley: University of California Press, 1990); *Essay on Ancient and Modern Judaism* (Chicago: University of Chicago Press, 1994).

Other important recent works include Glen W. Bowersock, *Fiction as History: Nero to Julian*, Sather Classical Lectures 58 (Berkeley: University of California Press, 1994); Niklas Holzberg, *The Ancient Novel: An Introduction*, trans. Christine Jackson-Holzberg (German original, 1986; London: Routledge, 1995); J. R. Morgan and Richard Stoneman, eds., *Greek Fiction: The Greek Novel in Context* (London: Routledge, 1994); James Tatum, ed., *The Search for the Ancient Novel* (Baltimore: Johns Hopkins University Press, 1994). An analysis of the ancient novel is the basis for Richard I. Pervo, *Profit with Delight: The Literary Genre of the Acts of the Apostles* (Philadelphia: Fortress, 1987).

Raoul Mortley estimates that only 5 percent of Hellenistic literature has survived, and it suggests "history had become entertainment rather than science," more like modern news becoming "infotainment" (*The Idea of Universal History from Hellenistic Philosophy to Early Christian Historiography,* Texts and Studies in Religion 67 [Lewiston, N.Y.: Edwin Mellen, 1996], 4, 9).

46. Gabba, "True History and False History."

47. T. P. Wiseman, "Practice and Theory in Roman Historiography," *History* 66 (1981): 375–93, here 386.

48. Mortley, *Idea of Universal History*, 33–40. For an overall description of the fragmentary historians see T. J. Luce, *The Greek Historians* (London: Routledge, 1997), 105–22.

49. Jacoby, *Fragmente* 115.24: τάς τε τῶν Ἑλλήνων καὶ Βαρβάρων πράξεις, rendered "the doings of Greeks and barbarians" by Shrimpton, *Theopompus the Historian* (197). The (appended) ending of the Gospel of John (21:25) reflects a similar culture: if everything Jesus did were written down, the world could not hold the books.

50. See Kenneth S. Sacks, *Diodorus Siculus and the First Century* (Princeton: Princeton University Press, 1990); "Diodorus and His Sources: Conformity and Creativity," in *Greek Historiography*, ed. Simon Hornblower (Oxford: Oxford University Press, 1994), 213–32.

Popular Hellenistic historians wrote for a pan-Hellenic audience that "expected to be entertained as well as instructed," which stimulated a variety of kinds of histories: rhetorical, ethical, biographical, patriotic, and "tragic."[51]

For the sake of those who nonetheless still appeal to the professed historiographical methods of Thucydides and Polybius, we must look more closely at the rhetoric of such historiography, before returning to the more popular historians. A. J. Woodman has examined ancient Greco-Roman writers of history to discern their rhetorical understanding of their work. He states his conclusions succinctly:

> Historiography was regarded by the ancients as not essentially different from poetry: each was a branch of rhetoric, and therefore historiography, like poetry, employs the concepts associated with, and relies upon the expectations generated by, a rhetorical genre.... [S]tyle was used by historians to denote the attitude which they adopted towards their material.[52]

Woodman begins with a careful study of Thucydides, already called the "father of history" by Cicero. Whereas Herodotus had "regarded Homer as a historical source and his narrative in some sense a true record of events which actually took place," and had freely used direct speech, "putting into the mouths of historical characters words which they did not utter," Thucydides, in contrast, is often "regarded as the first 'scientific' historian" and is "commonly believed to have set standards of objectivity, accuracy and truth against which all subsequent historians should be judged but which none was ever able to match."[53]

Woodman provides a fresh translation of Thucydides' comments on method, long misused by scholars. Thucydides begins with the speeches and admits

> it was difficult to recall the actuality (τὴν ἀκρίβειαν αὐτήν) of what was said when I heard it myself...; but the speeches have been rendered in accordance with what I thought each person would have said (namely, that which was generally necessary [τὰ δέοντα] given their circumstances at the time), keeping as closely as possible to the general gist (τῆς ξυμπάσης γνώμης) of what was actually (ἀληθῶς) said.
>
> As for the events which took place..., I did not consider it right to describe them either on the basis of what I learned from just anybody or in accordance with what I thought, but from personal experience and after investigating with as much accuracy (ἀκριβείᾳ) as possible each event reported by others. (I.22.1–2)[54]

The necessary conclusion Woodman reaches is that "the majority of each speech ...is the creation of the historian himself." Woodman notes Finley's contention that the speeches already were understood in antiquity as inventions. Thus Woodman posits: "Verbatim speeches and classical historiography are a contradiction in terms."[55]

---

51. Luce, *Greek Historians*, 108, 111–22.
52. A. J. Woodman, *Rhetoric in Classical Historiography: Four Studies* (London: Croom Helm; Portland, Ore.: Areopagitica Press, 1988), x.
53. Ibid., 3, 4, 5, 6.
54. Ibid., 10.
55. Ibid., 13; I. M. Finley, *Ancient History: Evidence and Models* (New York: Viking, 1985), 53 n. 64.

Woodman analyzes Thucydides' statement of purpose directed to those ὅσοι βουλήσονται τῶν γενομένων τὸ σαφὲς σκοπεῖν, who want "to view τὸ σαφές of the things that happened." This is not to be taken as a statement about "complete accuracy" or "the truth." Since Plutarch later compared Thucydides' narrative with the vividness (ἐνάργειαν) of a graphic painting, a better translation for τὸ σαφές would be "realistic," in the sense of "both vivid and probable," which makes it seem "true and reliable to scholars."[56]

Woodman then discusses Dionysius's comparison in *Letter to Pompey* 3 of Thucydides and Herodotus regarding the attitude (διάθεσιν) "the historian himself adopts towards the events he describes." In epideictic rhetoric the goal is to persuade the audience toward a certain point of view, either to praise or to blame, to celebrate or to denounce someone. In that sense, "historiography was itself a form of epideictic," and Dionysius clearly "envisaged the genre [of history] as essentially encomiastic." Dionysius regarded Herodotus "as an encomiastic historian," whereas Thucydides' treatment of Athens was rather critical. The contrast between Herodotus and Thucydides then is the difference between two types of epideictic rhetoric, one of praise and the other of blame.[57] Woodman confirms his interpretation in section 3 of Cicero's *De Oratore*, which "contrasts truth (*ueritas*) with prejudice (*gratia, amor*)," suggesting that he "saw the truth in terms of impartiality." Cicero does not, as is often contended, "present truth as the opposite of what we would call fiction."[58] The issue is not accuracy, but point of view. Lucian's view of writing history further reinforces what Woodman finds in Cicero: "The preface was where a historian was expected to profess impartiality."[59]

In order to better assess Luke's preface in light of these rhetorical conventions of ancient historiography we must first note more specifically how these conventions manifested themselves in the Hellenistic historians. The best preserved of the Hellenistic historians are Polybius (second century B.C.E.), Diodorus Siculus (mid–first century B.C.E.), and Dionysius of Halicarnassus (late first century B.C.E.).

As the major surviving historian from the second century, Polybius is an important transitional figure for evaluating later historians. Not only did he, like Thucydides, claim to be impartial, Polybius redefined the historian's task to include explanations for the narrated events. When reasons were beyond human access, such as with natural disasters, Polybius appealed to God and Fortune (ὁ θεός and ἡ τύχη). In the process of establishing his own credentials, Polybius was

---

56. Woodman, *Rhetoric*, 23, 25, 28.

57. Ibid., 41, 42, 44. Woodman suggests this is the likely reason Thucydides has long appealed to modern historians, who have tended to view his critical approach as close to their own "scientific" approach to history. For a description of the rhetorical categories, see George Kennedy, *New Testament Interpretation through Rhetorical Criticism* (Chapel Hill: University of North Carolina Press, 1984), 19. For Dionysius as encomiastic see David L. Balch, "Two Apologetic Encomia: Dionysius on Rome and Josephus on the Jews," *JSJ* 13 (1982): 102–22.

58. Woodman, *Rhetoric*, 73, 83.

59. Ibid., 87.

highly critical of his predecessors, especially those who relied on the (written) memoirs of others as primary sources for writing history. A good historian begins with personal experience, then adds insights from interviewing eyewitnesses, and finally considers other written accounts. The value of actual experience (ἐμπειρία) was not for "factual accuracy . . . from on-the-spot inspection," but to enable the historian to "know what things are worth discussing," and to examine eyewitnesses effectively, in order to achieve "accuracy" (ἀκριβεία).[60]

Polybius expressed stringent criteria for his speeches. He criticized the practice of others for "inventing words to suit every sort of occasion," but he too acknowledged:

> Of course to select from time to time the proper and appropriate language is a necessary part of our art. But as there is no fixed rule to decide on the quantity and quality of the words to be used on a particular occasion, great care and training is required if we are to instruct and not mislead our readers.

Polybius explained that this required historians "to state clearly the position, the aims, and the circumstances of those deliberating; and then, recording the real speeches made, to use the causes which contributed to the success or failure of the several speakers."[61] Apparently, "the real speeches made" (τοὺς κατ' ἀλήθειαν ῥηθέντας λόγους) were the sources for "the proper and appropriate language" (τοὺς ἁρμόζοντας καὶ καιρίους) that the historian selects.[62] Polybius thus insisted that the selections he made were from "real speeches," although Walbank disputes the literal meaning "the actual words spoken" (τοὺς κατ' ἀλήθειαν εἰρημένους) and suggests something closer to Thucydides, "the sense of what was said."[63] Later Hellenistic historians seemed to follow the dictum of Thucydides to use "realistic" speeches that give the "gist" of what was said.[64]

Two of the crucial terms in the statements about speeches are κατ' ἀλήθειαν and ἀκριβεία/ἀκριβῶς. The best way to render κατ' ἀλήθειαν appears to be "realistic," rather than "real" or "actual," and ἀκριβεία/ἀκριβῶς has less to do with factual "accuracy" than with sufficient detail.[65] The issues raised by these terms keep reappearing in subsequent historians.

---

60. Polybius, *History* 12.1–4; Kenneth S. Sacks, *Polybius on the Writing of History* (Berkeley: University of California Press, 1981), 49, 50–51, 57.

61. Polybius, *History* 12.1.5–6, 8.

62. Sacks, *Polybius,* 79–81.

63. Frank W. Walbank, "Speeches in Greek Historians," in *Selected Papers: Studies in Greek and Roman History and Historiography* (Cambridge: Cambridge University Press, 1985), 242–61.

64. Kenneth S. Sacks, "Rhetorical Approaches to Greek History Writing in the Hellenistic Period," *SBLSP* (1984): 123–33, revised as "Rhetoric and Speeches in Hellenistic Historiography," *Athenaeum* 64 (1986): 383–95.

65. The literature on these terms is extensive and cannot be summarized here. See especially, Walbank, "Speeches"; Sacks, "Rhetoric and Speeches"; Stanley E. Porter, "Thucydides 1.22.1 and Speeches in Acts: Is There a Thucydidean View?" *NovT* 32 (1990): 121–42; Earle Hilgert, "Speeches in Acts and Hellenistic Canons of Historiography and Rhetoric," in *Good News in History: Essays in Honor of Bo Reicke,* ed. Ed. L. Miller (Atlanta: Scholars Press, 1993), 83–109. See also David Balch in this volume (chap. 9).

Dionysius of Halicarnassus likewise comments about his approach to speeches. Scholars have tended to treat him primarily as a teacher of rhetoric. Cary judges his *Antiquities* to be "an outstanding example of the mischievous results of that unnatural alliance between rhetoric and history which was the vogue after the time of Thucydides," and seems most offended by Dionysius's handling of speeches: "In conformity with the rhetorical tradition, he interlarded his narrative with speeches which he managed to insert on every possible occasion from the third book onward,"[66] that is, after the mythological section. Michael Grant provides a more balanced assessment: "Linking rhetoric with political leadership and personal behaviour, [Dionysius] looked favourably upon the political and analytic role of speeches, and inserted (and invented) them when a classical model seemed to fit the situation."[67] The result of the "interlarding" of the narrative with speeches was that speeches "constitute about one-third of the text,"[68] about the same ratio as in the Book of Acts.[69]

Dionysius writes the history of Rome up to the point where Polybius begins. He categorizes Polybius among those historians who "wrote with great exactness" about what they themselves had experienced (διὰ τὴν ἐμπειρίαν ἀκριβῶς ἀνέγραψε, I.6.2). The early period others had passed over deserved a similarly detailed (ἀκριβῶς) portrayal, inasmuch as the very aim of all history is truth and justice (I.6.3, 5). Dionysius then, by citing his sources, counters the potential criticism that he invented this material. He used "narratives and records" (λόγοι τε καὶ ὑπομνηματισμοί), writings for which he first had to learn the language, as well as what he "received orally from men of the greatest learning" (τὰ παρὰ τῶν λογιωτάτων ἀνδρῶν…διδαχῇ παραλαβών), and the rest came from reading previous histories (I.7.2–3). Dionysius's claim to give an accurate, or detailed (ἀκριβῶς), account, when applied to the speeches in his sources, meant he "could paraphrase, recast and adorn them," utilizing classical rhetorical models.[70]

Dionysius's main criticism of Thucydides was that his composed speeches did not fit the occasion, thus failing the decisive criterion of appropriateness (τὸ πρέπον). By Dionysius's day history writing no longer had a place for epideictic rhetoric, which was best suited for ceremonial settings. Real history required oratory fit for public deliberation, before either a jury or a public assembly. In

---

66. Earnest Cary, introduction to LCL, vol. 1, xvi.

67. Michael Grant, *Greek and Roman Historians* (London: Routledge, 1995), 102.

68. Stephen Usher, "The Style of Dionysius of Halicarnassus in the 'Antiquitates Romanae,'" *ANRW* 2.30.1 (1982): 817–38, here 833.

69. According to data in Marion L. Soards, *The Speeches in Acts: Their Content, Context, and Concerns* (Louisville: Westminster/John Knox, 1994), 1. Soards himself makes no comparisons, but cites later (183) Horsley's judgment that the "major speeches" in Acts constitute many times the density of speeches in the histories of Tacitus, Herodotus, Thucydides, Polybius, and Josephus's *Jewish War* (G. H. R. Horsley, "Speeches and Dialogue in Acts," *NTS* 32 [1986]: 609–14), with no mention of Dionysius. Horsley, however, was counting the *number* of speeches, whereas Usher and Soards estimate the *amount* of speech material in the texts.

70. Usher, "Style," 833.

Dionysius's reading of Thucydides[71] historical speeches must be "suitable for debate."[72] By the rhetorical standards of first-century historiography, Polybius's call for using "words actually spoken" was an exception to the dominant pattern, and was possible only because Polybius limited history to what the historian could verify by "autopsy." Polybius's protest against invented speeches had little "effect in changing the current attitude towards writing history."[73]

Diodorus Siculus was not as prominent a historian as either Polybius or Dionysius, but he provides important confirmation about the historiographical ethos of the first century, as well as preserving material from earlier writers. Sacks argues that Diodorus reflects "the intellectual and political attitudes of the late Hellenistic period," especially in his treatment of two essential conventions of historical writing, the introductory prologues and the use of speeches.[74] Diodorus's prologue, written or revised after the work was finished, echoes the prologue of Polybius. Whereas Polybius claimed his distinctive purpose was to show the reader how τύχη (Fortune) guided all the world's affairs toward a common goal (I.4.1–2), for Diodorus, Divine Providence directed the whole of human affairs, making historians servants of Divine Providence (ὑπουργοὶ τῆς Θείας προνοίας, *Bibliotheke* I.1.3). Diodorus lauds history writing because it puts words in harmony with deeds (συμφωνούντων τῶν λόγων τοῖς ἔργοις), and makes full use of rhetoric to both instruct and entertain.

The sweeping scope of Diodorus's universal history, beginning with earliest civilization and covering the inhabited world, meant some parts had to be presented in summaries. Nonetheless, Diodorus claims, even "in the case of things that happened so long ago, we shall give an accurate account, beginning with the earliest times" (ὡς ἂν ἐνδέχηται περὶ τῶν οὕτω παλαιῶν, ἀκριβῶς ἀναγράψομεν ἀπὸ τῶν ἀρχαιοτάτων χρόνων ἀρξάμενοι, I.6.2, LCL). After his "accurate" (ἀκριβῶς), or better, "detailed" summary of the origins of the universe and of human culture, Diodorus then attempts to set out "a full account" concerning "events handed down to memory that happened in the known world" (περὶ τῶν πράξεων τῶν παραδεδομένων μὲν εἰς μνήμην, γενομένων δὲ ἐν τοῖς γνωριζομένοις τόποις τῆς οἰκουμένης, διεξιέναι πειρασόμεθα, I.9.1).

In subsequent books Diodorus uses a briefer preface. The opening of Book 2 is especially pertinent to our interest in Luke-Acts:

> The preceding book (ἡ πρὸ ταύτης βίβλος), being the first (πρώτη) of the whole work, embraces the facts (πράξεις) which concern Egypt, among which are included... And in this present Book we shall set forth the events which took place in Asia in the ancient period, beginning with the time when the Assyrians were the dominant power. (II.1.1a, 3, LCL)

---

71. Dionysius, *On Thucydides;* see W. Kendrick Pritchett, *Dionysius of Halicarnassus, "On Thucydides": English Translation... with Commentary* (Berkeley: University of California Press, 1975).

72. Sacks, "Rhetoric and Speeches," 388–89.

73. Walbank, "Speeches," 260.

74. Sacks, *Diodorus Siculus,* 5.

The gist of this prologue recapitulates the ending of Book 1:

> Now regarding Egypt, the events which history records (ἰστορουμένων) and the things that deserve to be mentioned (μνήμης ἀξίως), this account is sufficient. We shall present in the next Book . . . the events and legendary accounts next in order (τὰς ἑξῆς πράξεις καὶ μυθολογίας). (I.98.10)

This use of *prooemia* reflects the conventions of Diodorus's day, but they are written in his own style and language and are not mere imitations taken from earlier historical writings.[75]

By the time of Lucian's *How to Write History* (better, *How History Should Be Written*) in the second century C.E., the encomiastic tendency in historiography apparently had become so prevalent that he argues for a return to the methodological principles of Thucydides: that speeches "should conform to the speaker and the situation,"[76] that the historian should rely on autopsy as much as possible, and that history should be written more to be useful than to be enjoyable.[77]

Lucian took a satirical approach to the flood of amateur historians that emerged after a Roman military defeat in 162 C.E. He criticizes the many (οἱ πολλοί) who fail to maintain the distinction between history and encomium, as well as the many (οἱ πολλοί) who applaud them (5, 7, 11, 13). Encomium seeks to entertain by heaping praise on the victors, whereas history is supposed to educate by telling the truth. Among Lucian's specific criticisms are beginning with a formal "frigid" preface, then suddenly shifting to the vernacular, and the fad of imitating Thucydides, especially in unrealistic speeches. Lucian's prescription for good history writing emphasizes the beginning (ἀρχή), the arrangement (τάξις), and the proportion (μέτρος) of what is presented, as well as knowing what to include, leave out, and how to put it together (6).

Lucian describes the best writers as able to achieve powerful expression (δύναμιν ἑρμηνευτικήν) through hard work and "imitation of the ancients." Lucian is thus not against imitation, only against the pretense that results from overdone rhetorical flourishes. For instance, Lucian satirizes the eyewitness claims of one historian this way: he described so vividly (οὕτως ἀκριβῶς) the details of a battle scene, but the audience "knew for a fact" (ἀκριβῶς εἰδώς) that he had not seen so much as a painting of a battle.[78]

Lucian's model of a good historian is someone who first assembles the facts (τὰ πράγματα) with much care, preferably as an eyewitness, or at least by relying on those who are impartial. The historian makes notes (ὑπόμνημα) before producing an orderly arrangement (ἐπιθεὶς τὴν τάξιν), which he then enhances stylistically (47–48). "All this should be [done] in moderation," by a clear mind

---

75. Ibid., 9–22.
76. Sacks, "Rhetoric and Speeches," 386.
77. Usher, "Style," 837.
78. Lucian, *How to Write History* 29, 34.

"accurately centered" (ἀκριβεῖ τὸ κέντρον), to let "fact...speak for itself" (49–50). Finally, a preface in proportion to the subject matter is added to instruct the audience about the importance of what is to follow, with a gentle transition to the body of the narrative (διήγησις, 55). If someone must be introduced to make a speech, it should be suitable, clear, and unbiased, but within these restraints the historian is allowed to display his rhetorical skills (58). These guidelines provide the rule and standard of impartial history (κανὼν καὶ στάθμη ἱστορίας δικαίας, 63).

Lucian himself did not write a major historical work, but chose rather to compose "True Histories," masterful parodies of the trends in "historical" writing of the day. He began with a proper rhetorical preface (῞Ωσπερ...οὕτω δὴ...ἡγοῦμαι...) that sets the reader up for his entertaining "imaginary travels." Unlike his contemporaries, he is truthful enough to say, "I am a liar..., I am not telling a word of truth." He concludes the preface with a fine parody:

γράφω τοίνυν περὶ ὧν μήτε εἶδον μήτε ἔπαθον μήτε παρ' ἄλλων ἐπυθόμην, ἔτι δὲ μήτε ὅλως ὄντων μήτε τὴν ἀρχὴν γενέσθαι δυναμένων. διὸ δεῖ τοὺς ἐντυγχάνοντας μηδαμῶς πιστεύειν αὐτοῖς.

I am writing about things which I have neither seen nor experienced nor learned from others — which, in fact, do not exist at all and, in the nature of things, cannot exist. Therefore my readers should on no account believe in them.

The reader, then or now, who has any experience reading "historical" prefaces recognizes all the essential motifs Lucian spoofs.

Lucian's "lie" is successful because his fantastic voyage "is narrated in a fashion which makes it seem credible." Although it is throughout a parody of Homer's *Odyssey*, Lucian "has the narrator relate his adventures in a matter-of-fact style, which sounds like an eyewitness report," using "many details which are realistic and believable in terms of actual experience."[79]

Lucian's parody suggests a critique of popular culture in which the lines between "history" and fiction had become seriously blurred. G. W. Bowersock compares Lucian's "True Stories" (Ἀληθῆ Διηγήματα) to its contemporary, Celsus's "True Discourse" (Ἀληθῆ Λόγος), in which "the alleged truth is embedded in the fiction" Celsus creates to expose the Christian Gospels as fiction.[80] Bowersock sees here evidence for a second-century C.E. "problem that conspicuously unsettled thoughtful people of the time," a problem rooted in Greek culture. Lucian recognized that Herodotus, the "Father of History," was as much a teller of tales as was Homer.[81] Lucian's parody is equally heir to both, and Lucian's disclaimer, that nothing he says is true, is of course itself not true. Bowersock finds in these two writers a sign of the times:

---

79. Aristoula Georgiadou and David H. J. Larmour, "Lucian and Historiography: 'De Historia Conscribenda' and 'Verae Historiae,'" *ANRW* 2.34.2 (1994): 1448–1509, here 1489, 1491–92.

80. Bowersock, *Fiction as History*, 2–4.

81. Ibid., 1, 4.

It is symptomatic of the time that both Celsus and Lucian should proclaim truth even as they immerse themselves in fiction, that they should attack fiction by creating fiction, that they should confuse lies and admitted fabrication. Lucian makes it clear that it would surely be reassuring to his cultivated readers to know at the outset that what they are reading is all mendacious. Yet, as they read on, they discover that in some respect it is not. This is the reverse of the experience of readers like Celsus confronted with the Gospel narratives. There they are under the impression that this is an accurate record of what happened, but as they read on, they have the disquieting feeling that some of it may or must be mendacious. Celsus and Lucian thus give us two sides of the same coin, and this coin is perhaps the most important currency in the intellectual commerce of the Roman Empire.[82]

The cultural skepticism of the second century C.E. about historical truth and fiction reflects centuries of historiographical developments. The prefaces from the "historical" writings during this period express the rhetoric of these concerns. The preface of Luke is no exception. Before we assess Luke's place within this tradition, one final component requires greater attention, the legacy of Josephus as a contributor to the development of Hellenistic historiography.

Josephus and Hellenistic Historiography

In our initial look at prefaces in Greek historical writings, we noted the prefaces in the two books of Josephus's *Against Apion*. Both prefaces are retrospective. The first one refers to Josephus's *Antiquities* and the second preface refers to "the first volume." Both prefaces likewise contain the same dedication to Epaphroditus, called κράτιστε in the first preface, the same term used in the preface of Luke for the dedication to Theophilus. Features of these two prefaces obviously call to mind the two prefaces of Luke and Acts.[83]

Josephus also provides a digression in section 10 (1.53–56) that defends his work in the *Antiquities* against the charge that it reads like a schoolboy's exercise. In his defense he uses standard historiographical rhetoric. He sought to present παράδοσιν πράξεων ἀληθινῶν ("actual facts"), by learning about them ἀκριβῶς, either from παρηκολουθηκότα τοῖς γεγονόσιν ("following closely what happened") or παρὰ τῶν εἰδότων πυνθανόμενον ("inquiring from those who knew"). Of the war itself he was πολλῶν μὲν αὐτουργὸς πράξεων, πλείστων δ᾽ αὐτόπτης ("actor in many events and eyewitness of most"). The reader recognizes all the regularly professed qualifications for writing history. However, *Against Apion* is not itself a historical narrative. The narrative that best typifies classical historiography is Josephus's *History of the Jewish War against the Romans*. He insists he has no intention of "exaggerating the deeds

---

82. Ibid., 6–7.
83. See the comparative analysis in F. Gerald Downing, "Redaction Criticism: Josephus' *Antiquities* and the Synoptic Gospels (II)," *JSNT* 9 (1980): 29–48, especially the summary on p. 31 of the very few terms from Luke's preface that lack a parallel in Josephus.

of my compatriots," but will recount the actions of both sides μετ' ἀκριβείας (*War* 1.9), just the claim of "impartiality" that Woodman said historiography demanded. The irony of course is that Josephus, the Jewish military officer, had switched his allegiance from Jerusalem to Rome before becoming a historian.

As Harry Attridge notes, Josephus's claim "to detached, non-partisan objectivity is hardly supported by the details of the narrative."[84] Attridge offers this further assessment about Josephus:

> Jewish traditions have been hellenized, often with a dramatic or romantic tendency. Similar novelistic characteristics have been found in other sections of the historian's work.
>
> Josephus was also concerned with rhetorical effects and, like classical historians generally, freely composed speeches for his leading characters through which his own interpretation of events is presented.[85]

In an earlier treatment of Josephus's *Antiquities*, Attridge identified "an affinity with the rhetorical ideals represented by Dionysius." In the case of Josephus the result was "an apologetic plea for the Jewish people and their customs." Josephus also saw in "the theology of the Deuteronomistic history" an interpretive scheme similar to the role of God's providence (πρόνοια), which is prominent in Dionysius.[86]

Gregory Sterling has recently offered an alternative interpretation of Josephus's historiography. He argues that some works of Jewish history fit a pattern he calls "apologetic historiography," defined as "the story of a subgroup of people in an extended prose narrative written by a member of the group who follows the

---

84. Harold W. Attridge, *The Interpretation of Biblical History in the "Antiquitates Judaicae" of Flavius Josephus*, HDR 7 (Missoula, Mont.: Scholars Press, 1976), 50.

85. Harold W. Attridge, "Jewish Historiography," in *Early Judaism and Its Modern Interpreters*, ed. R. A. Kraft and G. W. E. Nickelsburg (Atlanta: Scholars Press, 1986), 326. Robert Hall suggests that Josephus's ability to write credible narrative was a skill acquired as part of "standard Roman rhetorical education" ("Josephus, *Contra Apionem*, and Historical Inquiry in the Roman Rhetorical Schools," in *Josephus' "Contra Apionem,"* ed. Louis H. Feldman and John R. Levinson, AGJU 34 [Leiden: Brill, 1996], 229–49, here 249).

86. Attridge, *Interpretation of Biblical History*, 51–52, 86, 164. David Balch ("Two Apologetic Encomia") describes another example of Josephus's use of rhetoric that has a parallel in Dionysius. See also Balch's more sustained comparison suggested in "Comments on the Genre and a Political Theme of Luke-Acts: A Preliminary Comparison of Two Hellenistic Historians," *SBLSP* 28 (1989): 343–61.

The influence of Deuteronomistic historiography on Luke-Acts is beyond the scope of this particular study, but see esp. David Moessner, *Lord of the Banquet: The Literary and Theological Significance of the Lukan Travel Narrative* (Minneapolis: Fortress, 1989; Harrisburg, Pa.: Trinity Press International, 1998); also Daryl D. Schmidt, "The Historiography of Acts: Deuteronomistic or Hellenistic?" *SBLSP* 24 (1985): 417–27; Brian S. Rosner, "Acts and Biblical History," in *The Book of Acts in Its First-Century Setting*, vol. 1: *The Book of Acts in Its Ancient Literary Setting*, ed. Bruce W. Winter and Andrew D. Clarke (Grand Rapids, Mich.: Eerdmans, 1993), 65–82; Thomas Römer and Jean-Daniel Macchi, "Luke, Disciple of the Deuteronomistic School," in *Luke's Literary Achievement: Collected Essays*, ed. C. M. Tuckett, JSNTSup 116 (Sheffield: Sheffield Academic Press, 1995), 91–109. For Luke's imitation of the LXX see Eckhard Plümacher, *Lukas als hellenistischer Schriftsteller: Studien zur Apostelgeschichte* (Göttingen: Vandenhoeck & Ruprecht, 1972). Plümacher also sees similarities with Dionysius's use of speeches in "Die Missionsreden der Apostelgeschichte und Dionys von Halikarnass," *NTS* 39 (1993): 161–77. The English translation appears as chapter 10 in this volume.

group's own traditions but Hellenizes them in an effort to establish the identity of the group with the setting of the larger world."[87] Sterling traces this genre, derived from Greek ethnography, to Berossus in the fourth century B.C.E. It developed mostly as a tradition within Jewish historiography, with its "greatest representative" in the *Antiquities* of Josephus. While he acknowledges Josephus's indebtedness to Dionysius, Sterling sees important differences:

> Yet for all his structural and historiographical dependence on Dionysius, Josephus clearly distances himself from the Greek tradition in the writing of the A[ntiquitates]. This can be seen from the polemics against Occidental historians within the A[ntiquitates] and even more from the sustained attack against Greek historiography and defense of Oriental — especially Jewish — historiography that opens C[ontra] A[pion]. Josephus thus exploited Dionysius but maintained his distance when forced to declare his allegiances.

Josephus's distinct achievement in *Antiquities* is that it "more successfully Hellenizes the Jewish story in form than any of its predecessors."[88]

As a near-contemporary of the author of Luke-Acts, Josephus highlights for us one way in which the Hellenistic culture intersected with Jewish approaches to writing. Further exploration of this nexus will surely add insight to the issues explored here.

Implications for Reading Luke-Acts

A wide range of concluding observations can be made from the data considered here, so we must be selective.[89] We began by setting aside the question of genre. The consensus among historiographers seems to be that "history" was not a narrowly defined genre in ancient Greek writing, but rather was on a wide spectrum of prose writing styles. Furthermore, the framework for making such distinctions at the time was based on rhetorical categories, not literary ones. Rhetoric has been called "the monarch of Hellenic education," and during the Hellenistic period history "was perhaps the most widely practiced and abundantly produced form of literature."[90] It thus seems unlikely that attempts to settle once for all whether Luke and/or Acts are really "history" or "biography," or something else, can be successful.

---

87. Gregory E. Sterling, *Historiography and Self-Definition: Josephos, Luke-Acts, and Apologetic Historiography,* NovTSup 64 (Leiden: Brill, 1992), 17.

88. Gregory E. Sterling, "Luke-Acts and Apologetic Historiography," *SBLSP* 28 (1989): 326–42, here 332–36.

89. The sense of "reading" mentioned in the subhead is not that of a general literary approach, e.g., that of Charles H. Talbert, in *Reading Luke* and *Reading Acts,* in Reading the New Testament Series (Crossroad), but closer to that of Kurz, *Reading Luke-Acts: Dynamics of Biblical Narrative.* See also F. Gerald Downing, "Theophilus's First Reading of Luke-Acts," in *Luke's Literary Achievement: Collected Essays,* ed. C. M. Tuckett, JSNTSup 116 (Sheffield: Sheffield Academic Press, 1995), 91–109.

90. Connor, "Historical Writing," 470.

If we treat Luke's opening sentence as the ancient equivalent of a title page, it is difficult to overlook the amount of historiographical language.[91] By itself, however, this observation is not a transparent clue to the author's purpose, nor a narrow signal to the reader how to interpret what follows. Historiographical rhetoric was highly conventional and used in a variety of literary settings (as Lucian's "True Stories" remind us). The mere presence of a word such as ἀκριβῶς can hardly bear the weight often placed on it. It fits with other clues in the preface that together belong with a "narrative" mode — the author does indeed call this a διήγησις. But a narrative, any narrative, is always put together ("ordered") by someone from some perspective. Whenever "events fulfilled among us" constitutes a narrative, the result is never limited to "accurate facts." Finally, the preface itself is clear about its overall goal — to be convincing, to provide ἀσφάλεια.

How does this kind of preface affect the way the narrative is read? The narrative itself begins, without transition: "Once upon a time..." (Ἐγένετο ἐν ταῖς ἡμέραις...). The stylistic contrast with the preface could hardly be greater. Luke 1:5 transports the reader back to an earlier world, when Herod was king of Judea and "there happened to be this priest named Zechariah." As the opening of the narrative further unfolds the informed reader soon recognizes that this narrative world resembles the biblical narrative world. The motifs are familiar to anyone who has heard the stories of ancient Israel: a divine messenger appears to a childless couple, "Fear not, she will bear a son, and you shall name him..."[92]

---

91. In addition to the key terms already discussed that are typical of historical writing, e.g., διήγησις, πράγματα, αὐτόπται, παρηκολουθηκώς, ἀκριβῶς, καθεξῆς, it is equally important to note typical rhetorical features of historiographical prefaces, such as πολλοί, ἀρχή, and πᾶς. A striking parallel is preserved from an author contemporary to Luke-Acts, Philo of Byblos. Although *The Phoenician History* is lost, the surviving fragments include this preface preserved by Eusebius, composed in a single sentence:

Τούτων οὕτως ἐχόντων ὁ Σαγχουνιάθων, ἀνὴρ δὴ πολυμαθὴς καὶ πολυπράγμων γενόμενος καὶ τὰ ἐξ ἀρχῆς..., παρὰ πάντων εἰδέναι ποθῶν, πολυφροντιστικῶς ἐξεμάστευσεν τὰ Τααύτου....

Since these things were so, Sanchuniathon, truly a man of great learning and curiosity, who desired to learn from everyone about what happened from the first..., quite carefully searched out the works of Taautos....

See Harold W. Attridge and Robert A. Oden, Jr., *Philo of Byblos, "The Phoenician History": Introduction, Critical Text, Translation, Notes*, CBQMS 9 (Washington, D.C.: Catholic Biblical Association of America, 1981), 28, 29. For an overall assessment of Philo's historiography, see R. A. Oden, Jr., "Philo of Byblos and Hellenistic Historiography," *Palestine Exploration Quarterly* 110 (1978): 115–26.

92. A sample of LXX motifs in Luke 1:7–13: καὶ ἦν Σαρα στεῖρα (Gen. 11:30); ὤφθη δὲ αὐτῷ ἄγγελος κυρίου (Exod. 3:2); Μὴ φοβοῦ, Αβραμ (Gen. 15:1); ἰδοὺ Σαρα ἡ γυνή σου τέξεταί σοι υἱόν, καὶ καλέσεις τὸ ὄνομα αὐτοῦ Ισαακ (Gen. 17:19). Raymond Brown notes that 90 percent of the vocabulary of Luke 1–2 is found in the LXX (*The Birth of the Messiah: A Commentary on the Infancy Narratives in the Gospels of Matthew and Luke*, new updated edition, ABRL [New York: Doubleday, 1993], 623). A strong case is made for Luke's Septuagintal imitations in Fearghus Ó Fearghail, "The Imitation of the Septuagint in Luke's Infancy Narrative," *Proceedings of the Irish Biblical Association* 12 (1989): 58–78. Ó Fearghail calls the ἐγένετο constructions Septuagintalisms that are also Lucanisms. In addition there are "Lucan-created septuagintal-type" expressions in Luke 1–2 that have no exact LXX parallels, but are surely meant to sound Septuagintal, e.g., Luke 1:6b,

This style of biblical language dominates Luke 1–2 and gradually recedes after that, but traces remain throughout Luke and into Acts.[93]

In the rhetoric of historiographical prefaces, I noted the importance attached to choosing the beginning of the narrative. Luke would seem to have fallen prey to one of Lucian's complaints: a formal preface suddenly shifting to a vernacular narrative.[94] Lucian in fact spoofs just such a style in his mythic "True History," with the narrative proper beginning, "Once upon a time," after a preface that parodies the formalities of pretentious histories.

Luke's narrative opening is not an arbitrary "once upon a time" in the distant past. It is a past moment of biblical proportions. Telling it in the same Septuagintal style used for the epic stories of Israel's origins conveys to the reader something of the significance of the events described, presented as "fulfilled among us." These events happen to characters whose portraits are composites of biblical heroes.[95] The characters so described are actors in events of momentous significance.[96]

The author's claim to have "followed everything closely from the beginning" appears to mean from the point at which it is necessary to begin this story. The opening scenes then imitate the style of the Septuagint so completely that the reader would not likely make any association with the "eyewitnesses" mentioned in the preface.[97] The author has thus established clear literary license in how this story is going to be told. It will be an orderly account, following the dictates of narrative logic.

Nowhere is the Septuagintal language more prominent than in the Lukan canticles, composed almost entirely of expressions from the LXX. Raymond Brown further notes that they can be easily detached from their present liter-

---

7b (59, 62). Ó Fearghail gives extensive Septuagintal examples, both direct parallels and Lukan imitations.

93. David L. Mealand reminds us that some of the "common LXX" stylistic features identified in Acts can be found in other Hellenistic historians ("Hellenistic Historians and the Style of Acts," *ZNW* 82 [1991]: 42–66). He includes redundant participles (e.g., "rising, answering, going") and the infinitive with ἐν τῷ.

94. In his criticism of unsuccessful attempts of most (οἱ πολλοί) historians, Lucian characterizes one, a military surgeon, as an "amateur" (ἰδιώτης), who began with a "frigid" preface, than suddenly shifted to vernacular language (*How History Should be Written* 13, 16). Downing ("Theophilus's First Reading," 97) associates these amateurs with the "technical" writers described by Alexander (*Preface*).

95. Ó Fearghail, "Imitation of the Septuagint," 72–73, cites numerous parallels. S. John Roth argues that the paradigmatic characters of the early chapters establish the LXX as Luke's primary intertext, which conditions how the authorial audience perceives later characters in the narrative (*The Blind, the Lame, and the Poor: Character Types in Luke-Acts*, JSNTSup 144 [Sheffield: Sheffield Academic Press, 1977], esp. 88–94).

96. For the paradigmatic use of historical figures in Hellenistic narratives, see William S. Kurz, "Narrative Models for Imitation in Luke-Acts," in *Greeks, Romans, and Christians: Essays in Honor of Abraham J. Malherbe*, ed. David L. Balch, Everett Ferguson, and Wayne A. Meeks [Minneapolis: Fortress, 1990], 171–89).

97. This sudden shift complicates any attempt to describe the authorial audience(s): literate enough, as was Theophilus, to appreciate the preface, yet familiar with the storytelling mode of Jewish scriptures.

ary context and seem to function similarly to the speeches in Acts: "They give voice to general sentiments that are appropriate for the dramatis personae in the setting in which they are placed."[98] Both the birth-story canticles and the speeches in Acts incorporate earlier materials, but in neither case is there reason to think these are reports of historical utterances.[99]

The use of Septuagintal portraiture is not limited to the opening of Luke's Gospel. In the final recounting of Paul's "conversion" in Acts 26:16–18, the commission charge is directly reminiscent of the commissionings of Jeremiah and Ezekiel.[100] The use of Septuagintal language to portray Paul's Gentile mission is part of a stylistic strategy[101] that contributes to the sense of divine direction in the narrative.[102]

Paul's speech in Acts 26 exemplifies well how the speeches in Acts fit within the rhetoric of Hellenistic historiography. An overall consideration of the speeches is beyond the scope here, but this speech can serve to illustrate the matter.[103]

---

98. Brown, *Birth of the Messiah*, 251, 347, 645.

99. Ibid., 239, 347. Brown thinks "there is every reason to believe that Luke himself composed many or all the speeches he has placed on the lips of Peter and Paul in Acts" (239), whereas the awkward fit of the canticles suggests Luke did not compose them himself. George A. Kennedy concurs, e.g., regarding the Magnificat: "This amounts to prosopopoeia, the exercise of the rhetorical schools in which a historical or mythological character is imagined in some situation and his or her feelings expressed" (*New Testament Interpretation through Rhetorical Criticism* [Chapel Hill: University of North Carolina Press, 1984], 107).

100. See Benjamin J. Hubbard, "Commissioning Stories in Luke-Acts: A Study of Their Antecedents, Form, and Content," *Semeia* 8 (1977): 103–26, esp. 120–21; idem, "The Role of Commissioning Accounts in Acts," in *Perspectives on Luke-Acts*, ed. Charles H. Talbert (Danville, Va.: Association of Baptist Professors of Religion, 1978), 187–98. The following are examples of Luke's composite of prophetic language in Acts 26:16–18, which has no parallels in the two earlier accounts of Paul's conversion (Acts 9:3–9; 22:6–11): στῆθι ἐπὶ τοὺς πόδας σου (Ezek. 2:1); ἐξαιρετσθαί σε (Jer. 1:8); εἰς ἔθνη (Jer. 1:5); οὓς ἐξαποστέλλω ἐγώ σε (Jer. 1:7; Ezek. 2:3); εἰς φῶς ἐθνῶν ἀνοῖξαι ὀφθαλμοὺς (Isa. 42:6–7); τὸ σκότος εἰς φῶς (Isa. 42:16). The phrase "from darkness to light" had become "stereotypical conversion language" (Beverly Roberts Gaventa, *From Darkness to Light: Aspects of Conversion in the New Testament*, Overtures to Biblical Theology 20 [Philadelphia: Fortress, 1986], 87). The combination of light and voice is conventional in theophanies (Marvin W. Meyer, "The Light and Voice on the Damascus Road," *Forum* 2,4 [1986]: 27–35).

101. Samples of this widely recognized phenomenon are plentiful in the literature. For two approaches, see John Drury, *Tradition and Design in Luke's Gospel: A Study in Early Christian Historiography* (Atlanta: John Knox Press, 1976); Craig A. Evans and James A. Sanders, *Luke and Scripture: The Function of Sacred Tradition in Luke-Acts* (Minneapolis: Fortress, 1993). The classical case for Septuagintal imitation in the speeches in Acts is still Plümacher, *Lukas als hellenistischer Schriftsteller*, 38–79. For an overall review of Plümacher's approach see Soards, *The Speeches in Acts*, 135–43.

102. See John T. Squires, *The Plan of God in Luke-Acts*, SNTSMS 76 (Cambridge: Cambridge University Press, 1993); David P. Moessner, "The 'Script' of the Scriptures in Acts: Suffering as God's 'Plan' (βουλή) for the World for the 'Release of Sins,'" in Witherington, *History, Literature, and Society in the Book of Acts*, 218–50. For the larger context, see G. W. Trompf, *The Idea of Historical Recurrence in Western Thought: From Antiquity to the Reformation* (Berkeley: University of California Press, 1976). For other prophetic elements in Acts' treatment of Paul, see David P. Moessner, "Paul and the Pattern of the Prophet Like Moses in Acts," *SBLSP* 22 (1983): 203–12.

103. The literature on the speeches is covered well by Soards, *The Speeches in Acts*. A cautious survey of both the ancient evidence and modern scholarship is provided by Conrad Gempf, "Public Speaking and Published Accounts," in Winter and Clarke, *Book of Acts in Its Ancient Literary Setting*, 259–303. For additional items that compare Acts 26 with Acts 9 and 22, see Ronald D. Witherup,

The prophetic language in 26:16–18 is only one of the noteworthy features of this speech. Paul gives a second retelling of the experience narrated in chapter 9, which he described somewhat differently, to a different audience, in chapter 22. Read in light of the rhetoric of Hellenistic historiography, the progression of these three accounts is not primarily a matter of discrepancies to be solved, but of narrative strategy. Witherup notes the shift in focus from the narrative account to the two speeches:

> The greater role which Paul plays in each successive account of his conversion / call, the less is played by Ananias (and by Paul's companions). Paul increasingly shows his ability to live up to his commission as he moves from helpless victim, to a defense before his fellow Jews, to a full-blown defense before the civil authorities. ...In each case the brightness of the light increases, the companions recede into the background, and the immediacy of Paul's revelation is heightened.[104]

Daniel Marguerat likewise contrasts how the two speeches reinterpret the narrative account. The first speech (Acts 22) presents "Paul's uninterrupted faithfulness to the Jewish tradition," in order "to interpret the Damascus road event as a fulfilment of the apostle's Jewishness." In the second speech, he is "no longer...crushed down by the light: in Acts 26, he is rather rereading this numinous encounter as a prophetic call to become himself a light, that is, a bearer of salvation beyond Israel."[105]

The narrative effect of Paul's speech in Acts 26 is to make the entire episode of his blindness highly symbolic: "Luke works a further, stunning variation on the motif of blindness and vision. All reference to blindness and seeing on Saul's part has been dropped and is transposed to the recipients of his mission, the people of Israel and the Gentiles."[106] Paul's eyes were opened in Acts 9 so that he could be sent to open the eyes of others. The voice commissioning him is none other than that of Jesus of Nazareth (26:9), who began his own mission, in Luke's account, at Nazareth, by claiming to fulfill Isaiah's promise: "...sent...to proclaim...recovery of sight to the blind" (Luke 4:18; Isa. 61:1). Paul's defense speeches are now over, and he journeys to Rome for one last chance "to convince them about Jesus." Some are convinced, some are not, which prods Paul to conclude that Isaiah was again right about this people: "They have shut their eyes" (Acts 28:27; Isa. 6:10). The result is good news: "God's salvation (τὸ σωτήριον τοῦ θεοῦ) has been sent to the Gentiles" (Acts 28:28).

"Functional Redundancy in the Acts of the Apostles: A Case Study," *JSNT* 48 (1992): 67–86, and Daniel Marguerat, "Saul's Conversion (Acts 9, 22, 26) and the Multiplication of Narrative in Acts," in *Luke's Literary Achievement: Collected Essays*, ed. C. M. Tuckett, JSNTSup 116 (Sheffield: Sheffield Academic Press, 1995), 127–55. On this speech itself, see John J. Kilgallen, "Paul before Agrippa (Acts 26,2–23): Some Considerations," *Biblica* 68 (1988): 170–95. Long ago van Unnik recognized the need to treat the speeches "within the framework of ancient historiography and Greek rhetorical theory," one of the shortcomings of Dibelius's approach ("Luke's Second Book," 58).

104. Witherup, "Functional Redundancy," 78, 79.

105. Marguerat, "Saul's Conversion," 147, 152.

106. Dennis Hamm, "Paul's Blindness and Its Healing: Clues to Symbolic Intent (Acts 9, 22 and 26)," *Biblica* 71 (1990): 63–72, here 66–67. None of these observations is noted by Soards.

Luke's second volume thus closes by echoing the words of Isaiah that frame Luke's first volume. John the Baptist is identified as Isaiah's "voice of one crying out in the wilderness," whose message is: "Everyone will see God's salvation (τὸ σωτήριον τοῦ θεοῦ)" (Luke 3:4–6; Isa. 40:3–5). In the opening infancy canticles, when Simeon first sees the infant Jesus, he praises God: "My eyes have seen your salvation (τὸ σωτήριόν σου), which you prepared for all peoples, a light for revelation to the Gentiles" (Luke 2:28–32). Simeon's added commentary can be seen as prophetic of the plot of Luke-Acts: he is "destined [to cause] the falling and rising of many in Israel, to be a sign spoken against" (ἀντιλεγόμενον, Luke 2:34).

Acts ends with the fulfillment of Simeon's double-edged prophecy. In hindsight Paul remembers those who opposed him (ἀντιλεγόντων), and his audience gives him one last chance to tell them about this sect they know to be "everywhere spoken against" (γνωστὸν ἡμῖν ὅτι πανταχοῦ ἀντιλέγεται). Paul explains the apparent lack of success by citing Isa. 6:9–10, as noted above, and then declares what they ought to know: "God's salvation has been sent to the Gentiles" (γνωστὸν ἔστω ὑμῖν ὅτι τοῖς ἔθνεσιν ἀπεστάλη τοῦτο τὸ σωτήριον τοῦ θεοῦ, Acts 28:28, in the manner of Peter's opening speech in Acts: τοῦτο ὑμῖν γνωστὸν ἔστω, 2:14). Paul's final words, "And they [emphatic] will listen" (αὐτοὶ καὶ ἀκούσονται), once more echo the prophetic call of Ezekiel heard in Acts 26:16–18, beginning with στῆθι ἐπὶ τοὺς πόδας σου (Ezek. 2:1), ἐξαποστέλλω ἐγώ σε (Ezek. 2:3). Ezekiel was warned not to be dismayed when his audience failed to listen (Ezek. 2:5–7). He was then consoled: "If I had sent (ἐξαπέστειλα) you to other peoples, they would listen" (οὗτοι ἂν εἰσήκουσαν, Ezek. 3:6).

We have already noted features of Paul's concluding speech in Acts that suggest its appropriateness as the ending of Luke's second volume. Scholars nonetheless have often been troubled by the seemingly unfinished ending of Acts.[107] Rhetorical considerations, however, further support the appropriateness of this ending. A metrical analysis of Greek prose rhythms (prosody) in Luke-Acts indicates that the ending of Acts (28:28–31) has the same elo-

---

107. For a sample of the many proposals, see G. W. Trompf, "On Why Luke Declined to Recount the Death of Paul: Acts 27–28 and Beyond," in *Luke-Acts: New Perspectives from the Society of Biblical Literature Seminar*, ed. Charles H. Talbert (New York: Crossroad, 1984), 225–39; H. van de Sandt, "Acts 28,28: No Salvation for the People of Israel? An Answer in the Perspective of the LXX," *ETL* 70 (1994): 341–58. From the perspective of an appropriate plot ending, along the lines suggested above, see Kurz, *Reading Luke-Acts*, 28–31. For the theological issues involved with "Jewish rejection" and the ending of Acts, see Daryl D. Schmidt, "Anti-Judaism and the Gospel of Luke," in *Anti-Judaism and the Gospels*, ed. William R. Farmer (Harrisburg, Pa.: Trinity Press International, 1999), 63–96. The classical hypotheses for the abrupt ending are stated succinctly, and rejected, by Conzelmann: (1) Luke had planned to write a third volume; (2) Acts was composed before Paul's trial had been completed; (3) according to Roman law, the case would have been dismissed after two years if the plaintiff had failed to appear by that time; (4) Paul's martyrdom was originally narrated, but was then removed (*Acts of the Apostles* [Hermeneia; Philadelphia: Fortress, 1987], 228). William F. Brosend proposes that an abrupt ending was modeled on the gospel of Mark ("The Means of Absent Ends," in *History, Literature, and Society in the Book of Acts*, 348–62).

quence of rhetorical style as the two prefaces do, a style associated with public oratory.[108]

Daniel Marguerat offers a different kind of rhetorical explanation for the ending of Acts, the rhetoric of silence, contending there is no inadvertence here on the part of the author, who rather "organizes a concerted displacement of the reader's expectation which he has methodically built up to that point."[109] Luke was following a convention of Hellenistic historiography that an appropriate ending was as crucial as a well-chosen beginning. An appropriate ending, however, does not mean closure must be achieved by actually narrating the anticipated events.

The language of the concluding verse echoes major themes in Luke-Acts. Paul, like Jesus, preaches and teaches. Paul's preaching (κηρύσσων τὴν βασιλείαν τοῦ θεοῦ) continues the characteristic activity of Jesus (κηρύσσων... τὴν βασιλείαν τοῦ θεοῦ, Luke 8:1, also 4:43) and of his disciples (ἀπέστειλεν αὐτοὺς κηρύσσειν τὴν βασιλείαν τοῦ θεοῦ, Luke 9:2), including Jesus' postresurrection activity (λέγων τὰ περὶ τῆς βασιλείας τοῦ θεοῦ, Acts 1:3). Paul's teaching (διδάσκων τὰ περὶ τοῦ κυρίου Ἰησοῦ Χριστοῦ) adds new content to what Jesus had taught, typically left unspecified in the preface of Acts (περὶ πάντων...ὧν ἤρξατο ὁ Ἰησοῦς ποιεῖν τε καὶ διδάσκειν, Acts 1:1). Even Apollos had been teaching ("accurately" to be sure) about Jesus (ἐδίδασκεν ἀκριβῶς τὰ περὶ τοῦ Ἰησοῦ, Acts 18:25).

What is the "accurate" teaching about Jesus, as Luke understands it in Acts? If the ending of Acts is a fit conclusion to the whole of Luke-Acts, what is its message? How should the reader hear Paul's last words, "the Gentiles will listen"? Does this good news of "God's salvation" mean bad news for those in the narrative who have not listened? What does the use of Isa. 6:9–10 suggest about Luke's understanding of the narrative audience of "Jews" to whom Paul directs Isaiah's words? These questions remain among the most disputed regarding Luke-Acts. The considerations presented above, focused on Luke's preface, imply ways of answering these questions that can only be summarized here.

The role of "anti-Judaism" in Luke-Acts has become one of the major ways to address the above questions, with no consensus forthcoming.[110] The narrative sequence of Luke-Acts, read in light of Luke's preface, strongly emphasizes continuity, not discontinuity, at the end of Acts. It would seem difficult to miss "salvation for all" as a major theme of Luke-Acts, and even more difficult to see how the narrative could accomplish this goal at the exclusion of "Israel" or "the Jews." The "events fulfilled among us" are thoroughly rooted in the antici-

---

108. Folker Siegert, "Mass Communication and Prose Rhythm in Luke-Acts," in *Rhetoric and the New Testament*, ed. Stanley E. Porter and Thomas H. Olbricht, JSNTSup 90 (Sheffield: Sheffield Academic Press, 1993), 42–58.

109. Daniel Marguerat, "The End of Acts (28.16–31) and the Rhetoric of Silence," in *Rhetoric and the New Testament*, 74–89, here 75; see revised version, chap. 12 in this volume.

110. Both an array of responses and my critique are presented in Schmidt, "Anti-Judaism and the Gospel of Luke."

pated "consolation of Israel" (Luke 2:25), which was always destined, in Luke's understanding, as good news for all people (2:10, 31; 3:6). Jesus understood this from the beginning (4:21), emphasized it at the end (24:47), and for this purpose commissioned Paul (Acts 26:17), who is still testifying to it in the closing scene of Acts (28:23). Luke's orderly account assumes all along that only "some were convinced" by this argument (28:24), although Luke's rhetoric often engages in hyperbole, as when Jesus' first audience shifts suddenly from "all spoke well of him" (Luke 4:22) to "all were filled with rage" (4:28).[111]

In the narrative of Acts, Paul talks about turning to the Gentiles, but he is never pictured as successful at it. After his failure in Athens (Acts 17:32), he goes right back to the synagogue (18:4), where he provokes opposition that again makes him claim: "From now on I'm going to the Gentiles" (18:6) — and goes next door to someone religiously sympathetic! When Paul gets to Ephesus, the pattern repeats itself with Paul debating Jews in the synagogue (18:19). In the final scene in Rome, "local leaders of the Jews" came to Paul's quarters to continue the debate. The refrain at the end of Acts, that the Gentiles "will listen," is not a definitive turning *away from* Israel. It is a projected hope, once again echoing Ezekiel's commissioning that others would listen (οὗτοι ἂν εἰσήκουσαν), when "the house of Israel does not" (Ezek. 3:6–7). Acts thus ends on the same hermeneutical note that has framed all of Luke-Acts, an appropriate note for "a narrative of events fulfilled among us."

Paul has the last word, preaching and teaching "with all boldness, unhindered" (μετὰ πάσης παρρησίας ἀκωλύτως, Acts 28:31). Luke thus concludes on a note that has sounded often in Acts — that Christians need boldness in public discourse — from the opening speech of Peter (ἐξὸν εἰπεῖν μετὰ παρρησίας, 2:29; 4:13), reinforced by the early community (μετὰ παρρησίας πάσης λαλεῖν, 4:29, 31), even to Apollos (18:26), but especially characteristic of Paul from the beginning (ἐπαρρησιάσατο ἐν τῷ ὀνόματι τοῦ Ἰησοῦ, 9:27, 28; 13:46; 14:3; 19:8; 26:26). The theme of παρρησία, boldness in public speaking, is the antithesis of Paul's disclaimer of something "done in a corner" (26:26), a pejorative dismissal of those who avoid public scrutiny. Malherbe describes the philosopher's παρρησία as "outspokenness [that] betokened a fearlessness in pointing out human shortcoming" with "confidence in his right to do so" and "backed by character."[112]

---

111. Richard Ascough notes that "Luke's presentation of crowds has a close affinity with crowd scenes in the ancient Greek novels" ("Narrative Technique and Generic Designation: Crowd Scenes in Luke-Acts and in Chariton," *CBQ* 58 [1996]: 69–81, here 69).

112. See Abraham Malherbe, " 'Not in a Corner': Early Christian Apologetic in Acts 26:26," *The Second Century* 5 (1985/86): 193–210, here 208. Marguerat renders the term as "total freedom of speech" ("End of Acts," 88), which misses its association with frank philosophical rhetoric. The full expression used here has historiographical parallels in Josephus, Dionysius, and Diodorus (see D. L. Mealand, "The Close of Acts and Its Hellenistic Greek Vocabulary," *NTS* 36 [1990]: 583–97, supplementary note on παρρησία, 596–97). See also S. C. Winter, "ΠΑΡΡΗΣΙΑ In Acts," in *Friendship, Flattery, and Frankness of Speech: Studies on Friendship in the New Testament World*, ed. John T. Fitzgerald, NovTSup 82 (Leiden: Brill, 1996), 185–202, who argues that this term views the final scene of Acts more favorably than earlier encounters in synagogues: "Acts depicts the Jews in

The last word of the narrative is ἀκωλύτως, "unhindered."[113] When added to "all boldness," it provides a strong rhetorical ending both for the narrative of Acts and for Luke and Acts together. What started out so humbly and (rhetorically) modestly in Luke 1:5, and then built on what the first book "began" (Acts 1:1), has concluded with a rhetorical flourish and a strong apologetic appeal: preaching God's kingdom and teaching about Jesus, not in a corner, but in Rome itself, boldly and freely, with a confident rhetoric to face whatever challenges lie ahead. Not bad for an amateur historian!

Conclusion

Only a brief assessment is possible here. The preface of Luke, read in light of the rhetoric of Hellenistic historiography, deepens the reader's appreciation for the conventions of narrative writing. To be sure, this does not make Luke another Thucydides or Polybius, or even Dionysius or Josephus. The judgment of van Unnik is still valid: this author knew "the rules of the game," and indeed, applied them mostly "with propriety."[114] We are more aware today, however, that the conventions of Hellenistic historiography inspired a wide range of narrative writings, with varying degrees of verisimilitude and styles. Richard Pervo has reminded us that ancient narratives were written as much for enjoyment as for other purposes.[115] Without accepting his thesis fully, we can nonetheless appreciate the insights he provides about the novelistic touches in many scenes in Acts.

Luke's contemporaries included writers of "historical" narratives who yielded to rhetorical excesses, and some who responded with parodies. The conventions of "history writing" must have been well-known to literate persons in the Hellenistic world and easily recognizable, whether in novels, biography, history, or some hybrid genre.

Luke's preface suggests obvious influences from the rhetorical conventions of Hellenistic historiography. That makes Luke a writer of "historical" narrative, but not necessarily a "historian." Luke-Acts appropriately belongs within the rather wide spectrum of "Hellenistic historiography." The conventions reflected

---

Rome as distinct, even isolated from their coreligionists. They behave like philosophers, not like an angry mob, and carry on debates in a Roman 'household' " (202).

113. The word represents part of the vocabulary in the ending of Acts, reflecting a civil law scenario of someone facing criminal charges who is free to lease his own accommodations and to exercise his rights undisturbed (Mealand, "Close of Acts").

114. "Luke's Second Book," 59.

115. Pervo, *Profit with Delight*. Dibelius had noted the fragmentary historian Duris (Jacoby, *Fragmente*, no. 76, frag. 1), who expected historians to include both μίμησις and ἡδονή (Dibelius, *Studies*, 142 n. 11, where the terms are translated "dramatic clarity" and "entertainment"). Pervo attributes his title to the poet Horace, but Polybius also recommended that history should provide "at the same time both profit and delight" (ἅμα καὶ τὸ χρήσιμον καὶ τὸ τερπνόν, *Plb.* 1.4.11; cited in Palmer, "Acts and the Ancient Historical Monograph," in Winter and Clarke, *Book of Acts in Its Ancient Literary Setting*, 1–29, here 29).

in Luke's preface signal the use of "historical" narrative models, without limiting the source of such models.[116] Thus the choice between "Deuteronomistic or Hellenistic" influences on Luke must be answered "both."[117]

The variety of evidence considered in this study of Luke's preface fully supports Philip Satterthwaite's balanced conclusions:

> At point after point Acts can be shown to operate according to conventions similar to those outlined in classical rhetorical treatises. There are some aspects which it is hard to explain other than by concluding that Luke was aware of rhetorical conventions.... The preface, in particular, seems to make an implicit claim to be operating within classical conventions. That is not to say that other influences have not been at work. The Old Testament has obviously exerted considerable influence on Acts; and this may have extended to narrative techniques.... In general it seems fair to speak of a considerable indebtedness to classical rhetoric; that is, he gives clear indication of having received the kind of (rhetorical) education one would expect in a Greco-Roman writer of this period who embarked on a work of this sort. Luke, however, is not a slave of classical conventions.... [The evidence] suggests Luke's freedom in regard to the conventions in which he had been educated, which implies a considerable mastery of those conventions.[118]

The emerging consensus about these conclusions can now form the basis for further probing insights into the narrative of Luke-Acts.[119]

---

116. The contributors to Winter and Clarke, *Book of Acts in Its Ancient Literary Setting,* represent well the range of options for Acts: it is at the same time "a short historical monograph" (Palmer, 1, recognizing that the novel was also a form of history, 3), partly "shaped by the template provided by the biographical tradition relating to Socrates" (Alexander, 31). Yet clearly "in writing Acts, Luke used biblical language and models" (Rosner, 65). These are complementary, not contradictory, observations.

117. Schmidt, "The Historiography of Acts: Deuteronomistic or Hellenistic?"

118. Philip Satterthwaite, "Acts against the Background of Classical Rhetoric," in Winter and Clarke, *Book of Acts in Its Ancient Literary Setting,* 337–79, here 378–79.

119. I express my appreciation to the editor of this volume, David Moessner, for numerous suggestions that helped sharpen the focus of this essay.

The Material Claims of the Prologues and Ancient Greek Poetics

Chapter 3

The Claims of the Prologues and Greco-Roman Rhetoric

The Prefaces to Luke and Acts in Light of Greco-Roman Rhetorical Strategies

Vernon K. Robbins

This essay is the result of a request by the editor of this volume to describe the Greco-Roman rhetorical strategies in the prefaces to Luke and Acts. Such a task, one might suppose, is quite easy. After all, a person of no less stature than Friedrich Blass described the preface to Luke as a "remarkable specimen of fine and well-balanced structure, and at the same time of well-chosen vocabulary."[1] In addition, H. J. Cadbury made it commonplace to think of Luke and Acts as part of the Greek literary world and to consider the preface to Luke as establishing an undeniable place for Luke and Acts in the literary tradition of Greek historiography.[2]

But things have changed. A significant challenge now stands before interpreters to take a more nuanced view of these writings and their prefaces. Two decades ago, Charles H. Talbert initiated a major debate by concluding that Luke and Acts are more accurately described as biographical writings about a founder and his successors than historiographical writings about Christianity as a political, religious movement.[3] In a context in which many interpreters are

---

1. F. Blass, *Philology of the Gospels* (London: Macmillan, 1898), 7. Cf. C. H. Talbert, *Reading Luke: A Literary and Theological Commentary on the Third Gospel* (New York: Crossroad, 1982), 10–11: "The style [of ancient prefaces] was often highly rhetorical. This is certainly true of 1:1–4.... The exalted style of 1:1–4 simply conforms to cultural expectations for a rhetorical beginning."

2. H. J. Cadbury, "The Purpose Expressed in Luke's Preface," *The Expositor* 8/21 (1921): 431–41; idem, "Commentary on the Preface of Luke," in *The Beginnings of Christianity*, pt. 1: "The Acts of the Apostles," vol. 2: *Prolegomena*, ed. F. Jackson and K. Lake (London: Macmillan, 1922), 489–510; idem, "The Knowledge Claimed in Luke's Preface," *The Expositor* 8/24 (1922): 401–20; idem, *The Making of Luke-Acts* (New York: Macmillan, 1927), 344–48, 358–59; idem, "'We' and 'I' Passages in Luke-Acts," *NTS* 3 (1956–57): 128–32.

3. C. H. Talbert, *What Is a Gospel? The Genre of the Canonical Gospels* (Philadelphia: Fortress, 1977); idem, "Biographies of Philosophers and Rulers as Instruments of Religious Propaganda in Mediterranean Antiquity," *ANRW* II.16.2 (1978): 1619–51; idem, "Once Again: Gospel Genre," *Semeia* 43 (1988): 53–74; idem, "Biography, Ancient," *ABD* 1.745–49.

ignoring the substance of his insights, he has raised the question whether interpreters can think that Luke and Acts use political history (the subject matter
proper of Greco-Roman historiography) as the host genre for their presentation
of the character of the individuals and peoples (the subject matter proper of
Greco-Roman biography) who populate Luke and Acts.[4] It should be obvious,
he proposes, that Luke and Acts use the medium of the words and deeds of Jesus
and of specific followers to communicate their view of God, the world, the nature
of history, and the nature of the future. Richard Pervo, in turn, has exhibited
dimensions of Acts that are closer to ancient romance literature than to historiography.[5] The novelistic aspects of Acts, then, must be given as much attention
as events that can be interpreted in the context of specific political events in the
Mediterranean world.[6] In the midst of this broader genre discussion, Loveday
C. A. Alexander has performed the most comprehensive and systematic analysis of prefaces in Greek, Roman, and Hellenistic literature in recent times and
concluded that

> the conventions employed in the [Lukan] Gospel preface do not accord with the
> common classification of Luke's work with Greco-Roman historiography: the scope
> and scale are wrong, dedication is not normally found in historical writings, the
> customary topics for historical prefaces do not appear, and both the style and the
> motifs of the Lucan preface are better paralleled elsewhere, in the broad area of
> Greek literature (too broad to be called "genre") which I have called "the scientific
> tradition."[7]

In turn, she concludes that

> the opening conventions used in the Book of Acts are not sufficient to establish
> the genre of the work as "history" within the frame of reference defined by Greek
> literary convention.[8]

In addition, Alexander has argued that Socratic intellectual biography is a very
important tradition for understanding the portrayal of Paul in Acts.[9] Gregory L.
Sterling has refined the historiographical approach through careful investigation

---

    4. C. H. Talbert, "The Acts of the Apostles: Monograph or 'Bios'?" in *History, Literature, and
Society in the Book of Acts*, ed. B. Witherington (Cambridge: Cambridge University Press, 1996),
58–72.
    5. R. Pervo, *Profit with Delight: The Literary Genre of the Acts of the Apostles* (Philadelphia:
Fortress, 1987).
    6. See S. P. Schierling and M. J. Schierling, "The Influence of the Ancient Romances on the
Acts of the Apostles," *The Classical Bulletin* 54 (1978): 81–88.
    7. L. C. A. Alexander, "The Preface to Acts and the Historians," in Witherington, *History,
Literature, and Society in the Book of Acts*, 77–78; cf. idem, *The Preface to Luke's Gospel: Literary
Convention and Social Context in Luke 1.1–4 and Acts 1.1*, SNTSMS 78 (Cambridge: Cambridge
University Press, 1993).
    8. Alexander, "The Preface to Acts," 101.
    9. L. C. A. Alexander, "Acts and Ancient Intellectual Biography," in *The Book of Acts in Its
Ancient Literary Setting*, vol. 1 of *The Book of Acts in Its First-Century Setting*, ed. B. W. Winter and
A. D. Clarke (Grand Rapids, Mich.: Eerdmans, 1993), 31–63.

of a subgenre he calls "apologetic historiography."[10] In addition, Kota Yamada has identified a subgenre he calls "rhetorical historiography"[11] in an attempt to adapt historiographical terminology to the nature of Luke and Acts.

Given the deep-seated disagreements over the nature of Luke and Acts, it may be futile to try to enter, or reenter,[12] the debate with a goal of changing anyone's mind. Yet one of the characteristics of works like Luke and Acts is the variegated texture of their discourse — they inherently defy simple classification.[13] Precisely because they contain multiple generic features that interact dynamically with one another, they regularly evoke new insights from highly disciplined and well-informed interpreters. If Luke and Acts were simple writings, most interpreters would have walked away from them long ago. The work of both Sterling and Yamada calls attention to the argumentative nature of the discourse in Luke and Acts: to them Luke and Acts function in a historiographical mode that employs selective, conventional strategies of persuasion for specific purposes. Alexander, however, has made her case, and continues to make it, with an argument that one of the most noticeable features of the prefaces to Luke and Acts is their absence of rhetorical pretension or flourish.[14] For her the prefaces exhibit an absence of rhetorical skill characteristic of literature that she describes as scientific discourse of the Mediterranean world. Talbert, in addition, emphasizes that the character of individuals and peoples is the primary medium Lukan discourse uses to communicate its view of the world. For him the discourse uses human agency in a powerful and important way. Pervo, in turn, emphasizes the exciting, adventurous, and entertaining aspects of Acts. For him Lukan discourse is not only informational or edifying, but has a quality that appeals to the aesthetic and adventuresome dimensions of human life.

The question is if it might be possible, at least implicitly, to address all four of the primary issues under debate — argumentative historiography, absence of developed rhetorical statement, biography, and novelistic literature — in a manner that advances the discussion of the nature of Luke and Acts rather than simply activates usual disagreements among interpreters. Among other things, I am concerned that some who defend the historiographical nature of Luke and Acts leave the impression, whether they mean to or not, that Lukan discourse is virtually equivalent in kind to the writing present in Herodotus, Thucydides,

---

10. G. E. Sterling, *Historiography and Self-Definition: Josephos, Luke-Acts, and Apologetic Historiography*, NovTSup 64 (Leiden: Brill, 1992).

11. K. Yamada, "A Rhetorical History: The Literary Genre of the Acts of the Apostles," in *Rhetoric, Scripture and Theology: Essays from the 1994 Pretoria Conference*, ed. S. E. Porter and T. H. Olbricht, JSNTSup 131 (Sheffield: Sheffield Academic Press, 1996), 230–50; idem, "The Preface to the Lukan Writings and Rhetorical Historiography," in *The Rhetorical Interpretation of Scripture: Essays from the 1996 Malibu Conference*, ed. S. E. Porter and D. L. Stamps, JSNTSup 180 (Sheffield: Sheffield Academic Press, 1999), 154–72.

12. See V. K. Robbins, "Prefaces in Greco-Roman Biography and Luke-Acts," *Perspectives in Religious Studies* 6 (1979): 94–108 = *SBLSP* 2 (1978): 193–207.

13. See the comment of Alexander, "The Preface to Acts," 102 n. 69, that Acts and some other Hellenistic Jewish writings "tend to fall at the overlap between history and biography."

14. Ibid., 97, 101.

and Polybius. It is not. This, as I understand it, is the issue that Alexander has attempted to address in her comprehensive study of prefaces in Mediterranean antiquity, and it would be beneficial if current interpreters would build on the implications of her study. The likelihood, as Alexander has shown through her extensive gathering and analysis of prefaces in Mediterranean writings, is that the author of Luke and Acts writes at a "middlebrow" social and cultural level, rather than at the level of the literary elite.[15] This level of writing regularly exhibits an overly formal approach in the preface, at the same time that it reveals an absence of truly sophisticated rhetorical skill.

Unfortunately, some current interpreters of Luke and Acts overlook the profound implications of Alexander's results.[16] One of the reasons may be her choice of the term "scientific" to describe the kind of literature that contains prefaces most analogous to the preface to Luke. Perhaps a better description of the literature with analogous prefaces is "profession-oriented writings." This literature is written by and for networks of people in "the world of the crafts and professions" in Mediterranean society: artisans, tradesmen, businessmen, businesswomen, physicians, engineers — people at the level of the professions and guilds — rather than networks of people in the literary circles of Mediterranean society.[17] This literature exhibits either limited access or indifference to literature produced by the major literary circles.[18] The result is literature that transmits data within a targeted sector of society for the purpose of advancing specific practices and points of view among those for whom it is written and to whom it is read. In other words, this is not truly "public" literature, intended for those who have access to the major literary collections of the time. Rather, it is writing for networks of people who exchange goods and services with one another regularly because they share a belief that Jesus of Nazareth and his followers are continuing the history of Israel.

The beginning of Luke evokes this story of Israel as the angel, in the opening chapter, tells Zechariah that his son John will "turn many of the sons of Israel to the Lord their God" (1:16). Soon after this, the angel Gabriel appears to Mary and tells her that the Lord God will give her son Jesus "the throne of his father David, and he will reign over the house of Jacob forever; and of his kingdom there will be no end" (1:32–33). This perception of the continuation of the story of Israel reaches a high point in Luke when Jesus tells his disciples that he assigns to them, as his Father assigned to him, "a kingdom, that you may eat

---

15. L. C. A. Alexander, "Luke's Preface in the Context of Greek Preface-Writing," *NovT* 28 (1986): 48–74; idem, *Preface to Luke's Gospel.*

16. See the following in W. J. McCoy, "In the Shadow of Thucydides," in Witherington, *History, Literature, and Society in the Book of Acts,* 30: "...the prologue or exordium in Lk. 1.1–4 reflects Luke's rhetorical interests....He writes in a clear and direct manner in this sentence, as Quintilian required in an exordium (*Inst. Or.* 4.1.34)."

17. Alexander, "Luke's Preface," 66–71; cf. Robbins, "The Social Location of the Implied Author of Luke-Acts," in *The Social World of Luke-Acts: Models for Interpretation,* ed. J. H. Neyrey (Peabody, Mass.: Hendrickson, 1991), 305–32.

18. Alexander, "Luke's Preface," 67.

and drink at my table in my kingdom and sit on thrones judging the twelve tribes of Israel" (22:29–30). The preface to Acts evokes a continuation of the story of Israel through Jesus' disciples, when the disciples ask Jesus if he will restore the kingdom of Israel at this time (Acts 1:6). Jesus' response reconfigures their perception of the kingdom of Israel by introducing a program whereby the words and deeds of Jesus will be taken to the end of the earth (1:8). The narrative enacts this program, then, until the final verse when Paul, evidently at the end of the earth in Rome, preaches the kingdom of God and teaches about the Lord Jesus Christ openly and unhindered (28:31).

To address the rhetorical qualities of the level of writing Alexander perceives to be present in Luke and Acts, I will approach the prefaces to Luke and Acts from the perspective of "progymnastic" rather than "fully" rhetorical discourse. The term "progymnastic" comes from the contents of the handbooks called *Progymnasmata* (Preliminary exercises), which rhetoricians wrote for grammarians who were preparing students at the end of secondary education for advanced instruction in rhetoric.[19] Progymnastic rhetoric specializes in "the 're-performance' of well-known traditions."[20] Within this overall approach, it "uses specific personages for its context of communication," makes traditions either generally or specifically argumentative in nature, and envisions a process of "rhetorical elaboration" (ἐργασία) that "works a tradition toward the form of an essay or speech that presents a complete argument."[21] The present essay, therefore, contains insights gleaned primarily from the *Progymnasmata* of Theon and Hermogenes, and it includes data from other rhetorical manuals only as a way of filling out the meaning of what is in the *Progymnasmata*. The challenge is to identify both what is present and what is absent in the prefaces to Luke and Acts, for the purpose of understanding more fully the nature of Lukan discourse. A truly careful description of Lukan discourse holds the potential for deeper understanding of the power of this mode of writing in relation to other modes of writing in the New Testament. In other words, we can provide a new description of early Christianity based on the discourse it generated to communicate its vision of God, the world, and human life in this world and beyond.[22] If we obtain new insights about discourse in the New Testament, we can transmit a fuller understanding of the nature of Christianity to people who will face the challenges of the twenty-first century.

One of the features of the debate during the past twenty years has been continuous appeal to literature outside of Luke and Acts. This has been very fruitful, revealing dimensions of Luke and Acts that had not been prominent. The time

19. B. L. Mack and V. K. Robbins, *Patterns of Persuasion in the Gospels* (Sonoma, Calif.: Polebridge Press, 1989), 31–35.

20. V. K. Robbins, "Progymnastic Rhetorical Composition and Pre-Gospel Traditions: A New Approach," in *The Synoptic Gospels: Source Criticism and the New Literary Criticism*, ed. C. Focant, BETL 110 (Louvain: Louvain University Press, 1993), 112.

21. Robbins, "Progymnastic Rhetorical Composition," 119–31.

22. V. K. Robbins, *The Tapestry of Early Christian Discourse: Rhetoric, Society and Ideology* (London: Routledge, 1996), 240–43.

might be right, however, to correlate more of these observations with the inner texture of Luke and Acts. In this way it may be possible to discover anew how this discourse attains its persuasive power and attracts such loyal advocates. What features within the discourse encourage readers to consider the portrayal of people and events to be virtually fully trustworthy, reliable, and true — indeed, almost without flaw? Why do some readers, on the other hand, express uncertainty about the reliability of Luke and Acts? Why do some readers consider Luke's account to claim more about earliest Christianity than it reliably delivers? The answer, as we will see, lies in the dialogical relation of the different modes of discourse. While one reader responds to portions of Luke and Acts that sound like historical description, another reader responds to portions that sound like popular adventure stories. Still other readers will respond to specific guidelines for obedient action, while others will respond to stories that challenge stereotypes and reconfigure dispositions and attitudes. The key to the persuasiveness of Luke and Acts lies in the interweaving of multiple kinds of discourse into a two-volume story about Jesus and his followers.

The Preface to Luke

Rationale (1:1)

The first line of the Lukan preface is a natural place to begin. As L. C. A. Alexander has explained, the message of the first clause is something like, "Since many have tried to put together an account of the business that has happened among us..."[23] But this is not a proper representation of the voice of the narrator. Rather, the inscribed author narrates in a formal manner, more appropriately represented by translating the Greek into, "Inasmuch as (ἐπειδήπερ) many have undertaken the task of compiling an account of the matters which have come to fruition in our midst..."[24] In rhetorical terms, the opening clause is a rationale — it explains the reason why the author has written the following discourse. In his *Progymnasmata*, Hermogenes of Tarsus presents the rationale as the first step in reconfiguring the statement of an authoritative individual into an argumentative elaboration.[25] The *Rhetorica ad Herennium* II.18.28, in turn, gives the rationale primary position in moving a proposition toward "the most complete and perfect argument." Aristotle, indeed, saw that the rationale was the crucial feature for moving assertions into the realm of logical reasoning and argumentation (*Rhet.* 1.1.3–11; 1.2.8–22).

---

23. Alexander, *Preface to Luke's Gospel*, 113. Cf. Talbert, *Reading Luke*, 7: "If we take ἐπειδήπερ as causal, then 'inasmuch as' would mean 'because,' and Luke would be using the work of previous writers positively to justify his own venture."

24. Alexander, *Preface to Luke's Gospel*, 113.

25. R. F. Hock and E. N. O'Neil, *The Chreia in Ancient Rhetoric*, vol. 1: *The Progymnasmata* (Atlanta: Scholars Press, 1986), 177.

NT writings show that early Christian writers differed both in the subject matter to which they gave highest priority and in the reasons for which they wrote. Sometimes the writers only subtly express their reasons; at other times they make their reasons explicit. The Gospel of John, for example, exhibits a writer (perhaps the author of a Signs Gospel incorporated into the Gospel of John) whose focus was on the many signs Jesus performed (John 20:30). Within this focus, the Gospel of John transmits an explicit reason for its composition. A display of both the unexpressed presuppositions and the explicit statements produces the following chain of reasoning:

> **Rule:** Believing that Jesus is the Christ, the Son of God, produces life in his name.

> **Case:** Experiencing signs that Jesus performed, either by reciting or hearing them from a written account, produces belief that Jesus is the Christ, the Son of God.

> **Result:** Therefore, I have written these signs (selected from many that exist) so that you may believe that Jesus is the Christ, the Son of God, and believing you may have life in his name.

The premises underlying the author's writing exhibit three convictions: (1) that extraordinary religious benefits come to people who believe in Jesus' special relation to God; (2) that signs performed by Jesus have special potential for eliciting belief; and (3) that Jesus performed many other signs before his disciples that the author, under the appropriate circumstances, could "re-perform" in writing. The reasoning in this author's statement has an explicit sacred texture that concerns the nature of Jesus as a holy person and the means by which people can invite God's powers of human redemption into their lives.[26]

Many interpreters have noticed that the Lukan preface does not contain such an explicit sacred texture.[27] It mentions neither Jesus nor God. Moreover, it does not mention faith or belief; the gospel; eternal life; salvation; or the kingdom of God. The preface, then, does not contain some of the most common vocabulary within early Christian discourse. Rather, it uses compound compositions and verbs with complex expressions that make its meanings significantly obscure. The crucial words in the preface for describing the subject matter of the discourse are "of the matters which have come to fruition in our midst" (περὶ τῶν πεπληρο-φορημένων ἐν ἡμῖν πραγμάτων). Following Cadbury, Alexander points out that the natural clause for comparison in Lukan discourse is Luke 2:15: "...this thing that has happened which the Lord has made known to us."[28] Luke 2:15 speaks clearly about its subject matter, while Luke 1:1 is overly formal discourse that obscures rather than reveals its subject matter. Did the author want, with the perfect participle πεπληροφορημένων, to characterize the "matters" as events

---

26. V. K. Robbins, *Exploring the Texture of Texts* (Valley Forge, Pa.: Trinity Press International, 1996), 121–22, 125–26.

27. See Alexander, *Preface to Luke's Gospel*, 124: "Luke goes out of his way to avoid explicitly Christian language in the preface."

28. Ibid., 113.

that "fulfill" the promises of God found in the scriptures?[29] If so, he does not clearly say so in the opening clause of his preface.

This aspect of the Lukan preface comes even more to light when the opening clause is compared to the opening of Josephus's *Jewish War.* Josephus, like Luke, opened his preface with a rationale (obscured by the translation in the Loeb Classical Library). It also describes the subject matter of the ensuing narrative, but in contrast to Luke, it states the subject matter clearly:

> Since the war of the Jews against the Romans — the greatest not only of the wars of our own time, but, so far as accounts have reached us, well-nigh of all that ever broke out between cities or nations — has not lacked its historians. (Josephus, *J.W.* 1.1)

Josephus announces his topic immediately and clearly: "the war of the Jews against the Romans." If one were to argue that Josephus's *Jewish Antiquities* rather than *Jewish War* is more analogous to Luke and Acts, the comparison is even more revealing. First, the preface to the *Antiquities,* like most prefaces to histories, is very long — clearly imitating the scope of historical prefaces in a manner that the preface to Luke does not. Second, the preface to the *Antiquities* clearly describes the subject matter of the account as "our entire ancient history and political constitution" (1.5: ἅπασαν τὴν παρ' ἡμῖν ἀρχαιολογίαν καὶ [τὴν] διάταξιν τοῦ πολιτεύματος). Some interpreters have argued that the Gospel of Luke must be historiography rather than biography, because it does not refer to Jesus in the preface.[30] The truth is that the preface to Luke does not state its subject matter clearly, whether it be historiography, biography, or novel; it is more concerned with formality than being explicitly informative. An additional comparison sheds more light on the preface. Acts 15:24–26 recites a letter the apostles and elders sent with Judas and Silas as they accompanied Paul and Barnabas. Like the preface to Luke, this letter begins with a rationale:

> Since (ἐπειδή) we have heard that some persons from us (τινὲς ἐξ ἡμῶν) have troubled you with words, unsettling your minds, although we gave them no instructions, . . . (15:24)

This rationale shows that the preface to Luke, which addresses another person directly ("you, most excellent Theophilus," 1:3) and uses a first-person singular construction to refer to the author's involvement in the composition ("it seemed good to me also," 1:3), exhibits the influence of both oratorical and epistolary prefaces.[31] But, once again, the unusual feature in Luke 1:1 is its extraordinary formality. The letter in Acts 15 opens with ἐπειδή, the less formal conjunction that Josephus used to open his *War.* Like the Lukan preface, however, the opening clause in Acts 15:24 only describes in a general manner the subject matter it

---

29. D. P. Moessner, "The 'Script' of the Scriptures in Acts," in Witherington, *History, Literature, and Society in the Book of Acts.*

30. E.g., T. Callan, "The Preface of Luke-Acts and Historiography," *NTS* 31 (1985): 578.

31. Robbins, "Prefaces in Greco-Roman Biography."

addresses. The reason is simple, and undoubtedly it is the reason for the general mode of the opening clause to Luke: one need not describe one's subject matter explicitly to an audience "in the know" about the subject matter under discussion. This is one of the important results of Alexander's investigation of prefaces in Mediterranean antiquity. If one is writing a truly "public" treatise, one will clearly announce the subject matter of that treatise. If, on the other hand, one is writing at a "profession-oriented" level, the audience will know basic things about the subject matter. Thus, one will not need to describe the subject matter with great specificity. A general reference in the preface will function perfectly well.

The preface to Luke, like the letter in Acts 15:24–29, begins with statements that presuppose that the recipient(s) will already know basic things about the subject matter. The preface to Luke builds on conversations that have occurred at previous times. This becomes clear in the final line of the preface, in which the writer asserts that the one to whom he is writing has already been informed about the things he is addressing (1:4). For this reason, the writer simply "points" to the subject matter. There is no reason to describe it for the "general public." Like the continuation of a previous conversation, the preface to Luke begins with a generally argumentative tone (presenting a rationale), adopts an extraordinarily formal style, and describes the subject matter in a mode characteristic of an epistle addressed to people already knowledgeable about the subject matter to be discussed.

Argument from Comparison (1:2)

The preface continues with an argument from comparison:

> ...just as the original eyewitnesses and ministers of the word handed [the tradition] to us,...

A comparison (παραβολή) supports an argument inductively (Aristotle, *Rhet.* 2.2–8). This means that its primary effect is to persuade a reader or hearer on the basis of similarity from particular to particular.[32] People are moved to belief when they see at least two examples that share something in common. Hermogenes, in his elaboration of the chreia — in this instance a brief saying attributed to Isocrates — features an argument from comparison (παραβολή) immediately after the rationale and argument from the opposite.[33] In this position, comparison builds on phenomena introduced in the rationale and the argument from the opposite.

Comparisons are highly complex figures of thought and argument, since they introduce dissimilarity at the same moment they introduce similarity. In an environment of similarity there are four kinds of argument: (1) from the similar

---

32. K. Demoen, "A Paradigm for the Analysis of Paradigms: The Rhetorical *Exemplum* in Ancient and Imperial Greek Theory," *Rhetorica* 15 (1997): 133.

33. Hock and O'Neil, *The Chreia*, 176–77; cf. *Rhetorica ad Herennium* 4.44.57.

or same; (2) from contrast, contrary, or opposite; (3) from greater to lesser; and (4) from lesser to greater.[34] Analysis of the preface to Luke from these four perspectives makes its complexity apparent.

First, since there is no "thus" in the preface after the "just as" clause (v. 2), the "just as" clause may be read as the last part of a comparison that begins with the "inasmuch as" clause (v. 1). Alexander introduces this possibility when she makes "the tradition" the subject of the third-person plural verb παρέδοσαν in her translation of v. 2.[35] With this translation, the comparison can be that "the matters which have come to fruition in our midst" (v. 1) are the same (option 1 above) as "the tradition that was handed down to us" (v. 2). As Alexander writes, "The tradition is simply there, to be received at its own valuation. . . ."[36] Just as the tradition was available to others who wrote it down, so it is available to the writer of Luke, who is in touch with the living tradition and has properly learned its "craft." Reading the comparison in this way can lead to the view that the preface to Luke presents at its outset a "tradition-based validation" of its contents.[37]

Second, the reader may merge vv. 1–2 so thoroughly — since "the tradition" in both instances is "the same" — that the comparison is perceived to lie between the narrative many "have compiled" (v. 1) and the "more accurate, orderly account" Luke has written (v. 3). Interpreters who understand the preface in this way modulate between presenting the argument from comparison as an argument "from lesser to greater" and "from contrast, contrary, or opposite." An argument from the opposite asserts that those other narratives were not well ordered and effective, but the accurate, orderly account in the Gospel of Luke is.[38] An argument from lesser to greater argues that if the works of the predecessors were good, because they were based on traditions from eyewitnesses and ministers of the word, Luke's account is better (because it is more accurate as

---

34. See Demoen, "A Paradigm," 136.

35. Alexander, *Preface to Luke's Gospel*, 116.

36. Ibid., 124–25.

37. Ibid., 82–85, esp. 84. Darrell L. Bock, *Luke*, vol. 1: *1:1–9:50* (Grand Rapids, Mich.: Baker Books, 1994), 57, reads the argument from comparison emphatically: "The term [καθώς] stresses the reliable basis on which these accounts rested: traditions passed down to reporters by the eyewitnesses and ministers of the Word. There is a two-step process described here; but the nature of the sources guarantees the quality. Luke is still describing the earlier accounts here, not his own study, which he will describe in 1:3–4." D. P. Moessner presents a somewhat different view in "'Eyewitnesses,' 'Informed Contemporaries,' and 'Unknowing Inquirers': Josephus' Criteria for Authentic Historiography and the Meaning of ΠΑΡΑΚΟΛΟΥΘΕΩ," *NovT* 38 (1996): 121: "Luke refers to another group of 'eyewitnesses' and/or 'attendants' upon whom he — in solidarity with the 'many' — is dependent for his information. . . ." In "The Meaning of ΚΑΘΕΞΗΣ in the Lukan Prologue as a Key to the Distinctive Contribution of Luke's Narrative among the 'Many,'" in *The Four Gospels 1992: Festschrift Frans Neirynck*, vol. 2, ed. F. van Segbroeck et al., BETL 100 (Louvain: Louvain University Press, 1992), Moessner argues that Luke is using comparison (Luke 1:2) both as affirmation and critique; both as (4) "from lesser to greater" and (2) "from contrast, contrary, or opposite."

38. J. A. Fitzmyer, *The Gospel according to Luke (I–IX)*, AB (New York: Doubleday, 1981), 292 (cf. 287, 298–99), exhibits evidence in support of the view that ἀνατάξασθαι διήγησιν means "to compile an orderly account."

a result of being better ordered). Luke T. Johnson's commentary reads the argument from comparison in the preface as an argument from the opposite, with a few qualifications included:

> Luke's language suggests dissatisfaction with the earlier attempts. Many had "put their hand to arranging," which suggests they did not quite succeed. Why? We must take seriously the force of the phrase "just as the eyewitnesses...handed on." Perhaps efforts such as Mark's were regarded by Luke as rhetorically ineffective because, too dependent on the way materials were transmitted by communities, they lacked a convincing sort of order. We remember the complaint by the second-century author Papias about Mark's lack of order (Eusebius of Caesarea, *Ecclesiastical History* 3, 39, 15). What this means — if we can judge from the improvement Luke himself made — is that they did not make sufficiently clear "connections" between events (cf. Lucian, *How to Write History*, 55). This was, in any case, the way that Eusebius understood Luke's prologue (*Ecclesiastical History* 3.24.14–16).[39]

I say of Johnson's analysis "with a few qualifications included," because his statement about the eyewitnesses and the use of "quite" and "sufficiently" slightly reduce the sharpness of the contrast. Finally, however, the series of negative phrases — "dissatisfaction," "did not quite succeed," "rhetorically ineffective," "lacked a convincing...order," "did not make sufficiently clear connections" — implies that the writings of the predecessors were not effective, unlike Luke's account.

Most recent interpreters are unwilling to state the contrast so sharply.[40] Talbert writes: "If there is any criticism of his predecessors implied, it is muted. It may very well be that his predecessors encouraged the evangelist to write by their example.... The absence of explicit critical comments about his predecessors sets Luke apart from most Greco-Roman prefaces."[41] Perhaps most common is an argument "from lesser to greater": the writing of the predecessors was good, but the Lukan account is better. This appears, for example, to be the position of Alexander. She agrees that some of the language in the preface is a "mild and ambiguous deprecation," but adds that the comments about the predecessors "are only there to reassure the reader that the subject is worth spending time on. The informational value of the clause lies more in the apparently incidental opportunity it gives the author to identify his subject matter."[42] Fred B. Craddock, perhaps as well as anyone, uses language that implies "from lesser to greater":

> Luke voices no criticism of the earlier narratives, but the thoroughness of his research, his recording the events "in order," and his desire to give the reader certainty in matters about which the reader was already informed combine to

---

39. L. T. Johnson, *The Gospel of Luke* (Collegeville, Minn.: Liturgical Press, 1991), 30.
40. Cf. R. A. Culpepper, *The Gospel of Luke*, New Interpreter's Bible 9 (Nashville: Abingdon, 1994), 40.
41. Talbert, *Reading Luke*, 7.
42. Alexander, *Preface to Luke's Gospel*, 116.

argue that Luke found in the prior accounts something confusing, erroneous, or incomplete.[43]

If interpreters perceive the argument from comparison in the preface to exist between the first two verses and the third verse, the emphasis is likely to lie either on an argument from lesser to greater or an argument from contrast, contrary, or opposite.

Third, an interpreter may consider the "just as [they]..." clause (v. 2) to reach its conclusion in "[so] I too..." (v. 3). In this instance, as in the first reading above, the comparison is an argument "from the same" or "from similarity." This way of reading the comparison focuses on Luke's credentials, rather than on the nature of the tradition itself. Robert Tannehill reads the argument in this way:

> The author's qualifications to write this work are presented in verse 3. The clause in verse 2 prepares for this by referring to the availability of a tradition that goes back to the original participants in the events. The "many" made use of this tradition "handed on to us" by the original eyewitnesses, and the author of Luke will too. The author does not claim to be an eyewitness, but he claims a foundation for his work in a reliable tradition that comes from a group of eyewitnesses.[44]

The point is that just as "they" handed on a reliable tradition, so Luke has access to reliable tradition as well. The emphasis is on the potential for Luke to write a trustworthy account. Thus, emphasizing the sequence "Just as [they]... [so] also I..." holds the potential for interpreting the argument from comparison as "from the same" or "from the similar."

The above analysis reveals why the comparison is one of the most disputed aspects of Luke's preface. Depending on how a reader hears the argument's construction, the comparison may emphasize the close association of the writer with "all his predecessors" (same or similarity) or the writer's dissociation from others who have written.[45] Absence of a clearly definable structure in this aspect of the preface makes the issue highly debatable. Recent interpretation, however, suggests that the comparisons are more "associative" than "dissociative" in tone. The major effect of the highly nuanced comparison is to link the writer with tradition that predecessors have handed down.

One of the noticeable differences between the preface to Luke and other contemporary prefaces is the absence of a statement like the following, which appears in Josephus's *Against Apion:*

> But since I see that a number of persons, influenced by malicious slander from certain people, discredit statements in my history concerning our antiquity and offer

---

43. F. B. Craddock, *Luke,* Interpretation (Louisville: John Knox Press, 1990), 18.

44. R. C. Tannehill, *Luke,* Abingdon New Testament Commentary (Nashville: Abingdon, 1996), 34.

45. See Ch. Perelman and L. Olbrechts-Tyteca, *The New Rhetoric: A Treatise on Argumentation* (Notre Dame, Ind.: University of Notre Dame Press, 1969), 190–92, 411–59, for association and dissociation.

as proof of the comparative modernity of our race the fact that it has not been considered worthy of mention by the best-known Greek historians, I consider it my duty to write briefly about all these points, to convict our detractors of oppro-brium and deliberate falsehood, to correct the ignorance of others, and to instruct whoever desires to know the truth about the antiquity of our race.[46]

This prose has a very different tone from the preface to Luke. Yet many inter-preters (including Fitzmyer) include this portion of Josephus's preface in their discussion of "close parallels." One of the major reasons is that *Against Apion* contains a retrospective preface, with direct address to Epaphroditus at the be-ginning of Book 2. The observation by Talbert (cited above) should be heeded, that one of the major differences between the Lukan preface and many other contemporary prefaces, except for the "profession-oriented" prefaces discussed by Alexander, is the absence of a strong "argument from the opposite."

The tone of the Lukan preface, in this regard, is also very different from Josephus's *War*:

[S]ome who have taken no part in the action but have collected from hearsay ca-sual and contradictory stories which they have then edited in a rhetorical style, while others who witnessed the events have, either from flattery of the Romans or from hatred of the Jews, misrepresented the facts, their writings exhibiting al-ternatively invective and encomium, but nowhere historical accuracy; in these circumstances I — Josephus, son of Matthias, a Hebrew by ancestry, a native of Jerusalem and a priest, who at the opening of the war myself fought against the Ro-mans and in the sequel was perforce an onlooker — propose to provide the subjects of the Roman Empire with a narrative of the facts by translating into Greek the account I previously composed in my vernacular tongue and sent to the barbarians in the interior.

The preface to Luke, in contrast, does not suggest that those who wrote other narratives were not in touch with eyewitnesses and reliable tradents of the tra-dition. Quite the opposite. The preface to Luke shows concern to exhibit that this writer can transmit the tradition as reliably as predecessors. The exigency he must overcome is precisely the one that Josephus aims at his detractors: they were not participants in the events themselves. Luke glosses this issue, since he cannot claim to have been a disciple who traveled with Jesus, or of being one of the seven selected by the church in Jerusalem to attend to the needs of the widows in the daily distribution (Acts 6:1–6). The primary goal of the argument from comparison in the preface to Luke, therefore, is to establish a firm link between the other people who handed on the tradition and the tradition this writer hands on in his account. The same subject matter, he claims, is avail-able to him that they had available to them. In fact, the predecessors are the source of much of the reliable subject matter. As the antecedent writers based their accounts on tradition handed down by eyewitnesses and ministers of the word, so the author of Luke has followed all things closely; namely, he has kept

---

46. Josephus, *Against Apion* 1.1.2–3, as quoted by Fitzmyer, *Luke*, 288.

in touch both with the tradition as people have handed it down and with things that happened afterward among the apostles.[47]

The Author's Explicit Assertion and Supporting Rationale (1:3–4)

Luke 1:3 contains the primary assertion in the preface: it seemed good to the author to write an account for Theophilus. Accompanying this assertion is an implication that the account follows with an accompanying rationale: (because) he has kept in touch with all things from the beginning. Verse 3, then, is an assertion that imitates an enthymeme, because it contains a statement that supports the assertion.[48] But what does this statement support? It does not explain why the author is writing. Rather, the statement supports an unexpressed assertion that this writer has the data available to write a well-informed account for Theophilus. The rationale in v. 3, as well as the rationale and the comparison in vv. 1–2, supports an unexpressed assertion that this writer is able to write a good account, because many already have written accounts based on reliable tradition (which are available to him), and he has kept in touch with all things from the beginning, both as they have been transmitted and as he has experienced them. Verse 1 and the dative participial clause in v. 3, then, are complementary rationales that support an unexpressed assertion that it is possible for this author to write an excellent, reliable account for Theophilus. Where, then, is the rationale for the assertion in v. 3 that it seemed good for the author to write this account? Verse 4 gives the reason: " ... so that you may (because I wanted you to) find out for certain about the things in which you have been instructed."[49]

Summary

In contrast to the usual way of understanding the preface as a two-verse protasis followed by a two-verse apodosis, it is necessary to understand the first two verses as a rationale and comparison that support an unexpressed assertion that the author has the data available to write a good, reliable account. The last half, then, contains an explicit assertion and rationale that have only a conjoined relation to the first half.

The Preface to Acts

The preface to Acts does not exhibit the extraordinarily formal features present in the preface to Luke. Rather, it summarizes aspects of the Gospel of Luke in a manner that reconfigures them as inaugural events for the actions of Jesus'

---

47. See Moessner, "'Eyewitnesses.'"

48. See G. A. Kennedy, *Aristotle on Rhetoric: A Theory of Civic Discourse* (New York: Oxford University Press, 1991), 297–98.

49. For this wording, see Alexander, *Preface to Luke's Gospel*, 137–38.

followers in the ensuing narrative. One of the goals of the preface to Acts is to provide a rationale for the presence of the eleven disciples, women, and Jesus' brothers and mother in Jerusalem. Another goal is to depict the followers of Jesus as obedient to Jesus' command and God's divine action. Still another goal is to introduce a program for the activity of Jesus' followers throughout Acts.

Summary of the Gospel of Luke (Acts 1:1–2)

The preface to Acts begins by presenting Theophilus with a summary of the Gospel of Luke. The inscribed author, narrating in first-person singular, describes the "first account" (τὸ πρῶτον λόγον) as a depiction of "all that Jesus began to do and to teach." Although some interpreters disregard the import of this opening statement,[50] it is clear that the author of the preface to Acts views the Gospel of Luke as a biographical account of Jesus' action and speech.

While the opening verse of the preface to Acts summarizes all that Jesus "began" (ἤρξατο) to do and to teach, it continues in the second verse by summarizing the end of the account in Luke, until the day, after having commanded through the Holy Spirit the apostles whom he had chosen, he was taken up. This clause within a clause represents a standard performance of the progymnastic rhetorical act of abbreviation (συστέλλειν),[51] abbreviating, in this case, the last ten verses of Luke (24:44–53). The writer writes freely in his own words, a skill acquired in the initial progymnastic exercise of recitation (ἀπαγγελία).[52] In other words, Acts 1:2 does not replicate any of the wording of Luke 24:44–53. The end of Luke does not use the term "the day" to introduce the setting of Jesus' ascension; it uses the verb ἀναφέρειν rather than ἀναλαμβάνειν to describe Jesus' ascent into the heavens (contrast Acts 1:11); it does not call Jesus' speech "commands"; it does not refer to the "Holy Spirit"; it does not refer to those gathered as "apostles"; and it does not speak of "those whom Jesus chose." The first two verses of the preface to Acts, then, present a concise summary of the "beginning and end" of the Gospel of Luke in words freely chosen by the writer.

Rationale for Staying in Jerusalem (Acts 1:3–5)

After the opening summary (1:1–2), formulated in direct address to Theophilus, the preface continues in a mode of progymnastic chreia composition, as it is taught in the *Progymnasmata* — namely prose featuring speech attributed to specific individuals.[53] With this compositional strategy, biographical prose becomes the medium for a chronological account of successors to Jesus' action and speech. Acts 1:3–5 is an expanded chreia introduced with a dative-case relative

---

50. E.g., Callan, "The Preface of Luke-Acts," 581 n. 11.
51. Hock and O'Neil, *The Chreia*, 100–101.
52. Ibid., 94–95.
53. Ibid., 82–83.

pronoun, but handled in such a manner that the situation and the attributed speech can be recited in nominative case. This is a skill acquired by performing the inflection exercise (κλίσις) during progymnastic education.[54] Using the nominative case, the author has composed an expanded chreia (ἐπεκτείνειν) resembling the one Theon presents in his *Progymnasmata*.[55] The opening statement summarizes Jesus' time on earth "after his suffering" in terms of forty days in which he "presented himself alive by many proofs" and spoke "of the kingdom of God." While the Gospel of Luke describes Jesus' time of testing prior to his public words and deeds as "forty days in the wilderness" (4:2), it does not indicate that Jesus appeared to women and the apostles during forty days prior to his ascension (24:1–53). It appears that the "beginning" of the account of the words and deeds of Jesus in Luke has influenced the summary of the "ending" of the account in Acts. The description of Jesus' action and speech is similar to Theon's summary of Epameinondas's "display of outstanding deeds of great courage" prior to the poignant statement he makes while he is dying.[56] The differences are twofold: (1) the expanded chreia in Acts focuses on the period after Jesus' death and resurrection rather than on his initial earthly ministry; and (2) part of Jesus' persona is both to teach and to act well, not simply to act with great courage. The description of Jesus' teaching is especially interesting, since neither the term "kingdom" nor the phrase "kingdom of God" occurs in Luke 24, although they occur frequently throughout the rest of Luke. In the Gospel of Luke, Jesus teaches disciples primarily about scripture and his suffering and death rather than the kingdom of God (24:25–27, 32, 44–46).

The preface to Acts, then, describes the teaching of Jesus during the interim period between the resurrection and ascension in terms of that teaching's content prior to Jesus' suffering and death. Here again we see biographical dimensions at work. The nature of Jesus during his lifetime was both to perform mighty works and to teach the kingdom of God. In biographical writing, one can expect that an individual's persona during his lifetime will be appropriate to attribute (μετ' εὐστοχία ἀναφερομένη)[57] to him after his resurrection. The persona follows that person wherever he or she goes.

As the expanded chreia continues, it introduces a context for Jesus' poignant speech, just as Theon's expanded chreia creates a context for poignant speech by Epameinondas.[58] Again the handling of content within the preface to Acts is instructive. The narrational prose in Acts 1:4 uses the mode of indirect speech, approximating the content of Luke 24:49, to establish a context for attributing direct speech to Jesus about John's baptizing with water and about Jesus' followers being baptized with the Holy Spirit. Speech attributed to Jesus in Luke 24:49 — "And behold, I send the promise of my Father upon you; but stay in the

---

54. Ibid., 94–99.
55. Ibid., 100–103.
56. Ibid.
57. Ibid., 82–83.
58. Ibid., 100–103.

city, until you are clothed with power from on high" — is presented as indirect speech in Acts 1:4 — "And while staying with them he charged them not to depart from Jerusalem, but to wait for the promise of the Father." This indirect speech establishes the context for Jesus' direct speech: "which," he (Jesus) said, "you heard from me, because John baptized with water, but you will be baptized with the Holy Spirit not many days from now."

This speech embedded within speech is unusual, and it occurs as a result of attributing to Jesus the rationale that explains why his followers should stay in Jerusalem. In the Gospel of Luke (3:16), the statement about John baptizing with water and Jesus baptizing with the Holy Spirit is attributed to John, not to Jesus. Acts presents this saying two more times, and each instance is instructive in seeing how speech attributed to one person may travel in biographical narrative. In Acts 11:15–16, Peter says: "As I began to speak, the Holy Spirit fell on them just as on us at the beginning. And I remembered the word of the Lord, how he said, 'John baptized with water, but you shall be baptized with the Holy Spirit.'" Peter attributes the saying to Jesus rather than John, just as the narrator of Acts attributes it to Jesus in Acts 1:4–5 — in a context in which the narration exhibits the fulfillment of the prophecy of John.

Later in the narrative (Acts 19:1–7), this process moves one step further.

> [Paul] said to [disciples of Apollos]: "Did you receive the Holy Spirit when you believed?" And they said, "No, we have never even heard that there is a Holy Spirit." And he said, "Into what then were you baptized?" They said, "Into John's baptism." And Paul said, "John baptized with the baptism of repentance, telling people to believe in the one who was to come after him, that is, Jesus." On hearing this, they were baptized in the name of the Lord Jesus. And when Paul had laid his hands upon them, the Holy Spirit came on them; and they spoke with tongues and prophesied.

In this setting, the narrator of Acts attributes speech to Paul that exists partly as narration in Luke 3:3 — "And he went into all the region about the Jordan, preaching a baptism of repentance for the forgiveness of sins" — and partly as speech attributed to John the Baptist — "He who is mightier than I is coming, the thong of whose sandals I am not worthy to untie; he will baptize you with the Holy Spirit and with fire" (Luke 3:16). Paul recites John's speech in his own words, much like the inscribed author of Acts narrates speech of Jesus in his own words. John, according to the Gospel of Luke, did not literally tell people to "believe in the one who is to come after me." Paul, however, attributes this wording authoritatively to John (Acts 19:4). We see not only story as fulfillment of earlier prophetic speech but also different wording, handed on authoritatively by followers of Jesus who adapt the message to their favorite terminology. By this means, Christian discourse gradually modulates speech attributed to predecessors into speech that perpetuates later terminology and meaning.

The goal of the sequence (1:3–5), then, is to provide a reason for Jesus' followers to remain in Jerusalem. One can think of at least two reasons for such a rationale. First, one might imagine that Jesus' followers would have departed

Jerusalem immediately to preach the gospel to all nations. But the Gospel of Luke (21:12–19) does not contain the assertion of Mark 13:10 that "first it is necessary to preach the gospel to all nations." Second, one might imagine that Jesus' followers would go to Galilee after Jesus' death, where they expected to see him (as he had told them). But in the Gospel of Luke the personage at the empty tomb does not direct followers to Galilee, but directs them to remember that Jesus had told them in Galilee that the Son of Man would rise up.[59] The Gospel of Luke focuses on Jerusalem and vicinity as the place where Jesus appears after his resurrection. In accord with this emphasis, Jesus' command to his followers has an apotreptic feature ("do not depart from Jerusalem," Acts 1:4; cf. Luke 24:49) and a protreptic feature ("wait for the promise of the father," Acts 1:4; cf. Luke 24:49). These features combine with the rationale that "you will be baptized with the Holy Spirit before not many days" (Acts 1:5; cf. Luke 24:49).

A Program of Action for Jesus' Followers (Acts 1:6–8)

Acts 1:6–11 presents the result ("therefore," οὖν) of Jesus' command to his followers. Again the unit is composed like an expanded chreia. In this instance, the scene begins with a question from Jesus' followers: "Lord, will you at this time restore the kingdom to Israel?" This question recalls the scene at the Last Supper in which Jesus told the disciples he would assign them the kingdom his Father had assigned to him (Luke 22:28–30). The disciples, then, simply want a "yes" or "no" answer, presupposing that they know what the restoration of the kingdom will mean — that they will eat and drink at table and sit on thrones judging the twelve tribes of Israel, as in Luke 22:30. In the terms of Theon's *Progymnasmata*, Jesus treats the question not as a simple question (κατ᾿ ἐρώτησιν) that calls only for a "yes" or "no" answer, but as an inquiry (κατὰ πύσμα) requiring a substantive answer.[60] The answer Theon provides clarifies the matter by providing both a positive assertion and a negative clarification.[61] In Acts 1:7–8, Jesus responds with a negative assertion ("It is not for you to know times or seasons which the Father has fixed by his own authority") and a positive clarification ("But you will receive power when the Holy Spirit comes upon you; and you will be my witnesses in Jerusalem and in all Judea and Samaria and to the end of the earth"). Jesus' response does not answer whether or not Jesus will restore the kingdom to Israel, nor does it provide a rationale for the followers not knowing times or seasons the Father has established. Rather, the question provides the context for Jesus to reconfigure the program of the kingdom so it coheres with the command he had given in Acts 1:4. The disciples must not depart from Jerusalem, because

---

59. Cf. Mark 16:7 // Matt. 28:7 and Mark 14:28 // Matt. 26:32 with Luke 24:6–7 and 22:31–34).

60. Hock and O'Neil, *The Chreia*, 84–87.

61. *Positive:* A woman who has intercourse with her husband may go immediately in purity to the Thesmophorion. *Negative:* But a woman who has intercourse with a man who is not her husband is never able in purity to go to the Thesmophorion. See ibid., 87.

they will be baptized with the Holy Spirit so they may be "witnesses in Jerusalem and in all Judea and Samaria and to the end of the earth."

A new program of action emerges in this chreia statement, attributed to Jesus. If there is to be a time when the apostles will eat and drink at Jesus' table in the kingdom, and sit on thrones judging the twelve tribes of Israel, this is not it. A new program has emerged, and this program guides the ensuing narrative. In this way the program of Acts is authorized by Jesus himself, the founder and validator of the Christian movement.

Jesus' Ascension as Divine Action Witnessed by His Followers (Acts 1:9–11)

Immediately after Jesus' speech introduces a program for his followers' activity, Jesus' action becomes passive — he experiences something done to him (by God), rather than doing something himself. The result is a "passive" chreia:[62] Jesus is lifted up and a cloud takes him out of sight (1:9). Luke 24:50–51, in contrast, presents Jesus as the subject of all the action except his final ascent into heaven. He leads the disciples out, lifts up his hands, blesses them, parts from them, and is carried up into heaven. In Acts, Jesus' followers are active as Jesus experiences divine action upon himself. They look on as he is lifted up, and they gaze into heaven after a cloud takes him out of sight (1:9–11). The effect is to transform speech of Jesus that describes his followers as witnesses (Acts 1:8) into an action of the witnesses themselves, who are moving beyond Jesus' words, deeds, death, and resurrection. As they witness Jesus' ascension and gaze into heaven with wonderment, the issue is what this might mean for their future.

The final two verses address the witnesses' future, as two men in white robes ask a question that reorients the apostles' wonderment toward the return of Jesus. By means of these two men, Acts 1:10–11 presents a commentary (ἐπιφώνησις)[63] on the event. By contrast, "bystanders" do not interpret Jesus' ascension in Luke 24:50–53. The reader learns of "great joy" among the followers of Jesus that leads them to "bless God" continually in the Temple. But this is standard reaction to the miraculous in the Gospel of Luke, not an interpretation for what will unfold in Acts. The commentary in Acts gives "divine" insight into the event. Just as God has taken Jesus into heaven, as witnessed by his followers, so God will send Jesus back to earth at some future time, which only God knows (cf. Acts 1:7). The correlation of Jesus' ascent with his return in Acts 1:10–11 is part of the reconfiguration of the episode for its new context, the beginning of the acts of Jesus' followers, in which they receive the power to become Jesus' witnesses to the end of the earth. From the perspective of Acts, the issues are what Jesus' followers will do now that Jesus has gone, and what God and Jesus will do concerning the restoration of the kingdom to Israel. The issue is not

---

62. Ibid., 88–89, 96–99.
63. Ibid., 98–101.

simply Jesus' ascent into heaven as the last act of his resurrected life, but Jesus' ascent as an event his "witnesses" observe and as an event that establishes a model for Jesus' return.

Authoritative Pronouncement and Divine Action
Produce Obedient Response (Acts 1:12–14)

The final unit in the preface to Acts (1:12–14) is not a chreia but a narrative (διήγημα),[64] which Theon defines as an explanatory account of matters which have occurred, or an account of matters as if they have occurred.[65] A narrative contains six elements: (1) one or many characters; (2) the act of the character(s); (3) the place of the act; (4) the time of the act; (5) the manner of the act; and (6) the reason. The characters in this narrative are eleven apostles, women — including the mother of Jesus — and the brothers of Jesus (1:13–14). The act is devotion to prayer, and the place is the upper room in Jerusalem where they had been staying. The time is immediately after Jesus' ascension into heaven, and the manner is "with one accord." The reason is not stated in the unit itself, but is evident from the information provided in 1:4–5.

In contrast to the previous units in the preface to Acts, this unit uses key words from its counterpart at the end of Luke (24:52) as a beginning for amplification. The key words are "they returned to Jerusalem" (ὑπέστρεψαν εἰς Ἰερουσαλήμ, Luke 24:52 // Acts 1:12). Similar to previous units, however, the episode is substantively reconfigured for its new setting. Luke 24:52–53 gives the impression that Jesus' followers return to the Temple. Acts 1:13 has them return to the upper room. The account in Acts amplifies their return to this venue, lists the people who gather, and describes their activity as "devotion to prayer with one accord."

With this unit, the preface to Acts makes a transition to the narrative account. Whether Acts 1:12–14 is the final unit of the preface or the introductory unit in the account of Jesus' followers in Jerusalem is not certain. The final unit adopts a "narrative" mode, which differs from the "chreia" mode that characterizes every other unit in the preface. This means that the unit contains neither attributed speech, either as authoritative pronouncement or commentary, nor poignant action that introduces a decisive thought. The major portion of the preface prepares the reader for the ensuing account by attributing speech to various personages. The initial speech is by Jesus (1:4–5); followers ask Jesus a question (1:6); Jesus responds to his followers (1:7–8); and two men in white robes interpret the meaning of the ascension for Jesus' followers (1:11). In contrast, Acts 1:12–14 contains no attributed speech. Rather, it shows how the directives, rationale, program beyond Jerusalem, and commentary on Jesus' ascension produce a decisive response by Jesus' followers to the authoritative

---

64. J. R. Butts, *The "Progymnasmata" of Theon: A New Text with Translation and Commentary* (Ann Arbor, Mich.: University Microfilms, 1987), 290–401.

65. Ibid., 291.

pronouncements in the preceding units. With one accord, Jesus' followers and family return to Jerusalem, to the upper room, and devote themselves to prayer, awaiting their baptism with the Holy Spirit.

Conclusion

The claim of the preface to Luke is solidarity with others who have written narratives about the Christian movement. My analysis reveals an absence of significant concern to correct what others have written. Interpreters often have overlooked that the major exigency the author had to overcome was that he could write a good, reliable account for Theophilus. The major interest is in writing a "continuous" account — one that tells the story from the beginning to Rome. The preface to Acts builds on this interest, exhibiting how the words and deeds of Jesus' followers in Acts "grow out" of the words and deeds of Jesus in the Gospel.

Chapter 4

The Appeal and Power of Poetics (Luke 1:1–4)

Luke's Superior Credentials (παρηκολουθηκότι), Narrative Sequence (καθεξῆς), and Firmness of Understanding (ἡ ἀσφάλεια) for the Reader

David P. Moessner

Luke's Gospel prologue (Luke 1:1–4) has little to do with literary "genre" and everything to do with the distinctive *scope* and *sequence* of the account that follows. Rather than pinpoint the precise "type" or "subtype" of his narrative (διήγησις, 1:1),[1] Luke assumes that his audience already possesses some familiarity with the "events" or "matters" (πράγματα) that "have come to full fruition in our midst!" (1:1b) and is intent, instead, to commend his rendering of these matters vis-à-vis the many other accounts and oral reports that are already at hand (πολλοί...λόγων, 1:1, 3–4; cf. ἐπεχείρησαν, 1:1, and Theophilus's "instruction," κατηχέω, 1:4). By implication, his is a superior narrative account of happenings that seem to matter so much.[2]

In fact, the contours of his version would appear so critical that Luke appeals, in the first instance, to "eyewitnesses and attendants to this word" that ground his account with the many, and yet, in the next breath, sets his construal apart as instrumental in providing Theophilus with a certainty concerning these matters that Theophilus apparently lacks (1:3; ἡ ἀσφάλεια, 1:4) — this despite the many versions that, at least in theory, would be available to one so prominent as "your excellency" (κράτιστε, 1:3b; cf. κράτιστε, Acts 23:26 and 24:3 [Felix]; 26:25 [Festus]).[3] Bluntly stated, Luke must promote his own version because he

---

1. E.g., L. C. A. Alexander, "The Preface to Acts and the Historians," in *History, Literature, and Society in the Book of Acts*, ed. B. Witherington III (Cambridge: Cambridge University Press, 1996), 73–103. Alexander concludes that the Gospel prologue points to scientific or technical traditions and treatises, whereas the Acts prologue seems to introduce a continuation of the "first volume" as biography. This divergence of genre thus signals a unity which cannot be realistically predicated at either the narrative (plot) level or the generic level. But see p. 102: "There is sufficiently varied use of prefaces among Hellenistic Jewish writers to provide a literary context for Luke's."

2. As I shall argue below, the claim to an "improved" or "better" version is part of a larger topos occurring often in Hellenistic *prooemia*.

3. See, e.g., Josephus (*Against Apion* I.50), where Titus and Vespasian play the roles of guarantor as well as patron, perhaps even promoting distribution of Josephus's *War*.

is not fully satisfied with the narrative accounts of the "many." As we shall see, the central claims of his Gospel prologue evoke the terms and debates of the poetics of narrative (διήγησις) of the Greco-Roman period. The reason therefore that modern commentators continue to disagree over the generic markers of Luke's introductory statements is that they have missed the essential rubric of these opening claims. The scope of this essay permits a detailed discussion of only two of these terms, παρηκολουθηκότι and καθεξῆς (1:3), along with several related terms, ἀρχή, ἄνωθεν, ἀκριβῶς, and ἀσφάλεια (1:2, 3, 4). But I shall demonstrate that Luke uses his *prooemium* to place his work within debates of contemporary poetics concerning what constitutes "good" narrative. On the basis of those criteria, he presents his narrative as a worthy and legitimate reconfiguration of the "many" other attempts. Finally, in an epilogue, I suggest that, a generation later, the rather odd defense in the Papias fragment (*Ecclesiastical History* III.39.15–16) of Mark's "narrative" over against Matthew's echoes the arguments of poetics in Luke's Gospel prologue. Ironically, Mark receives his due based on the widely accepted criteria that Luke's prologue (and subsequent text) had already established for the Gospel narratives.

My thesis, then, is that Luke 1:1–4 can best be illuminated by contemporary Hellenistic writers' references to their own superior credentials in producing alternative versions of traditions, themes, or periods of history, and so on, ostensibly well represented in current literature. Justification for a "new" compilation often includes — whether explicitly or implicitly — criticism of the others' narrative sequences, starting points, and scope. As the epistemological hinge and hermeneutical lens for Luke's distinctive enterprise, παρηκολουθηκότι (1:3) is the most promising place to begin.

Παρηκολουθηκότι as a Term of Superior Credentials (Luke 1:3)

It is hard to overestimate the importance of this perfect participle, which authenticates Luke as a composer of διήγησις and promotes him vis-à-vis the "many others" and the tradents of oral λόγοι who have instructed the likes of Theophilus. L. Alexander in her groundbreaking *The Preface to Luke's Gospel* refers to this participle as making "some sort of epistemological claim about the status of the material presented,"[4] while earlier in the twentieth century Cadbury had contended that proper interpretation of the *whole* of the prologue depended on its precise meaning.[5]

---

4. L. C. A. Alexander, *The Preface to Luke's Gospel: Literary Convention and Social Context in Luke 1.1–4 and Acts 1.1*, SNTSMS 78 (Cambridge: Cambridge University Press, 1993), 133–34.

5. See H. J. Cadbury, "The Knowledge Claimed in Luke's Preface," *Expositor* 8 (1922): 401–20; cf. J. A. Fitzmyer, *The Gospel according to Luke (I–IX)*, AB 28 (Garden City, N.Y.: Doubleday, 1981), 1.296: "It is the crucial word in the modern interpretation of the Lucan prologue."

Possible Meanings of Παρακολουθέω

παρηκολουθηκότι can*not* mean one who has "followed up," "traced," "investigated," "informed himself about," "gone back and familiarized himself with," and so on. As Cadbury demonstrated in several articles, παρακολουθέω always has the sense of staying current or abreast of something (or someone) that is developing, increasing, or occurring over time.[6] Moreover, in the *Festschrift* for Professor Smit Sibinga,[7] I have shown that the usual appeal to Josephus's *Against Apion* I.53, in support of the current, "orthodox" rendering of παρακολουθέω as "investigate"[8] or to "go back over" something (as in Bauer and many commentaries) is fundamentally wrong; in fact, by παρηκολουθηκότες in I.53, Josephus means almost the opposite (see "παρακολουθέω in Josephus," below).

παρηκολουθηκότι may mean:

1. One who has followed *with the mind* a speech; a text,[9] through reading or hearing; a teaching[10] (meaning hence approximates "observant," "adherent of"); a habit[11] (habitual behavior) or ritual[12] as a religious observant; events; persons; movements of history.[13]

2. One who has physically accompanied (a) person(s) at their side or in their entourage; or something that has been alongside or accompanied other things; or a nonliteral use of "having accompanied" or "attended" in the negative sense of

---

6. In addition to Cadbury's "The Knowledge Claimed" (n. 5), see idem, "The Purpose Expressed in Luke's Preface," *The Expositor* (June 1921): 431–41; idem, "Commentary on the Preface of Luke," in *The Beginnings of Christianity* (New York: Macmillan, 1922–33), 2, appendix C (489–510); idem, "'We' and 'I' Passages in Luke-Acts," *NTS* 3 (1956–57): 128–32. Cf., e.g., E. Trocmé, *Le "Livre des Actes" et L'Histoire* (Paris: Presses Universitaires de France, 1957), 122–29, who follows Cadbury's interpretation.

Among many who hold to the now classic meaning of "investigate" are R. J. Dillon ("Previewing Luke's Project from His Prologue [Luke 1:1–4]," *CBQ* 43 [1981]: 218–19); I. I. du Plessis ("Once More: The Purpose of Luke's Prologue [Luke I 1–4]," *NovT* 16 [1974]: 266–67); A. J. B. Higgins ("The Preface to Luke and the Kerygma in Acts," in *Apostolic History and the Gospel*, ed. W. W. Gasque and R. P. Martin [Grand Rapids, Mich.: Eerdmans, 1970], 79–82); F. H. Colson ("Notes on St. Luke's Preface," *JTS* 24 [1923]: 304, 309); M. Devoldère ("Le prologue du troisième évangile," *NRT* 56 [1929]: 714–19); V. Hartl ("Zur synoptischen Frage: Schliesst Lukas durch 1,1–3 die Benutzung des Matthäus aus?" *BZ* 13 [1925]: 334–37); E. Haenchen ("Das 'Wir' in der Apostelgeschichte und das Itinerar," *ZTK* 58 [1961]: 363–65); J. Kürzinger ("Lk 1,3:...ἀκριβῶς καθεξῆς σοι γράψαι," *BZ* 18 [1974]: 253–54); W. Grundmann (*Das Evangelium nach Lukas*, THKNT [Berlin: Evangelische Verlagsanstalt, 1961], 44); I. H. Marshall (*The Gospel of Luke*, NIGTC [Exeter: Paternoster, 1978], 42–43); Fitzmyer (*The Gospel according to Luke [I–IX]*, 296–97); E. Schweizer (*The Good News according to Luke* [Atlanta: John Knox Press, 1984], 12).

7. D. P. Moessner, "'Eyewitnesses,' 'Informed Contemporaries,' and 'Unknowing Inquirers': Josephus' Criteria for Authentic Historiography and the Meaning of ΠΑΡΑΚΟΛΟΥΘΕΩ," *NovT* 38 (1996): 105–22.

8. See, e.g., NRSV: "having investigated everything."

9. In addition to the passages treated below, see esp. Dionysius of Halicarnassus (*De Thucydide* 9) and discussion in "Extratextual Evidence for the Significance of καθεξῆς," below.

10. E.g., 1 Tim. 4:6 or 2 Tim. 3:10.

11. E.g., Josephus, *Against Apion* II.5. K. H. Rengstorf, ed., *A Complete Concordance to Flavius Josephus* (Leiden: Brill, 1973–83), lists "habit" as a distinct referent for παρακολουθέω.

12. E.g., Josephus, *Antiquities* 12.259; cf. 2 Tim. 3:10.

13. In addition to the passage of Josephus treated below, see, e.g., 2 Tim. 3:10; Josephus, *Life* 357; Demosthenes, *De Corona* 53; idem, *De Falsa Legatione* 257; UPZ 71,20; PSI IV.411,3.

pestering or insulting someone.[14] Prior to the Papias fragment, the positive sense of a disciple or student "physically accompanying / following" a teacher cannot be adduced. In fact, before this reference to Mark not having "followed him [i.e., the Lord]" (*Eccles. Hist.* III.39.15), there is no demonstrable instance of positive physical "accompaniment."[15] Rather, if not neutral, the sense may be negative, as in "dogging" someone or "accompanying with malevolent intent."[16]

3. Something that has followed logically in the intransitive sense of "result from."[17]

Since παρηκολουθηκότι in Luke 1:3 has the dative direct object πᾶσιν, sense 3 can be ruled out.

Likewise, sense 2 can be eliminated since:

(*a*) Luke aligns himself with the "us" (καθὼς παρέδοσαν ἡμῖν, 1:2) who have received tradition "delivered over" by others. Moreover, this traditional material comes from those, unlike him, who were "eyewitnesses" or "attendants" of the traditions ἀπ᾽ ἀρχῆς ("from the origins" / "from the beginning").

(*b*) The credibility of πᾶσιν as masculine plural (i.e., "all" the eyewitnesses and attendants [ὑπηρέται] as tradents of "the word" [1:2]) becomes stretched beyond rhetorical believability even if Luke is indicating that he has physically accompanied only some of the apostles and teachers. To claim to have followed all of them, and yet, possibly through the first-person "we" narration of Acts 16ff. to indicate having only followed Paul (cf. 26:16 — Paul as ὑπήρέτης), produces at best a confused profile of his qualifications to compose διήγησις, particularly when Luke describes his narrative as concerning "events that have come to fruition in *our* midst" (1:1).[18]

(*c*) The syntax and balanced period of the *prooemium* point in the last half (1:3–4) to the author's intention to reconfigure traditions in which Theophilus has been instructed; Luke's credentials must therefore indicate how he is qualified to reorder those traditions delivered by the eyewitnesses and attendants who have already set the standard concerning the integrity of their material. In order to accomplish his goal of giving Theophilus the "certainty" of understanding these traditions' true significance (ἡ ἀσφάλεια, 1:4), Luke finds it necessary to compose another narrative, *not* simply to correct the accuracy of individual

---

14. E.g., Aristophanes, *The Ecclesiazusae* 725:10; Plato, *The Sophist* 266a; Demosthenes, *Oration* (against Meidias) XXI.14.69; Philemon 124; Demosthenes, *De Corona* 162; Aristotle, *Historia Animalium* 496a29; Josephus, *Antiquities* 14.438; idem, *Jewish War* 1.455.

15. Cf. Eusebius, *Ecclesiastical History* III.39.4 (παρηκολουθηκώς ... τοῖς πρεσβυτέροις); III.39.15 (παρηκολούθησεν αὐτῷ [i.e., the Lord]); see epilogue below. Neither Bauer nor Liddell and Scott, for instance, attests this positive sense in their many examples of "physical accompaniment."

16. See, e.g., Josephus, *Jewish War* 6.251.

17. E.g., *PSI* 3.168.24; PRein. 18.15.

18. The rather late appearance of the "we" in Acts 16, in fact, becomes even more mysterious if Luke is claiming that he had physically accompanied several eyewitnesses / attendants (ὑπηρέται) "for some time back" / "from the top" (ἄνωθεν, Luke 1:3). Although "we" narration may be treated as a separate convention, distinct from the "I" and "us" of the prologues, it can still be read as including the inscribed author of the prologues, as was done, for instance, in the early church; see, e.g., Irenaeus, *Adversus Haereses* 3.1.1; Tertullian, *Adversus Marcionem* 4.2.2.

traditions of the "many" or of the "oral" tradents. Hence his relation to the various traditions would accord well with an author "having followed" (with his mind) all the matters (παρηκολουθηκότι…πᾶσιν), together with the sense of ἀκριβῶς to mean "with understanding."[19] Luke is claiming the competence to reconfigure the events or matters of the many by virtue of his "having followed with understanding" all these as well as other traditions. Otherwise, ἀκριβῶς sits rather awkwardly with παρηκολουθηκότι as connoting physical accompaniment. In fact, neither Bauer nor Liddell and Scott attests *physical* "following," whether closely or accurately; both establish that ἀκριβῶς goes hand in hand with verbs of perception and cognition, commensurate with παρακολουθέω as "following with the mind."[20] (For παρακολουθέω used with ἀκριβῶς, see below.)

(d) Finally, the recurrence of πάντα in the Acts prologue as "*all* that Jesus *began* to do and teach" (Acts 1:1) reinforces its dynamic sense and referent in the Lukan prologue as *all* the events / matters (πράγματα) that have been "delivered over" to the "us" (1:2), including traditions / matters / reports that are circulating as sources of instruction (cf. λόγοι, 1:4). That "eyewitnesses" are linked to these πράγματα "from the beginning" (ἀπ' ἀρχῆς, 1:2) in the Lukan prologue and that the opening of Acts takes great pains to define this beginning *with respect to the apostles as eyewitnesses*, points to a common πάντα as the material linking both volumes (ἀρξάμενος ἀπὸ — "the baptism of John," Acts 1:5 → 1:22). The further fact that the closing πράγματα of the Gospel are repeated and refigured as the opening πράγματα of Acts[21] graphically portrays this common πάντα of traditions.

Παρηκολουθηκότι *in Luke 1:3 must therefore mean "one who has followed with the mind" all the traditions of the* πράγματα *that have been "delivered over from those tradents of the word from the beginning." But what more precisely does this mean?*

Παρακολουθέω in Prologues

Most instructive are the ways that ancient Greek authors of historiography, philosophical essays, and scientific or technical prose and treatises employ παρακολουθέω in prefaces to provide a rationale for and/or legitimation of their undertaking.

Polybius, *The Histories* I.1–15

In this first of two introductory books to his larger forty-volume history, Polybius is justifying the *scale, starting point,* and *sequence* of his composition.[22] Παρακο-

---

19. See esp. Dionysius of Halicarnassus, *De Thucydide* 9, and "Extratextual Evidence," below.

20. See Bauer, who lists the verbs ἀκούειν, προσέχειν, γινώσκειν, κατανοεῖν, εἰδέναι, ἱστορῆσαι, ἐκτίθεσθαι, etc.; Liddell and Scott, s.v., εἰδέναι, ἐπίστασται, καθορᾶν, μαθεῖν.

21. Luke 3:21–24:53≈Acts 1:1–2; Luke 24:13–43≈Acts 1:3; Luke 24:36–49≈Acts 1:4–5; Luke 24:50–51≈Acts 1:6–11; Luke 24:52–53≈Acts 1:12–14; notice the special catena of Acts 1:5 ↔ Luke 24:47 → Luke 3:16.

22. See appendix 1, below. All translations are from the Loeb Classical Library, unless otherwise indicated.

λουθέω functions as a fulcrum to tie the reader (1) to the nature, scope, and authorial intention for the work as a whole, on the one side, and (2) to the author's special credentials, on the other.

1. In order for the reader to gain an overall grasp or synopsis (σύνοψις) of Rome's supremacy — the main purpose of Polybius's enterprise — they will have to follow (παρακολουθέω) the earlier events of Rome's rise by integrating them into the sequel (ἐν τοῖς ἑξῆς, I.12.7–8; cf. καθεξῆς, Luke 1:3). That is, the reader must follow (παρακολουθέω) the sequence of Polybius's διήγησις. Only in this way will clarity (σαφέστερον κατανοεῖν; cf. ἐπιγινωσκειν…ἀσφάλειαν, Luke 1:4) emerge, which Polybius argues is critical and which motivates him to write in the light of "others'" accounts.

The reason is as profound as it is obvious. Polybius writes an extended, multivolume narrative which in effect is a mimesis of the workings of Fortune (τύχη) in the rise of Roman power. Polybius's narrative must "re-present" in its scope and its multiple narrative connections the grand sweep of Fortune in her multifarious interconnecting "performances." Both the whole and parts of Polybius's narrative must reflect the total purpose (συντέλεια) and all of the "operations" that Polybius in his study of history has discerned as the master orchestration of Fortune. It is not just that contemporary treatments of recent wars, as for instance in Josephus's *Against Apion*, are inadequate or misrepresent the truth. Rather, "above" and "beyond" that rationale, no reader can discover the greater truth of the grander purpose — not to mention the significance of various events — without a "synoptic" view of *all* the events, including those extending back to a logically conceived "beginning" (ἀρχή), which have combined to produce this "complete" whole. To say it another way, the poetics of Polybius's narrative are constitutive of his own "synopsis" of reality. Both the scope and the sequence of Roman ascendancy must be reconstrued through a new narrative "road," which will "guide my readers…to a true notion (ἀλήθινα ἐννοία) of this war" (I.15.13).

2. It is already clear that παρακολουθέω also links the reader's "following" to the narrator's credentials to "lead." Throughout his forty volumes Polybius draws attention to his keen study of the rise of Rome, which occurred both through firsthand witness of many of the events themselves and through careful study of government documents and earlier histories. We learn, for instance in III.4–5, that in composing the history from the Second Punic War to the end of the Third Macedonian War (220–168 B.C.E.), Polybius learned through his own experiences of turbulent times following "the last conquest" of 168 that he must describe the aftermath of Rome's rule as well as have readers "follow" (παρακολουθέω) him back to the earlier "beginning" of 264 B.C.E., to bring this new state of affairs into proper perspective. Polybius's active engagement both as eyewitness and as an informed contemporary follower of the rise of Rome produced his special qualifications to compose a narrative. Polybius can lead his readers precisely because of his "mind's own ability to follow" the rise of Rome's preeminence.

In sum, Polybius was an avid student of history. He assumed that his readers would be so engaged. Thus, the emphasis in Polybius's use of παρακολουθέω in his extended preface is on the mind finding new vistas of understanding which will occur by "following" the distinctive scope and sequence of his narrative. Παρακολουθέω thus ties the *readers' ability to follow to the author's peculiar competence to lead.*

Theophrastus, *The Characters*, Prooemium (4)

Although some four times longer than the Gospel prologue, Theophrastus's concentrated preface, by coordinating common concerns with similar vocabulary, produces intriguing parallels with Luke 1:1–4.[23] (1) Like Luke (1:1), Theophrastus begins with a summary of the content before proceeding to his credentials. (2) Like Luke (1:3), Theophrastus addresses his patron/dedicatee in the vocative (cf. esp. Acts 1:1 — ὦ θεόφιλε) by way of introducing his qualifications, which are (*a*) careful observation (συνθεωρήσας; cf. Luke 1:3 — παρηκολουθηκότι) (*b*) for a long period of time (ἐκ πόλλου χρόνου; cf. Luke 1:3 — ἄνωθεν), (*c*) with great carefulness or diligence (ἀκριβεία; cf. Luke 1:3 — ἀκριβῶς). Such qualifications are then linked to the desired impact on the reader. It is only as the reader follows the author's composition that true understanding (i.e., the author's!) of the subject matter ensues. Again, the word παρακολουθέω ties the edification of the reader to the author's special competence and unparalleled literary results. Unlike Luke and Polybius, however, Theophrastus does not mention "others'" attempts and therefore does not have to legitimate his own reworking of a conventional topos.

Strabo, *Geography* 1.1.14–15, 22–23; 1.2.1

In this extended *prooemium* (I.1–2),[24] Strabo delineates the scope and nature of his subject matter to justify the illumination he intends for his readers. Unless his readers follow (παρακολουθέω) the peculiar scope and sequence of his treatise, they will not be able to attain a "clear exposition" (σαφῶς ἐξειπεῖν). Moreover, they will be in no position to judge whether his own undertaking — which both adds to the information of his predecessors and criticizes certain insights — has been worth the effort. For instance, it would be futile, he claims, to present the ways that geography bears on the political life of the nations without treating the influence of the celestial world on these affairs. Without that critical component, the readers would not be able to follow (παρακολουθέω) his text and gain an accurate understanding (ἅπαντα ἀκριβοῦν) of the subject matter.

Once again, the pivotal term linking the author's purpose to the readers' experience of the author's qualifications is παρακολουθέω. For as Strabo invites his

---

23. See appendix 2 for translation.
24. See appendix 3 for translation.

readers to "follow," he stresses more than previously cited authors the high level of education which is required of them; he envisions as primary reader the "person of public life" or the "statesman" (τὸ πολιτικόν). Only a reader schooled in "virtue" and "practical wisdom" will be able to appreciate the additions that Strabo makes to the "many" before him, and to "follow" Strabo's criticisms of certain predecessors (including Polybius!), by following (παρακολουθέω) the structured arrangement (σύνταξις) of his arguments. Hence, similar to Polybius and Theophrastus, παρακολουθέω again links the author's qualifications to expectations placed on the readers. Only "schooled" readers will be able to follow the distinctive scope and sequence that motivated Strabo to put together a new, rhetorical sequence (ὑπόθεσις) in the first place. Thus both *formal* (literary) and *material* rationale are linked to παρακολουθέω.

Apollonius of Citium, *Commentary on the "De Articulis" of Hippocrates* I

> In order that every detail may be thoroughly easy for you to follow (εὐπαρακολού-θητά), I shall set out the text . . . and methods of operation . . . some of which I have performed myself, while others I observed as a student of Zopyrus in Alexandria. And Posidonius, who studied with the same doctor, would testify with us that this man performed cures with the highest degree of fidelity to Hippocrates. (End of preface)

Prefaces in the scientific or technical prose traditions are generally much shorter and follow a standard sequence, containing (1) a statement of the author's decision to write; (2) the subject and contents, or scope, of the book; (3) second-person address of dedication; (4) the nature of the subject matter; (5) mention of others who have written on the subject, whether predecessors and/or rivals; (6) assessment of the author's qualifications; and, (7) general remarks on methodology.[25]

Παρακολουθέω or cognate εὐπαρακολουθέω are found in several of these prefaces, usually tying the author's distinctive credentials and literary product, as in the first three examples above, to the desired impact on the reader. In the example of Apollonius, both "hands-on" experience as well as faithfulness to a tradition mark him as qualified to lead the reader through a new path of understanding.[26]

---

25. Alexander, *Preface,* 69–91. See n. 4 above. The last two categories emerge in the late and post-Hellenistic period, and by the first century C.E. listing the "author's qualifications" was "well established in the scientific tradition" (87). In her more recent contribution to this volume, Alexander amends the sevenfold scheme to six categories, subsuming the "subject and contents" as part of the "nature and sources" of the subject and changing "general methodological remarks" to "the intended effect of the book" on the reader.

26. Alexander, *Preface,* 96, also points to the following examples: εὐπαρακολούθητος — Hero of Alexandria, *Belopoeica* W 73.11 ("so that the tradition may be easy to follow for all"); Dioscorides, *De Simplicibus* (=Eup Bk. I pref. [M. Wellmann vol. III]) p. 151.5; παρακολουθέω — Diocles of Carystus, *Letter to Antigonus* [c. 300 B.C.E., short treatise on hygiene] ("And you, if you are persuaded by what I say, will be able to understand their accuracy" [ἀκριβείᾳ]).

Summary

Παρακολουθέω (or εὐπαρακολουθέω) has the following characteristics in the prefaces studied.

1. It spans different genres, historiography, philosophical and moral treatises, and scientific and technical prose, to link the author's distinctive credentials and rationale for writing to the specific goals the reader is to achieve by "following" (παρακολουθέω).

2. It occurs in a variety of socio-literary circumstances when an author refers to others' writings on the same topic, whether in cases of inadequate rival versions (Polybius), unprecedented or perhaps allegedly unrivaled undertakings (Theophrastus), or in supplementing and correcting certain aspects of previous and/or rival treatments (Strabo).[27]

3. It parallels Luke's concerns to link his competence to the writing's salutary impact on readers (Luke 1:3–4). Strabo would appear, at first glance, to provide the closest parallel to Luke's usage of παρακολουθέω in 1:3. Strabo justifies his version by referring to supplemental and complementary material, while at points correcting impressions of those he otherwise follows rather closely.

Yet Polybius's rationale seems much closer to Luke's. Like Polybius, (a) Luke emphasizes the unique subject matter that consists of matters / events in history that have come to a certain τέλος[28] or completion/fruition (πεπληροφορημένα, 1:1). And although Luke does not articulate the basis for this "fulfillment" as Polybius does in his references to Fortune, throughout his two volumes Luke does refer to a "divine necessity" or "plan" as the source of coherence for the matters/events (πράγματα, 1:1).[29] (b) Luke refers to a "beginning" that is critical as a base point for the narrative, and records his own credentials in relation to that ἀρχή: παρηκολουθηκότι ἄνωθεν. Yet neither Polybius nor Luke was an eyewitness or an engaged contemporary of their "beginning point." Moreover, both trace events even further back so the reader will better appreciate the significance of the "beginning" for the rest of the narrative. (c) Luke ties his new narrative sequence, as well as its scope, to the deliberate enlightenment of readers, which includes a firmer grasp of individual events as they relate to a larger whole. (d) Unlike Polybius, Luke does not explicitly challenge another account.[30] Yet the consistent linkage of scope and sequence, the author's creden-

---

27. With regard to scientific texts, see ibid., 76–77: "It is a particular feature of the post-Hellenistic prefaces regularly to place this theme at the beginning of their work and to make the work of others the explicit basis of the author's own decision to write. This basis is by no means always polemical . . . " (76).

28. *The Histories* I.3.4. But see also the many times Luke uses the τελέ-ο word group and synonyms in what has come to be called his theology of promise / prophecy and fulfillment.

29. Already, however, the passive voice of πεπληροφορημένα is suggestive. For "the plan (βουλή) of God," see Luke 7:30; Acts 2:23; 4:28; (5:38); 13:36; 20:27; (27:42–43). See, e.g., D. P. Moessner, "The 'Script' of the Scriptures in Acts: Suffering as God's 'Plan' (βουλή) for the World for the 'Release of Sins,'" in Witherington, *History, Literature, and Society in the Book of Acts*, 218–50.

30. See, e.g., Book 12 of *The Histories*, where Polybius challenges both the facts as well as the methods of other historians.

tials, and the impact on the reader, which παρακολουθέω provides, indicates that in Luke's mind all is not well with the "many's" accounts. On this score also, Luke closely parallels Polybius.[31]

Yet for all these similarities between Luke's use of παρηκολουθηκότι and the authors reviewed, the striking difference between Luke 1:3 and other occurrences of παρακολουθέω in prefaces is that the word, in claiming the ability to "follow," is predicated of Luke the author and not of his readers. More than that, the perfect tense suggests previous activity or ability on the part of Luke, the *consequence* of which has become crucial to his qualifications to tender yet another narrative version, rather than a present ability "to follow with the mind" the sequence of his own account. Do not, in fact, these differences sever the linkage of παρακολουθέω in Greco-Roman prefaces with the oeuvre of Luke's writing to Theophilus?

First, Polybius's use of the aorist infinitive in I.12.7 (παρακολουθῆσαι) applies to any reader, including himself, since it is only through "following" through reading the specific "arrangement" (οἰκονομία, I.13.9) of connected events *in and through the narrative itself* that any person can attain a sufficient point of view (σύνοψις, I.4.1) to bring intelligibility to the rise of Rome (see esp. I.13.9). Only the narrative with its multivalent connections is epistemologically adequate to the task! To underscore this point Polybius repeats this argument, with παρακολουθέω, within the composition itself, "breaking frame" (III.32.2) in a digression against detractors who contend his multivolume work is too difficult to read (δυσανάγνωστον).[32]

Even more important, however, Josephus uses the perfect participle παρηκολουθηκότες of *himself* in arguing for the superiority of his credentials and narrative over against rival accounts of the war with Rome. Later in the same work, *Against Apion*, he employs the present infinitive in clarifying how he (similar to Polybius with Rome's past) could "follow" events hundreds or more years removed from Israel's current events.

Παρακολουθέω in Josephus

Against Apion I.53–56

The cluster of παράδοσις, ἀκριβῶς, and πράξεις with the perfect participle of παρακολουθέω provides striking parallels to Luke 1:1–4.[33] The context of Josephus's argument vis-à-vis "others'" accounts is that Greek history writers show much less regard for historical records and historical accuracy than other

---

31. Interestingly, more like Theophrastus's *Characters*, the resulting generic shape of Luke's two volumes has produced something "new," for which the church's separation of Acts from the Gospels in the New Testament canon is the most glaring evidence.

32. Cf. παρέκβασις, III.33.1. "How much easier it is to acquire and peruse forty Books, all as it were connected by one thread, and thus to follow clearly [παρακολουθῆσαι σαφῶς, III.32.2] events in Italy, Sicily... than to read or procure the works of those who treat of particular transactions."

33. See appendix 4 for translations of this and the following section of *Against Apion*.

peoples, but especially compared with the Jews and the long-standing tradition that has formed Josephus as a writer.[34] He expatiates on how he is more qualified to write the history of the war with Rome than others who have "never visited the sites nor were anywhere near the actions described" (I.46). Josephus, on the contrary, has "composed [ἐποιησάμην; cf. Acts 1:1] a veracious account," as "one present in person at all the events" (πράγμασιν αὐτὸς ἅπασι παρατυχών, I.47). So confident is he of his final narrative account of the events (ἐποιησάμην τῶν πράξεων τὴν παράδοσιν, I.50) that, in countering his critics, he can call as witnesses (μάρτυρες, I.50; cf. Acts 1:8), if need be, no less than Vespasian or Titus, commanders in chief of the war. Other notables who have read Josephus's War have already "borne testimony" (ἐμαρτύρησαν, I.52) to its "safeguarding of the truth" (I.49–52).

Poignant parallels notwithstanding, Josephus's relationship to the "other" history writers would seem the obverse of Luke's relation to the "many." Josephus makes eyewitness claims for all the events he recounts in his War, whereas Luke refers to another group of "eyewitnesses" upon whom he depends for information. Prima facie, it would seem that Luke fits into Josephus's second category of writers who must "inquire" (πυνθάνομαι, I.54) from "those who know"/"are in the know."[35]

But when Josephus in the same passage applies his credential of having followed recent events to the ancient events of the Antiquities — justifying his qualifications for that work as well — we see how close his use of this term is to Luke's claim in the Gospel prologue. But how can a historian "follow" (παρακολουθέω) ancient events when separation of time precludes the ability "to follow with the mind" or to stay informed about happenings as they unfold? Since Josephus could not make the same "eyewitness" claims, would he not perforce have to describe himself as an "inquirer," one who must study and research (πυνθάνομαι) ancient documents and other pertinent sources?[36] Josephus continues to answer in I.54: He has met his own criterion of providing a

---

34. Cf. T. Rajak's comment ("Josephus and the 'Archaeology' of the Jews," JJS 33 [1982]: 465–77: "The real home of the sort of claim which he makes about accurate reproduction of a sacred tradition seems to be among the later Greek exponents of Oriental cultures ... generally native in origin but using the Greek language ... closer to Josephus in function than the students of early Greek tradition" (472).

35. For a fuller discussion of all eight uses of παρακολουθέω in Josephus's extant works, see Moessner "'Eyewitnesses,' 'Informed Contemporaries'" (cited in n. 7 above).

36. It is tempting to understand I.53–54 as a straightforward chiasm with the author treating the following topics: (a) "following" events as they occur; (b) "inquiring" (after the event) from "those who knew/know them"; (b') Antiquities as an "inquiry" into the scriptures "from those [the authors, eyewitness sources, etc.] who knew them"; (a') War as recounting events by one who "followed" them as they occurred. Is this not the general sense of Josephus's claims? Yet neither in this passage nor in Ant. 1.5 does Josephus speak of "inquiring" or "seeking information" (πυνθάνομαι) from the scriptures. Rather, he "translates" them. His means of presenting an accurate account of ancient events leaps over the inquiry stage directly to the following stage. This leap is all the more striking given the necessity, in the opening of the treatise, of πυνθάνεσθαι τὴν ἀλήθειαν ("inquiring after the truth") through studying the primeval histories of other nations (Against Apion I.6). But this difference in referent between other nations', including "Greek," historiography, and Josephus's own

reliable (ἀκριβῶς) account of ancient events because he "translated our sacred scriptures" (ἐκ τῶν ἱερῶν γραμμάτων μεθηρμήνευκα, I.54). All the same, how can his translation of Jewish scripture be deemed a "following" (παρακολουθέω) when hundreds of years removed from the events he "translates"? "In my *Antiquities,* as I said, I have given a translation of our sacred books; being a priest and of priestly ancestry, I am well-versed in the philosophy of those writings" (γενομονὼς ἱερεὺς ἐκ γένους καὶ μετεσχηκὼς τῆς φιλοσοφίας τῆς ἐν ἐκείνοις τοῖς γράμμασι). Years of training and immersion (μετέχω) in Israel's texts have formed Josephus into one supremely qualified to comprehend, "to follow" these scriptures when he reads or translates them for a less informed audience. Josephus has superior credentials to *follow with his mind* the meaning of these texts as he follows the sequence of the texts themselves, since he, as he says in introducing his qualifications (I.42–46), by "instinct (σύμφυτον) with every Jew, from the day of his birth" has come to regard the scriptures "as the decrees of God, to abide by them, and, if need be, cheerfully to die for them" (I.42). Now in this same Book 1 of *Against Apion,* Josephus returns to a discussion of a historian's ability to "follow" (παρακολουθέω) ancient events of Israel as depicted in their scriptures, reminding us of Polybius's assertion concerning his knowledge of the early events in Rome's ascendancy.

Against Apion I.213–18

Within Book 1's survey of historical accounts of the Jewish nation, Josephus mentions the majority of writers' neglect of their scriptures (and history) — out of a variety of motives, including base character. But he also refers to three historians who out of the best intentions have become familiar with Israel's scriptures, but who still evince "the inability to follow the meaning of our records with complete reliability / accuracy" (οὐ γὰρ ἐνῆν αὐτοῖς μετὰ πάσης ἀκριβείας τοῖς ἡμετέροις γράμμασι παρακολουθεῖν) when they read them.[37]

He does not mean that their ability to read Hebrew was limited, since Josephus himself appears to rely heavily on an Alexandrian version of the Old Greek for his own "translation."[38] More to the point, as a priest from a line of priests, Josephus may "excuse" (οἷς συγγιγνώσκειν ἄξιον, I.218) a Demetrius, Eupolemus, or Philo for a lack of "insider" knowledge since they do not have the long years of training of one schooled in the ideas and way of life of these sacred writings.[39] However diligent and competent the three "exceptional" historians may be, their

---

saturation in the scriptural traditions of Israel's history illustrates precisely the distinction between πυνθάνομαι and παρακολουθέω.

37. Translation mine.

38. See, e.g., S. Z. Leiman, "Josephus and the Canon of the Bible," in *Josephus, the Bible, and History,* ed. L. H. Feldman and G. Hata (Detroit: Wayne State University Press, 1988), 50–58; cf. H. S. J. Thackeray, *Josephus: The Man and the Historian* (New York: Ktav, 1967), 73–99.

39. Cf. Rajak's assessment ("Josephus and the 'Archaeology' "), 474: "He [Josephus] is apparently so ill-informed abut those writers that he can confuse Demetrius the historian with his better-known Greek namesake, the politician and librarian, and can assume all three to be non-Jews. He did not,

ability to "follow" (παρακολουθέω) Israel's scriptures pales alongside one who for many years had been saturated (μετεσχηκώς, I.54) in the meaning of the scriptures and who thus did not need to "seek information" (πυνθάνομαι, I.53).

Summary

Παρακαλουθέω is a credentialing term in *Against Apion*, linking the author's superior qualifications to the desired impact of his works on readers. It functions, therefore, in the same manner as παρακαλουθέω in the prefaces of the multiple genres surveyed above. Just as, for example, Polybius stresses an ability to provide readers with the necessary perspective from which to interpret the parts and the whole, Josephus emphasizes in *Antiquities* his long-standing, deeply rooted expertise in the texts and traditions of his nation, which therefore, better than any rival, qualifies him to lead his readers *to* and *through* those traditions. In both of Josephus's historiographical works, παρακολουθέω connotes a credentialed expert whose mastery of the subject effects fundamental confidence for the reader. The writer's competence comes through "staying abreast" of events as they occurred, as in *War*, and/or through the ability to "comprehend immediately" the history of a people or nation by following their ancient texts, and thereby leading others into new territories of knowledge through the epistemological shaping of the expert's own account (*Antiquities*).[40]

Preliminary Conclusions for Παρηκολουθηκότι in Luke 1:3

Until relating παρηκολουθηκότι in more detail to the surrounding terms and syntax of Luke's prologue (Luke 1:1–4), we can draw only preliminary conclusions. But it has already become clear that of the authors investigated, Josephus sparks significant illumination.

The literary-historical claims are similar. It would appear that similar to Josephus in *Against Apion* I.54 and 213–18, Luke highlights the credentials of one steeped in the events, traditions, and reports that he orders into a narrative. This claim would explain how Luke could say, again like Josephus, that on the one hand, he "has followed" "from farther back"[41] or "for a long time"[42] events/matters which go back to eyewitnesses, perhaps long before he himself has begun to witness the "coming to fruition of these matters among us" (1:1b); and yet, on the other hand, how he as one formed with "informed familiarity" with all these traditions, is also in a position to assess and adjudicate the validity (ἀκριβῶς) of

---

then, regard Hellenistic Jewish historians as his precursors; and in reality such authors can hardly have shared Josephus's broad objectives."

40. For the view that, in his portraits of biblical heroes in the *Antiquities*, Josephus was "indebted to the two great Greek schools of historiography, the Isocratean and the Aristotelian," see L. H. Feldman ("Josephus' Portrait of Saul," *HUCA* 53 [1982] 45–99). Quotation from p. 96.

41. Liddell and Scott also include "from the beginning," as a translation with reference to "in narrative or inquiry," cited in conjunction with ἄρξεσθαι and ἐπιχειρεῖν.

42. Bauer lists Acts 26:5 and not Luke 1:3 under this definition.

any written narratives, oral teachings, or reports (λόγοι) that he may encounter. Luke's use of the perfect participle would capture both of these dimensions and explain the seeming discrepancy between being dependent on "eyewitness" traditions, but also proffering one's authority for an "improved" version of these same events. Neither author mentions a "tracing back" or "investigative research" in their activity of "following." Rather, immediate comprehension, whether of oral or written "texts," is underscored by the "informed familiarity" or the "staying abreast" of matters which παρακολουθέω entails.

The literary-social setting is intriguingly parallel.

1. Like Josephus in his *Antiquities*, Luke must distinguish his narrative from "others'" accounts when he could not claim "eyewitness" or "informed contemporary" status for the vast majority of the events. Moreover, like Josephus in *War*, Luke is writing to readers who might have some experience or information about events that have come to fruition in his and their midst (see περὶ…ἐν ἡμῖν…περὶ ὧν κατηχήθης, Luke 1:1, 4). In the midst of competing accounts, Luke had best not "get it wrong" nor disappoint his readers. Like Josephus, Luke draws on παρακολουθέω to signal his superior credentials.

2. Accordingly, like Josephus in *War*, Luke also employs παρακολουθέω when grounding a diverging epistemological configuration on the foundation of eyewitness evidence. Similar to Josephus's appeals to trustworthy witnesses, Luke in the Gospel preface, with its αὐτόπται καὶ ὑπηρέται (1:2), anticipates "witness" (μάρτυς) and "bearing testimony" (μαρτύρ-ειν/ουν) as a key component of his enterprise. As we saw above, in the preface of his "second" volume (see τὸν…πρῶτον λόγον, Acts 1:1) Luke will link "eyewitnesses and attendants" to the authoritative "apostolic" witness (ὧν ἤρξατο ὁ Ἰησοῦς…ἄχρι ἧς ἡμέρας…τοῖς ἀποστόλοις…οὓς ἐξελέξατο…μάρτυρες, Acts 1:1b–2, 8) before, in the second half of the sequel, he introduces Paul as his chief ὑπηρέτης καὶ μάρτυς (Acts 26:16). In other words, *in justifying his own beginning and ending points*, as well as the narrative's distinctive sequence, Luke is parading the confidence of eyewitness corroboration, *most especially as it pertains to the sequel volume*. In an epistemological predicament similar to Josephus's, with other accounts vying for a "following," that Luke invokes "eyewitnesses" can hardly be regarded an idiosyncratic ploy.

In short, both writers recruit a stock term from discussions of poetics and possibly also from rhetorical handbooks to assure readers of their impeccable credentials.

Καθεξῆς and the Argument from Sequence

If παρηκολουθηκότι points to Luke's qualifications, καθεξῆς encapsulates the formal argument of poetics. We have already seen that this linkage between superior credentials and superior sequence is hardly fortuitous. Indeed, it is in prefaces that παρακολουθέω links the author's sterling qualifications to the unrivaled *ordering* of the text, which enables the reader to "follow" with unparalleled understanding. We should not be surprised, then, that in his prologue Luke offers this same catena of claims. As the syntax mimetically reveals, καθεξῆς forms the middle term tying the reader's "better grasp" (ἀσφάλεια, Luke 1:4) of the "matters come to fruition" to the author's select qualifications (παρηκολουθηκότι ἄνωθεν πᾶσιν ↔ καθεξῆς ↔ τὴν ἀσφάλειαν, 1:3–4). Because of Luke's special credentials to comprehend "the matters that have come to fruition" (1:1), he reconfigures them into a peculiarly well-ordered sequence, including (more) appropriate starting and ending points. In asserting such a claim, Luke not only draws on conventional topoi from Hellenistic prefaces, but in a way familiar from Polybius, illustrates how readers will be rewarded if they but "follow" the distinctive connections, the καθεξῆς, that set his two volumes apart.

The "Intratextual" Evidence for the Significance of καθεξῆς

καθεξῆς in Greek literature often bears a sense synonymous with ἐφεξῆς, "in order, in a row, one after another."[43] But when we see that "logical progression" — whether within temporal, or spatial, or textual contexts — can be the primary referent for its sequential sense, then we must investigate more precisely what Luke is referring to.[44]

Chronological Referent (Luke 8:1; Acts 3:24).

In Luke 8:1, the text states that "he himself [Jesus] went on through cities and villages" accompanied by the Twelve and some women "afterward" or "in the following sequence" of Jesus' public ministry.

---

43. So Liddell and Scott, who point, e.g., to Plutarch, *Moralia* 2.615c (ed. D. A. Wyttenbach); Aelianus, *Varia Historia* 8.7.

44. Bauer emphasizes "succession" in his definition, meaning "in order, one after the other of sequence in time, space or logic." Of the seven occurrences in the NT and subapostolic literature treated by Bauer, five are in the NT, and all occur in Luke and Acts. Among the growing literature on καθεξῆς, see, e.g., Cadbury, "Commentary on the Preface," 504–5 (he translates the word as "seriatim"/"continuously"); J. Kürzinger, "Lk 1,3:...ἀκριβῶς καθεξῆς σοι γράψαι" ("a specific sequence announced in advance by the evangelist"/"hereinafter"); G. Klein, "Lukas 1,1–4 als theologisches Programm," in *Zeit und Geschichte: Dankesgabe an Rudolf Bultmann*, ed. E. Dinkler (Tübingen: J. C. B. Mohr [Siebeck], 1964), 193–216 ("complete, well-ordered chronological sequence"); M. Völkel, "Exegetische Erwägungen zum Verständnis des Begriffs ΚΑΘΕΞΗΣ im lukanischen Prolog," *NTS* 20 (1973–74): 289–99 ("continuity within a logical whole" [toward a correct understanding of the events]); G. Schneider, "Zur Bedeutung von καθεξῆς im lukanischen Doppelwerk," *ZNW* 68 (1977): 128–31 ("coherent, logical presentation" [to secure greater certainty for the reader]); D. L. Tiede, *Luke* (Minneapolis: Augsburg, 1988), 37 ("coherence" [with respect to the purpose of the narrative]); D. P. Moessner, "The Meaning of ΚΑΘΕΞΗΣ in the Lukan Prologue as a Key to the Distinctive Contribution of Luke's Narrative among the 'Many,'" in *The Four Gospels 1992: Festschrift Frans Neirynck*, ed. F. van Segbroeck et al., BETL 100 (Louvain: Louvain University Press, 1992), 2.1513–28; R. Tannehill, *The Narrative Unity of Luke-Acts* (Minneapolis: Fortress, 1990), 2.144–45 ("narrative order" [toward a unified story]); G. H. Whitaker, "The Philology of St. Luke's Preface," *Expositor* 7 (1920) 262–72, 380-384 ("bringing out continuity"); F. Mussner, "Καθεξῆς im Lukasprolog," in *Jesus und Paulus: Festschrift für Werner Georg Kümmel*, ed. E. E. Ellis and E. Grässer (Göttingen: Vandenhoeck & Ruprecht, 1978), 253–55 ("continuous without gaps").

In Acts 3:24, Peter mentions that "all the prophets who have spoken from Samuel and those on down (οἱ καθεξῆς) have also proclaimed these days," which will bring a prophet like Moses (Acts cites Deut. 18:15–19 and Lev. 23:29). In both these instances, however, logical "order" or "coherence" is not completely absent since, for example, in Acts 3 all the prophets proclaimed the message of Moses, of the coming of a prophet "like him." The prophets after Samuel are not only his chronological but his *logical* "successors," as well. By highlighting the message of all the prophets "in order," Peter is referring not just to an interesting historical sequence but also is making sense of signs and wonders of the last days (cf. 2:17–21) of the prophet like Moses that are happening in his audience's own midst (e.g., 3:1–26).

Spatial/Geographical Referent (Acts 18:23)

After spending time in Antioch, Paul departs to "pass through the region of Galatia and Phrygia from place to place in sequence (καθεξῆς), strengthening (ἐπιστηρίζω) all the disciples." This retracing of his itinerary, albeit in reverse (see 16:6), is hardly unprecedented. In Acts 14:21–28 Paul and Barnabas retrace in *reverse order* the cities they have just visited — Lystra, Iconium, Antioch of Pisidia, Perga of Pamphilia, and Antioch of Syria — "strengthening (ἐπιστηρίζω) the disciples, exhorting them to remain in the faith" (14:22a). Again in 15:36, following the apostolic assembly, Paul (and now Silas) go over the same route as on the first journey through Syria and Cilicia, including Derbe and Lystra (14:8–20) and other cities (16:4). Before this return, Paul says to Barnabas: "Come, let us return and visit the brothers and sisters in every city (κατὰ πόλιν) in which we proclaimed the word of the Lord to see how they are doing" (15:36). So when in 18:23 the narrator states that Paul, after again spending time in Antioch of Syria, passes καθεξῆς through Galatia and Phyrgia — part of the new regions covered after the first journey — and then adds the phrase, "strengthening the disciples," we can discern a rationale consistent with the "order" of Paul's previous movements. Consequently, καθεξῆς in 18:23 is dynamically equivalent to "corresponding to each city" (κατὰ πόλιν, 15:21, 36; 20:23), or to "one city after the other," *in the same sequence* in which Paul had earlier visited that region.

•

To sum up, in both Acts passages and to a lesser degree in Luke 8,[45] καθεξῆς connotes a sequence which is *logical* given the larger configuration of the narrative. Both chronological and spatial-geographical movements become meaningful within a poetics of coherence.

---

45. This difference is due in part to the use of καθεξῆς as the third term of an idiom meaning "afterward" or "subsequently" (ἐν τῷ καθεξῆς), and possibly also to Luke's greater dependence on formulated tradition in the Gospel, compared to a more distinctive use of καθεξῆς in the sequel.

Narratological Referent (Acts 11:4)

Peter lays out καθεξῆς the story of his visit to Cornelius when believers among "the circumcision" dispute with him, accusing him of eating with "those of the uncircumcision" (Acts 11:1–3). By comparing Peter's account in 11:4–18 with the narrator's much longer version in 10:1–48, we can observe that καθεξῆς denotes a "narratological" sense of the Cornelius visit within the larger frame of meaning created by the diegetic connections of the two-volume Luke-Acts:

1. Peter's recounting καθεξῆς is neither a chronological improvement nor an abbreviated, simplified version of the narrator's account. Peter begins with his own vision of "the sheet with unclean food" (11:5–10) over against the narrator's depiction of Cornelius at prayer and the visitation by an angel/messenger (10:1–3). Moreover, when we see that Peter dwells on his vision at Joppa — utilizing six verses (11:5–10) compared to the narrator's relatively short eight-verse version (10:10–16, 28) — we see that Peter concentrates on the way he came to understand the significance of what God had done at Cornelius's home (11:17). Rather than sorting out the complex, intersecting sequences of dreams and movements in the narrator's account,[46] the emphasis in Peter's response is on the vision of unclean food as the hermeneutical catalyst to comprehending the import of the Holy Spirit's descent on the uncircumcised in Cornelius's home (10:44–45). Seen from the end, Peter's vision becomes a decisive revelation of God's purposes for the Gentiles.

2. The strategic role of Peter's vision is borne out through two explicit references in Peter's defense to two "beginnings" within the diegetic sequence which, in turn, correspond to the beginning points of narration in each volume. Through this structural mimesis these seminal events are tagged hermeneutically as determinative in enabling the reader to discern a larger narrative plan.

(a) *Pentecost as the* ἀρχή *of the "falling" of the Holy Spirit on the uncircumcised.*

As I began to speak the Holy Spirit fell upon them just as also upon us in the beginning (ἀρχή).... If then God had given to them the same gift as God had also given to us who had believed in the Lord Jesus Christ, who was I that I could hinder God? (Acts 11:15, 17)

While Peter was still speaking these words the Holy Spirit fell upon all those who were hearing the word. Those believers from among the circumcised who had come with Peter were amazed that even upon the Gentiles the gift of the Holy Spirit had been poured out; for they were hearing them speaking tongues and magnifying God. (10:44–46)

When the day of Pentecost was arriving... all of them were filled with the Holy Spirit and began to speak in other tongues as the Spirit was giving them to utter.... Change your way of thinking, he said, and let each of you be baptized

---

46. The NRSV's rendering of καθεξῆς as "step by step" gives the impression that Peter's explanation of the many happenings that led to his "staying and eating with the uncircumcised" provides the substantive response to the theological criticism. This rendering, though slightly better than the RSV's "in order," is still misleading.

into the name of Jesus Christ for the release of your sins and that you might receive the gift of the Holy Spirit. For the promise is both for you and your children
and for all who are far away, all whomever the Lord our God calls. (2:1a, 4, 38–39)

Peter's reference in 11:15 to the "beginning" demonstrates the legitimacy of
his lodging and eating with the noncircumcised, for they had received the same
Spirit. The "beginning" of Pentecost led eventually to the Gentiles also receiving
the Spirit. But in what sense for Peter is Pentecost a "beginning"? Did Pentecost "begin" a plan of God that would lead — from within the "logic" of the
scheme — to the "falling" of the Spirit upon Gentiles? Is Peter suggesting that
from his vision of unclean food, he could now, in retrospect, portray himself as
one who had been standing in the way of this plan? The narrator's sketch of
Peter's progressive understanding indicates precisely this new view that transforms Peter's grasp of God's intention for the Gentiles "from the beginning," and
of his own inattention to this plan.

Through the verb διακρίν-ω/ομαι and paronomastic parody, the narrator
links Peter's "discrimination" against the "unclean" ("uncircumcised") to the criticism of the Jerusalem "circumcision," on one side, and to the Spirit's instruction
that Peter not "make a distinction," on the other. In the narrator's account,
Peter, perplexed by the "vision," is told by the Spirit when Cornelius's messengers
arrive to "get up and go with them without doubting/hesitating" (διακρίνομαι
[mid.], 10:19–20).[47] But when he returns from Cornelius's house, "those of the
circumcision" in Jerusalem "criticize"/"dispute with" him because of that very
lack of hesitation (διακρίνομαι [mid.], 11:2). In the retelling that forms his
defense, however, Peter maintains that when the messengers were arriving the
Spirit told him "not to make a distinction"/"discriminate" (διακρίνω [act.]) between them and himself—a conscious conviction that Peter does not express in
the narrator's version until he begins to address Cornelius and his household in
Caesarea (10:28–29, 34–35, 43). Finally, at the apostolic assembly in Acts 15,
Peter reminds them that it was God who, "from the beginning days" (ἀφ ἡμερῶν
ἀρχαίων), had chosen him as the messenger through whom the Gentiles would
"hear the good news and believe" (15:7). Because of God's initiation, it would
be foolish for Jewish believers to require anything further for salvation, seeing
that it was God who had testified about the Gentiles' "qualification" by "giving
them the Holy Spirit just as He did to us." Interestingly, this gift of the Spirit (in
Cornelius's home) is interpreted with these words from Peter: "God who knows
the heart . . . did not discriminate [διέκρινεν (act.), 15:9] between us and them,"
since it was by God's "cleansing their heart through faith" that the Spirit had
come upon them.

We can conclude that as the narrative progresses, the chosen witnesses' roles
recede and God's enactment of this plan takes the forefront. Peter's harking back
to "the beginning" in his own defense in Acts 11 is telescoped with Pentecost in

---

47. According to Bauer, this sense for the middle voice first appears in the NT literature; cf.
Matt. 21:21; Rom. 4:20; etc.

Acts 15 as " the days of the beginning" when God had chosen him to take the message. By the time of the apostolic assembly of Acts 15, God is credited with showing no discrimination against the uncircumcised; God, not Peter (cf. 10:28–29), is the "knower of the heart," as Peter becomes the passive vehicle of God's plan of salvation. Peter even goes so far to say that "through the grace of the Lord Jesus we [circumcised believers] believe that we are saved in the same way that they are" (15:11).

Peter's "laying out" καθεξῆς (11:3) his lodging and eating with the uncircumcised delineates the significance of the Cornelius event within the larger plan of God, which itself is divulged through the narrative connections and sequences. Peter's hearers receive a minilesson on how to go back to the beginning of Acts to read it.

(b) *The "baptism of John" as the "beginning"* (ἀρχή) *of "witness" to the "falling of the Holy Spirit" upon the "uncircumcised."*

> I remembered the word of the Lord how he said, "John baptized with water, but you shall be baptized with the Holy Spirit." (Acts 11:16)

> You yourselves know the word which took place throughout the whole of Judea, *beginning* from Galilee after the baptism which John preached . . . and we are *witnesses* of all the things he [Jesus of Nazareth] did in the region of the Jews and in Jerusalem. . . . God raised this one on the third day and granted that he become manifest not to all the people, but to us as *witnesses* who were chosen by God, *who ate and drank with him* after he rose from the dead. . . . Can anyone hinder water for these folk to be baptized who have received the Holy Spirit just as we? (10:37, 41, 47)

> It stands written in the Book of the Psalms [that] . . . one of these men, therefore, who had gone with us during the whole time in which the Lord Jesus went in and out among us — *beginning* from the baptism of John until the day in which he was taken up from us — [one of these] must become together with us a *witness* to his resurrection. (1:20a, 21–22)

> And *while he was eating with them* he charged them not to depart from Jerusalem but to await the promise of the Father which "you heard from me, namely, John baptized with water, but not after many days you shall be baptized with the Holy Spirit. . . . You shall receive power when the Holy Spirit comes upon you and shall be my *witnesses* in Jerusalem, and in all of Judea, and Samaria, and to the end of the earth." (1:4–5, 8)

> And *he ate in their presence*. . . . "Thus it stands written . . . that a change of mind for the release of sins should be proclaimed in his [Messiah's] name to all the nations, *beginning* from Jerusalem, these things of which you are *witnesses*. And look, I am sending the promise of my Father upon you; you stay in the city until you are clothed with power from on high." (Luke 24:43b, 46b, 47b–49)

> Now while the people were in expectation and all were wondering in their hearts about John, that perhaps he himself might be the Messiah, John answered them all,

saying, "I myself baptize you with water; but one is coming who is mightier than I . . . he will baptize you with holy spirit and fire." (Luke 3:16)

. . . concerning those matters that among us have come to fruition, just as those who *from the beginning* were *eyewitnesses* and attendants of the word handed on to us, it seemed good to me also as one who has stayed abreast from way back and with understanding of all these matters, to write for you in a distinctive sequence, your excellency Theophilus, in order that you may gain a firm grasp of the true significance of the traditions which you have been taught. (Luke 1:1b–4)

The "logic" of Peter's answer to his critics in Acts 11:1–18 ties together all the passages above into a coherent plot line of the entire two volumes. The narrator has Peter take the reader back not only to Pentecost as the origin of his behavior with Cornelius, but to an even more fundamental beginning for the fruition of Pentecost — to the beginning of the first volume.

Between recounting the Spirit's "falling upon" the uncircumcised and his grasp of the momentous consequence for the "unclean," Peter recalls a "word of the Lord" (Acts 11:16). The reader is led inevitably to Acts 1:5, where the resurrected Jesus speaks the word in anticipation of "being taken up from" his followers (1:10).[48] This "word" in turn directs the reader to connect the dots of the thematic sequences into a coherent plan of God.

Jesus' injunction to wait for the "power from on High" (Acts 1:5; Luke 24:49) is forged both *forward and backward* in the narrative to highlight the significance of "witness."

The meal setting of Acts 1:5–8 echoes the more detailed version in Luke 24:36–49, in which Jesus "eats in [his disciples'] presence" and commissions them to be witnesses "to the nations" of scripture's plan for the "release of sins" through proclamation of the resurrected, crucified Messiah (24:44–49). But this confluence of "baptism of the Holy Spirit," "witness to the nations," "eating" with Jesus, and John the Baptist's role — at the closing pivot of the first volume and beginning of the second — takes the reader back also to the beginning of Jesus' public activity as initiated by the baptism of John.

It is John in Luke 3:16 who also utters the "word of the Lord" attributed to the resurrected Christ in Acts 1:5. John has challenged the people of Israel to a fundamental "change of mind" (μετανοία), with the caveat that God can easily make children of Abraham "out of stones" if Israel should take refuge in its special status (Luke 3:7–9). John's call to a changed mind-set toward Torah (3:2b, 10–14, 17–18) includes at its heart "all flesh seeing the saving action of God" (3:6, citing Isa. 40:5).

But this move back to the "beginning" of Jesus' public ministry in volume one hardly allows the reader to pass over the plot of the first volume, as though

---

48. It is not clear from the syntax whether "that which you heard from me" (Acts 1:4b) refers only to the promise of forthcoming "power from on high" (Luke 24:49b) so that Jesus' "word" about John baptizing with water introduced by ὅτι in 1:5 is a "new" word, or whether 1:5 restates the essential word of Luke 24 that Jesus is recalling. See esp. V. Robbins's contribution in this volume (chap. 3) on expansion through progymnastic reiteration.

the notions of "witness" and "baptism by the Holy Spirit" in Acts 1:5–8 were only forward-looking. On the contrary, as Acts moves forward, the link between "witness" and "eating with Jesus" continually pushes the reader back to the public activity of Jesus, "beginning from the baptism of John." A "witness to the resurrection" necessarily entails witness to the public ministry of Jesus, which climaxed in the scriptures' fulfillment of a suffering, rejected Messiah (Luke 24:44–48). This "from-the-beginning" eyewitness is already announced in the inscribed author's first-person preface as the basis upon which the compilation of this new narrative construal will take place (Luke 1:2). The *prooemium* signals nothing less than a base point and witness to that point, from and through which all narratological perspective must be anchored (κἀμοὶ παρηκολουθηκότι ἄνωθεν, 1:3).

> Scripture had even forecast a special role for Judas, "one of the twelve" and a "witness to the resurrection" "during the whole time that the Lord Jesus went in and out among us, beginning from the baptism of John" (Acts 1:15–17, 20–22).[49] Judas's role as "a guide to those who arrested Jesus" (Acts 1:16b) already had reached a semiclimax with Jesus and the rest of the Twelve *at table,* when Jesus had linked "the hand of the one who is about to betray" with his own (Luke 22:21–22). Jesus continues, as he breaks the bread and pours the wine, to depict the scenario of his rejection and denial by his own as "that which stands written" which is "coming to its intended goal" (Luke 22:37, quoting Isa. 53:12d). But unlike the rest of the eleven witnesses, when Judas failed to turn back (Luke 22:31–32; Acts 1:17–19), it was necessary — again according to the plan of scripture — to replace his spot in the ministry of "apostolic witness" with another "one of the twelve" (Acts 1:20–22).

Thus it comes as no surprise when, at Pentecost, Peter summons this "pre-ordained plan and prescience of God" (2:23) to call people to change their mind-set, so they might be baptized and receive the gift of the Holy Spirit (2:36–39; cf. vv. 25–28, 34–35a). Nor will it seem strange for the reader who has followed the diegetic sequence that Peter will hark back to his *eating and drinking with Jesus* as the watershed of witness "to all those far away," even to the "unclean" Gentiles (Acts 10:41, 13–15). For the reader overhears the murmuring (διαγογγύζω) complaints of the Pharisees and their scribes against Jesus' behavior (Luke 15:2) in the "criticizing" of the circumcised against Peter (Acts 11:3; cf. Luke 5:30; 7:34, 39; 19:7).[50]

To sum up,

1. The prologue of Acts, by aligning two beginnings in the larger plot sequence, binds the two volumes as the scriptural plan of God, enacted through apostolic witness.

---

49. For fuller discussion, see Moessner, "The 'Script' of the Scriptures," cited in n. 29 above.

50. When the issue of circumcised believers' social relations with Gentiles resurfaces in Acts, "certain ones" who teach the necessity of circumcision for salvation are depicted in part as "believers from among the party of the Pharisees" (15:1, 5).

2. Consequently the prologues to Luke and Acts create an "intratext," characterized by a primary and a secondary beginning (Luke 3; Acts 2), which are preceded by introductions of the major characters and anticipations of the main actions (Luke 1:5–2:52; Acts 1:6[15]–26).[51] We are reminded, in this respect, of Polybius's rationale for narrating back before the beginning, so readers might gain better perspective on the "workings of Fortune."[52] That Josephus calls on witnesses when invoking παρακολουθέω is also not far from mind.

3. Far from being a formal link only, eating and drinking with Jesus as a qualification for apostolic witness to the nations is developed through diegetic interconnections in Luke and Acts as an epistemological touchstone of the plan of God. As the falling of the Spirit at Pentecost was instrumental in illuminating the apostles of the plan of God as outlined at table, so also is the Holy Spirit critical in illuminating Peter to see the charge to eat unclean food as instrumental to this plan of the Spirit "falling upon" the Gentiles. In essence, Peter becomes a "guide" to those who would like a firm(er) grasp of the meaning of the events in the sequence, or καθεξῆς, of Luke's two-volume narrative.

The Foretextual Narratological Referent (Luke 1:3)

We have already seen that the Gospel prologue is linked to the plan of God through reference to a beginning and witnesses from that beginning. We can now establish that καθεξῆς denotes the sequence which issues in a distinctive narratological sense. Prior to narrating events in an omniscient third person, Luke in first person declares his intentions to provide a new perspective.

> Inasmuch as many have set out to compose a narrative concerning those matters that among us have come to fruition, just as those who *from the beginning* were *eyewitnesses* and attendants of the word handed on to us, it seemed good to me also as one who has stayed abreast from way back and with understanding of all these matters, to write for you in a distinctive sequence, your excellency Theophilus, in order that you may gain a firm grasp of the true significance of the traditions which you have been taught. (Luke 1:1–4)

1. *Paul as "witness" to Luke's* καθεξῆς *(Acts 26:4–6).* Paul, chief attendant and witness to the persecuted yet living Jesus (ὑπηρέτης καὶ μάρτυς, Acts 26:16), when put on trial before the governor Festus, harks back to a base point and witness "from" that point to defend the legitimacy of his witness to Israel's

---

51. Where the Acts prologue ends and the narrative begins are notoriously difficult to determine, especially given Luke's almost imperceptible transition from indirect discourse to direct discourse of the risen Jesus in 1:4b. The indeterminate boundary, however, does not affect the parallel to Polybius.

52. See Polybius, *The Histories* 12.5–7: "Such then was the occasion and motive of this the first crossing of the Romans from Italy with an armed force, an event which I take to be the most natural starting-point (ἀρχήν) of this whole work. I have therefore made it my serious base, but went also somewhat further back in order to leave no possible obscurity in my statements of general causes. To follow (παρακολουθῆσαι) out this previous history…seems to me necessary for anyone who hopes to gain a proper general survey (συνόψεσθαι) of their present supremacy." See also above, "Παρακολουθέω in Prologues."

Christ. Through this formal mimesis of authenticated witness to "the resurrection of Christ" (Acts 1:21–22), the narrator weaves the diegetic sequences of Paul's witness more tightly into the καθεξῆς of the plan of God and, by analogy, dovetails the inscribed author Luke more securely into this plot as well:

> All the Jewish people know my way of life from my youth, a life spent from the beginning (ἀπ' ἀρχῆς) among my nation and in Jerusalem; they have known about me from way back (ἄνωθεν), if they would but testify (μαρτυρεῖν), that I have lived according to the most accurately adherent (ἀκριβέστατης)[53] party of our religion, a Pharisee! Yet now I stand here being judged for the hope of the promise which was made by God to our patriarchs. (Acts 26:4–6)

We find a curious cluster of three words from Luke 1:1–4. Particularly suggestive is that "from the beginning" is not defined in strict chronological sense but "begins" with Paul's youth, which is significant for understanding the course and character of his whole life (cf. Acts 22:3). If any of the Jews were required to testify to his roots (ἄνωθεν), they would confirm Paul's assertion and could therefore be witnesses to Paul's life from this beginning.

The following parallel to the Gospel prologue results: (*a*) Like "the most excellent (κράτιστε) Theophilus," in need of a firmer grounding in the traditions in which he has been taught (ἐπιγνῷς…τὴν ἀσφάλειαν, Luke 1:4), so the "most excellent (κράτιστε) Festus" (26:25) needs to obtain more reliable (ἀσφαλής, 25:26) information about Paul in order to adjudicate the charges against him and to write his superior (γράψαι, 25:26; cf. γράψαι, Luke 1:3). (*b*) The governor Festus is in a situation not unlike the tribune in Jerusalem, who earlier needed to know "reliable facts"/"firm things" (γνῶναι τὸ ἀσφαλές, 21:34) to understand the opposition against Paul (21:33–34).[54]

The formal parallels, however, serve the scriptural plan of God. In the final trial scenes of Acts, Paul twice links his loyalty as a Pharisee to the appearance and mandate of the Lord Jesus, Israel's Messiah (22:3–21; 26:4–23). Out of his zeal for God he had persecuted the Way (22:3–4). But this Way (26:13; cf. 9:17, 27) led to a change of mind (μετάνοια), to a turning to God, and to a proclamation of what "the prophets and Moses said would come to pass" (26:19–23). With Paul on trial, the same way of the Lord adumbrated by John the Baptist is on trial (Luke 3:4–6).

Like Peter's defense, which re-configures salvation for the Gentiles in an overarching plan of God (Acts 11:1–18; 15:7b–11), Paul's defense speeches also

---

53. The sense of ἀκριβέστατης is "most exact/precise/accurate" while its referent, from the larger context of the trial settings (Acts 22–26), is adherence to the true traditions of Israel under dispute. The issue is which party or "school" of Israel exhibits the most reliable understanding of these traditions as demonstrated through adherence (see esp. Acts 23:6–10).

54. Between the tribune's and Festus's attempts to learn the facts comes "most excellent (κράτιστε) Felix" (23:26; 24:3), who realizes that the high priest's and elders' accusations against the Way are not accurate. Since "Felix knew (οἶδα) the things concerning this Way more accurately" (ἀκριβέστερον, 24:22) than Paul's accusers, he was able to "put off" the high priest's entourage and to delay the investigation. This delay allows Felix opportunity to learn from Paul more reliable information. But "desiring to do the Jews a favor," Felix leaves Paul in prison (24:27).

direct the reader to sort out καθεξῆς the significance of his witness in the larger plot. Of the many allusions, echoes, and parallels with main characters that en-rich a reader's view of Paul, one of the most prominent is the repetition of Paul's conversion, which leads back to Paul's first appearance during Stephen's witness (7:58–8:3). The repetition in Acts 22:6–16 makes this dovetailing imperative. Within the resonating voice — "Saul, Saul, why are you persecuting me?" (22:7 → 9:4) — Paul and the reader hear: "The God of your patriarchs has appointed you to know his will and to see the just one and hear a message from his mouth since you will be a witness (μάρτυς) for him to all peoples of the things you have seen and heard" (22:14–15). What Paul has just seen and heard on his way to Damascus, in chapter 9, is himself as chief persecutor struck down and blinded by the resurrected yet persecuted Jesus (9:3–9). Soon thereafter, an intermedi-ary, Ananias, will relate that it was the Lord Jesus who "appeared to him in order that he might look up to see and be filled with the Holy Spirit" (9:17b).

If the import of this seeing and hearing is missed the first time,[55] Paul in his defense refers to his return to Jerusalem from Damascus, when he is nearly killed by those behind the execution of Stephen (9:26–30).[56] There in the Temple, Paul again sees and hears the "just one" tell him to leave Jerusalem. Paul is directed to the "nations far off," since the Jewish people of Jerusalem

> "will not accept your testimony (μαρτύρια) about me." But I said, "Lord... when the blood of Stephen your witness (μάρτυς) was being shed, I myself was standing there and coaching them and keeping their garments as they were violently putting him to death." (22:17–21)

Paul as well as the reader must learn quickly "how many things he must suffer for the sake of my name" (9:16). To understand Paul's witness one must understand Stephen's witness, which climaxes by echoing Jesus' dying breath, "Lord Jesus, receive my spirit" (7:59≈Luke 23:46; cf. Acts 7:52 with Luke 23:47).

Analogous to the twelve witnesses of the suffering resurrected one, Paul, through the church's suffering, becomes the chief witness "to all the nations" of this same rejected, resurrected Messiah (Luke 24:47–48). The threefold esca-lation of the Lord's intervention in Peter's encounter with Cornelius is mimicked in the crescendo reached in Jesus' mandate to Paul.[57] In short, to figure out Paul's role and the accusations against him, Luke's readers must con-figure Paul's way with the *narrato-logical* Way of the Lord Jesus Messiah.

---

55. The reader, however, already knows from Ananias's vision that the Lord will "show [Paul] how many things he must suffer for the sake of my name." Paul's calling will be to bear this name as "a chosen vessel" to all peoples (9:15–16).

56. Cf. the Hellenists of Acts 9:29 with those of 6:1 and 6:9. The tables are turned on Paul the Hellenist (9:11; cf. 21:39), who had earlier led the pogrom against the Hellenist Stephen.

57. Compare the use of "Lord" in Acts 10:4, 14; 11:8 with 10:36; 11:16, 17; 15:11. In Acts 9:1–19, the "Lord" Jesus speaks to Paul in three verses but to Ananias in five verses. Ananias relays to Paul the details of Paul's calling. In 22:3–16 the Lord speaks to Paul in three verses, but does not speak to Ananias; Ananias's role as mediator (22:12–16) is simply anticipated in 22:10b. In the Temple sequel (22:17–21) the Lord speaks directly to Paul in two verses. In 26:9–18 Ananias disappears, while the Lord, in five verses, relates all details directly to Paul.

2. Apollos as corroborator of Paul's witness, and as a "type" of Theophilus.
In some ways more intriguing than the story of Paul's calling is the cameo
appearance of Apollos. Like Theophilus, he had already "been instructed"
(κατηχημένος, 18:25; cf. Luke 1:4) and would seem to have achieved the ideal
set for "your excellency" — "teaching accurately/with understanding (ἀκριβῶς)
the things concerning Jesus" (18:25). But Priscilla and Aquila "lay out the way
of God to him with greater understanding/more accurately" (ἀκριβέστερος,
18:26). Why? Apollos's knowledge of the way of the Lord lacks "reliable" or "informed understanding." Cohorts of Paul must take Apollos aside and give him
better understanding once they hear what he is preaching.

Clues to this mysterious encounter come with the narrator's disclaimer in
18:25b, and with the ensuing depiction of the "about twelve disciples" of John
the Baptist in 19:1–7. "Burning with zeal, [Apollos] was speaking and teaching
with understanding/accurately the things concerning Jesus, although he knew
only the baptism of John!" As with Peter's reference to the "word of the Lord"
in 11:16, so with Apollos the reader must go back to Luke 3 via Acts 1 to the
fundamental difference between John's baptism and the Messiah's baptism with
the Spirit. It is, as we have seen, this distinction which determines the content of
authentic witness. Whatever the details of Apollos's lack of understanding, that
only *after* the instruction of Priscilla and Aquila does he "completely refute"[58]
fellow Jews through the scriptures — echoing Paul's own witness in Corinth "that
the Messiah is Jesus" (18:28; cf. 18:5) — argues that Apollos for the first time
understands the Way of God as the way of Isa. 40:3–5 to "all flesh" through
the suffering Messiah's gift of the Spirit (Luke 3:3–6 → Acts 26:19–23). Luke's
way of confirming Apollos's *reliable* understanding is, of course, *narrato-logical*
through the following sequence: Pentecost comes to Ephesus among disciples of
John the Baptist who had "not even heard that there is a Holy Spirit," but who
had been baptized "into the baptism of John" (Acts 19:2b–3; cf. 18:25c!; Luke
3:16). "And when Paul laid his hands upon them, they began to speak in tongues
and to prophesy" (19:6). In sum, Apollos prefigures a Theophilus, Luke's readers,
who must follow the two-volume narrative καθεξῆς to gain the firmer grasp of
the Way of the Lord.[59]

---

58. The *hapax legomenon* διακατηλέγχομαι emphasizes the "complete or full refutation" of
others' arguments. The nuance of powerful refutation is also present (NRSV, "powerfully refute"),
but even *before* Priscilla and Aquila's instruction, the narrator had already described his argumentation as "powerful" (18:24b). Apollos now can provide a fuller and thus "complete" refutation, since
he has a "more informed/accurate" understanding.

59. See R. R. Creech, "The Most Excellent Narratee: The Significance of Theophilus in Luke-
Acts," in *With Steadfast Purpose: Essays on Acts in Honor of Henry Jackson Flanders, Jr.*, ed. N. H.
Keathley (Waco, Tex.: Baylor University Press, 1990), 107–26. Creech refers to Theophilus as "a
God-fearing Gentile...asked to consider Christianity" (126). See also F. G. Downing, "Theophilus's
First Reading of Luke-Acts," in *Luke's Literary Achievement*, ed. C. M. Tuckett, JSNTSup 116
(Sheffield: Sheffield Academic Press, 1995), 91–109, who writes that Luke reassures "Theophilus
and his Christian friends...that their faith is both entertaining and eminently respectable" (109).

"Extratextual" Evidence for the Significance of καθεξῆς

My scope allows treatment of only one writer, other than Luke, engaged in debates concerning the standards for "good" narrative in the Hellenistic period: Dionysius of Halicarnassus of the first century B.C.E. This influential rhetorician, historian, and literary critic permits a look at the role of a narrative's sequence in fostering clear understanding.[60]

In several literary-critical essays Dionysius treats the historian Thucydides' style and compositional techniques. I focus on his most detailed discussion in *De Thucydides* 9–12, in which Dionysius assesses Thucydides' "division" (διαίρεσις) and "order" (τάξις). These terms fall under the larger rubric of "arrangement" (οἰκονομία), which also encompasses Thucydides' "method of development" (ἐξεργάσια), discussed in chapters 13–20.

Before describing Thucydides' predecessors and critiquing his general approach to history (chaps. 5–6, 7–8), as well as his composition (9–20) and style (21–49), Dionysius recognizes that his often negative evaluation of this literary giant goes "against a prevalent opinion established through a long tradition and firmly entrenched in all men's minds" (chap. 2). As one historian criticizing another, it becomes evident that Dionysius views Thucydides from a pragmatic and rhetorically oriented approach, a view already in Dionysius's *Demosthenes* (chap. 10): "The orator's aim is to satisfy the special needs of his case, and he makes his style conform to this practical requirement, not solely to that of permanent literary value, which the historian [i.e., Thucydides] had in mind."[61] Accordingly it is Thucydides' "arrangement" which is especially vulnerable to the critic's knife; Dionysius finds Thucydides' *Peloponnesian Wars* a difficult text to follow. In the midst of demonstrating the inadequacy of the *Wars'* sequence, Dionysius combines three key terms that approximately a century later will reappear in Luke's prologue:

> He [Thucydides] wished to follow a new path, untrodden by others, and so divided his history by summers and winters. The result of this was contrary to expecta-

---

60. For a survey of Dionysius's work and influence, see, e.g., S. Usher, "Introduction," in *Dionysius of Halicarnassus: The Critical Essays in Two Volumes*, LCL 465 (Cambridge: Harvard University Press, 1974), 1.vii–xxx. Cf. W. K. Pritchett, *Dionysius of Halicarnassus: On Thucydides*, English translation, with commentary (Berkeley: University of California Press, 1975), esp. xiii–xxxvi; D. L. Toye, "Dionysius of Halicarnassus on the First Greek Historians," *American Journal of Philology* 116 (1995): 279–302.

61. Dionysius betrays a rhetorically oriented understanding of history writing that became more prominent during the Hellenistic period. Placing value on the immediate impact of Thucydides' style on the average hearer or reader differs considerably from a later critic, Lucian, who applauds Thucydides' determination to write for posterity (*How to Write History* §§38–40, 42). Although Lucian does not treat Thucydides' style per se, his commendation of lofty poetic language in, for instance, battle scenes, would seem to be an indirect defense of Thucydides' procedure. The praise recalls Theophrastus's positive views, which were opposed by Ephorus as well as Dionysius. On the rhetorical emphasis in the Hellenistic period, see E. Gabba, *Dionysius and "The History of Archaic Rome"* (Berkeley: University of California Press, 1991), esp. 60–92; M. Fox, "History and Rhetoric in Dionysius of Halicarnassus," *The Journal of Roman Studies* 83 (1993): 31–47; D. L. Balch, "Two Apologetic Encomia: Dionysius on Rome and Josephus on the Jews," *Journal for the Study of Judaism* 13 (1982): 102–22.

tions: the seasonal division of time led not to greater clarity (σαφέστερα) but to *greater obscurity* (δυσπαρακολουθητοτέρα). It is surprising how he failed to see that a narrative which is broken up into small sections describing the many actions which took place in many different places will not catch "the pure light shining from afar." ... Thus in the third book ... he begins his account of the Mytilenean episode, but before completing this he turns ... This in turn he leaves unfinished ... then from there he transfers his narrative (ἄγει τὴν διήγησιν) ... He then leaves this account, too, half-finished. ... What need I say further? The whole of the book is broken up in this way, and the continuity (τὸ διηνεκές) of the narrative is destroyed. *Predictably, we wander here and there, and have difficulty in following the sequence of the events described* (δυσκόλως ... παρακολουθοῦμεν ... τὰ πράγματα), *because our mind is confused by their separation and cannot easily or accurately* (ἀκριβῶς) *recall the half-completed references which it has heard.* ... It is clear that Thucydides' principle is wrong and ill-suited to history: for no subsequent historian divided up his narrative by summers and winters, but all followed the well-worn roads which lead to clarity (σαφήνειαν). (*De Thuc.* 9)

In the highlighted sentence, Dionysius faults Thucydides for the confused sequence of his narrative, which prevents clear understanding of the lasting significance of events. The readers cannot παρακολουθέω the πράγματα and therefore cannot reliably, with proper understanding (ἀκριβῶς), attain sufficient clarity (σαφήνεια) to determine their significance. Because the interconnections of the πράγματα — the relation of each part to other parts — are bewildering, so is their meaning in the *whole* narrative.

By contrast, as we have seen, Luke claims that he has "followed" the πράγματα of his narrative ἀκριβῶς and written in a narrative sequence (καθεξῆς) that will elucidate his readers (ἵνα ἐπιγνῷς ... τὴν ἀσφάλειαν).[62] ἡ ἀσφάλεια combines the senses of "clarity" (σαφήνεια) and "certainty" (ἀσφαλής), while the reader's ability to follow the narrative's sequence constitutes the term's referent.[63] We are again reminded of Polybius's link between παρακολουθέω and his own knowledge of the significance of events and interconnections that produced Roman hegemony, as well as the "arrangement" (οἰκονομία) carefully crafted to pass this knowledge to readers. But is Dionysius's criticism based on Thucydides' lack of knowledge or qualifications to write?[64]

---

62. I am not suggesting that ἀκριβῶς has this sense in all contexts. But D. L. Balch's conclusion in chapter 9 of this volume that ἀκριβῶς in Luke 1:3, modifying "to write," means "completely" or "in full detail" misses the more integral link between sense and referent, that is, the ability to follow a text with understanding.

63. See J. H. Ropes, "St. Luke's Preface: ἀσφάλεια and παρακολουθεῖν," *JTS* 25 (1924): 67–71: "σαφήνεια 'clarity' seems to go on all fours with Lk. 1:4. To 'learn clarity,' in the sense of 'gain clear knowledge,' and to 'know certitude,' in the sense of 'gain certain knowledge,' seem completely parallel. ... the 'certitude' intended is that of the person who is to know, not the objective 'certitude' of the facts or doctrines" (69). Ropes cites Wisd. of Sol. 18:6, which contains ἀσφαλῶς εἰδότες, as the closest biblical parallel.

64. Polybius became known as the "minority voice" in his insistence that a qualified historian travel to the sights as a "man of action," rather than become resident of a library! See, e.g., Usher, *Dionysius,* ix–x.

Dionysius moves immediately to link the faulty sequence and divisions of the text to Thucydides' beginning and ending. Because both the ἀρχή and the τέλος of the narrative are inappropriate to Thucydides' purpose and scope, the arrangement of parts and their sequences is jumbled. The reader cannot find causes and fundamental forces that coalesced to produce *the beginning* of the conflict:

> Some critics also find fault with the order (τάξις) of his history, complaining that he neither chose the right beginning (ἀρχήν) for it nor a fitting place to end it (τέλος). They say that by no means the least important aspect of good arrangement (οἰκονομίας ἀγαθῆς) is that a work should begin (ἀρχήν) where nothing can be imagined as preceding it, and end (τέλει) where nothing further is felt to be required.... The historian himself has provided them with the ground for this charge.... he does not begin his narrative from the true cause, in which he himself believes, but from the other point [chap. 10].... He ought to have stated at the beginning (ἀρξάμενον) of his enquiry into the true causes of the war the cause which he considered to be the true one: for not only was it a natural requirement that prior events should have precedence over later ones (τὰ πρότερα τῶν ὑστέρων ἄρχειν), and true causes be stated before false ones, but the start of his narrative would have been far more powerful (τε τῆς διηγήσεως εἰσβολὴ κρείττων ἂν ἐγίνετο μακρῷ) if he had adopted this arrangement (οἰκονομίας) [chap. 11].

Thucydides has himself to blame; he knew better than to start with an event less than the true cause! Dionysius charges that although Thucydides had set out to improve on other writers who had neglected events between the Persian and Peloponnesian Wars — a period which proved critical to the outbreak of the conflict — by beginning with the more popular explanation of the war's beginning he had failed dramatically. It is not that Thucydides was less qualified than the "others" or that Thucydides had depicted a period before a "beginning" (cf. Polybius and Luke), which would prove confusing to the readers. Rather, against his better judgment, Thucydides had selected the wrong ἀρχή, thereby making it impossible for the reader to interpret subsequent events "with understanding."[65] Moreover, Thucydides' ending is epistemologically unsatisfying:

> This, then, would have been sufficient in itself to prove that his own narrative is not organized in the best possible way, by which I mean that it does not begin at the natural starting point (τὴν κατὰ φύσιν ἐχέιν ἀρχήν); and there is a further impression that his history does not end at an appropriate finishing-point. For although the war lasted twenty-seven years and he lived to see its conclusion, he brought his narrative down only to the twenty-second year by concluding the

---

65. Dionysius (see *Pompeius* 3), like Lucian two centuries later, can critique a historian's selection and arrangement of events since he considers the historian's diegetic endeavors genuine *poiesis*, a creative composition reserved earlier by, e.g., Aristotle (*Poetics*), for non-historiographical writing, especially tragedy and epic. See Fox, "History and Rhetoric in Dionysius," 47: "History can never simply neutrally reflect *the facts*, and in this, he [Dionysius] resembles modern historical thinking.... the difference between idealization and historical reconstruction is one of historical context rather than method. What motivated Dionysius's version of Rome's beginnings was a desire to give an account which made sense in terms of what happened later in Rome's history...."

eighth book with the Battle of Cynossema, in spite of having expressed the intention in his introduction (προοιμίῳ) to include all (πάντα) the events of the war.[66]

A distinctive sequence to enable proper understanding, the authentic starting point and scope of "all" the events to produce confidence, and the author's intent, supported by his qualifications, to yield a better version vis-à-vis other writers — these concerns of poetics, applied by Dionysius to Thucydides, are precisely those addressed in Luke's short but concentrated *prooemium* in Luke 1:1–4. Although Luke does not employ τάξις or οἰκονομία in 1:3, in 1:1 he does refer to others' writing as a "compiling"/"ordering up" (ἀνατάξασθαι)[67] of a narrative whose final shape is a συντάξις, with a particular οἰκονομία. By writing σοι γράψαι ("to write for you") καθεξῆς (Luke 1:3), Luke indicates that both his ordering and arrangement of all events/matters fulfill a high standard of narrative that will deliver the desired benefits.

Conclusions for Παρηκολουθηκότι and καθεξῆς in Luke 1:3

1. Through intratextual evidence, we have seen that Luke ties his credentials of "steeped familiarity" and "staying abreast" (παρηκολουθηκότι) to having composed a narrative sequence (καθεξῆς) that will provide a firm(er) understanding of the significance of the events (ἵνα ἐπιγνῷς ... τὴν ἀσφάλειαν). By following the peculiar sequence and by relating matters to the larger plan of God — including various parts to seminal events (ἀρχαί) — readers imitate the author, who has followed all events/matters (πάντα) with reliable understanding (ἀκριβῶς). Luke's goal is that readers like an Apollos or Theophilus will gain the firm ground of understanding that will join them to the word or message, "just as those from-the-beginning eyewitnesses [like Peter] and attendants of (this) word [like Paul] delivered over to us" (Luke 1:2).[68]

2. We have also discovered that in Hellenistic authors and especially in prefaces, παρακολουθέω links the author's qualifications to the benefit for the reader, who follows the superior text that results. Luke is no exception (Luke 1:3 → 1:4). Polybius and Josephus present particularly illuminating parallels.

---

66. Earlier in his *Pompeius*, Dionysius had observed: "The concluding portion of his narrative is dominated by an even more serious fault. Although he states that he was an eye-witness of the whole war ... it would have been better, after describing all the events of the war, to end his history with a climax (τελεύτης), and one that was most remarkable and especially gratifying to his audience, the return of the exiles from Phyle, which marked the beginning of the city's recovery of freedom" (chap. 3).

67. Synonymous with συντάσσεσθαι, meaning "draw up, compile," as in writing a narrative (Bauer ad loc.).

68. See, e.g., Acts 2:22, 41; 10:36, 44, where the apostolic witness is outlined in Peter's speeches. Cf. the frequent variations of the phrase, "the word of God (the Lord)/the gospel/his grace," through the whole of Acts.

3. I have tested findings for παρακολουθέω and intratextual observations of Luke's sequential arrangement (καθεξῆς) by examining a debate of the Hellenistic period surrounding Thucydides. We discovered in Dionysius's critique a catena of concerns about poetics that will reemerge in Luke's prologue. Particularly telling is the link between παρακολουθέω and ἀκριβῶς, a connection based on the quality of the narrative's sequence, including its scope and starting point (ἀρχή), and judged on an author's ability to improve on other diegetic renderings of the same events.[69] To attribute Luke's use of these categories to Dionysius or other Hellenistic authors is unnecessary.[70] The analysis of παρακολουθέω revealed the conventional chain, from mentioning others' accounts, to the author's own credentials, to the resulting superior version, to the benefit to the reader. Luke is simply reflecting the topoi of the rhetorical schools in their debates over the epistemological contours of narrative (διήγησις).[71] The vocabulary of Luke 1:3 — and even the balance between other versions in 1:1–2 and Luke's own version in 1:3–4 — reflects debates on poetics in the Hellenistic era.

4. Finally, conclusions for the Gospel prologue have far-reaching implications for the story of Israel. The superior version proffered in Luke 1:1–4 is reconstituted in a secondary preface in Acts which breaks frame with "third-order discourse."[72] The movement from indirect to direct speech (Acts 1:4) in a short *prooemium* is unusual enough; but when the inscribed author ("I") joins a synopsis of the first volume — "all the things which Jesus began to do and to teach" (Acts 1:1) — to Jesus' continuing to teach and act, as the *prooemial* voice and hermeneut of the second volume (1:1 → 1:4b), then the reader receives an unexpected nudge that the plotting of the first narrative is not finished. The reader discerns that a narrative unity, vouchsafed by Jesus himself, is being established and extended beyond the ascension. From Luke's point of view, the matters referred to in Luke 1:3 are not exhausted by the events recounted in the Gospel volume. Luke's rendering includes what Jesus continued to do and to teach through his witnesses. The Jesus who "proclaims the good news of the kingdom of God" (Luke 8:1) speaks about the kingdom "between" volumes one and two (Acts 1:3), and continues to speak through Paul all the way to Rome (Acts

---

69. This interweaving of ἀρχή, narrative arrangement, and audience benefit means, of course, that the *prooemium* itself can be far more than an "address label" (L. Alexander). In fact, I have shown how concerns for poetics, stated in Luke 1:1–4, are woven within the narrative, whether explicitly (e.g., "beginning with the baptism of John") or implicitly in the arrangement of the plot (e.g., in the overlap of *pragmata* between volumes), such that Alexander's conclusion for Luke 1:1–4 must be revised to its very opposite.

70. I am not suggesting that Luke was himself a *rhetor* engaged in "school" debates, but that he reflects the issues current in educated society of the time. L. Alexander's conclusion regarding the "middlebrow" level of Luke's "atticizing" in Luke 1:1–4, that Luke is a writer at home in the "academic discourse of the technical and scientific traditions," is an important advance in understanding the author's world.

71. On Lucian of Samosata's reflections of those categories, see G. Avenarius, *Lukians Schrift zur Geschichtsschreibung* (A. Hain: Meisenheim a. Glan, 1956), esp. 30–35; H. Hohmeyer, *Lukian: Wie man Geschichte schreiben soll* (Munich: W. Fink, 1965), esp. 45–60.

72. I am indebted to L. Alexander's use of this phrase in describing the Gospel prologue; see her contribution to this volume, chap. 1.

28:31).[73] It is no accident that volume two begins with "the *promise* of the Father which you heard from me" and ends with "the *hope* of Israel," for which Paul is in chains (28:20) and yet, ironically, remains "unfettered" (28:31). From the beginning of the Gospel to the end of Acts, the author unfolds a carefully crafted plot of the overarching plan of God consummated in Jesus, Messiah of Israel.

This means that Acts is not simply a witness *to* the Gospel (or gospel) as the title to a recent theology of Acts would suggest,[74] but is a witness *of* the Gospel and, in Luke's own mind, part and parcel of what the church would later term a "Gospel." That the church in subsequent years apparently never read Luke's Gospel as Luke intended is due in no small measure to competing versions with more limited scope but with equal or greater authority, as well as to factors which will probably remain a mystery (see epilogue). Nevertheless, to speak of an organic unity in Luke and Acts does not necessitate a "one-flesh unity," to use the provocative image of R. Pervo (see chap. 5). The church's understanding of Acts as a *sequel* to Luke's Gospel, in which the living word of the gospel continues to be expressed in the church, approximates the relationship of parent to child, such that Acts continues one larger story of God's promise to Israel, her children, and "to all who are far away" (Acts 2:39). It is when the child is torn apart from the parent, when Gentile Christianity is "triumphally" severed from the hope of Israel, that an emaciated body called "the church" staggers onto the scene, "legitimated" through a mutilated corpus, and rending asunder "all that Jesus began to do and to teach."

Epilogue

Papias, bishop of Hierapolis at the turn of the first and second centuries, relayed John the Presbyter's words concerning criticism of Mark's Gospel current at that time.[75] Two statements in particular, as quoted by Eusebius, are rather odd:

(1) "Mark did nothing wrong (ἥμαρτεν) in thus writing down single points as he remembered them." (2) "For to one thing he gave attention, to leave out nothing of what he had heard (τοῦ μηδὲν ὧν ἤκουσεν παραλιπεῖν) and to make no false statements in them (ψεύσασθαί τι ἐν αὐτοῖς)" (*Eccl. Hist.* III.39.15 — Loeb translation). Mark's "mistake" is typically understood as hav-

---

73. Note the "proclaimer" in Paul's own summary of his career as witness (Acts 26:22–23).

74. *Witness to the Gospel: The Theology of Acts*, ed. I. H. Marshall and D. Peterson (Grand Rapids, Mich.: Eerdmans, 1998).

75. For critical assessments, see, e.g., J. Kürzinger, *Papias von Hierapolis und die Evangelien des Neuen Testaments*, EichM 4 (Regensburg: Pustet, 1983); U. H. J. Körtner, *Papias von Hierapolis: Ein Beitrag zur Geschichte des frühen Christentums*, FRLANT 133 (Göttingen: Vandenhoeck & Ruprecht, 1983); J. Munck, "Presbyters and Disciples of the Lord in Papias: Exegetic Comments on Eusebius, *Ecclesiastical History*, III,39," HTR 52 (1959): 223–43; L. C. A. Alexander, "The Living Voice: Scepticism towards the Written Word in Early Christian and in Graeco-Roman Texts," in *The Bible in Three Dimensions*, JSOTSup 87 (Sheffield: Sheffield Academic Press, 1990), 221–47.

ing produced a Gospel too short with a chronology too loose.[76] Compared to Matthew's Gospel, described immediately thereafter (III.39.16), Mark left out significant facts such as Jesus' birth, important teachings, and resurrection appearances. Moreover — according to this explanation — the episodic character of the events of Jesus' life strings words and deeds together too haphazardly to provide accurate information regarding the times and places of Jesus' public activities.

But one problem of this reading is what Papias then relates about Matthew's Gospel, that Matthew is neither a more complete nor a more "chronologically correct" version than Mark.

It will be helpful to quote the whole of Papias's words, as recorded by Eusebius, regarding Mark's and Matthew's Gospels:[77]

"And this the presbyter would say,

'Mark became Peter's interpreter/translator (ἑρμηνευτής); all of whatever he remembered he wrote down with understanding/reliably (ἀκριβῶς) — though not, to be sure, in an ordered account (τάξει) — of the things said or done by the Lord. For he had neither heard the Lord nor followed (παρηκολούθησεν) him, but later, as I have said, [followed] Peter. He [Peter] used to give teachings according to the needs of various situations, but not by presenting, as it were, a formal account (σύνταξιν) of the reports[78] concerning the Lord, so that Mark did not make a mistake in this manner by writing down single units (ἔνια) [teachings/reports] as he remembered them. For to one thing he committed himself: not to leave out anything of the things he had heard nor to distort anything through/among them (ἐν αὐτοῖς) [among the written units with their resulting sequence].' "

These things then are related by Papias about Mark; now about Matthew these things were said,

"Matthew therefore compiled a narrative (συνετάξατο) of the reports[79] in the Hebrew [Aramaic?] language, and each one interpreted/translated (ἡρμήνευσεν) them as each was able." (Translation mine)

When we see that Papias's defense reflects the standard concerns of poetics, the criticisms of Mark's undertaking assume a very different profile.

- One overarching purpose of Eusebius's *Ecclesiastical History* is to trace the succession of apostolic teaching up to his own day.[80] Accordingly, Eusebius takes pains to

---

76. See, e.g., B. Reicke's survey, *The Roots of the Synoptic Gospels* (Minneapolis: Fortress, 1986), 155–74, esp. 161–64. I am indebted to Reicke for pointing out the meaning of λόγια (see n. 84); cf. Kürzinger, *Papias von Hierapolis,* and Körtner, *Papias von Hierapolis,* contrary to, e.g., A. D. Baum, "Papias als Kommentator Evangelischer Aussprüche Jesu," *NovT* 38 (1996): 257–76.

77. Papias cites John the Presbyter. Identification of this "John" is not material to my thesis.

78. λογία here must refer to Peter's "teachings" (διδασκαλίαι) in the previous phrase, which in turn have been defined as "all of whatever" Mark "remembered and wrote down of the things said or done by the Lord" as Peter's "interpreter." In this context and in Book II.14–16 (see n. 82), "sayings"/"oracles" *by* the Lord is a mistranslation. See further, Reicke (*Roots,* 155–57), and nn. 84, 87 below.

79. See nn. 78, 87 for the sense as "reports," "oral presentations."

80. See, e.g., K. Lake's introductory comments to his translation in the Loeb edition: "The object of the whole book was to present the Christian 'Succession.'... whereas modern writers try to trace

delineate the writings that embody that teaching, including writings of successors to the apostles in major churches such as Clement of Rome and Ignatius of Antioch (III.37–38).[81] In Book 2, Eusebius cites Clement's *Hypotyposes*, which says that Mark, known in Rome as Peter's follower, was constrained by "hearers of Peter" to write down "the teaching given them orally" (τῆς διὰ λόγου παραδοθείσης)[82] (II.14–16), and that Peter later ratified Mark's work for "study in the churches" (II.15.2). In Book 3, Eusebius returns to Mark's Gospel, adding the "confirming testimony"[83] of Papias, whom Eusebius otherwise considers "a man of very little intelligence" (III.39.13). Pointing to the interviews conducted by Papias near the turn of the century with presbyters who "were followers of the apostles," Eusebius relates the bishop's quest, from the preface to Papias's five volumes, for the words (λόγοι) of the apostles:[84] "For I did not suppose that information from books would help me so much as the word of a living and surviving voice" (III.39.4).

- How and why, given the association of Peter with Mark's Gospel at least from the second century, could Mark's account be regarded a "mistake"? And how could Mark be charged with falsifying the words and deeds of Jesus? Is the case against Mark one of "mistaken" credentials, that Mark was not an apostle and therefore possessed inadequate authority to render a legitimate version? If so, we could expect Eusebius to use the confirming testimony of Papias as independent and even earlier evidence that Peter stood behind Mark's version. Instead, Eusebius appears far more interested in discrediting the millenarian belief in Christ's earthly thousand-year reign, as promulgated by John the Presbyter — in Eusebius's estimate the author of Revelation — and championed later by the "unintelligent" Papias. Eusebius, in beginning his citations of Papias, argues against Irenaeus's regard for Papias as a "hearer of John" (the apostle) and as "one of the ancients": "Papias himself, according to the preface of his treatises, makes plain that he had in no way been a hearer and eyewitness of the sacred Apostles, but teaches that he had received the articles of the faith from those who had known them" (III.39.2). The presbyter John — who connects Peter to Mark's Gospel — is not John the apostle, but is of the next generation. Eusebius then includes "other accounts" from Papias, "as though they came to him from unwritten tradition, and some strange parables and teachings of the Saviour, and some other more mythical ac-

---

the development, growth, and change of doctrines and institutions, their predecessors were trying to prove that nothing of the kind ever happened...and heresy was the attempt of the Devil to change it" (xxxiv).

81. "It is impossible for us to give the number and the names of all who first succeeded the Apostles....It was, therefore, natural...to record by name the memory only of those of whom the tradition still survives to our time by their treatises on the Apostolic teaching (ἔτι καὶ νῦν...τῆς ἀποστολικῆς διδασκαλίας ἡ παράδοσις φέρεται)" (III.37.4).

82. Peter's oral teachings/traditions about Jesus are described in the same sentence as "the unwritten teaching of the divine proclamation" (τῇ ἀγράφῳ τοῦ θείου κηρύγματος διδασκαλίᾳ); see nn. 78, 84, 87.

83. See *Eccles. Hist.* II.15.2.

84. Although the title of Papias's five volumes remains obscure (λογίων κυριακῶν ἐξηγήσεως), it would make more sense from Eusebius's perspective to understand the genitive λογίων κυριακῶν as "reports/traditions concerning the Lord." Eusebius is quick to point out that Papias did not actually hear the apostles speak their own words "but teaches that he had received *the articles of the faith* from those who had known them" (III.39.2, emphasis mine). The manner of Peter's teaching is described in II.14 as διὰ λόγου.

counts. Among them he says there will be a millennium after the resurrection of the dead. . . . I suppose he got these notions by a perverse reading of the apostolic accounts. . . . But he is responsible . . . that so many Christian writers after him held the same opinion, *relying on his antiquity*" (III.39.13).[85] When Eusebius finally mentions the material on Mark, he quotes Papias without comment; he has fulfilled his earlier promise to include the opinions of others and, after briefly mentioning Papias's familiarity with 1 John, 1 Peter, and the Gospel of the Hebrews, is ready to move on to the next book.[86]

- Within the Papias citation, emphasis is on Mark's method of writing as Peter's interpreter and translator. That Peter is closely associated with Mark and his Gospel is a given. Thus the unsurpassed authority of Peter per se does *not* justify Mark's "mistake." Rather, Mark followed a procedure commensurate with Peter's own preaching and teaching of "the things said or done by the Lord." "He [Peter] used to give teachings according to the needs of various situations, but not by presenting, as it were, a formal account (σύνταξιν) of the reports concerning the Lord, so that Mark did not make a mistake in this manner by writing down single units (ἔνια) [teachings / reports] as he remembered them."

- But a formal literary account (σύνταξις) is precisely what Matthew produced. He arranged (συνετάξατο) the words and deeds of Jesus into a narrative above reproach. Matthew's readers have no problem attaining a reliable (ἀκριβῶς) understanding of Jesus' words and deeds. Whereas Mark's readers have no difficulty "translating" his Greek text — but cannot configure Jesus' words and deeds due to the confusing sequence — Matthew's readers encounter difficulty only in translating and interpreting Hebrew or Aramaic: " . . . and each one interpreted / translated (ἡρμήνευσεν) them as each was able."[87]

---

85. Emphasis mine. Eusebius (III.28) also says that the heretic Cerinthus promoted a thousand-year reign of Christ on earth.

86. See III.24.16; cf. III.1.3; II.15.2, and his statement before introducing Papias (III.31.6): "We have now described the facts which have come to our knowledge concerning the Apostles and their times, the sacred writings which they have left us, those books which are disputed yet nevertheless are used openly by many in most churches, and those which are altogether fictitious and foreign to our historic orthodoxy. Let us now continue the narrative." Eusebius continues with Trajan's reign.

87. As others have noted, this phrase may indicate multiple translations of Matthew. See, e.g., Reicke (*Roots*, 157–60) and D. Farkasfalvy ("The Papias Fragments on Mark and Matthew and Their Relationship to Luke's Prologue: An Essay on the Pre-history of the Synoptic Problem," in *The Early Church in Its Context: Essays in Honor of Everett Ferguson*, ed. A. J. Malherbe, F. W. Norris, and J. W. Thompson, NovTSup 9 [Leiden: Brill, 1998], 100–106). But the "them" (αὐτά) represents the reports (τὰ λόγια) that Matthew has arranged, making the primary contrast — within Eusebius's juxtaposition of the two citations — the difficulty of translating Matthew's Hebrew / Aramaic over against Mark's Greek; see further n. 78. Farkasfalvy, without reference to Hellenistic poetics, mistakenly assumes that both Luke, in his prologue, and Papias's presbyter held Matthew as a Gospel model (*primum analogatum*, p. 106). Farkasfalvy's argument that multiple attempts to translate Matthew render it "secondary," placing Mark's status as a nonapostolic author in a far better light, cannot be sustained from within Eusebius's "arrangement." Eusebius is not concerned at the end of Book 3 to describe relationships among the Gospels, but to state which Gospels represent authentic portrayals, recognized by the church. As we have seen, in Eusebius's estimation, Matthew was written after both Mark and Luke, and the apostle John "testified to their truth," i.e., to all three of them before he wrote his "recollections" (III.24.6–7).

• Papias's defense, then, is clear. The "living voice" of Peter is summoned to justify Mark's inferior sequence. However faint, that voice reverberates through the
Gospel's "unordered" arrangement; however difficult it may seem for the reader
to gain reliable (ἀκριβῶς) understanding, the voice nevertheless rings true. Mark
diligently records Peter's teachings. With respect to scope and starting and ending points, Mark remembered and wrote down *everything* he heard Peter teach.
With respect to order, Mark imitates the one he followed (Peter), who himself had
"followed" (παρηκολούθησεν)[88] the Lord. Since Peter did not present the words
and deeds of Jesus in coherent, acceptable literary fashion, Mark likewise "did not
do anything wrong" in following the same procedure. Readers can be assured that
Mark remembered what Peter taught and that he did not distort Peter's teachings
by placing them in their present order. "For to one thing he committed himself: not
to leave out anything of the things he had heard nor to distort anything through /
among them (ἐν αὐτοῖς)."

Curiously absent — explicitly, at least — is mention of Luke's Gospel, especially since Eusebius in III.24 has already expatiated on relations among the
four Gospels, indicating that Mark and Luke "published" their Gospels before
Matthew. Yet Luke's Gospel is very much present. Three of the key terms or
cognates of Luke 1:1–4 — ἀκριβῶς, παρακολουθέω, σύνταξις / συντάξασθαι,
ἀνατάξασθαι — appear in Papias's comparison of Mark and Matthew. It is
Luke's "proper" narrative which has set the standard for critique. Eusebius even
suggests as much in III.24.14–16 when he assesses Luke's prologue:

Luke himself at the beginning of his own writing puts forward the reason for which
he had produced his own narrative arrangement (σύνταξις), explaining that while
many (πολλῶν) others had attempted rather rashly to write a suitable narrative
(διήγησιν) of the traditions (λόγων) of which he himself was fully certain (πε-
πληροφόρητο), he felt it necessary to release us from the doubtful judgments of
the others and related (παρέδωκεν) through his own Gospel the firm (ἀσφαλῆ)
account of those things of which he had ably grasped the truth by virtue of his
association and time with Paul and through his profitable conversations with the
rest of the apostles. This must suffice us for the present; *but at a more appropriate
time by citing the ancients we shall try to explain what has also been said about these
things by others.* (Translation and emphasis mine)

Eusebius's next mention of the "ancients" and the Gospels is Irenaeus's characterization of Papias! A generation or so after the writing of Luke's prologue,
church communities in Antioch, Smyrna, Rome, or Hierapolis,[89] and so on were
continuing to sort out the "living voice" from the growing clamor of claimant
voices and "forgeries of the heretics."[90] In certain quarters of the church toward
the end of the first century, Luke's Gospel had become the silent arbiter in the

---

88. In III.39.4 the perfect participle denotes "those who had followed the presbyters" (=apostles /
disciples who had followed Jesus); in III.39.7 the perfect participle again denotes "followers of the
apostles."

89. Four of the churches headed by disciples of the apostles who, according to Eusebius at the
end of Book 3, produced writings which authenticated the traditions of the apostles.

90. *Eccles. Hist.* III.25.7.

jostling for recognition by the "many." Luke's Gospel prologue thus represents an earlier stage of a complex trajectory which would eventuate in the church espousing some or rejecting others' narrative portrayals. By Papias's time the appeal and power of Luke's poetics claims were indeed provoking a "firmer grasp of the true significance of the traditions which you have been taught."

Appendix 1

Polybius, The Histories I.1–15

1.1 Had previous chroniclers neglected to speak in praise of History in general, it might perhaps have been necessary for me to recommend everyone to choose for study and welcome such treatises as the present, since there is no more ready corrective of conduct than knowledge of the past. But all historians ... have impressed on us that the soundest education and training for a life of active politics is the study of History.... **1.5** For who is so worthless or indolent as not to wish to know by what means and under what system of polity the Romans in less than fifty-three years have succeeded in subjecting nearly the whole inhabited world to their sole government — a thing unique in history? Or who again is there so passionately devoted to other spectacles or studies as to regard anything as of greater moment than the acquisition of this knowledge? ... **2.8** In the course of this work it will become more clearly intelligible by what steps this power was acquired, and it will also be seen how many and how great advantages accrue to the student from the systematic treatment of history. **3.1** The date from which I propose to begin (ἄρξει) is the 140th Olympiad.... **3.4** ever since this date history has been an organic whole (σωματοειδῆ), and the affairs of Italy and Africa have been inter-linked with those of Greece and Asia, all leading up to one end (τέλος). And this is my reason for beginning (τὴν ἀρχήν, 3.5) where I do.... **4.1** For what gives my work its peculiar quality, and what is most remarkable in the present age, is this. Fortune having guided almost all the affairs (πράγματα) of the world in one direction and having forced them to incline toward one and the same end, a historian should bring before his readers under one synoptical view (σύνοψιν) the operations by which she has accomplished her general purpose (πρὸς τὴν τῶν ὅλων πραγμάτων συντέλειαν, 4.2).... **4.3** I observe that while several modern writers deal with particular wars and certain matters connected with them, no one ... has even attempted to inquire critically when and whence the general and comprehensive scheme of events originated and how it led up to the end. I therefore thought it quite necessary (ἡμᾶς εἰδέναι ... ἀναγκαῖον, 4.4) not to leave unnoticed or allow to pass into oblivion this the finest and most beneficent of the performances of Fortune.... **4.10** Special histories therefore contribute very little to the knowledge of the whole and conviction of its truth. It is only indeed by study of the interconnection of all

the particulars (τῆς ἁπάντων πρὸς ἄλληλα συμπλοκῆς, 4.11)...that we are
enabled at least to make a general survey, and thus derive both benefit and
pleasure from history.... **5.1** I shall adopt as the starting-point (ἀρχήν) of this
book the first occasion on which the Romans crossed the sea from Italy.... The
starting-point must be an era generally agreed upon and recognized, and one
self-apparent from the events (πράγμασι, 5.4), even if this involves my going
back a little in point of date and giving a summary of intervening occurrences.
For if readers are ignorant or indeed in any doubt as to what are the facts from
which the work opens, it is impossible that what follows (τῶν ἑξῆς, 5.5) should
meet with acceptance or credence....

12.5 Such then was the occasion and motive of this the first crossing of the
Romans from Italy with an armed force, an event which I take to be the most
natural starting-point (ἀρχήν) of this whole work. I have therefore made it my
serious base, but went also somewhat further back in order to leave no possible
obscurity in my statements of general causes. To follow (παρακολουθῆσαι, 12.7)
out this previous history...seems to me necessary for anyone who hopes to gain
a proper general survey (συνόψεσθαι) of their present supremacy. My readers
need not therefore be surprised if, in the further course of this work (ἐν τοῖς
ἑξῆς, 12.7), I occasionally give them in addition some of the earlier history of
the most famous states; for I shall do so in order to establish such a fundamental
view (ἀρχάς, 12.9) as will make it clear (σαφῶς κατανοεῖν, 12.9) in the sequel starting from what origins and how and when they severally reached their
present position.... **13.2** To take them in order (κατὰ τὴν τάξιν) we have first
the incidents of the war between Rome and Carthage for Sicily. Next follows...
13.9 Thus there will be no break in the narrative (διηγήσεως) and it will be seen
that I have been justified in touching on events which have been previously narrated by others, while this arrangement (οἰκονομίας) will render the approach to
what follows intelligible and easy for students (τοῖς...φιλομαθοῦσιν...εὐμαθῆ
καὶ ῥᾳδίαν).... **14.1** An equally powerful motive with me for paying particular
attention to this war is that the truth (τὴν ἀλήθειαν) has not been adequately
stated by those historians who are reputed to be the best authorities on it, Philinus and Fabius. I do not indeed accuse them of intentional falsehood, in view
of their character and principles, but they seem to me to have been much in
the case of lovers; for owing to his convictions and constant partiality Philinus
will have it that the Carthaginians in every case acted wisely, well, and bravely,
and the Romans otherwise, whilst Fabius takes the precisely opposite view....
14.5 but he who assumes the character of a historian must ignore everything
of the sort, and often...speak good of his enemies...while criticizing and even
reproaching roundly his closest friends, should the errors of their conduct im-
pose this duty on him.... **14.6** If History is stripped of her truth all that is left
is but an idle tale.... **14.8** We must therefore disregard the actors in our narrative and apply to the actions such terms and such criticism as they deserve....
15.13 Now that I have said what is fitting on the subject of this digression, I
will return to facts (πράξεις) and attempt in a narrative that strictly follows the

order of events to guide my readers by a short road to a true notion (ἀληθινὰς ἐννοίας, 15.13) of this war. [End of *prooemium*.]

Appendix 2

Theophrastus, The Characters, *Prooemium*

I have often marvelled, when I have given the matter my attention... why it has come about that, albeit the whole of Greece lies in the same clime and all Greeks have a like upbringing, we have not the same constitution of character.[91] I there-fore, Polycles (ἐγὼ οὖν, ὦ Πολύκλεις), having observed (συνθεωρήσας) human nature a long time (ἐκ πολλοῦ χρόνου)... and moreover had converse with all sorts of dispositions and compared them with great diligence (ἐξ ἀκριβείας πολλῆς), have thought it incumbent upon me to write in a book (ὑπέλαβον δεῖν συγγράψαι) the manner of each several kind of men both good and bad. *And I will set down for you each in its place* (κατὰ γένος) [cf. καθεξῆς, Luke 1:3] the behaviour proper to them and the fashion of their life; for I am per-suaded, Polycles, that our sons will prove the better men if there be left them such memorials as will... make them choose the friendship and converse of the better sort, in the hope they may be as good as they. But now to my tale (λόγος) [cf. Luke 1:2]; and be it yours to follow with understanding (σὸν δέ παρακολουθῆσαί τε εὐμαθῶς) and see if I speak true (εἰδῆσαι εἰ ὀρθῶς λέγω) [cf. Luke 1:4 (ἐπιγνῷς...τὴν ἀσφάλειαν)]. First, then, I shall dispense with all preface and with the saying of much that is beside the mark (ἔξω τοῦ πράγματος) and treat of those (ποιήσομαι τὸν λόγον) [cf. Acts 1:1] that have pursued the worse way of life, beginning with (ἄρξομαι πρῶτον) [cf. Luke 1:1; Acts 1:1] dissembling and the definition of it... and thereafter I shall endeavor, as I purposed to do, to make clear (φανερὰ καθιστάναι) the other affections each in its own place (κατὰ γένος). [End of *prooemium*.]

Appendix 3

Strabo, Geography 1.1.14–15, 22–23; 1.2.1

1.1.14 So, if one is about to treat of the differences between countries, how can he discuss his subject correctly and adequately if he has paid no attention, even superficially, to any of these matters? For even if it be impossible in a treatise (ὑπόθεσις) of this nature, because of its having a greater bearing on affairs of state, to make everything scientifically accurate (ἅπαντα ἀκριβοῦν), it will nat-urally be appropriate to do so, at least in so far as the man in public life is able to follow the thought (παρακολουθεῖν). **1.1.15** Moreover, the man who has once

---

91. Italics mine. Text of LCL modified.

thus lifted his thoughts to the heavens will surely not hold aloof from the earth as a whole; for it is obviously absurd, if a man who desired to give a clear exposition (σαφῶς ἐξειπεῖν) of the inhabited world had ventured to lay hold of the celestial bodies and to use them for the purposes of instruction, and yet had paid no attention to the earth as a whole....

1.1.22 In short, this book of mine should be generally useful — useful alike to the statesman (πολιτικόν) and to the public at large — as was my work on *History*. In this work, as in that, I mean by "statesman," not the man who is wholly uneducated, but the man who has taken the round of courses usual in the case of freemen or of students of philosophy. For the man who has given no thought to virtue and to practical wisdom, and to what has been written about them, would not be able even to form a valid opinion either in censure or in praise; nor yet to pass judgment upon the matters of historical fact that are worthy of being recorded in this treatise.

1.1.23 And so, after I had written my *Historical Sketches*, which have been useful, I suppose for moral and political philosophy, I determined to write the present treatise (σύνταξις) also; for this work itself is based on the same plan, and is addressed to the same class of readers, and particularly to men of exalted stations in life....

1.2.1 If I, too, undertake (ἐπιχειροῦμεν) to write upon a subject that has been treated by many others (πολλοί) before me, I should not be blamed therefore, unless I prove to have discussed the subject in every respect (ἅπαντα) as have my predecessors. Although various predecessors have done excellent work in various fields of geography, yet I assume that a large portion of the work still remains to be done; and if I shall be able to make even small additions to what they have said, that must be regarded as a sufficient excuse for my undertaking.... I therefore may have something more to say than my predecessors. This will become particularly apparent in what I shall have to say in criticism of my predecessors, but my criticism has less to do with the earliest geographers than with the successors of Eratosthenes and Eratosthenes himself.... And if I shall, on occasion, be compelled to contradict the very men whom in all other respects I follow (ἐπακολουθοῦμεν) most closely, I beg to be pardoned.... Indeed, to engage in philosophical discussion with everybody is unseemly, but it is honorable to do so with Eratosthenes, Hipparchus, Poseidonius, Polybius, and others of their type.

Appendix 4

Josephus, Against Apion I.53–56

I.53 Nevertheless, certain despicable persons have essayed to malign my history, taking it for a prize composition such as is set to boys at school. What an extraordinary accusation and calumny! Surely they ought to recognize that it is the duty of one who promises to *present his readers with actual facts* (παράδοσιν πράξεων ἀληθινῶν) first *to obtain an exact knowledge* (ἐπίστασθαι ταύτας πρότερον ἀκριβῶς) *of them* himself, *either through having been in close touch with the events* (ἢ παρηκολουθηκότα τοῖς γεγονόσιν), *or by inquiry from those who knew them* (παρὰ τῶν εἰδότων πυνθανόμενον). **I.54** That duty (πραγματεία) I consider myself to have amply fulfilled in both my works. In my *Antiquities*, as I said, *I have given a translation of our sacred books* (ἐκ τῶν ἱερῶν γραμμάτων μεθηρμήνευκα); *being a priest and of priestly ancestry, I am well versed in the philosophy of those writings* (ἱερεὺς ἐκ γένους καὶ μετεσχηκὼς τῆς φιλοσοφίας τῆς ἐν ἐκείνοις τοῖς γράμμασι). **I.55** My qualification as historian of the war was that I had been *an actor in many* (πολλῶν μὲν αὐτουργὸς πράξεων), *and an eyewitness of most, of the events* (πλείστων δ' αὐτόπτης γενόμενος); in short, nothing whatever was said or done of which I was ignorant. **I.56** Surely, then, one cannot but regard as audacious the attempt of these critics to challenge my veracity. Even if, as they assert, they have read the *Commentaries* of the imperial commanders, they at any rate had no *first-hand acquaintance* (παρέτυχον) with our position in the opposite camp.

Josephus, Against Apion I.213–18

I.213 That the omission of some historians to mention our nation was due, not to ignorance, but to envy or some other disingenuous reason, I think I am in a position to prove. Hieronymus ... was a contemporary of Hecataeus. ... **I.214** Yet, whereas Hecataeus devoted a whole book to us, Hieronymus, although he had lived almost within our borders, has nowhere mentioned us in his history. So widely different were the views of these two men. One thought us deserving of serious notice; the eyes of the other, through an ill-natured disposition, were totally blind to the truth. **I.215** However, our antiquity is sufficiently established by the Egyptian, Chaldean, and Phoenician records, not to mention the numerous Greek historians. ... **I.217** The majority of these authors have misrepresented the facts of our primitive history (ἐξ ἀρχῆς πραγμάτων διήμαρτον), because they have not read (μή...ἐνέτυχον) our sacred books. ... **I.218** Demetrius Phalereus, the elder Philo, and Eupolemus are exceptional in their approximation to the truth (οὐ πολὺ τῆς ἀληθείας διήμαρτον), and [their errors] *may be excused* (οἷς συγγιγνώσκειν ἄξιον) *on the ground of their inability to follow quite accurately the meaning of our records* (οὐ γὰρ ἐνῆν αὐτοῖς μετὰ πάσης ἀκριβείας τοῖς ἡμετέροις γράμμασι παρακολουθεῖν).

Part II

Reframing the Heritage through Luke's Gospel–Acts

Chapter 5

Israel's Heritage and Claims upon the Genre(s) of Luke and Acts

The Problems of a History

Richard Pervo

Introduction

For the important question of what difference it makes to read each volume in light of the whole work, the issue of the genre(s) of Luke and Acts is almost an embarrassment. Robert Tannehill's valuable two-volume study of the narrative unity of Luke and Acts does not address the question of genre, and he is not alone, for much of the most fruitful literary, theological, and social analysis of "Luke-Acts" proceeds without profound reflection on its literary form or forms.[1] At the risk of appearing disloyal to the principles of this collection of essays, which I do not wish to be, or naughty, which I often am, I note that "Luke-Acts" is a modern construct, not yet seventy-five years old. From this perspective one could argue that the work belongs to a twentieth-century genre, and some seem to have followed this line.

Matters are not so simple. The hypothesis of Luke-Acts takes its origin from the indisputable fact of their linked prefaces and from the universal conclusion that both derive from the same author. Luke-Acts is, the argument runs, not a modern discovery, but the recovery of a unity lost long ago. Soteriological resolutions have their appeal. Parsons and Pervo have raised some embarrassing questions about this story of redemption.[2] In brief, the problem is why this essential unity was not generally observed and developed in the course of Christian

---

1. R. Tannehill, *The Narrative Unity of Luke-Acts: A Literary Interpretation*, 2 vols. (Philadelphia and Minneapolis: Fortress, 1986–90). One notable exception to this trend is Gregory E. Sterling, *Historiography and Self-Definition: Josephos, Luke-Acts, and Apologetic Historiography*, NovTSup 64 (Leiden: Brill, 1992).

2. M. Parsons and R. Pervo, *Rethinking the Unity of Luke and Acts* (Minneapolis: Fortress, 1993).

history.[3] Luke-Acts is essentially without support from the ancient manuscript and commentary traditions.

The major explanation for the "fall" has been that the two volumes belong to *different* genres, leading to the separation of the Gospel from its successor. In order to reassemble Humpty and Dumpty, modern proponents of generic unity must thus burn the bridge they crossed. Their apparent presumption is that early Christian theologians were mistaken in their estimates of Luke and Acts. Even when all the animus of Protestant historiography is set aside, it is true that, by our lights, early Christian theologians were mistaken about many things. Rarely, however, can they be accused of overlooking opportunities to discover unity and continuity. The opposite is more nearly true. A prime illustration of this propensity is the Book of Acts.[4]

Luke and Acts

No one, to my knowledge, denies that Luke and Acts should be read against one another, although commentaries that largely ignore the other volume continue to be written.[5] Hypotheses or conclusions about genre affect *how* this reading will take place. If the suggestion that the two books provide almost no illumination of one another may be set aside, it would also seem apparent that the view of this work as a continuous narrative, disrupted only by the requirement to move to a new roll of papyrus or something equally insignificant, should be rejected. This latter understanding does, however, appear to be a common, if covert, working hypothesis, abetted by the literary-critical view of works as autonomous artifacts — a view that gives powerful impetus to and receives stimulus from the hypothesis of Luke-Acts. By obliterating the possibility of generic difference, and by setting aside such vexing questions as the order of their composition, or whether the two volumes were separated by a period of time, possibly of place, or whether the actual author might have uncovered new sources, and the like, the ultra-unitarian approach raises the danger of not giving voice to possible differences between the books.

A great gain from a narrative orientation to Luke and Acts is the realization that the work of Luke has a plot (or plots), that one cannot determine the implied author's view of, for example, Pharisees by listing all of the references

---

3. Irenaeus and Tertullian, to name the leading examples, seize upon authorial continuity and the presumed link between Paul and Luke as a weapon against Marcion (and others). This primarily historical link does not constitute the "upon" which modern scholars build. For more on the early reception of Acts see below. See also C. K. Barrett, "The First New Testament?" *NovT* 38 (1996): 94–104.

4. One critical probe of the Lukan picture of unity is Paul J. Achtemeier, *The Quest for Unity in the New Testament Church* (Philadelphia: Fortress, 1987).

5. For example, C. K. Barrett's contribution to the International Critical Commentary, *A Critical and Exegetical Commentary on the Acts of the Apostles*, vol. 1: *Preliminary Introduction and Commentary on Acts 1–14*, vol. 2: *15–18* (Edinburgh: T. & T. Clark, 1994–98).

to them and adjudicating any dissonances, but that such groups or characters are components of a narrative strategy that must be examined in context.[6] One need not say how damaging this orientation is to the project of reading Luke and Acts as "objective" history. Recognition of this danger is one of the motives that has given rise to the most massive of recent "separatist" endeavors: *The Book of Acts in Its First-Century Setting*.[7] For the vast majority of the editors, authors, and contributors to this useful series the Book of Acts is simply facts. There is limited reflection on why the author has selected, from a multitude of data, these particular facts, whereas for literary criticism and theological analysis such selection is fundamental.[8] To state the matter quite sharply, defenders of Acts as a thoroughly (not a generally) reliable historical text must separate it generically from the Gospel because no intellectually respectable argument can be advanced that Luke has not constructed, probably revised, the life of Jesus. Equally authoritative alternative constructions are available, and the author was aware of some of them (Luke 1:1).

Genre, Again

Discussion of the genre(s) of Luke and Acts has long revolved around the question of accuracy, but this is, in my view, a false trail. One can learn very little about the accuracy of a text from its implicit or explicit genre. The tabloid newspapers displayed in American supermarkets present the most sensational and bizarre material as simple fact in the form of journalistic reports. Even the most scrupulous of historians will make mistakes or be misled by their sources, let alone by their biases, conscious or unconscious.[9] Luke and Acts stand somewhere on a gradient between pure fiction and absolute fact, on the one hand, and, on another, between the recording of tradition and invention. Tradition, however carefully preserved, is not to be confused with fact, and it is often difficult to identify the "free invention" of data.[10] Genre does provide useful hints about a writer's intentions.

6. This particular instance is inspired by D. W. Gowler, *Host, Guest, Enemy, and Friend: Portraits of the Pharisees in Luke and Acts* (New York: Peter Lang, 1991).

7. The general editor of this six-volume series, jointly published by Eerdmans and Paternoster Press, is Bruce Winter.

8. This is not to suggest that historians ought also to neglect the material their sources have selected or elected not to discuss!

9. A biblical example of historiographic bias is the Chronicler. "The Father of (Western) History," Herodotus, propounded the thesis that the conflict between Greeks and Persians was a battle between slavery and freedom. Only in recent times has this thesis been identified as prejudiced and misleading.

10. A relevant case is Livy's dramatic and romantic description of the Roman suppression of Dionysiac religion in 186 B.C.E. (39.8.3–39.9.1), which has provoked a host of scholarly discussions. For a recent example of the latter see E. S. Gruen, "The Bacchanalian Affair," in *Studies in Greek Culture and Roman Policy* (Leiden: Brill, 1990; Berkeley: University of California Press, 1996), 34–78. Another famous example is the little romance narrated by Josephus as explanation of an expulsion of Isis worshipers from Rome, *Ant.* 18:65–80.

This characterization constitutes most of the battleground, but it does not resolve the issues. Hans Conzelmann and Martin Hengel both view Luke and Acts as historical monographs, but greatly diverge in their estimates of their accuracy.[11] Just as it is impossible to provide adequate illumination for Luke and Acts by the consideration of any single genre, so it is also impossible to resolve disputes about accuracy by means of a generic classification.

The following brief review of the options proposed, much of which summarizes other surveys,[12] attempts to focus on the driving questions of this collection rather than the general theme of the genre(s) of Luke and Acts. Most comparisons look to narrative genres of the historical or biographical types, including biblical historiography, monograph, historical novel, apologetic history, general history, "Antiquities," and biography. A different, although not wholly unrelated, perspective has begun to emerge from examination of technical types of writing, less belletristic in style.[13]

There is a general consensus that Luke and Acts owe a substantial literary debt to the "Hellenistic Jewish" narrative tradition, including biblical narratives in Greek translation, Israelite books reflecting the influence of Hellenism, and texts written in Greek by Jewish authors during the Hellenistic and early Roman periods, that is, the LXX, Josephus, the fragmentary Hellenistic Jewish historians, and others.[14] To this inventory one must add their Hellenistic and Roman prototypes, including ethnographers, historians, antiquarians, and apologists. Biblical models provide two indisputable advantages. From them derives the integration of history and prophecy, theological models for the interpretation of history.[15] They also include texts with which Luke, who can imitate, cite, and allude to the LXX, was undoubtedly familiar. Yet the diversity of genre, content, theme,

---

11. For references to Conzelmann and his students see Parsons and Pervo, *Rethinking*, 26–27. M. Hengel, *Between Jesus and Paul*, trans. J. Bowden (Philadelphia: Fortress, 1983), 99, speaks of the two-volume work as "a 'monograph' with a purpose." Conzelmann is much more skeptical than is Hengel.

12. For more detail see Parsons and Pervo, *Rethinking*, 20–44. M. Dumais ("Les Actes des Apôtres: Bilan et orientations," in *"De bien des manières": La recherche biblique aux abords du XXIᵉ siècle*, ed. M. Gourgues and L. Laberge, LD 163 [Paris: Cerf, 1995], 307–64) devotes two pages (338–40) to the genre of Luke and Acts, concluding, "Le fait que le livre des Actes a eté attribué à des genres littéraires si différents — n'est-il pas un bon indice qu'il n'appartient pleinement à aucun d'entre eux?" Although inspired mainly by history and biography, Acts is a unique work (340).

13. The study of the genre(s) of Luke and Acts is particularly vexed by the tendency of the proponents of a particular model to reduce alternative proposals *ad absurdum* or to caricature them.

14. Among those "others" are Pseudo-Philo, which Eckhart Reinmuth has illuminatingly brought into the discussion: *Pseudo-Philo und Lukas* (Tübingen: J. C. B. Mohr [Paul Siebeck], 1994). Exploration of the lives of the prophets (on which see A. M. Schwemer, *Studien zu den frühjüdischen Prophetenlegenden Vitae Prophetarum*, 2 vols. [Tübingen: J. C. B. Mohr (Paul Siebeck), 1996]) and other narrative works included among the Pseudepigrapha and/or now appearing in the DJD remains a *desideratum*.

15. Brian S. Rosner's "Acts and Biblical History," in *The Book of Acts in Its First-Century Setting*, ed. B. W. Winter and A. D. Clarke, vol. 1: *The Book of Acts in Its Ancient Literary Setting* (Grand Rapids, Mich.: Eerdmans, 1993), 65–82, is a recent survey of the subject. See also, in the same volume, D. Peterson, "The Motif of Fulfilment and the Purpose of Luke-Acts," 83–104, who relates the practice to Greco-Roman historiography.

and viewpoint introduces complications. Did the author of Luke and Acts regard 2 Kings, Judith, 2–3 Maccabees, and Daniel, for example, as homogeneous grain from the mill of "Biblical History"? This is not an easy question to answer, but it is surely an important one. Recent research on the history of the canon demonstrates that much of the language about Luke's "scripture" requires more qualification and nuance than it has received.[16] Texts that found their way into the LXX also show tendencies to organize narrative histories around great figures, to mingle history with something like biography. This propensity may cast considerable light on Acts, but it does not, in my judgment, explain how the two books belong to a single genre.

The same observation applies to a number of monographs. To summarize observations made elsewhere, "monograph" is quite acceptable as a description for Acts, possibly even for Luke, but it lacks sufficient specificity. In this regard it has some of the merits and defects of that invaluable refuge, "narrative."[17] If Diodoros of Sicily displays a "monographizing tendency,"[18] and 3 Maccabees is a monograph,[19] as well as the works of Sallust and Tacitus's *Agricola*, the "genre" covers a wide ground. Defined broadly, "monograph" is not a genre, but a structure appearing in numerous genres.[20] Monography can also serve to explain the association or sequence of books on different topics. This factor is evident in technical and scientific works, the individual volumes of which are often monographs on a particular aspect of the discipline. These individual volumes could appear over a period of time.[21]

When Acts is considered by itself, the case for viewing it as a historical monograph, in the tradition of 2 Maccabees, is considerably more cogent. In a recent study of the question Darryl Palmer,[22] after sharply distinguishing between the two books, presses for such a definition and understanding of Acts, by which, he asserts, it may be understood as "dramatic" rather than "romantic" history

---

16. Robert Brawley's *Text to Text Pours Forth Speech: Voices of Scripture in Luke-Acts* (Bloomington: University of Indiana Press, 1995) displays considerable literary-critical sophistication that can, stimulated by modern use of the term, assume the existence of a first-century biblical "canon." That term is anachronistic, since it presumes authoritative persons or bodies who can promulgate rules. For a recent survey of the concept see L. M. McDonald, *The Formation of the Christian Biblical Canon* (Peabody, Mass.: Hendrickson, 1995).

17. So invaluable is that refuge that I shall use it myself, below.

18. E. Plümacher ("Lukas als griechischer Historiker," *Realencyklopädie der classischen Altertumswissenschaft Supplementband* 14.235–64, here 263) points to *Diod. Sic.* 16.1. See also C. W. Fornara, *The Nature of History in Ancient Greece and Rome* (Berkeley: University of California Press, 1983), 43.

19. H. Conzelmann, *Acts of the Apostles,* translated and edited by E. J. Epp with C. Matthews, Hermeneia (Philadelphia: Fortress, 1987), xl.

20. The same may be said of historical novels.

21. One example is the second-century *Oneirocritika* of Artemidoros, in five books. Books 1–3 are dedicated to Cassius Maximus (Maximus of Tyre?). The preface to Book 3 indicates that it is an afterthought. Books 4 and 5, however, while linked to the others, are dedicated to his son; 4.84 promises another volume. The preface to Book 5 indicates that this was late in coming.

22. Darryl W. Palmer, "Acts and the Ancient Historical Monograph," in Winter and Clarke, *The Book of Acts in Its Ancient Literary Setting,* 1–29.

(for whatever comfort this distinction may bring).[23] He also observes that "the history of an incipient religious movement is an unprecedented subject for an ancient monograph. But the way has been prepared by the religious content of the Hellenistic Jewish historical monographs."[24] Just how these works play the role of John the Baptizer is worthy of further discussion.

Examination of general or antiquarian models takes its departure from the view of Luke and Acts as a comprehensive project, analogous to the story of a nation or race. This approach reinforces and builds on the Lukan object of linking the Jesus movement in a formal way to the story of Israel, a story of which it is an integral and climactic component, and to the pursuit by some philosophers and historians of the unity underlying human diversity, a subject often glossed in Lukan studies as "universalism."[25] The various general or universal histories tend (if Diodoros be taken as exemplary) toward the status of macrogenres, allowing the possibility that Luke and Acts could represent distinct literary types. Examination of the prototypes quickly reveals that the two volumes to Theophilus could constitute chapters within a general history, but that the narrowness of their scope is one obstacle to the comparison. Luke and Acts have something in common with at least some of the diverse sources exploited by general historians like Alexander Polyhistor.[26]

Much can also be learned from the type known as "Antiquities," notably the works of Josephus and Dionysius of Halicarnassus.[27] "Antiquities" provided a format for explaining one national group to outsiders by describing its growth and development. Although Luke does not directly address outsiders, his method follows some of the same paths.[28] Differences include, once more, a much smaller size, a narrow scope, and an unusual, if not inappropriate, subject. The two surviving examples of this type focus on the traditional realms of war and politics, neither of which was of much use to the narrator of a movement that was neither ethnic nor coterminous with a political unit. G. E. Sterling's hypothesis of "apologetic historiography"[29] represents a turn, on the one hand, toward more

---

23. E. Plümacher has also pointed to the "dramatic episodic style" of Luke and Acts. (His views are now also available in a convenient English summary, "Luke as Historian," *ABD* 4.398–402.) Curtius Rufus and, in particular, Livy, provide examples of this episodic orientation. "Dramatic" (or "tragic") history is not, as Plümacher recognizes, a genre, but a *mode* of writing.

24. Palmer, "Acts and the Ancient Historical Monograph," 29.

25. On the subject of Lukan "universalism" see Parsons and Pervo, *Rethinking*, 84–114.

26. Polyhistor is the source, by way of Eusebius et al., for the fragments of Hellenistic Jewish historians, available in the modern edition of C. Holladay, *Fragments from Hellenistic Jewish Authors*, vol. 1: *Historians*, SBLTT 20 (Chico, Calif.: Scholars Press, 1983). Among those who have explored their relevance to the form of Luke and Acts are Pervo (*Profit with Delight: The Literary Genre of the Acts of the Apostles* [Philadelphia: Fortress, 1987]) and Sterling (*Historiography and Self-Definition*).

27. D. Balch is preparing a major work on this subject. See his "Acts as Hellenistic Historiography," *SBLSP* 24 (1985): 429–32; idem, "Comments on the Genre and a Political Theme of Luke-Acts," *SBLSP* 28 (1989): 343–61; and idem, "The Genre of Luke-Acts: Individual Biography, Adventure Novel, or Political History?" *Southwestern Journal of Theology* 33 (1991): 5–19.

28. See Parsons and Pervo, *Rethinking*, 29 n. 41.

29. Sterling, *Historiography and Self-Definition*. The same term is used by L. T. Johnson in his

technical types of writing, and, on the other, toward continuation of the logical and time-honored comparison between the Lukan corpus and Josephus. By
tracing the origins of his subject to Greek ethnography and by including within
his purview many works of a rather modest size and some of a less intellectually
elevated character, Sterling has provided apologetic writings with a range, background, and depth of understanding that transform the adjective from something
of a vague catchall into a more precise category for research.

The inventory of texts surveyed by Sterling displays considerable overlap with
those examined by Pervo, who began not with predecessors but successors, which
he found in the apocryphal Acts rather than in Eusebius and other ecclesiastical
historians.[30] This research focused on elements in Acts for which historians in
the classical tradition provided limited warrant.[31] Pervo argued for the presence
of important prototypes in Jewish (and other) historical novels.[32] Both he and
Sterling single out as their leading example the work of Artapanus, which, they
ruefully admit, is fragmentary and known only at thirdhand.[33]

A major obstacle to finding generic identity in Luke and Acts is the facil-
ity with which Luke, like Matthew, Mark,[34] and John, can be associated with
ancient biography.[35] Charles Talbert, who wrote a pioneering study of the literary and structural affinities between Luke and Acts, has taken this bull by the
horns.[36] One object of his analysis is demonstrating the importance of establishing legitimacy by claiming authentic transmission of tradition through valid
leaders. Loveday Alexander, informed by a careful study of Diogenes Laertios,

---

Sacra Pagina commentaries, *The Gospel of Luke* and *The Acts of the Apostles* (Collegeville, Minn.:
Liturgical Press, 1991–92), 3–10 and 3–9, respectively.

30. R. Pervo, "The Literary Genre of the Acts of the Apostles," Ph.D. diss., Harvard University,
1979, of which *Profit with Delight* represents a substantial revision. Although Acts constituted one
of Eusebius's sources, it was scarcely his model. Eusebius viewed himself as the first to tread the
path (*H.E.* 1.1.3). On the topic see A. Nobbs, "Acts and Subsequent Ecclesiastical Histories," in
Winter and Clarke, *The Book of Acts in Its Ancient Literary Setting*, 153–62, who labors to establish
links. In my view those who wish to relate Luke and Acts to the traditions of "Antiquities" and/or
philosophical succession would do well to pay close attention to Eusebius and his successors, whose
use of these genres is indisputable.

31. These features will be addressed below.

32. For a recent study of this, and related, material see L. W. Wills, *The Jewish Novel in the
Ancient World* (Ithaca, N.Y.: Cornell University Press, 1995).

33. Novels of various kinds have also been introduced into the discussion of the Gospel genre.
Papers on this subject have been presented in the SBL section on Ancient Fiction and Early Jewish and Christian Literature. See also Richard A. Burridge, *What Are the Gospels? A Comparison
with Graeco-Roman Biography*, SNTSMS 70 (Cambridge: Cambridge University Press, 1992), who
treats novels among those genres "proximate" to biography, and M. A. Tolbert, *Sowing the Word*
(Minneapolis: Fortress, 1989), who compares Mark with Xenophon's *An Ephesian Tale*.

34. In a nuanced study of the genre of Mark, Adela Y. Collins inclines to regard the earliest
Gospel as a type of monograph rather than a biography (*The Beginning of the Gospel: Probings of Mark
in Context* [Minneapolis: Fortress, 1992], 1–38).

35. Acts 1:1, Τὸν μὲν πρῶτον λόγον ἐποιησάμην περὶ πάντων, ὦ Θεόφιλε, ὧν ἤρξατο ὁ Ἰησοῦς
ποιεῖν τε καὶ διδάσκειν, all but defines Luke as biographical. From this data an ancient editor would
be likely to extract the title λόγος ἁ περὶ τῶν πράξεων καὶ διδαχῆς τοῦ Ἰησοῦ.

36. C. Talbert, *Literary Patterns, Theological Themes, and the Genre of Luke-Acts*, SBLMS 20
(Missoula, Mont.: Scholars Press, 1974), followed and refined by a number of essays and articles.

subjected this hypothesis to a fresh review that moves beyond the frequently cited strictures of David Aune.[37] At the narrative level she finds the model wanting. More significant, in her view, are the various school traditions and their *Sitze im Leben*, in particular traditions about Socrates. Although narrative has been one of Talbert's enduring concerns, by reflecting on school traditions he has also introduced the subject of technical works. L. C. A. Alexander also gave new impetus to this discussion in her study of the preface to Luke, in which she finds closer affinities to the *prooemia* of *wissenschaftlich* works than those of historians proper.[38] For Alexander this finding has implications both for the question of genre and for efforts to profile the author's intellectual and social background. In a learned and interesting paper presented at the international SBL meeting at Louvain in August 1994, Hubert Cancik discussed Luke and, primarily, Acts within the context of ancient institutional histories, a perspective applied to philosophical, as well as to national, subjects, with affinities to technical as well as to more literary works.[39]

Where, amid these diverse proposals, can common ground be found? From a strictly generic approach, stronger arguments can be made for division. The Gospel, by itself, can without great difficulty be associated with representative works of the biographical tradition, while Acts has many features of the historical monograph. In conflict with strictly generic approaches, narrative studies readily identify numerous shared themes within a continuous plot line. Advocates of general, antiquarian, or apologetic history have the merit of attempting to reconcile these conflicting results. The debate becomes less confusing when one recognizes that these genres are marked less by particular features and style than by their scope and objectives.

In the Greco-Roman world, genre was intimately bound up with style and, to a large degree, with content. Among items that distinguish Luke and Acts from learned historiography are the persistent use of an omniscient narrator,[40] the

---

37. L. C. A. Alexander, "Acts and Ancient Intellectual Biography," in Winter and Clarke, *The Book of Acts in Its Ancient Literary Setting*, 31–63. Aune discusses the genre of Luke and Acts in *The New Testament in Its Literary Environment*, Library of Early Christianity 8 (Philadelphia: Westminster, 1987), 17–157. Note in particular p. 141.

38. Loveday Alexander, *The Preface to Luke's Gospel: Literary Convention and Social Context in Luke 1.1–4 and Acts 1.1*, SNTSMS 78 (Cambridge: Cambridge University Press, 1993). I reviewed this work in *JBL* 114 (1995): 522–24.

39. "Kultur-Religions-Institutionsgeschichte in der antiken Historiographie: Philologische Bermerkungen zum lukanischen Geschichtswerk," published as "The History of Culture, Religion, and Institutions in Ancient Historiography: Philological Observations Concerning Luke's History," *JBL* 116 (1997): 673–95.

40. Since so much of Luke's reputation as an historian is based on the prefaces to Luke and Acts, it is important to underline the obvious literary observation that the narrator of the prefaces ("extradiegetic narrator") cannot be identified with the narrator of the text. The former is limited; the latter is omniscient. Appeals to the prefaces in defense of the author's method, goals, and reliability — in the factual, not the literary, sense — evaporate the instant this distinction is grasped. See now L. C. A. Alexander, "The Preface to Acts and the Historians," in *History, Literature, and Society in the Book of Acts*, ed. B. Witherington III (Cambridge: Cambridge University Press, 1996), 73–103.

volume of dialogue and direct speech,[41] techniques of plotting and structure, the quantity and quality of entertaining narrative,[42] limitations of style,[43] the nature of the subject,[44] and the presence of what I describe as "fiction."[45] These are compelling reasons for including more "popular" texts on the menu of works to be compared with Luke and Acts.[46] There is another: popular texts were much less likely to be concerned with the fine points of generic distinction than were more sophisticated literary compositions.

To summarize: There is tension between evident generic disunity and indisputable thematic unity. With reference to the scope of each book and the division between them, the case for the monograph is strong. From the perspective of episode, style, and narrative technique historical novels cannot be neglected. Those who look to more general histories and antiquities correctly sense the compass of Luke and Acts. Apologetic history is not an inappropriate label for the author's aim.

---

41. On the matter of direct speech alone I should be willing to rest my case that surveys of the genre(s) of Luke and Acts need to extend beyond the realm of learned historiography.

42. "Profit with delight" was a cliché in antiquity, used even by writers of technical prose. Few authors wished to claim that their material was useless and dull. There are, however, varieties of pleasure. For an important discussion of the different ways in which pleasure entered ancient discussions of historiography, see C. W. Fornara, *The Nature of History in Ancient Greece and Rome*, 120–34. D. Palmer concludes his study of Acts ("Acts and the Ancient Historical Monograph") as a historical monograph with these words: "Even Polybius, in supporting the merits of universal history, believes that the reader should 'derive from history at the same time both profit and delight'" (29, citing Polyb. 1.4.11). Palmer's first prepositional phrase is not gratuitous, for Polybius there argues that monographs *cannot* provide profit with delight. Pleasure derives from the grasp of connections among masses of facts. This is not the same type of delight found, for example, in Acts 16:16–40 and 19:13–17.

43. It is often implied that Luke could write high-quality prose but chose not to. If true, this would have ramifications for audience and thus for genre. In fact, it does not seem to be true. Alexander's study of the preface(s) comes to the conclusion that the author's ambitions exceeded his ability. The attempted period in Acts 24:5–8 is another example of biting off more than one can chew. It does not seem likely that the author had substantial rhetorical training.

44. The chief social function of Greco-Roman historiography was character formation, in particular the development of aristocratic military and political leaders.

45. "Fiction" is a slippery and, to some, an inflammatory concept. In the case of factual narrative this is exacerbated in the Greco-Roman world by the propensity of authors to describe actual events (for example, a shipwreck one experienced, or, quite commonly, sieges) in terms of literary models and stereotypes. The composition of appropriate speeches was a responsibility rather than a license of historians. In addition, ancients debated the propriety of extracting history from myth and legend. The legend of Saul's conversion (Acts 9:1–9a) is, by critical standards, a fiction in that someone probably composed it along conventional lines. (It is also "truth" in that it presents what this change of perspective meant for those who transmitted it.) Few believe that the author of Acts was that "someone." I should not, therefore, classify this as a Lukan fiction. Acts 9:23–25, which must derive, directly or indirectly, from 2 Cor. 11:32, very probably *is* a Lukan fiction, since the themes and motifs accord with others in Acts. A clear-cut example of what I label "fiction" may be found in Acts 23:13–35. Gerd Lüdemann (*Early Christianity according to the Traditions in Acts*, trans J. Bowden [Philadelphia: Fortress, 1989], 242–47) attempts to fit his recognition of this passage as "novelistic" (246–47) into a redaction-critical framework. It does not constitute his strongest case.

46. These matters may appear superficial to modern scholars, but they were not extraneous to those who discussed genre in antiquity.

Common Ground

In terms of the object of Luke and Acts I believe there is general consensus that these works can be called "legitimating narrative." "Narrative" is something of a weasel word, but it is sufficient in that it reflects the intention to make a case by telling a story (or stories), rather than by means of a treatise or a dialogue.[47] "Legitimating" serves to express the purpose of the work, whether this is construed more precisely as the legitimacy of Pauline Christianity (possibly in rivalry to other manifestations) or generally as the claim of the Jesus movement to the Israelite heritage.[48] The adjective also characterizes Luke and Acts as midway between an evangelist like the author of Mark and an apologist like Justin.[49] Such median points are rife with tensions, vexed with ambiguities, and characterized by fluidity. It is not, therefore, surprising that scholars can find evidence to describe Luke as a proponent of early catholicism or of charismatic fervor, as a social radical or as a social conservative, as relegating eschatology to a corner or as preserving apocalyptic theology. The tensions are present, even if, as I believe is most likely, Luke tends more toward Justin than toward Montanism. Formal apologies are ostensibly addressed to "outsiders." Luke and Acts are not.[50] The legitimating function of these works has as its object followers of Jesus, rather than polytheists or "Jews," to use a shorthand expression for the (presumably vast) majority of Israelites who did not accept claims that Jesus was the Messiah. Arguments for legitimacy imply suggestions of illegitimacy. What and whom do Luke and Acts seek to legitimate, and how? Against what and whom are these claims made, and how? "What/whom" and "how" should not be sundered. One of the major goals of generic study is to illuminate the matter of "how."

Luke and Acts certainly seek to legitimate a social body comprised of both "Jews" and Gentiles, and do so by the erection of a symbolic universe that includes theological views, notably a christology. The intellectual grounds for the Lukan argument take the shape of a case for continuity from Adam (and the

---

47. Justin's *Apologies* and the *Dialogue with Trypho* are apt comparisons.

48. "Legitimating" is not a synonym for "apologetic" but a concept derived from the sociology of knowledge set forth in P. L. Berger and T. Luckmann, *The Social Construction of Reality* (Garden City, N.Y.: Doubleday, 1967), and is intimately related to the notion of a "symbolic universe." The seminal application of this concept to Lukan studies is P. F. Esler's important *Community and Gospel in Luke-Acts*, SNTSMS 57 (Cambridge: Cambridge University Press, 1987). See, in particular, pp. 16–23, and p. 45. Esler points to the *Res Gestae* of Augustus (p. 18). To this one might add the *Aeneid* of Virgil and Livy's histories, which perform similar functions, among others. With regard to the social-scientific study of our texts note also the contributions to J. H. Neyrey, ed., *The Social World of Luke-Acts: Models for Interpretation* (Peabody, Mass.: Hendrickson, 1991).

49. "Legitimating" is, from the social-scientific perspective, a proper task of the second and later generations of a movement, although it may well begin at the time of origin.

50. Contrast Epaphroditus, the patron and dedicatee of several of Josephus's works, who is to be supplied with desired information, with the at least somewhat "informed" Theophilus of Luke 1:4. For a pointed discussion of the role of "apologetic" in Luke and Acts see Esler, *Community and Gospel*, 205–19.

God who brought Adam to life) to Paul (and beyond). Biblical, general, and antiquarian history come into play at this point. Vindication through "miracle" constitutes the leading (not the only) psychological and empirical factor. Here the governing model is "aretalogy," which may be expressed in a number of literary forms. The two happily coincide when Jesus does what Moses and Elijah did, and Peter and Paul follow suit. Luke thus had to utilize both the popular arguments for legitimating a new or newly arrived cult and at the same time to claim that the cult was of venerable antiquity. The project may seem rather self-contradictory, but it was far from unheard of. Sarapis did the same,[51] as did one emperor after another from Augustus onward. The argument that a phenomenon is no novelty but rather a return to the good old days is not of recent vintage. Prior to the Industrial Revolution it was de rigueur.

The Other

This Lukan program was not self-evident. One major problem Luke and many others, including Paul, faced was why, if Jesus were the Messiah of Israel, most Israelites had refused to accept this claim. The only possible defense at that time was to "blame it on the Jews," to attempt to prove that large numbers of them, at the very least, had missed the boat. One may wonder why I am making such trite observations. My response is that a good deal of the apologetic written about "Luke-Acts and the Jews" seems to treat the matter from the perspective of the twentieth century, which has seen the fruit of supersessionist claims harvested in the Holocaust.[52]

From a narrative perspective, "the other" in Luke and Acts moves in a line that is conclusive, if crooked, from the leaders and some others ("the people" often excluded) in Jerusalem toward "the Jews" in the Diaspora.[53] To speak of

---

51. A leading example is the history of the cult of Sarapis at Delos, which moved in the course of a century from marginal existence in rented quarters (see Acts 28:30) to public recognition and regulation (see the Edict of Milan). Much of this story is told, from an insider viewpoint, in the famous "Sarapis Aretalogy" from Delos (IG XI.4, 1299), most recently edited by H. Engelmann, *The Delian Aretalogy of Sarapis* (Leiden: Brill, 1975). For a fresh discussion of a range of evidence see L. M. White, *Building God's House in the Roman World: Architectural Adaptation among Pagans, Jews, and Christians* (Baltimore: Johns Hopkins University Press, 1990), 31–40. This story (present in both prose and poetic editions) stresses the strict succession, from knowledgeable father to carefully instructed son, of a cult brought from Memphis (the "Jerusalem" of Egyptian religion) to Delos.

52. From the perspective of modern apologetics in a pluralistic age the challenge to "mainstream" Christians is "legitimating" Judaism, that is, repudiating supersessionism. Luke's perspective was just the opposite, for Judaism required no legitimation. However odd, even perverse, its social practices or beliefs might seem, and however inclined toward revolt Jews might be, their religion was the faith and practice of an ancient people. For Luke the problem was not whether the door should be left open for future Jewish adherents, a development he would doubtless have welcomed, but the legitimacy of the movement he represented.

53. An important exception is the people of Nazareth, Luke 4:16–30. One of Luke's shortcomings as a historian is his failure to clarify why the general public turns against Jesus (Luke 23:13–23, which is atypical) and Peter (Acts 12:1–5).

"the Jews" is to identify a distinct social group different from one's own.[54] One expects that Luke and Acts, as narrative, will identify and criticize opponents by describing their behavior. Rhetorical education had long before developed vilification to a fine art, let alone whatever contributions popular polemic could make — and these were not negligible. If this were what we regard as a "family fight," we should expect the antagonism to be all the greater. Trotskyists classically reserve their most potent venom for Stalinists, and vice versa; both, as claimants to the authentic heritage of Marx and Lenin, often appear to despise social democrats more than capitalists.

If "the Jews" wish to have Paul executed for his labors on behalf of the hope of Israel (Acts 25:24; 26:6–7), they are not part of Israel. The claims of Acts are exclusive. I find it unlikely that "the Jews" would be employed if ethnic and/or observant Jews constituted a large part of the "Christian" community envisioned by Luke and Acts.[55] They rather appear to have been in danger of becoming a neglected minority, toward whom the narrator would extend some sympathy and protection.[56] Nonetheless, any who use "Jew" as a self-designation would find Luke and Acts painful reading, then and subsequently.[57] Luke does wish to legitimate the Jesus movement against its critics, most of whom, Jew or Gentile, find their best ammunition in Israel's "no." Nonetheless, he has come perilously close to producing, quite unwillingly, one book portraying the culmination of a "religion" and another describing the birth of a new cult. Unity and continuity were not unimportant elements of the Lukan program. The various fault lines that appear in the discussion of the generic, narrative, and theological unities of Luke and Acts, including claims on Israel's heritage, reveal both success and failure in repairing these with plaster. The first of these artisans was the author of Luke and Acts. There has been no lack of successors.

---

54. Forty-two of 119 occurrences of οἱ Ἰουδαῖοι in the NT are in Acts 9:22–28:19. Sixty are found in John. "The Jews" as opponents of Paul first emerge in Acts at Damascus (9:22–23; cf. 12:3, 11, of "the Jews" as wishing Peter dead [Jerusalem]). Paul's opponents in various Diaspora cities can be characterized as "the Jews," as are those in Jerusalem (chaps. 22–26), and his audience at Rome (chap. 28). This is in obvious conflict with Paul's own spoken claims to be a Jew and a Pharisee (22:3, etc.). The most likely explanation of these apparent anachronisms is the tension between the narrator's desire to find continuity and the social situation the narrative addresses.

55. Although Acts 28:23–28 states that some of Paul's Jewish hearers believed in his message, the closing announcement is directed to the entire body, who are further distinguished by reference to "your" ancestors, a distinction corrected in much of the manuscript tradition (see also the addition of "Jews and Greeks" [from 19:10?] in 28:30 by several witnesses). Here, if anywhere, the social situation of the implied author should dominate the narrative.

56. Such a viewpoint would help to explain the social significance of Acts 21:20–25. For neglect of "minorities" see also Acts 6:1–7. Among those who would strongly dissent from this view of Jews as a minority are J. Jervell and P. Esler.

57. Paul might be enrolled in this number. He uses οἱ Ἰουδαῖοι only in the famous 1 Cor. 9:20. (In my view 1 Thess. 2:14 is a later interpolation reflecting a perspective like that of Luke and Acts, from which it may derive.) Translation of the expression as "(the) Judeans" will not work for most of the references in Acts.

Sequels and Replacements

One approach to the question of genre is to examine not only predecessors but also successors. Using later texts to explain earlier works that may, in fact, have influenced them is an approach that NT scholars have come to find methodologically questionable, but we have been less prone to accept that the explication of phenomena within their context requires examination of subsequent no less than prior events. My object is to look for direct and indirect successors and sequels to Luke and Acts. Sequels to the Gospel genre included abbreviation, amalgamation, and development of certain traditional complexes, such as the "infancy stories," passion narratives, and, most prolifically, "Sayings Gospels" and postresurrection dialogues.[58] Harmonies, culminating in the *Diatessaron* of Tatian, sought to preserve the unity of the gospel message.

Marcion was one successor who utterly rejected the Lukan synthesis, offering an expurgated edition of the Gospel and a collection of Pauline letters.[59] It is tempting to see Marcion's work as a replacement of Luke and Acts, as well as of the LXX, but one cannot be certain, for Marcion may not have known when he formulated his system and scripture.[60]

An interesting successor to the Gospel of Luke is the so-called *Protevangelium Jacobi*, a popular and influential work[61] of the later second century that was subject to much editing in antiquity.[62] Although this text makes use of the gospels that later became canonical, Luke is its major source and model.[63] Its style is very similar to Luke's "biblicizing Greek." Angelophanies are numerous.[64] The

---

58. Examples of these types may be found in the standard handbook, *New Testament Apocrypha,* vol. 1: *Gospels and Related Writings,* ed. Wilhelm Schneemelcher, revised edition translated and edited by R. McL. Wilson (Louisville: Westminster/John Knox, 1991). Note also J. K. Elliott, *The Apocryphal New Testament* (Oxford: Clarendon Press, 1993). For a comprehensive review of the subject see H. Koester, *Ancient Christian Gospels: Their History and Development* (Philadelphia: Trinity Press International, 1990).

59. Although he has long and justifiably been chastised for his editorial activities, Marcion was not the last person to edit a text in accordance with his understanding of its original aims, then to use the result to support his understanding.

60. Scholarly tradition affirms that Marcion rejected the Book of Acts. So, for example, Harnack (*Marcion: The Gospel of the Alien God,* trans. J. E. Steely and L. Bierma [Durham, N.C.: Labyrinth Press, 1990], 175 n. 12), who writes of Marcion's rejection of Acts but gives no evidence. Tertullian, *Adv. Marc.* 5.1.6, which is cited in this connection, does not say that Marcion rejected Acts but that he should have accepted it, as it was written by Luke. (After proving, by reference to Genesis 49:11 and other texts, that the OT prophesied Paul, Tertullian goes on to say that if Marcion does not accept these figures, he should accept Acts. Since Marcion despised all figurative interpretation, this is a joke.) Behind the theory that Marcion rejected Acts is the assumption that both Luke and Acts were equally known and associated with one another at that time.

61. More than 147 manuscripts exist, some from the fourth, one possibly from the third, century.

62. This title originated in the West at the time of its first printing in the sixteenth century. For a summary of the scholarly discussion see O. Cullmann in Schneemelcher-Wilson, *New Testament Apocrypha,* 1.414–38, and W. Vorster, "James, Protevangelium of," *ABD* 3.629–32.

63. For the use of Luke see W. Vorster, "The Protevangelium of James and Intertextuality," in *Text and Testimony,* ed. T. Baarda et al. (Kampen, 1988), 262–75.

64. For example, 4.2; 11.2. In 14.2 there is a dream angelophany of the Matthean sort.

characters offer aria-like canticles at appropriate moments.[65] The author has, like Luke, drawn heavily on 1 Samuel. Whereas Judith has inspired Luke's Anna (Luke 2:36–38), the *Protevangelium* finds in Susanna a model for the Virgin.

In addition to the development of Lukan literary and narrative interests, the *Protevangelium* devotes attention to theological problems. At the level of inter-textuality, potential conflicts between Matthew and Luke are resolved, and the two are harmonized into a single story.[66] One of those problems is the clash be-tween Davidic descent and the virgin birth. The *Protevangelium* places Mary in the Davidic lineage (10.1). Questions about the virgin birth itself, a theme that lacks perfect clarity in Matthew and Luke, are answered with concrete proof that Mary's virginity remained after delivery.[67] There is no room for embarrassing gos-sip. Mary, like Samuel, was reared in the Temple. No longer able to remain there when she approached puberty, she was assigned to a widower with sons (Joseph). Apologetic interests also contribute to the removal of poverty, birth among ani-mals, and adoration by shepherds. Mary's family is quite wealthy; Joseph is a building contractor.[68] At least one "historical" hyperbole is corrected: the univer-sal census (Luke 2:1) is reduced to a local enrollment (17.1). The *Protevangelium Jacobi* witnesses to the use of Luke's Gospel as a source for data and as a model for the generation of legends as narrative creations inspired by scriptural mate-rial. Except for some details, such as birth in a cave, there is no sound basis for the detection of tradition beyond texts known to us.[69]

Acts was rather better endowed with successors. At some level the various major (and minor)[70] apocryphal "Acts" were successors and, at least sometimes, rivals to the work that became canonical. In composing a Gospel, Luke was an imitator of others. Acts provided the distinction, or downfall, of making him an object for imitation.[71] Because of its content and subject, the *Acts of Paul* is a

---

65. For example, 2.1; 3.1–3; 6.2.

66. It would be difficult to maintain that the author of the *Protevangelium* regarded Matthew and Luke as "canonical," for he alters both, eliminating, for example, the flight into Egypt (Matt. 2:13–21). On the other hand, acceptance of the story of Herod's murder of all male infants requires attention to the survival of John (chap. 22). Alterations of Luke are not infrequent. Swaddling of the infant Jesus in a cattle pen is made into a means for concealing him from Herod's agents (22.2). Vestiges of the annunciation to shepherds is barely visible behind 18.2 (which may be later).

67. At 19.3 a certain Salome (who has appeared without introduction) says, in clear imitation of John 20:25, ἐὰν μὴ βαλῶ τὸν δάκτυλόν μου καὶ ἐρευνήσω τὴν φύσιν αὐτῆς, οὐ μὴ πιστεύσω ὅτι παρθένος ἐγέννησεν. Aurelio de Santos Otero calls this a "frase de una crudeza extraordinaria" (*Los Evangelios Apocrifos* [Madrid: Biblioteca de Autores Cristianos, 1956], 179). After this exploration proves the point, Salome's arm becomes useless, but is quickly restored through touching the infant Jesus.

68. 1.1; 9.2. Zechariah no longer belongs to the minor orders of priests. He is, in fact, high priest (8.2).

69. Like Luke 1–2, *Protevangelium Jacobi* has nothing negative to say about "Jews." Rather re-markably, for a text of its era, the people of Israel, including in particular the priests, are pious and attentive to their obligations. The sole exception is the wicked king Herod, imported from Matthew 2.

70. The (late) *Acts of Barnabas* may be the closest imitation of the canonical book among the apocryphal "Acts."

71. Luke 1:1 does not exclude the possibility that Acts had narrative (i.e., extensive and written)

natural target for close scrutiny. Given the vagaries of its text, which was often revised and is now available only in segments from various editions, the *Acts of Paul* can be viewed as either a sequel to or a replacement of the Lukan text.[72] Criticism from the opposite angle emerged in what is reluctantly designated as Jewish Christianity and Judeo-Christianity. The Pseudo-Clementines, in which Paul does not take the role of hero, exhibit awareness of Acts and, not surprisingly, deliberate revisions of its story.[73] A somewhat more neutral motive for overlooking Acts, although useful in opposing Marcion,[74] was the view that each apostle left Jerusalem after the ascension to evangelize a particular region.[75] The narrative expression of this belief is the "apostolic lottery," which probably constituted the opening section of a number of "Acts."[76] It is hardly fortuitous that Acts 1:15–26 describes a lottery.[77]

The period from c. 125 to 225 thus indicates repeated attempts, in some circles, to provide an alternate portrait. Acts is, in each of these constructions (not all of which were "heretical"), the problem, either because it did not get Paul "right" (see Marcion; *Acts of Paul;* sources of the Pseudo-Clementines), or because it devoted too much attention to Paul and too little to the others. Irenaeus exhibits the eventual orthodox solution: four Gospels, Acts, and epistles of both Paul and others. The "storm center" identified by van Unnik in 1966 was a mere squall compared to the tempest that raged in the middle-third of the second century.[78] This rough sketch of reception history indicates that Luke's

---

prototypes, but all of the available evidence reveals imitation of Acts rather than hypothetical earlier sources used by both. This common view would, by silently eliminating the πολλοί of Luke 1:1 from application to Acts, raise questions about the view that the preface to Luke encompasses both books.

72. The thesis that *Acts of Paul* is a sequel is developed by R. Bauckham, "The Acts of Paul as a Sequel to Acts," in Winter and Clarke, *The Book of Acts in Its Ancient Literary Setting,* 105–52. A case for viewing it as a competitor to Acts is set forth in R. Pervo, "A Hard Act to Follow: *The Acts of Paul* and the Canonical Acts," *Journal of Higher Criticism* 2.2 (1995): 3–32. It no longer seems possible to contend that the author of the *Acts of Paul* did not know Acts (a position long espoused by W. Rordorff), although it is possible that the *Acts of Paul* may have been the better known of these two works among second-century Christians.

73. F. Stanley Jones can demonstrate critical revision of the canonical Acts in the Pseudo-Clementines: "A Jewish Christian Reads Luke's Acts of the Apostles: The Use of the Canonical Acts in the Ancient Jewish Christian Source behind Pseudo-Clementine *Recognitions* 1.27–71," *SBLSP* (1995): 617–35.

74. The received title of the canonical book, "Acts of the Apostles," which could scarcely be original (it would exclude Paul), is probably anti-Marcionite.

75. Justin also seems implicitly to reject the account of Acts in his description of the mission of the Twelve, *1 Apol.* 39.3: "For a band of twelve men went forth from Jerusalem, and they were common men, not trained in speaking, but by the power of God they testified to every race of humankind…" (trans. E. R. Hardy, in *Early Christian Fathers,* ed. C. Richardson (New York: Macmillan, 1970 [=LCC 1]), 266. It is astonishing that this passage has often been invoked to prove the *use* of Acts by Justin. The *Epistula Apostolorum* (probably c. 150 C.E.) may well know Acts but brings Paul into even closer proximity with the Twelve.

76. For this "lottery" see *Acts of Thomas* 1 and *Acts of Andrew and Matthias* 1. The problem is complicated by the loss of the opening sections of all but the *Acts of Thomas.*

77. The legend of the division of the world into territories for each apostle may antedate Luke and Acts.

78. W. C. van Unnik, "Luke-Acts, a Storm Center in Contemporary Scholarship," in *Studies in Luke-Acts,* ed. L. E. Keck and J. L. Martin (New York: Abingdon, 1966), 15–31.

second volume was often viewed as a sequel attractive in form but questionable in content.[79]

If Luke and Acts experienced various attempts at replacement, the author could hardly complain, for he, himself, was attempting to replace presumably inadequate "narratives."[80] Was the second volume also a "replacement"? Of what? The most likely candidate would be the letters of Paul.[81] What has the author replaced? To a large degree Acts, when set against the letters, "replaces" conflicts among followers of Jesus with conflicts between those followers and Jews. The critical tradition has, since F. C. Baur, portrayed Luke as the painter of a fictional portrait of early Christian unity, "harmonizing Peter and Paul," and so on. When addressed in the light of the question governing the present collection, it appears that Luke was seeking to clarify the emergent church's claims on Israel's heritage in a more adequate fashion than had Paul's letters to communities largely composed of Gentile converts. A similar purpose is visible in Ephesians, which is no less interested in unity than is Luke. These claims are shaped in terms of a post-Pauline conflict and reflect a post-Pauline situation, which may well have included a substantial influx of "Jews" (and, possibly, "Jewish sympathizers")[82] in the aftermath of the first revolt, when the existence of diverse Jewish sects was becoming less tolerable and lines were being drawn and redrawn.

Conclusion

Reflection on the question of genre in the light of Luke's predecessors and successors offers support to the view that Acts is a sequel rather than a second volume. Two quite dissimilar books would concede the existence of "two stories," the story of Jesus and the story of the church, the story of a "reform" movement

---

79. I say "sequel" because use and imitation of Acts indicates that it was viewed as separable, if not separate, from the Gospel, as does the use of Luke by Marcion, Irenaeus, and Tatian. This is not to overlook the important argument of F. Bovon ("The Synoptic Gospels and the Non-canonical Acts of the Apostles," *HTR* 81 [1988]: 19–36) that the various "Acts" are developments of the Gospel genre.

80. Luke 1:1.

81. One "assured conclusion" of NT research being subjected to considerable challenge is the dogma that Luke had no access to Pauline letters. For an example see L. Aejmelaeus, *Die Rezeption der Paulusbriefe in der Miletrede* (Helsinki: Suomalienen Tiedeakatemia, 1987). I do not believe that a respectable argument can be advanced for the hypothesis that Luke had never heard that Paul wrote letters.

82. Historically considered, there were doubtless "Jewish sympathizers" of many sorts at different periods. Their motives need not always have been religious. As in the case of the Pharisees, it is necessary to distinguish between the gathering of historical data about such persons, whether to illuminate Luke (where no religious motives are assigned to the "God-fearing" centurion of 7:1–10) and Acts (where the concept is essentially religious), or for other reasons, and the narrative function of these characters in Acts, which is a part of the author's literary strategy. The revealing social-scientific analysis of Esler (*Community and Gospel*) is a great advance upon naive historicism, but he is reluctant to concede much value to literary studies (see his *The First Christians in Their Social Worlds* [London: Routledge, 1994], 17).

or sect within emergent Judaism and the story of an explosion of Gentile converts who worshiped Jesus Christ the Lord, that is, the rise of a new cult. Early "Christians"[83] were united in the conviction that there was one story. Marcion resolved the issue by editing the Gospel of Luke to describe the birth of a new religion, the theological meaning of which was proclaimed by the Apostle, now audible in his letters.

Luke's solution was the production of two books that also move from Jesus to Paul. The "second" story becomes a logical outcome of the first, which often foreshadows and anticipates it. The two have become less one flesh than parent and child. For some the sequel conceded too much to Paul, for others too little, while yet others found it neglectful of other apostles. A number of writers viewed Luke and Acts as two stories, the second of which, in particular, was inadequate. Irenaeus fashioned them, with other ingredients, into one story again, and as "the etiological or foundational myth of gentile Christianity"[84] they have made an indelible (and by no means wholly lamentable) mark on Christian history.

---

83. The term "Christians," which, like the *titulus* on the cross, reflects Hebrew, Greek, and Latin features, is, of course, familiar to Luke (Acts 11:26), at the inception of Paul's Gentile mission, but scarcely preferred. Since polytheist authors did not, as a rule, speak of Jewish sects, the term probably indicates a distinct cult.

84. L. T. Johnson, *The Writings of the New Testament* (Philadelphia: Fortress, 1986), 204.

Section A

Hellenistic Jewish Narrative:
"Events that have come to fruition"
(Luke 1:1)

Chapter 6

Promise and Fulfillment in Hellenistic Jewish Narratives and in Luke and Acts

William Kurz

Introduction

Within the overall series objective of studying the Acts of the Apostles in re-lation to the Gospel of Luke, and in comparison with other writings from the Lukan environment which had similar purposes and used similar procedures, I will investigate the motif of promise and fulfillment in Hellenistic Jewish narra-tives and the particular relationship between the Gospel of Luke and Acts. Some Hellenistic Jewish narratives, such as the *Letter of Aristeas,* did not seem to relate closely enough to promise-and-fulfillment motifs to include in this essay. Those narratives that are included — Luke, Acts, 1 and 2 Maccabees, the *Jewish War* and *Antiquities of the Jews* of Josephus, and the Septuagint versions of Tobit and Judith — differ significantly in genre, ranging from ancient historiography to fic-tion. They differ in taking a more obviously biblical approach (Luke and Acts, 1 Maccabees, Tobit) to having a more Hellenistic emphasis (2 Maccabees, Jose-phus, *Jewish War* and *Antiquities of the Jews*). From the start it must be specified that the term "Hellenistic Jewish narratives" has been stretched to include orig-inal Semitic narratives current in Greek translation as part of the Greek Bible at the time of Luke and Acts, such as Judith, Tobit, and 1 Maccabees. The only extant complete narratives written originally in Greek, besides Luke and Acts, were 2 Maccabees and the published Greek works of Josephus.[1]

---

1. In response to a 1996 Catholic Biblical Association paper based on an earlier version of this essay, Anthony Saldarini recalled the fact of translation from Semitic originals to help explain the paucity of some Hellenistic elements. For a convenient edition of fragments, see Carl R. Holla-day, *Fragments from Hellenistic Jewish Authors,* vol. 1: *Historians,* SBLTT 20 (Chico, Calif.: Scholars Press, 1983).

Because of its well-known narrative of the Septuagint translation, the *Letter of Aristeas* was initially investigated as one of these Hellenistic Jewish narratives. That narrative, however, plays a minor role in what is usually and better categorized as an epistle with strong Hellenistic wisdom and symposium motifs.

The motif of promises or prophecies and their fulfillment is a literary device for making sense of disparate episodes. It is not only a key intertextual motif within the Jewish scriptures, in both the Hebrew and more extensive Greek collections, but also between the scriptures and the two Lukan narratives, and between the Lukan Gospel and Acts. To varying degrees, this motif is also important in other Hellenistic Jewish narratives being considered.

Promise-and-Fulfillment Themes in Luke and Acts

Space permits only a brief recollection of the study of promise and fulfillment in Luke and Acts. The two most obvious levels are, first, the fulfillment of *biblical* promises and, second, the fulfillment of prophecies and promises made by *characters*, by Simeon, Jesus, the apostles, and so on. For example, the biblical promises to Abraham are a major theme in the Gospel infancy narratives. Prophecies by Jesus, such as passion predictions, are sometimes fulfilled later in the Gospel, in Acts, beyond Acts, or in the eschatological future.[2] The Lukan version of the Last Supper (Luke 22:14–38) provides examples of fulfillment of both biblical prophecies and of Jesus' own prophecies.

Promises Made in Jewish Scriptures, Fulfilled in Luke and Acts

A consensus has emerged that Luke and Acts are thoroughly inspired by biblical motifs, vocabulary, writing styles, models, promises and prophecies, and other devices.[3] The two volumes are grounded in God's saving history from the creation and Adam in Genesis (e.g., in Luke 1–3) to the eschatological parousia of the Son of Man (as in Luke 21).[4] Already the preface to the Gospel makes a biblical allusion — granted, in nonbiblical Hellenistic idiom — to "events that have been fulfilled among us" (τῶν πεπληροφορημένων ἐν ἡμῖν πραγμάτων, Luke 1:1). The style switches dramatically after the elegant Hellenistic periodic preface to a "barbaric" biblical style, from verse 5 through the rest of Luke 2, for the account of the announcements, births, and childhoods of John the Baptist

---

2. See William S. Kurz, S.J., *Reading Luke-Acts: Dynamics of Biblical Narrative* (Louisville: Westminster/John Knox, 1993), 57, 72, 142, 148; idem, "Acts 3:19–26 as a Test of the Role of Eschatology in Lukan Christology," *SBLSP* (1977): 309–23; John T. Carroll, *Response to the End of History: Eschatology and Situation in Luke-Acts,* SBLDS 92 (Atlanta: Scholars Press, 1988), 107–14.

3. For example, see Craig A. Evans and James A. Sanders, *Luke and Scripture: The Function of Sacred Tradition in Luke-Acts* (Minneapolis: Fortress, 1993); and Craig A. Evans and W. Richard Stegner, eds., *The Gospels and the Scriptures of Israel,* JSNTSup 104 (Sheffield: Sheffield Academic Press, 1994).

4. E.g., the Lukan genealogy grounds Jesus' human ancestry in "Adam [son] of God" (Luke 3:38); the eschatological sermon in Jerusalem culminates in the cosmic signs and glorious return of Jesus as eschatological judge (Luke 21:25–28). See William S. Kurz, "Luke 3:23–38 and Greco-Roman and Biblical Genealogies," in *Luke-Acts: New Perspectives from the Society of Biblical Literature Seminar,* ed. Charles H. Talbert (New York: Crossroad, 1984), 169–87; and idem, *Reading Luke-Acts,* 10–11, 57, 72, 142, 148.

and Jesus — an account full of allusions to biblical models and promises, as is the resurrection chapter (Luke 24).[5]

Regarding the Third Gospel's references to the fulfillment of scriptures and to God's saving plan, Fitzmyer points to the use of the terms πληροῦν and πίμπλαναι from the infancy narrative onward.[6] Especially noteworthy is the redactional use of fulfillment terms at turning points in both volumes: at Luke 9:51 ("And it happened in the fulfillment of the days of his being taken up..." [ἐν τῷ συμπληροῦσθαι τὰς ἡμέρας]) and Acts 2:1 ("And in the day of Pentecost being fulfilled..." [ἐν τῷ συμπληροῦσθαι τὴν ἡμέραν).[7] In Jesus' "inaugural address" at Nazareth, explicit mention is made that "Today this scripture [Isa. 61:1–2; 58:6] has been fulfilled (Σήμερον πεπλήρωται ἡ γραφὴ αὕτη) in your hearing" (Luke 4:21). Acts 2:16 explicitly claims that the Pentecost phenomena are the fulfillment of "what was said through the prophet Joel" (Joel 3:1–5 [LXX] in Acts 2:17–21). Overall, for example in Luke 4:21, 18:31, 21:22, 22:37, and 24:44, the notion of fulfillment in Luke shows the continuity of God's will as opposed to pagan notions of blind fate or chance.[8]

In the body of his Gospel (Luke 3–23), the author shares and sometimes augments the biblical allusions of both his main sources — the one responsible for readings common to all three Synoptic Gospels, and the one common only to Matthew and Luke ("Q") — as well as Luke's exclusive ("L") sources and materials. For example, as in Luke's other Gospel sources, John the Baptist fulfills the prophecy of "Isaiah the Prophet" (Luke 3:4–6). But Luke adds, in Luke 4:21, cited above, the mixed quotation of Isa. 61:1–2 (LXX) with 58:6.

Explicit mention of Old Testament predictions includes Luke 18:31, "Behold we are going up to Jerusalem, and all those things written through the prophets regarding the Son of Man will be fulfilled." In the Lukan Last Supper, after warning the disciples to be prepared, Jesus combines personal prophecy with reference

---

5. See William S. Kurz, "Narrative Approaches to Luke-Acts," *Biblica* 68 (1987): 195–220, esp. 206–8; idem, *Reading Luke-Acts*, 11–12, 19–23, 164–66; David E. Aune, *The New Testament in Its Literary Environment*, Library of Early Christianity (Philadelphia: Westminster, 1987), 66–67; cf. 82, 128.

6. Joseph A. Fitzmyer, *The Gospel according to Luke (I–IX): Introduction, Translation, and Notes*, AB 28 (Garden City, N.Y.: Doubleday, 1981), 1.292–93. Note also the recent argument (with references) explicitly linking the use of scriptures in Luke and Acts with the notion of God's plan, and with the related Hellenistic notion of providence: David P. Moessner, "The 'Script' of the Scriptures in Acts: Suffering as God's 'Plan' (βουλή) for the World for the 'Release of Sins,'" in *History, Literature, and Society in the Book of Acts*, ed. Ben Witherington III (Cambridge: Cambridge University Press, 1996), 218–50. Cf. John T. Squires, *The Plan of God in Luke-Acts* (Cambridge: Cambridge University Press, 1993), comparing God's plan with the programmatic role of providence and the relationship to portents, epiphanies, prophecy, and fate in Hellenistic historiography.

7. Especially in Acts 2:1, ἐν τῷ συμπληροῦσθαι τὴν ἡμέραν τῆς πεντηκοστῆς, the primary linguistic reference is probably to the arrival of the feast of Pentecost on the fiftieth day, but my translation suggests a double entendre: that the deeper meaning of the Jewish Pentecost is fulfilled in the events of Acts 2.

8. Gustav Stählin, "Das Schicksal im Neuen Testament und bei Josephus," in *Josephus-Studien: Untersuchungen zu Josephus, dem antiken Judentum und dem Neuen Testament. Otto Michel zum 70. Geburtstag gewidmet*, ed. Otto Betz, Klaus Haacker, and Martin Hengel (Göttingen: Vandenhoeck & Ruprecht, 1974), 319–43, here 327. Cf. G. Delling, "πληρόω," *TWNT* 6.292–95.

to scripture: "For I tell you that this which has been written ought to be fulfilled in me (τοῦτο τὸ γεγραμμένον δεῖ τελεσθῆναι ἐν ἐμοί): 'And he was reckoned among the lawless,' for that [which is written] about me is nearing accomplishment (τὸ περὶ ἐμοῦ τέλος ἔχει)" (22:37).

Predictions of sufferings in Luke 21 use explicit fulfillment language: "...because these are the days of punishment to fulfill all those things written (ὅτι ἡμέραι ἐκδικήσεως [Deut. 32:35; Hos. 9:7; Jer. 46:10] αὗταί εἰσιν τοῦ πλησθῆναι πάντα τὰ γεγραμμένα)" (21:22). In language heavy with biblical resonance, Jesus predicts in v. 24 that Jerusalem will fall by the sword (Jer. 21:7), be taken captive (αἰχμαλωτισθήσονται) by the nations (Ezra 9:7), and trampled by the Gentiles (Zech. 12:3 [LXX]; Ps. 79:1; Dan. 9:26; 1 Macc. 3:45, 51) "until the times of the Gentiles are fulfilled" (πληρωθῶσιν καιροὶ) (Dan. 12:7; Tob. 14:5).

After Jesus' resurrection, angelic witnesses and the risen Jesus refer to previous predictions. All these references are distinctive to Luke. For example, the unrecognized Jesus calls the disciples on the way to Emmaus "slow of heart to believe all the things which the prophets said. Did not the Christ have to (ἔδει) suffer and enter into his glory?" He then applies the scriptures to himself. "And beginning from Moses and from all the prophets, he interpreted for them in all the scriptures those things about himself" (24:25–27).

In a final appearance, the risen Jesus refers both to his own prophecies and prophecies of scripture. " 'These are my words which I spoke to you while I was still with you, that all those things written in the Law of Moses and the prophets and the psalms about me must be fulfilled (δεῖ πληρωθῆναι).' Then he opened their minds to understand the scriptures. And he said to them, 'Thus it is written that the Messiah will suffer and rise from the dead on the third day, and there will be preached in his name repentance unto the forgiveness of sins to all the nations [or Gentiles], beginning from Jerusalem' " (24:44–47).

There is also consensus that Acts emphasizes fulfillment of biblical promises and prophecies, especially in the speeches.[9] The speeches clearly proclaim that the age of fulfillment has dawned (see Acts 2:16 cited above). Acts 3:18, in a literal translation, reads: "What God has foretold through the mouth of all the prophets (ἃ προκατήγγειλεν διὰ στόματος πάντων τῶν προφητῶν), that his Christ would suffer, he thus fulfilled" (ἐπλήρωσεν οὕτως). Acts 3:24 reads: "And all the prophets from Samuel and those following, as many as spoke, also announced (κατήγγειλαν) these days."

The Acts speeches also argue strongly that various events, such as the death of Jesus, were determined "by the set plan and foreknowledge of God" (τῇ ὡρισμένῃ βουλῇ καὶ προγνώσει τοῦ θεοῦ, 2:23). This set plan and foreknowledge apply, for example, to the Davidic descent of the Messiah (2:30–31), to the Messiah's ministry (2:22), to his death (2:23 and 3:13–14), to his resurrection (2:24–31; 3:15; 4:10), to his exaltation at God's right hand (2:33–36; 3:13;

---

9. E.g., see Kurz, *Reading Luke-Acts*, 77–81, 142–43, 153–55; cf. 181–82.

4:11; 5:30–31), to the Spirit as a sign of Christ's power and glory (2:33), and to the completion in Christ's return (3:21; cf. 10:42, "the one appointed by God [ὁ ὡρισμένος ὑπὸ τοῦ θεοῦ] as judge of the living and the dead").

Further references to fulfillment of scriptural prophecies include Acts 13:29, "As they finished (ἐτέλεσαν) all those things written about him [Jesus], having taken him down from the tree they laid him in a tomb." The speech of Peter to Cornelius in Acts 10:43 concludes, "To this all the prophets witness (πάντες οἱ προφῆται μαρτυροῦσιν) that everyone believing in him [Jesus] receives forgiveness of sins."

Another major motif in the Gospel and Acts that involves fulfillment of OT prophecy is the centrality of Jerusalem in God's plan, which was also pointed out by Fitzmyer. Thus, "events that have come to fulfillment among us" (Luke 1:1) include the stage-by-stage spread of God's word from Jerusalem to Judea and Samaria (Acts 8:1, 5, 26), to Caesarea Maritima (8:40), and Galilee (9:31), to Damascus (9:2), to Phoenicia, Cyprus, and Antioch in Syria (11:19), to the Roman provinces of Cilicia, Galatia, Asia, Macedonia, and Achaia, and finally to Rome (Acts 1:8; 23:11c; 28:14). The fate of Jerusalem is also seen as a fulfillment of God's OT plan, for example, of Isa. 49:6 that "my salvation may reach to the end of the earth" (see Luke 2:32; Acts 13:47), or of Isa. 2:3 (=Mic. 4:2) that "out of Zion the Law shall go forth, and the word of the Lord from Jerusalem." And although the expression itself is not used, Jerusalem functions as the "navel of the earth" (Ezek. 38:12; cf. 5:5; *Jub.* 8:19).[10]

One of the most consequential themes for the plotting of Luke and Acts is that of fulfillment of God's biblical promises to Abraham, a fulfillment that takes place from the beginning in various characters and situations. Thus the introductory Lukan infancy account emphasizes the Abrahamic promises in the songs of Mary (Luke 1:55) and "prophecy" (1:67) of Zechariah (1:72–73). Whether people are children of Abraham is a major theme of the Baptist's preaching (Luke 3:8). The Lukan portrayal of Jesus' healings and conversions is the only one to emphasize the recipients as daughters or sons of Abraham (Luke 13:16; 19:9).

In Acts, the promise to Abraham is partially fulfilled in Moses, according to the speech of Stephen — "As the time of the promise which God swore to Abraham drew near..." (7:17). The speech depicts fulfillment of the promises according to a divinely planned periodization of Moses' life (Acts 7:20, 23, 30; compare the similar periodization which Luke 21 provides for the end times). The climax of this fulfillment of Abrahamic promises through Moses (and ultimately in Jesus) comes in Acts 7:37: "This is the Moses who said to the sons of Israel, 'God will raise up (ἀναστήσει) a prophet like me from among your brothers.'"

Acts 7:37 reiterates the earlier statement in 3:22–23: "For Moses said that the Lord our God will raise up (ἀναστήσει) for you a prophet like me from

---

10. Fitzmyer, *Luke I–IX*, 168.

among your brothers and sisters: listen to him according to whatever he says to you. For it shall be that every soul which does not heed that prophet will be cut off out of the people." This principle functions as a plotting strategy for the rest of Acts, demonstrating that Jews who refuse to accept the resurrected Jesus excommunicate themselves from God's people (cf. the climactic Acts 28:24–28, foreshadowed by Acts 17:4 and contrasted with 13:46 and 18:6). Jews who reject the Christian message are judged unworthy, and the message is taken to the Gentiles. This principle is a Lukan response to whether God kept the promises to the children of Abraham, given the large numbers from Israel that had not accepted the resurrected Messiah and therefore the fulfillment of biblical promises according to the Christian message.

Prophecies Made and Fulfilled within the Gospel

The predictions most central to the plotting of the Gospel are, as expected, Jesus' passion predictions, which foretell his death and resurrection. But the predictions also refer to aspects of plot development in Acts. Besides passion predictions which Luke shares with the "triple tradition" — Luke 9:22 parallels the first Markan passion prediction, Luke 9:44 the second, and Luke 18:31–33 the third — he includes several more: 9:31; 12:50; 13:33–35; 17:25; and the retrospective 24:6–7, 25–27, and 44–47, not to mention foreshadowings of the passion in the infancy narrative (such as Simeon's prophecy in 2:34–35).

Luke 9:22 is the first prophecy of Jesus' passion, and it is explicit: "...the Son of Man ought ($\delta\epsilon\hat{\iota}$) to suffer many things and be rejected by the elders and chief priests and scribes and be killed and on the third day be raised." Luke 9:31 adds a peculiarly Lukan (and implicit) passion prediction, along with reference to scripture at the transfiguration, where Moses and Elijah are shown "speaking about [Jesus'] departure, which he was about to fulfill in Jerusalem ($\tau\grave{\eta}\nu$ ἔξοδον αὐτοῦ, ἣν ἤμελλεν πληροῦν ἐν Ἰερουσαλήμ)." The second passion prediction from the triple tradition is Luke 9:44: "The Son of Man is about to be delivered into the hands of humans (μέλλει παραδίδοσθαι εἰς χεῖρας ἀνθρώπων)." An additional Lukan prediction comes within the eschatological comments in Luke 17:25: "But first he ought ($\delta\epsilon\hat{\iota}$) to suffer many things and be rejected by this generation." The third prediction from the triple tradition in Luke 18:31–33 is quite detailed: "Behold we are going up to Jerusalem, and all the things written by the prophets about the Son of Man will be completed (τελεσθήσεται πάντα τὰ γεγραμμένα διὰ τῶν προφητῶν). For he will be handed over to the Gentiles and ridiculed and insulted and spit upon, and after they scourge him they will kill him, and on the third day he shall arise." In Luke 24:6–7, the angel announces that Jesus has been raised: "Remember how he spoke to you while yet being in Galilee, saying that the Son of Man ought ($\delta\epsilon\hat{\iota}$) to be handed over into the hands of sinful men and be crucified and on the third day arise."

An important concentrated source in the Lukan Gospel of the motif of prophecy, or promise and fulfillment, is its special redaction of the account of the Eucharist of the new covenant in 22:14–38.[11] The opening of Jesus' farewell address clearly foreshadows his impending death: "With great longing I longed to eat this passover with you before I die" (22:15b). Then come two prophecies, "I will not eat it again until it is fulfilled (πληρωθῇ) in the kingdom of God" (v. 16); and "from now on I will not drink from the fruit of the vine until the kingdom of God comes" (v. 18). The elements of the following institution of the Eucharist include promise, prophecy, and covenant, with the command to repeat the action liturgically (vv. 19b–20): "This is my body which is given for you [prophecy]. Do this in memory of me.... This is the cup of the new covenant in my blood which is poured out for you [prophecy]."[12]

Further intra-Gospel prophecies in this farewell are the prediction of Jesus' betrayal and the woe — a negative promise admittedly fulfilled after the Gospel — to his betrayer (22:21–22): "For the Son of Man goes as it is determined (κατὰ τὸ ὡρισμένον), but woe to that man through whom he is betrayed." There is a special prophecy and promise for Peter: although Satan has desired to sift him like wheat, "I have prayed for you that your faith may not give out. And you, when you have repented, strengthen your brothers" (vv. 31–32, whose fulfillment begins in Luke 24 but is completed in Acts). A further prophecy, that Peter will deny knowing Jesus three times before the cock crows, follows Peter's protest (vv. 33–34).

Promised Fulfilled in Acts, and after Acts

A striking prophecy that receives its complete fulfillment only in Acts is the angel's annunciation to Mary, that her son "shall be called the Son of the Most High, and the Lord shall give him the throne of his father David, and of his kingdom there shall be no end" (Luke 1:32–33).

The main part of the Gospel contains other promises fulfilled in Acts. Luke 21:18's promise that "not a hair of your head" will suffer harm is echoed in Paul's reassurance to his shipmates in the storm (Acts 27:34). The prophecy of Jesus' return in the parousia (Luke 21:27) receives angels' reassurance of fulfillment after Jesus' ascension (Acts 1:9, 11).[13] Jesus' promise to disciples in Luke 21:15 that he would give them wisdom persecutors could not withstand is fulfilled in Stephen (Acts 6:10). At the Last Supper in Luke 22:29–30, Jesus makes promises to the disciples in solemn covenant language, not to be fulfilled in their eschatological fullness until after the events of Acts: "And I appoint

---

11. William S. Kurz, "Luke 22:14–38 and Greco-Roman and Biblical Farewell Addresses," *JBL* 104 (1985): 251–68; idem *Farewell Addresses in the New Testament* (Collegeville, Minn.: Liturgical Press [Michael Glazier], 1990), 52–70.

12. With most scholars I accept the authenticity of the debated sections of vv. 19b–20; but even if they are not original most of my thesis holds, in any case for the canonical level of Luke. See esp. Bruce M. Metzger, *A Textual Commentary on the Greek New Testament*, 2d ed. (Stuttgart: German Bible Society, 1994), 148–50.

13. See Kurz, *Reading Luke-Acts*, 148.

(διατίθεμαι) to you as my Father has appointed to me a kingdom...and you will sit on thrones judging the twelve tribes of Israel."

At the end of Luke, not only are Jesus' death and resurrection recounted, but the prophecy includes also Christian mission in his name, fulfillment of which does not occur until Acts. In addition, Jesus orders his disciples to wait in Jerusalem for their heavenly empowerment, for the promise (ἐπαγγελίαν) Jesus sends from the Father (Luke 24:49); this is also fulfilled in Acts. This remarkably detailed set of promises and prophecies summarizes much of the plot at the end of the Gospel and especially of the Acts of the Apostles.

A major Gospel theme not fulfilled until after Acts is the punishment of Jerusalem. In Luke 13:34–35 Jesus laments over Jerusalem, "who kills the prophets and stones those sent to you," and about his desire to gather her children — "but you [pl.] did not want [it]." Then he prophesies, "Behold your house shall be forsaken," and warns followers that they will not see him until they say, "Blessed is the one coming in the name of the Lord." In Luke 19:41–44, Jesus weeps over the lost chances and coming punishment of Jerusalem. "If you had only known in this day what was for peace; but now it is hidden from your eyes" (v. 42). Jesus makes explicit mention of the coming siege of Jerusalem (v. 43), and the dashing of her children to the ground (cf. Psalm 137:9). His explanation of the destruction is that hearers "did not know the time of your visitation" (v. 44), a thematic allusion to the failure to recognize when a promise or prophecy is being fulfilled (see esp. Acts 13:27).

On Jesus' way to The Skull, it is only in Luke where Jesus tells the women of Jerusalem to weep rather for themselves and their children. "For behold the days are coming," Jesus says, when the sterile will be blessed and people will call the mountains to "fall upon us" (Luke 23:28–30; Hos. 10:8). Finally, in Acts 6:14 Stephen is accused of claiming that Jesus would destroy Jerusalem. All these prophetic references by Jesus and his followers to the destruction of Jerusalem, which are also expressed in past biblical prophecy, clearly function as devices pointing beyond Acts to the destruction of the year 70, justifying the Christian response to this catastrophe and using it as evidence of fulfillment of God's wrath.

Another cluster important to Luke and Acts are references from Psalm 118 to Jesus as the stone rejected by the builders (Luke 20:17; Acts 4:11), which are closely related to the ending of Paul's Antioch of Pisidia speech (Acts 13:40–41). Paul claims that justification not possible through the law of Moses is available to everyone who believes in Jesus (vv. 38–39), and the speech ends with a warning: "Therefore see to it lest that said in the prophets comes upon you (βλέπετε οὖν μὴ ἐπέλθῃ τὸ εἰρημένον ἐν τοῖς προφήταις)" (v. 40). Verse 41 cites Hab. 1:5, warning despisers who do not heed or believe the work God is doing "in your days (ἐν ταῖς ἡμέραις ὑμῶν)...even if someone narrates it to you (ἐάν τις ἐκδιηγῆται ὑμῖν)." The pattern is clear: God's prophetic words from the past and their present fulfillments are not being heeded, which leads to judgment on the present "despisers." The rejection of Jesus recounted in Acts is presented as fulfillment of ancient biblical prophecies, and the punishment for this rejection, to take place after the ending of Acts, fulfills still other biblical warnings.[14]

Most scholars see Acts 1:8 as not only a prophecy by Jesus but also as a partial preview of the plot to come: You will receive power — the Holy Spirit comes in Acts 2 — and be my witnesses in Jerusalem (Acts 2–7), Judea and Samaria (Acts 8–9), and to the end of the earth (Acts 10–28, esp. chaps. 26–28).[15]

Promise-Fulfillment Themes in 1 Maccabees

At first reading, 1 Maccabees, compared to Luke and Acts, seems to use little promise-and-fulfillment language. Closer analysis, however, reveals both the fulfillment of biblical prophecies and prophecies within the narrative. The text also implies fulfillment in indirect and allusive ways, clear enough for audiences steeped in scripture. The biblical style, narrative structure, and language of 1 Maccabees imply that the history of the Maccabees continues the biblical history.

An example of explicit fulfillment of *biblical prophecies* is 1 Macc. 7:16–17. After reporting that the priest Alcimus killed sixty Hasideans — who had trusted him because he was a "priest of the seed of Aaron" — the narrator quotes Ps. 79:2–3 as fulfilled "according to the word which he [God?] had written (κατὰ τὸν λόγον, ὃν ἔγραψεν αὐτόν)."

The use of biblical types for the heroes of 1 Maccabees shows that God guides events and that they fulfill a biblical plan of salvation. Thus Mattathias is modeled after the type of Phinehas, the zealous priest who defended the law from abuse, even to the point of killing the abuser (1 Macc. 2:23–26; Num. 25:6–15). The farewell speech of the patriarch Mattathias to his sons (1 Macc. 2:49–70), who would win battles and lead the people in the rest of the account, strongly implies that God's saving plan would be fulfilled in them.

A major structuring principle of this speech is the enumeration of biblical ancestors and forebears, listed as exempla of virtues for the sons to follow (2:51–61). Even the narrative introduction, which Dimant argues is modeled on Jacob's testament in Genesis 49, sets the stage not only for the virtues exemplified in the list, but also for the overall plot.[16] The list is introduced by an exhortation

---

14. See Jerome Neyrey, *The Passion according to Luke: A Redaction Study of Luke's Soteriology,* Theological Inquiries (New York: Paulist, 1985), 108–28.

15. E.g., compare Rudolf Pesch, *Die Apostelgeschichte,* vol. 1: *Apg 1–12,* EKKNT 5.1 (Neukirchen-Vluyn: Neukirchener, 1986), 65, 69–70, and the distinctions in Robert C. Tannehill, *The Narrative Unity of Luke-Acts: A Literary Interpretation,* vol. 2: *The Acts of the Apostles,* FFNT (Minneapolis: Fortress, 1990), 17–18.

16. See Devorah Dimant, "Use and Interpretation of Mikra in the Apocrypha and Pseudepigrapha," in *Mikra: Text, Translation, Reading, and Interpretation of the Hebrew Bible in Ancient Judaism and Early Christianity,* ed. Martin Jan Mulder (Philadelphia: Fortress; Assen, the Netherlands: Van Gorcum, 1988), 379–419, esp. 394–95. Mattathias emphasizes the difficulties his sons

to "remember the deeds of your fathers" (cf. Sir. 44:1 [LXX], "Let us now praise famous men [ἄνδρας], and our fathers [each] in [his] generation").

Especially important for 1 Maccabees' justification of the Hasmonean priesthood is the reference to "Phinehas our father," who because of his zeal "received a covenant of everlasting priesthood" (v. 54).[17] Also of importance for what will happen in 1 Maccabees are Abraham's fidelity in testing (v. 52);[18] Joseph's preservation of the commandment in distress (v. 53); Joshua's ascent to judgeship for keeping God's word (v. 55); Caleb's testimony in the assembly (v. 56); David's mercy and eternal kingdom (v. 57); Elijah's great zeal for the law (v. 58); the belief and salvation of Hananiah, Azariah, and Mishael (v. 59); and Daniel's innocence and consequent deliverance from lions (v. 60).[19]

A broader plotting convention implying fulfillment of promises is portrayal of the Maccabees in language reminiscent of earlier Israelite achievements (compare 1 Macc. 5:48 with Num. 20:17–20; 21:22),[20] or in terms of Davidic messianic hopes coming to partial accomplishment in Maccabean deeds and successes.[21] The book as a whole, beginning from the revolt of Mattathias and ending with the Hasmonean John Hyrcanus, justifies the Hasmonean dynasty by portraying its rise and solidification in terms reminiscent of biblical judges and kings.[22] Thus God chose to free Judah from foreign oppression through Judas Maccabeus, often against overwhelming odds, as God had done through the judges (see esp. 1 Macc. 3:16–22).[23] The final images of peace and prosperity in

---

face and their need to be zealous for the Torah and covenant, giving examples of zeal with corresponding outcomes. "Thus the list illustrates the principle, and serves as its model" (394). Listed good deeds are examples of *zeal* for Torah, though the term "zeal" is only used in 2:24, 26–27, 58.

17. Ibid., 395. Phinehas's zeal comes from the Hebrew in Num. 25:13, with the phrase "covenant of everlasting priesthood" also from Numbers. (Compare the use of "zeal" for Elijah and Mattathias in 1 Macc. 2:26.) Zeal functions as the chief virtue at the beginning of this exhortation.

18. Ibid., 394. Compare Sir. 44:20 (LXX), "and in testing he was found faithful," an allusion to Gen. 22:1, "God tested Abraham," and Neh. 9:8, "you found his heart faithful."

19. Ibid., 395, summarizes the technique throughout this list: first, an explicit element (a name) is introduced and the most typical aspect about his life is summarized, using terms from the original source. Such lists *actualize* major biblical tenets.

20. Ibid., 407. Judas's request recalls the Israelites passing through the land of the Edomites and Amorites in Num. 20:17–20; 21:22: not only does it have the same motifs but some of the biblical text is interwoven. Deut. 2:26–29 is the basis, with details from other texts, and the refusal echoes that of the Amorites in Deut. 2:30. Thus 1 Maccabees implies that Judas enacts patterns of biblical history.

21. See the apparent allusions to David in the description of the rise of Maccabeus in 1 Macc. 3:1–4, cited below. See Jonathan A. Goldstein, *1 Maccabees: A New Translation with Introduction and Commentary*, AB 41 (Garden City, N.Y.: Doubleday, 1976), 10–11, 244, 240–41, 248.

22. Compare the theme of the Maccabeans avenging their brother John in 1 Macc. 9:38 and 42 with the revenge of Levi and Simeon for the rape of their sister Dinah (Gen. 34:25–29), and the allusions to Amos 8:10 in "the wedding was turned into mourning..." (1 Macc. 9:41). Goldstein, *1 Maccabees*, 526, also notes that 1 Maccabees ends (16:23–24) in the style of 2 Kings 20:20, by stating that the rest of the king's deeds are written in chronicles.

23. Note especially the principle: "There is no difference in the sight of heaven to save by many or by few: for not in multitude of the army is victory of battle, but the power is from heaven" (1 Macc. 3:18b–19). Note also the biblical pattern of dividing groups into companies (1 Macc. 3:55; cf. also the feeding of the five thousand), and having those with heavy obligations and the fearful leave the army before the battle (1 Macc. 3:56, following Deut. 20:5–8).

1 Macc. 14:8–9, 12, 15 can be viewed as fulfilling Lev. 26:4; Zech. 8:12; Ezek. 34:27; Zech. 8:4; Isa. 52:1; and perhaps Isa. 60:10.[24]

For *predictions within the narrative* fulfilled later in the account, see especially the thematic clustering in Mattathias's farewell, which establishes the plot of events to come through prophecies, promises, and commands to his sons, the heroes of most of the remaining narrative.[25] Thus Mattathias's exhortation to fight for the law is obeyed and accomplished throughout 1 Maccabees. The exhortation to give their lives for the covenant is fulfilled in the deaths of Judas and all his brothers, including lastly Simon, and also of some Hasmoneans from the next generation. The death of the sons receives special emphasis, as when Simon reminds the people, "You know how many things I and my brothers and the house of my father have done on behalf of the laws.... For this reason all my brothers have perished for the sake of Israel, and I alone am left" (13:3–4).

Mattathias's prediction that "Simon...will be to you as a father" (2:65) is realized in Simon's reign (chaps. 13–16). Mattathias's designation of Judas as commander (2:66) comes to pass immediately after Mattathias's death, and is first signaled by a poem to Maccabeus which seems to echo the David story: "And Judas called Maccabeus, his son, arose in his place, and all his brothers helped him...and they waged the war of Israel with gladness, and he broadened the glory for his people and put on a breastplate like a giant and girded on his war armor...and he was like a lion in his deeds" (3:1–4).

1 Maccabees also contends that events show that God gave both leadership and the high priesthood to the Hasmoneans, in whom Jewish hopes have been fulfilled. But the book cannot explicitly claim messianic fulfillment. Rather 1 Macc. 14:41 notes "that Simon should be their governor and high priest forever, until a trustworthy prophet should arise" (εἰς τὸν αἰῶνα ἕως τοῦ ἀναστῆναι προφήτην πιστόν). The term "forever," which justifies the dynasty stemming from Simon, is limited temporally (as were the dynasties in the Northern Kingdom) by the possibility that a true prophet might anoint another dynasty.[26]

Promise-and-Fulfillment Themes in 2 Maccabees

2 Maccabees has a different theology from 1 Maccabees, to the extent that some scholars see the two accounts as competing and as trying to supplant the

---

24. See Goldstein, *1 Maccabees*, 491: "Simon's donations parallel both those of Solomon (1 Kings 6–7) and of Greek communal benefactors (e.g., Pseudo-Plutarch, *Vitae decem oratorum* 852b)."

25. Ibid., 8, 12–13, makes the distinction that since 1 Maccabees presumes at least a temporary cessation of prophecy after the last of the canonical prophets (cf. 4:46; 9:27; 14:41), it does not call these sayings prophecies but simply predictions.

26. Goldstein interprets "until a true prophet arise" as a compromise with other sects who may have expected a miraculous reappearance of the Davidic dynasty or coming of the Son of Man (see Ezra 2:63 and Neh. 7:65; Goldstein, *1 Maccabees*, 507, esp. 508).

other.[27] It is also written in a different style from 1 Maccabees. Whereas 1 Maccabees is written in biblical style as a continuation of the biblical histories to the time of the Hasmoneans, 2 Maccabees is filled with Hellenistic language, style, concerns, and conventions — carried over in this epitomizer's condensation of the original five volumes of Jason of Cyrene. 2 Maccabees sounds less like biblical history, nor is it as explicitly dependent on such biblical motifs as promise and fulfillment. Promise-and-fulfillment themes, however, are not without importance.

One major aspect of promise and fulfillment centers around the martyrs, who died horrible but heroic deaths to be faithful to God's law in the face of human persecution. There are repeated promises that at the resurrection bodily members and limbs now being torn or cut off will be restored. Thus in 2 Macc. 7:9, the second brother prophesies that God "will resurrect us to an eternal revivification of life (εἰς αἰώνιον ἀναβίωσιν ζωῆς ἡμᾶς ἀναστήσει)." Goldstein points to the redundancy and attributes it to an allusion to Dan. 12:2 (LXX; "will be resurrected to eternal life").[28]

Neil McEleney points out that the mother's philosophical thoughts in 2 Macc. 7:22–23 are related to Ps. 139:13–16; Wis. 7:1–2; and Qoh. 11:5:[29] "I do not know how you appeared in my womb, nor did I grant the spirit and life to you.... Therefore since it is the creator of the world who shapes the origin of man (ἀνθρώπου γένεσιν), as he finds out the origin of all things, he with mercy will give back to you the spirit and life...." Compare Qoh. 11:5 (LXX), "As there is none who knows what is the way of the spirit, how the bones grow in the womb, so you do not know the works of God...."

In 2 Macc. 7:14, the fourth brother contrasts the brothers' anticipated resurrection with the denial of resurrection for Antiochus. The brother dies in hopes "of being resurrected by him [God]; but for you [Antiochus] there will be no resurrection unto life (πάλιν ἀναστήσεσθαι ὑπ᾽ αὐτοῦ· σοὶ μὲν γὰρ ἀνάστασις εἰς ζωὴν οὐκ ἔσται)." Goldstein again attributes the redundancy of "resurrection unto life" to an allusion to Dan. 12:2 (LXX), as well as to the Greek of Isa. 14:20–21, interpreted as meaning that Antiochus and his children will have no resurrection (esp. Isa. 14:21: "Prepare your children to be slain for the sins of your [their] father, in order that they may not rise and inherit the land": ἑτοίμασον τὰ τέκνα σου σφαγῆναι ταῖς ἁμαρτίαις τοῦ πατρός σου [some manuscripts have αὐτῶν], ἵνα μὴ ἀναστῶσιν καὶ τὴν γῆν κληρονομήσωσιν).[30] The fulfillment of these promises, in which author and presumably the intended audience believe, remains, at the time of writing, in the

---

27. E.g., Goldstein, 1 Maccabees, 4, 33–34; idem, 2 Maccabees: A New Translation with Introduction and Commentary, AB 41A (Garden City, N.Y.: Doubleday, 1983), 82; George W. E. Nickelsburg, Jewish Literature between the Bible and the Mishnah: A Historical and Literary Introduction (Philadelphia: Fortress, 1981), 121.

28. Goldstein, 2 Maccabees, 305; cf. 64, 55 n. 2. See Goldstein, 1 Maccabees, 12, and 2 Macc. 7:9, 11, 14, 23, 29, 36; 12:43–45; 14:46.

29. N. McEleney, "1–2 Maccabees," NJBC 444.

30. Goldstein, 2 Maccabees, 306. Greek from Rahlfs LXX text and apparatus.

indefinite eschatological future.[31] There is also expectation in 2 Macc. 2:4–8 as the prophet Jeremiah hides the ark of the covenant on the mountain of Moses, not to be found until a time of righteousness.

Some prophecies of characters within 2 Maccabees are fulfilled later in the narrative, as were the passion predictions of Jesus in Luke. An example early in the narrative are the pathetically described prayers of the pious for deliverance of the Temple, fulfilled when the Greek commander, Heliodorus, is diverted by a divine epiphany (2 Macc. 3:24–40).

The most emphatic examples in 2 Maccabees of fulfillment within the narrative are prophecies, promises, and warnings (i.e., negative promises) uttered by the seven sons martyred by the cruel tyrant Antiochus.[32] Goldstein points out many allusions in the sons' statements (2 Macc. 7:16–19) to Dan. 8:24–25.[33] The author of 2 Maccabees has added biblical dimensions to the sons' prophecies through scriptural language and allusions. The sons' warning that Antiochus will be forced in death to confess that God alone is God (7:17, 19; esp. 7:31–37) is fulfilled. As Antiochus lies dying with excruciating bowel pain and swarming with worms, with rotting skin and a stench his army could not endure (9:4b–10; cf. v. 28), he confesses his sin and God's authority (9:11–18).

Other significant examples of fulfillment include purification of the Temple (10:1–8) and the foiling of Nicanor (chaps. 14–15), culminating in the sung praises to one "who has kept his place undefiled" (15:34).

Promise and Fulfillment in Josephus's *Jewish War* and *Antiquities of the Jews*

Like 2 Maccabees, the histories of Josephus comply explicitly with the standards and expectations of Greco-Roman historiography. The *Jewish War* (henceforth

---

31. Nickelsburg argues that the treatment of resurrection has roots in Second Isaiah (*Jewish Literature*, 121). He refers specifically to suffering-vindication in Isaiah 52–53; to Antiochus's arrogance and punishment in 2 Maccabees 9 as related to Isaiah 14 (see pp. 86, 88, 178–79); to the Mother of Seven as equivalent to Second Isaiah's Mother Zion awaiting return of her dispersed sons (2 Macc. 7:17–29; cf. Isa. 49:14–23; 54:1ff.; 60:4–9). To the Mother of Seven's language Nickelsburg compares the interpretation of Second Isaiah in Baruch 4:17–29 (see pp. 112–13). To resurrection as new creation, he compares Second Isaiah's creation-redemption in 43:1–2, 6–7; 44:1–2; 46:3–4.

32. See Nickelsburg, *Jewish Literature*, 120, with special reference to 2 Macc. 7:17, 19, 31, 35–37. Cf. McEleney, "1–2 Maccabees," 444, who writes that the vivid account in 2 Macc. 9:9–12 is heavily theological and echoes Isa. 66:24. See esp. Isa. 14:11, "Your glory has gone down to Hades, your great gladness; under you they shall spread rottenness, and your covering shall be a worm" (κατέβη δὲ εἰς ᾅδου ἡ δόξα σου, ἡ πολλή σου εὐφροσύνη· ὑποκάτω σου στρώσουσιν σῆψιν, καὶ τὸ κατακάλυμμά σου σκώληξ). Cf. Sir. 7:17; 19:3; Jth. 16:17. For similar descriptions of deaths of God's enemies, see Josephus, *Ant.* 17.6.5, 168–69, on Herod the Great, and Acts 12:23 on Herod Agrippa.

33. "You wield power" (2 Macc. 7:16) alludes to "his power shall be great" (Dan. 8:24); "work your will" (v. 17) to "he shall work his will"; "they [mutilations] pass belief" (v. 18) to "he shall cause destruction past belief" (Dan. 8:24; cf. Deut. 28:59, "The Lord will make your afflictions pass belief"); "having dared to contend with God" (v. 19) to "he shall rise against the Prince of princes" (Dan. 8:25) (Goldstein, *2 Maccabees*, 306–7).

War) conforms more to a "pragmatic" military and political history, as represented by Polybius, and the *Antiquities of the Jews* (henceforth *Ant.*) follows the rhetorical historiography of Josephus's model, *Roman Antiquities* of Dionysius of Halicarnassus.[34] Nevertheless, the histories of Josephus also maintain the biblically prominent belief in promise and fulfillment, a belief which they sometimes recast in Hellenistic terminology.

Reasons for this become more evident when we consider Josephus and Luke-Acts from the perspective of "apologetic historiography.".[35] Since these narratives, in telling the story of a subgroup within Roman culture, follow the group's traditions, but Hellenize them to describe the group's identity within the larger world, promise and fulfillment are important in relating the group's history to God's plan.[36] Therefore it is necessary first to consider briefly how Josephus recasts biblical motifs in Hellenistic terms before investigating his two uses of promise and fulfillment — relating scripture to his narrative, and relating characters within his narrative to later fulfillment.

Recasting Biblical Motifs in Hellenistic Terms

The primary source of Josephus's belief in providence and the divine governance of history — the Bible — enunciates this belief primarily through covenantal motifs like promises, or prophecies, and fulfillment. To express this belief in his Greek writings, Josephus draws from Greek historiographical terminology for fate and providence, but also varies usage between *War* and *Antiquities*. In *War*, he makes heavy use of τύχη (fortune) and εἱμαρμένη (destiny) to suggest that God's favor in history is being shown to the Romans. From this perspective he criticizes the revolutionary theologies that opposed Rome. In *Antiquities*, Josephus leans more on πρόνοια (providence) terminology as a substitute for the biblical theology of covenant and to express his belief in God's universal moral control. Josephus attributes God's favor to the Jews to their exemplary virtue, which was most like that of God.[37] In the biblical section of *Antiquities* (Books 1–10), Josephus paraphrases the Bible with exegetical adjustments for his Greek audience. He combines the retributive theology of

---

34. Harold W. Attridge, "Jewish Historiography," in *Early Judaism and Its Modern Interpreters*, ed. Robert A. Kraft and George W. E. Nickelsburg (Philadelphia: Fortress; Atlanta: Scholars Press, 1986), 311–43, here 327.

35. Gregory E. Sterling, *Historiography and Self-Definition: Josephos, Luke-Acts, and Apologetic Historiography*, NovTSup 64 (Leiden and New York: Brill, 1992).

36. Ibid., 17. See pp. 308–10 on Josephus's definition of Judaism in historical terms. He defines the Jewish people through their own record rather than through Gentile misconceptions, but nevertheless in terms understandable to the Greek world.

37. Attridge, "Jewish Historiography," 326–27; cf. idem, *The Interpretation of Biblical History in the "Antiquitates Judaicae" of Flavius Josephus*, HDR 7 (Missoula, Mont.: Scholars Press, 1975), 71–144.

Deuteronomistic history with a πρόνοια concept of providence from Hellenistic historiography.[38]

Gustav Stählin notes that when Josephus uses Hellenistic terms, such as εἱμαρμένη and τύχη, so often in *War*, he usually means providence.[39] In *Antiquities*, the term "providence" refers primarily to God's retributive justice, intervening on behalf of the righteous or against the wicked.[40] In fact, this notion of retributive providence gives Josephus a theological framework for his biblical exegesis (*Ant.* 1.14). The main lesson is that those who follow God's will succeed and are rewarded, whereas those who depart from strict observance of God's laws find their efforts ending in disaster.[41] The two major demonstrations of retributive providence are *reversals* (περιπέτειαι), especially miraculous rescues or horrific punishments, and *prophecy* (προφητεία), which for this essay is the most important aspect.[42]

One important question relating to promise, or prophecy, and fulfillment is Josephus's treatment of prophecy and prophets after the close of the Hebrew Bible. It is true that Josephus mentions in *Contra Apion* 1.41, at the time of Artaxerxes, successor to Xerxes, an end to the succession of prophets.[43] But whereas 1 Maccabees frequently refers to the (at least temporary) cessation of prophecy (e.g., 1 Macc. 4:46; 9:27; 14:41), Josephus's paraphrases of these passages in *Antiquities* routinely edit out such references. Thus, where 1 Macc. 4:44–47 referred to storing the profaned altar stones "until there should come a

---

38. Sterling, *Historiography and Self-Definition*, 297. On pp. 309–10, Sterling notes that in the more pro-Roman *War*, providence sustains Rome, whereas in the *Antiquities*, providence generally sustains Israel (but the examples are from Israel's ancient [biblical] past).

39. Stählin, "Schicksal," 336 (see n. 8 above for citation). But Stählin sharply distinguishes Josephus's use of such terms from the prophets' use, and accuses Josephus in some cases of going beyond Hellenistic language to borderline syncretism (334–38). He suggests that the turning point seems to be Josephus's μετάνοια to the Romans, with the corresponding claim that τύχη has gone to the Roman side (*War* 5.367, 2.360). Sometimes Josephus attributes this to God's will (*War* 3.354, 5.412; "Schicksal," 341). Josephus finds God closely bound to the τύχη of Rome and especially of Titus (341–42), whence his uncharacteristic expressions for τύχη (342). However, because of Josephus's own situation and his link to the Romans, he seems to go beyond Pharisaism and comes precariously close to syncretism (342). Luke never writes about τύχη and εἱμαρμένη the way Josephus does (343).

Attridge, however, disagrees with syncretistic interpretations of Josephus (*Interpretation of Biblical History*, 19–21, esp. 20–21 n. 3; and 154–55 n. 2). Attridge counters that Josephus does not just syncretistically import alien notions: he avoids fatalism and transforms Hellenistic antiquarian rhetorical historiography into truly theocratic (and Jewish) history, eliciting a religious response (εὐσεβεία) to these facts of providence (182–84).

40. Attridge, *Interpretation of Biblical History*, 92 n. 1, argues that *pronoia* in the *Antiquities* refers not to God's plan for history, but to God's constant care that retributive justice be done among humans. He also believes that Josephus applies this concept of providence or forethought not only to God but to human leaders like Moses and others (71–72).

41. Cited by Maren R. Niehoff, "Two Examples of Josephus' Narrative Technique in His 'Rewritten Bible,'" *JSJ* 27/1 (February 1996): 31–45, here 33.

42. Attridge, *Interpretation of Biblical History*, discusses reversals (91–99) and prophecy (99–104; cf. 151).

43. Gerhard Delling, "Die biblische Prophetie bei Josephus," in Betz, Haacker, and Hengel, *Josephus-Studien*, 109 (see n. 8 above for full citation); cf. Rudolf Meyer, "Bemerkungen zum literargeschichtlichen Hintergrund der Kanontheorie des Josephus," in Betz, Haacker, and Hengel, *Josephus-Studien*, 319–43.

prophet to tell what to do with them," *Ant.* 12.318 simplifies this to: "He [Judah] also pulled down the altar, and built a new one of various stones which had not been hewn with iron" (LCL).[44] 1 Macc. 9:27 mentions the cessation of prophets: "Thus there was great distress in Israel, such has had not been *since the time that prophets ceased to appear* among them." *Ant.* 13.5 ignores this prophetic reference: "After this calamity had fallen the Jews, which was greater than any they had experienced *since their return from* Babylon . . ."[45] In fact, Josephus refers to postbiblical prophets, and refers to the high priest John Hyrcanus as a prophet (*War* 1.68–69). "He was the only man to unite in his person three of the highest privileges: the supreme command of the nation, the high priesthood, and the gift of prophecy (προφητείαν)."[46] Sid Leiman argues that Josephus usually distinguishes these individuals from the succession of literary prophets which had ended, allowing for isolated instances of prophecy, but not literary prophecy. He also notes that Josephus usually uses different terminology. The term to refer to prophecy before Artaxerxes is προφήτης; after Artaxerxes Josephus uses μάντις, or a related Greek term.[47]

We have seen how in the biblical section of *Antiquities* Josephus tries to justify God's ways to Greeks, or to make theological corrections, or to find Hellenistic language to express the biblical account.[48] Therefore much of the biblical dynamic of promise (or prophecy) and fulfillment does get translated into the *Antiquities*, although sometimes under Greco-Roman guise. What follows are a few examples, some well-known, illustrating Josephus's use of prophecy-and-fulfillment motifs in *War* and *Antiquities*.

Promise-Fulfillment in Josephus, *Jewish War*

Scriptural Prophecies Fulfilled in or beyond the Narrative

A well-known example, both in the ancient world, where it was referred to by other Roman historians, and among contemporary treatments of Josephus is the

---

44. Texts from 1 Maccabees (and also *Antiquities*) were cited in Isaiah M. Gafni, "Josephus and I Maccabees," in *Josephus, the Bible, and History*, ed. Louis H. Feldman and Gohei Hata (Detroit: Wayne State University Press, 1989), 116–31, here 118. Gafni also refers to passages from 1 Maccabees on p. 128 n. 21.

45. Cited in ibid., 119; Gafni's emphasis.

46. Josephus, *The Jewish War, Books I–III*, trans. H. St. J. Thackeray, LCL 2 (Cambridge: Harvard University Press, 1967), 34–35.

47. Sid Z. Leiman, "Josephus and the Canon of the Bible," in Feldman and Hata, *Josephus, the Bible, and History*, 50–58, here 56; cf. 58 n. 42 and its references. The word "usual" accounts for the exceptional applications of the term "prophet" to postbiblical figures listed by David E. Aune, "The Use of προφήτης in Josephus," *JBL* 101 (1982): 419–21, esp. *War* 6.286 (LCL, "numerous prophets who led people astray") and *Ant.* 1.240–41 (LCL, "Cleodemus the prophet [προφήτης]" [but this is quoting Alexander Polyhistor]).

48. See Sterling, *Historiography and Self-Definition*, 222–24, on fragmentary Hellenistic Jewish predecessors to Josephus; see pp. 295–97 on theological control portrayed as providence, especially in rewarding virtue and punishing vice.

"ambiguous oracle" prophecy. Apparently based on Num. 24:17, the prophecy stated that someone "from their [the Jews'] country" would become ruler of the world (*War* 6.313). Though the Jews interpreted this messianically, Josephus, who portrayed himself as a prophetic messenger (*War* 3.350–54, 400–401), applies the prophecy to Vespasian, who was named emperor while in Judea and who thus came "from their country" as a world ruler (*War* 6.312–13; cf. 3.352, 4.601–4).[49]

Another significant example is Josephus's claim that the building of the Egyptian temple of Onias fulfilled Isaiah's prophecy: "There had, moreover, been an ancient prediction (πρόρρησις) . . . by one named Esaias, who had foretold the erection of this temple in Egypt by a man of Jewish birth" (*War* 7.432, LCL; cf. Isa. 19:18–19).

Characters' Prophecies Fulfilled in or beyond the Narrative

As treated above under Hellenistic recasting of biblical motifs, a significant element in the *Jewish War* are Josephus's references to postbiblical prophecies, even when not using biblical prophetic terminology. Notable is his well-known portrayal of himself as a prophet; more specifically, as a successor to prophets in distressing times.[50] His self-portrait shows a strong predilection for the tradition of Jeremiah. Thus, Josephus provides an emphatic portrait of himself as a prophet of the destruction of Jerusalem, with significant allusions to the life and reception of Jeremiah in similar situations (*War* 3.400–402; 5.391–93).[51]

Promise and Fulfillment in Josephus, *Antiquities of the Jews*

Scriptural Prophecies Fulfilled in or beyond the Narrative

As one would expect, especially in the sections of the *Antiquities* that rewrite the biblical narratives, Josephus makes numerous references to fulfillment of biblical prophecies. Stählin points out one example, the claim of *Ant.* 8.418 that Ahab has fulfilled the prophecies of Elijah and Micaiah ben Jimla (1 Kings 21:19; 22:20).[52] Delling refers to several instances.[53] A good example is Josephus's statement in *Ant.* 7.214 that the prophecy of Nathan in 7.152 has been fulfilled: "And this [Absalom's publicly lying with David's concubines] came about in

---

49. See Paul W. Barnett, "The Jewish Sign Prophets, A.D. 40–70, Their Intentions and Origins," *NTS* 27 (1981): 679–97, esp. 686, and Stählin, "Schicksal," 332–33. Cf. Francesco Lucrezi, "Un' 'ambigua profezia' in Flavio Giuseppe," *Atti della Accademia di Scienze morali e politiche della Società Nazionale* 90 (1979): 589–631.

50. David Daube, "Typology in Josephus," *JJS* 31/1 (1980): 18–36, here 20.

51. Ibid., 20; cf. Stählin, "Schicksal," 333; Reinhold Mayer and Christa Möller, "Josephus — Politiker und Prophet," in Betz, Haacker, and Hengel, *Josephus-Studien*, 284.

52. Stählin, "Schicksal," 332.

53. Delling, "Prophetie bei Josephus," esp. 111–13.

accordance with the prophecy which Nathan had made when he revealed to David that his son would one day rise up against him" (LCL). Josephus's version of Nathan's prophecy went beyond the original in 1 Sam. 12:11 — "I will take your wives...and give them to your neighbor," fulfilled in 16:21–22 — to specify that "his wives would be violated *by one of his sons*" (emphasis mine). Josephus also mentions fulfillments of several of Elijah's prophecies, in *Ant.* 9.27 (the death of Ahab's son Ochozias [Ahaziah]); 9.119–20 (Jehoram's death in Naboth's field); 9.124 (the manner of Jezebel's death); and 9.129 (the perishing of Ahab's house).

Characters' Prophecies Fulfilled in or beyond the Narrative

Perhaps more significant for Josephus's purposes than showing fulfillment of biblical prophecies is relating prophecies within his account to their providential fulfillment. The relationship of providence to prophecy is stated clearly in Solomon's speech at the Temple dedication (*Ant.* 8.109–10), in which Solomon demonstrated God's providence by the fulfillment of prophecies of his father David. Soon after, the prophecy of Ahijah to Jeroboam is said to be fulfilled through the arrogance of Rehoboam (8.218).[54] The theme is again developed at the end of Book 10, where the fulfillment of Daniel's prophecies foretelling destructions of Jerusalem by Antiochus Epiphanes and by the Romans is asserted to demonstrate God's providence. The assertion is made particularly against the Epicurean denial of providence (esp. *Ant.* 10.278–81). That God's retribution has been fulfilled as foretold proves that God exercises providential care.[55]

Promise and Fulfillment in Tobit

Tobit provides an example of how a different category of narrative — fiction — uses the promise-and-fulfillment strategy. I will consider the same strategies in Tobit as I did for Luke and Acts: first, how prophecies from *scripture* are fulfilled either in or beyond the narrative; and second, how prophecies by *characters* within the narrative are fulfilled. Because Tobit has a fictional setting in the eighth century B.C.E., centuries earlier than its composition, probably in the second century B.C.E., it is not surprising to find *ex eventu* prophecies written in light of their "fulfillments," that is, in light of what is known to have happened.

Scriptural Prophecies Fulfilled in or beyond the Narrative

Of major influence on the Book of Tobit are the biblical prophets. Thus the descriptions of Israel's exile in Tob. 1:3–10, 3:1–5, 14:3–4, as well as of the return

---

54. Ibid., 100.
55. Ibid., 102–4.

from exile in Tobit 13–14, are heavily influenced by the writings of the prophets Jeremiah, Ezekiel, and Deutero- and Trito-Isaiah. The plot exploits information and themes gleaned from these prophets, such as the abandonment of the Jerusalem Temple by the tribe of Naphtali (Tob. 1:4–5); Israel's exile as punishment (3:4–5); and the prophesied destruction of Nineveh and Jerusalem, Judah's exile and return, the destruction of the Temple and building of a replacement, and the final restoration of Jerusalem and the conversion of the Gentiles (14:4–7).

Other influences from the prophets include explicit references by the character Tobit. In 2:6, Tobit says: "I remembered the prophecy of Amos, how he said, 'Your feasts shall be turned into mourning...'" (Amos 8:10). This reference illustrates the sorrow at the murdered and unburied Jew that interrupted Tobit's Pentecost feast, increasing the pathos. But the change of perspective from Amos's judgment on Israel to Israel's suffering seems irenic, and leaves God more on Israel's side. In Tobit's farewell instructions to his son Tobiah in 14:4, he refers, depending on the manuscript, to the prophet Nahum or Jonah in warning Tobiah to move out of Nineveh. In the Sinaiticus manuscript, Tobit says, "I believe the word of God about Nineveh, as Nahum said" (Rahlfs). In the Vaticanus manuscript, Tobit says, "I am persuaded by as much as [ὅσα] Jonah the prophet said about Nineveh" (Rahlfs).[56]

A different but also mostly ornamental reference to the prophets comes in Tobit's instructions to Tobiah in 4:12. Tobit tells Tobiah that he should wed within their tribe, "For we are sons of the prophets. Remember, my son, Noah, Abraham, Isaac, and Jacob, our fathers from of old, that they all took wives from among their brothers." Being a son of the prophets is mentioned as an incentive not to marry a foreign woman, and several ancestors are cited as examples.

Characters' Prophecies Fulfilled in or beyond the Narrative

In several instances Tobit refers to prophecies fulfilled later in the narrative or beyond. Some work strictly within the story as plot devices. Others are *ex eventu* references to events known to have occurred.

In 5:20–22, Tobit prophesies to his wife Anna that their son will return safely, and gives a reason which, in view of his ignorance of the angel Raphael's identity, is full of irony: "For a good angel will keep him company." This prophecy is fulfilled in Tobit 11. In 11:7–8, Raphael promises Tobiah that his father will regain his sight after Tobiah anoints him with fish gall. Raphael recounts details that the narrator will repeat when recounting the fulfillment: when Tobit's eyes smart "he shall rub them," which will scrape off the white film so that "he will see you." All is fulfilled almost immediately a few verses later in 11:11–13.

Tobit's farewell to Tobiah (chap. 14) is based on the motif of Deuteronomistic

---

56. The fact that, in Jonah, Nineveh is spared would presumably be viewed from this perspective as a temporary reprieve in light of the author's *ex eventu* awareness of its eventual destruction.

retribution and makes significant use of *ex eventu* prophecies and fulfillments.[57] In a prophetic warning, Tobit instructs Tobiah to move his family from Nineveh to Media after Tobit's and Anna's deaths. This is fulfilled at the end of the book (14:15), when Tobiah hears that Nineveh has been destroyed and rejoices over its fate. After Jonah (or Nahum) predicts the destruction of Nineveh in 14:4, 14:4b–5a prophesies that brethren in Jerusalem will be scattered (=Deut. 30:2–3 [LXX]; cf. Luke 21) "from the good land" (=Deut. 1:35; 3:25; 4:21, 22; and often). Jerusalem will become desolate. The house of God will be burned and remain desolate for a time, but the people will return and rebuild the Temple, "but not like the first." All the Jewish people will then return from their places of captivity, and Jerusalem and the house of God will again be glorious "as the prophets have spoken."

Tob. 14:6–7 makes the eschatological prediction that all nations shall convert, and that Israelites shall "dwell forever in the land of Abraham," referring to the promise to Abraham in Deut. 1:8 and elsewhere concerning "the land which the Lord your God swore to give to your fathers, Abraham, Isaac, and Jacob." For this wording compare the references in Deut. 12:10–11 (LXX) that they shall dwell in the land, receive their inheritance, find their promised rest, and dwell in security (ἀσφάλεια). This word ἀσφάλεια is a *hapax legomenon* both in Deuteronomy and in Tobit, and in the rest of the Pentateuch occurs only in Lev. 26:5.[58]

Promise and Fulfillment in Judith

A second fictional narrative, Judith, can also be compared to Luke and Acts with respect to its use of promise and fulfillment.[59]

Scriptural Prophecies Fulfilled in or beyond the Narrative

As the farewell song by Tobit provided many key elements in that work, so does Judith's song of triumph, which is modeled on other songs by biblical heroines such as Miriam (Exodus 15) and Hannah (1 Samuel 2). Like these songs, Judith's song repeats the theme at the heart of much biblical narrative: that God's power,

---

57. See Alexander A. DiLella, "The Deuteronomic Background of the Farewell Discourse in Tob. 14:3–11," *CBQ* 41/3 (July 1979): 380–89.

58. Ibid., 383.

59. There is much scholarly indecision about the time and circumstances of the composition of the Book of Judith, though it was probably written originally in Hebrew and survives only in three slightly different Greek recensions, in one Syriac and in two Latin versions, and in some later Hebrew recensions. Because scholars find both Persian and Maccabean elements in the book, George Nickelsburg suggests that the story has two stages: that it originated in the Persian era and was rewritten in Hasmonean times ("Stories of Biblical and Early Post-biblical Times," in *Jewish Writings of the Second Temple Period: Apocrypha, Pseudepigrapha, Qumran Sectarian Writings, Philo, Josephus*, ed. Michael E. Stone, CRINT 2.2 [Philadelphia: Fortress; Assen: Van Gorcum, 1984], 46–52, esp. 51).

as God of the lowly, depends not on numbers (Jth. 9:11).[60] Though this theme does not usually occur in Judith as explicit biblical promise or prophecy, it relates to a similar idea of God's providence working through and for the chosen people.

The book's typology of the heroine Judith, as a weak human vessel — not a member of the warring class or army, but a woman — carrying God's power, relates to implied promises that God's power will work through human weakness. This typology is shared, for example, by Deborah and Jael (Judges 4–5).[61] Jael's slaying of the oppressing general may well be a prototype for Judith's assassination of Holofernes. Such typology remains only implicitly promise and fulfillment.

Such themes and typology lend a paradigmatic quality to Judith in showing how God acts in history. Promise and fulfillment are only implicit in such a paradigm but the paradigm belongs to the biblical worldview that God acts providentially on people's behalf at crisis points in Jewish history. Especially striking are the paradigmatic uses of activism seen in both Judith and Mattathias (and in Phinehas, a prototype for them both). The treatment of Levi's slaughter at Shechem in *Testament of Levi* and *Jubilees* glorifies a somewhat similar activism.[62]

Nickelsburg suggests that Judith recalls several ancient heroes of Israel. If the book has a Hasmonean date, the name "Judith" seems an obvious allusion to Judas Maccabeus.[63]

Characters' Prophecies Fulfilled in the Narrative

A key statement in Judith is the mock prophecy of Holofernes: "Who is God except Nebuchadnezzar? He will send his power and will destroy them [Israelites] from the face of the earth, and their god shall not deliver them" (6:2–3).[64] With this gauntlet cast between God and Nebuchadnezzar, the prophecy guides most of the events to follow.

Another key statement is Judith's prophetic critique that people cannot test or force God's hand with oaths or prayer (8:11–17). Instead, Judith recalls that the people once were exiled because they worshiped false gods. Since the present generation has remained faithful they can hope for God's deliverance, and can view the crisis as a test and pedagogical admonishment rather than as punishment and destruction (8:18–27). This prophetic critique and Judith's related promise that "the Lord will visit (ἐπισκέψεται) Israel by my hand" (8:33) are

---

60. Ibid., 46.

61. Ibid., 48, suggests that Judith combines several heroines: Deborah and Jael; the woman of Thebez (Judg. 9:53–54); and the woman of Abel at Beth-maacah (2 Sam. 20:14–22).

62. Ibid., 48.

63. According to Nickelsburg, Jth. 13:7 recalls Samson in Judg. 16:28; Jth. 13:6–8 recalls 1 Sam. 17:51, in which David beheads Goliath with Goliath's sword; Jth. 9:2–3, 8–10; 13:6–8 recalls the patriarch Simeon (ibid., 49 n. 86).

64. See ibid., 46.

fulfilled when the enemy general is overcome and the enemy routed (Judith 13–15).

Conclusion

The influence of fulfillment of promises or prophecies on the Lukan Gospel is clear. So is the influence of fulfillment motifs on the Acts of the Apostles. Both books make intensive reference to fulfillment of biblical prophecies. Both also contain frequent prophecies by characters like the prophet Simeon and Jesus in Luke, and like Jesus, Peter, and Paul in Acts. In addition, evidence seems to support the interrelationship of Luke and Acts through the influence of the promise-and-fulfillment motif on the transitions between the two books, and through frequent fulfillments in Acts of prophecies given in the Gospel. In many ways, the plot of the Lukan Gospel has not been completed at its end, but several strands require the continued narrative of Acts for their realization. One especially important strand is the place of Jerusalem in both Luke and Acts and its punishment, which was foretold by Jesus.

Even the initial promises of Simeon that Jesus will be both a "glory for his people Israel" and a "light for the nations" require the reports of Acts for their accomplishment. For despite Jesus' resurrection, by the end of the Gospel he can hardly be called the glory of the people Israel. Beyond Jesus' immediate disciples, significant numbers of people have not yet accepted Jesus. It takes large numbers of Jewish conversions in Acts — at Pentecost and after the healing of the lame man in Acts 2–3 — before Jesus can realistically be referred to as a glory for Israel. Accounts in the early chapters of Acts confirm the importance of Jerusalem that the Gospel had underlined, through such means as the inclusio of beginning and ending in the Temple. And only a few Gentiles in the Gospel are affected by Jesus; missionary outreach does not begin until Acts 8–13.

To name other key examples, the biblical promises relating to Abraham and the double Jewish rejection of the "prophet like Moses" — first in Jesus, then in the apostles — require Acts for their fulfillment. Many of the key sets of prophecies by Jesus, such as the eschatological scenarios in Luke 21 and the Last Supper predictions of Luke 22, look toward accounts of their fulfillment in Acts. Significant prophesied events like the destruction of Jerusalem and cosmic signs have to wait for their fulfillment even beyond Acts.

These patterns of prophecy and fulfillment from Hebrew scriptures to Luke to Acts and beyond, in the light of related patterns in other Hellenistic Jewish literature, also shed light on the meaning and significance of "Israel" at the end of Acts.[65] Since Luke and Acts fairly consistently preserve Jewish connections for

---

65. See the annotated bibliography in Joel B. Green and Michael C. McKeever, *Luke-Acts and New Testament Historiography*, IBR Bibliographies 8 (Grand Rapids, Mich.: Baker Books, 1994), sec. 5.5, "Judaism, the Jewish People, and the Gentiles," 61–71.

the phrase "the people," and since they consistently place prophecies concerning the people Israel on a continuum from Hebrew scripture to the Gospel to Acts, it seems clear that Christians in Acts are considered to have inherited the biblical name and promises concerning "the people" and, hence, "Israel." A similar sense of continuity with the biblical people Israel runs through 1 and 2 Maccabees, Josephus's *Jewish War* and *Antiquities of the Jews*, and Septuagint versions of Tobit and Judith.

But unlike authors of those Hellenistic Jewish narratives, the author of Luke and Acts has a further pressing problem — competing claims to the heritage of Israel between Jews who have accepted Jesus as their Messiah, and the apparently much greater numbers in both Jerusalem and the Diaspora who have not. This issue is further complicated with the incorporation of uncircumcised Gentiles into this people after Acts 10–11.

We have seen how the quotation from Deut. 18:19 and Lev. 23:29 in Acts 3:23 is meant to explain some Jews' refusal to listen to Jesus as their self-excommunication from the people of God, from Israel. It is also well-known how Acts 10–11 and Acts 15 tried to provide biblical warrant to scriptural and contemporary visions (as to Peter and Cornelius) for including uncircumcised Gentiles into "the people," in effect, into Israel.

Thus at the end of Acts, when Paul quotes Isa. 6:9–10 as the Holy Spirit's words "to your ancestors" (Acts 28:25–27), preceding promises give this Isaiah passage the sense of Paul's final drastic warning to the Jews of Rome — who still remain members of God's people — not to resist the message and excommunicate themselves from "the people" (Acts 3:23). In this sense, it seems that the question of Israel remains "open."[66]

The survey of other Hellenistic Jewish narratives confirms the likelihood that it is not eisegesis to find promise-and-fulfillment plotting in the two Lukan volumes, and from the first narrative to the second. Though the forms and frequency of such plot devices varied greatly among these various historical and fictional narratives, most exhibit some dependence on plotting in light of biblical promises and God's plan for Israel. 1 Maccabees portrays much of the history of the Maccabees in terms reminiscent of biblical judges and David. The martyr theology and expectations of resurrection in 2 Maccabees probably draw on Daniel 12. Josephus recasts many biblical motifs, including promise and fulfillment, in Hellenistic terms, especially by subsuming promise and fulfillment under the broader notion of God's retributive providence. In his rewriting of the Bible in *Antiquities*, Josephus frequently underlines how later events fulfill earlier prophecies. Much of the fictional plot of Tobit is structured and enhanced with the help of *ex eventu* scriptural prophecies. Judith is portrayed in light of biblical heroines Deborah and Jael, and her song echoes those of Miriam and Hannah.

---

66. See esp. Vittorio Fusco, "Luke-Acts and the Future of Israel," *NovT* 38 (1996): 1–17; cf. Darryl W. Palmer, "Mission to Jews and Gentiles in the Last Episode of Acts," *RTR* 53 (1993): 62–73.

To a lesser but still meaningful extent, the significance of fulfillment of characters' predictions within the narratives can also be found. 1 Maccabees clusters predictions in Mattathias's farewell that structure much of the ensuing narrative about his sons. Predictions in 2 Maccabees of punishment for Antiochus are fulfilled later. Josephus portrays himself as a prophet like Jeremiah whose predictions (especially concerning Vespasian) are later fulfilled. Prophecies by characters in Tobit motivate their fulfillment shortly thereafter. Judith's prophetic critique of the people and her prophecy that the Lord will visit Israel by her hand are plot devices fulfilled in her overcoming of the enemy Holofernes.

Luke and Acts shared with most of these works from Hellenistic Judaism an immersion in the biblical sense of God's providence and plan as demonstrated in promises and prophecies and their fulfillment. Such a widespread and deep-seated biblical worldview provides confirming evidence for the narrative linkage between the Lukan Gospel and Acts. Not only do the events in Acts fulfill the prophecies made by characters in the Lukan Gospel, but Luke and Acts together continue the biblical history of the fulfillment of God's promises.

Chapter 7

Acts and the Fragments of Hellenistic Jewish Historians

Carl R. Holladay

The importance of Greek-speaking Judaism for understanding Luke-Acts has long been recognized. Almost forty years ago, J. C. O'Neill argued that Acts is best read as an apologetic work from the early second century.[1] He devotes an entire chapter to "the debt to Hellenistic Judaism," in which he sees a close correlation between the situation of Diaspora Jews in the pre-Christian period and that of the author of Acts.[2] Convinced by P. Dalbert of the thoroughly missionary character of much of the writing from Diaspora Jews,[3] O'Neill writes:

> The Judaism of the Dispersion had for at least three centuries been confronted with the sort of missionary problem which the Church faced in the first century of its life. It had produced a large body of missionary literature written in Greek which employed a developed apologetic to convince its Gentile readers of the truth of the Jewish faith.[4]

He then seeks to show that "a number of features of Acts [can] best be explained by assuming that the Church to which Luke belonged had learnt much of both its missionary strategy and its missionary theology from the Synagogues of the Dispersion" (147). According to O'Neill, Luke's choice of genre reflects this debt. "In choosing to write a history of the foundation period of the Church Luke has chosen the basic method which the Greek-speaking Jewish apologists had chosen before him" (149). In support of this he cites a number of examples where Greek-speaking Jews chose to recount the biblical story as part of their apologetic efforts. As further support of Luke's indebtedness to his Hellenistic Jewish predecessors, O'Neill points to "(1) the way Acts commends the heroes of the faith; (2) the appeal to the State; (3) the approach to the philosophers; and (4) the theology of conversion" (150).

---

1. *The Theology of Acts in Its Historical Setting* (London: SPCK, 1961).

2. Ibid., 146–65.

3. P. Dalbert, *Die Theologie der hellenistisch-jüdischen Missionsliteratur unter Ausschluss von Philo und Josephus* (Hamburg-Volksdorf: Herbert Reich, 1954).

4. O'Neill, *Theology of Acts,* 146–47. Parenthetical references in text are to O'Neill's volume.

O'Neill sees similarities between forms of heroic depiction in the episodes in Acts 14 and 28, where Paul and Barnabas are treated as gods by the Lystrans and the Maltese. He argues that Moses is similarly portrayed by Artapanus as one whose achievements earned him divine honors among the Egyptians. Even more striking, he insists, is the similarity between Artapanus's account of Moses' miraculous escape from prison and the three prison escapes in Acts 5, 12, and 16 (152–53).

According to O'Neill, Hellenistic Jewish writers also provide precedents for the strategies used in Acts to portray Christianity favorably before political authorities. Such strategies included arguing for distinctive political rights, showing rulers the risk in opposing or alienating their religious constituencies, convincing political leaders of the benefits of following the law. Examples from Philo, Josephus, Wisdom of Solomon, and the *Letter of Aristeas* are correlated with various episodes in Acts that show similar concerns (153–57).

O'Neill sees philosophical indebtedness reflected in Acts 14 and 17, where God is presented in ways reminiscent of certain Greek philosophical traditions. In both instances, Luke was using "well-tried arguments developed by Greek-speaking Jewish apologists" (157–58).

O'Neill thinks that Luke derived conversion language, especially repentance (μετανοέω and μετάνοια), "from the language of proselytism developed in Hellenistic Judaism" (160). Examples are adduced from Wisdom of Solomon, *Sibylline Oracles, Prayer of Aseneth,* and Philo's *Concerning the Virtues.*

More recently, Hellenistic Jewish writings have figured prominently in the work of G. E. Sterling, who places Luke-Acts within the tradition of apologetic historiography represented especially by Josephus, but also by the earlier "historians" Demetrius, Artapanus, Pseudo-Eupolemus, and Eupolemus.[5] Especially useful is the way Sterling sketches the broader historical and literary context out of which apologetic historiography emerges. He fully documents how Jews writing during the Hellenistic period shared the concerns of authors from other national and cultural traditions, such as Hecataeus of Abdera, Megasthenes, Berossus, and Manethon. As they became increasingly aware of each other's national histories and cultural traditions, these writers developed accounts of their own traditions that helped not only their fellow citizens but also outsiders to understand who they were. Naturally such literary endeavors drew on a wide range of oral and written sources, and their success depended heavily on the author's imaginative ability to shape these disparate sources into a coherent story. Heroic figures of the past inevitably played central roles in these accounts, and these authors employed different strategies in sketching the portraits of figures whom they considered influential and noteworthy. When Jewish writers enter the contest, they work with the biblical history at their disposal — the Sep-

---

5. *Historiography and Self-Definition: Josephos, Luke-Acts, and Apologetic Historiography,* NovTSup 64 (Leiden: Brill, 1992).

tuagint. This story provides the cast of characters for shaping their accounts. Sometimes they follow it quite closely, at other times loosely.

Sterling advances the discussion considerably by the detailed treatment he gives to these Jewish authors. He carefully places each in his own social-historical context and dutifully attends to the array of critical problems inherent in dealing with texts that have been transmitted through several hands. He gives special attention to the ways these authors appropriate the biblical story. Once Sterling has established the probable extent of each author's work and how the work handled the biblical traditions, he then seeks to assess the significance of each work. Given its setting within the larger historiographical tradition of the Hellenistic world, Sterling seeks to determine what each work was trying to accomplish and how well it succeeded.

Of the four fragmentary Hellenistic Jewish historians he studied, Sterling concludes:

> The four authors whom we have considered undertook the task of restating their history in terms which were heavily influenced by Hellenism. In some ways, their works are a refutation of the notion that the LXX was designed for pagans, or at least a witness of its failure. I have argued that these four oeuvres all stand within the same literary tradition. This is supported by our model for genre analysis. They all share the same basic content: they retell their own story. They all go about this in the same general way: they retell their native traditions in an extended prose narrative.... While they vary in their fidelity to the Bible...they all use it as their basic point of reference. The specific devices they utilize to shape their individual versions cover a wide range.... Regardless of the specific conventions, they all self-consciously use Greek literary modes for their *Geschichten*. What gives them a sense of unity in this diversity is that they all wrote *ad maiorem Iudaeorum gloriam*. They are national historians — *tout-à-fait* — who claim the superiority of the Jewish nation over both other Oriental people and Greeks.[6]

In this essay, I presuppose Sterling's extensive treatment of these four authors and attempt to press the investigation a little further. Stated in the broadest possible terms, the question is: In what ways do these four fragmentary Hellenistic Jewish historians inform our understanding of Acts? Apart from individual motifs or specific cases of parallel phrasing, do they provide useful comparisons for Acts? To what extent are all five texts engaged in the same enterprise? And, is this enterprise "history" in any meaningful sense? How does each of them read and appropriate scripture, and do we learn anything from their use of scripture that appreciably broadens our understanding of Luke's use of scripture? What about the literary horizons of these five texts? Do these Jewish authors tell their story, or retell the biblical story, in ways that illuminate Acts or that help us understand certain features of Luke's narrative technique? Would we be significantly poorer in our understanding of Acts had none of these texts survived?

---

6. Ibid., 223.

Demetrius

Two things well-known about Demetrius are his biblicism and his fascination with chronology. By the former is meant not only his focused interest in the biblical text but also his relative conservatism in handling it. All four of the undisputed fragments either treat biblical incidents or summarize biblical events.[7] The two disputed fragments treat biblical themes as well.[8]

Demetrius tends to follow the biblical text rather closely. His summary of events from Genesis 27–50 in Frg. 2 touches some of the high points of the narrative,[9] yet he omits numerous episodes.[10] Even with these omissions, however, he follows the biblical order. In a couple of instances, he picks up details, usually chronological details, from other parts of the story and inserts them at a different place.[11] There is very little, if anything, in Demetrius that could be called haggadic. Most everything found in his fragments is either drawn from the Bible or can be inferred from the Bible. In the textual tradition of Demetrius there are several instances in which the biblical text is contradicted,[12] yet because these are such obvious factual mistakes, editors have consistently emended the text

---

7. Frg. 2 in 139 lines summarizes Genesis 27–50, although it concludes with a lineage that extends to Moses. Frg. 3, comprising twenty-six lines, treats events in the life of Moses, including his slaying the Egyptian, fleeing to Midian, and especially his marriage to Zipporah. Using chronological calculations Demetrius shows that Moses and his wife Zipporah were contemporaries. Frg. 4 summarizes in seven lines the incidents involving bitter and sweet water at Marah and Elim found in Exod. 15:22–27. Frg. 6 gives a ten-line chronological summary of events (apparently based on 2 Kings 17; 18:13–19:37; 24–25) from the fall of Samaria until the reign of Ptolemy IV Philopator (221–205 B.C.E.).

Note: All references to the fragments in this paper are based on the numbering system in C. R. Holladay, *Fragments from Hellenistic Jewish Authors, Volume I: Historians*, SBLTT 20, Pseudepigrapha Series 10 (Chico, Calif.: Scholars Press, 1983) = *FHJA* in this article.

8. Frg. 1 gives a seven-line summary of Abraham's sacrifice of Isaac; Frg. 5 in five lines explains how the Israelites fleeing Egypt unarmed eventually obtained weapons.

9. Demetrius mentions the following events: Jacob's departure to Haran prompted by Esau's "hidden resentment" and the need to obtain a wife; Jacob's marriage to Leah and Rachel; the birth of Jacob's children; Jacob's desire to return to Isaac in Canaan; wrestling with the "angel of God"; arrival in Shechem; the rape of Dinah by Shechem, son of Hamor, and the revenge by Simeon and Levi; arrival at Bethel, finally at Ephrath (Bethlehem); the birth of Benjamin and the death of Rachel; arrival at Mamre in Hebron; death of Isaac; selling of Joseph to Egypt; Joseph's interpretation of the king's dreams; Joseph's rule over Egypt; Joseph's marriage to Asenath; famine; Joseph's treatment of Benjamin; Jacob's arrival in Egypt; why Joseph didn't send for his brothers earlier; Jacob's death in Egypt; and Joseph's death.

10. Omissions include: Esau's marriage to Ishmael's daughter; Jacob's dream at Bethel; Jacob's meeting of Rachel; Jacob's fleeing with family and flocks; Laban's overtaking Jacob; Jacob and Laban's making a covenant; Jacob's sending presents to appease Esau; Jacob's meeting Esau; Esau's descendants; the clans and kings of Edom; Joseph's relationships with his brothers; Judah and Tamar; Joseph and Potiphar's wife; the dreams of the two prisoners; Joseph's brothers' trip to Egypt and return; most of the Benjamin story; Jacob's last words to his sons; Joseph forgiving his brothers.

11. In Frg. 2.12 he mentions two years of famine, a detail drawn from Gen. 45:6, while he is discussing Genesis 41.

12. For example, Zilpah is identified as the handmaid of Rachel rather than Leah (2.3); Dan is born to Leah instead of Rachel's handmaid Bilhah (2.5); Leah is said to have borne Jacob seven sons, not six (2.14); Dan is omitted from the list of children given in 2.8.

to produce readings that conform more closely to the biblical account. In other instances, Demetrius appears to have misread the text.[13]

Another way of describing Demetrius's biblicistic interest is to classify him as an exegete; or, to characterize his primary interest as being exegetical.[14] It is difficult to be much more concrete about what prompted this exegetical activity. Are these questions raised by outside critics, the likes of Celsus and Porphyry later? Or are they questions raised by Jews who are critically reading their own Bible, perhaps in translation, for the first time? Do they reflect internal debates within the Jewish community? Or, are they simply the questions Demetrius himself asks? Most likely, they are insiders' questions, although they may well have been prompted by conversations with non-Jews within various Egyptian settings.

The other hallmark of Demetrius's work is chronography, and his efforts in this regard have been variously evaluated. To be sure, he spent a lot of time hunting for chronological references in the Bible, adding and subtracting years, and calculating birthdates. Much here is dry and uninteresting to many modern readers. But he is also making some creative moves. As B. Z. Wacholder observes, "The writings of Demetrius marked the first stage of Hellenistic biblical chronology. He established the so-called *annus Adami* and divided biblical history into epochs, assigning absolute dates to the flood, the patriarchs, the exodus, and the destruction of the Northern and Southern kingdoms."[15]

As is evident, especially from Frg. 2.18 and Frg. 6, Demetrius has gleaned

---

13. He apparently thinks Luz is located in Bethel (εἰς Λουζὰ τῆς Βαιθήλ, 2.10), whereas the LXX gives Bethel as an alternate name for Luz (εἰς Λουζα…ἥ ἐστιν Βαιθηλ, Gen. 35:6). He identifies Jacob's wrestling opponent as an "angel" (ἄγγελος, 2.7; similarly Josephus, *Ant.* 1.331–34), whereas MT and LXX read "man." There is some confusion in reporting Jacob's subsequent arrival in the land of Canaan. Gen. 33:18 in LXX reads: καὶ ἦλθεν Ιακωβ εἰς Σαλημ πόλιν Σικιμων, ἥ ἐστιν ἐν γῆ Χανααν. In Demetrius this becomes: καὶ ἐλθεῖν αὐτὸν τῆς Χαναὰν γῆς εἰς ἑτέραν πόλιν Σικίμων, which seems to be a terribly confused rendering of the LXX. In his rendering of Gen. 35:16, he takes the transliterated form in the LXX (χαβραθα) as a place-name (2.10). This is not a clear case of misreading since the LXX itself seems to confuse the MT. Another confusion of place-names also occurs in 2.11, when he reports that Jacob went "to Mamre in Hebron" (εἰς Μαμβρὶ τῆς Χεβρὼν), whereas the LXX identifies Mamre as an alternate name of Hebron (εἰς Μαμβρη εἰς πόλιν τοῦ πεδίου [αὕτη ἐστὶν Χεβρων] ἐν γῆ Χανααν, Gen. 35:27). Demetrius gives a slightly different twist to Gen. 46:31–34, where Joseph instructs his brothers how to introduce themselves to Pharaoh. Demetrius uses the story to explain why Joseph had not sent for his aged father.

14. N. Walter includes Demetrius, along with Aristobulus and Aristeas, among Hellenistic Jewish exegetes (*Jüdische Schriften aus hellenistisch-römischer Zeit*, 2d ed., vol. 3, pt. 2 [Gütersloh: G. Mohn, 1980], 280–92). See Sterling, *Historiography and Self-Definition*, 166 n. 165. Understanding Demetrius as an exegete helps make sense of his "question-and-answer" approach to the biblical text. Adopting the well-established scheme of *aporia-lusis*, Demetrius spots problems of various sorts in the text and proposes solutions to them. Most of the problems are chronological, e.g., how twelve children could have been born to Jacob within seven years, or reconciling the generational differences between Moses and Zipporah. But he also tackles other types of problems. Puzzled by the dubious morality of young Joseph prospering in Egypt for nine years without notifying his aged father in Canaan, Demetrius devises a solution based on Gen. 46:31–34: his family consisted of shepherds, and Egyptians despise shepherds. Anticipating a long line of puzzled readers of Exod. 17:8–13 who wonder how the Israelites could have become sufficiently armed to fight Amalek, Demetrius explains that they took the arms of those (Egyptians) who had drowned.

15. *Eupolemus: A Study of Judaeo-Greek Literature* (Cincinnati: Hebrew Union College-Jewish Institute of Religion, 1994), 103–4.

from the Bible several chronological benchmarks: Adam, the flood, the call of Abraham, several pivotal events relating to Egypt (the arrival in Egypt by Joseph, his brothers, and finally Jacob), the exodus, the wilderness wandering, and later events in Israel's history relating to captivities (the fall of Samaria, Sennacherib's invasion of Judah, the siege of Jerusalem by Nebuchadnezzar). Moreover, he brings his calculations to the time of Ptolemy IV Philopator (220–204 B.C.E.), which probably means that he has extended his chronological scheme to his own time.

But he has done more. He has also calculated the length of these periods, and has done so on the basis of the LXX. Thus, from Adam until the arrival of Joseph's brothers in Egypt he figures at 3,624 years; from the flood until Jacob's arrival in Egypt — 1,360 years; from the time of Abraham's call until his successors arrived in Egypt — 215 years (Frg. 2.18). At the other end of the spectrum, he has calculated the length of time between the fall of Samaria and Nebuchadnezzar's siege of Jerusalem (128 years), and the period from the fall of Samaria until his own time (573 years).

If we try to imagine what is driving him to do this, the most plausible explanation is that Demetrius is doing what others, such as Manetho and Berossus, had done — trying to demonstrate the antiquity of his own tradition. Following the LXX gives him a distinct advantage, since its chronology yields a considerably earlier date for Adam. And yet, Demetrius makes no explicit claims that this is what he is about, as do some of the other Hellenistic Jewish authors.

But is there more to it? Do these calculations create dispensations or periods of history that are operating as part of some larger scheme? Wacholder thinks so. "A close reading of the fragments," he writes, "indicates that each computation was but part of general explanations intended to make the scriptural events appear 'rational' and part of a preconceived plan."[16] But is this actually the case? I find nothing in the fragments that clearly suggests this. If we assume, for the moment, that all six fragments are authentic and read them in the usually assigned order, they begin with the call of Abraham (Frg. 1), treat Jacob and Joseph to the time of Moses (Frg. 2), touch events in the life of Moses, the exodus, the wilderness (Frgs. 3, 4, and 5), and conclude with the two captivities (Frg. 6). But I find no indications that these scattered events are seen as part of a "preconceived plan," or even as part of a continuous story. Language of promise-fulfillment is absent. Even the connections made within the Bible itself linking events to each other are absent in Demetrius.

To what extent are Demetrius and Acts engaged in the same enterprise? Scripture functions as an important basis for each, but it does so in different ways. The language of promise-fulfillment that dominates Acts and helps shape the story at several levels is absent in Demetrius. Demetrius does not read scripture looking for promises that are later fulfilled or even for language that helps him interpret events in his own time. Unlike Luke, Demetrius does not quote

---

16. Ibid., 100.

scripture. Echoes of scripture are heard in his summarizing history. He reads scripture, summarizes it, puzzles over it, sees different kinds of questions arising from it, and attempts to give "rational" explanations of these problems.

One point of common interest, of course, is Demetrius's and Luke's interest in summarizing the biblical story. The summaries in Acts 7 and 13 provide the most useful parallels to Demetrius. Yet these Lukan summaries, taken together, reflect a "preconceived plan" of history that culminates in Christ. The biblical events that are mentioned are seen as part of a coherent salvation history in which divine promises are fulfilled in subsequent events. Such interests are absent in Demetrius. It is not even clear that Demetrius is rehearsing the events of biblical history as part of his ancestral history. He does not relate the events as part of "our history." Instead, he distances himself from the biblical story. It is there to be read, used, and explained, but it does not create the kind of enthusiasm that leads to embellishment. The biblical characters whom Demetrius mentions, if anything, remain smaller than life. Much of the pathos of the Bible evaporates in Demetrius's retelling. Three times Demetrius mentions an "angel of God" — once in his summary of the sacrifice of Isaac, repeating what he finds in the Bible (Frg. 1); twice in his account of Jacob's wrestling match (Frg. 2.7). In the latter instance, he mythicizes the LXX, which identifies the adversary as a "man" (ἄνθρωπος). This is what is meant by characterizing Demetrius as "rational."[17]

It might also be worth noting glaring differences. Luke nowhere exhibits an interest in chronology comparable to Demetrius. Computing the length in years of various periods of history is not one of Luke's concerns. He does periodize in different ways, for example, in Luke 16:16, but not in the way Demetrius does. Nor does Luke display Demetrius's "exegetical" interests. He obviously cites scripture often, but he does not feel compelled to explain exegetical problems that arise in scripture, chronological or moral. Scripture does not send Luke to the calculator the way it does Demetrius. Nor does it prompt him to devise ingenious explanations that will somehow harmonize what he reads. Instead, scripture prompts Luke to ask, "What did God promise?" and "How has God's promise been fulfilled?" Luke's penchant for shaping his narrative in light of biblical events, using biblical imagery to sketch character portraits or scenes within the narrative, should be seen as an extension of this fundamental way of reading scripture.

There are, however, some interesting points of convergence. The Lukan genealogy in Luke 3 traces the lineage of Jesus to Adam, and begins by giving Jesus' age as thirty years. Demetrius exhibits only slight interest in genealogy, the one exception being Frg. 2.19, but his chronological scheme does have the effect of linking his own time to that of Adam. Whether Luke's interest in providing chronological markers along the way, or in giving the age of Jesus, places him

---

17. For a more detailed characterization of Demetrius, see my remarks in "Demetrius the Chronographer as Historian and Apologist," in *Christian Teaching: Studies in Honor of LeMoine G. Lewis*, ed. E. Ferguson (Abilene, Tex.: Abilene Christian University, 1981), 124–25.

within Demetrius's tradition is doubtful. Demetrius may also be instructive in evaluating some of the chronological problems in Luke-Acts, such as the problem of dating the census under Quirinius (Luke 2:1–2). Admittedly, the text of Demetrius is corrupt at numerous points, but there appear to be cases where he confuses events. For example, depending on how the text is read, in Frg. 6 he appears to equate the fall of Samaria with the invasion of Sennacherib.

How, then, does Demetrius inform our reading of Acts? Like Luke, Demetrius is engaged in interpreting his native tradition in response to a larger set of concerns. They are both trying to make their own histories intelligible, both to themselves and to their readers, who are probably sympathetic readers. Yet they both appear to be aware of larger audiences. At least, they do their work with a conspicuous level of cultural awareness. Even if Demetrius's work will never be read by a larger circle of outside readers, he probably writes with Eratosthenes in mind. Similarly, Luke clearly knows enough Hellenistic conventions to make him aware of literate users of those conventions, both Greeks and Romans. Scripture is important for both, but in quite different ways. Each reads scripture and relates to it differently. They represent two fundamentally different ways of construing scripture. Compared with Luke, Demetrius is a much flatter writer. The kind of excitement and adventure we find in Acts nowhere appears in Demetrius. Admittedly, we have only a few fragments from Demetrius, but as brief as they are they do not exhibit Luke's flair for the dramatic. Luke and Demetrius both portray God as actively present within Israel's history, although this takes a slightly different form. Demetrius mentions God several times (Frg. 1; Frg. 2.7, 10; Frg. 4) but in each instance he is repeating what the Bible says. For Luke, God is not only an active participant in the biblical story but in the events that he narrates as well.

Artapanus

Only three fragments of Artapanus's work *Concerning the Jews* survive — a very brief fragment treating Abraham, a slightly longer one treating Joseph, and a fragment of over two hundred lines treating Moses. But in spite of the brevity of these fragments, we get a fairly clear sense of the overall complexion of the work. The topics he treats are biblical, and there is a paraphrastic quality about his work. Yet it is not a biblical paraphrase like *Jubilees*. Students of Artapanus have always been struck by the liberties he takes with the biblical text. Some have even wondered whether these fragments could have been written by a loyal Jew. But given the fragments' propensity to glorify Jewish heroes, there is little doubt of their Jewish origin.

When scholars place Artapanus within the tradition of popular, romantic literature, they are recognizing his distinctive flair for recasting the biblical story. The Bible provides him with the basic materials, such as story line and heroic figures, but he feels free to incorporate nonbiblical features from a variety of traditions at his disposal.

Since Artapanus focuses on three biblical characters, his resonance with Acts would appear to be those places in Acts, most notably the speeches, where summaries of biblical history appear.[18] And he is instructive in this regard. But perhaps as instructive as anything else for our understanding of Acts is Artapanus's storytelling technique, or, as O'Neill observes, the way he depicts heroic figures.[19]

The clearest instance in which Acts and Artapanus converge is the prison escape reported in Frg. 3.23–26. It is one of many instances in Frg. 3 where Artapanus departs from the biblical account. In certain respects, the biblical story line provides only the faintest outline for Artapanus's treatment of Moses, which covers material found in Exod. 1:1–15:19. Just prior to this episode, Artapanus has reported Moses' flight to Arabia, his marriage to Raguel's daughter, and a much reduced version of the burning-bush episode. After the prison-escape episode, Artapanus resumes the biblical story line, but gives a considerably modified version of Moses' spectacular feats in the presence of Pharaoh, the plagues, and the exodus.

The account is brief enough to quote in full:

> Upon learning of the arrival of Moses, the king of the Egyptians summoned him and inquired of him why he had come. Moses replied that he had come because the Lord of the universe had commanded him to liberate the Jews. Upon learning this, the king imprisoned him. When night came, all the doors of the prison opened of their own accord, and some of the guards died while others were overcome with sleep; also, their weapons broke into pieces. Moses left the prison and went to the palace. Finding the doors open, he entered the palace and aroused the king while the guards were sleeping on duty. Startled at what happened, the king ordered Moses to declare the name of the god who had sent him. He did this scoffingly. Moses bent over and spoke into the king's ear, but when the king heard it, he fell over speechless. But Moses picked him up and he came back to life again. He wrote the name on a tablet and sealed it securely, but one of the priests who showed contempt for what was written on the tablet died in a convulsion. (Frg. 3.22b–26)

The resemblance between this episode and Peter's escape from prison in Acts 12 has long been recognized.[20] In fact, as O. Weinreich conclusively demonstrated, the prison-escape scenes in Acts 5, 12, and 16 belong to a literary topos widely attested in antiquity.[21] As R. Pervo says,

---

18. See R. Pervo, "Narrative Theology: Two (Too?) Enlightened Popularizers: Artapanus and Lucas," paper presented at the Annual Meeting of the Society of Biblical Literature, November 1997, 27.

19. O'Neill, *Theology of Acts*, 152–53.

20. For example, F. J. Foakes Jackson and K. Lake, *The Beginnings of Christianity* (London: Macmillan, 1933), 4.135; E. Haenchen, *The Acts of the Apostles: A Commentary* (Oxford: Blackwell, 1971), 384 n. 3.

21. "Gebet und Wunder: Zwei Abhandlungen zur Religions- und Literaturgeschichte," in *Religionsgeschichtliche Studien* (Darmstadt: Wissenschaftliche Buchgesellschaft, 1968), 147–79.

The prison-escape scene in Acts 5 participates, along with related incidents in chapters 12 and 16, in one of the most widespread stock incidents of aretaological literature. More than thirty such tales can be studied, in Acts and Apoc. Acts, Dionysiac literature, Jewish narrative, historical and romantic novels, and novellas.[22]

In spite of its relative brevity, Artapanus's version of Moses' prison escape exhibits the basic form typical of such stories as well as many of the distinctive features found in such stories. The form usually begins with a confrontation between a religious figure — either a god or a representative of a god — and a resistant king portrayed as opposing God (θεομάχος). As a repressive measure, the king imprisons the religious figure. Details of the imprisonment may vary, but a description of security measures is usually given — the prisoner is bound or chained, guards are posted, and so on. The escape is narrated, usually with recurrent features. It often occurs at night, is precipitated or accompanied by extraordinary events, such as an earthquake, dazzling light, or doors that open of their own accord (αὐτομάτως). Some confirmation of the escape usually follows, and, as a rule, the cause of the religious figure is vindicated and the king is punished for opposing God.

The prison-escape topos is widely attested in literature featuring Dionysus; in fact, the earliest such occurrences are in Dionysiac circles. Artapanus may very well have flourished in an Egyptian setting in the mid–second century B.C.E., when the worship of Dionysus enjoyed widespread popularity. In such a setting he might easily have encountered these traditions and drawn on them for his portrait of Moses. As is evident from his use of the cultural-benefactor topos, Artapanus was well aware of traditions that circulated around other figures, such as Isis, Osiris, and Sesostris, and he appropriated these in his depictions of Joseph and Moses. His use of the prison-escape topos cannot easily be traced to the Bible. Figures such as Joseph, Jeremiah, and Daniel are imprisoned, but none of them escapes from prison in ways reported in these classic prison escapes. This use provides a clear instance in which Artapanus utilizes a stock literary device that was already well developed among Greek authors as a way of enhancing the status of a biblical hero.

The strategic literary function of Acts 12 within the overall narrative is now more widely appreciated. As O. W. Allen, Jr., has shown, the death of Herod is not simply an odd historical footnote supplied by Luke to anchor the story in secular history; instead, it plays a pivotal role in extending Luke's theological and literary purpose.[23] Since Peter's prison escape in Acts 12 is a necessary prelude to the death of Herod, it too plays a central role in advancing Luke's literary purpose. Taken together, both episodes assist Luke in showing how God deals with those who attempt to thwart the achievement of God's purpose.

---

22. *Profit with Delight: The Literary Genre of the Acts of the Apostles* (Philadelphia: Fortress, 1987), 21.

23. *The Death of Herod: The Narrative and Theological Function of Retribution in Luke-Acts*, SBLDS 158 (Atlanta: Scholars Press, 1997).

Between chapters 5 and 12, the Gospel makes dramatic strides — geographically and numerically — and with chapter 12 the scene returns to Jerusalem. Actions taken by the authorities reach a new high as Herod orders the execution of James. The level of authority has increased — from Jewish leaders in Jerusalem to Herod Agrippa I, the king. By arresting Peter, he focuses on a single significant leader, whereas the earlier prison-escape scenes deal with the apostles as a group, or with Peter and John, along with the apostles. The level of incarceration is also intensified. Not just "overnight custody," nor even a "public prison" this time, but Peter is "seized" and placed in prison, guarded by four squads of soldiers (12:4). Such security is required because the imprisonment occurs during Passover.

The prison escape of Acts 12 advances beyond the two previous imprisonment episodes in virtually every detail. The level of resistance that prompts the imprisonment is much higher — the death of the apostle James, a member of the inner circle, at the hands of the king. The focus narrows to Peter, the apostolic spokesperson of the Christian movement, rather than the apostles as a group. The actions now taken against Peter are more drastic. Earlier, he is placed in a public prison and released at night by an angel of the Lord. Here he is under extraordinarily heavy guard — four squads of soldiers — bound with two chains, sleeping between two guards. The events of the release are given with photographic detail. The words and movements of the angel are carefully recorded. The miraculous escape from chains and sleeping guards is followed by the automatic opening of the iron gate leading into the city. Peter's own emotions are given in greater detail — his sense of disbelief at what is happening, his interpretive comments confirming all this to be the Lord's work. The level of public confirmation is higher: by killing the guards Herod publicly acknowledges the truth of Peter's escape.

The points of correspondence between Artapanus and Acts are remarkable: the religious hero is pitted against a villainous king; the imprisonments occur at night; doors open of their own accord (αὐτομάτως); in Artapanus the guards' weapons break into pieces, while in Acts 12 Peter's chains fall off; the king acts inappropriately with respect to the deity. In Artapanus, Pharaoh scoffs at the divine name, and on hearing it whispered in his ear falls over speechless. This presumably means that Pharaoh died, since Moses brings him back to life again (ἀναβιῶσαι). A similar fate befalls a sacrilegious priest. In Acts, Herod dies horribly because he fails to give "the glory to God" (Acts 12:23).

To suggest that Luke depended directly on Artapanus is probably going too far, even though there is no reason, in principle, why this could not have occurred. Artapanus is certainly early enough to have functioned as a source for Luke. And there is firm evidence that the story circulated well beyond Egypt. After all, Artapanus was preserved by Alexander Polyhistor, who flourished in Rome in the mid–first century B.C.E. Luke's use of Artapanus may not be as farfetched as it seems, especially when one considers other possibilities. Since the Bible contains no prison-escape stories like these, it obviously did not serve as a source for Luke in this instance, even though it did supply abundant imagery for him in other respects. Given the widespread popularity of this topos, however, it may be safer to assume that Luke appropriated it from a much broader range of narrative traditions and techniques. It may simply have been a stock narrative device so widely known and used that no specific source needs to be sought.

Apart from this specific episode, Artapanus and Acts may be compared in other ways as well. Broadly speaking, their contexts and overall purposes appear to have much in common. Many things about Artapanus remain puzzling, but no one seriously disputes that he was engaged in religious propaganda of some sort. In his writings, he glorifies Israel's past, using commonly understood forms of heroic typification to present the figures of Israel's past. His purpose is clear: to present Abraham, Joseph, and Moses as worthy competitors of similar figures from other traditions, such as Sesostris, Dionysus, Isis, and Osiris. Luke is engaged in a similar enterprise — presenting a credible account of the origin and development of the Jesus movement. He does so by presenting what Jesus "did and taught," then shows how Jesus' deeds and words were continued in the lives of his followers, most notably Peter and Paul. Both Artapanus and Luke are enthusiastic promoters of the traditions they represent.

Both Artapanus and Luke employ narrative as a means of portraying their respective traditions. But they share more than this simple choice. They also tell their stories in remarkably similar ways. Artapanus exercises great freedom with the biblical tradition, now supplementing, now modifying, sometimes with breathtaking boldness. Luke exercised similar freedom with the Markan story line, and there is no reason to assume that he drastically altered his method in composing Acts. Like other historians and storytellers, he composed speeches to fit both speaker and occasion. Accordingly, Lukan scholars have long read the speeches in Acts as Lukan compositions that tell us more about Luke's theological outlook and literary purpose than they do about the speaker.

Luke's literary creativity is seen in other ways as well. His skill in shaping scenes, portraying characters, and developing plot is now widely recognized. In doing so, he employs literary conventions but is not bound by them. He has a clear sense of the distinctive elements of the story he wishes to tell, and he employs a dazzling array of narrative devices to achieve his purpose. Perhaps this, as much as anything else, Luke has in common with Artapanus.

Artapanus and Acts may be said to share a sense of the dramatic, and this is seen in the way they construct their narratives. The prison-escape scene provides a concrete example, but the similarity can be shown in other ways as well. As brief as Artapanus's treatment of Moses is, we can see the general shape of the narrative. As Exodus 1 reports, a new king arises, and Artapanus amplifies the narrative to show how Moses was adopted by Merris, the king's daughter, and rose to prominence in Egypt. Artapanus first rehearses Moses' achievements as cultural benefactor, which earn him the highest esteem among the Egyptians. Naturally this makes Chenephres, the local ruler of Memphis, jealous, and he becomes the main adversary of Moses, resisting him at every turn. Frg. 3.7–18 reports Chenephres' unsuccessful efforts to block Moses' rising career as an Egyptian hero. The first episode, Moses' battle against the Ethiopians, only confirms the mismatch: Chenephres sends Moses with an army of ill-trained farmers against the mighty Ethiopians, but Moses wins the ten-year battle hands down, even earning the love and esteem of the Ethiopians and turning them into his followers — they adopt from him the practice of circumcision. Not to be outdone, Chenephres tries again. Feigning pleasure at Moses' successes, Chenephres begins to plot his overthrow. Ostensibly following Moses' lead, he works to strengthen religious institutions throughout Egypt — rebuilding a temple at Diospolis, introducing oxen to till the land, and dedicating a temple to Apis. In doing so, he attempts to suppress the earlier religious reforms of Moses. Even so, he meets rejection from the Egyptians, thereby intensifying his efforts to kill Moses. He develops a plan to have Moses assassinated by Chanethotes while both are attending the funeral of Merris. But Moses learns of the plot in advance and manages to escape. On Aaron's advice he flees to Arabia. En route, Chanethotes makes yet another attempt on Moses' life, only to be outwitted, outfought, and finally killed by Moses.

In Acts the characters are different, as is the basic story line. But certain features of Acts resonate with Artapanus. Chenephres plays the role of ὁ θεομαχῶν, always resisting but never besting the religious hero Moses. Moses' adventures range from heroic feats in the battlefield to impressive performances in the royal palace, and he never suffers a serious setback. On the contrary, he moves from success to success. Plots against his life are thwarted, even as they are against Paul in Acts. Those who resist God's appointed representative Moses, especially those in high places, come to ignominious ends, as does Herod in Acts. As the prison escapes in both texts illustrate, attempts to imprison are met with dramatic rescues. And in both instances, the power of God is visibly at work in effecting the release and vindicating the cause of God's representative.

Pervo rightly emphasizes the entertainment value of this mode of storytelling.[24] Adventure is surely there, and the story is told in a way that excites the reader. But the story does more than entertain. It also advances a point of view. In both Artapanus and Acts, God is clearly on the side of the lead characters, and the narrative road is littered with the bodies of God-fighters.

It is in this sense that Acts stands in the tradition of Artapanus. Not that they are both "historians" in any definable sense. Nor are both engaged in producing "romantic" literature. Rather, they both cast their respective stories — their "religious histories" — in narrative form, and tell their stories in the triumphalist fashion that typifies national romantic literature.

---

24. Pervo, *Profit*, esp. 12–57.

Eupolemus

We have roughly the same amount of material from Eupolemus as we do from Artapanus (some 250 lines), slightly more than we have from Demetrius (about 200 lines). Most of it is concentrated in Frg. 2, which is aptly summarized by Eusebius's title: "Eupolemus' remarks concerning David and Solomon who ruled the Hebrews and his remarks concerning Jerusalem." Frg. 3, which consists of only four lines, continues his interest in Solomon, while Frg. 4 summarizes Jeremiah's prophetic activity prior to Nebuchadnezzar's capture of Jerusalem: his prophetic denunciation of idol worship by the Jews; his resistance of "Jonacheim," king of Judah; his prediction of the fall of Jerusalem; and his rescue of the ark and tablets from the Temple. Frg. 5 gives a chronographical summary that calculates the number of years from Adam and the exodus respectively until the reign of Demetrius I Soter. Frg. 1, which portrays Moses as cultural benefactor, is exceptional in its treatment of earlier biblical events.

Compared with Demetrius and Artapanus, Eupolemus presents a different configuration of interests. Frg. 5 suggests that he shares Demetrius's chronographical interests, at least to some extent. Elsewhere he displays an interest in calculating the length of activity for various biblical figures.[25] In one sense, Eupolemus is more fascinated with numbers than Demetrius is.[26] But there is a crucial difference. The biblical account does not present number puzzles for Eupolemus as it does for Demetrius. When Demetrius reads the Bible, he detects certain exegetical cruxes in the text relating to numbers. By contrast, the Bible presents no such problems for Eupolemus. He does not read the Bible and scratch his head, as Demetrius does, trying to make the numbers fit.

But neither does Eupolemus flatten the biblical narrative as Demetrius does. In some ways, he is much closer to Artapanus in the way he relates to the biblical story. To be sure, the Bible provides the basic story line. The sequence of events sketched in Frg. 2 follows the biblical story: Moses, Joshua, Samuel, Saul, David, and Solomon. And yet Eupolemus is not bound by the biblical story line in his portrait of biblical figures. His portrait of Moses as *Kulturbringer* in Frg. 1 moves well beyond the biblical portrait; indeed, there is nothing in the biblical portrait of Moses that specifically supports any of the claims in Frg. 1, except his role as lawgiver. His portrait of David in Frg. 2.30.3–8 also moves well beyond the biblical account. David's realm in Eupolemus stretches from Egypt to the Euphrates, and as far north as Phoenicia. Like the biblical account, Eupolemus reports David's victories over the Syrians, Idumeans (Edomites), Ammonites,

---

25. Moses prophesied forty years, Joshua prophesied thirty years, Saul died after ruling twenty-one years (Frg. 2.1–2); David reigned forty years, then transferred power to the twelve-year-old Solomon (Frg. 2.8); Solomon lived fifty-two years, reigning peacefully forty years (Frg. 3).

26. Frg. 2 is replete with statistics relating to the building of the Temple: the number of workers supplied by Vaphres, king of Egypt (Frg. 2.32.1); the amount of supplies needed from Souron, king of Tyre (Frg. 2.33.1); the dimensions of the Temple (Frg. 2.34.1–18).

and Moabites, but he goes beyond the Bible in reporting David's victories over the Assyrians, Phoenicians, Itureans, Nabateans, and Nabdeans.[27]

Similar revisionist tendencies are reflected in his portrait of Solomon. Following the biblical account, Eupolemus reports Hiram's assistance in building the Temple, although Hiram's biblical status as "king of Tyre" is expanded by Eupolemus to "king of Tyre, Sidon, and Phoenicia." Even though Eupolemus's version of the exchange of letters between Solomon and Hiram is more formalized than biblical counterparts, it has a solid biblical basis (Frg. 2.33.1–34.3; cf. 1 Kings 5:1–12; 2 Chron. 2:1–16). Yet Eupolemus feels no reluctance in supplying a similar exchange of letters between Solomon and Vaphres, king of Egypt (Frg. 2.31.1–32.1), thereby enhancing the extent of Solomon's influence. Though brief, the letters are subtly crafted. Solomon addresses Vaphres as "king of Egypt," but he is addressed by Vaphres as "the great king." Moreover, Solomon's accession prompts a day of celebration throughout Egypt, and Vaphres acknowledges the greatness of Solomon's God. Solomon thus emerges as a world ruler, whose peers are the king of Egypt and the king of Tyre, Sidon, and Phoenicia.

Eupolemus's elaborate description of the Temple continues to enhance Solomon's status. The Temple exceeds its biblical counterpart in almost every respect: its dimensions are larger, it is more lavishly gilded, its costs are fantastically large. There is even some doubt whether Eupolemus's description is based on that of 1 Kings and 2 Chronicles. Wacholder may be right in seeing it as a "futuristic Temple" reflecting Ezekiel's idealized version.[28]

As these examples of biblical embellishment show, Eupolemus clearly begins with the biblical text, but he certainly does not end there. "Biblicist" may accurately describe Demetrius, but not Eupolemus. Sterling rightly characterizes Eupolemus as a "revisionist who uses the biblical text for his own purposes. It is his own agenda which best explains the form his narrative took. It is fair to say that Eupolemus is a Hellenistic redaction of Chronicles in much the same way Chronicles revises Kings."[29]

Yet, for all of his "haggadic" tendencies, Eupolemus is no clone of Artapanus. In Artapanus, we find local, especially Egyptian, traditions interwoven with biblical traditions. His portrait of Moses as *Kulturbringer* is more fully elaborated than that of Eupolemus, and Moses comes out looking more like an Egyptian hero. Such tendencies are not as clearly visible in Eupolemus. There is some indication that he may have drawn on other sources besides the biblical text,

---

27. Why Eupolemus gives such an exaggerated account of David's reign is not altogether clear. Political motives may have been at work. We are relatively confident in attaching the work to the Eupolemus who belonged to the prominent Accos priestly family and flourished in Palestine in the period immediately following the Maccabean revolt. This greatly expanded role of David in Eupolemus's history might well have served to justify Hasmonean expansionistic policies. Or Eupolemus might have simply extended the Chronicler's tendency to enlarge the accomplishments of the Davidic monarchy.

28. Wacholder, *Eupolemus*, 201.

29. Sterling, *Historiography and Self-Definition*, 218.

such as Ktesias, possibly Herodotus,[30] but if so, such borrowing is slight. It would be better to characterize Eupolemus as a biblical paraphraser or even a biblical expansionist, someone who takes the biblical story as a starting point but freely expands and embellishes it, using his own imagination and creative powers. In Artapanus we see evidence of dramatic, narrative powers that we do not see in Eupolemus. Artapanus's rehearsal of Moses' exploits over the Ethiopians, or of Moses' confrontation with Pharaoh, reflects a storytelling technique, or a tradition of storytelling, not found in Eupolemus. In this sense Artapanus is closer to the tradition of Hellenistic novel and romance than Eupolemus. And while Eupolemus is not the "dry chronographer" Demetrius is, his interest in straightforward, historical narrative seems much closer to Demetrius, even though he feels far less compelled to stick to the biblical story.

To be sure, the personalities that emerge in Eupolemus's account, especially Moses, David, and Solomon, are sketched in terms more heroic than the biblical account. And yet, there is a sense in which Eupolemus's portraits of David and Solomon simply continue tendencies already present in the biblical account, especially reflected in the way Chronicles reinterprets Kings. We see no discernible tendency in Eupolemus to supply miraculous events or to enhance such elements that he finds in the biblical text. He reports that "by the will of God" Saul was chosen by Samuel to be king, but this is surely a suitable way of paraphrasing 1 Sam. 8:4–22; 9:27–10:27. Certain features of the angel's appearance to David in connection with his desire to build the Temple are problematic (Frg. 2.30.5–6). Eupolemus conflates the biblical account in which David communicates with the Lord about the need for a temple (2 Samuel 7 and 1 Chronicles 17) and the biblical account of David's census and the angel's appearance at the threshing floor of Araunah the Jebusite, where David is instructed to erect an altar to the Lord (2 Samuel 24; 1 Chronicles 21). In Eupolemus it is the angel who forbids David from building the Temple because of his warfare, whereas in the biblical account this message is mediated to David by a "word of the Lord" (1 Chron. 22:8; 28:3). This is an understandable extension of the angel's role, and in no substantial way does Eupolemus embellish or flatten the angel's role. In Souron's letter to Solomon, he acknowledges that God chose Solomon to be king, but this simply makes explicit what is asserted in the biblical account (2 Chron. 2:12).

A slight heroizing tendency is perhaps seen in Eupolemus's treatment of Jeremiah. As with his treatment of David and Solomon, Eupolemus expands the biblical story. He reports that Jeremiah "caught the Jews sacrificing to a golden idol whose name was Baal," a nonbiblical detail, as are the report of Jonacheim's attempt to burn Jeremiah alive and Jeremiah's prediction that the Jews would cook for the Babylonians and dig trenches in the Tigris and Euphrates (Frg. 4.3). Similarly, his report of the Medes' participation in the destruction of Jerusalem is not found in the Bible (Frg. 4.4). The details of Nebuchadnezzar's campaign again are fictional, as is the tradition that Jeremiah rescued the Temple ves-

---

30. Ibid., 217–18.

sels (see 2 Macc. 2:1–10). Eupolemus's treatment of Jeremiah in Frg. 4 simply reinforces what we have seen earlier — a "haggadic" tendency to paraphrase, expand, and freely embellish the biblical account.

How does Eupolemus inform our reading of Luke-Acts? As we saw with Artapanus, Eupolemus exhibits remarkable freedom vis-à-vis the Bible. Even though the Bible supplies the main story line and subject matter for Eupolemus, he quite readily revises it in the interest of heroic presentation. He does not see his task as that of an epitomizer. Rather, he amplifies freely, anachronizes often. He makes little effort to distinguish between the political and geographical realities of the Bible and those of his own time.[31] He betrays no sense that he will be found out as he obliterates such distinctions, or even as he magnifies the accomplishments of Moses, David, Solomon, and Jeremiah. Both Artapanus and Eupolemus are instructive in this regard, for they provide some context within which to evaluate Luke's summaries of Israel's history such as we find in Acts 7 and 13. The well-known discrepancies between Stephen's summary of Israel's history and the biblical account may appear less problematic when placed beside Eupolemus's use of the Bible. Rather than evaluating Luke's summaries of biblical history against the LXX tradition as we know it or assuming that there was a relatively fixed canonical version of this history, we may need to envision a much more fluid state of affairs. Accordingly, rather than evaluating the differences between Acts 7 and the LXX as places where Luke "got it wrong," we should perhaps see traditions of "biblical summaries" such as those we find in Eupolemus (and Artapanus) lying behind and informing Acts 7.[32]

Another point worth noting are the distinctive features of Eupolemus's characterization of Moses' and Joshua's work as "prophesying" (Frg. 2b.30.1). Like the biblical account, he calls Samuel a prophet; he mentions Nathan the prophet (Frg. 2b.34.4); he obviously devoted attention to Jeremiah's prophetic activity. There is also the problematic title, *Concerning the Prophecy of Elijah*, which Eusebius gives for Eupolemus's work. Though widely believed to be incorrect, and, at most, the title of a section of the larger work, Wacholder argues for its plausibility.[33] If he is correct, the prophet Elijah may have fascinated Eupolemus every bit as much as he did other writers of the period.[34] Taken together, these various references to prophecy incline F. Fallon and H. W. Attridge to think that perhaps Eupolemus "wrote in part to clarify the place of prophecy in the Jewish state."[35] Such interest in prophecy resonates with the distinctive Lukan empha-

---

31. The difficulties with Eupolemus's geographical divisions are well-known: they are full of anachronisms and appear to reflect political and geographical realities during the Maccabean period rather than the Davidic monarchy. See *FHJA*, 1.140 n. 20.

32. See M. Hengel's reminder to assess "accuracy" in Luke-Acts in terms of how he compares with other Hellenistic authors: he is neither more nor less "accurate" in his handling of various geographical, political, or other historical information (*Acts and the History of Earliest Christianity* [Philadelphia: Fortress, 1979], esp. 60–62).

33. Wacholder, *Eupolemus*, 23–24.

34. See references in ibid., 23–24.

35. "The Genuine Eupolemus," paper, Harvard New Testament Seminar, March 2, 1970, 8.

sis on prophecy. Eupolemus's distinctive characterization of Moses and Joshua as prophets resonates with Luke's penchant for casting Jesus, Peter, Stephen, and Paul into prophetic molds.[36] More specifically, Eupolemus's designation of Moses as a prophet anticipates the distinctive role the prophetic figure Moses plays in Luke's understanding of Jesus' role and Israel's response to the apostles' preaching, especially as reflected in Acts 3:22–36 and Acts 7:37–43.

Also worth noting is the way Eupolemus portrays Israel's heroes vis-à-vis other nations. As *Kulturbringer*, Moses benefits the Phoenicians and Greeks through his invention of the alphabet. Clearly, other peoples are presented in a subordinate role to the Jews, an emphasis reflected elsewhere in Eupolemus. Most of the people David encounters he subdues, even forcing Souron, king of Tyre and Phoenicia, to pay tribute. Exceptionally, he concludes a friendship treaty with Vaphres, king of Egypt (Frg. 2b.30.4). His reach extends to "Elana, a city in Arabia," where he commissions ships to be built to assist in transporting building materials for the Temple to Jerusalem (Frg. 2b.30.7). He also has power to send miners to the island of Ophir in the Red Sea.

Unlike David, Solomon is not portrayed as a military expansionist; his position is already well established, thanks to David's victories. The cultivation of foreign powers, begun by David, is continued by Solomon, especially seen in the correspondence with Vaphres, king of Egypt, and Souron, king of Tyre, Sidon, and Phoenicia. Both kings are deferential toward Solomon, fully recognizing his superiority. Solomon, in return, is the essence of diplomacy, even journeying to the mountain of Lebanon with the Sidonians and Tyrians. He is presented as being unusually generous and magnanimous. Not only does he return the Egyptians and the Phoenician workers to their homelands after the building of the Temple, but he also gives each worker a ten-shekel bonus. He expresses his appreciation to Vaphres and Souron by sending generous portions of gifts, even sending Souron a golden pillar that was set up in the Temple of Zeus in Tyre.

While no single figure in Luke-Acts is depicted in precisely the ways that Eupolemus depicts Moses, David, and Solomon, Luke's cosmopolitan outlook is strongly reminiscent of Eupolemus. For Eupolemus, Moses, David, and Solomon are more than national heroes; their fame and achievements reach well beyond Israel's borders. Eupolemus makes a concerted effort to make these connections explicit: Moses as cultural benefactor, David and Solomon as world rulers. In Luke-Acts, this cosmopolitan outlook takes a different form. The Jesus movement begins in Jerusalem, gradually spreads through Judea, Samaria, Galilee, and Syria (interestingly enough, geographical areas Eupolemus reports; see Frg. 4.5), eventually moves westward through Asia, Greece, and finally to Rome. At each stage, of course, leading characters interact with clearly identified political figures, representatives of the Roman Empire, and while the reader never doubts

---

36. See L. T. Johnson's emphasis on Luke's use of prophetic models for portraying Jesus and the leading spokespersons in Luke-Acts (*The Acts of the Apostles*, Sacra Pagina 5 [Collegeville, Minn.: Liturgical Press, 1992], 12–14).

the ultimate power of Rome, neither is there any doubt who the true victors are. Representatives of the Jesus movement, including Peter, Stephen, Philip, and Paul, encounter authority figures in the Roman world in many different ways, but like David's enemies and Solomon's foreign partners, these authority figures yield to the power and persuasion of Christ's representatives.

Even Eupolemus's portrait of Jeremiah retains this triumphal element. Nebuchadnezzar, allied with Astibares, king of the Medes, conquers Jerusalem because of the sins of idolatrous Jews. But Jeremiah foresaw it; he thwarted the king's attempt to burn him alive; he accurately predicted that his countrymen would cook and dig ditches for the Babylonians; and while Nebuchadnezzar made off with all the Temple treasure, he was unable to seize the ark and the tablets of the law. These Jeremiah rescued.

Luke depicts the ultimate victory of the Christian movement in ways not altogether different. Paul's trials and imprisonment unfold methodically. Plots are discovered. Dramatic rescues occur — from prison, snakebite, and the raging sea. Ultimately he reaches Rome and stands trial, but the final scene is one of vindication. Like the city of Jerusalem, Paul is captured, but the most valuable things are rescued from the enemy's hands.

There is one critical difference between Eupolemus and Luke-Acts — their view of the Jerusalem Temple. The Temple looms large in Eupolemus, even larger than it does in 1 Kings and 2 Chronicles. Those who link Eupolemus's priestly status with his glorified portrait of the Temple are probably right, especially if he worked in the aftermath of the Maccabean revolt. Cleansing the Temple and restoring it to its former glory would be motivated by such grand descriptions as the one created by Eupolemus, especially if it takes on the idealized form of Ezekiel's Temple. The Temple appears not to be eschatological, yet that does not keep it from serving as a future ideal. The Temple's grandeur and glory, as sketched by Eupolemus, underscore even more the tragedy of its fall to Nebuchadnezzar.

No such devotion to the Temple is found in Luke-Acts. If Stephen's speech in Acts 7 is indeed an anti-Temple piece, it represents a fundamentally different set of loyalties. The gradual displacement of the Temple as the defining locus of Jewish worship that we see in the earlier chapters of Acts reflects an entirely different evaluation of its significance. Thus we see nothing of the glorification of the Temple in Luke-Acts comparable to what we find in Eupolemus, although we do find the progress of the "sect of the Nazarenes" sketched in similarly idealized terms. Its numerical growth, geographical spread, the respect it gains from political figures all serve as rough counterparts to Eupolemus's revisionist portrait of Israel's history under David and Solomon.

As noted before in reference to Demetrius, the chronographical interests reflected in Frg. 5 of Eupolemus appear to have no real counterpart in Luke-Acts, unless it is the way Israel's history is periodized. However, what this chronological summary does show is Eupolemus's concern to understand the biblical story as a whole, and to see it as a continuous story that can be divided into periods and counted by years, reaching into his own time. N. Dahl's suggestion that Luke intended to write a continuation of biblical history tends to place Luke and Eupolemus within the same tradition.[37] Even though Luke does it quite differently from Eupolemus, he appears to be responding to the same impulse. This is especially the case if Eupolemus's work included an account of the Maccabean period.[38]

Pseudo-Eupolemus

In many ways, we are on shaky ground with two fragments focusing on Abraham, attributed since J. Freudenthal to the anonymous Samaritan author Pseudo-Eupolemus.[39] They exhibit many problematic features, some of them perhaps attributable to Alexander Polyhistor.[40] They are especially remarkable for the peculiar blend of traditions that they represent. Their subject matter is the biblical figure Abraham, with the biblical account of Genesis 5–14 supplying the basic story line. They provide a very compressed account of these chapters, but Pseudo-Eupolemus is no mere summarizer. In some ways, he renders the Greek version of these chapters into a plausible summary. This is especially true of his account of the origins of Babylon from the time of the flood forward (Frg. 1.2–

---

37. "The Purpose of Luke-Acts," *Jesus in the Memory of the Early Church* (Minneapolis: Augsburg, 1976), 88.

38. Wacholder, *Eupolemus*, 25.

39. These two fragments featuring Abraham are usually attributed to the author designated Pseudo-Eupolemus, or simply Anonymous. According to Eusebius, the first fragment, comprising some fifty-seven lines, comes from a work by Eupolemus entitled *Concerning the Jews of Assyria* (περὶ Ἰουδαίων τῆς Ἀσσυρίας, Frg. 1.2). Freudenthal contested this attribution, however, because it links Abraham with the "temple Argarizin," presumably the temple at Mount Gerizim, and identifies the latter as the "mountain of the Most High (ὄρος ὑψίστου)." (See Freudenthal, *Alexander Polyhistor* [Breslau: H. Skutsch, 1875], 85–86). Such a positive view of the Samaritan temple he could not reconcile with the glorious picture of Solomon's Temple in the other Eupolemus fragments, especially in light of the known hostility between Jews and Samaritans during the mid–second century B.C.E. Accordingly, he assigned it to an unknown Samaritan author and coupled it with another ten-line fragment about Abraham which Eusebius traced to "some anonymous writings" (Frg. 2). The two fragments have some important discrepancies, but they also have much in common. Scholarly opinion remains divided, however. R. Doran, for one, sees nothing in Frg. 1 that is distinctively Samaritan and thinks it belongs with the other Eupolemus fragments ("Pseudo-Eupolemus," in *Old Testament Pseudepigrapha,* ed. J. H. Charlesworth [Garden City, N.Y.: Doubleday, 1985], 2.873–79). G. Sterling, on the other hand, remains convinced by Freudenthal (*Historiography and Self-Definition,* 190). I too remain convinced of the Samaritan outlook of Frg. 1 and connect it with Frg. 2 (*FHJA* 1.158–59). Though, see below, n. 48.

40. Eusebius's suggested title (see n. 39) is problematic. No Samaritan author would entitle a work περὶ Ἰουδαίων. Nor has it been easy to see how Abraham would be treated in a work on Assyria, unless τῆς Ἀσσυρίας somehow describes the region of Babylon. Polyhistor may well have supplied the title "On the Jews," and "of Assyria" may simply locate the "city of Babylon." Yet "Assyria" does figure in the Genesis 10 genealogy (10:11) as the region to which Nimrod the γίγας went after he established Babel, Erech, and Accad in the land of Shinar. Frg. 1 links the building of the "well-known tower" with the giants who survived the flood. In this way, Pseudo-Eupolemus connects the founding of the city of Babylon with the descendants of Noah, which, of course, makes it easier to locate the birth of Abraham in Babylon.

3). Other features of his account also resonate closely with the biblical account. Yet he is not content to stick to the biblical account, either in its narrative details or sequence. Nor does he ever claim that he is doing so. He gives a simplified version of Abraham's migration from Babylon. The biblical sequence unfolds in three stages: from Haran to the land of Canaan (Gen. 12:1–9), from Canaan to Egypt (Gen. 12:10–20), from the Negeb back to Canaan (Gen. 13:1–18). Pseudo-Eupolemus's Abraham journeys from Babylon to Phoenicia, then to Egypt. The Phoenician section draws largely on Genesis 14, while the Egyptian section depends on Gen. 12:10–20.

There is some indication that Pseudo-Eupolemus is working with an "Abraham template" that informs, and maybe even dictates, his reading of the biblical account.[41] The profile of his understanding of Abraham is quite clear: a Babylonian stage, a Phoenician stage, followed by an Egyptian stage. That Abraham originated in Babylon he could easily deduce from Genesis 10–11, and his account of the giants as survivors of the flood who built the "well-known tower," and who were scattered throughout the earth after its destruction by God is a plausible rendering of the Greek version of Genesis 10.[42] Placing Abraham in the tenth generation after the flood also represents a plausible rendering of the genealogical table in Gen. 11:10–30. Dating Abraham to the "thirteenth generation," while problematic grammatically, may represent an alternative tradition tracing Abraham's genealogy to Enoch, who, according to Genesis 5, is three generations before the flood. The Babylonian section concludes with the innovative claims about Abraham's surpassing nobility and wisdom and his discovery

---

41. For a reconstructed summary of Pseudo-Eupolemus's story, see Sterling, *Historiography and Self-Definition,* 193–94.

42. Most likely, Pseudo-Eupolemus is dependent on a Greek version of Genesis, which identifies Nimrod as a γίγας (Gen. 10:9) and which also identifies the Rephaim in Gen. 14:4 as γίγαντες. Also, Gen. 10:10 links Nimrod with the founding of "Babel, Erech, and Accad, all of them in the land of Shinar." Genesis 10 also reports that he subsequently built other cities, including Nineveh in Assyria (Gen. 10:11). Also worth noting is that Nimrod, according to Gen. 10:8, is the son of Cush, one of the sons of Ham. The lineage of Canaan, another son of Ham, is given in Gen. 10:15, where he is said to be the father of Sidon, and the one through whom the "families of the Canaanites spread abroad" (Gen. 10:18). The "territory of the Canaanites" is then described as extending "from Sidon, in the direction of Gerar, as far as Gaza, and in the direction of Sodom, Gomorrah, Admah, and Zeboiim, as far as Lasha" (Gen. 10:20). Earlier, the descendants of Japheth were located in the coastlands (Gen. 10:5), while those of Shem occupied the territory "Mesha in the direction of Sephar, the hill country of the east" (Gen. 10:30). Informed by this geography of Genesis 10, Pseudo-Eupolemus would quite logically identify all the territory extending from Sidon in the north all the way to the Dead Sea as a single territory, which Gen. 10:19 (LXX) identifies as "the territory of the Canaanites" (τὰ ὅρια τῷ Χαναναίων) inhabited by the "families of the Canaanites" (αἱ φυλαὶ τῶν Χαναναίων).

Given the LXX version of Genesis 5–11, Pseudo-Eupolemus's summary is entirely plausible. Immediately after the flood, Nimrod "the giant" is introduced as one of the descendants of Cush, the son of Ham, and the "beginning of his kingdom" was located in "Babel . . . in the land of Shinar" (Gen. 10:10), where the Bible locates the tower episode (Gen. 11:2). Pseudo-Eupolemus's claim that the tower "fell" (πεσόντος) may derive from the name given to the tower in the LXX: σύγχυσις, "tumult." Since Gen. 11:10–32 rehearses the descendants of Shem and in the tenth generation places Terah's family in "Ur of the Chaldeans," Pseudo-Eupolemus's account represents an apt summary, although he is more explicit in claiming that Abraham was born there.

(or mastery) of astrology and Chaldean science and the reassurance that these were related to, perhaps even derived from, his pursuit of piety that won him divine approval.[43]

With Abraham's Babylonian roots firmly established, along with his role as savant extraordinaire, Pseudo-Eupolemus then moves to stage two: Phoenicia.[44] There is nothing in Genesis 5–14 explicitly related to Phoenicia, although there is much about Canaan and the Canaanites, which the LXX sometimes renders as Phoenicia and Phoenicians (Exod. 6:15; 16:35). But this seems slim reason for turning Abraham's trip to "the land of Canaan" (cf. Gen. 12:4–9) into a sojourn in Phoenicia. Possibly the biblical account is being bent toward some independent account of Phoenician history and culture similar to that of Philo of Byblos. In any case, Abraham is portrayed as transmitting his knowledge of Babylonian science to the Phoenicians, which has no counterpart in the Bible.[45] To fill

---

43. Pseudo-Eupolemus moves beyond the biblical account in claiming that "Abraham excelled all men in nobility and wisdom" (εὐγενείᾳ καὶ σοφίᾳ). Here begins his portrayal of Abraham as *Kulturbringer*, the one who "discovered both astrology and Chaldean science" (τὴν ἀστρολογίαν καὶ Χαλδαϊκὴν εὑρεῖν). Whether Pseudo-Eupolemus is actually positing Abraham as the original discoverer of "astrology and Chaldean science," or simply claiming that he "sought and obtained knowledge" of these things (R. Doran, *OTP* 2.880), depends on how one understands εὑρεῖν, and also how this claim is to be related to his later claim that Enoch was the original discoverer (Frg. 1.8). Conceivably, Pseudo-Eupolemus is presenting Abraham as one who gained expertise in Babylonian astrology and who did so as an exercise in piety. After all, he is presented as being "eager in his pursuit of piety" (τὴν εὐσέβειαν ὁρμήσαντα), which would seem to imply that his learning about the heavens and their operation was related to this devotion to God. Which was the cause, which the effect is not clear, whether he came to know God through his quest of the heavens, or whether his knowledge of God prompted his search of the heavens. In either case, it gained him favor with God (εὐαρεστῆσαι τῷ θεῷ). Pseudo-Eupolemus presents a strong claim in behalf of "astrology," the science of the heavens, and provides an alterative view to other Jewish traditions where such knowledge is viewed negatively (see *FHJA* 1.180–81 n. 12 for references). Also worth noting is the way Abraham's "pursuit of piety" (τὴν εὐσέβειαν ὁρμήσαντα) forms the basis of his acceptance by God (εὐαρεστῆσαι τῷ θεῷ). One might well deduce this from Gen. 11:31–12:9, although nothing is said there about Abraham's motivations or aspirations, or about God's assessment of his actions. Possibly, Gen. 15:6 informs Pseudo-Eupolemus at this point. To say that Abraham's piety prompted God's pleasure is not too far removed from a faith that is reckoned by God as righteousness. The language is different, but the connection anticipates the Pauline link between faith and justification in Romans 4.

44. Frg. 1.4 begins Pseudo-Eupolemus's paraphrase of God's call of Abraham reported in Genesis 12. God's injunction to Abraham in Gen. 12:1 is understood as a divine command, or, more accurately, as a series of divine commandments (τὰ προστάγματα τοῦ θεοῦ). But whereas the Bible reports that Abraham experienced God's call in Haran, Pseudo-Eupolemus locates it in Ur. And where the Bible reports Abram and his family journeying from Haran to "the land of Canaan" (Gen. 12:5), a journey that took them first to "Shechem, to the oak of Moreh" (Gen. 12:6), then to "the hill country on the east of Bethel" (Gen. 12:8), and then "by stages toward the Negeb" (Gen. 12:9), Pseudo-Eupolemus gives a much simpler itinerary: Abraham goes from Ur of the Chaldees to Phoenicia (εἰς Φοινίκην) and dwells there (κατοικῆσαι). This introduces the "Phoenician" section of Pseudo-Eupolemus's portrait of Abraham, where the patriarch is presented as *Kulturbringer* to the Phoenicians as well as military hero.

45. Living among the Phoenicians, Abraham teaches them "the movements of the sun and moon, and everything else as well" (τροπὰς ἡλίου καὶ σελήνης καὶ τὰ ἄλλα πάντα διδάξαντα τοὺς Φοίνικας, Frg. 1.4). Thus having learned (discovered?) Babylonian astrological science, Abraham transmits it to the Phoenicians. Pseudo-Eupolemus makes no mention of Abraham's transmitting knowledge of the alphabet to the Phoenicians (see Eupolemus, Frg. 1), although this may be implied

out this heroic picture of Abraham among the Phoenicians, Pseudo-Eupolemus gives his own version of the war between the four foreign kings, chief among them King Chedorlaomer of Elam, and the five kings of the regions around the Dead Sea, most notably Sodom and Gomorrah, as recorded in Gen. 14:1–12.[46] In Pseudo-Eupolemus's version, the Armenians wage war against the Phoenicians and capture Abraham's nephew in the process, which prompts Abraham to launch a rescue mission. Abraham thus emerges as the military hero who frees the Phoenicians from the control of the Armenians. Unlike the biblical account where Abraham defeats the army of Chedorlaomer with 318 trained men of his own household, Pseudo-Eupolemus's Abraham whips the Armenians assisted by nothing more than "his household servants." His attitude toward his defeated enemies also represents a variation of Gen. 14:21–24. Abraham emerges as generous and humane victor.

The Melchizedek episode of Gen. 14:17–20 also functions as part of the Phoenician segment, with the intriguing variation reporting Abraham's being generously received by "the city at the temple Argarizin."[47] The probable explanation is that Pseudo-Eupolemus has understood "King Melchizedek of Salem" to mean that this enigmatic "priest of God and king as well" exercises his sacerdotal functions at the Samaritan site of Mount Gerizim. This Pseudo-Eupolemus achieves by transferring the biblical descriptive title "of God Most High" to

---

in τὰ ἄλλα πάντα. In any case, as teacher of the Phoenicians, Abraham "gained the favor of the king" (εὐαρεστῆσαι τῷ βασιλεῖ).

This portrait of Abraham as cultural benefactor of the Phoenicians bears striking similarity to Artapanus's portrait of Abraham, Joseph, and Moses: Abraham taught the Egyptians astrology, Joseph introduced many inventions to Egypt that endeared him to the Egyptians, and Moses also introduced many useful inventions to the Egyptians, including philosophy. But unlike Artapanus, Pseudo-Eupolemus stresses Abraham's piety and devotion to God. Abraham's original pursuit of astrological learning either derives from, or leads to, his devotion to God; in either case, they are connected. Moreover, Abraham moves from Babylon to Phoenicia in response to God's commands. Like his biblical counterpart, Pseudo-Eupolemus's Abraham is fully obedient to God. When Pseudo-Eupolemus claims that Abraham taught the Phoenicians "movements of the sun and moon, and all other things," we are tempted to hear missionary overtones and to see Abraham being depicted as imparting to the Phoenicians religious knowledge — what he knows about God. But this is probably stretching it. No such explicit claim is made, and there is a sense in which Abraham is being presented as cultural benefactor to the Phoenicians in a purely secular sense, at least to this point.

46. In the biblical account, the four foreign kings, in capturing Sodom and Gomorrah, also capture Lot, Abraham's nephew, the event that prompts Abraham to gather his 318 trained men and launch a rescue operation against the enemy forces, in which he defeats the forces of Chedorlaomer and his allies (Gen. 14:13–17). Moreover, in the biblical account, Abraham's encounter with Melchizedek in Gen. 14:17–24 occurs as the sequel to Abraham's rescue of Lot and his defeat of the foreign kings.

47. In the biblical account, Abraham is welcomed by the king of Sodom at the Valley of Shaveh, identified as the King's Valley, and here "King Melchizedek of Salem," also identified as "priest of God Most High" (ἱερεὺς τοῦ θεοῦ τοῦ ὑψίστου), sets before him bread and wine and gives Abraham a blessing from the "God Most High," who is identified as "maker of heaven and earth" and the one responsible for Abraham's military victory. In response, Abraham gives Melchizedek "one-tenth of everything" (Gen. 14:20). Then the king of Sodom asks Abraham to hand over to him those whom he captured in battle while retaining the goods, i.e., the booty. Abraham responds that he swore before God to take nothing, not even thread or sandal thong, and insists on taking what his young men, and the other young men who had joined him, have eaten (Gen. 14:21–24).

the mountain site, thus his explanatory identification of the location as the "mountain of the God Most High." The biblical Melchizedek extends a blessing to Abraham from "God Most High," who is given credit for Abraham's victory, and in response Abraham gives Melchizedek a "tenth of everything." In Pseudo-Eupolemus, however, Abraham *receives* gifts from Melchizedek, a reversal effectively elevating Abraham to a status higher than Melchizedek. It is only fitting, however, for Abraham whose piety had earlier won approval from God now to receive honor from a king duly certified as a "priest of God," and to do so at his sacred site.[48]

The Egyptian stage in Pseudo-Eupolemus's portrait is also triggered by a famine (Gen. 12:10).[49] As before, Pseudo-Eupolemus aptly summarizes the biblical account (Gen. 12:10–20) in reporting that the Egyptian king married Sarah because Abraham had said she was his sister (Gen. 12:11–16), although he is more protective than the Bible in his assurance that the marriage was not consummated sexually. As in the biblical account, the king's actions result in dire consequences, prompting him to summon his diviners, who inform him of Sarah's true status. Pseudo-Eupolemus skips the biblical conclusion where Abraham is expelled from the country by Pharaoh (Gen. 12:18–20) and reports instead Abraham's stay in Heliopolis, where he lived with the Egyptian priests. As with the Phoenicians earlier, Abraham functions as *Kulturbringer* among the Egyptian priests, teaching them "many new things," but especially introducing them to "astrology and other such things." Among the Egyptian priests Abraham is keen to clarify the true origins of astrological science. While he and the Babylonians had discovered these things, the original discovery (εὑρηκέναι πρῶτον) he traces back to Enoch and "not the Egyptians."[50]

---

48. It is Pseudo-Eupolemus's treatment of this episode that has prompted his identification as a Samaritan author. But does it actually present a view of events that constitutes a Samaritan outlook? Not necessarily. True, Abraham is received favorably by the "city at the temple Argarizin," but if Melchizedek is identified with the sacred Samaritan site as its priest and king, he shows his gratitude on behalf of the city to Abraham. In this case, the Samaritan cult could be seen as owing its survival to the heroic feats of Abraham. Accordingly, they would be indebted to Abraham. Abraham emerges as their savior, the one who rescued them from the terrible onslaught of the Armenians, and they, in turn, through the actions of Melchizedek, acknowledge his heroic actions by showing their gratitude. In one sense, Pseudo-Eupolemus might be showing that the Samaritans owe the survival of their cult to the actions of Abraham, not that Abraham is relating to them approvingly. Thus it is not at all clear from this incident that the version of events narrated by Pseudo-Eupolemus is demonstrably "Samaritan" in outlook.

49. Pseudo-Eupolemus reverses the biblical order of events, where a famine prompts Abraham to journey to Egypt immediately after his travels in "the land of Canaan" (Gen. 12:10).

50. By this point, several claims have been made about the discovery of astrology. Earlier, its discovery is located firmly in Babylon, and Abraham is associated with its discovery, either as the prime agent or as a recipient of this knowledge. He is responsible for transmitting it first to the Phoenicians, then to the Egyptians. But by the end of the fragment, Pseudo-Eupolemus is keen to show that Abraham himself recognized that the discovery was actually earlier, having originated with Enoch, who, according to Genesis 5, was three generations earlier than Abraham. It would seem, then, that Pseudo-Eupolemus is less interested in presenting Abraham as the *first* discoverer of astrology than in portraying him as *Kulturbringer* first to the Phoenicians, then to the Egyptians.

The genealogical information at the end of the fragment, where Pseudo-Eupolemus introduces two traditions, one from the Babylonians, the other from the Greeks, has many puzzling features. Reconstructing his intended genealogical table is difficult because the connecting points are not always clear. Yet some things seem clear. The Babylonian genealogical tradition appropriately begins with Belus and proceeds by showing that the Phoenicians came next, followed by the Ethiopians and the Egyptians. What is significant is the order of the nations: Babylonians, Phoenicians, Ethiopians, and Egyptians. What "the Babylonians say" thus reinforces the order of Pseudo-Eupolemus's Abraham story, which may suggest that Pseudo-Eupolemus's portrait of Abraham has been constructed to fit Babylonian tradition.

The second genealogical tradition, what "the Greeks say," reinforces Pseudo-Eupolemus's final claim about Enoch. Accepting the Greek claim that Atlas discovered astrology, Pseudo-Eupolemus then identifies Atlas with the biblical figure Enoch. How he does this is not altogether clear, although he does mention the next link in the genealogy from Genesis 5 — Methuselah, who, we are told, "learned all things through the help of the angels of God." He concludes with the cryptic note, "and thus we gained our knowledge."[51]

Though Pseudo-Eupolemus does not elaborate further on Enoch, we can safely assume a knowledge of Enoch traditions comparable to what we find in *1 Enoch* 41–44 and 72–82, where Enoch is introduced to the mysteries of heaven, and 1QapGen 2:19–26.

Frg. 2, which is much shorter, also focuses exclusively on Abraham. Like Frg. 1, it traces Abraham's origins to "giants living in Babylonia," but it reverses the order of events reported in Frg. 1. In Frg. 1 the giants who survived the flood built the tower, which was destroyed by God's action, after which they scattered throughout the earth. In Frg. 2 the giants living in Babylonia were destroyed "by the gods" because of their wickedness. One of the giants, Belus, escaped and

---

51. How are the two genealogical traditions related? One possibility is that the Greek tradition is intended to supplement the Babylonian tradition, thereby providing the earlier stages of the genealogy. This would lend further support to the overall portrait, where Abraham finally introduces Enoch as the original discoverer of astrology. The Babylonian tradition supports the first part of the Abraham story — Abraham the Babylonian transmitting knowledge to the Phoenicians and the Greeks. The Greek tradition supports the second part — Abraham claiming that Enoch actually discovered astrology.

Yet one of the most intriguing features of these two genealogical traditions is the way other genealogical information is integrated. Belus is identified with the Greek mythical figure Kronos, who occupied an important role in Greek mythic accounts of cosmogony. Similarly, Cush is identified as the Greek figure Asbolus. Finally, the Greek mythic figure Atlas is identified with the biblical figure Enoch.

Ordinarily, Pseudo-Eupolemus's treatment of this genealogical information is understood as a bow to Euhemerism, the school of Greek thought that gave a rational account of the origin of the gods. According to this view, human beings who accomplished extraordinary things were elevated to divine status after their death. Accordingly, Pseudo-Eupolemus's efforts represent an attempt to synchronize genealogical information found in Genesis 5 and 10 with nonbiblical genealogical traditions. Even more, it represents a rationalizing move: mythical figures from Babylonian and Greek traditions are demythologized as they are brought into connection with the biblical genealogy.

came to dwell in Babylon where he built a tower and lived. The name of the tower is derived from Belus. Frg. 2 implies that Abraham originated in Babylon, where he learned astrology and thereafter transmitted this knowledge first to the Phoenicians, and finally to Egypt. In spite of some discrepant features between Frgs. 1 and 2, their common focus on Abraham, the circumstances surrounding his Babylonian origins, and his role as *Kulturbringer* to the Phoenicians and Egyptians suggest that they derive from the same work.

In spite of their brevity, the two Pseudo-Eupolemus fragments provide a fairly clear indication of the author's interests and his method of heroic characterization. He displays an openness to nonbiblical traditions comparable to, and in some ways even surpassing, Artapanus. He displays none of the chronographical interests that typified Demetrius and that were found in Eupolemus. The *Kulturbringer* topos is a critically important interpretive category for him as it was for Artapanus especially, but for Eupolemus as well. As with them, this topos functions in Pseudo-Eupolemus as a way of establishing respectability by setting Abraham on the world stage. In this case, the world stage has three loci: Babylon, Phoenicia, and Egypt. Abraham emerges as a prominent figure in each setting, exhibiting qualities of surpassing worth and performing deeds that set him apart from the citizens of each country. In both Phoenicia and Egypt he interacts with the king of each country, is found "well-pleasing" to one and supplies the wife for another, without serious repercussions. In both instances, he is defined over against religious authorities, receiving honors from the "priest and king" of one — Melchizedek — and living among the priests in the other. Abraham's native tradition, which is never really specified, proves to be superior to other native traditions because it is linked to earlier patriarchal figures, most notably Enoch and Methuselah.

Comparisons with Luke-Acts are obviously limited because of the brevity of the fragments. The most obvious points of contact are their respective treatments of Abraham. Like Pseudo-Eupolemus, Acts 7:2 locates Abraham in Mesopotamia and pushes the call of Genesis 12 back beyond Haran to the "country of the Chaldeans." But the portrait of Abraham in Acts 7:2–8 exhibits none of the syncretistic tendencies that are so prominent in Pseudo-Eupolemus. By contrast, Acts follows the biblical account much more closely, although like Pseudo-Eupolemus, Acts does more than simply summarize the biblical story. It too is informed by other motives, which are fairly clear.

There is a sense in which the literary tasks of Pseudo-Eupolemus and Acts are similar. As we noticed in Eupolemus, the world stage is conceived in rather broad terms. In this instance, it comprises Babylon, Phoenicia, and Egypt. As was the case with Eupolemus, there appear to be anachronistic concerns. The heightened interest in Phoenicia and Egypt, along with the role of the Armenians in the story, probably reflect the political realities of the Hellenistic period. Sketching Abraham as *Kulturbringer* to the Phoenicians and Egyptians of an earlier period obviously has benefits during a period when Seleucids and Egyptians are the dominant powers. Even so, Abraham is sketched as a cosmopolitan figure, interacting with kings and priests wherever he goes, winning favor and distinction along the way.

A similar conception of the world is shared by Luke-Acts, although Luke is less interested in depicting ancient biblical heroes in this way. Of greater concern is to portray Peter and Paul, especially Paul, in this way. There are some remarkable similarities between Pseudo-Eupolemus's portrait of Abraham and Luke's portrait of Paul. Pseudo-Eupolemus's template is *Kulturbringer*, whereas Luke's is not, but Luke is no less interested in demonstrating Paul's distinctive contribution as the transmitter of Israel's traditions to the nations.

Conclusion

Relating these antecedent Hellenistic Jewish traditions to Acts is complicated by a number of factors, not the least of which is their fragmentary form. Equally problematic is that we are twice removed from them. Distortions certainly occurred when they were first quoted by Alexander Polyhistor, and further distortion doubtless occurred when Eusebius abstracted them from Polyhistor. Even with all of the complexities of the textual tradition of Acts, we are still in the position of thinking about Acts as a single, comprehensive story supported by a unified textual tradition. Thus when we compare Acts with snippets from four separate authors, our perspectives are bound to be distorted. The partial state of the Hellenistic Jewish evidence thus inevitably renders our judgments partial.

This obviously affects the conclusions we draw. As we have seen, in the textual tradition as we have it, Demetrius contains numerous discrepancies from the biblical text. What we have from Demetrius convinces us that he was a close, careful reader of the Bible, and consequently we cannot imagine that such blatant mistakes could be his. And we confidently edit the texts accordingly. But in doing so, we may be clarifying a distorted picture. Are the errors traceable to Demetrius? to Polyhistor? or even, in some cases, to Eusebius? Dozens of such instances confront us in these texts, and at every turn, we must take this into account in our comparative work. Before we generalize about Artapanus's treatment of Abraham, Joseph, and Moses, and conclude that these were his heroes par excellence, we must remember that the survival of these three was purely accidental, nothing more.

Even though these texts are fragmentary, they appear to be representative enough of the larger works from which they survive to enable us to make some fairly confident judgments. We have enough of Artapanus to know that he had a different mind from Demetrius. They both read the Bible, but how they construed it and what they did with it are poles apart. We also have enough of Eupolemus and Pseudo-Eupolemus to draw similar conclusions. And in this respect, we are entirely justified in comparing these four authors with Acts, and such comparisons, as we have seen, can be quite informative. In some cases, they enable us to see what is distinctive about Acts even more clearly. In none of these four authors, for example, do we find anything approaching Luke's scheme of promise and fulfillment, even though they have already begun to conceptualize the biblical story in ways that the Bible itself does not. Yet we find genuine resonance between the way Luke envisions his aetiological myth and that of these four authors, in spite of their broad diversity. O'Neill is right to see connections between Acts and the form of heroic characterization we find in Artapanus, and to a lesser extent in Eupolemus and Pseudo-Eupolemus.[52] The prison-escape scene in Artapanus and Acts 12 presents a point of striking convergence and invites us to think about connections between these two authors, or the traditions they represent, in much more concrete terms. Such obviously similar use of a well-established literary topos should tell us something about literary conventions that Luke had at his disposal and perhaps even something about common features of their literary horizons.

---

52. O'Neill, *Theology of Acts*, 150, 152.

Chapter 8

"Opening the Scriptures"

The Legitimation of the Jewish Diaspora and the Early Christian Mission

Gregory E. Sterling

For one land does not hold the Jews since they are so numerous. For which reason they reside in many of the most desirable lands of Europe and Asia — both on islands and on the mainlands. Although they consider the sacred city in which the holy temple of the Most High God stands to be their mother city, each holds that the lands they have inherited from their parents, grandparents, great grandparents, and earlier ancestors are their home countries in which they were born and raised.

Philo, *Against Flaccus* 45–46

In his response to Christianity's first intellectual pagan critic, Origen argued that the gospel produces sages. As an example he cites a text from Acts: "Stephen, who undoubtedly took [this information] from old writings which have not become accessible to most, testifies to the great learning of Moses in the Acts of the Apostles. For he says: 'and Moses was educated in all of the wisdom of the Egyptians.'"[1] While the apologist is primarily concerned with Moses, his comments on Stephen are fascinating. What writings did Origen think Stephen had read? Is he remembering the descriptions of Moses' Egyptian education in Greek-speaking Jewish authors?[2] The possibility raises an important but overlooked body of material for understanding the longest and most difficult speech in Acts.

In what has become a classic essay on the speeches in Acts, Martin Dibelius put his finger on one of the key difficulties posed by the Stephen speech: "The irrelevance of most of this speech has for long been the real problem of exegesis.... From 7.2–34 the point of the speech is not obvious at all; we

---

1. Origen, *c. Celsum* 3.46. I have used the text in P. Koetschau, *Origines Werke*, vol. 1: *Die Schrift vom Martyrium, Buch I–IV Gegen Celsus*, GCS 2 (Leipzig: J. C. Hinrich, 1899). All translations are my own unless otherwise noted.

2. Ezekiel, *Exagoge* 36–38; Philo, *Moses* 1.20–24; Josephus, *Ant.* 2.236. Cf. also Artapanus Frg. 3 (Eusebius, *PE* 9.27.4). C. K. Barrett, *The Acts of the Apostles*, 2 vols., ICC (Edinburgh: T. & T. Clark, 1994–), 1:356, considers this a possibility.

are simply given an account of the history of Israel."[3] How does the story of Abraham, Joseph, and the detailed biographical material on Moses relate to the charges of 6:11, 13–14? One of the standard responses to textual incongruities such as this is to attribute the material to a source which the author has taken over but failed to contextualize fully. In the last half of the twentieth century, scholars have attempted to find the basis for the speech in a wide range of traditions that share common exegetical or thematic concerns. These include the Essenes,[4] the Nasaraioi,[5] the Samaritans,[6] a sectarian Jewish Christian sect,[7] Hellenistic Jewish homilies,[8] or a Christian version of a Hellenistic Jewish homily which has undergone a Deuteronomistic revision.[9] The fundamental difficulty

---

3. M. Dibelius, *Studies in the Acts of the Apostles* (New York: Charles Scribner's Sons, 1956), 167. Cf. the similar complaint of K. Lake and H. Cadbury in F. J. Foakes Jackson and K. Lake, *The Beginnings of Christianity: The Acts of the Apostles*, 5 vols. (London: Macmillan, 1920–33; reprint, Grand Rapids, Mich.: Baker Books, 1979), 4.69, and H. Conzelmann, *Acts of the Apostles*, Hermeneia (Philadelphia: Fortress, 1987), 57.

4. E.g., O. Cullmann, "The Significance of the Qumran Texts for Research into the Beginnings of Christianity," *JBL* 74 (1955): 213–26, esp. 220–24, and A. F. J. Klijn, "Stephen's Speech-Acts vii 2–53," *NTS* 4 (1957–58): 25–31. For a critique see H. Braun, *Qumran und das Neue Testament*, 2 vols. (Tübingen: J. C. B. Mohr [Paul Siebeck], 1966), 2.157–58, 181–83. Cf. also H. Ringgren, "Luke's Use of the Old Testament," *HTR* 79 (1986): 227–35, esp. 234–35, who appeals to CD 2.14–6.11 as a parallel use of the OT.

5. M. Simon, *St. Stephen and the Hellenists in the Primitive Church* (London: Longmans, Green, 1958), 78–97, esp. 90–94.

6. E.g., A. Spiro in J. Munck, *The Acts of the Apostles*, revised by W. F. Albright and C. S. Mann, AB 31 Garden City, N.Y.: Doubleday, 1967), 284–300; M. H. Scharlemann, *Stephen: A Singular Saint*, AnBib 34 (Rome: Pontifical Biblical Institute, 1968), 34–56; R. Scroggs, "The Earliest Hellenistic Christianity," in *Religions in Antiquity: Essays in Memory of Erwin Ramsdell Goodenough*, ed. J. Neusner, Studies in History of Religions 14 (Leiden: Brill, 1968), 176–206, who argues that the speech arose in the Hellenistic Christian mission to the Samaritans; L. Gaston, *No Stone on Another: Studies in the Significance of the Fall of Jerusalem in the Synoptic Gospels*, NovTSup 2 (Leiden: Brill, 1970), 155–61; C. H. H. Scobie, "The Origins and Development of Samaritan Christianity," *NTS* 19 (1973): 390–414; idem, "The Use of Source Material in the Speeches of Acts iii and vii," *NTS* 25 (1978–79): 399–421, who thought the sermon was the product of a Christian mission to Samaria; O. Cullmann, *The Johannine Circle* (Philadelphia: Westminster, 1975), 39–53, who argued for the origins in heterodox Judaism, which served as the nexus for both Acts 7 and the Gospel of John. Major critiques include: R. Plummer, "The Samaritan Pentateuch and the New Testament," *NTS* 22 (1976): 441–43, who answers Scobie; E. Richard, "Acts vii: An Investigation of the Samaritan Evidence," *CBQ* 39 (1977): 190–208; G. Schneider, *Die Apostelgeschichte*, 2 vols., HTKNT 5.1–2 (Freiburg, Basel, and Vienna: Herder, 1980–82), 1.448–52; and W. Litke, "Acts 7:3 and Samaritan Chronology," *NTS* 42 (1996): 156–60.

7. T. L. Donaldson, "Moses Typology and the Sectarian Nature of Early Christian Anti-Judaism: A Study in Acts 7," *JSNT* 12 (1981): 27–52, reprinted in *New Testament Backgrounds: A Sheffield Reader*, ed. C. A. Evans and S. Porter (Sheffield: Sheffield Academic Press, 1997), 230–52.

8. Dibelius, *Studies in the Acts of the Apostles*, 169; Ernst Haenchen, *The Acts of the Apostles: A Commentary* (Philadelphia: Westminster, 1971), 288–89; C. K. Barrett, "Old Testament History according to Stephen and Paul," in *Studien zum Text und zur Ethik des Neuen Testaments: Festschrift zum 80. Geburtstag von Heinrich Greeven*, ed. W. Schrage, BZNW 47 (Berlin: Walter de Gruyter, 1986), 66; idem, *The Acts of the Apostles*, 1:338. J. W. Bowker, "Speeches in Acts: A Study in Proem and Yellammedenu Form," *NTS* 14 (1967): 96–111, esp. 107, argues that Acts 7 is an example of a proem homily.

9. O. H. Steck, *Israel und das gewaltsame Geschick der Propheten: Untersuchungen zur Überlieferung des deuteronomistischen Geschichtsbildes im Alten Testament, Spätjudentum und Urchristentum*, WMANT 23 (Neukirchen-Vluyn: Neukirchener Verlag, 1967), 265–29, esp. 267; U. Wilckens, *Die*

with all source criticism in Acts is that the author has so completely rewritten all preexisting material that it is impossible to separate source from redaction on stylistic grounds. It is therefore predictable that a good number of other scholars have contended that the speech is a Lukan composition.[10] This has led them to attempt to find the unity of the speech and explain how it functions within the context. Responses range from accentuating the motif of Israel's rejection of God's representatives[11] to a positive emphasis on the Jewishness of Stephen,[12] and even to a tragic portrayal which demonstrates how the optimistic promises to Israel have failed to find fulfillment as a result of Israel's own opposition.[13]

I share the view that the speech is a Lukan composition; however, I think that the author may have had models for writing the speech. By model I do not mean that the author incorporated a preexisting source. Rather, I mean that the author knew narratives which retold the story of Israel in ways analogous to what we have in the speech. I will argue that these earlier retellings shaped the way that the author read and understood the LXX. Just as we do not read scripture in a vacuum today, neither did the author of Luke-Acts learn the LXX *tabula rasa.* The models I have in mind are the Hellenistic Jewish historians.

There are at least two reasons why on a priori grounds these neglected texts deserve to be considered. First, there is an *opinio communis* that the author of Acts was either a Hellenistic Jew or a God-fearer who had been attached to a Jewish synagogue. It is at least reasonable to examine texts which we know were associated with the Greek Diaspora. Second, a minimalist interpretation of Acts 6–7 associates Stephen with the Hellenists; a maximalist reading identifies him as one of the Hellenists.[14] If the author wanted to maintain any degree of verisimilitude, Stephen should speak like a Greek-speaking Jew. It is therefore

Missionsreden der Apostelgeschichte: Form- und traditionsgeschichtliche Untersuchungen, 3d ed., WMANT 5 (Neukirchen-Vluyn: Neukirchener Verlag, 1974), 208, 213–20; G. Schneider, "Stephanus, die Hellenisten und Samaria," in *Les Actes des Apôtres: Traditions, redaction, théologie,* ed. J. Kremer, BETL 48 (Louvain: Louvain University Press, 1979), 215–40, esp. 224–37; idem, *Die Apostelgeschichte,* 1:448. E. Larsson, "Temple Criticism and the Jewish Heritage: Some Reflections on Acts 6–7," NTS 39 (1993): 379–95, esp. 384–85, argues for a pre-Lukan Christianized version of a Hellenistic Jewish homily, but does not posit Deuteronomistic influence.

10. E.g., J. Bihler, *Die Stephanusgeschichte in Zusammenhang der Apostelgeschichte,* Münchener Theologische Studien 1.16 (Munich: Max Hueber, 1963), 86; J. Kilgallen, *The Stephen Speech: A Literary and Redactional Study of Acts 7,2–53,* AnBib 67 (Rome: Biblical Institute Press, 1976), 121–63, esp. 121, 163; E. Richard, *Acts 6:1–8:4: The Author's Method of Composition,* SBLDS 41 (Missoula, Mont.: Scholars Press, 1978), whose work has been significant for the formation of my own judgment; M. Sabbe, "The Son of Man Saying in Acts 7,56," in Kremer, *Les Actes des Apôtres,* 245–49; C. C. Hill, *Hellenists and Hebrews: Reappraising Divisions within the Earliest Church* (Minneapolis: Fortress, 1992), 67–101; and S. Légasse, *Stephanos: Histoire et discours d'Étienne dans les Actes des Apôtres,* LD 147 (Paris: Cerf, 1992), 149–77.

11. J. J. Kilgallen, "The Function of Stephen's Speech (Acts 7, 2–53)," *Bib* 70 (1989): 173–93, who does make a serious attempt to explain the relevance of Abraham (180), Joseph (181), and more weakly the expansive section on Moses (176); and E. Richard, "The Polemical Character of the Joseph Episode in Acts 7," *JBL* 98 (1979): 255–67.

12. E.g., D. D. Sylva, "The Meaning and Function of Acts 7.46–50," *JBL* 106 (1987): 269 n. 2.

13. R. C. Tannehill, "Israel in Luke-Acts: A Tragic Story," *JBL* 104 (1985): 79–81, who points to a number of reversals in the text (7:4 vs. 43; 7:7 vs. 42; 7:8 vs. 51).

14. On the identity of the Hellenists as Greek-speaking Jews from the Diaspora see M. Hengel,

quite reasonable to look in the direction of Hellenistic Jewish authors to see if
we can determine how their retellings of the LXX might have served as a model
for the Stephen speech.[15]

The Legitimation of the Jewish Diaspora

Jews in the Diaspora faced issues that their compatriots in Judea and Jerusalem
did not. One of the most significant was the establishment of their identity in
a place removed from the Temple. What did lifelong separation from the center of Judaism mean for their identity as Jews? For most the issue was not an
either/or decision (i.e., either Jerusalem was or was not the center of Jewish
life), but a both/and (i.e., Jerusalem was the center of Judaism and yet residence in the Diaspora did not diminish Jewish identity). This was not an issue
which a Diaspora Jew who reflected on Jewish identity could dodge. It is worth
pointing out that both of the major literary representatives of Greek-speaking
Judaism addressed it. Philo confronted it while the Temple was standing. His
response was to present the Jews scattered throughout the empire as a single
nation, united on the grounds of religion: Jerusalem with the Temple was the
mother city ("metropolis"), and the Diaspora consisted of colonies. He wrote of
Jerusalem: "She is, as I have said, my native city, the mother city not of one
country, Judea, but of a great many others as a result of the colonies which she
has sent out at different times. . . . "[16] Josephus, writing after the destruction of
the Temple, faced a slightly different issue: how important was the land for Jewish identity? His response was to downplay the significance of land theology in
his retelling of Israel.[17] Both writers insisted on full Jewish identity for those living in the Diaspora. There were other ways in which the same case could be
made.[18] The most important for our purposes was the attempt to legitimize life

---

Between Jesus and Paul: Studies in the Earliest History of Christianity (Philadelphia: Fortress, 1983),
4–11.

15. There have been some attempts to take these authors into account, most notably R. Pervo,
Profit with Delight: The Literary Genre of the Acts of the Apostles (Philadelphia: Fortress, 1987), 115–21,
and my *Historiography and Self-Definition: Josephos, Luke-Acts, and Apologetic Historiography,* NovTSup
64 (Leiden: Brill, 1992), 363–65. M. Soards, *The Speeches in Acts: Their Content, Context, and Concerns* (Louisville: Westminster/John Knox, 1994), 157–60, points to the importance of the material,
but does not develop it.

16. Philo, *Embassy* 281. For an exposition of Philo's views see H. A. Wolfson, *Philo: Foundations of
Religious Philosophy in Judaism, Christianity, and Islam,* 2 vols. (Cambridge: Harvard University Press,
1947), 2.241–48, 396–426, and H.-J. Klauck, "Die heilige Stadt: Jerusalem bei Philo und Lukas,"
KAIROS 28 (1986): 129–51.

17. B. Halpern-Amaru, "Land Theology in Josephus' *Jewish Antiquities*," *JQR* 71 (1980): 201–29,
and idem, *Rewriting the Bible: Land and Covenant in Post-biblical Jewish Literature* (Valley Forge, Pa.:
Trinity Press International, 1994), 95–115, 165–69.

18. Some authors spiritualized the sacrifices, e.g., Philo. Cf. V. Nikiprowetzky, "La spiritualization
des sacrifices et le culte sacrificiel au temple de Jérusalem chez Philon d'Alexandrie," *Semitica* 17
(1967): 97–116, reprinted in *Études philoniennes*, Patrimoines Judaïsme (Paris: Cerf, 1996), 79–96.

in the Diaspora by making connections between Israel's early heroes and locales in the Diaspora.[19]

Cleodemus Malchus

The first example of this approach is a fragment attributed to a Cleodemus the prophet, surnamed Malchus, which Alexander Polyhistor cited, from whom Josephus in turn quoted in his *Antiquities* (1.239–41), from whom Eusebius extracted the material in his *Praeparatio evangelica* (9.20.2–4).[20] That Polyhistor cited it provides our only firm evidence for dating: it was prior to c. 50 B.C.E. While some have disputed the Jewish identity of the author, the appeal to Abraham makes more sense for a Jewish or Samaritan author than for any other. Since the fragment claims to deal with the Jews, I prefer to think of a Jewish author.[21]

The fragment relates an ethnographic genealogy of Abraham's descendants through Keturah. According to Cleodemus, Abraham and Keturah had three sons who each became the founder of an important locale: Sures of Assyria, Iapheras of Africa, and Iaphras of the city of Ephra (presumably a city in Africa).[22] The two African colonists, Iapheras and Iaphras, fought with Heracles against Libya and Antaeus, the Libyan giant.[23] The alliance between Jews and Greeks was sealed when Heracles married the daughter of Iaphras from which union came the later kings of Libya. The Greek mythological hero is thus connected to Abraham.

---

19. N. Walter, *Fragmente jüdisch-hellenistischer Historiker*, 2d ed., Jüdische Schriften aus hellenistisch-römischer Zeit 1.2 (Gütersloh: Gerd Mohn, 1980), 117, has also recognized the practice. More recently B. Bar-Kochva, *Pseudo-Hecataeus: Legitimizing the Jewish Diaspora*, Hellenistic Culture and Society 21 (Berkeley: University of California Press, 1996), 232–48, has argued that Pseudo-Hecataeus made a similar case by appealing to the migration of Jews to Egypt under the leadership of Hezekias the priest. I have not included Pseudo-Hecataeus since the appeal is not to an ancient hero.

20. For these fragments I have used the edition of C. R. Holladay, *Fragments from Hellenistic Jewish Authors*, vol. 1: *Historians*, SBLTT 20 (Chico, Calif.: Scholars Press, 1983), 245–59. For recent discussions see Walter, *Fragmente jüdisch-hellenistischer Historiker*, 115–20; R. Doran, "The Jewish Hellenistic Historians before Josephus," ANRW 2.20.1 (1987): 255–57; and E. Gruen, *Heritage and Hellenism: The Reinvention of Jewish Tradition*, Hellenistic Culture and Society 30 (Berkeley: University of California Press, 1998), 151–53.

21. Frg. 1 (Josephus, *Ant.* 1.240); Frg. 2 (Eusebius, PE 9.20.3). For the arguments with bibliography see Holladay, *Fragments from Hellenistic Jewish Authors*, 1.245–46, 248–49.

22. There are a number of problems with the orthography of the names and their identifications. The names of the three sons vary in Josephus and Eusebius: Iepheras, Sures, and Iaphras (Josephus, *Ant.* 1.241 [Frg. 1A]); Apher, Assouri, and Aphran (Eusebius, PE 9.20.3 [Frg. 1B]). According to Gen. 25:1–4, Abraham and Keturah had six sons: Zemran, Ieksan, Madan, Madiam, Iesbok, and Soue (LXX). The second son, Ieksan, had three sons including a son named Daidan who in turn begat five sons including Assouriim. The fourth son, Madiam, had five sons including Gaipha and Apher. Josephus, *Ant.* 1.238–41, has a slightly different genealogy. He informs us that the sixth son, Soue (=Souos in Josephus), had two sons including Dadanes, who in turn had three sons including Assouris. The three sons named in Cleodemus Malchus appear to be Soue (the sixth son in the LXX), Gaipha (Abraham's grandson through Madiam, the fourth son in the LXX), and Apher (Abraham's grandson through Madiam, the fourth son in the LXX).

23. Cf. Diodorus Siculus 1.21.4; 1.24.1; 4.17.4–5; Plutarch, *Sertorius* 9.4–5, for the tradition. For a discussion see Holladay, *Fragments from Hellenistic Jewish Authors*, 1.258–59 n. 15.

Why interweave Greek mythology and biblical figures in order to make Abraham the ancestor of the Assyrians and Carthaginians? While the fragment is too brief to permit firm conclusions, we can draw some reasonable conclusions about the geographical interests. The fragment has a distinct geographical focus: it associates Abraham with Libya. Three pieces of evidence support this conclusion. First, Libya is the central geographical location in the fragment. We might wonder whether the larger text was just as concerned with Assyria since it is also mentioned. I am skeptical that it was. The reference to Assyria is due to the genealogical connection between Sures and Assouris.[24] The reference was too obvious to pass; however, the text that we have only mentions it in passing. The fulcrum of the fragment is Libya. Second, the fragment probably comes from Polyhistor's Λιβυκά rather than his Περὶ Ἰουδαίων since Josephus failed to name it and Eusebius, who consistently lifted material from Polyhistor, cited Josephus rather than the Roman when he quoted it.[25] This suggests that the work that Alexander Polyhistor cited dealt principally with Libya; otherwise he would have most likely cited it in his work Περὶ Ἰουδαίων as he did other Jewish works. Third, Josephus introduced the fragment in this way: "It is reported that this Heophren [=Iapheras] campaigned against Libya and occupied it. His grandsons took up residence in it and named it Africa after his name."[26] The historian corroborates his interpretation by citing the fragment. He understood that the fragment related the *origo* of Jews in Libya.

The limited evidence that we have suggests that the work dealt with the Jewish community in Libya. Why? Was it to enlarge the figure of Abraham as a *Kulturbringer* by associating him with yet another locale, even if through his descendants?[27] While I think that this purpose must play some role since it is a ubiquitous feature of such works, it is worth pointing out that Abraham and his descendants are not credited with any specific cultural contributions in this fragment. This leads me to ask whether we should nuance our reading of this fragment to accentuate what the text does affirm, namely the founding of the Jewish community in Libya — perhaps Carthage in particular — through the migration of Abraham's descendants.[28] If this was turned *ad extra* it must have

---

24. The relationship of Abraham to the Assyrians varies in the tradition: in the LXX Assouriim is Abraham's grandson through Daidan (Gen. 25:3); in Josephus, Assouris is Abraham's great grandson through Souos and Dadanes (*Ant.* 1.238); in Eusebius, Assouri is Abraham's son through Keturah (PE 9.20.3).

25. So also Walter, *Fragmente jüdisch-hellenistischer Historiker*, 115; Holladay, *Fragments from Hellenistic Jewish Authors*, 1.245; and Doran, "The Jewish Hellenistic Historians before Josephus," 256. For the Λιβυκά, see F. Jacoby, *Die Fragmente der griechischen Historiker*, 3 vols. in 16 pts. (Leiden: Brill, 1923–69), no. 273, Frgs. 32–47.

26. Josephus, *Ant.* 1.239.

27. For a provocative statement supporting this perspective see Gruen, *Heritage and Hellenism*, 152–53.

28. So also Walter, *Fragmente jüdisch-hellenistischer Historiker*, 116. Holladay, *Fragments from Hellenistic Jewish Authors*, 1.246, lists both Samaria and Carthage as possible locales for the author, although he appears to incline to the latter. Doran, "The Jewish Hellenistic Historians before Josephus," 256, prefers Carthage.

functioned apologetically: the Jews were not newcomers to the city but ancient residents whose associations reach back as far as the fabled Hellenistic founding myths. If it was addressed *ad intra* it must have been an attempt to build self-identity: the Jewish community had a right to be there since the community was founded by a direct descendant of Abraham. In either case it appears to offer legitimation for the Jewish community in Libya by associating their origins with an ancestor.

Pseudo-Eupolemus

The second example consists of the first and third fragments which Eusebius cited from Polyhistor's work (*PE* 9.17.1–9; 9.18.2).[29] Polyhistor attributes the first to Eupolemus and the third to some anonymous writings in spite of the similarity between the two. The agreements demonstrate that the two belong together, although the specific relationship is a point of debate.[30] Fortunately for our purposes we need only posit that they attest a work composed sometime prior to Polyhistor, probably in the early second century B.C.E.[31] It is certain that they do not come from Eupolemus since they have an explicit orientation away from Jerusalem and toward Samaria (see below). The author is therefore anonymous and as we will see, probably a Samaritan.

These fragments concentrate on Abraham who is cast in the role of a *Kulturbringer*, a common depiction of an ancient ancestor in apologetic historiography. Drawing on only Frg. 1, we may summarize the material as follows. Abraham was born in the tenth generation after the tower of Babel in Camerine (=Ur). After he learned astrology, God instructed him to migrate to Phoenicia where he enlightened the inhabitants by teaching them astrology. Following a rout of the Armenians who had invaded Phoenicia, Abraham was honored by Melchizedek at Mount Gerizim. He then made his way to Egypt where, after recovering his wife from a lustful but innocently ignorant Pharaoh, he offered the Egyptian priests instruction in astrology. The fragment ends with a genealogy which situates the Phoenicians and Egyptians in the biblical material.

The fragments have a distinct double-edged geographical orientation. On the one hand, there is a pronounced bias in favor of Samaritan concerns. The first hint appears in the consistent use of "Phoenicia" for Canaan. This appears to reflect the Samaritans' proximity to and ties with the Phoenicians.[32] The hint becomes an open claim when we are told that Abraham was entertained "by

---

29. For the text see Holladay, *Fragments from Hellenistic Jewish Authors*, 1.157–87. Cf. also Walter, *Fragmente jüdisch-hellenistischer Historiker*, 137–43; Doran, "The Jewish Hellenistic Historians before Josephus," 270–74; Sterling, *Historiography and Self-Definition*, 187–206; and Gruen, *Heritage and Hellenism*, 146–50.

30. For details see my *Historiography and Self-Definition*, 191–93.

31. Ibid., 190–91.

32. So also Walter, *Fragmente jüdisch-hellenistischer Historiker*, 138, and Holladay, *Fragments from Hellenistic Jewish Authors*, 1.181 n. 13. For the tie see Josephus, *Ant.* 11.344 and 12.260. The Samaritans claimed to be Sidonians.

the city at the temple Argarizin which is interpreted 'mountain of the Most High.' "[33] Given the polemical nature of the rival claims for temple sites, it is difficult to overlook the Samaritan insistence on Gerizim as the sacred site. This is reinforced by the implicit identification of Argarizin with Salem (versus Salem = Jerusalem) when the fragment states that Melchizedek honored Abraham (at Argarizin).[34] While the identification of Salem varied in the tradition — a fact that made the debate about its identity problematic — the specific identification of it with Mount Gerizim is an explicit Samaritan claim. I find it difficult to think that anyone other than a Samaritan (or perhaps, a proto-Samaritan) would make such an identification.[35] Finally, the fragment rearranges the order of the biblical text by placing the story of Gen. 14:1–24 (PE 9.17.4–6) before that of Gen. 12:10–20 (PE 9.17.6–8). This has the effect of giving priority to Phoenicia over Egypt. On the other hand, this priority points to the negative polemic in the fragment. The critique becomes explicit in the concluding genealogy when Canaan is presented as the father of the Phoenicians and of Mizraim, who is the father of the Egyptians. The Egyptians are thus one step behind the Phoenicians in culture and one generation behind in age.

Why make this case? The polemical nature of the geographical data suggests that there is a political aspect to the argument: the Seleucids are favored over the Ptolemies. The fragments also make cultural claims: some think that Pseudo-Eupolemus used pagan material as confirmation of the biblical tradition, others that he demythologized the pagan material polemically, and still others that he accentuated the superiority of the Jews.[36] There is another dimension to the fragments as well, the geographical aspect. Like Cleodemus Malchus, this work addresses the issue of the *origo* of a specific people: Abraham came to Phoenicia (not Canaan or Judea), and more specifically to the temple at Mount Gerizim. What can this be but an argument for the legitimation of the Samaritan community who wanted to anchor their roots in the story of their ancestors?

Artapanus

The third example is the most extensive and most significant. We have three fragments from Artapanus, all preserved by Polyhistor.[37] In this instance we may know more of the full work since the fragments are internally linked by means

---

33. Frg. 1 (Eusebius, *PE* 9.17.5).
34. Frg. 1 (Eusebius, *PE* 9.17.6).
35. As opposed to Gruen, *Heritage and Hellenism*, 147–48.
36. For a summary with bibliography see ibid, 149–50.
37. Holladay, *Fragments from Hellenistic Jewish Authors*, 1.189–243; Walter, *Fragmente jüdisch-hellenistischer Historiker*, 121–36; idem, "Jüdisch-hellenistische Literatur vor Philo von Alexandrien (unter Ausschluß der Historiker)," *ANRW* 2.20.1 (1987): 98–99; Doran, "The Jewish Hellenistic Historians before Josephus," 257–63; Sterling, *Historiography and Self-Definition*, 167–86; and Gruen, *Heritage and Hellenism*, 150–51 (Frg. 1), 87–89 (Frg. 2), 155–60 (Frg. 3).

of transitional genealogical introductions and end with a summary statement.[38] Like the two preceding works we can only date this work with certainty between the two known termini: the LXX and Polyhistor. Since the focus of the fragments is unambiguously on Egypt, the author was probably an Egyptian Jew.

The first fragment is a brief recapitulation of the career of Abraham in Egypt. Like Pseudo-Eupolemus, Artapanus claims that Abraham taught the Egyptians astrology. The second fragment celebrates the career of Joseph who, since he cannot be a *Kulturbringer* in the sense that he brings culture from one civilization to another, is cast as an "inventor" or "discoverer." The greatest panegyric, however, is reserved for Moses in Frg. 3. The Jewish legislator is presented as the "discoverer" of many features of Egyptian civilization. The fragment is extensive enough that we could call it a short "romance." Artapanus draws on not only the biblical text, but more significantly the traditions of heroes of other civilizations whose careers are paralleled and exceeded by Moses.

As in the other two examples noted, the geographical focus is unambiguous. In this instance it is on Egypt, which is evident in a number of ways. It cannot be an accident that Artapanus has selected the careers of the three Hebrew ancestors who were active in Egypt. In the case of Abraham, Artapanus has made his orientation quite clear by only discussing — if Polyhistor has not misled us by his condensation — Abraham's activities in Egypt. This is reinforced by the fact that the Moses fragment appears to end with the crossing of the Red Sea, marking the departure from Egypt as the terminus of the story. The only statements that follow this final scene are a brief note about the manna during the forty years in the wilderness and a description of Moses built on Deut. 34:7. Since this text marks the end of the Torah, it probably had a similar function for Artapanus.[39] Within these limits, Artapanus has expanded the biblical material to underscore the Jewish presence in Egypt. In the case of Abraham he has done this in two ways: he claims that Abraham spent twenty years in Egypt and that some of his retinue remained in Egypt when he returned to Syria. The latter is a clear apologetic claim attempting to extend the Jewish residence in Egypt to the earliest possible period. Philo of Alexandria makes the same claim in one of his apologetic treatises.[40] It is another example of the *origo* motif. In the cases of Joseph and Moses Artapanus has again expanded the biblical narrative by making them the founders of all that is worthwhile in Egyptian civilization, even Egyptian religion!

There is a consensus that Artapanus wrote *ad maiorem Iudaeorum gloriam*. While it is possible that he wrote in order to rebut defamatory presentations such as those of Manethon, I think it more probable that he wrote for a Jewish audience; at least there is no evidence that pagans read Jewish works in this

---

38. Frg. 2 (Eusebius, *PE* 9.23.1) and Frg. 3 (Eusebius, *PE* 9.27.1–3, esp. 1). For the concluding summary see Frg. 3 (Eusebius, *PE* 9.27.37).

39. Cf. Walter, *Fragmente jüdisch-hellenistischer Historiker,* 122, 123.

40. Philo, *Hypothetica* (Eusebius, *PE* 8.6.1).

period. But why would he write such a story for the Jewish community? Artapanus offered a history of the Jews in Egypt as a means of providing Egyptian
Jews with a sense of identity. Jews living in Egypt had an illustrious past, a past
which was in no way inferior to that of other nations. He demonstrated this by
incorporating the traditions of other national heroes. The combination of Jewish
and foreign traditions showed how Jews could integrate into the larger society
without forfeiting their own identity. In this way he legitimated the Egyptian
Diaspora.

Summary

These three Greek-speaking Jews/Samaritans of the Diaspora share a number
of perspectives and techniques. They all used the biblical stories about their
ancestors as a basis for creative stories about the origins of their respective communities. Why? Each lays claim to cultural superiority for the Jewish people as
a means of developing a healthy identity. Their effort is evident in the incorporation and subordination of non-Jewish traditions within the ancestral stories.
At the same time, they did not make these claims globally, but within specific
geographical limits. The use of the *origo* motif and the focus on specific locales
suggests that each of these authors wanted to legitimate their own community's
existence. They did this by anchoring their past in the lives of their most illustrious heroes. The specific focus did not negate the legitimation of other Jewish
communities, but validated their own. The community had a legitimate right
to exist in a foreign land where they were not cultural inferiors, but equals or
superiors to the people around them.

The Legitimation of the Early Christian Mission in Acts 7

How do these texts illuminate the Stephen speech? Or to frame the question
more specifically: How does the understanding of ancient Jewish history in these
Hellenistic Jewish historians explicate the understanding of Jewish history in
Acts 7? Before we can answer the question we need to explore the possibility
that the author of Acts knew Hellenistic Jewish interpretative traditions. While
this will not determine whether the author used the traditions we have sketched,
it will assist us in weighing the probability of such a use.

Hellenistic Jewish Exegetical Traditions in the Stephen Speech

The Stephen speech is a learned recitation of select sections of the LXX. In order
to clarify the relation between the speech and the biblical text on the one hand
and to Hellenistic Jewish interpretations of the LXX on the other, I have set the
evidence out in an appendix. When there is a clear citation of the LXX I have
set the text of Acts 7:2–50 in bold font. When the speech paraphrases the LXX,

I have italicized the text. Otherwise I have noted the appropriate references in the LXX and in Hellenistic Jewish authors. I have only listed Hellenistic Jewish authors when they and the speech of Acts agree in disagreeing with the LXX. I do not intend to suggest that the author of Acts knew these specific works, but that the author of Acts and these Hellenistic Jews knew and used similar exegetical traditions when they retold the LXX. There are eight noteworthy examples, although not all of these are of equal weight.

1. Acts suggests that God appeared to Abram (ὤφθη τῷ πατρὶ ἡμῶν Ἀβραάμ) in Mesopotamia (Acts 7:2). The LXX does not support this; rather Gen. 12:1 reads: καὶ εἶπεν κύριος τῷ Αβραμ. The phrase in Acts comes from Gen. 12:7 when Abram was in Canaan. The author may have paraphrased Gen. 12:1 with a phrase that he considered synonymous or confused the two incidents. It is worth noting that Philo of Alexandria makes the same move: he cites Gen. 12:7 in association with the initial call rather than the later event. This could be a coincidental exegetical agreement; however, there are other agreements in the same context.

2. It is well-known that the author of Acts telescoped the call of Abram by locating it in Ur (Acts 7:2) rather than in Haran where the LXX places it (Gen. 11:27–12:3). This was a fairly well-known tradition in Hellenistic Jewish authors: Pseudo-Eupolemus, Philo, and Josephus all attest it. Since there is nothing in the biblical text that requires the rearrangement, it is likely that the tradition was the lens by which many Jews read or heard the text, including the author of Acts.

3. There is a third agreement in connection with the call of Abraham. Acts tells us that Abraham left Haran after the death of Terah (Acts 7:4). This, however, stands in tension with the chronological information in the LXX. According to the latter, Terah was 70 when Abram was born (Gen. 11:26). Abram was 75 when he set out for Canaan (Gen. 12:4), making Terah 145. Since Terah died in Haran at 205 years of age (Gen. 11:32), he lived 60 years after Abram left. Those who have argued for the Samaritan origin of the speech have been quick to point out that the Samaritan Pentateuch says that Terah died at 145 years of age or when Abram left Haran. This might well be a Palestinian text tradition. There is, however, another possibility. Philo makes the same argument: "It is likely that no one who is well-read in the sacred laws is ignorant of the fact that Abraham first left the land of Chaldea and then resided in Haran and after his father died he also transferred from that country. . . ."[41] It may be that both Philo and the author of Acts either made a simple narrative assumption without doing the arithmetic made possible by the hints in the text[42] or that they drew on a common tradition that had already made this assumption.

4. The Joseph material contains some phenomena similar to what we found

---

41. Philo, *Migration* 177.

42. So Barrett, "Old Testament History according to Stephen and Paul," 61, and Litke, "Acts 7:3 and Samaritan Chronology," 159.

in the Abraham traditions. As with Abraham's call, the author of Acts collapses the story of Joseph's entry into Egypt by dropping all mention of the Ishmaelites / Midianites and simply affirming that the brothers sold Joseph into Egypt (Acts 7:9). Demetrius condenses the story in the same way. This could either be an example of a common attempt to compress a much larger story or a common report of a tradition which had already condensed the text.

5. Acts claims that God gave Joseph not only grace but σοφία (Acts 7:10), a quality never ascribed to Josephus in the LXX. Philo and Joseph likewise emphasize Joseph's σοφία. The ubiquity of such a virtue in the Hellenistic world is sufficient to explain its appearance in all three authors.

6. The agreements in the Moses material are more significant. Acts alters the birth story of Moses in two ways: it omits any reference to the Egyptian midwives and uses the language of exposure (ἐκτίθημι) to describe the fate of Jewish children and Moses (Acts 7:19, 21). The same alterations appear in Ezekiel and Philo, who also omit any reference to the midwives and use the language of exposure (ὑπεκτίθημι [Ezekiel] and ἐκτίθημι, ἔκκειμαι [Philo]). There seems to have been a tradition among Hellenistic Jews in Egypt that recast the birth story of Moses to reflect the well-known practice of exposure.

7. The most obvious instance of dependence is the education of Moses. Like Ezekiel, Philo, and Josephus, Acts emphasizes Moses' Egyptian education (Acts 7:22). This runs counter to some of the Semitic presentations of Moses, which emphasize his Hebrew education.[43] Since Origen knew Philo's works and through Philo's library may have known Ezekiel, he could have had such writings in mind when he made his comments on Acts 7.[44]

8. The author of Acts uses a well-known schema to describe Moses' early years: ἐγεννήθη...ἀνετράφη...ἐπαιδεύθη (Acts 7:20–22), a schema he will use again in connection with Paul (Acts 22:3). This is a standard encomiastic pattern which is widely attested.[45] It is, however, worth noting that Philo uses the same pattern in regard to Moses. He summarized the first treatise in his *Life of Moses* in the preface to the second treatise with these words: "The former treatise dealt with the birth (γένεσις) of Moses and his upbringing (τροφή), also with his education (παιδεία) and office as ruler (ἀρχή)...."[46] It is likely that Hellenistic Jews commonly used standard encomiastic patterns to present their ancestral heroes.

It thus appears that there is evidence to think that the author of Acts knew Hellenistic Jewish traditions about the call of Abraham and the Egyptian career of Moses. The Joseph material is too inconclusive to be persuasive. While these do not exhaust the possible traditions the author knew, they at least point to the

---

43. E.g., *Jub.* 47:9.
44. Origen, *c. Celsum* 3.46. See the opening paragraph.
45. For details see W. C. van Unnik, *Tarsus or Jerusalem: The City of Paul's Youth* (London: Epworth, 1962), 18–27.
46. Philo, *Moses* 2.1.

presence of a common body of exegetical traditions in Greek-speaking Jewish circles.[47]

The Legitimation of the Diaspora

But does the author know and use traditions that make claims of legitimation for locales outside Jerusalem and Judea? There is one clear use of an exegetical tradition and one intriguing possibility of a pattern that made such a claim. The speech relates the death and burial of not only Jacob, but of his sons: "And Jacob went down into Egypt and died, he and our fathers. They were brought to Shechem and placed in the tomb that Abraham bought for a sum of silver from the sons of Hamor in Shechem" (Acts 7:15–16).[48] This narrative stands in tension with the LXX in several details. According to the LXX, Jacob was buried near Hebron (Gen. 49:29–32; 50:13) not in Shechem. Jacob, not Abraham, purchased land in Shechem from the sons of Hamor (Gen. 33:18–20); Abraham purchased a burial plot near Hebron from Ephron (23:1–20). Why the confusion in Acts? According to the LXX, Joseph was buried in Shechem in the plot of land Jacob purchased from the sons of Hamor (Josh. 24:32). Perhaps the author of Acts confused burial traditions.[49] While this is possible, it is important to note a well-known tradition that situates the burial of Joseph's brothers in Hebron.[50] Josephus even claims that the tomb could be seen in his day.[51] The claim that they were buried in Shechem may therefore be a rival claim. Those who have argued for a Samaritan background to the speech have understandably pointed to the importance of Shechem for the Samaritans. This is a quite reasonable appeal even though we do not know of a Samaritan text which makes this identification; however, it is another matter to claim that the larger speech has an underlying Samaritan source.[52] This draws too much from too little. What we can say is that Acts 7:15–16 is the earliest evidence for the tradition attested in later texts which locates the tomb of Jacob's sons in Shechem.[53] The tradition probably had its origins among the Samaritans who used it as a counter to the

---

47. Another noteworthy pattern is the parallel between Acts 7:36 and the *Assumption of Moses* 3.11.

48. The most helpful analysis of this material is still J. Jeremias, *Heiligengräber in Jesu Umwelt (Mt. 23,29; Lk. 11,47): Eine Untersuchung zur Volksreligion der Zeit Jesu* (Göttingen: Vandenhoeck & Ruprecht, 1958), 36–38.

49. So Barrett, *The Acts of the Apostles,* 1.351.

50. E.g., *Jub.* 46:9–10; *T. Reuben* 7:1–2; *T. Levi* 19.5; *T. Judah* 26.4; *T. Issachar* 7.8; *T. Zebulon* 10.7; *T. Dan* 7.2; *T. Naphtali* 7.1–3; *T. Gad* 8.3; *T. Asher* 8.1–2; *T. Benjamin* 12.1–4; Josephus, *War* 4.530–32; *Ant.* 2.199.

51. Josephus, *War* 4.532.

52. Scobie, "The Use of Source Material in the Speeches of Acts iii and vii," 409, goes so far as to claim that Shechem as the site of the true sanctuary "gives the historical section of Acts 7 a remarkable and hitherto unnoticed underlying unity." This unity was unnoticed because it does not exist.

53. For the later Christian tradition see Jerome, *Ep.* 57.10; Syncellus, p. 284 (Dindorf).

Judean tradition that the twelve were buried in Hebron.[54] The competitive traditions of the Judeans and Samaritans demonstrate that each vied to legitimate
their sacred site through the geographical details of the sacred story.

There is one other possibility, although it is more tenuous. It is worth noting
that the rehearsal of Israel's early history in Acts 7 selects the same material
and same balance of material as we find in Artapanus. That is to say that the
three fragments of Artapanus which deal with Abraham (Frg. 1), Joseph (Frg. 2),
and Moses (Frg. 3) are paralleled here by the careers of Abraham (Acts 7:2–8),
Joseph (Acts 7:9–16), and Moses (Acts 7:17–43). Just as Abraham and Joseph
are preliminary to the main presentation of Moses in Artapanus, so the account
in Acts 7 expands the Moses traditions beyond the more cursory retellings of
the earlier figures. The result is that both authors focus on Egypt, although Acts
is far less exclusive than Artapanus. As I have already indicated, I do not want
to imply that the author of Acts knew Artapanus — although I do consider this
a possibility on larger grounds — but that the author of Acts knew retellings of
Israel which concentrated on the history of the Jews in Egypt.[55]

The Legitimation of the Early Christian Mission

Why would the author incorporate both a tradition arguing for the legitimacy
of Shechem as a sacred site and a history of the Jews in Egypt which probably
argued for the legitimacy of Egyptian Judaism? I suggest that the author wanted
to argue for the legitimacy of the Christian mission beyond Jerusalem and drew
from the histories of Hellenistic Jews, who had already made similar geographical arguments. The author of Acts differs from the traditions we have examined
in at least one important aspect: the Hellenistic Jewish authors legitimated specific communities; the author of Acts legitimated a mission which transcended
the Temple and Jerusalem. What they share is that they all accomplish their
legitimations by making connections between Israel's ancestral heroes and geographical locales beyond the immediate vicinity of the Temple and homeland.
For all of these texts it is not a matter of either the Temple/Jerusalem or the
Diaspora, but of both the Temple/Jerusalem and the Diaspora. The use of the
same strategy to make this both/and case argues for the dependence of Acts on
the established Jewish Diaspora tradition.

Acts does this by emphasizing God's dealings with Israel away from the

---

54. One of the most sane assessments of this material is F. S. Spencer, *The Portrait of Philip in
Acts: A Study of Roles and Relations,* JSNTSup 67 (Sheffield: Sheffield Academic Press, 1992), 70–81.

55. This is quite different than the old Alexandrian source theory. See B. W. Bacon, "Stephen's
Speech: Its Argument and Doctrinal Relationship," in *Biblical and Semitic Studies: Critical and His-
torical Essays by the Members of the Semitic and Biblical Faculty of Yale University* (New York: Charles
Scribner's Sons, 1901), 213–76; W. Soltau, "Die Herkunft der Reden in der Apostelgeschichte,"
ZNW 4 (1903): 144–46; and more recently, L. W. Barnard, "Saint Stephen and Early Alexandrian
Christianity," NTS 7 (1960/1961): 31–45, who argues for the influence of Acts 7 on the *Epistle of
Barnabas.*

Temple.[56] We see this in a number of ways. There is a greater preoccupation with the concept of land (γῆ) here than anywhere else in Luke-Acts: nine of the fifty-seven uses of the term in the two volumes are clustered here. Nor are the references restricted to Israel (7:3, 4): they refer to Chaldea (7:3, 4), Egypt (7:6, 36, 40), and Midian (7:29, 33). Events are situated in the following locales:

Locale	Coverage in Text
Mesopotamia	7:2–3
Haran	7:4a–c
This land	7:4d–5, 7d–e, 11b–12a, 14, 45–50
Egypt	7:6, 9–11a, 12b–13, 15, 17–28, 35–36c
Shechem	7:16
Midian	7:29–34
Wilderness	7:36d–44

More important, the Stephen speech emphasizes God's dealings with Israel's heroes away from the Temple and surrounding area. If we restrict our survey to the explicit statements, we find the following: God appeared to Abraham in Mesopotamia (7:2); God did not give Abraham a single foot of ground in the homeland (7:5), making Abraham the first Jew without a homeland; God was with Joseph in Egypt (7:9); and God appeared to Moses in the form of the angel in Midian (7:30, 35). Even more telling is the treatment of "place" (τόπος). The term appears in both the charges leveled against Stephen and the speech proper. It occurs in the accusations where it denotes the Temple (6:13, 14). In the speech proper it surfaces three times. The first is the promise to Abraham, which combines Gen. 15:13–14 with Exod. 3:12. The author alters the citation of the latter by replacing "mountain" with "place," thus changing the reference from Mount Horeb to the Temple (Acts 7:7). This appears to run counter to the *Tendenz* we have noted of locating activities outside the land.[57] It does fit quite nicely with the broader assessment of the Temple in Luke-Acts as a sacred place. However, the next time a reference to Sinai occurs, the Stephen speech permits Horeb to stand as the "place" (Exod. 3:5). God said to Moses: "Loose the sandals from your feet, for the place (τόπος) where you are standing is sacred land (γῆ ἁγία)" (Acts 7:33). This recalls the language of the charge that Stephen spoke "against this holy place (κατὰ τοῦ τόπου τοῦ ἁγίου [τούτου])" (Acts 6:13).

---

56. This has been noted by a number of scholars, e.g., Gaston, *No Stone on Another,* 156–57; W. D. Davies, *The Gospel and the Land: Early Christianity and Jewish Territorial Doctrine* (Berkeley: University of California Press, 1974; reprint, Sheffield: JSOT, 1994), 267–74, esp. 269–72; Schneider, "Stephanus, die Hellenisten und Samaria," 234; F. F. Bruce, "Stephen's Apologia," in *Scripture: Meaning and Method (Essays Presented to Anthony Tyrell Hanson for His Seventieth Birthday)* (Pickering: Hull University Press, 1987), 40; K. Haacker, "Die Stellung des Stephanus in der Geschichte des Urchristentums," *ANRW* 2.26.2 (1995): 1535–40; and Donaldson, "Moses Typology and the Sectarian Nature of Early Christian Anti-Judaism," 236. As opposed to Larsson, "Temple-Criticism and the Jewish Heritage," 385–88, 392–94.

57. A. J. McNicol, "Rebuilding the House of David: The Function of the Benedictus in Luke-Acts," *Restoration Quarterly* 40 (1998): 35–37, makes the intriguing suggestion that the place refers to the Jerusalem church. I am not sure that we should assign an eschatological meaning to the biblical citations in this context.

The implication is that there is more than one holy place.[58] This is confirmed by the third use of the term at the end of the sermon in the Isaiah citation: "Heaven is my throne, the earth is the footstool of my feet. What house will you build for me, says the Lord? Or what is the place (τόπος) of my rest?" (Acts 7:49). The point is that God cannot be confined to a single holy place: the Temple is holy, but so is Mount Sinai.

The Stephen speech was not the first to make such arguments. The Hellenistic Jewish historians had been making similar arguments for several centuries. The author of Acts used these retellings as models to argue a new case, that is, the Christian mission. For his Jewish predecessors the heroes of ancient Israel demonstrated God's dealings outside the land where the Temple would one day stand. For the author of Acts they served as a means of legitimating a mission beyond territory where the Temple once stood. It therefore makes perfectly good sense to retell the story of Israel's earliest heroes when confronting the issue of expansion beyond the Temple and its environs.

The Legitimation of the Early Christian Mission in Luke-Acts

This is not the first time in Luke-Acts that the author has used this hermeneutical strategy. In the inaugural sermon of Jesus in Luke 4:16–30, Jesus appealed to Elijah and Elisha as a warrant for his activities in Capernaum since true to the aphorism, "no prophet is acceptable in his own hometown," the residents of Nazareth rejected him (Luke 4:23–27). Most interpreters also understand the references to point beyond the immediate context to anticipate the later Gentile mission.[59] In both cases, Jesus' mission in Capernaum and the Gentile mission, the appeal is to ancient geography: Elijah journeyed to the widow of Zarepath in Sidon, and Elisha healed Naaman who came from Syria. Just as in Acts 7, the appeal is to ancient figures — here appropriately prophets. Whether the prophet moved beyond the borders of Israel or a foreigner came to Israel from the outside, the point is the same: the mission of Christianity cannot be restricted geographically.

The author of Luke-Acts was, however, careful where he[60] situated the mission in the story. There are several hints in Luke that suggest the author deliberately withheld the Gentile mission until Acts. First, it is well-known that the "Bethsaida section" of Mark (6:45–8:26) is missing where we would ex-

---

58. As opposed to Larsson, "Temple Criticism and the Jewish Heritage," 388.

59. L. C. Crockett, "Luke 4:25–27 and Jewish-Gentile Relations in Luke-Acts," *JBL* 88 (1969): 177–83, argued that the text also anticipated Jewish-Gentile relations. While these are logically presupposed by the Gentile mission, the point of the text is the extension of the prophetic mission beyond Israel.

60. The author uses the masculine gender in self-reference (Luke 1:3). I use the masculine gender as a means of replicating the claim of the implied author.

pect it between Luke 9:17 and 18. Some have argued that the third evangelist had a different edition of Mark than the canonical version we now have.[61] I find this difficult to accept since the material is thoroughly Markan and was known to Matthew. I think that it is more likely that the third evangelist has deliberately excised it, perhaps for several reasons.[62] One of these was the concern to limit the geographical extent of Jesus' mission. By dropping this material, Jesus remained in Galilee. The third evangelist did not need Mark 7:1–23 with its justification of the Gentile mission; he held this until Acts 10:1–11:18. Second, the third evangelist omitted the charge that Jesus spoke against the Temple at his trial (Mark 14:58 // Matt. 26:61 // John 2:19) in Luke 22:66, 67. Why? The evangelist knew that the Jewish Temple was linked to the question of the early Christian mission. He therefore held the charge until Acts 6:14 where he addressed it in the following speech. Such evidence suggests that Acts — at least in rough form — was already planned when Luke was composed. This means that the two-volume work was planned as a single work in two parts rather than two separate works or a first independent work with a sequel.[63]

If this is correct, the Stephen speech assumes an important position in Luke-Acts: it stands on the cusp where Jewish Christianity and Gentile Christianity meet. We should therefore read the speech of Stephen as a suprahistorical speech, that is, as a speech which is designed to justify not Stephen as an individual martyr, but Stephen as a representative of the early Christian mission. Or to put it in the specific terms of the Acts narrative, the speech is an attempt to legitimate the early Christian mission in the four major narratives that directly follow it in the transitional section of Acts (8:4–12:25).[64] Taking the geographical comments in Acts 1:8 as a rough guide to the structure of the work, the work falls into three major units: 2:1–8:3, Jerusalem; 8:4–12:25, Judea and Samaria; 13:1–28:31, the ends of the earth. The section on Judea and Samaria is set off in several ways. First, Acts 8:1 echoes 1:8 as a means of signaling the transition from Jerusalem to Judea and Samaria. Lest we forget the geographical orienta-

---

61. The most important recent advocate of this view is H. Koester, *Ancient Christian Gospels: Their History and Development* (London: SCM; Philadelphia: Trinity Press International, 1990), 284–86.

62. For a summary of some options with bibliography see J. A. Fitzmyer, *The Gospel according to Luke*, 2 vols., AB 28, 28A (Garden City, N.Y.: Doubleday, 1981–85), 1.770–71.

63. As opposed to M. C. Parsons and R. I. Pervo, *Rethinking the Unity of Luke and Acts* (Minneapolis: Fortress, 1993), who provide the most important recent challenge to the standard view.

64. See also Dibelius, *Studies in the Acts of the Apostles,* 169–70, for the function of Acts 7, and pp. 138, 140, 169 where he deals with the broader phenomenon; Klijn, "Stephen's Speech," 26, who argues that it reflects a mission within the orb of Judaism, not the later Gentile mission; Haenchen, *The Acts of the Apostles,* 289; Davies, *The Gospel and the Land,* 272, who understands it to address the relationship between Christianity and Judaism; Donaldson, "Moses Typology and the Sectarian Nature of Early Christian Anti-Judaism," 234, who thinks that it introduces and defends the mission to the Samaritans and Diaspora Judaism; Bruce, "Stephen's Apologia," 40, who calls it a manifesto of Hellenistic Christianity; and Barrett, *The Acts of the Apostles,* 1.340, who thinks that it addresses the relationship between Christianity and Judaism.

tion of the work, we are reminded again in 9:31. Second, the unit is marked by a framing device: just as the section on Jerusalem ended in persecution including the death of a significant martyr (Stephen), so does the Judean-Samaritan section (James).

There is, however, a difference between the way the two martyr stories function: the Stephen story serves as a closing marker and sets up the next four narratives; the James story only serves as a closing marker. This is clear from the intertextual connections between the Stephen story and the four major narrative strands that flow from it. The first is connected in the person of Philip (Acts 8:4–40) who was one of the seven (Acts 6:5). The second is connected through the person of Saul (Acts 9:1–30) who was an accomplice to Stephen's violent death (Acts 7:58; 8:1, 3). When the narrative relating Saul's Damascus experience begins, it recalls the events surrounding Stephen's death (ὁ δὲ Σαῦλος ἔτι ἐμπνέων ἀπειλῆς [Acts 9:1]). When Saul returned to Jerusalem, he debated Stephen's former opponents in the synagogue (Acts 9:29; cf. 6:9–10). Lest any doubt remain, the author has Paul make the connection between Stephen's death and his call/conversion explicit in a later speech (Acts 22:20–21). The third narrative strand (9:32–11:18) recounts the activities of Peter, who began an itinerant mission (διέρχομαι in 9:32 as in 8:4). Eventually a report of his activities found its way back to those who had remained in Judea (11:1; cf. 8:1). The fourth narrative strand (Acts 11:19–30) has an explicit transition statement which connects the activities of the missionaries with Stephen's death (Acts 11:19). In this way we understand that all of the succeeding narratives are grounded in the Stephen episode. How? I suggest that the speech constitutes the argument for the legitimation of the actions in these narratives. It may even be that the reference to Shechem anticipates the Samaritan mission and the Egyptian orientation anticipates the Ethiopian eunuch. Whether such specific associations are present or not, the general orientation is clear.

If this is correct, then it also has implications for two other issues relating to the speech: the place of the Temple and the anti-Judaism of the speech. Does the Stephen speech sound a more critical note than the remainder of Luke-Acts vis-à-vis the Temple? The traditional answer has been yes.[65] In recent years several have challenged this view, arguing that the speech makes the case that the Christian mission transcends the Temple, but does not reject it.[66] If I am correct about the use of the Abraham, Joseph, and Moses traditions, then the speech is not intended to reject the Temple but to qualify it by arguing that just as Judaism could extend beyond the Temple, so could Christianity. This in turn means that the geographical aspect of the speech — including the comments on

65. For contemporary examples of this view see Bruce, "Stephen's Apologia," 40, 48, and Barrett, *The Acts of the Apostles,* 1.373–76.

66. E.g., Sylva, "The Meaning and Function of Acts 7:46–50," 261–75, and F. D. Weinert, "Luke, Stephen, and the Temple in Luke-Acts," *BTB* 17 (1987): 88–90.

the Temple — is not anti-Jewish.[67] It is, rather, Judaism extended geographically and ethnically.

Conclusions

The Stephen speech permits us an opportunity to peer behind the Christianity of the author of Acts into the world of Judaism which nourished him. Probably a Diaspora Jew, the author learned to understand the LXX through earlier retellings — whether histories or homilies — which created a perspective by which he read the scriptures. One of these lenses was the legitimacy of life under God outside the land of Israel. The strategy this took was the association of an ancestral hero with the geographical area in which the Diaspora community resided. I have suggested that the author knew of at least Samaritan and Egyptian Jewish models for such an understanding, although I am suspicious on a priori grounds that he knew more. This hermeneutic offered a biblical warrant for the early Christian mission beyond Jerusalem. Rather than puzzling over the relevance of Acts 7:2–34, we should realize that it has been placed in the narrative at a critical point. It demonstrates that the mission was in harmony with God's dealings with the ancestors, who offer a warrant for a geographically unlimited mission. It also reminds us that the two-volume work we call Luke-Acts was carefully planned and written.

---

67. I have not dealt with all aspects of the speech, e.g., the christological dimension. I have deliberately restricted my comments to the geographical dimension. I first presented this as a paper to the Luke and Acts Group of the Society of Biblical Literature in November 1997. I want to thank the members of the group and the guests whose comments and questions contributed to the final draft of this contribution.

EXEGETICAL TRADITIONS IN ACTS 7:2-50

Acts 7:2–50	LXX Verbal Citation/ Paraphrase	LXX Story as Basis	Greek-Speaking Jewish Texts That Share a Common, Divergent Tradition
2 Ἄνδρες ἀδελφοὶ καὶ πατέρες, ἀκούσατε. Ὁ θεὸς τῆς δόξης	Ps. 28:3		
ὤφθη τῷ πατρὶ ἡμῶν Ἀβραὰμ ὄντι ἐν τῇ Μεσοποταμίᾳ πρὶν ἢ κατοικῆσαι αὐτὸν ἐν Χαρράν	Gen. 12:7		Philo, Abr. 77; Pseudo-Eupolemus Frg. 1 (=PE 9.17.3–4); Philo, Abr. 60–88, esp. 72; Josephus, Ant. 1.154
3 καὶ εἶπεν πρὸς αὐτόν· ἔξελθε ἐκ τῆς γῆς σου καὶ [ἐκ] τῆς συγγενείας σου, καὶ δεῦρο εἰς τὴν γῆν ἣν ἄν σοι δείξω.	Gen. 12:1		
4 τότε ἐξελθὼν ἐκ γῆς Χαλδαίων κατῴκησεν ἐν Χαρράν.	Gen. 11:31		
κἀκεῖθεν μετὰ τὸ ἀποθανεῖν τὸν πατέρα αὐτοῦ μετῴκισεν αὐτὸν εἰς τὴν γῆν ταύτην εἰς ἣν ὑμεῖς νῦν κατοικεῖτε,		Cf. Gen. 11:32 Gen. 12:5	Philo, Migra. 177
5 καὶ οὐκ ἔδωκεν αὐτῷ κληρονομίαν ἐν αὐτῇ οὐδὲ βῆμα ποδὸς	Deut. 2:5		
καὶ ἐπηγγείλατο δοῦναι αὐτῷ εἰς κατάσχεσιν αὐτὴν καὶ τῷ σπέρματι αὐτοῦ μετ' αὐτόν,	Gen. 17:8; 48:4		
οὐκ ὄντος αὐτῷ τέκνου.		Gen. 15:2; cf. 11:30	

6 ἐλάλησεν δὲ οὕτως ὁ θεὸς ὅτι
ἔσται τὸ σπέρμα αὐτοῦ πάροικον
ἐν γῇ ἀλλοτρίᾳ
καὶ δουλώσουσιν αὐτὸ
καὶ κακώσουσιν ἔτη τετρακόσια·
7 καὶ τὸ ἔθνος ᾧ ἐὰν δουλεύσουσιν
κρινῶ ἐγώ,
ὁ θεὸς εἶπεν, —
καὶ μετὰ ταῦτα ἐξελεύσονται
καὶ λατρεύσουσίν μοι ἐν τῷ τόπῳ τούτῳ.
8 καὶ ἔδωκεν αὐτῷ διαθήκην περιτομῆς·
καὶ οὕτως ἐγέννησεν τὸν Ἰσαὰκ
καὶ περιέτεμεν αὐτὸν τῇ ἡμέρᾳ τῇ ὀγδόῃ,
καὶ Ἰσαὰκ τὸν Ἰακώβ,
καὶ Ἰακὼβ τοὺς δώδεκα πατριάρχας.
9 Καὶ οἱ πατριάρχαι ζηλώσαντες τὸν Ἰωσὴφ
ἀπέδοντο εἰς Αἴγυπτον.
καὶ ἦν ὁ θεὸς μετ' αὐτοῦ
10 καὶ ἐξείλατο αὐτὸν ἐκ πασῶν τῶν θλίψεων αὐτοῦ
καὶ ἔδωκεν αὐτῷ χάριν καὶ σοφίαν
ἐναντίον Φαραὼ βασιλέως Αἰγύπτου
καὶ κατέστησεν αὐτὸν ἡγούμενον ἐπ' Αἴγυπτον
καὶ [ἐφ'] ὅλον τὸν οἶκον αὐτοῦ.
11 ἦλθεν δὲ λιμὸς ἐφ' ὅλην τὴν Αἴγυπτον
καὶ Χανάαν
καὶ θλῖψις μεγάλη,
καὶ οὐχ ηὕρισκον χορτάσματα οἱ πατέρες ἡμῶν.
12 ἀκούσας δὲ Ἰακὼβ ὄντα σιτία εἰς Αἴγυπτον
ἐξαπέστειλεν τοὺς πατέρας ἡμῶν πρῶτον.

Gen. 15:13–14; cf. Exod. 2:22

Gen. 15:14
Exod. 3:12

Gen. 17:10–11

Gen. 21:1–4
Gen. 25:24–26
Gen. 29:31–30:24

Gen. 37:11

Gen. 37:25–28, 36

Gen. 39:2, 3, 21, 23

Gen. 39:1–41:46

Gen. 39:21
Gen. 41:43, 41
Gen. 45:8; Ps. 104:21

Gen. 41:53–57
Gen. 42:5
Gen. 41:57

Gen. 42:1

Gen. 42:1–28

Demetrius Frg. 2 (=PE 9.21.11)

Philo, Ios. 106;
Josephus, Ant. 2.87

EXEGETICAL TRADITIONS IN ACTS 7:2-50

Acts 7:2–50	LXX Verbal Citation/ Paraphrase	LXX Story as Basis	Greek-Speaking Jewish Texts That Share a Common, Divergent Tradition
13 καὶ ἐν τῷ δευτέρῳ ἀνεγνωρίσθη Ἰωσὴφ τοῖς ἀδελφοῖς αὐτοῦ	Gen. 45:1	Gen. 43:1–44:34	
καὶ φανερὸν ἐγένετο τῷ Φαραὼ τὸ γένος [τοῦ] Ἰωσήφ.		Gen. 45:16	
14 ἀποστείλας δὲ Ἰωσὴφ	Gen. 45:27		
μετεκαλέσατο Ἰακὼβ τὸν πατέρα αὐτοῦ καὶ πᾶσαν τὴν συγγένειαν		Gen. 45:9–13, 21–24, 27	
ἐν ψυχαῖς ἑβδομήκοντα πέντε.		Gen. 46:27; Exod. 1:5	
15 καὶ κατέβη Ἰακὼβ εἰς Αἴγυπτον	Gen. 46:3; Deut. 26:5	Gen. 46:1–7	
καὶ ἐτελεύτησεν αὐτὸς καὶ οἱ πατέρες ἡμῶν,		Gen. 49:33 Gen. 50:26; Exod. 1:6	
16 καὶ μετετέθησαν εἰς Συχὲμ καὶ ἐτέθησαν ἐν τῷ μνήματι		Josh. 24:32	
ᾧ ὠνήσατο Ἀβραὰμ τιμῆς ἀργυρίου παρὰ τῶν υἱῶν Ἑμμὼρ ἐν Συχέμ.		Gen. 49:29–32; 50:13; cf. 23:16–20; 33:19	
17 Καθὼς δὲ ἤγγιζεν ὁ χρόνος τῆς ἐπαγγελίας ἧς ὡμολόγησεν ὁ θεὸς τῷ Ἀβραάμ,		Cf. Exod. 2:24	
ηὔξησεν ὁ λαὸς καὶ ἐπληθύνθη ἐν Αἰγύπτῳ	Exod. 1:7; cf. Gen. 47:27		

18 ἄχρι οὗ ἀνέστη βασιλεὺς ἕτερος
[ἐπ' Αἴγυπτον]
ὃς οὐκ ᾔδει τὸν Ἰωσήφ.
19 οὗτος κατασοφισάμενος τὸ γένος ἡμῶν
ἐκάκωσεν τοὺς πατέρας [ἡμῶν]
τοῦ ποιεῖν τὰ βρέφη ἔκθετα αὐτῶν
εἰς τὸ μὴ ζῳογονεῖσθαι.
20 Ἐν ᾧ καιρῷ ἐγεννήθη Μωϋσῆς
καὶ ἦν ἀστεῖος τῷ θεῷ·
ὃς ἀνετράφη μῆνας τρεῖς ἐν τῷ οἴκῳ τοῦ πατρός,
21 ἐκτεθέντος δὲ αὐτοῦ

ἀνείλατο αὐτὸν ἡ θυγάτηρ Φαραὼ
καὶ ἀνεθρέψατο αὐτὸν ἑαυτῇ εἰς υἱόν.
22 καὶ ἐπαιδεύθη Μωϋσῆς
[ἐν] πάσῃ σοφίᾳ Αἰγυπτίων,

NOTE: ἐγεννήθη...ἀνετράφη...ἐπαιδεύθη
ἦν δὲ δυνατὸς ἐν λόγοις καὶ ἔργοις αὐτοῦ.
23 Ὡς δὲ ἐπληροῦτο αὐτῷ τεσσερακονταετὴς χρόνος,
ἀνέβη ἐπὶ τὴν καρδίαν αὐτοῦ
ἐπισκέψασθαι τοὺς ἀδελφοὺς αὐτοῦ
τοὺς υἱοὺς Ἰσραήλ.
24 καὶ ἰδών τινα ἀδικούμενον
ἠμύνατο καὶ ἐποίησεν ἐκδίκησιν τῷ καταπονουμένῳ
πατάξας τὸν Αἰγύπτιον.
25 ἐνόμιζεν δὲ συνιέναι τοὺς ἀδελφοὺς [αὐτοῦ] ὅτι
ὁ θεὸς διὰ χειρὸς αὐτοῦ δίδωσιν σωτηρίαν αὐτοῖς·
οἱ δὲ οὐ συνῆκαν.

Exod. 1:8

Exod. 1:9–22

Exod. 2:2
Cf. Exod. 2:3

Exod. 2:5
Exod. 2:10

Exod. 2:11

Exod. 2:11–12

Ezekiel, Exagoge 12–13, 16;
Philo, Mos. 1.8, 10, 11, 14

Ezekiel, Exagoge 16;
Philo, Mos. 1.10, 11, 14

Ezekiel, Exagoge 36–38;
Philo, Mos. 1.20–24;
Josephus, Ant. 2.236;
cf. Artapanus Frg. 3 (PE 9.27.4)
Cf. Philo, Mos. 2.1

EXEGETICAL TRADITIONS IN ACTS 7:2-50

Acts 7:2-50	LXX Verbal Citation/ Paraphrase	LXX Story as Basis	Greek-Speaking Jewish Texts That Share a Common, Divergent Tradition
26 τῇ τε ἐπιούσῃ ἡμέρᾳ ὤφθη αὐτοῖς μαχομένοις καὶ συνήλλασσεν αὐτοὺς εἰς εἰρήνην εἰπών· ἄνδρες, ἀδελφοί ἐστε· ἱνατί ἀδικεῖτε ἀλλήλους; 27 ὁ δὲ ἀδικῶν τὸν πλησίον ἀπώσατο αὐτὸν εἰπόν· **τίς σε κατέστησεν ἄρχοντα καὶ δικαστὴν ἐφ᾽ ἡμῶν;**		Exod. 2:13–14	
28 μὴ ἀνελεῖν με σὺ θέλεις ὃν τρόπον ἀνεῖλες ἐχθὲς τὸν Αἰγύπτιον;	Exod. 2:14		
29 ἔφυγεν δὲ Μωϋσῆς ἐν τῷ λόγῳ τούτῳ καὶ ἐγένετο πάροικος ἐν γῇ Μαδιάμ, οὗ ἐγέννησεν υἱοὺς δύο.		Exod. 2:15 Exod. 2:21–22	
30 Καὶ πληρωθέντων ἐτῶν τεσσεράκοντα ὤφθη αὐτῷ ἐν τῇ ἐρήμῳ τοῦ ὄρους Σινᾶ **ἄγγελος ἐν φλογὶ πυρός βάτου.** 31 ὁ δὲ Μωϋσῆς ἰδὼν ἐθαύμαζεν τὸ ὅραμα, προσερχομένου δὲ αὐτοῦ κατανοῆσαι ἐγένετο φωνὴ κυρίου·	Exod. 3:2	Exod. 3:2–4	
32 ἐγὼ ὁ θεὸς τῶν πατέρων σου, ὁ θεὸς Ἀβραὰμ καὶ Ἰσαὰκ καὶ Ἰακώβ. ἔντρομος δὲ γενόμενος Μωϋσῆς οὐκ ἐτόλμα κατανοῆσαι.	Exod. 3:15, 16	Exod. 3:6	

33 εἶπεν δὲ αὐτῷ ὁ κύριος·	Exod. 3:5
λῦσον τὸ ὑπόδημα τῶν ποδῶν σου,	
ὁ γὰρ τόπος ἐφ᾽ ᾧ ἕστηκας γῆ ἁγία ἐστίν.	
34 ἰδὼν εἶδον τὴν κάκωσιν τοῦ λαοῦ μου	
τοῦ ἐν Αἰγύπτῳ καὶ τοῦ στεναγμοῦ αὐτῶν ἤκουσα,	Exod. 3:7
καὶ κατέβην ἐξελέσθαι αὐτούς·	Exod. 3:8
καὶ νῦν δεῦρο ἀποστείλω σε εἰς Αἴγυπτον.	Exod. 3:10
35 Τοῦτον τὸν Μωϋσῆν ὃν ἠρνήσαντο εἰπόντες·	Exod. 2:14
τίς σε κατέστησεν ἄρχοντα καὶ δικαστήν;	
τοῦτον ὁ θεὸς [καὶ] ἄρχοντα καὶ λυτρωτὴν	
ἀπέσταλκεν σὺν χειρὶ ἀγγέλου	
τοῦ ὀφθέντος αὐτῷ ἐν τῇ βάτῳ.	
36 οὗτος ἐξήγαγεν αὐτοὺς	
ποιήσας τέρατα καὶ σημεῖα	Exod. 3:2
ἐν γῇ Αἰγύπτῳ	Exod. 3:10, 11, 12
καὶ ἐν ἐρυθρᾷ θαλάσσῃ	Exod. 7:3; Deut. 34:11
καὶ ἐν τῇ ἐρήμῳ ἔτη τεσσεράκοντα.	Exod. 14:15–31
NOTE: ἐν γῇ Αἰγύπτῳ... καὶ ἐν ἐρυθρᾷ θαλάσσῃ...	Num. 14:33
καὶ ἐν τῇ ἐρήμῳ	
37 οὗτός ἐστιν ὁ Μωϋσῆς ὁ εἴπας τοῖς υἱοῖς Ἰσραήλ·	
προφήτην ὑμῖν ἀναστήσει ὁ θεὸς	Deut. 18:15
ἐκ τῶν ἀδελφῶν ὑμῶν ὡς ἐμέ.	
38 οὗτός ἐστιν ὁ γενόμενος ἐν τῇ ἐκκλησίᾳ	
ἐν τῇ ἐρήμῳ μετὰ τοῦ ἀγγέλου τοῦ λαλοῦντος αὐτῷ	
ἐν τῷ ὄρει Σινᾶ καὶ τῶν πατέρων ἡμῶν,	
ὃς ἐδέξατο λόγια ζῶντα δοῦναι ἡμῖν,	
39 ᾧ οὐκ ἠθέλησαν ὑπήκοοι γενέσθαι	
οἱ πατέρες ἡμῶν,	
ἀλλὰ ἀπώσαντο καὶ ἐστράφησαν	
ἐν ταῖς καρδίαις αὐτῶν εἰς Αἴγυπτον	Num. 14:3

Ass. Mos. 3.11

EXEGETICAL TRADITIONS IN ACTS 7:2–50

Acts 7:2–50	LXX Verbal Citation/ Paraphrase	LXX Story as Basis	Greek-Speaking Jewish Texts That Share a Common, Divergent Tradition
40 εἰπόντες τῷ Ἀαρών· ποίησον ἡμῖν θεοὺς οἳ προπορεύσονται ἡμῶν· ὁ γὰρ Μωϋσῆς οὗτος, ὃς ἐξήγαγεν ἡμᾶς ἐκ γῆς Αἰγύπτου, οὐκ οἴδαμεν τί ἐγένετο αὐτῷ.	Exod. 32:1		
41 καὶ ἐμοσχοποίησαν ἐν ταῖς ἡμέραις ἐκείναις καὶ ἀνήγαγον θυσίαν τῷ εἰδώλῳ καὶ εὐφραίνοντο ἐν τοῖς ἔργοις τῶν χειρῶν αὐτῶν.		Exod. 32:4, 8	
42 ἔστρεψεν δὲ ὁ θεὸς καὶ παρέδωκεν αὐτοὺς λατρεύειν τῇ στρατιᾷ τοῦ οὐρανοῦ καθὼς γέγραπται ἐν βίβλῳ τῶν προφητῶν· μὴ σφάγια καὶ θυσίας προσηνέγκατέ μοι ἔτη τεσσεράκοντα ἐν τῇ ἐρήμῳ, οἶκος Ἰσραήλ; 43 καὶ ἀνελάβετε τὴν σκηνὴν τοῦ Μόλοχ καὶ τὸ ἄστρον τοῦ θεοῦ [ὑμῶν] Ραιφάν, τοὺς τύπους οὓς ἐποιήσατε προσκυνεῖν αὐτοῖς, καὶ μετοικιῶ ὑμᾶς ἐπέκεινα Βαβυλῶνος.	Amos 5:25–27	Deut. 17:3	
44 Ἡ σκηνὴ τοῦ μαρτυρίου ἦν τοῖς πατράσιν ἡμῶν ἐν τῇ ἐρήμῳ καθὼς διετάξατο ὁ λαλῶν τῷ Μωϋσῇ ποιῆσαι αὐτὴν κατὰ τὸν τύπον ὃν ἑωράκει·		Exod. 27:21, etc. Exod. 25:40	
45 ἣν καὶ εἰσήγαγον διαδεξάμενοι οἱ πατέρες ἡμῶν μετὰ Ἰησοῦ ἐν τῇ κατασχέσει τῶν ἐθνῶν, ὧν ἐξῶσεν ὁ θεὸς ἀπὸ προσώπου τῶν πατέρων ἡμῶν ἕως τῶν ἡμερῶν Δαυίδ,		Josh. 3:14; 18:1 Deut. 7:1, 22	

46 ὃς εὗρεν χάριν ἐνώπιον τοῦ θεοῦ
καὶ ᾐτήσατο εὑρεῖν σκήνωμα τῷ οἴκῳ Ἰακώβ.
47 Σολομῶν δὲ οἰκοδόμησεν αὐτῷ οἶκον.

48 ἀλλ᾽ οὐχ ὁ ὕψιστος ἐν χειροποιήτοις κατοικεῖ,

καθὼς ὁ προφήτης λέγει·
49 ὁ οὐρανός μοι θρόνος,
ἡ δὲ γῆ ὑποπόδιον τῶν ποδῶν μου·
ποῖον οἶκον οἰκοδομήσετέ μοι, λέγει κύριος,
ἢ τίς τόπος τῆς καταπαύσεώς μου;
50 οὐχὶ ἡ χείρ μου ἐποίησεν ταῦτα πάντα;

Ps. 131:5; cf. 2 Kgdms. 7:2

3 Kgdms. 6:2;
1 Para. 22:6

3 Kgdms. 8:2;
Isa. 57:15

Isa. 66:1–2

Philo, Cher. 99–100;
Josephus, Ant. 8.108

Engaged in a Public Enterprise
in the Context of Greco-Roman Prototypes:
"Events that have come to fruition...
of all that Jesus began to do and to teach"
(Luke 1:1–Acts 1:1)

Chapter 9

ἀκριβῶς...γράψαι (Luke 1:3)

To Write the *Full* History of God's Receiving All Nations

David L. Balch

Jacques Dupont[1] suggests that Luke wrote the second volume, Acts, because of an interest in the Gentile mission. I want to support his thesis by arguing that the theme belongs within the context of Hellenistic historians, including Luke, writing speeches. First, I will sketch differences among contemporary scholars about the source and function of speeches in Hellenistic historians, and interpret what historians mean when they claim to write ἀκριβῶς, which I translate "fully" (Luke 1:3). Second, the "reception" of Gentiles / foreigners is central to the speeches constructed by the author of Luke-Acts, one means of communicating the purpose of the two-volume history. Third, the theme of a people's reception of foreigners is common among Hellenistic Jewish historians (2 Maccabees and Eupolemus) who wrote in Jerusalem, which raises the question whether speeches constructed by the Gentile Luke correspond to debates in the earliest Jewish church in Jerusalem.

Modern and Ancient Debates Concerning the Historicity and Function of Speeches in Hellenistic Historiography

This first section is a sketch of polarized scholarly opinion, concluding with a suggestion about the translation of ἀκριβῶς in Luke 1:3. Some New Testament scholars prefer to understand Luke's method of presenting speeches as analogous to that of Thucydides (c. 455–400 B.C.E.) and Polybius (c. 200–118 B.C.E.), aspects of whose style were apparently adopted by Julius Caesar (100–44

I gave this paper at the international Society of Biblical Literature meeting in Lausanne, Switzerland, July 1997, a paper invited by Professor Daniel Marguerat, whom I thank for his hospitality.

1. Jacques Dupont, "Le salut des Gentiles et la signification théologique du Livre des Actes," in *Études sur les Actes des Apôtres*, LD 45 (Paris: Cerf, 1967), 393–415, a reprint from *NTS* 6 (1959–60): 132–55. English translation: "The Salvation of the Gentiles and the Theological Significance of Acts," in *The Salvation of the Gentiles: Essays on the Acts of the Apostles* (New York: Paulist, 1979), 11–33.

B.C.E.) and Sallust (86–35 B.C.E.).[2] Others understand our author to have created nonhistorical speeches more in the manner of Dionysius (fl. 30–7 B.C.E.) and Josephus (c. 37–c. 100 C.E.).[3]

The speeches in Thucydides' *History* are not entirely subjective — a mouthpiece for his own views — nor are they correctly described as true to the situation, what a speaker would or ought to have said on particular occasions.[4] According to Walbank, Thucydides "does his best to remain anchored to τά ἀληθῶς λεχθέντα" ("what was really said"; *Hist.* 1.22.1).[5] Many scholars perceive a tension between this criterion and Thucydides' attempt "to make the speakers say what was in my opinion demanded of them by the various occasions, of course adhering as closely as possible to the general sense..." (*Hist.* 1.22.1). Gempf understands Thucydides to be describing a continuum between two poles: on the one hand, he does not supply the speaker's exact words but rather those which he thinks appropriate; on the other hand, he does not lose track of "the general sense" (τῆς ξυμπάσης γνώμης).[6]

Walbank thinks that "Polybius is an honest man" who

> in speeches made at gatherings in Greece or before the Senate at Rome...allows us to hear the genuine voice of leading Greek statesmen of the time and to share in their dilemmas and clashes of policy. Only in this way could the *History* become that handbook of political and moral instruction for a Greek public which Polybius intended it to be.[7]

Human beings are rational, historians assumed, and actions are the result of conscious decisions that are themselves influenced by speeches or dialogues. One must then know who spoke persuasively, the arguments that were used, and whether the resulting actions were successful or not. Polybius's intent is to let the reader see these orators, hear their persuasive speeches, and know the results. In digressions, Polybius discusses his method of writing history. The method is not like tragedy, in which the poet tries "to imagine the probable utterances

---

2. Conrad Gempf, "Public Speaking and Published Accounts," in *The Book of Acts in Its First-Century Setting,* vol. 1: *The Book of Acts in Its Ancient Literary Setting,* ed. Bruce W. Winter and Andrew D. Clarke (Grand Rapids, Mich.: Eerdmans, 1993), 259–303, at 282–83.

3. On Josephus, see ibid., 288–91. Cf. Charles H. Talbert, "The Acts of the Apostles: Monograph or *Bios?*" in *History, Literature, and Society in the Book of Acts,* ed. Ben Witherington III (Cambridge: Cambridge University Press, 1996), 58–72.

4. Frank W. Walbank, "Speeches in Greek Historians," in *Selected Papers: Studies in Greek and Roman History and Historiography* (Cambridge: Cambridge University Press, 1985), 242–61, at 244. Gempf, "Public Speaking," 267–68. See Daryl Schmidt's essay in chap. 2 of this volume.

5. Walbank, "Speeches," 246.

6. Gempf, "Speaking," 268. Cf. W. J. McCoy, "In the Shadow of Thucydides," in Witherington, *History, Literature, and Society in the Book of Acts,* 3–23, at 11–13 with n. 50; his n. 60 discusses the debated relationship between narrative and speeches. Witherington himself, in an editor's addendum (pp. 23–32) is one-sided: "...Thucydides was claiming that he presented his speech-makers as saying what it seemed like that they did say (not what they ought to have said), adhering as closely as he could to what he knew of what they actually spoke" (25). Cf., however, Dionysius, *Thuc.* 18.7 (quoted below) and George A. Kennedy, *The Art of Persuasion in Greece* (Princeton: Princeton University Press, 1963), 47–51.

7. Walbank, "Speeches," 253, 260.

of his characters or reckon up all the consequences probably incidental to the occurrences with which he deals." Polybius, in contrast, "simply records what really happened and what really was said (τῶν δὲ πραχθέντων καὶ ῥηθέντων κατ᾽ ἀλήθειαν αὐτῶν μνημονεύειν πάμπαν), however commonplace" (*Hist.* 2.56.10).[8] The historian is concerned with causes, so that the reader can feel either legitimate pity or proper anger (*Hist.* 13). The final criterion of good and evil lies not in what is done, but in the different reasons and purposes (αἰτίαις καὶ προαιρέσεσι) of the doer (*Hist.* 16). Similarly,

> The peculiar function of history is to discover, in the first place, the words actually spoken, whatever they were (τοὺς κατ᾽ ἀλήθειαν εἰρημένους, οἷοί ποτ᾽ ἂν ὦσι, γνῶναι λόγους), and next to ascertain the reason why what was done or spoken led to failure or success. For the mere statement of a fact may interest us but is of no benefit to us: but when we add the cause of it, study of history becomes fruitful. . . . But a writer [Timaeus] who passes over in silence the speeches made and the causes of events and in their place introduces false rhetorical exercises and discursive speeches,[9] destroys the peculiar virtue of history. (*Hist.* 12.25b.1–2, 4)

But Wiedemann argues that Polybius attacks Timaeus for his inappropriate high-flown rhetoric, not his rhetoric as such.[10] Polybius writes:

> I may be justly pardoned if I am found to be using the same style, or the same disposition and treatment, or even actually the same words as on a previous occasion. . . . For in all such matters the large scale of my work is a sufficient excuse. It is only if I am found guilty of deliberate mendacity,[11] or if it be for the sake of some profit, that I do not ask to be excused. . . . (*Hist.* 29.12.10–11)[12]

As Gempf comments, this means Polybius did not aim at verbatim accuracy, a practice similar to one pole of the well-known Thucydidean statement.

Wiedemann does not use Walbank's (modern?) criterion of "honesty" in interpreting Polybius. Statements which Walbank interprets as Polybius's attack on the use of rhetoric Wiedemann understands as literary criticism, an objection to the use of speeches on inappropriate occasions or with inappropriate style and diction (*Hist.* 36.1.3–4) — inappropriate, that is, for written discourse.[13] History is the prose form closest to poetry, and where the subject is grand, the grand

---

8. Paton's translation in LCL. On the uncertain text, see Walbank, "Speeches," 249 n. 50.

9. There is a difference between historians and speechwriters; the former "attempt to see the majority of places and peoples with one's own eyes (αὐτόπτη) (*Hist.* 12.28.11; 28a.4). But Dionysius (Pomp. 6.3) too admires Theopompus, a professional historian, because he was an eyewitness (αὐτόπτης) of many events. See *Denys d'Halicarnasse: Opuscules rhétoriques*, vol. 5: *L'Imitation (Fragments, Épitomé), Première Lettre à Ammée, Lettre à Pompée Géminos, Dinarque*, ed. Germaine Aujac (Paris: Les Belles Lettres, 1992), 97.

10. Thomas Wiedemann, "Rhetoric in Polybius," in *Purposes of History: Studies in Greek Historiography from the 4th to the 2nd centuries* B.C., ed. H. Verdin, G. Schepens, and E. de Keyser, Studia Hellenistica 30 (Louvain, 1990), 289–300, at 300.

11. This is his charge against Timaeus (*Hist.* 12.25k.1).

12. Cited by Gempf, "Speaking," 273–74, and by Wiedemann, "Rhetoric," 289.

13. Wiedemann, "Rhetoric," 290 n. 2, citing Aristotle, *Rhet.* 1413a12.

style — including set speeches — is appropriate: "Grand speeches are a sign that the subject matter, the actual battle, was historically important."[14]

Wiedemann sees a closer relationship between Polybius's history and rhetoric than many other scholars, but no one disagrees about the close relationship between the two in Dionysius of Halicarnassus, *Roman Antiquities*. Intriguing, however, is Sacks's insight concerning how Lucian (c. 120–80 C.E.) and Dionysius interpreted Thucydides. Dionysius's criterion is appropriateness to situation and speaker (τὸ πρέπον). For example, because Thucydides could not have been present at the Melian Dialogue, Dionysius asks whether he made it appropriate to the circumstances and befitting the persons at the conference (Dionysius, *Thuc.* 41.3–4).[15]

> Dionysius has already argued that Thucydides had no access to first-hand information as to what was actually said at Melos; nevertheless Dionysius would judge him by Thucydides' declared standard [1.22], which modern scholars interpret to mean a general fidelity to the actual words spoken.[16]

Sacks focuses on the Thucydidean phrase τῶν ἀληθῶς λεχθέντων, which is often casually translated, "what was actually said." He shows, however, that for Dionysius and Lucian, "true" or "real" speeches (ἀληθινοὶ λόγοι) are words spoken in a law court or public assembly, actual ("true") agonistic speeches, not speeches merely written down, nor epideictic ones.[17] The two poles of the Thucydidean ideal — what was truly said as well as what was demanded by the various occasions — are identified: both refer to what was rhetorically appropriate in forensic or deliberative situations. Sacks concludes: "Thucydides' expression is no longer a claim to recording actual speeches with accuracy; instead it becomes a simple declaration of the general types of speeches his history will include: the agonistic type delivered publicly in hopes of carrying an issue."[18] This manner of understanding Thucydides gains additional importance in light of the fact that "Polybius was largely unread by later generations."[19]

A term in Luke's preface (1:3) helps place our author within this general historiographical tradition. ἀκριβῶς in the preface is usually translated "accurately,"

---

14. Wiedemann, "Rhetoric," 297.

15. *Denys d'Halicarnasse: Opuscules rhétoriques*, vol. 4: *Thucydide, Seconde Lettre à Ammée*, ed. Germaine Aujac (Paris: Les Belles Lettres, 1991). Also H. Usener and L. Radermacher, *Dionysii Halicarnasei quae exstant*, vol. 6: *Opusculorum volumen secundum* (Stuttgart: Teubner, 1965), and *Dionysius of Halicarnassus: The Critical Essays*, ed. Stephen Usher, Loeb Classical Library (Cambridge: Harvard University Press, 1974), vol. 1.

16. Kenneth Sacks, "Rhetoric and Speeches in Hellenistic Historiography," *Athenaeum* 64 (1986): 383–95, at 392.

17. Sacks, "Rhetoric and Speeches," 388, 392, citing Dionysius's rhetorical works I Ammaeus 3; Lysias 6; Isocrates 2; Isaeus 6 and 20; Demosthenes 4. Nevertheless, Sacks observes (389 n. 35; cf. 388 n. 30) that Dionysius says he will also employ epideictic speech, since he includes political debates and writes for the entertainment of his readers (*Ant. Rom.* 1.8.3). I have shown that Dionysius did employ epideictic (an encomium of Rome) in "Two Apologetic Encomia: Dionysius on Rome and Josephus on the Jews," *JSJ* 13/1–2 (1982): 102–22.

18. Sacks, "Rhetoric and Speeches," 392–93.

19. Ibid., 394.

but should rather be translated "fully." Dionysius uses this root several times in his preface: there is no accurate/full (ἀκριβής) history of Rome in Greek, only brief, summary epitomes (ὅτι μὴ κεφαλαιώδεις ἐπιτομαὶ πάνυ βραχεῖαι; Ant. Rom. 1.5.4). Each of the earlier historians wrote few things and not accurately/fully (ὀλίγα καὶ οὐδὲ ἀκριβῶς...ἀνέγραψεν, 1.6.1, my translation). Some Romans wrote accurately/fully (ἀκριβῶς ἀνέγραψε, 1.6.2) in Greek of events at which they had been present, but only in a summary way (κεφαλαιωδῶς) of the founding of the city. Three times in his preface (1.5.4; 6.1, 2), Dionysius contrasts "full" with brief summaries, and twice (1.6.1, 2) "fully" is governed by the verb "to write."

Dionysius writes two books narrating the sedition of the plebeians against the patricians (6.92–8.62). He comments on his method in 7.66.1–3,[20] claiming that he has supplied the cause and the outcome. Romans did not change their government from kings to consuls by force, but by the persuasion of words (ἀλλὰ λόγοιος πείσαντες μεθήρμοσαν); therefore, Dionysius felt it necessary to report the speeches (7.66.3).

> 3. ...I might express my surprise that some historians, though they think themselves obliged to give an exact account of military actions (τὰς ἐν τοῖς πολέμοις πράξεις ἀκριβῶς οἴνται δεῖν ἀναγράφειν) and sometimes expend a great many words over a single battle..., [including] the exhortations of the generals,...yet when they come to give an account of civil commotions and seditions, do not consider it necessary to report the speeches by which the extraordinary and remarkable events were brought to pass (πολιτικὰς δὲ κινήσεις καὶ στάσεις ἀναγράφοντες οὐκ οἴονται δεῖν ἀπαγγέλλειν τοὺς λόγους δι᾽ ὧν αἱ παράδοξοι καὶ θαυμασταὶ πράξεις ἐπετελέσθησαν)....5. Therefore, I have chosen to make my narration accurate rather than brief (ἀκριβεστέραν μᾶλλον ἢ βραχυτέραν ποιήσασθαι τὴν διήγησιν). (7.66.3–5)[21]

In 7.66.3, "fully" is again governed by the verb "to write."[22] When military historians write "fully," they include the exhortations of the generals, but Dionysius complains that they leave speeches out of their narratives of civic events. Using the same contrast, he claims to have made his "narrative fuller rather than

---

20. See Clemence Elizabeth Schultze, "Dionysius of Halicarnassus and His Audience," in *Past Perspectives: Studies in Greek and Roman Historical Writings*, ed. I. S. Moxon, J. D. Smart, and A. J. Woodman (Cambridge: Cambridge University Press, 1986), 1–41, 126–27, 132, based on her dissertation at Oxford.

21. Cary's translation in LCL. Eckhard Plümacher, "Die Missionsreden der Apostelgeschichte und Dionys von Halikarnass," *NTS* 39 (1993): 161–77, at 167 (translated in this volume as chap. 10) cites *Ant. Rom.* 7.66.3: speeches are causes.

22. The definition in Dionysius, *Pomp.* 6.7–8, is the most extensive. He praises Theopompus for having "achieved exactness (ἀκριβῶς ἐξείργασται),...the ability, in the case of every action, not only to see and to state what is obvious to most people, but to examine even the hidden reasons for actions (ἐξετάζειν καὶ τὰς ἀφανεῖς αἰτίας τῶν πράξεων) and the motives of their agents, and the feelings in their hearts...and to reveal all the mysteries of apparent virtue and undetected vice. Indeed I feel in some way that the fabled examination before the judges of the other world, which is conducted in Hades upon the souls that have been released from the body, is of the same searching (ἀκριβής) kind...." This is not accomplished as well by any of the other historians (συγγραφέων; trans. Usher in LCL, "Critical Essays," 2.394–95).

briefer" (7.66.5), that is, to have included the civic speeches of the plebeians
and patricians — for example, those of Brutus and Coriolanus.[23]

Dionysius's preface to Book 11 exhibits the whole complex of terms in these
debates; I have underlined the terms that Luke uses again a century later:

1. I shall now endeavour to relate from the beginning (ἐπεχείρησαν...ἐξ ἀρχῆς
...διελθεῖν) in what manner they attempted to do away with this domination
[the decemvirate]..., who the leaders were in the cause of liberty, and what their
motives and pretexts were (αἰτίας καὶ προφάσεις). For I assume that such information is necessary and an excellent thing for almost everyone (μαθήσεις ἅπασι),
but particularly for those who are employed either in philosophical speculation
or in the administration of public affairs (πολιτικὰς ... πράξεις). 2. For most
people (πολλοῖς) are not satisfied with learning this alone from history (ἱστορίας),
that the Persian War, to take that as an example, was won by the Athenians
and Lacedaemonians..., but they wish also to learn from history of the places
where those actions occurred (τοὺς τόπους ἐν οἷς αἱ πράξεις), to hear of the
causes (αἰτίας) that enabled those men to perform their wonderful and astonishing exploits, to know who (τίνες) were the commanders of the armies, both
Greek and barbarian (τε βαρβαρικῶν καὶ τῶν Ἑλληνικῶν), and to be left ignorant of not a single incident.... 3. For the minds of all men (παντὸς ἀνθρώπου)
take delight in being conducted through words to deeds (διὰ τῶν λόγων ἐπὶ τὰ
ἔργα) and not only in hearing the words spoken but in seeing the deeds [transla-
tion modified]. Nor, indeed, when they hear of political events, are they satisfied
with learning the bare summary and outcome of the events (τὸ κεφάλαιον αὐτὸ
καὶ τὸ πέρας τῶν πραγμάτων), as for instance, that the Athenians agreed with
the Lacedaemonians to demolish the walls of their city...; but they at once demand to be informed also of the necessity which reduced the Athenians to submit
to such dire and cruel calamities, what the arguments were that persuaded them
(δι' ἃς...ὑπέμεινε), and by what men those arguments were urged (καὶ τίνες οἱ
πείσαντες αὐτοὺς λόγοι καὶ ὑπὸ τίνων ῥηθέντες ἀνδρῶν), and to be informed of
all the *circumstances* that attended those events (καὶ πάντα ὅσα παρηκολούθει[24]
τοῖς πράγμασι διδαχθῆναι). 4. Men who are engaged in the conduct of civil affairs
...take pleasure in a comprehensive survey of all the circumstances that accompany events (τὸ μὲν ἥδεσθαι τῇ παντελεῖ θεωρίᾳ τῶν παρακολουθουντῶν τοῖς
πράγμασι κοινόν). And, besides their pleasure, they have this advantage, that in
difficult times (ἀναγκαίους καιροὺς) they render great service to their countries as
the result of the experience thus acquired and lead them as willing followers to that
which is to their advantage, through the power of persuasion (διὰ τοῦ λόγου)....

---

23. I analyze one aspect of this narrative in "Political Friendship in the Historian Dionysius
of Halicarnassus," in *Greco-Roman Perspectives on Friendship,* ed. John T. Fitzgerald, SBLRBS 34
(Atlanta: Scholars Press, 1997), 123–44, another aspect in "Rich and Poor, Proud and Humble
in Luke-Acts," in *The Social World of the First Christians: Essays in Honor of Wayne A. Meeks,* ed.
L. Michael White and O. Larry Yarbrough (Minneapolis: Fortress, 1995), 214–33. This last article
quotes Jürgen von Ungern-Sternberg, "The Formation of the 'Annalilstic Tradition': The Example of
the Decemvirate," in *Social Struggles in Archaic Rome: New Perspectives on the Conflict of the Orders,*
ed. K. A. Raaflaub (Berkeley: University of California Press, 1986), 77–104, at 100: Because it is
interested in providing practical examples for the statesman and citizen, Roman historical tradition
is separate from the historical novel. Luke-Acts belongs to the former genre, not the latter.

24. This form is Cary's conjecture; all the MSS and Jacoby read παρακολουθεῖ.

5. It is for these reasons, therefore, that I have determined to report in accurate detail [fully] all the circumstances (ἔδοξεν ἅπαντα ἀκριβῶς διελθεῖν τὰ γενόμενα) which attended the overthrow of the oligarchy, in so far as I consider them worthy of notice (λόγου...ἄξια). 6. I shall begin my account (λόγον... ἀρξάμενος) of them, however, not with the final incidents..., but I shall begin with the first insults (ἤρξατο πρῶτον) the citizens suffered at the hands of the decemvirate. These I shall mention first (πρῶτον), and then, relate in order (ἐφεξῆς) all the lawless deeds committed under that regime. (Dionysius, Ant. Rom. 11.1.1–6)[25]

Here "fully" is governed by the verb "to go through" (διελθεῖν; 11.1.5). Not only Dionysius, but Luke too addresses a person interested in the civic effects of these speeches and deeds, the most excellent Theophilus. Not only Dionysius's audience but also Luke's wants to hear the narrative from the "beginning" and "in order." They do not want to know only what happened, but where the actions happened, the causes, and who spoke and acted. Neither audience wants a bare summary of events or merely to hear the disastrous or successful outcome. Rather they want to know which speakers employed what arguments to persuade audiences as well as the circumstances that attended the events.

This meaning also fits references in Dionysius's evaluation of the earlier historian Thucydides. When Thucydides narrates (3.36–49) the Mytilenean episode of 427 B.C.E., because he divides his history by summers and winters, he narrates half of it and then turns to other events, so that the reader cannot ἀκριβῶς recall the "half-completed sequence of events" (Dionysius, Thuc. 9.8). Although Usher (LCL) translates "accurately," "fully" better fits the contrast to "half-completed" narration. Again, when both cities had suffered major disasters, the Athenians sent ambassadors to Sparta to sue for peace, but

Thucydides (2.59) does not give the names of the ambassadors or the speeches (λόγους) they made there, nor the name of the opposing speakers whose arguments persuaded (ὑφ᾽ ὧν πεισθέντες) the Lacaedaemonians to reject an armistice. His narrative is a rather jejune and careless affair (φαύλως...καὶ ῥαθύμως), as if the episode were a minor one of no importance. (Dionysius, Thuc. 14.3 [trans. Usher, LCL])

On a less important occasion, however, Thucydides records the speech and gives the reasons (14.3). Dionysius asks: "If it was necessary to render an accurate (ἀκριβῶς...εἰρῆσθαι) account of the latter, why did he neglect the former so carelessly (ῥαθύμως)?" (15.1). Again, "to tell fully" is contrasted with a historical narrative that omits the speeches. Further, as Plümacher points out, Dionysius's critique of the famous funeral speech by Pericles (Thucydides, Hist. 2.35–46) is that Thucydides did not place it on an important occasion.[26] Few Athenians died in the first Peloponnesian invasion, and those few had done nothing distinguished (Dionysius, Thuc. 18). But later when there was an important occa-

---

25. Plümacher, "Die Missionsreden," 167, cites Ant. Rom. 11.1.3 on "persuasive words."
26. Ibid., 168; also 170–71.

sion, when Athenians under Demosthenes opposed Lacedaemonians at Pylos and were victorious, he wrote no funeral speech (Thucydides, *Hist.* 4.9–23, 26–40)!

> But it seems likely (and I shall speak my mind), that the historian composed this funeral eulogy and assigned it to Pericles because he wished to make full use of his character; and since that statesman died during the second year of the war and did not witness any of the misfortunes that befell the city after that time, he reserves this minor and uninspiring event for him to adorn with exaggerated praise. (Dionysius, *Thuc.* 18.7)[27]

These texts support Schultze's conclusion: "*Akribeia* often seems to relate to fullness rather than to precision or discrimination. *Akribeia* and completeness go together, while in contrast are lack of care and a summary treatment."[28] Not only Dionysius but also Polybius affirms that he writes "fully," in numerous and lengthy books that explain consequences and causes:

> It might be said by some of these who look on such things without discernment, that these are matters which it was not necessary for me to treat in such detail (ἐξαρκριβοῦν).... [But] writers and readers of history should not pay so much attention to the actual narrative of events as to what precedes, what accompanies, and what follows each. For if we take from history the discussion of why, how, and wherefore each thing was done, and whether the result was what we could have reasonably expected, what is left is a clever essay but not a lesson, and while pleasing for the moment of no possible benefit for the future. For this reason I must pronounce those to be much mistaken who think that this my work is difficult to acquire and difficult to read owing to the number and length of the Books it contains....
>
> [T]he most essential part of history is the consideration of the remote or immediate consequences of events and especially that of causes. (Polybius 3.31.2, 11–13; 32.1, 6 [trans. Paton, LCL])

---

27. Biography focuses on a single person such as Pericles; history does (or should) not. Acts is not biography but history; the narrative does not primarily concern the persons Peter or Paul, e.g., we do not hear of Paul's death because his biography is not the center of the history. Contrast the view of Talbert (n. 3 above). Dionysius's observation on Pericles' *epitaphios* also makes Witherington's view (n. 6 above) of speeches in Thucydides problematic.

28. Schultze, "Dionysius," 126. I agree with Schultze's contrast between "fullness" and modern historical "precision." But Dionysius, *Pomp.* 6 (quoted in n. 22 above), associates "examination" (ἐξετάζειν) of causes, motives, and feelings with "fullness"; therefore, I disagree with Schultze's contrast between "fullness" and "discrimination." In an epilogue (206), the three editors of the volume (Moxon, Smart, and Woodman) agree with Schultze: "It is self-evident that ancient readers relished the detailed description of battle-scenes, so it is hardly surprising if historians sought to provide them. Yet Schultze also observes that in Dionysius's opinion ἀλήθεια is closely associated with ἀκρίβεια, and that the latter seems to refer to fullness and completeness rather than to precision or discrimination. If we assume that Dionysius was reflecting the common view...this raises once more the central question of what truth is." Cf. A. J. Woodman, *Rhetoric in Classical Historiography: Four Studies* (London and Sydney: Croom Helm, 1988).

This notion of "fullness" should be added to meanings given by W. Rhys Roberts, *Dionysius of Halicarnassus, "On Literary Composition"* (London: Macmillan, 1910), 286, and by Jacobus van Wyk Cronjé, *Dionysius of Halicarnassus, "De Demosthene": A Critical Appraisal of the Status Quaestionis Followed by a Glossary of the Technical Terms*, Spudasmata 39 (Zurich: Georg Olms, 1986), 179–80.

And as we have seen in Polybius 12.25b.1–2, 4 quoted above, the words spoken are among the causes that have consequences.

Finally, the verb διακριβοῦν also occurs in the preface to 2 Macc. 2:28:[29]

> To go through each matter fully/accurately we leave to the historian [Jason] (τὸ μὲν διακριβοῦν περὶ ἑκάστων τῷ συγγραφεῖ παραχωρήσαντες), but we have worked to complete an orderly epitome (τὸ δὲ ἐπιπορεύεσθαι τοῖς ὑπογραμμοῖς τῆς διαπονοῦντες). (My translation)

The τὸ μὲν... τὸ δὲ construction contrasts the task of the historian with that of the epitomizer; the central task of the former is "to *write fully* concerning each matter." The phrase διακριβοῦν περὶ ἑκάστων in 2 Maccabees 2 corresponds to Thucydides' phrase (ἀκριβείᾳ περὶ ἑκάστου; *Hist.* 1.22). The epitomizer then observes (v. 29) that when one builds a new house, the architect must be concerned with the whole house (ἀρχιτέκτονι τῆς ὅλης καταβολῆς φροντιστέον), but the decorator and painter, on the other hand, must examine only what is necessary for aesthetics, "which is how I judge our task" (v. 29). Then this author once more contrasts the tasks of a historian with those of an epitomizer. The historian is critically to judge traditional reports and to research each part (πολυπραγμονεῖν ἐν τοῖς κατὰ μέρος τῷ τῆς ἱστορίας ἀρχηγέτῃ καθήκει; v. 30). The epitomizer wants only to tell the story, even when this would be too short for a historian (v. 31). The author then proceeds immediately into the "narrative" (v. 32).

The epitomizer shortens Jason's five-volume historical work, which narrated each event "fully." This raises a question for my thesis, since writing "fully" for Dionysius includes supplying appropriate speeches for the characters — but this epitome, which shortens the fuller history, also has speeches. However, most of the direct speeches occur in chapter 7, those of the brothers (7:2, 6, 30–38) and the mother (7:22–23, 27–29).[30] Habicht perceives three layers in the book: (1) Jason, the historical source, wrote in 161 or 160 B.C.E.; (2) the epitomizer wrote in 124 B.C.E.; and (3) later additions were made, especially chapters 7 and 12–15.[31] He argues that chapter 7 is a magnification of Eleazar's martyrdom in chapter 6, so belongs to the third layer. In contrast to Jason, chapter 7 stresses belief in the resurrection, and it is the only chapter in which the Temple does not play a role. To Habicht's reasons I add that chapter 7 is the only chapter with longer deliberative speeches, not characteristic of an epitomizer.[32]

---

29. I thank Hubert Cancik for this observation. See his *Mythische und historische Wahrheit: Interpretationen zu Texten der hethitischen, biblischen und griechischen Historiographie*, SBS 49 (Stuttgart; Katholisches Bibelwerk, 1970), 111. He compares Aristotle, *Poet.* 9.1–3.

30. There are also, for example, a young man's speech to Heliodorus (3:33–34); Eleazar's speech (6:24–28); Maccabeus's indirect speech to his companions that evolves into direct speech (8:16–20); two verses from an arrogant then repentant king Antiochus (9:4, 12); direct speech in the Nicanor story (14:25, 33, 35; 15:2, 4, 5, 14, 16, 21, 22–24); and prayers (1:24–29; 15:22–24, 34).

31. Christian Habicht, "2. Makkabäerbuch," in *Jüdische Schriften aus hellenistisch-römischer Zeit* (Gütersloh: Gerd Mohn, 1979), 1.167–285, at 171–76.

32. Thus I disagree with Robert Doran, *Temple Propaganda: The Purpose and Character of 2 Mac-*

Luke claims to do the opposite of the epitomizer of Jason's history. By claiming ἀκριβῶς...γράψαι, Luke is claiming to be a historian who will treat each
event "fully." I propose that Luke 1:3 be translated: "I, too, having mentally followed[33] all things from the beginning with respect to cause and effect, decided
to write you in a full and orderly manner, most excellent Theophilus," meaning that unlike his predecessors (such as Mark) who wrote briefly, Luke would
include speeches that indicate the causes and consequences of the events of salvation history. Luke proposes to write ἀκριβῶς so that Theophilus may know
certainty (ἀσφάλειαν) concerning the words (περὶ...λόγων) that he has been
taught (1:4), in some sense over against the πολλοί who have already written
narratives (1:1) that Luke wants to replace. The Lukan churches probably did
want those briefer narratives replaced. This translation — based on an investigation of how the words in Luke's preface are used in Dionysius's and Polybius's
prefaces and digressions on historical method — can also be supported by looking at the actual form of Luke-Acts, at the speeches which Luke adds to the
narrative.

I conclude that the historians Polybius, Dionysius, and Luke, in contrast to
the epitomizer who wrote 2 Maccabees, share certain presuppositions: (1) a narration of deeds alone, that is, a brief epitome, would (or should, they argue)
not interest their readers. For Luke's readers, a Gospel like Mark, which may
have been the Lukan congregations' original Gospel, would be inadequate.[34]
(2) Historians and their readers wanted to know why events happened and their
consequences, that is, who persuaded whom to do what, and whether the actions were a success or failure. Historians and their rhetorically sensitive readers
wanted the narratives to be written ἀκριβῶς, fully, to include the persuasive
speeches that caused the events narrated. (3) Whether the historian should be

---

cabees (Washington D.C.: Catholic Biblical Association, 1981), 22–23, who argues that chap. 7 is
not a later insertion by a redactor.

33. Liddell, Scott, Jones, s.v. παρακολουθέω: "II. metaph., follow closely...2. of an audience,...
follow with the mind...4. of a logical property...; of notions, inseparably connected; of cause and
effect..." David P. Moessner, "'Eyewitnesses,' 'Informed Contemporaries,' and 'Unknowing Inquirers': Josephus' Criteria for Authentic Historiography and the Meaning of ΠΑΡΑΚΟΛΟΥΘΕΩ," NovT
38 (1996): 105–22, at 112–13, 115, 119, 120–22, shows that this root does not mean to go back
over the affairs of an earlier period, but rather means that Josephus has superior credentials to follow
(with his mind) the meaning of biblical texts, or that he "follows" events as they unfold or develop,
in contrast to "inquiry" from others, indicated by the root πυνθάνομαι.

It simply does not mean "to inquire," "to investigate," "to study," "to conduct research," etc.,
whether directly or indirectly through following a text....

παρακολουθέω in [Josephus,] Ag[ainst]. Ap[ion]. 1.53 cannot bear this connotation
and, in fact, means something almost the opposite — one who "follows with the mind"
concurrently / as a contemporary. (121)

Dionysius writes this verbal root twice in the preface to Ant. Rom. 11.1.3–4.

34. Contrast Loveday Alexander, The Preface to Luke's Gospel: Literary Convention and Social
Context in Luke 1.1–4 and Acts 1.1, SNTSMS 78 (Cambridge: Cambridge University Press, 1993),
114–15, 135, who denies that Luke is criticizing predecessors. She also thinks (14) that Luke's preface is "detachable," a contrast to the interpretation given above, which explains why the author
would write such a preface anticipating speeches in the narrative.

an epitomizer or should write lengthy narratives was a matter of debate both in prefaces and in digressions that discussed historiographical method, debates referred to by Polybius, 2 Maccabees, Dionysius, and Luke. The verbs that govern ἀκριβῶς in these contexts are (ἀνα)γραφεῖν and διελθεῖν. In Luke 1:3 ἀκριβῶς means "fully," not "accurately," and is governed by the infinitive γράψαι, not by the participle παρηκολουθηκότι. Luke is not claiming "to have followed accurately," but "to write a full narrative."[35] Polybius, Dionysius, and Luke share a basic rhetorical purpose — to include speeches in their narratives that caused the events they narrate, so that their readers know not only what happened, but why, and who persuaded or failed to persuade their audiences to make decisions that led to acts that were successful or disastrous. Luke's preface means that the interpreter must pay careful attention to the speeches, for through them readers learn the who, how, where, and why of the events that the historian narrates[36] as well as whether they have good reasons to imitate the characters' successful actions or to avoid their failures.[37] (For a note on the grammar of Luke 1:3, see the appendix to this article.)

The Reception of Gentiles / Foreigners in the Speeches of Luke-Acts

Plümacher argues on the basis of Acts 10 and 13 that the mission speeches in Acts are causes.[38] Luke writes that "while Peter was still speaking…, the Holy Spirit fell on them" (Acts 10:44a), "on all those hearing the word" (10:44b). The narrator risks the reader (mis)understanding that the Holy Spirit also fell on the Jewish Christian companions of Peter, since the two are not distinguished until 10:45, which then observes that believers among the circumcised are astounded that the Spirit is poured out also on the nations (τὰ ἔθνη). The narrator

---

35. For different reasons, J. Kürzinger, "Lk 1,3: …ἀκριβῶς καθεξῆς σοι γράψαι," BZ 18/2 (1974): 249–55, at 254, inclines to the construal of ἀκριβῶς with γράψαι, as does David P. Davies, "The Position of Adverbs in Luke," in Studies in New Testament Language and Text: Essays in Honour of George D. Kirkpatrick, ed. J. K. Elliott, NovTSup 44 (Leiden: Brill, 1976), 106–21, at 115: "It is fairly certain that ἄνωθεν goes with παρηκολουθηκότι and καθεξῆς with γράψαι. The question is whether ἀκριβῶς modifies the participle or the infinitive. Usage suggests that since adverbs of manner are usually in pre-position, and always with the infinitive, it should be taken with γράψαι, giving the translation 'to write an accurate and orderly account' (contra RSV and NEB)." For further discussion, see the appendix at the conclusion of this article and Moessner, chap. 4 in this volume.

36. Speeches are the adverbs of ancient historical narratives.

37. David P. Moessner, "Re-reading Talbert's Luke: The Bios of 'Balance' or the 'Bias' of History?" in Cadbury, Knox, and Talbert: American Contributions to the Study of Acts, ed. Mikeal C. Parsons and Joseph B. Tyson (Atlanta: Scholars Press, 1992), 203–28, at 208–10, emphasizes the historian Luke's narrative sequence (kathexes) as well as the interest in cause and effect.

38. Plümacher opposes M. Dibelius, Aufsätze zur Apostelgeschichte, 5th ed. (Göttingen: Vandenhoeck & Ruprecht: 1968), 121, 142, translated as Studies in the Acts of the Apostles (New York: Scribners, 1956), 138, 166, who denied that the mission speeches were related to Greco-Roman historiography.

wants to connect the first-ever outpouring of the spirit on the Gentiles with the proclamation of the word, which is the source of the epoch-making event.

In Acts 13:16–41, Paul delivers a speech to Jews in the synagogue in Pisydian Antioch. The first result is that the hearers invite him to preach the same sermon again the next sabbath (v. 42), at which time nearly the whole city comes "to hear the word of the Lord" (v. 44). When Paul speaks, the Jews speak against (ἀντέλεγον) and blaspheme the word of God (vv. 45–46), but the Gentiles praise it (v. 48). Both the failure and the successful persuasion have consequences: "Since you thrust it [the word of God] from yourselves,... behold we turn to the Gentiles" (v. 46). Here again, the word evokes key choices in salvation history, in this instance a division prophesied by Simeon in the infancy narrative: "Behold, this child is set for the fall and rising of many in Israel, and for a sign that is spoken against (ἀντιλεγόμενον) ..., that thoughts (διαλογισμοί) out of many hearts may be revealed" (Luke 2:34b, 35b).[39]

Other speeches in this two-volume work could be examined from this perspective. The author may well have revised a first edition of the Gospel and added the infancy narrative[40] with its hymns/speeches — that have many connections backward to the Septuagint and forward to the speeches of Acts. The Gospel should not begin (see n. 77) in the wilderness by the Jordan River (despite Mark 1:4; Luke 3:3; Acts 10:37), but rather with a priest seeing an angel in the Temple in Jerusalem announcing a new Elijah who will prepare a people for the Lord (Luke 1:5). The climactic hymn in the infancy narrative is delivered by a prophet in the Temple in Jerusalem (Luke 2:29–35). If Q was one of Luke's sources, the author refused to employ its "sermon on the plain" first (Matthew 5–7//Luke 6:17–49), but placed it two chapters later in order to construct a programmatic inaugural speech, delivered not on some indeterminate Galilean level place, but rather at Jesus' birthplace in a synagogue after reading Torah (Luke 4:18–27), a speech resulting in an initial rejection generated by this proclaimed word from the prophet Isaiah (4:28–30, with the hearers rejecting the interpretation of Isa. 61:1–2; 58:6; cf. Luke 24:44–45).[41] Luke placed this composition before Jesus' own words in Q. Luke also constructed a farewell address for Jesus at Passover in Jerusalem (Luke 22:14–38), the only farewell address in the synoptics, appropriately spoken reclining at a symposium, appropriately, that is, for a Greco-Roman congregation who heard the Gospel read in the dining rooms and courtyards of such houses, with appropriate disputes over status, authority, and mission, appropriate for the author who was writing to stimulate a church to accept all equally in their house-church Eucharists.[42]

---

39. Cf. Dionysius, *Pomp.* 6 (quoted in n. 22 above) and Acts 28:22.

40. Fitzmyer, *The Gospel according to Luke (I–IX)*, 310–11.

41. Marion L. Soards, *The Speeches in Acts: Their Content, Context, and Concerns* (Louisville: Westminster/John Knox, 1994), fails to investigate speeches in the Gospel of Luke or any connection the hymns in the infancy narrative might have to speeches in Acts, and second, he fails to investigate any relationship to speeches in Greco-Roman historiography beyond formal rhetorical categories.

42. See Carolyn Osiek and David L. Balch, *Families in the New Testament World: Households and House Churches* (Louisville: Westminster/John Knox, 1997), chaps. 1 and 8, esp. pp. 204–6.

The foundational speech of the church was placed in the Temple in Jerusalem on a great holy day, Pentecost (Acts 2), not at some unworthy time or place
like a Galilean or Judean village. Luke places Stephen's review of the history of
Israel precisely at the juncture when Jesus' disciples are driven out of Jerusalem
into the Diaspora (Acts 7); Stephen gives this Bible survey course just before he
is lynched, another speech that failed to persuade but still generated response.
Athens, which Paul himself mentions only once (1 Thess. 3:1; on Paul's mood
afterward see 1 Cor. 1:17–2:5), is the site for his major speech to Stoic and Epicurean philosophers: Paul addresses the intelligentsia of the ancient world on
the Areopagus, their home turf (Acts 17). Dionysius would have approved the
location and the event. Luke reported the speech to Stoics neither in nearby
commercial Corinth, which was indeed an important site for the historical Paul's
mission speeches, nor in Thessalonica (see 1 Thess. 1:9–10). Athens, not Corinth or Thessalonica, was the center of the intellectual world of antiquity. Paul
too, like Peter, must make his own speech at Pentecost — in Hebrew in the
Temple in Jerusalem (Acts 20:16 and Acts 22). He must deliver his final proclamation in the political center of the world, Rome itself, not in some Caesarean
or Ephesian jail or in Spain.

Not only the occasions, but the content of the speeches are appropriate. The
content is appropriate for Gentile Christians living in multiethnic cities of the
Greco-Roman world, although perhaps not historically appropriate (in a modern sense) for a synagogue sermon in a homogeneous Galilean village of Jewish
peasants in the first third of the first century c.e.[43] I agree with Wilckens that
Peter's sermon to Cornelius (Acts 10:34–43) is a virtual outline of the Gospel of
Luke with its distinctive emphases.[44] It is not a mission sermon, but belongs to
another genre; it is not kerygma, but catechesis to Christian congregations.[45] I
emphasize a few of Wilckens's arguments. The author of this sermon expands
the Jesus kerygma in comparison to other mission sermons, and begins with
"you know" (ὑμεῖς οἴδατε; 10:37), which Wilckens argues is addressed not
to Cornelius's unconverted household, but to the readers of Acts. This is what
Christian preaching should be.[46] The sermon is addressed to Christians, just as
Theophilus, addressed in the prologue (Luke 1:4), had already been taught ("cat-
echized," although this transliteration is anachronistic). At the beginning of the
sermon (vv. 34–35, "in every nation") and at its conclusion (v. 43, "everyone
who believes"), Peter refers to the Gentile mission. *Christians* must be told re-

---

43. But see Josephus, *Life* 65–66: Galilean peasants set Herod's Tiberian palace on fire because it
had representations of animals forbidden by the law. Tension between rural Galilean Jewish peasants
and Hellenized Jewish urban dwellers was high. On the chronology of prophets, bandits, and mes-
siahs, see J. D. Crossan, *The Historical Jesus: The Life of a Mediterranean Jewish Peasant* (New York:
Harper, 1991), appendix 2.

44. Ulrich Wilckens, "Kerygma und Evangelium bei Lukas (Beobachtungen zu Acta 10,34–43),"
ZNW 49 (1958): 223–37, at 229.

45. Ibid., 236–37. This rejects the view of C. H. Dodd that all the "mission" sermons have the
same outline and make the same points.

46. Ibid., 226.

peatedly that "in every nation, anyone who fears him and does what is right is acceptable to him" (NRSV). *Christians*, reclining in the dining rooms of their Greco-Roman houses and enjoying their status as they hear the Gospel, must hear catechetical instruction concerning "Jesus Christ: he is Lord *of all!*" (v. 36; see 1 Cor. 11:21–22).[47] As this sermon begins and concludes, so the Gospel of Luke begins and Acts concludes (Luke 2:31–32; 3:6; Acts 28:29–30); the latter point is the one made by Dupont.

The church expands from the Jewish to the Gentile world, a growth that is not the result of fortuitous circumstances, Dupont observes, but is a program assigned to Christ and Paul by the scriptures.[48] I will only quote Dupont's conclusion, then give the briefest summary of his argument: "The practical point of the argumentation in all these various speeches is always the same, namely that the message of salvation is to be announced to all men and all nations."[49] I have argued that speeches were the means by which Hellenistic historians informed their readers of the who, why, when, and where of the events they narrated, which may strengthen Dupont's point that the creation and redaction of these speeches reveals the purpose of the author of both volumes.[50]

Dupont observes that Acts ends on a triumphant note: the Gentiles will listen (Acts 28:28), and Paul "receives all," as a few manuscripts add, "both Jews and Greeks" (28:30), an interpretation of Isa. 6:9–10.[51] This interest corresponds to the beginning of the first edition of the Gospel. Luke 3:1–5 lengthens the quotation of Isa. 40:3 in Mark 1:3 to include Isa. 40:4–5, "and all flesh (πᾶσα σάρξ) will see the salvation (τὸ σωτήριον) of God." Dupont observes that the neuter gender of "salvation" is particularly Lukan (2:30 and Acts 28:28). Its use opens the Gospel and concludes Acts.[52] These words are not just the rhetoric of Paul and John the Baptist, but are the words of God revealed to the prophet Isaiah;[53]

---

47. See Osiek and Balch, *Families in the New Testament World*, chap. 8.

48. Dupont, "Salvation of the Gentiles" (see n. 1 above), 13. On the institutional aspects of this growth, see Hubert Cancik, "The History of Culture, Religion, and Institutions in Ancient Historiography: Philological Observations Concerning Luke's History," *JBL* 116/4 (1997): 681–703.

49. Dupont, "Salvation of the Gentiles," 32.

50. See Emilio Gabba, *Dionysius and the History of Archaic Rome* (Berkeley: University of California Press, 1991), 69, on how Dionysius wrote history and especially speeches: "The historian should, with speeches, concern himself with portraying a coherent image.... One should bear this conclusion in mind when reading the work of Dionysius and particularly when examining the policy speeches attributed to major historical personalities." Luke similarly is a historian and rhetorician.

51. On the debated question whether the Gentile mission originated because of Jewish rejection of the gospel or rather because of Jewish acceptance of the gospel, see Charles H. Talbert, "Once Again: The Gentile Mission in Luke-Acts," in *Der Treue Gottes Trauen: Beiträge zum Werk des Lukas für Gerhard Schneider*, ed. Claus Bussmann and Walter Radl (Freiburg: Herder, 1991), 99–109; also Daryl Schmidt, chap. 2 in this volume, and Schmidt's "Anti-Judaism and the Gospel of Luke," in *Anti-Judaism and the Gospels*, ed. William R. Farmer (Harrisburg, Pa.: Trinity Press International, 1999), 63–96.

52. Dupont, "Salvation of the Gentiles," 15.

53. See Talbert, "Once Again: The Gentile Mission," 101–4, who shows that whether words were spoken by a Greek sibyl or a Hebrew prophet, both Greek and Jewish readers could and would understand this idea.

ultimately, the speech of God causes these events of salvation history, inspired speech verbalized by human prophets and apostles (compare Isa. 55:10–11).

The Gospel concludes and Acts is introduced with a similar emphasis. In direct speech, the narrator reports the contents of the resurrected Jesus' Bible study with the apostles, adding a third item to traditional christological interpretation of the scriptures, that "repentance and forgiveness of sins should be preached in his name to all nations (εἰς πάντα τὰ ἔθνη) beginning from Jerusalem" (Luke 24:47). Similarly, Acts opens with an emphasis on the apostles being Christ's witnesses "as far as the ends of the earth" (ἕως ἐσχάτου τῆς γῆς; 1:8), the exact phrase quoted by Paul after the conclusion of his later speech in Antioch (Acts 13:47). The audience in the synagogue has rejected the message Paul proclaimed — "Behold, we turn to the Gentiles" — which the author supports by quoting Isa. 49:6, including precisely the phrase used in Acts 1:8.[54] Dupont argues that the parallelism in the Isaiah quotation is theological. "Gentiles" is parallel with "the ends of the earth," interpreted as a prophecy of the third messianic task listed by Jesus at the end of the Gospel.

Dupont suggests several factors pointing to Luke's construction of Jesus' inaugural speech in Luke 4, which concludes by referring to stories of Elijah (1 Kings 17) and Elisha (2 Kings 5). True, in the immediate context, the references respond to townspeople's jealousy of miracles Jesus performed in Capernaum, but the contrast between Israel and Syrians (Luke 4:26–27) functions as a contrast between Israel and the nations. Similarly, Peter's inaugural speech quotes Joel 3:5, but Peter's quotation includes a contrast between "you and your children" on the one hand, and "those who are far off" on the other (Acts 2:39, an allusion to Isa. 57:19).[55] Further, at the conclusion of Peter's second speech, a similar contrast appears:

> You are the sons of the prophets and of the covenant that God struck with our fathers when he told Abraham, "In your descendants all the nations of the earth will be blessed" [cf. Gen. 22:18; 26:4]. It is first of all for your sake that God raised up his servant and sent him to bless you. (Acts 3:25–26)

A primary concern in the inaugural speeches of Jesus and Peter, which open the two volumes, focuses on this contrast between Jews and Gentiles.

> It is significant that Luke has inserted these pointers at the end of the first two great speeches in Acts. The similarity with the conclusion of the inaugural discourses of Jesus and Paul indicates that Luke is composing these speeches purposely. We discover a genuine consistency in Luke's thinking which enables him to grasp and express a profound unity in the various stages of the salvation history he is writing.[56]

Conversion of the Gentile Cornelius constitutes the culmination of Peter's apostolic career. His speech has been briefly analyzed above, with the argument that

---

54. Dupont, "Salvation of the Gentiles," 18.
55. Ibid., 23.
56. Ibid., 24.

in outline it constitutes the Gospel of Luke in miniature, with both the speech and Gospel emphasizing the inclusion of all nations. After Peter opens the door, Paul does the rest. He gives his inaugural in chapter 13, discussed above, and addresses Stoics in chapter 17, with a by now familiar conclusion: "God has overlooked the times of ignorance, but he now makes known to all people everywhere (τοῖς ἀνθρώποις πάντας πανταχοῦ) that they must repent..." (17:30). And like Peter's final speech, Paul's closes and opens with this theme, this time expressed philosophically: "God made out of one every nation of humans dwelling upon the entire face of the earth" (17:26). Not only must repentance and forgiveness be preached in God's name to all nations, but the preaching has not been forbidden by Rome (ἀκωλύτως, 28:31; the final word of the two volumes).[57]

The speeches at the Jordan River, in Nazareth, in Jerusalem/Bethany, at Pentecost, in Caesarea, in Antioch of Pisidia, on the Areopagus, and in Rome all encourage the church to accept foreigners, interpreting the who, how, why, when, and where of salvation history "fully" (ἀκριβῶς).

Hellenistic Jewish History, Written in Jerusalem, on Receiving Foreigners

I have argued that historians, including Luke, composed speeches that were not verbatim reports, but that like adverbs modify the verbal events of the narrative (n. 36). Second, I have argued that one focus of Luke's speeches in both volumes concerns the problematic relation between religious and ethnic groups, Jews and Gentiles. Third, I ask the *modern* question whether there is correspondence between the speeches that the historian Luke constructed, writing perhaps in a city like Antioch, Philippi, Ephesus, or Rome, and the debates that occurred among the earliest Christians in Jerusalem? Were Luke's speeches more like those of Polybius or Dionysius? In sketching an initial response to this question, I observe that Hellenistic Jewish historians *in Jerusalem* debated exactly this question.[58]

The theme of God's people and of their relationship to other ethnic and religious groups is woven through the narrative of 2 Maccabees[59] and Luke-Acts.

---

57. See David L. Balch, "Paul in Acts: '...You teach all the Jews...to forsake Moses, telling them not to...observe the customs' (Act. 21,21)," in *Panchaia: Festschrift für Klaus Thraede*, JAC 22 (Münster: Aschendorf, 1995), 11–23.

58. For the theme in Dionysius, see D. L. Balch, "Cultural Ideology: a Comparison of the Historian Dionysius of Halicarnassus, *Roman Antiquities*, and Luke-Acts," in *The Book of Acts in Its First-Century Setting*, vol. 6: *The Book of Acts in Its Theological Setting*, ed. Bruce W. Winter (forthcoming). These comments are excerpted from my article, "Attitudes toward Foreigners in 2 Maccabees, Eupolemus, Esther, Aristeas, and Luke-Acts," in *The Early Church in Its Context: Essays in Honor of Everett Ferguson*, ed. A. J. Malherbe, F. W. Norris, and J. Thompson, NovTSup 90 (Leiden: Brill, 1998), 22–47.

59. Christian Habicht, "2. Makkabäerbuch" (cited n. 31), 173–75, dates the source, Jason of Cyrene, between 161 or 160 and 152 B.C.E., therefore a contemporary of Judas the Maccabee, and the epitomizer to 124 B.C.E. Joseph Sievers, *The Hasmoneans and their Supporters: From Mattathias to*

The orthodox (see Acts 15:1; 22:3) Christian apostle Peter phrases the problem sharply when he arrives at the house of a Roman centurion, Cornelius, in Caesarea, "You yourselves know that it is unlawful for a Jew[ish disciple of Jesus] to associate with or to visit a Gentile" (more literally translated "foreigner" or "alien"; ἀθέμιτόν ἐστιν ἀνδρὶ Ἰουδαίῳ κολλᾶσθαι ἢ προσέρχεσθαι ἀλλοφύλῳ;[60] Acts 10:28a, NRSV). The final term occurs also in 2 Maccabees. When Maccabeus and his followers recovered the Temple and city, "they tore down the altars that had been built in the public square by the foreigners (ὑπό τῶν ἀλλοφύλων)...; it happened that on the same day on which the sanctuary had been profaned by foreigners (ὑπό ἀλλοφύλων), the purification of the sanctuary took place..." (2 Macc. 10:2a, 5a).[61] The early reign of Antiochus IV Epiphanes is described in 4:10; Jason bought the high priesthood and shifted his compatriots over to the Greek way of life. "There was such an extreme of Hellenization and increase in the adoption of foreign ways (ἀκμή τις Ἑλληνισμοῦ καὶ πρόσβασις ἀλλοφυλισμοῦ) because of the surpassing wickedness of Jason, who was ungodly and no true high priest..." (2 Macc. 4:13).

But Eupolemus,[62] who wrote in Greek in Jerusalem in the mid–second century B.C.E., gives very different accents. This ambassador presents his people in a favorable light for foreigners. Solomon is a "friend" of the king of Egypt and the king of Tyre to whom he writes letters referring to "the Most High God" who "commanded me to build a temple to the God who created heaven and earth" (trans. Holladay, 119, 121). Both write in return, acknowledging God and responding to Solomon's requests for help building the Temple. These "nations (τὰ ἔθνη) supplied the labor" for the Temple (Frg. 2.34.4), after which "Solomon returned the Egyptians and the Phoenicians each to their own countries" (Frg. 2.34.17; Holladay, 125, 131).

2 Maccabees and Eupolemus both focus their narratives on the Temple, but their stories about foreigners — the nations — differ. In 2 Maccabees we hear about many foreigners who are blasphemous, barbarous, murderous, and licentious, who bring prostitutes and pork into the Temple and are intent on murdering all Jews, but in Eupolemus about nations who help build the Temple and celebrate Solomon, approved by a great God (Frg. 2.32.1). Hasmoneans

---

the Death of John Hyrcanus I, South Florida Studies in the History of Judaism 6 (Atlanta: Scholars Press, 1990), 6, dates Jason's history between c. 155 and c. 106 B.C.E. and the epitomizer between 124 B.C.E. and 70 C.E., probably in the first third of that time span (7 n. 28). Jan Willem van Henten, The Maccabean Martyrs as Saviours of the Jewish People: A Study of 2 and 4 Maccabees, JSJSupp 57 (Leiden: Brill, 1997), 50–57, 296, argues that the author wrote in Judea around 124 B.C.E.

60. This term occurs 269 times in the LXX, very often for "Philistines" but also for "Greeks." See R. de Vaux, "Les Philistins dans la Septante," in Wort, Lied und Gottespruch: Beiträge zur Septuaginta (Festschrift for Joseph Ziegler), ed. Josef Schreiner (Würzburg: Echter, 1972), 1.185–94.

61. Compare the decree of Antiochus III: "It is unlawful for any foreigner (ἀλλοφύλῳ) to enter the enclosure of the temple which is forbidden to the Jews, except to those of them who are accustomed to enter after purifying themselves in accordance with the law of the country" (Josephus, Ant. 12.145 [trans. Marcus, LCL]).

62. Text, translation, and notes in Holladay, Fragments from Hellenistic Jewish Authors, 1.93–156.

in Jerusalem narrated very different legends about foreigners. Maccabeans generated conflicting images of the other.

This ambivalence is also present in the bilingual Book of Esther. The Greek Esther is concluded by a colophon which assigns it to Lysimachus and dates it to 78–77 B.C.E. in Jerusalem. The colophon also assumes that the Hebrew Esther was still unknown in Alexandria, which would then have been written a little earlier: Bickerman suggests about 100 B.C.E. in the reign of Alexander Jannaeus.[63]

Bickerman cautions[64] about naively labeling any of these books pro- or anti-Gentile. The authors believed that God protects the chosen people. There was no essential conflict between Jews and Greeks (e.g., 2 Macc. 12:30; 3 Macc. 3:8; Esther 9:15), but on the other hand, Esther, especially Additions A and F, could excite animosity among Gentiles (*Megillah* 7a).[65] The themes concerning foreigners are similar to 2 Maccabees, although more alienated.

Evil suppresses Judaism, but going beyond 2 Maccabees, the Greek interpreter/translator (Addition F11) of Esther emphasizes that Gentiles plan utterly to destroy all Jews (e.g., Esther A6; 3:6–7, 13; F5).[66] Being Jewish (Ἰουδαῖος) is problematic (3:4; 4:13; 5:9, 13), for this nation differs from all the nations (πάντα τὰ ἔθνη; 3:8; B5). The conflict no longer focuses on specific customs such as a refusal to eat pork offered to Zeus, but concerns being Jewish as such. In the Hebrew Esther, the possibility of extermination had been an historical accident, the result of an all-powerful despot who agrees to the wish of an adviser without even knowing the victims.[67] The Greek additions dramatically increase the emphasis on slander, threatened holocaust, and denial of more generalized anti-Jewish accusations. The author confesses hatred of the lawless and uncircumcised, of every stranger (παντὸς ἀλλοτρίου; C26).

In partial summary, the conception and experience of foreigners in the Hebrew Esther differs from that in the Greek additions, and both differ dramatically from Eupolemus, Judas Maccabeus's ambassador to Rome, who also wrote after an intense crisis, projecting different images of outsiders. Jewish literature from

---

63. Elias Bickerman, "The Colophon of the Greek Book of Esther," in *Studies in Jewish and Christian History,* Arbeiten zur Geschichte des antiken Judentums und des Urchristentums 9 (Leiden: Brill, 1976), 225–45, at 232, 239–40, and "Notes on the Greek Book of Esther," in ibid., 246–74, at 252, 258. If the Greek Esther originated in Jerusalem as its colophon claims (see Bickerman, "Colophon," 240, 244), the possibility that 2 Maccabees might have been redacted there is higher. Hans Bardtke, "Zusätze zu Esther," *JSHRZ* 1 (1973): 15–62, at 25, argues that the occasion of the Greek additions was the successful outcome of the Maccabean struggle in the second century B.C.E., and that these additions are older than 2 Maccabees, which he dates to the first century B.C.E. Bardtke (57–59) disagrees with Bickerman's later dating of Esther's colophon to 87–77 B.C.E.

64. Bickerman, "Notes," 274.

65. Bickerman, "Colophon," 243 n. 100. "Lysimachus made of the Greek Esther a document stressing mutual hatred between the Jews and the Gentiles," but under Alexander Jannaeus, "the simple dichotomy of his book was already out of fashion" (Bickerman, "Colophon," 243; idem, "Notes," 268).

66. Text in R. Hanhart, ed., *Esther,* Septuaginta 8/3 (Göttingen: Vandenhoeck & Ruprecht, 1966).

67. Bickerman, "Notes," 265.

Jerusalem in the Maccabean age exhibits a spectrum of alienation from and/or integration with Hellenistic culture, persons, and rulers.

Dates assigned the *Letter of Aristeas* to Philocrates differ from 250 B.C.E. to C.E. 100. Tcherikover denies that it is a letter of propaganda directed to Greeks, insisting rather that it was written by a Jewish author, learned in philosophical literature, to Jewish readers.[68] The high priest Eleazar (*Letter of Aristeas* 3) chooses seventy-two Jerusalem elders as translators of the Hebrew Bible into Greek, elders who know both Jewish and Greek literature (121). They had "the middle way as their commendable ideal; they forsook any uncouth and uncultured attitude of mind (τὸ...βάρβαρον τῆς διανοίας); in the same way they rose above conceit and contempt of other people...." (122). Tcherikover observes that the author here defends the elders of Jerusalem who know Greek culture and criticizes the Hasidim,[69] analogous to the differentiation in Jerusalem discussed above between Eupolemus the ambassador and the Greek additions to Esther. As in Eupolemus, in the *Letter of Aristeas* the high priest in Jerusalem is a true friend of King Ptolemy and Queen Arinoe and the children (41; cf. 318), who cherish piety for "our God" to the extent that they give silver to repair the Temple (42) and recognize the "holy words" of Torah (31, 177). The high priest sends these elders / ambassadors "for the common benefit of all his countrymen" (126).

The author's aim is to encourage Jews to accept Greek culture (2, 6–7, 121, 124, 321–22) and to deny that there is an abyss between the two, even in theology.[70] Hellenistic culture is presented as monotheistic, without any attempt to emphasize its moral and religious depravity. Aristeas, the Jewish author disguising himself literarily as a Greek (40), takes the opportunity to ask Ptolemy II (285–247 B.C.E.) to release one hundred thousand Jewish slaves, describing the king and God as follows:

> As a man of mature and generous mind, release the [Jewish] men confined under such hardships. The same God who gave the Jews their Law is the one who directs your kingdom...for the God who watches over and creates all things is the God whom they worship, the God whom all men worship, the God whom we ourselves worship, your Royal Highness, except that we address him by other names such as Zeus and Dis. (15–16; cf. 19, 37, 189)

The main passage on Torah concerns kosher food (128–72). Regulations concerning forbidden food are allegories given by Moses in a symbolic manner (150), which have a profound meaning (143). Moses was not concerned for mice and the weasel (144). Birds which may be eaten are pure since they feed on grain, whereas forbidden, unclean ones are birds of prey, a distinction that promotes righteousness and discourages violence against others (147–48). The prescrip-

---

68. V. Tcherikover, "The Ideology of the Letter of Aristeas," *HTR* 51 (1958): 59–85, at 62, 66, 83; A. Pelletier, *Lettre d'Aristée à Philocrate*, SC 89 (Paris: Cerf, 1962).

69. Tcherikover, "Ideology," 67–68, 83.

70. Ibid., 69.

tion concerning animals "chewing the cud and parting the hoof" (Lev. 11:3) was given with a view to truth, "a token of right reason" (161).

In summary, an Alexandrian Jewish author encourages knowledge of both Hebrew and Greek culture, disparaging (possibly Hasidic, possibly some Maccabean) negative attitudes in Jerusalem toward others, a radical contrast with the Greek additions to Esther. Jews and Greeks worship the same God, whom the Greeks name Zeus, an attitude close to that of Eupolemus, who tells of Solomon and the kings of Syria and Egypt praising the same one God. Discussing passages in Torah concerning kosher food, the author deemphasizes "meat, drink, and clothes," a qualitative contrast to 2 Maccabees. The Bible should be in Greek, the author writes, and a Septuagint reading is preferred to the Hebrew, a contrast with the method of ben Sirach's grandson. God blesses the human race and fulfills the prayers of the deserving, a universalism also in contrast to 2 Maccabees. Nevertheless, Aristeas assumes (139–41) that Jews are not "mingling" with any other peoples.

This sketch yields the conclusion that there was a spectrum of attitudes in Maccabean Jerusalem concerning relationships with foreigners, a spectrum from left to right that includes: (1) the *Letter of Aristeas* — whose narrative concerns, but was not written, in Jerusalem — which understands the high priest and Ptolemy to worship the same God, the latter calling God Zeus, and deemphasizes and transforms the meaning of distinctive customs such as kosher foods, with one result that Jews and Gentiles may associate in a symposium. Judaism is a philosophy, not practice focused on food and drink. (2) Eupolemus likewise pictures rulers in Jerusalem and Alexandria honoring the same God, including the latter sending "the nations" to help construct the Jerusalem Temple. (3) 2 Maccabees rather characterizes most foreigners as Hellenizing polytheists who bring pork and prostitutes into the Temple, the Jewish alternative to which is martyrdom or war. (4) Additions A and F to Esther distinguish Jews totally from others, who are perceived as intent on destroying all Jews. Given this spectrum, we students of Luke-Acts would be mistaken to write in the singular of "the" Maccabean or of "the" Jewish attitude toward foreigners. But the important conclusion is that the author of Luke-Acts was certainly correct to imagine that debates concerning Jews' relationships with foreigners occurred in Jerusalem, debates narrated by Hellenistic Jewish historians.

Conclusions

Far from Jerusalem, the Gentile historian Luke wrote of conflict in Jerusalem concerning whether the church should accept foreigners into membership. He constructed debates among the Jewish Christians Peter, James, and Paul, analogous to debates in Dionysius of Halicarnassus, *Roman Antiquities,* and in Josephus, *Jewish Antiquities,* concerning citizenship in Rome or in the Jewish commonwealth.[71] The vocabulary and issues that Luke assigns to these three leaders of

---

71. See Balch, "Paul in Acts," 13–14.

the church correspond to the diverse attitudes in 2 Maccabees, Eupolemus, the Greek additions to Esther, and the *Letter of Aristeas,* the first three of which may have been written in Jerusalem. The Alexandrian Jewish writer Aristeas imagines similar tensions in the same city. In other words, debates on this subject did indeed occur in Jerusalem, as Luke suggests. Luke constructs speeches by Simeon, Jesus, Peter, and Paul to unite and explain "fully" the meaning of the two-volume history, to give answers to questions about who, where, when, why, and how the "word of the Lord" was accepted or rejected and about who "caused" the events of salvation history — questions still intensely debated by modern historians.

In relation to the focus on Israel of all the essays in this volume, we have seen Simeon bless Jesus and tell his mother, Mary, that "this child is destined for the falling and the rising of many in Israel, and to be a sign that will be opposed" (ἀντιλεγόμενον; Luke 2:34, explicitly fulfilled in Acts 13:45 and 28:19). Speeches, the prophesied and proclaimed word of God that Luke has added to this "full" history, generate a division in Israel. Stephen proclaims a Moses who prophesied to the Israelites, "God will raise up a prophet for you from your own people as he raised me up" (Acts 7:37, quoting Deut. 18:15), a proclamation that is rejected by those who hear him, also by Saul, who however is later baptized and who himself proclaims the message (Acts 7:58 and 9:18, 20). Peter's sermon in Caesarea, "the message God sent to the people of Israel" (Acts 10:36), evokes the conversion of Cornelius as well as the opposition of some believers in Jerusalem (10:44–48 and 11:1–3). Paul too proclaims that of King David's "posterity God has brought to Israel a Savior, Jesus, as he promised; before his coming John had already proclaimed a baptism of repentance to all the people of Israel" (Acts 13:23–24). As Plümacher observes, Paul's speech persuades some and generates rejection from others in the synagogue in Antioch of Pisidia (13:44–52). Paul proclaims that God "exalted" Israel (ὕψωσεν) in Egypt (Acts 13:17). God has also "exalted the humble (ὕψωσεν ταπεινούς) Mary" (Luke 1:52) and raised Jesus up, who is therefore "exalted" (ὑψωθείς) at the right hand of God (Acts 2:33). This prophesied message (re)proclaimed in Luke's history brings "certainty" (ἀσφαλῶς) to Israel (Acts 2:36), the certainty that Luke promised.

Appendix

For my interpretation in section 1 above ("Modern and Ancient Debates") to be possible, ἀκριβῶς must be governed by γράψαι. This is disputed by Janse,[72] who refers to Wackernagel's law that enclitics in Indo-Germanic languages are readily

---

72. Mark Janse, "The Prosodic Basis of Wackernagel's Law," in *Actes du XV Congrès International des Linguistes* (Sainte-Foy, Québec: Université Laval, 1993), 19–22; idem, "La position des pronoms personnels enclitiques en Grec néo-testamentaire à la lumière des dialectes néo-Helléniques," in *La Koiné greque antique,* vol. 1: *Une langue introuvable?* ed. Claude Brixhe, Études anciennes 10 (Nancy, France: Presses Universitaires, 1993), 83–121; idem, "La Koiné au contact des Langues Sémitiques de la Septante au Nouveau Testament (Questions de Méthode)," in *La Koiné grecque antique,* vol. 3: *Les contacts,* ed. Claude Brixhe, Études anciennes (Nancy, France: Presses Universitaires, 1998), 99–111; idem, "L'importance de la position d'un mot 'accessoire' (à propos de Luc 1,3)," *Biblica* 77/1

attached to the first word of a clause, even when they occur prior to the word on which they depend syntactically. Wackernagel's law applies regularly when the first word of a clause is emphasized or focalized.[73] Janse argues that the enclitic personal pronoun σοι (Luke 1:3) is occasioned by the focalization of the adverb καθεξῆς, which means that this adverb is the first word of the clause, literally translated, "orderly to you to write," which means further that the preceding adverbs, ἄνωθεν and ἀκριβῶς belong to a different clause, governed by the participle παρηκολουθηκότι.[74] Luke 1:3 would be divided into clauses as follows: ἔδοξε κἀμοί // παρηκολουθηκότι ἄνωθεν πᾶσιν ἀκριβῶς // καθεξῆς σοι γράψαι.

I accept an alternative suggestion Janse made to me by E-mail:[75] the enclitic σοι focalizes both the adverbs ἀκριβῶς and καθεξῆς, which form a complex unit,[76] and this focalization of the complex unit explains the position of σοι before and not after γράψαι. Luke formed this complex unit in relation to contemporary historiographical theory and practice: historians must "begin" at an indisputable point, narrate events that "follow,"[77] and write "fully." Luke mentions these three historical tasks in the prologue. As Polybius and Dionysius demand, Luke claims "fully, in order to you to write" (Luke 1:3).

(1996): 93–97, with further bibliography in nn. 15, 17; idem, "Adams, Wackernagel's Law, and the Placement of the Copula *esse*," in *Kratylos: Kritisches Berichts und Rezensionsorgan für Indogermanische und Allgemeine Sprachwissenschaft* 42 (1997): 105–15; idem, "Convergence and Divergence in the Development of the Greek and Latin Clitic Pronouns," in *Stability and Change of Word-Order Patterns over Time*, ed. R. Sornicola, E. Poppe, and A. S. Ha-Levy (Amsterdam: Benjamins, forthcoming). I thank the editor of *Biblica*, Jean-Noël Aletti, for pointing out Janse's work to me, and the author himself for corresponding about the grammar. See also n. 35 above.

73. Janse, "L'importance de la position," 95.

74. Janse, "La position des pronoms," 98, and "L'importance de la position."

75. Janse's published works argue against this option; I thank him for observing the possibility.

76. Janse, "La position des pronoms," 96, gives the example of Acts 20:23: δέσμα καὶ θλίψεις με μένουσιν. The enclitic personal pronoun με follows and focalizes the first three words as a complex unit. Janse, "Convergence and Divergence," no. 34c, gives the possible example of Luke 7:44 in codex Bezae (D): ὕδωρ ἐπὶ πόδας μοι οὐκ ἔδωκας. The enclitic personal pronoun μοι may focalize the first three words as a complex constituent.

77. Polybius in his prologue argues that the beginning of a history is crucial:

Thus we must first state how and when (πῶς καὶ πότε) the Romans established their position in Italy, and what prompted them afterwards to cross to Sicily, the first country outside Italy where they set foot. The actual cause (αἰτίαν) of their crossing must be stated without comment; for if I were to seek the cause of the cause and so on, my whole work would have no clear starting-point (ἀρχῆς) and principle. The starting-point must be an era generally agreed upon and recognized and one self-apparent from events. . . . For if there is any ignorance or indeed any dispute (ἀμφισβητουμένης) as to what are the facts from which the work opens (ἀρχή), it is impossible that what follows (ἑξῆς) [cf. Luke 1:3] should meet with acceptance or credence; but once we produce in our readers a general agreement on this point they will give ear to all the subsequent narrative. (1.5.2–5)

But there was a dispute about the relationship between John the Baptist and Jesus, one of the reasons Luke added chap. 1. The "beginning" in Luke 1:5 (v. 2: ἀρχή) is different from the one in Acts 10:37, which agrees rather with Luke 3:3; both Luke 3 and Acts 10 present Jesus' baptism by John as the beginning. Polybius's comment on the relationship between the "beginning" and what subsequently "follows" explains Luke's interest in the prologue to write the Gospel in "order" (καθεξῆς). Luke modified the "beginning," so that the narrative "follows." Compare Dionysius, *Rom. Ant.* 11.1.6 (quoted above).

Chapter 10

The Mission Speeches in Acts and Dionysius of Halicarnassus

Eckhard Plümacher

If I am not mistaken, the debate concerning the literary genre of the Lukan historical work or Acts of the Apostles has intensified during the past two decades. Previously, the usual premise was that the Lukan work, and especially Acts, should be viewed within the context of ancient historical writing. For example, scholars defined the overall work as "popular 'general history' written by an amateur Hellenistic historian with credentials in Greek rhetoric,"[1] or classified Acts as a historical monograph similar to the works of Sallust and commensurate with the program Cicero presents in *Epistulae ad Familiares* 5.12.2–3.[2] This consensus, however — if ever it genuinely existed — was broken first by Charles H. Talbert, who viewed the double work within the context of biography, especially that of philosopher biographies.[3] And recently, Acts has once again been associated with the apocryphal "Acts" and viewed as a kind of historical novel.[4] All this notwithstanding, I do think it quite in order that we continue to view Luke as a historian (or at least as someone who wanted to be such). In what follows, I would like to demonstrate the legitimacy of this view by focusing on one specific phenomenon within the Lukan historical writing, namely, on the function the author of Acts ascribes to what are known as the mission speeches.[5] General

---

Seminar paper presented to the SNTS Luke-Acts Seminar at Bethel, Germany, July 31, 1991, and first published as "Die Missionsreden der Apostelgeschichte und Dionys von Halikarnass," *NTS* 39 (1993): 161–67. My thanks to the translator of the original article, Dr. Doug Stott, and to the editor for translating the excursus which has been added for this publication. This essay is dedicated to my daughter Johanna.

1. D. E. Aune, *The New Testament in Its Literary Environment* (Philadelphia: Westminster, 1987), 77.

2. See H. Conzelmann, *Acts of the Apostles* (Philadelphia: Fortress, 1987), xli; Plümacher, "Die Apostelgeschichte als historische Monographie," in *Les Actes des Apôtres: Traditions, rédaction, théologie,* ed. J. Kremer, BETL 48 (Gembloux, Belgium: Duculot, 1979), 457–66.

3. See, e.g., his book *Literary Patterns, Theological Themes, and the Genre of Luke-Acts,* SBLMS 20 (Missoula, Mont.: Scholars Press, 1974).

4. R. I. Pervo, *Profit with Delight: The Literary Genre of the Acts of the Apostles* (Philadelphia: Fortress, 1987).

5. Acts 2:14–39; 3:12–26; 4:9–12; 5:29–32; 10:34–43; and 13:16–41.

consensus holds that the speeches in Acts represent not accounts of actual addresses, but products from the hand of the author of Acts himself. Many of these speeches stand at pivotal junctures within the events portrayed in Acts, and initiate the reader into the "suprahistorical significance of the historical moment" and "render visible the powers at work behind these events." This insight itself is not new, and I can refer the reader simply to the pioneering essay by Martin Dibelius on "The Speeches of Acts and Ancient Historical Writing," from which these citations are taken.[6] Dibelius also recognized that "despite various peculiarities," Luke was essentially composing in the great tradition inaugurated by Thucydides, insofar as he integrated such speeches into his work in the first place, and insofar as he did so in a certain way.[7]

Still, not all the speeches in Acts derive from that particular historiographical tradition going back ultimately to Thucydides. This applies especially to the mission speeches, for which Dibelius, for example, denied any connection with Greco-Roman historical writing.[8] Although the mission speeches stand at significant turning points in Luke's portrayal of early Christian history, they do not illuminate the suprahistorical significance of these turning points in the manner of Thucydides, but draw the reader's attention *verbaliter* to what in Luke's opinion has moved early Christian history forward and determined its course, namely, the witness to Jesus in the mission proclamation of the apostles and Paul.

We owe this insight into the function of the mission speeches primarily to Ulrich Wilckens,[9] who, however, arrived at this understanding less as a result of his otherwise detailed exegesis of the pertinent pericopes within Acts[10] than from a consideration of the theology and conception of the overall Lukan work. His main insight was that the Lukan Spirit brackets the time of Jesus with the present. Wilckens recognized further that Luke associated the promise of the bestowal of the Spirit with "the commission to 'witness' to Jesus," which in the salvific-historical epoch of church history then became the "decisive instrument in attaining salvation." Since, however, "in its initial, determinative form this testimony to Jesus was actually that of an eyewitness account," the apostles became the authorized bearers of the proclamation, and it was their proclamation that became the "real moving force behind church history." "In this epoch, too, God himself is guiding salvation history, and is using the testimony of the apostles as

---

6. M. Dibelius, *Aufsätze zur Apostelgeschichte*, 5th ed. (Göttingen: Vandenhoeck & Ruprecht, 1968), 120–62; citations on 121 and 142.

7. Ibid., 142. Concurring scholars include O. Luschnat, "Thukydides der Historiker," *PRE* (Supplement) 12.1085–1354, here 1299–1301. Concerning the difficulties of understanding the author of Acts as an (indirect!) successor of Thucydides, related to interpretive possibilities of Thucydides' discourse passage 1.22.1 (see also Luschnat, "Thukydides," 1162–83), see recently S. E. Porter, "Thucydides 1.22.1 and Speeches in Acts: Is There a Thucydidean View?" *NovT* 32 (1990): 121–42.

8. "In any event, we are dealing here with a tradition that has nothing to do with ancient historical writing" (Dibelius, *Aufsätze*, 142).

9. *Die Missionsreden der Apostelgeschichte: Form- und traditionsgeschichtliche Untersuchungen*, 3d ed., WMANT 5 (Neukirchen-Vluyn: Neukirchener Verlag, 1974).

10. Wilckens discusses in detail the structure, organization, and framework of the discourses, as well as questions regarding the content of each discourse and their traditio-historical background.

his primary instrument. The function of the speeches in Acts within the overall literary composition of the work becomes comprehensible from the perspective of Luke's theological conception here. As the salvific-historical moving force, the apostles' testimony to Jesus not only must become visible, but must actually be delivered verbally as well."[11]

Although the question of the function of the mission speeches can be posed legitimately from the perspective of the "theological conception" of the author of Acts, the critique to which Wilckens, too, has been subjected in this regard[12] suggests examining more closely than did Wilckens himself whether the mission speeches themselves confirm his views concerning their function. The following discussion will undertake this examination by focusing on two texts.

First concerning Acts 10. The events Luke reports are guided by the *providentia specialissima* and lead to the conversion of a Roman centurion, Cornelius. In this story, the author of Acts arrives at what is probably the most momentous turning point in his story of early Christianity: henceforth Gentiles, too, will be able to join the church. However, before arriving at this goal for the entire episode — namely that Cornelius, to use a Lukan expression, "is added" — Luke has Peter deliver one of the mission speeches (10:34–43). It is not until Peter has finished the speech, indeed, even while he is uttering its final words, ἔτι λαλοῦντος τοῦ Πέτρου τὰ ῥήματα ταῦτα ("while Peter was still speaking these words," v. 44a), that this goal is reached: the Holy Spirit falls upon Cornelius and his companions, indicating that henceforth nothing stands in the way of the baptism of non-Jews (vv. 47–48).

The extremely tight syntactical connection Luke establishes in 10:44a between Peter's presentation of the mission kerygma on the one hand, and the outpouring of the Spirit on the other, ἔτι λαλοῦντος τοῦ Πέτρου...ἐπέπεσεν τὸ πνεῦμα τὸ ἅγιον ("while Peter was still speaking...the Holy Spirit came down," v. 44a), already shows that the discourse in 10:34–43 is an integral part of the turning point Luke is portraying and does not represent, for example, merely a pious rhetorical addendum. Of particular significance, however, is that in v. 44b Luke does not refer — as the course of events would have suggested — to Cornelius and his companions as those who receive the Spirit, but to πάντας τοὺς ἀκούοντας τὸν λόγον ("all who were listening to the speech"). In so doing, he runs the risk of a misunderstanding on the part of his readers, as if the Spirit was also bestowed on the Jewish Christians listening to Peter's proclamation and who have accompanied the apostle since v. 23, that is, on people who

---

11. Wilckens, *Missionsreden*, 95–96.

12. Thus G. Delling, in his review of Wilckens's book, objected to Wilckens's interpretation of Acts 10:34–43: "The events of Acts 10 do indeed involve a turning point; but apart from vv. 34f....of the discourse, this turn comes to expression especially in the *other* content of Acts 10f." (*TLZ* 87 [1962]: 840–43, here 841; my emphasis). C. Burchard even rejected in its entirety Wilckens's view "that the purpose of the discourses is to present the word as *movens* of salvific history" (*Der dreizehnte Zeuge: Traditions- und kompositionsgeschichtliche Untersuchungen zu Lukas' Darstellung der Frühzeit des Paulus*, FRLANT 103 [Göttingen: Vandenhoeck & Ruprecht, 1970], 142 n. 27).

had, after all, been Christians for some time.[13] Only the following verse eliminates the possibility of this misunderstanding by differentiating precisely between
those "circumcised believers" who are astonished at the events and the ἔθνη
("Gentiles") who actually receive the Spirit. Why does Luke formulate the story
in this way? Not from carelessness. Rather, he is apparently concerned with establishing a substantive connection between this epochal occurrence of the first
outpouring of the Spirit on Gentiles, on the one hand, and the proclamation of
the mission kerygma which precedes it, on the other. Only if the apostolic testimony to Jesus is proclaimed and heard can these decisive events take place.
This, however, means nothing other than Luke did indeed want his readers to
understand Peter's discourse in 10:34–43[14] as the last, but indispensable catalyst
for the epoch-making events he portrays in chapter 10.

The setting of Acts 13:14–52 is Pisidian Antioch, where Luke has Paul deliver the corresponding speech (vv. 16–41), the initial result of which is merely
that the (Jewish) listeners ask Paul to deliver the same discourse on the next sabbath (λαληθῆναι αὐτοῖς τὰ ῥήματα ταῦτα ["to speak these words to them"],
v. 42). By the next sabbath, however, the number of those wanting to hear Paul
has grown unexpectedly. Now not only the Jews themselves, but virtually the
entire city has assembled ἀκοῦσαι τὸν λόγον τοῦ κυρίου[15] ("to hear the word
of the Lord," v. 44). Because Luke has already had Paul give a thorough presentation of the mission kerygma a few verses previously, and because from v. 42
the reader already knows that Paul will merely repeat what he said earlier, Luke
has no need to present it again *verbaliter;* the simple reference suffices that Paul
does indeed preach (τὰ ὑπὸ Παύλου λαλούμενα ["the words spoken by Paul"],
v. 45). This time, Paul's preaching has a considerable effect. The Jews "begin to
contradict him and blaspheme" (ἀντέλεγον…βλασφημοῦντες, v. 45), while τὰ
ἔθνη ("the Gentiles") exhibit the opposite reaction. Precisely that which the Jews
blaspheme (τὸν λόγον τοῦ θεοῦ ["the word of God"], cf. v. 46), the Gentiles
praise, namely, τὸν λόγον τοῦ κυρίου ("the word of the Lord," v. 48). Luke has
Paul himself relate the momentous consequences, and he does so — differently
than in chapter 10 — *expressis verbis.* In an epochal change of plans, the Christian missionaries will henceforth turn their attention to the ἔθνη, and will do so
not because the Jews, generally speaking, have already and for long enough been
hostile, but because they were unwilling to accept the witness to Jesus which
Paul has just delivered (ἐπειδὴ ἀπωθεῖσθε αὐτὸν [τὸν λόγον τοῦ θεοῦ]…ἰδοὺ
στρεφόμεθα εἰς τὰ ἔθνη ["since you reject it (the word of God)…we now turn
to the Gentiles"], v. 46). Just as in chapter 10, but now even more clearly, a

---

13. At least one exegete has fallen prey to this misunderstanding: H. H. Wendt, *Die Apostelgeschichte,* 5th ed., KEK 3 (Göttingen: Vandenhoeck & Ruprecht, 1913), 185. G. Schneider, *Die
Apostelgeschichte,* vol. 2, HTKNT 5/2 (Freiburg, Basel, and Vienna: Herder, 1982), 80, does in any
case see the possibility of such a misunderstanding.

14. "τὸν λόγον evidently means the mission sermon just delivered by Peter" (E. Haenchen, *Acts
of the Apostles* [Philadelphia: Westminster, 1971], 353).

15. That is, "the preaching of Christ" (ibid., 413).

mission speech proves to be the decisive *movens* of the history of the church, moving the Jews to reject the kerygma and prompting the Christian missionaries to the decision to make the church into a church primarily of Gentiles.

These two examples show that one does not have to rely only on an interpretation of Luke's theological conception or on exegetical instinct to determine the function of the mission speeches in Acts in the way Wilckens has done (and correctly, in my opinion). Each text in its position reveals that, in Luke's opinion, it was the speeches of the apostles and Paul that directed the development of early Christianity at the turning points of its history.

Since this is the case, one can take the next step with a good exegetical conscience and ask which models Luke may have been following here. In this regard, I have already drawn attention to Dionysius of Halicarnassus[16] and would like to provide a broader foundation for those earlier insights.

At the beginning of the eleventh book of his *Roman Antiquities*, Dionysius reflects on the best way to do justice to his readers' expectations. A concise presentation of the *bruta facta* alone is doubtless not to their taste, as he makes clear in a six-line résumé of the Persian War. Rather, readers want to learn details as well as τὰς αἰτίας ἀκοῦσαι δι᾽ ἃς τὰ θαυμαστὰ καὶ παράδοξα ἔργα ἐπετέλεσαν ("to hear of the causes that enabled men to perform their astonishing and extraordinary exploits," 1.2). A few lines later, Dionysius speaks about the manner in which the historian is to write about "political events" (πολιτικὰς πράξεις), asserting anew that readers are not satisfied merely with learning τὸ κεφάλαιον αὐτὸ καὶ τὸ πέρας τῶν πραγμάτων ("the bare summary and outcome of the events"). For example, the historian cannot simply report that at the end of the Peloponnesian War the warring parties agreed to raze the long walls, to dismantle the Athenian fleet, to relocate a Spartan garrison to Athens, and to introduce an oligarchy there in place of democracy — and to do all this without any final battle. No, readers also want to know what conditions forced the Athenians to submit to such gruesome conditions and, in general, to learn about everything that may have played a role in these events. Dionysius then mentions one additional ingredient of history which in his opinion readers expect in any portrayal of the kind of cataclysm the end of the Peloponnesian War represented for Athens: τίνες οἱ πείσαντες αὐτοὺς [τοὺς Ἀθηναίους] λόγοι καὶ ὑπὸ τίνων ῥηθέντες ἀνδρῶν ("what speeches that persuaded them [the Athenians] were delivered at that time and by whom," 1.3). In our context, it is of significance that Dionysius calls these speeches πείσαντες αὐτοὺς λόγοι ("speeches that persuaded them"), a specification apparently intended to show that the λόγοι expected by readers do not involve merely arbitrary embellishments, but precisely those speeches that prompted the Athenians to submit to their "harsh defeat" (ταῦτα τὰ δεινὰ καὶ σχέτλια) without further struggle, speeches that

---

16. *Lukas als hellenistischer Schriftsteller: Studien zur Apostelgeschichte,* SUNT 9 (Göttingen: Vandenhoeck & Ruprecht, 1972), 36; "Apostelgeschichte," *TRE* 3 (1978): 483–528, here 505.

were thus of historically determinative significance.[17] This means, however, that the speeches to which Dionysius draws attention are to be viewed as part of those αἰτίαι ("causes") which he has just discussed and which, being responsible for certain θαυμαστὰ καὶ παράδοχα ἔργα ("astonishing and extraordinary deeds"), are not to be withheld.

In *Ant.* 7.66, Dionysius's understanding of such speeches as determinative factors (i.e., αἰτίαι) emerges much more clearly. Dionysius's portrayal of the class wars that convulsed Rome after the collapse of the kingship is both unusually thorough and replete with speeches. He ends this portrayal by justifying its excessive length[18] with the assertion: ποθεῖ γὰρ ἕκαστος ἐπὶ τοῖς παραδόξοις ἀκούσμασι τὴν αἰτίαν μαθεῖν ("for everyone, upon hearing of extraordinary events, desires to know the cause that produced them," 66.1). For just that reason, he writes a few lines later, he decided not to pass over the αἰτίαι, but to report "all" of them (ἁπάσας, 66.2). Since the class wars were not decided by weapons, ἀλλὰ λόγοις πείσαντες ("but by the persuasion of words"), he considered it "absolutely necessary" (παντὸς μάλιστα ἀναγκαῖον) "to report the speeches" (τοὺς λόγους αὐτῶν διεξελθεῖν) delivered by the leaders of the opposing parties (66.3).

But Dionysius is not finished yet. After explaining why he proceeds as described in composing his own historical work, he expresses his critical amazement that other historical writers (τίνες) have not done this. He charges them with having reported the most minute details while considering it unnecessary to provide depictions of political events, which, along with those particular speeches, set the most extraordinary and remarkable events into motion: πολιτικὰς δὲ κινήσεις καὶ στάσεις ἀναγράφοντες οὐκ οἴονται δεῖν ἀπαγγέλλειν τοὺς λόγους δι᾽ ὧν αἱ παράδοξοι καὶ θαυμασταὶ πράξεις ἐπετελέσθησαν ("yet when they come to give an account of civil commotions and seditions, do not consider it necessary to report the speeches by which the extraordinary and remarkable events were brought to pass," 66.3).

Who, however, are these τίνες whom Dionysius accuses of neglecting the historiographical task of transmitting such historically significant speeches? The only real possibility is Thucydides. Dionysius, himself probably a teacher of rhetoric by profession, and in any case the author of a series of rhetorical writings,[19] devoted a special study to Thucydides — Περὶ Θουκυδίδου — a treatise joining fundamental admiration for the great Athenian with criticism that does not shy away from the occasional acerbic judgment. Thus Dionysius claims to have noted, among other things, that Thucydides does not always treat with appropriate care the material critical in portraying certain events. With respect to unimportant matters, Dionysius alleges, Thucydides writes with undue verbosity,

---

17. The parallelism with ἀλλὰ λόγοις πείσαντες ("but by persuasion of speeches," 7.66.3) also shows that this interpretation is accurate; see the discussion below.

18. 7.66.1: ἐμήκυνα δὲ τὸν ὑπὲρ αὐτῶν λόγον ("I have related these [things] at length").

19. See in this regard W. Schmid and O. Stählin, *Geschichte der griechischen Literatur* II.1, HKAW VII/1 (Munich: Beck, 1920), 466–72.

whereas precisely where such thoroughness would be in order he fails to put forth the necessary effort.[20] The reproach — πλείονας τοῦ δέοντος λόγους ἀποδιδοὺς τοῖς ἐλαττόνων δεομένοις ("giving more space to matters that demand less") — recalls the τίνες of *Ant.* 7.66.3 who, to Dionysius's chagrin, pass over what he considers to be important material while elsewhere becoming infatuated with details, καὶ περὶ μίαν ἔστιν ὅτε μάχην πολλοὺς ἀναλίσκουσι λόγους ("and sometimes expend a great many words over a single battle").

Dionysius tries in the following chapters of his tractate to demonstrate this criticism in individual examples from Thucydides' work; in the process, he also speaks about Thucydides' speeches. Dionysius's critique of the Epitaphios, which he finds misplaced since it is not at a turning point (chap. 18), is not pertinent to our own context and can thus be disregarded. Dionysius adduces two other passages from Thucydides in support of his own critique, however, and these are of significance.

The first (*Peloponnesian War* 3.36–49) recounts the treatment the Athenians wish to accord the inhabitants of Mytilene, which had seceded and then was retaken in the summer of 427 B.C.E. Initially the assembly decides to kill or to enslave them all, but subsequently regrets the brutal decision and rescinds it after further debate. That Thucydides reports only the speeches delivered during the second session, and not those delivered during the first, demonstrates to Dionysius that Thucydides himself was inclined τιθέναι μὲν ἃς οὐκ ἔδει, παραλιπεῖν δὲ ἃς ἔδει λέγεσθαι ("to take up nonessentials and to omit essentials"). The decision to extinguish an entire city through murder and enslavement Dionysius found of greater import than the decision to grant mercy. Hence he thought Thucydides should have complemented his portrayal of the first assembly with speeches rather than the second assembly, at which merely μετάνοιά τις ὑπεισῆλθε τοὺς πολλούς ("a change of heart gradually came over the majority"). Unfortunately, the great historian did just the opposite, as Dionysius relates with regret, by τοὺς μὲν ἐν τῇ προτέρᾳ ῥηθέντας ὑπὸ τῶν δημαγωγῶν λόγους παρέλιπεν ὡς οὐκ ἀναγκαίους... τοὺς δ' ἐν τῇ ὑστεραίᾳ πάλιν ὑπὸ τῶν αὐτῶν ῥηθέντας... παρέλαβεν ὡς ἀναγκαίους ("he omits as unnecessary the speeches made by the demagogues in the first meeting... but he finds it necessary to include the speeches made by the same men at the second meeting").[21] Again we notice the similarity with *Ant.* 7.66.2–3, in which Dionysius emphasizes that he has not omitted (παρέλιπον) anything essential for the reader, namely, the αἰτίαι ("causes") of events, since he considered it "absolutely necessary" (παντὸς μάλιστα ἀναγκαῖον) to include the speeches of the various parties which were ultimately determining the course of events.

Dionysius's criticism of the other Thucydides passage shows clearly that in his own historical writing, what he theoretically demands of others, or as critic thinks one should demand, he carries out. In 2.59.1–2, Thucydides recounts

---

20. *De Thuc.* 13 (839).
21. *De Thuc.* 17 (848).

with exceptional brevity the occasion when the peace emissaries Athens had dispatched to Sparta in the summer of 430 b.c.e. return without having accomplished anything. Dionysius charges Thucydides with failing to report the essentials — neither the identity of the Athenian emissaries, nor the speeches they must have delivered in Sparta, nor also those of their opponents — speeches which in Dionysius's opinion persuaded the Spartans that it would be better not to comply with the Athenians' wishes (οὔτε τοὺς ἀποσταλέντας ἄνδρας εἴρηκεν οὔτε τοὺς ῥηθέντας ἐκεῖ λόγους ὑπ᾿ αὐτῶν οὔτε τοὺς ἐναντιωθέντας, ὑφ᾿ ὧν πεισθέντες Λακεδαιμόνιοι τὰς διαλλαγὰς ἀπεψηφίσαντο ["he does not give the names of the ambassadors or record the speeches they made there, nor the names of the opposing speakers whose arguments persuaded the Lacedaemonians to reject an armistice"]).[22] What Dionysius finds lacking is virtually verbatim the same thing he presents in Book 11 of the Antiquitates as the essential ingredient of appropriate historical writing, writing that does not omit the αἰτίαι of events. The reader should learn τίνες οἱ πείσαντες αὐτοὺς λόγοι καὶ ὑπὸ τίνων ῥηθέντες ἀνδρῶν ("what the speeches were that persuaded them, and by what men those speeches were delivered," 1.3). Like Thucydides, the unnamed historical writers in Ant. 7.66.3 had also failed to discharge this historiographical task, namely, ἀπαγγέλλειν τοὺς λόγους δι᾿ ὧν αἱ παράδοξοι καὶ θαυμασταὶ πράξεις ἐπετελέσθησαν ("to report the speeches by which the extraordinary and astonishing events were brought to pass").[23] And Dionysius was convinced that Thucydides' apparently inappropriate report in Peloponnesian War 2.59.1–2 must have involved events whose considerable significance certainly merited the historian's literary attention. He goes on to criticize Thucydides for narrating inappropriately and carelessly, as if he were reporting merely small, unimportant matters: φαύλως δέ πως καὶ ῥαθύμως ὡς περὶ μικρῶν καὶ ἀδόξων πραγμάτων ταῦτα εἴρηκε ("His narration is rather insipid and careless, as if the episode were minor and without importance").[24] We thus have good reason to conclude that Dionysius's reproach of his colleagues in Ant. 7.66.3 was in fact directed at none other than Thucydides himself.[25]

In summary, several observations show clearly that the Lukan conception of the mission speeches as factors determining the course of history is identical with that of Dionysius. These observations are Dionysius's reasoning concerning the correct way to report the end of the Peloponnesian War (11.1.2–3), the

---

22. De Thuc. 14 (842–43). Dionysius admits that Thucydides is capable of proceeding differently, and precisely this fact provokes his criticism (14–15 [843–44]).

23. See 11.1.2: The readers of a ἱστορία demanded καὶ τὰς αἰτίας ἀκοῦσαι, δι᾿ ἃς τὰ θαυμαστὰ καὶ παράδοξα ἔργα ἐπετέλεσαν ("to hear of the causes that enabled men to perform their astonishing and extraordinary exploits").

24. De Thuc. 14 (843).

25. In this case, τίνες would represent "an indefinite substitute for an all-too-clear singular" (E. Schwyzer and E. Debrunner, Griechische Grammatik, vol. 2, Handbuch der Altertumswissenschaft II 1.2 [Munich: Beck, 1950], 45). This is not the place to discuss whether Dionysius's charges against Thucydides are justified or not (probably the latter is the case), though see W. K. Pritchett, Dionysius of Halicarnassus: On Thucydides (Berkeley: University of California Press, 1975), 64–70.

justification he offers for his extensive portrayal of the early republican class wars (7.66), his astonishment and displeasure concerning those historians who fail to report speeches in the way he considers appropriate (7.66.3–4), and finally his relevant criticism of Thucydides (*De Thuc.* 14; 17). These texts leave no doubt that, like the author of Acts, Dionysius was already convinced that at important turning points of history, such as the end of the Peloponnesian War or the entry of the *plebs* into Roman politics, it was speeches that determined the course of history. Because of their function as αἰτίαι of events, such speeches were to be transmitted by the writer of history — de facto, of course, styled by the author himself and placed into the mouths of these protagonists of history.[26]

The significance Dionysius ascribed to the structuring of such speeches can hardly be overestimated. In the prologue to the *Antiquitates,* he defined the form of his own historical work as ἐξ ἁπάσης ἰδέας μικτὸν ἐναγωνίου τε καὶ θεωρητικῆς καὶ διηγηματικῆς ("as a mixture of narrative, reflection, and political speeches," 1.8.3). That ἐναγώνιος does indeed imply this sense, namely that of a political speech, emerges from Dionysius's own rhetorical writings, where ἐναγώνιοι λόγοι refer to deliberative and forensic speeches, "speeches which involve decisions of state and thus are of central importance to the historical narrative." Such is the assessment of Kenneth S. Sacks, who, investigating these connections in Dionysius, came to the conclusion that "it is, after all, the agonistic style which is the true stuff of decision-making situations and hence of history writing; a consideration which Dionysius himself expresses in the *prooemium* to his own historical work."[27]

Admittedly, there is little chance that Luke was dependent on Dionysius. Such direct influence is unlikely, especially since at least one additional historian shared the views expressed by Dionysius and implemented by Luke concerning the value of citing historically determinative speeches. Livius[28] followed this principle in composing his own works — writings with which Dionysius was not familiar.[29] Just which historical writers might have influenced Luke's approach to

---

26. Accordingly, Dionysius writes the following in his *prooemium*, *Ant.* 1.8.2: ἀφηγοῦμαι δὲ τούς τε ὀθνείους πολέμους τῆς πόλεως ἅπαντας ...καὶ τὰς ἐμφυλίους στάσεις ὁπόσας ἐστασίασεν, ἐξ οἵων αἰτιῶν ἐγένοντο καὶ δι᾽ οἵων τρόπων τε καὶ λόγων κατελύθησαν ("I relate all the foreign wars of the city ... and all the internal seditions with which she was agitated, showing from what causes they sprang and by what methods and by what arguments [namely, delivered in speeches] they were brought to an end").

27. "Rhetorical Approaches to Greek History Writing in the Hellenistic Period," *SBLSP* 23 (1984): 123–33, here 129, 131. Cf. idem, "Rhetoric and Speeches in Hellenistic Historiography," *Athenaeum* (Paris), n.s., 64 (1986): 383–95.

28. He was a master at composing speeches whose literary function consisted in setting into motion critical historical processes (several examples are included in Eckhard Plümacher, *Lukas als hellenistischer Schriftsteller: Studien zur Apostelgeschichte* (Göttingen: Vandenhoeck & Ruprecht, 1972), 36–37). Unlike Dionysius, however, Livy did not reflect on this in his works; such was not customary for Roman historians. "If we wish to study the methodological considerations and practices of the various [Roman] historians, we must deduce their methods from the actual portrayals themselves" (E. Burck, "Grundzüge römischer Geschichtsauffassung und Geschichtsschreibung," *GWU* 25 [1974]: 1–40, here 10 = idem, *Vom Menschenbild in der römischen Literatur: Ausgewählte Schriften,* vol. 2 [Heidelberg: Winter, 1981], 72–117, here 82).

29. E. Schwartz, "Dionysius von Halikarnassos," *PRE* 5.934–61, here 946. Cf. A. Klotz, "Livius

the mission speeches is not especially important. What is important is that we are able to discern what kind of historical writing influenced Luke here, namely, political writing. To that extent, one can certainly agree with David L. Balch when at the end of his comparison of Luke and Dionysius he summarizes: "Luke-Acts is written in the genre of Greco-Roman political historiography."[30]

In this connection, I would like to draw attention to yet another point of comparison between the Lukan mission speeches and Dionysius's views of political speeches as αἰτίαι of history. As Ernst Haenchen has put it in an accurate and much-cited dictum, "Luke the historian is wrestling, from the first page to the last, with the problem of the *mission to the Gentiles without the law.*"[31] That mission had brought about the condition of the Lukan church as one consisting almost exclusively of Gentile Christians. Its continuity with its ἀρχή, its Jewish Christian beginnings, and, beyond that, with the Jewish people of Israel, to whom the promises were, after all, initially given, had been called into question (or even been disputed?). Luke writes in order to resolve the identity crises that had emerged among his congregations in this situation. To this end, Luke became a church historian; by doing so, he could demonstrate the legitimacy of the Gentile church by showing the legitimacy of the events through which the church had come to its present status.[32] The mission speeches represent one essential element in this demonstration. They are delivered by the apostles (and Paul), who themselves were eyewitnesses to the Jesus events and in any case guarantors of tradition. As such, the speeches contain the unadulterated Jesus kerygma, which Luke always introduces in Acts whenever the development of the church

---

und seine Vorgänger," in *Neue Wege zur Antike* II.11.3 (Leipzig and Berlin: Teubner, 1941), 201–303, here 218–72.

30. "Comments on the Genre and a Political Theme of Luke-Acts: A Preliminary Comparison of Two Hellenistic Historians," *SBLSP* 28 (1989): 343–61, here 361 (see also D. Balch's more recent contribution to this volume in chap. 9 [ed.]). To be sure, the question arises whether the "Greco-Roman political historiography" as genre can be characterized in the strict sense as a specific generic type (*Gattung*). Certainly it cannot be denied that Dionysius of Halicarnassus in his *Antiquitates* pursued politically motivated goals (namely, "apologetic" [see below]), as Polybius earlier also had done in his universal history. The latter notwithstanding, Dionysius belongs in the context of rhetorically oriented historiography and not, as with Polybius, in the more pragmatic-factually oriented. It is different again with the author of Acts. Although not in every respect, nevertheless in his presentation he is indebted in a wide variety of ways to tragic-pathetic (i.e., mimetic) historiography (see E. Plümacher, "ΤΕΡΑΤΕΙΑ: Fiktion und Wunder in der hellenistisch-römischen Geschichtsschreibung und in der Apostelgeschichte," *ZNW* 89 [1998]: 66–90). Therefore one should always keep this observation in mind: "Rhetorical, tragic (i.e., mimetic), and factually oriented (i.e., pragmatic) historiography are the main lines of Hellenistic historiography. From the very beginning, however, they do not exist as ideal-types nor develop into discrete modes of their own; rather, from early on they begin to overlap and combine with each other with the result that a large number of historians can be mentioned, whose presentations exhibit not only rhetorical but also tragic and 'pragmatic' elements — to be sure, in a wide range of combinations" (K. Meister, *Die griechische Geschichtsschreibung: Von den Anfängen bis zum Ende des Hellenismus* [Stuttgart: Kohlhammer, 1990], 80–81).

31. *Acts of the Apostles*, 100 (emphasis in the original).

32. See in this regard Plümacher, *TRE* 3.518–20; idem, "Acta-Forschung 1974–1982," *TRu*, n.s., 48 (1983): 1–56, here 45–46, and especially the bibliographical information supplied in both references.

is about to take a significant step toward the Gentile church. In fact, Luke not only introduces this kerygma as present at such junctures, he also suggests that its very pronouncement is what first precipitates and sets this development in motion. An event inaugurated by the Jesus-witness itself could not possibly be illegitimate and, consequently, according to the author of Acts, neither could the result of such an event, in this case the Gentile church itself. This means, however, that Luke appeals to speeches delivered in the ideal early period of the church — especially speeches which were instrumental in opening the church to Gentiles — in order to resolve a basic problem of the church of his own age, namely, that of identity and legitimacy.

•

It may not be redundant at this point to elaborate on the content of the procla-mation, as well as on those who deliver the mission speeches of Acts 10:34–43 and 13:16–41. As requested for this volume, these remarks are intended to bring into bolder relief the relation of these speeches to the Jesus tradition of Luke's first volume.

First, attention should be directed to the focus of the two mission speeches which, as in the rest of the speeches, appeals to events of Jesus which Luke has already described in his Gospel (see Acts 10:37–42; 13:23–31).[33] Jesus' baptism (10:38); the witness to Jesus of John the Baptist (13:25); Jesus' Spirit-empowered deeds of mercy and of healing the infirm during his itinerant (διέρχεσθαι) pub-lic ministry (10:38; 13:31); the sentencing by Pilate (13:28); crucifixion, death, burial (10:39; 13:29), and resurrection (10:40–41; 13:30); the resurrection appear-ances (10:40–41; 13:31); as well as the commissioning of the apostles as witnesses (10:42a) — to be sure, all of these appear in such abbreviated form that familiarity with the preceding πρῶτος λόγος ("first volume") becomes indispensable to under-standing the passages in Acts.[34] By virtue of these multiple lines of connection, one has a basis to regard the Lukan volumes as a carefully crafted literary unity.

It should further be noticed that in both speeches, the pointedly provocative rehearsals of Jesus' activities and fate can hardly be intended as edifying ornamen-tation; rather, in the context of legitimation in which both speeches have been instrumental in spawning seminal developments in the growth of the church, this appeal to specific events in Jesus' ministry takes on a substantive function — ma-terially significant in the transformation of an early community of Jewish believers to a predominantly Gentile church. The more distinctive role this appeal assumes

---

33. See M. Korn, *Die Geschichte Jesu in veränderter Zeit: Studien zur bleibenden Bedeutung Jesu im lukanischen Doppelwerk,* WMANT, 2d ser., no. 51 (Tübingen: Mohr, 1993), 215–16; see also K. Kliesch, *Das heilsgeschichtliche Credo in den Reden der Apostelgeschichte,* BBB 44 (Cologne and Bonn: Hanstein, 1975), 77–78, who offers a synopsis of the "Jesus kerygma" presented in the mission speeches.

34. Korn (*Geschichte Jesu,* 216) observes correctly: "The Jesus kerygma of the speeches is pre-sented only in skeletal form.... This skeleton is enfleshed for the reader of Acts only through the Gospel of Luke which, not incidentally, is referred to at the beginning of Acts as the prerequisite for a second book which now follows" (Acts 1:1–2). In this same vein, it should come as no surprise that in Acts 10:37–42a the basic conception of the course of Jesus' public ministry corresponds to that which Luke has already described in his Gospel; see U. Wilckens, "Kerygma und Evangelium bei Lukas (Beobachtungen zu Acta 10,34–43)," *ZNW* 49 (1958): 223–37, esp. 235–36.

becomes evident when one keeps in mind that these words of the proclaimers, which thrust the events of Jesus' life before their audiences as still present and pertinent, can hardly then be construed as a recollection of bare facts. Rather, they are historical events pregnant with meaning, especially as their relevance emerges from the rhetoric of Acts 13:16–41 (cf. also 10:43!): the events of Jesus' ministry are dovetailed into the larger context of the history of the people of God (13:17–23). In light of the argument developed from scripture (13:27, 29, 32–37), they must be viewed within the scheme of promise and fulfillment and acknowledged as events of salvation history. But as such, these events of Jesus, fully integrated into the roles of Peter and Paul in their proclamation as "witness to Jesus," insofar as they become catalysts for further events render these new moments in the church's preaching as saving events: legitimation begets legitimation.

The speakers of these mission addresses, the apostles as well as Paul, possess a gift of legitimation — their own unique legitimation — which surpasses even the gifts of the Spirit which empower their testimony to Jesus. With respect to the events which they proclaimed of Jesus' ministry, "beginning from the baptism of John until the day he was received up from us" (Acts 1:22), they were "eyewitnesses" (10:39–41; 13:31). To be sure, Paul is an "eyewitness" only in an indirect sense, although he can still claim to be a direct witness *of* and *to* the Resurrected One (9:1–6, 17; 22:6–10, 14–15; 26:12–16); otherwise, however, concerning the integrity of this "testimony," he must rely on his frequent contacts with the apostles, whose testimony he *expressis verbis* appeals to in 13:31.[35] That this special "eyewitness" authority can only stimulate more possibilities for further legitimation, and through the mission speeches lend greater credence to the significance of the events of Jesus' ministry for the church's development, is self-evident.

Finally, it should be noted that it is completely fitting that the mission speeches of the apostles and Paul follow the same outline[36] and, despite numerous differences in detail, convey fundamentally the same message. The witness to Jesus — which stands at the beginning of the church's history, steers the development, and accords the church legitimacy — must be substantively the same, since otherwise the unambiguous proclamation of the early church which authenticates later developments and events would be placed in jeopardy.[37]

•

Just as Luke turned his attention in Acts to the beginnings of church history, so also Dionysius in the *Antiquitates* to the early history of Rome. Dionysius, too, is

---

35. The literature treating Luke's notion of "witness" is rather extensive. Here can be mentioned only G. Schneider, "Die zwölf Apostel als 'Zeugen': Wesen, Ursprung und Funktion einer lukanischen Konzeption," in *Christuszeugnis der Kirche: Theologische Studien*, ed. P.-W. Scheele and G. Schneider (Essen: Fredebeul & Koenen, 1970), 39–65; E. Nellessen, *Zeugnis für Jesus und das Wort: Exegetische Untersuchungen zum lukanischen Zeugenbegriff*, BBB 43 (Cologne and Bonn: Hanstein, 1976), as well as the relevant passages in Korn (*Geschichte Jesu*, 193–213).

36. See E. Schweizer, "Zu den Reden der Apostelgeschichte," *ThZ* 13 (1957): 1–11, and Wilckens, *Missionsreden* (see n. 9), 54–55.

37. The element of "sheer repetitiveness" which M. L. Soards ("The Speeches in Acts in Relation to other Pertinent Ancient Literature," *ETL* 70 [1994]: 65–90 [quote, p. 90]) correctly sees as influencing the speeches in Acts, including the mission speeches, is the result of Luke's understanding of the uniform character of the early church's kerygma.

driven not by any antiquarian interest, but rather, as he discloses *expressis verbis* in his prologue, by apologetical considerations, namely, to counter anti-Roman propaganda. During his own time this anti-Romanism was enjoying considerable popularity among his fellow Greeks, and, to Dionysius's indignation, was even being disseminated by writers of history (τῶν συγγραφέων τινές).[38] Two reproaches were making the rounds. First, that the Romans originally were merely a homeless, wandering people of barbarian or even slave origins. Second, that Rome became a world power not as the result of any particular piety (εὐσέβεια), righteousness (δικαιοσύνη), or any other virtue (ἀρετή), but merely by chance and through the injustice of fate, which arbitrarily bestows the highest gifts on the most unworthy, gifts which by all rights belong not to the Romans — these most barbaric of all the barbarians — but alone to the Greeks.[39]

In his *Antiquitates*, Dionysius tries in every respect to demonstrate the falsity of such defamation. The entire first book addresses the assertion that the ancestors of the Romans were in reality true Greeks, and numerous excursuses address the kinship between the Roman and Greek institutions, or even the superiority of the former over the latter.[40] Just how unwarranted is the charge that fate allowed Rome to rise undeservedly to power Dionysius's readers can see from its history. From the very beginning, the city produced myriad (μυρίαι) individual examples of the ἀνδρῶν ἀρετάς ("heroic exploits"), who were "more devout" (εὐσεβέστεροι), "more righteous" (δικαιότεροι), "demonstrated more lifelong self-control" (σωφροσύνῃ πλείονι παρὰ πάντα τὸν βίον χρησάμενοι), and were more courageous than anything found in any Greek or barbarian city history.[41]

One of the examples of Rome's moral superiority over Greece, from which Dionysius deduces Rome's right to world dominion, involves the manner in which the class struggles (in his opinion) were conducted and resolved during the period of the oldest republic. That the opposing parties refrained from using violence against one another Dionysius initially describes as a τῆς Ῥωμαίων πόλεως μέγα ἐγκώμιον ("as a Roman act certainly deserving of praise"). He points out that they resolved their disputes ὥσπερ ἀδελφοὶ ἀδελφοῖς ἢ παῖδες γονεῦσιν ἐν οἰκίᾳ σώφρονι περὶ τῶν ἴσων καὶ δικαίων διαλεγόμενοι ("conferring together about what was fair and just, like brothers with brothers or children with their parents in a well-governed family"), without inflicting permanent damage on each other, but πειθοῖ καὶ λόγῳ ("by persuasion and reason"). Then, however, he continues by qualifying such actions as absolutely exemplary: (ἐγκώμιόν ἐστι) καὶ ζηλοῦσθαι ὑπὸ πάντων ἀνθρώπων ἄξιον ("this is an ex-

---

38. 1.4.2; 5; cf. 1.89.1–2; 2.17; 7.70.1. On history writers, see 1.4.3; cf. Livius 9.18.6.

39. 1.4.2. Concerning the anti-Roman propaganda, see Schwartz, *PRE* 5.959–60; H. Fuchs, *Der geistige Widerstand gegen Rom in der antiken Welt*, 2d ed. (Berlin: de Gruyter, 1964), 13–19; 40–47.

40. See Schwartz, *PRE* 5.960.

41. 1.5.2–3; cf. 20.6.1, where Dionysius has Pyrrhus admit that in the war against Rome he fought "against people who were more pious than the Greeks and more just" (πρὸς ἀνθρώπους ὁσιωτάτους [conj. ὁσιωτέρους] Ἑλλήνων καὶ δικαιοτάτους [conj. δικαιοτέρους]).

ample worthy of emulation by all humanity").[42] Given what Dionysius says in his *prooemium*, it is clear that the entire passage of 7.66.4–5 is addressing the Greeks. Still, rather than leaving this insight to the reader, he prefers to state it explicitly himself, revealing thereby just how important the insight was to him. That which in early republican Rome the *patres* and *plebs* had avoided in so exemplary a fashion, namely, ἀνήκεστον δ᾽ ἢ ἀνόσιον ἔργον μηθὲν ὑπομεῖναι δρᾶσαι κατ᾽ ἀλλήλων ("inflicting irreparable damage on one another during their disputes"), was allegedly common among the Greeks: διὰ Κερκυραῖοί τε κατὰ τὴν στάσιν εἰργάσαντο καὶ Ἀργεῖοι καὶ Μιλήσιοι καὶ Σικελία πᾶσα καὶ συχναὶ ἄλλαι πόλεις ("such as the Corcyraeans committed at the time of their sedition, and also the Argives, the Milesians, and all Sicily, as well as many other states," 66.5).

From the *prooemium* and certainly no less from individual reflections dispersed throughout the *Antiquitates*, we can thus conclude that Dionysius, no differently than Luke, wrote in order to address problems of legitimacy.[43] Just as Luke found himself confronted with the question concerning the legitimacy of a church that, contrary to its own Jewish Christian beginnings, had become a Gentile church, so Dionysius was confronted with the problem generated for Rome by Greek intellectuals who disputed its right to power with historical and moral arguments.

---

42. 7.66.4–5. By acting as Dionysius asserts, the Romans resembled their own ancestor Romulus in fulfilling a political ideal which, as Dionysius remarks in 2.18.1, was seldom actualized in political life, since "all statesmen chatter about it but few succeed in making it effective: first, the favor of the gods ... next, moderation and justice, as a result of which the citizens, being less disposed to injure one another, are more harmonious" (θρυλοῦσι μὲν ἅπαντες οἱ πολιτικοί, κατασκευάζουσι δ᾽ ὀλίγοι, πρῶτον μὲν τὴν παρὰ τῶν θεῶν εὔνοιαν ... ἔπειτα τὴν σωφροσύνην τε καὶ δικαιοσύνην, δι᾽ ἃς ἧττον ἀλλήλους βλάπτοντες μᾶλλον ὁμονοοῦει). Cf. also 2.62.5.

43. One additional goal of the *Roman Antiquities* was in any case to provide "a παράδειγμα of classicism" (Schwartz, *PRE* 5.934; cf. 938–39). In addition, Dionysius, like Horace, Livy, or Virgil, may also have been trying to function as a propagandist for the Augustean ideology of the principate. P. M. Martin has shown that the entire first book of the *Antiquitates* can be read as "a hymn to *concordia* and a demonstration *ad absurdum* of the folly of civil wars" ("La propagande augustéenne dans les Antiquités romaines de Denys d'Halicarnasse [Livre I]," *Revue des études latines* 49 [1971]: 162–79). Is the passage in *Ant.* 7.66.4 also to be understood in this sense? Dionysius not only relates that the opposing parties in the class struggle renounced the use of violence, he also gives precise details: The δημοτικοί did not attempt to rise up against the πατρίκιοι, kill many of the κράτιστοι, and seize their property. Nor did those with rank and status (i.e., the patricians) try to destroy the δημοτικόν through their own power or with foreign support (ξενικαὶ ἐπικουρίαι). The following, however, did take place during the civil war: murder of senators, proscriptions, and even the mobilization of a foreign power, namely, Egypt, against Rome — thus the suggestion of Octavian's propaganda, which Virgil renders as follows: *Hinc ope barbarica variisque Antonius armis / ... / Aegyptum viresque Orientis et ultima secum / Bactra vehit, sequiturque — nefas — Aegyptia coniunx* ("here Antonius with barbaric might and varied arms ... brings with him Egypt and the strength of the East and utmost Bactra; and there follows him — o shame! — his Egyptian wife" (*Aeneid* 8.685–88). We recall that Dionysius praised the ancestors' renunciation of violence as "worthy of emulation by all humankind" (ζηλοῦσθαι ὑπὸ πάντων ἀνθρώπων ἄξιον). One might conclude that he saw his age characterized by the peaceful accord he advocates, and that he wanted to legitimate (similar to Livy; cf. F. Altheim, *Römische Geschichte*, vol. 2 [Berlin: de Gruyter, 1948], 123–25) the *consensus universorum* or *omnium* on which the principate of Augustus was ideologically based (see in this regard H. U. Instinsky, "Consensus universorum," *Hermes* 75 [1940]: 265–78; Altheim, *Geschichte*, 103–31) by demonstrating its foreshadowing in the early Roman Republic. Dionysius's goal, however, delineated *expressis verbis*, was the legitimation of Roman rule, not that of the principate.

As we saw, both Luke and Dionysius tried to resolve these problems through recourse to history, which in their opinion should and could adequately legitimate the current state of affairs.

For Luke, speeches — the mission speeches — played a monumental role in this process of legitimation. Because they were the decisive factors in the developing legitimation of unfolding events, Luke transmitted (i.e., shaped) them. The same applies to Dionysius.

As I have already shown, Dionysius saw in the class struggles of the earliest republic a luminous example of the moral superiority of Rome over Greece, moral superiority lending legitimacy to Roman rule. For Dionysius, this superiority resulted from the nonviolent fashion in which the disputes between the *patres* and *plebs* were resolved, a fashion the opposite of that in many Greek states. What, however, was able to move the Roman ancestors to the nonviolence generating such moral superiority? Dionysius poses this question as well, and also uses it to justify the considerable length of his own portrayal of the class struggles. He wanted, he says in 66.1, to prevent anyone from wondering *how* the *patres* came to grant the *plebs* such power without, as was the case in other many other states (πόλεις), being coerced into doing so through murder and exile of aristocrats (πῶς ὑπέμειναν οἱ πατρίκιοι τηλικαύτης ἐξουσίας ποιῆσαι τὸν δῆμον κύριον, οὔτε σφαγῆς τῶν ἀρίστων ἀνδρῶν γενομένης οὔτε φυγῆς, οἷον ἐν ἄλλαις πολλαῖς ἐγένετο πόλεσι ["how the patricians ever consented to grant the populace with such great power, when there had been no murdering or banishing of the best citizens, as has happened in many other states"]). As a historian dedicated to discovering the αἰτίαι,[44] Dionysius does not withhold the answer to this question: It was the persuasive speeches of the respective leaders that brought about the nonviolent change (λόγοις πείσαντες μεθήρμοσαν).[45] Precisely because these speeches functioned as αἰτίαι, the historian was bound to include them and make them available to readers (66.3).[46] This means, however, that once again the author of the *Antiquitates* ascribes to the speeches of the participants in the class struggles the same function Luke ascribed to his own mission speeches. For both historians, the speeches in question are not only, as we saw above, the actual *movens* of events. In both cases, they are simultaneously the *movens* of events that — albeit in different ways — possessed the power to lend legitimacy to present circumstances. The Jesus-witness which comes to expression in the mission speeches led to the Gentile mission; as such, it also was able to legitimate the results of that mission, namely, the Gentile church. The speeches delivered during the class struggles resulted in the latter's nonviolent resolution. In a similar way, the speeches transformed those struggles

---

44. He does not want to accuse himself: "I left out the causes for their making these concessions" (δι᾽ ἃς δὲ συνεχωρήθη ταῦτ᾽ αἰτίας παρέλιπον, 66.2).

45. See 66.5, where Dionysius relates that the disputes were resolved "by persuasion and reason" (πειθοῖ καὶ λόγῳ).

46. Dionysius then includes the reflection on the duty of the historian to transmit such historically determinative speeches.

into a prime example of the moral superiority of Rome, which is well-suited to serve Dionysius's larger purpose for the *Antiquitates* in arguing for the legitimacy of Roman rule.

This concludes my considerations. Let me emphasize again that the above discussion does not allow us to conclude that the author of Acts was in any way dependent on Dionysius. What the two writers share are views that were probably widespread within the broad sphere of Hellenistic historiography, though even this assumption would be difficult to verify given the fragmented condition of Hellenistic history writing available to us. For just that reason, however, a consideration of the comparatively voluminous work of Dionysius is of value. One should not be "scared off" by the fact that Dionysius was long ridiculed as a "pedantic *graeculus*," a "small soul,"[47] an "extraordinarily slow-witted mind," or as "a man at birth whom the muses scowled at with angry eyes."[48] This applies especially to the scholar interested in Acts, particularly since Acts itself, albeit some time ago, was said to owe its own existence merely to an instance of "tactlessness" (though "of world-historical dimensions").[49] I in any case found consideration of the work of this "pedantic *graeculus*" extremely helpful, and I hope that by drawing attention to the considerable historiographical (and not merely literary) features he shares with Luke, I have shown that the work of Luke belongs not in the context of biography, and certainly not in the context of the novel, but rather in the sphere of the writing of history.

---

47. Schwartz, *PRE* 5.958, 934.

48. E. Norden, *Die antike Kunstprosa*, 3d ed., 2 vols. (Leipzig and Berlin: Teubner, 1915–18), 1.79; 2.884–85.

49. F. Overbeck, *Nachlass*, A.207, Collectaneen zu den Synoptikern, s.v. Lucasevangelium (Charakteristik): Historicismus, n. 2 (cited after J.-C. Emmelius, *Tendenzkritik und Formengeschichte: Der Beitrag Franz Overbecks zur Auslegung der Apostelgeschichte im 19. Jahrhundert*, FKDG 27 [Göttingen: Vandenhoeck & Ruprecht, 1975], 182).

Chapter 11

A Theology of Sea Storms in Luke-Acts

Charles H. Talbert and J. H. Hayes

This essay deals with the theology, implicit and explicit, in the narratives about sea storms in Acts 27 and Luke 8:22–25. It attempts to answer two questions: (1) What theological content would ancient Mediterranean listeners have heard in these narratives? and (2) How do the theological implications of these two stories fit into the Lukan whole?[1]

Theological Content in Acts 27 and Luke 8:22–25

Acts 27

We begin with Acts 27. What theological content would an ancient listener have heard in this narrative? The attempted answer to this question will be developed in three stages: (1) composition, (2) comparative materials, and (3) context.

Composition

Acts 27 belongs to a large thought-unit dealing with Paul's journey from Caesarea to Rome. It consists of introductory (27:1–8) and concluding (28:11–16) itineraries enclosing three episodes (27:9–20; 27:21–44; 28:1–10).

Introductory Itinerary (27:1–8)

    1. To Myra in a ship of Adramyttium (1–5)

    2. To Fair Havens on a ship of Alexandria (6–8)

EPISODE ONE (27:9–20)

    1. Paul's prediction (27:10) based on the time of year (27:9) is disregarded because of greed (27:11) and an unsatisfactory harbor (27:12).

---

1. This way of framing the aim of the paper relegates to irrelevance much secondary literature which either focuses on the question of sources or treats the text of Luke-Acts as something other than a religious document (e.g., a secular narrative).

267

2. Paul's prediction is fulfilled in three paragraphs:

    (*a*) the south wind blew gently (27:13)

    (*b*) a tempestuous wind struck (27:14–17)

    (*c*) they were violently storm-tossed so that all hope was abandoned (27:18–20).

EPISODE TWO (27:21–44)

    1. Paul's prediction (27:21–22, 26) is based on an angelic message (27:23–25).

    2. Paul's prediction is fulfilled in three paragraphs:

        (*a*) about midnight, Paul gives a warning (27:27–32)

        (*b*) as day was about to dawn, Paul gives encouragement (27:33–38)

        (*c*) when it was day, all escaped to land (27:39–44)

EPISODE THREE (28:1–10)

    1. Paul is protected from the effects of snakebite (28:1–6)

    2. Paul prays effectively for healing (28:7–10)

Concluding Itinerary (28:11–16)

    1. To Puteoli on a ship of Alexandria (28:11–14)

    2. To Rome via the Appian Way (28:15–16)

Acts 27 comprises the introductory itinerary and the first two episodes of the larger thought unit.

Comparative Materials

Acts 27 is an example of the type-scene involving sea storm and shipwreck.[2] Narratives of storm and shipwreck are widespread in Mediterranean antiquity. Among the extensive remains we may mention the following:[3]

1. Greek — Homer, *Odyssey* 4.499–511; 5.291–453; 12.403–28; Aeschylus, *Agamemnon* 647–66; Herodotus, *Histories* 7.188–92; 8.12–14; Euripides, *Daughters of Troy* 77–86; *Iphigeneia in Taurica* 1391–1498; *Helen* 400–413; Apollonius Rhodius, *Argonautica* 2.1093–1121; Polybius, *Histories* 1.37; *Ninus Romance* C; Chariton, *Chaereas and Callirhoe* 3.3; Chion of Heraclea, 4; a fragment of the romance, *Herpyllis*; Dio Chrysostom, *Oration* 7.2–7; Xenophon of Ephesus, *Ephesian Tale* 2.11; 3.2; 3.12; Lucian, *Toxaris* 19–21; *The Ship* 7–9; Aelius Aristides,

---

2. The language of type-scene is that of Pamela Thimmes, *Studies in the Biblical Sea-Storm Type-Scene* (San Francisco: Mellen, 1992).

3. The following accounts of sea storms and shipwrecks were collected by J. H. Hayes as part of a project sponsored by the Spire for Individualized Research at Wake Forest University in the summer of 1994.

Sacred Tales 2.12–14; 2.64–68; Achilles Tatius, *Leucippe and Clitophon* 1.1; 3.1–5; the anonymous romance, *Apollonius King of Tyre* 11–12; Heliodorus, *Ethiopian Story* 1.22; 5.27; Quintus of Smyrna, *The Fall of Troy* 14.359–527.

2. Roman — Plautus, *The Rope* 62–78; Virgil, *Aeneid* 1.122–252; 3.253–75; 5.14–43; Ovid, *Metamorphoses* 11.477–574; *Tristia* 1.2.1–110; Curtius, *History of Alexander* 4.3.16–18; Phaedrus, *Fables* 4.23; Petronius, *Satyricon* 114; Seneca, *Agamemnon* 456–578; Lucan, *Civil War* 4.48–120; 5.560–677; 9.319–47; 9.445–92; Statius, *Thebaid* 5.360–421; Valerius Flaccus, *Argonautica* 1.614–58; Silius Italicus, *Punica* 17.244–90; Tacitus, *Annals* 2.23–24.

3. Jewish — Jonah 1:3–17; the *Testament of Naphtali* 6:1–10; Josephus, *War* 1.279–80; *Life* 13–16.

4. Christian — *Acts of Philip* 3.33–36; Pseudo-Clementine *Homilies* 1.8.

Practice in composing such narratives was part of the rhetorical training in the Roman imperial period.[4] Such stories shared numerous elements: for example,[5] (*a*) a warning not to sail (Polybius; Chion; *Herpyllis;* Aelius Aristides); (*b*) sailing in a bad season (Polybius; Chion; Dio Chrysostom; Lucian); (*c*) unusually chaotic winds (Homer; Herodotus; Apollonius Rhodius; *Herpyllis;* Lucian; Aelius Aristides; Achilles Tatius; *Apollonius King of Tyre;* Virgil; Ovid; Petronius; Seneca; Lucan; Statius); (*d*) darkness during the storm (Homer; Herodotus; Apollonius Rhodius; Chariton; *Herpyllis;* Aelius Aristides; Achilles Tatius; *Apollonius King of Tyre;* Heliodorus; Virgil; Ovid; Curtius; Petronius; Seneca; Lucan; Juvenal); (*e*) horrendous waves (Herodotus; *Herpyllis;* Lucian; Achilles Tatius; Virgil; Ovid; Lucan); (*f*) sailors scurrying about (Aelius Aristides; Achilles Tatius; Heliodorus; Virgil; Curtius; Petronius; Tacitus; Jonah); (*g*) cargo or tackle thrown overboard (Lucian; Achilles Tatius; Heliodorus; Tacitus; Juvenal; Jonah; Josephus; *Acts of Philip*); (*h*) control of the ship given up and its being driven by the winds and waves (Homer; Herodotus; Apollonius Rhodius; Chariton; *Herpyllis;* Lucian; Achilles Tatius; Heliodorus; Virgil; Ovid; Petronius; Lucan; Juvenal; *T. Naphtali*); (*i*) the ship's frame or hull breaking up (Homer; Aeschylus; Euripides; Apollonius Rhodius; Xenophon; Lucian; Achilles Tatius; *Apollonius King of Tyre;* Virgil; Ovid; Petronius; Jonah; *T. Naphtali*); (*j*) passengers abandoning all hope (Homer; Herodotus; Apollonius Rhodius; *Herpyllis;* Lucian; Achilles Tatius; Virgil; Ovid; Petronius; Lucan; Valerius Flaccus; *Acts of Philip*); (*k*) the ship wrecking on rocks or a shallow beach (Homer; Aeschylus; Herodotus; Euripides; Apollonius Rhodius; Polybius; *Ninus;* Dio Chrysostom; Xenophon; Lucian; Achilles Tatius; Heliodorus; Plautus; Virgil; Seneca; Lucan; Tacitus); (*l*) survivors drifting on planks (Homer; Euripides; Apollonius Rhodius; Xenophon; Lucian; Achilles Tatius; *Apollonius King of*

---

4. M. P. O. Morford, *The Poet Lucan: Studies in Rhetorical Epic* (New York: Barnes and Noble, 1967), 32–36; Susan Marie Praeder, "The Narrative Voyage: An Analysis and Interpretation of Acts 27–28," Ph.D. diss., Graduate Theological Union, 1980, 243. The Elder Seneca, *Controversiae* 7.1.4 and 8.6, illustrates the use of stylized sea-storm episodes in his declamations.

5. The list that follows is a part of a larger collection compiled by J. H. Hayes, summer, 1994, as part of his individualized research project.

Tyre; T. Naphtali); (m) swimming to shore or to another ship (Homer; Ninus; Xenophon; Lucian; Achilles Tatius; Phaedrus; Josephus); (n) helpful, simple folk on shore (Dio Chrysostom; Petronius).

The common elements justify one's calling such accounts type-scenes (i.e., a literary convention with recurring elements and functions). So predictable were these accounts that they became the object of satire (Juvenal, Satires 12.17–82; Lucian, On Salaried Posts in Great Houses 1–2) and parody (Lucian, True Story 1.5–6).

Some of these sea stories functioned merely as a record of historical events (e.g., Tacitus, Annals 2.23–24); others served primarily as entertainment (e.g., Petronius, Satyricon 114). Certain narratives, however, taught either theological or moral lessons. Examples of moral lessons taught by sea narratives include:[6] (a) reckless pride leads to destruction (Polybius, Histories 1.37; cf. Acts 27:9–12); (b) wealth is a burden and is a transient possession (Phaedrus, Fables 4.23; cf. Acts 27:18, 38); (c) a true friend is willing to risk his life for the other (Lucian, Toxaris 19–21; cf. Acts 27:31–32); (d) only the true philosopher is calm in a crisis (Lucian, Peregrinus 43–44; the story of Pyrrho in Diogenes Laertius, Lives of Eminent Philosophers 9.68; cf. Acts 27:33–36); (e) when in crisis, pray (T. Naphtali 6:1–10; cf. Acts 27:23–26). Most of these moral points function in subsidiary roles in Acts 27.

The theological functions of sea narratives, viewed in terms of causality,[7] fall into four categories:[8]

1. Storm caused by gods or God and outcome also due to gods or God, whether deliverance or death (Homer, Odyssey 4.499–511; 5.291–453; Aeschylus, Agamemnon 647–66; Herodotus, 7.188–92; Euripides, Daughters of Troy 77–86; Iphigeneia in Taurica 1391–1489; Apollonius Rhodius, 2.1093–1121; Chariton, 3.3; Virgil, Aeneid 1.122–252; Seneca, Agamemnon 456–578; Statius, Thebaid 5.360–421; Valerius Flaccus, 1.614–58; Silius Italicus, 17.244–90; Jonah 1:3–17).

2. Storm caused by gods or God and outcome due to mortals on the ship (Euripides, Helen 400–413; Plautus, The Rope 62–78).

3. Storm due to other than a divine cause and outcome due to gods or God (Herpyllis; Lucian, On Salaried Posts 1–2; The Ship 7–9; Aelius Aristides, Sacred Tales 2.12–14; Achilles Tatius, 1.1; 3.1–5; Virgil, Aeneid 3.253–75; Ovid, Tristia 1.2.1–110; T. Naphtali 6:1–10; Josephus, Life 13–16; Acts of Philip 3.33–36).

4. Storm due to other than a divine cause and outcome due to natural or human agents (Apollonius Rhodius, Argonautica 4.1228–47; Polybius, 1.37; Ni-

---

6. Luke T. Johnson, The Acts of the Apostles (Collegeville, Minn.: Liturgical Press, 1992), 451, recognizes some of these moral lessons.

7. Ancient Mediterranean peoples debated various theories of causation. Sometimes the categories "natural" and "divine" were used. See R. M. Grant, Miracle and Natural Law in Graeco-Roman and Early Christian Thought (Amsterdam: North Holland Publishing, 1952).

8. This typology was suggested by C. H. Talbert and developed by J. H. Hayes during the summer of 1994 as part of the Spires Program for Individualized Research at Wake Forest University.

nus C; Chion, 4; Dio Chrysostom, *Oration* 7.2–7; Xenophon, *An Ephesian Tale*
2.11; 3.2; 3.12; Lucian, *Toxaris* 19–21; *True Story* 1.5–6; 2.47; Aelius Aristides, *Sacred Tales* 2.64–68; *Apollonius King of Tyre* 11–12; Heliodorus, 1.22;
5.27; Virgil, *Aeneid* 5.14–43; Ovid, *Metamorphoses* 11.472–574; Quintus Curtius, *Alexander* 4.3.16–18; Phaedrus, *Fables* 4.23; Petronius, *Satyricon* 114; Lucan,
5.560–677; 9.319–47; Tacitus, *Annals* 2.23–24; Josephus, *War* 1.279–80).

The first of these categories of narratives of sea storms has received attention
of late. Gary Miles and Garry Trompf in 1976[9] and David Ladouceur in 1980[10]
have called attention to the Mediterranean assumption that nature is a vehicle
of divine justice and, if so, then storm and shipwreck can be understood as divine
judgment on the wicked; and conversely, the absence of storm and shipwreck
can be seen as evidence of absence of guilt. It is against this background, they
claim, that Acts 27 is to be understood.

The Elder Seneca, in his stylized declamations written in the early first century c.e., includes one that is relevant to our concerns (*Controversiae* 7.1 [LCL]).
A son is unjustly convicted of parricide (the attempted murder of his father). As
punishment, he is put on a boat whose rigging was removed. He immediately
finds himself in a storm. Seeing this, his brother says: "The sea . . . is waiting for a
parricide" (i.e., to punish the criminal). Then he prays: "I commend him to you,
Fortune — if he is innocent" (7.1.4). "The seas roll savagely, hurricanes press
the ship's sides with the rush of their spray, the boat is beaten on every side
by dangers; but innocence is safe" (7.1.10). The boat is "equipped by heaven;
suddenly sails have appeared, suddenly the ship begins to ride higher and right
itself. Innocence is a great shield in danger" (7.1.10). This vindication by heaven
is met with wonder: "O seas that are more fair than trials" (7.1.11). In the first
century c.e. the assumption that divine justice sometimes acts through the sea
is common enough that it can be used in the teaching of declamation. If this
is really the backdrop of Paul's shipwreck scene, in what way does this cultural
assumption serve as the key to Acts 27?

Acts 27 belongs to category 3 of ancient sea-storm type-scenes: the storm
is due to natural causes, the outcome is due to the divine will. In Acts 27 the
narrator makes no mention of divine action in sending the storm. Rather there
are references that indicate the natural causes of the storm: (*a*) the time of
year (27:9 — "the time of the fast had already gone by,[11] so Paul warned them");
(*b*) the apparent greed of the pilot and owner of the ship who want to sail despite
the bad time of the year[12] (27:11 — "the centurion paid more attention to the

---

9. Gary Miles and Garry Trompf, "Luke and Antiphon," *HTR* 69 (1976): 259–67.

10. David Ladouceur, "Hellenistic Preconceptions of Shipwreck and Pollution as a Context for
Acts 27–28," *HTR* 73 (1980): 435–49.

11. The fast refers to the Day of Atonement, 10th Tishri. For Jews, the Feast of Booths five days
after the fast marked the end of the season for sailing. Generally, from May 27 (?) until September 14
was regarded by Mediterranean people as the safe season for sea travel.

12. Since grain was needed in Rome, Claudius had instituted a policy to secure a regular supply.
Suetonius, "Claudius" 18.2, says Claudius assumed the expense of any loss suffered by ship owners
due to winter storms. Pliny the Elder, *Natural History* 2.47.125, says that not even the fury of storms

pilot and the owner of the ship than to what Paul said"); (c) the search for a
suitable harbor in which to spend the winter (27:12 — "Since the harbor was
unfavorably situated for spending the winter, the majority planned to put out to
sea ... in the hope of reaching Phoenix, a port in Crete"); (d) the fact that other
ships had spent the winter in a safe harbor (28:11 — "Three months later we
set sail on a ship that had wintered at the island"). All of these details make
the same point. The storm and shipwreck were not due to divine judgment but
rather to a natural cause, namely, the time of the year. Such a depiction of Paul's
experience of storm and shipwreck could be understood as a protection against
possible misunderstanding in terms of category 1: since one cannot escape divine
justice, the storm is caused by God as a judgment on a guilty party, Paul. That
the narrator was aware of such a possibility is evidenced by the views espoused
by his characters in 28:4b: "This man must certainly be a murderer; though he
escaped the sea, justice has not allowed him to remain alive."

Over against any impression that Paul was judged guilty by God because he
was involved in a storm and shipwreck, Acts 27 makes explicit that the storm
and shipwreck were due to the time of the year (27:9). Over against any claim
that Paul's escape from the dangers of the deep was due to human prowess,
Acts 27 makes explicit that the deliverance was in accord with the divine plan
(27:23–25; 19:21–22; 23:11). The effect of the former is to declare that Paul's
involvement in storm and shipwreck was not evidence of his guilt. The effect
of the latter is to say that Paul's preservation is part of the divine plan to carry
the gospel to Rome by means of this innocent man. You cannot stop the divine
plan! This seems likely to be the way an ancient Mediterranean listener would
have heard the narrative, given the cultural conventions about sea storms and
shipwrecks.

Context

The reading suggested above on the basis of comparative material is reinforced
by an examination of the immediate contexts of Acts 27. Two contexts should be
considered: (1) Acts 28:1–10, the narrative which follows chapter 27 and which
goes together as part of the larger thought-unit of 27:1–28:16, and (2) Acts
23:12–26:32, the large thought-unit which precedes chapter 27.

Acts 28:1–10 constitutes Episode Three in the thought-unit of 27:1–28:16
and consists of two parts: 28:1–6 and 28:7–10. In the first part, Paul is bitten by
a viper (v. 3) which causes the natives to think he is a murderer who, though
he escaped from the sea, has now been caught by divine justice (v. 4). When he
is not affected by the snakebite, the natives change their opinion (v. 5). He is
not a murderer; he is a god. Two observations emerge from vv. 3–4. First, there
is an explicit statement by the characters of the Mediterranean assumption that

---

closed the sea, because of avarice (David W. J. Gill and Conrad Gempf, eds., *The Book of Acts in Its
Graeco-Roman Setting* [Grand Rapids, Mich.: Eerdmans, 1994], 22).

the animal kingdom, often a serpent, functioned as a vehicle of divine justice. Second, the serpent bite is explicitly understood as a corollary to involvement in storm and shipwreck. Both are believed by the natives to function in the same way, as divine judgment.

Three examples from the Greco-Roman world illustrate one or both dimensions of the case. (*a*) In *The Greek Anthology* 7.290, we read:

> The shipwrecked mariner had escaped the whirlwind and the fury of the deadly sea, and as he was lying on the Libyan sand not far from the beach...naked and exhausted by the unhappy wreck, a baneful viper slew him. Why did he struggle with the waves in vain, escaping then the fate that was his lot on the land? (LCL)[13]

Here both dimensions are combined: snakebite and shipwreck as vehicles of divine destiny.

(*b*) Heliodorus, *An Ethiopian Story* 2.20, tells of a brigand, Themouthis, making his escape, who lay down to sleep, "but the sleep he slept was the final sleep, the brazen sleep of death, for he was bitten by a viper."[14]

(*c*) An Egyptian papyrus of the fourth to fifth centuries c.e., cited by Cadbury, reads:

> A son having murdered his own father and fearing the laws fled into the desert. As he passed through the mountains he was pursued by a lion; and being pursued by a lion he went up into a tree, and finding a snake as he went up into a tree and being unable to go up on account of the snake he came down again. Wrong doing does not escape the attention of god. The divine always brings the wicked into Dike.[15]

Similar assumptions are expressed in Jewish sources as well.[16] (*a*) In the Tosefta, *Sanhedrin* 8:3 [E], R. Simeon ben Shatah (c. 80 c.e.) said he saw a man with a sword running after a fellow. The two ran into a deserted building. When Simeon entered, he saw the one slain and the other with the sword dripping blood. The rabbi comments: "But He who knows the thoughts of man will exact punishment from the guilty. He did not move from the spot before a snake bit him and he died."[17] (*b*) The Jerusalem Talmud, *Berakoth* 5:1 [XIV.D], contains a tradition about R. Haninah ben Dosa (before c.e. 70) who, when praying, was bitten by a snake but did not interrupt his prayers. Not only was the rabbi not affected by the bite but the snake died at the entrance to its den. In the Babylonian Talmud, after these events Haninah is reported to have said: "It is not the

---

13. Sometimes a villain escaped judgment by the sea because he was destined for a further punishment (e.g., Caesar escapes by being hurled to shore by a miraculous tenth wave [Lucan, *Civil War* 5.672–77] because the parricide was being saved for the death he deserved). See Morford, *The Poet Lucan*, 34.

14. B. P. Reardon, ed., *Collected Ancient Greek Novels* (Berkeley: University of California Press, 1989), 392.

15. Henry J. Cadbury, *The Book of Acts in History* (London: Black, 1955), 27.

16. L. H. Silberman, "Paul's Viper: Acts 28:3–6," *Forum* 8 (1992): 247–54.

17. *The Tosefta: Neziqin*, trans. Jacob Neusner (New York: KTAV, 1981), 223.

snake that kills, but sin" (*b. Berakoth* 33a).[18] A righteous man is unaffected by
snakebite, just as a wicked man is punished by it.

This latter point corresponds to the Jewish mind-set found in Dan. 6:22,
in which Daniel says to the king: "My God sent his angel and shut the lions'
mouths . . . *because* I was found blameless before him." That this idea is not limited to a Jewish context is evidenced by the Greco-Roman tradition found in
Horace, *Odes* 1.22. There the poet proves his righteousness with the news that
while he was strolling unprotected through the woods, a wolf fled from him,
leaving him unharmed. The animal kingdom, like the sea, punishes the wicked
as the agent of divine justice. It does not, however, harm the righteous.

The same cultural mind-set is reflected in Christian sources as well. In the
Acts of John a villain lusted in vain after the married Drusiana. When she died,
he bribed the steward of her husband to open the tomb so he could have his
way with the corpse. When they entered, but before the act could occur, a serpent appeared and slew the steward with a single bite. The narrator describes
this judgment as "such as they deserve to suffer who do such deeds" (70–71).
The apostle John, however, who then entered the tomb, was unharmed by the
serpent (75).[19]

There seems to be no other way to read Acts 28:1–6 in a Mediterranean
context. The natives think Paul guilty when he is bitten; they change their minds
when he is unaffected. So Paul is declared innocent by God! Neither storm nor
serpent bite is to be taken as God's judgment on Paul. Quite the contrary, God
protects and vindicates his upright one.

Acts 28:7–10 functions in two ways. First, it refutes the natives' wrong belief
that Paul is a god (v. 6). How? In v. 8, in connection with the healing of Publius's
father, Paul "prays" for the healing. A god does not pray for a healing but heals
out of himself (cf. Luke 8:46). Likewise, a magician with pretensions to deity
would not pray but would regard the miracle as his own doing. This is made clear
by Philostratus, *Life of Apollonius of Tyana* 8.7.9. In Apollonius's defense before
Domitian, he contends that he is no magician even though he has eradicated
the disease causing a plague in Ephesus. Why? Because he "prayed" to Hercules
for the healing. A magician would not do this because he would consider it his
own achievement. Contrary to the natives' opinion, Paul is neither a god nor a
pretender to divine honors (=a magician; cf. Acts 8:10).

Second, the four-verse unit indicates that Paul is a righteous man. James
5:16b–18, in the context of prayers for healing, uses Elijah as an example to
indicate that "the fervent prayer of a righteous person is very powerful" (NAB).
John 9:31, again in the context of healing, has the formerly blind man declare:
"We know that God does not listen to sinners, but if one is devout and does
His will, He listens to him." That Paul's prayer is answered is an indication that

---

18. *The Babylonian Talmud: Seder Zera'im*, ed. I. Epstein, trans. M. Simon (London: Soncino
Press, 1948), 204.

19. M. R. James, *The Apocryphal New Testament* (Oxford: Clarendon, 1955), 245–46.

he is regarded as righteous by God. Paul is not a god but he is a righteous man. Acts 28:1–10 declares Paul innocent by God's decree. This declaration parallels the same point in chapter 27. Acts 27 says Paul is not guilty even if he was in a storm and shipwreck. Acts 28 says Paul is not guilty even if he was bitten by a serpent. Both affirm that Paul is God's servant, a righteous man whose prayers are answered. By God's decree, Paul is innocent.

Acts 23:12–26:32 forms the second part of chapter 27's immediate context as the immediately preceding large thought-unit. This unit is subdivided into four scenes, each dealing with Paul's status before Roman authorities.

SCENE ONE (23:12–35)

> The plot (23:12–15)
>
> The plot is discovered (23:16–22)
>
> The plot is foiled (23:23–35) and Paul is declared innocent (23:29)

SCENE TWO (24:1–27)

> Felix hears charges against Paul (24:1–9)
>
> Felix hears Paul's defense (24:10–21)
>
> Felix disposes of Paul's case by delay, putting off the Jews (24:22–23) and Paul (24:24–27)

SCENE THREE (25:1–12)

> Festus hears charges against Paul (25:1–7)
>
> Festus hears Paul's defense (25:8) and appeal to Caesar (25:9–11)
>
> Festus disposes of Paul's case by agreeing to send him to Caesar (25:12)

SCENE FOUR (25:13–26:32)

> Agrippa hears charges against Paul: privately (25:13–22) and publicly (25:23–27), including a statement of Paul's innocence by Festus (25:25)
>
> Agrippa hears Paul's defense (26:1–23)
>
> Agrippa and others, after dialogue with him (26:24–29), give their judgment that Paul is innocent (26:30–32)

The thrust of the large thought-unit, 23:12–26:32, is that Paul is declared innocent by human authorities (Acts 23:29; 25:25; 26:31; 26:32). This means that the last sections of Acts are concerned to declare Paul's innocence. His innocence is recognized and declared by both human authorities (23:12–26:32) and divine authority (27:1–28:10). The storm and shipwreck function as part of this overall design. At the same time, the deliverance from the storm and shipwreck are understood as part of God's vindication of God's messenger, enabling Paul to carry the gospel to Rome (Acts 19:21–22; 23:11).

Luke 8:22–25

It is time to turn to Luke 8:22–25 to ask what theological overtones an ancient listener would have heard. Again, remarks that follow will be developed in terms of composition, comparative materials, and context.

Composition

This is a miracle story with the usual three parts: problem (vv. 22–24a), miracle (v. 24b), and reaction to the miracle (v. 25). Its obvious point is that Jesus has power over the wind and the sea.

Comparative Materials

Ancient listeners might have heard a range of implications.

1. When Luke 8:25b gives as the reaction to the miracle the question, "Who then is this, who commands even the winds and the sea, and they obey him?" echoes from the LXX could have been heard. Psalm 88:9 (LXX; MT 89:9) reads: "Thou rulest the power of the sea, and thou calmest the tumult of its waves." Psalm 106:29–30 (LXX; MT 107:29–30) reads: "And he commands the storm, and it is calmed into a gentle breeze, and its waves are still. And they are glad, because they are quiet; and he guides them to their desired haven." Of course, the one about whom the LXX speaks is Yahweh. The story, then, applies to Jesus the attributes of the Lord. Who is Jesus? Jesus is one with Yahweh's power.

2. The question, "Who is this?" might have evoked other echoes as well. Two biographies of Pythagoras offer relevant data about the popular belief that would have been "in the air" in Luke's time. Porphyry, *The Life of Pythagoras* 29, says of the philosopher that "he calmed storms on rivers and seas, for the comfort and safe passage of his friends."[20] Similar feats were performed by his followers Empedocles, Epimenides, and Abaris. Iamblichus, *The Life of Pythagoras* 28, says that one sign of the philosopher's divinity were his "tranquilizations of the waves of rivers and seas, in order that his disciples might the more easily pass over them."[21] Among others who did such things was Empedocles of Agrigentum, surnamed the "wind-stiller." In *Life of Pythagoras* 3, moreover, a story is recounted of a shipboard journey Pythagoras took during the time for travel to be suspended. "The sailors considered that contrary to their expectations, the voyage had proceeded without interruptions, as if some deity had been on board."[22] Again, echoes that might have been heard in Luke 8:22–25 relate to one who had the marks of divinity.

---

20. Kenneth Sylvan Guthrie, ed., *The Pythagorean Sourcebook and Library* (Grand Rapids, Mich.: Phanes Press, 1987), 129.

21. Ibid., 91.

22. Ibid., 60.

3. It is even possible that the question of the identity of Jesus, the storm-stiller, could have had apologetic overtones. Plutarch, in his "Life of Caesar," 38.2–4, tells the story of how Caesar, disguised as a slave, went on board a ship. When a strong wind arose so that the ship could make no progress, the captain was about to turn around. Caesar then disclosed himself and said: "Come, good man, be bold and fear naught; thou carryest Caesar and Caesar's fortune in thy boat" (LCL). The sailors forgot the storm and tried to force their way through the waves with the oars. The project proved impossible, and Caesar reluctantly allowed the captain to put about and return to port. In such a story, one hears that Caesar is only a man, although he tries to act like a god. In his pretensions to divinity, he is an impostor — unlike Jesus.[23] Such stories about Caesar were likely to have circulated long before Plutarch wrote.

"Who is this that commands the wind and the sea and they obey him?" An ancient listener would have heard in the story a claim for Jesus' divine authority. Luke 8:22–25, like Acts 27, belongs to category 3 of sea-storm type-scenes: the cause of the storm may be other than the divine (here, actually the demonic), but the outcome is due to divine power. The divine power in Luke 8:22–25 is located in the person of Jesus. Contrast Acts 27:1–28:10 in which divine power is located outside of Paul. Indeed, that Paul is delivered from storm and shipwreck in Acts 27 is due to the divine power of the Lord, a power demonstrated in Luke 8:22–25.

Context

Luke 8:22–25 is part of a large thought-unit, 8:22–9:6, in which four miracle stories demonstrate Jesus' power (8:22–25; 8:26–39; 8:43–48; 8:40–42, 49–56). These stories are followed by 9:1–6, in which Jesus gives power and authority to the Twelve for their mission work.[24] Luke 8:22–25's function in this thought-unit is to say that Jesus' power includes authority over the sea. His "sent ones" are, therefore, not outside the sphere of his control and protection when they travel on the sea. Moreover, the exorcism story in 8:26–39, set in Gentile territory, in which demons, resident in unclean swine, try to escape Jesus' power by rushing into the waters of the lake, functions in part to say that demons are by no means eluding the authority of the one to whom even wind and water hearken. Jesus is Lord of the sea and its storms. His "sent ones" may have faith that they are safe in his power for the assigned tasks that lie before them.

---

23. It is possible that Acts 28:11 reflects the same type of polemic in its context: "Three months later we set sail on a ship that had wintered at the island, an Alexandrian ship with the Twin Brothers as its figurehead." While Paul and his company were tossed about on the sea and finally delivered by the God to whom Paul belonged, the Twin Brothers, those famed deliverers of travelers in peril at sea, spent the winter in the safe harbor at Malta (so J. H. Hayes).

24. Charles H. Talbert, *Reading Luke* (New York: Crossroad, 1982), 95–97.

Do Acts 27 and Luke 8:22–25 Fit into the Lukan Whole?

The theological perspectives of Acts 27 and Luke 8:22–25 fit nicely into the Lukan whole. Three dimensions of the overall vision of Luke-Acts can be employed to demonstrate this claim: (1) the divine plan, (2) the use of fore-shadowing in Luke-Acts, and (3) the use of correspondence between events in Luke and those in Acts.

The Divine Plan

According to Luke-Acts there is a divine plan that stands behind the events of history.[25] It is spoken of as the *boulē tou theou* in Luke 7:30; Acts 2:23; 4:38; 5:38–39; 13:36; 20:27. It is referred to as God's *thelēma* in Luke 22:42; Acts 21:14; 22:14. It is described as God's *exousia* in Acts 1:7.

Events of history happen according to the divine plan in Luke-Acts. This is sometimes described with the term *dei*, as in Luke 2:49; 4:43; 9:22; 13:33; 17:25; 21:9; 22:37; 24:7; 24:26; 24:44; Acts 1:16; 1:21; 3:21; 4:12; 9:16; 17:3; 23:11; 27:24. It is referred to by *kata to horismenon* in Luke 22:22; by *ho horismenos hupo tou theou* in Acts 10:42; and by *ho horisen* in Acts 17:31. In Acts 26:16 the term used is *procheirisasthai*; in Acts 22:14 it is *proecheirisato*. The expression is *en anagkaion* in Acts 13:46. In Luke 9:31; 9:44; 24:21; Acts 17:31; 26:22–23, the word *mellei* that refers to the fact that events happen according to the divine plan.

The realization of the divine plan is often spoken of in terms of fulfillment. Luke 1:20; 4:21; 21:24; Acts 1:16; 3:18; 13:27, all use *plēroun*. Luke 9:51 uses *sumplērounthai*. Luke 18:31 and 22:37 employ *telein*.

The divine plan can be known by humans. The scriptures of Israel make it known, as in Luke 4:18–19; 24:45–47; Acts 13:23, 32–33, 37; 15:15; 28:25–27. Angelic announcement reveals the plan as well, as in Luke 1:13–17; 1:30–33; Acts 10:3–8, 22, 30–33; 27:23–25. Living humans prophesy in ways that make the divine will known, as in Luke 1:29–32, 34–35; Acts 21:10–11. Both the pre-Easter Jesus (Luke 9:22, 44; 18:31–33; 11:13) and the risen Christ (Luke 24:49; Acts 1:4–5, 8) express the divine purpose. Sometimes God's purpose is made manifest by special appointment, as in Acts 22:14. The will of God, which lies behind and determines the course of history, is made known to humans in various ways.

What has been said about the Lukan understanding of the divine plan for history would have been intelligible to a Mediterranean hearer. The belief that divine necessity controls human history, shaping the course of events, was a widespread assumption in Mediterranean antiquity.

---

25. For what follows, see C. H. Talbert, "Once Again: The Gentile Mission in Luke-Acts," in *Der Treue Gottes Trauen*, ed. Claus Bussmann and Walter Radl (Freiburg: Herder, 1991), 101–4. John T. Squires, *The Plan of God in Luke-Acts* (Cambridge: Cambridge University Press, 1993), offers the fullest treatment of the Mediterranean backgrounds of the concept.

A pagan like Polybius reflects this conviction. Early in his career, Polybius saw that Roman power was irresistible and, as a Stoic, he believed the Roman order was part of a divine providence that ruled the world. This belief he expounded in his *Histories*.

> Fortune (*tyche*) having guided almost all the affairs of the world in one direction and having forced them to incline towards one and the same end, a historian should bring before his readers under one synoptical view the operations by which she has accomplished her general purpose. (1.4.1–2, LCL)

A Jew like Josephus shared this cultural belief. As a Jew, however, he believed that the divine necessity derived from the personal will of God, who is a living person and not a neutral necessity. So in *Antiquities* 10.8.2–3 §142, for example, he tells of the fulfillment of Jeremiah's prophecy of the fall of Jerusalem, and says that these events manifest the nature of God, "which foretells all which must (*dei*) take place, duly at the appointed hour" (LCL). Pagan and Jew alike believed that history unfolded according to a divine necessity or compulsion that could be expressed in terms of *dei* or *deon esti*. A Jew would have heard the idea in terms of his belief in a personal deity, but the cultural context was agreed that history unfolded according to a divine necessity. It was in these terms that Luke's language about the divine plan would have been heard.

It was also believed in Mediterranean antiquity that the divine will could be disclosed to and known by humans. This idea was often connected with oracles in the pagan sphere and with prophecy in the Jewish culture. Indeed, oracles and prophecy not only revealed the divine plan but advanced it. History moved along its appointed course as a fulfillment of oracles and prophecy. This was true for pagan (e.g., Lucian, *Alexander the False Prophet*; Suetonius, *Life of Vespasian*; Apuleius, *Golden Ass*) and for Jewish settings (the Deuteronomic history; Qumran; Josephus, *Antiquities*).

A major motif of fulfillment of prophecy exists in Luke-Acts. The prologue speaks of "the things fulfilled (*peplērophoremenon*) among us" (Luke 1:1). There follows a narrative that is literally controlled by a prophecy-and-fulfillment pattern. Prophecy is given by the scriptures of Israel, by living prophets, and by heavenly beings. The prophecies disclose the divine will and the fulfillment of prophecy moves the story to another stage. In this regard the Lukan writings would have been perfectly intelligible to the Mediterranean hearer, whether Jewish or pagan.

Within this scheme, the narrative of Acts 23:12–28:16 fits nicely. In Acts 23:11 a prophecy of the risen Christ controls the rest of the book: "The following night the Lord stood by him and said, 'Take courage. For just as you have borne witness to my cause in Jerusalem, so you must (*dei*) also bear witness in Rome.'" In Acts 27:23–26 Paul speaks to the terrified sailors and passengers on board the storm-driven ship:

> I urge you now to keep up your courage; not one of you will be lost, only the ship. For last night an angel of the God to whom I belong and whom I serve stood before

me and said, "Do not be afraid, Paul. You are destined (*dei*) to stand before Caesar; and behold, for your sake, God has granted safety to all who are sailing with you." Therefore, keep up your courage, men; I trust in God that it will turn out as I have been told. We are destined (*dei*) to run aground on some island. (NAB)

If the storm and shipwreck of Paul's journey to Rome are due to natural causes and not divine judgment, his deliverance is part of the divine plan that he preach the gospel in Rome before Caesar. In this regard, Acts 27 fits into the scheme of Luke-Acts.

Foreshadowing in Luke-Acts

In Luke-Acts, as in other texts of Mediterranean antiquity, there is frequent use of foreshadowing. In Greek and Roman epics, for example, one finds devices to forecast the future, both the future that finds fulfillment within the narrative and the future whose fulfillment is beyond the narrative.[26] Sometimes the foreshadowing is done by the author, sometimes by a divine being within the narrative, and sometimes by a mortal character (all of which are found in Luke-Acts). These foreshadowings frequently take the form of prophecies of the future: for example, in the *Aeneid* 7.652–53, the author hints that Lausus will meet his death; in the *Aeneid* 11.587–94, the goddess Diana's words to Opis foreshadow the later death of Camilla with the attendant death of her slayer; and in the *Aeneid* 12.725–38, Andromache foresees the future fate of Astyanax and of the Trojans in general. A Greco-Roman hearer of Luke-Acts, therefore, would have understood the evangelist's use of foreshadowing.

The closest parallels to the Lukan use of foreshadowing by prophecy, however, are from the LXX. Luke's repeated use of prophecy fulfillment, for example, functions as foreshadowing by divine forecast, sometimes within a dream or vision, sometimes apart from a dream or vision.[27] This reflects the same practice in the LXX.

1. Take the matter of foreshadowing by divine forecast. In 2 Samuel 11 David sins against Uriah. In chapter 12, Nathan the prophet confronts David. In 12:10–12, 14, there is a prophecy of the consequences of David's sin (foreshadowing by divine forecast): (*a*) the sword will never depart from David's house (v. 10); (*b*) God will raise up evil against David out of his own house (v. 11a) and will take David's wives and give them publicly to another (vv. 11b–12); (*c*) the child to be born of the illicit union with Bathsheba will die (v. 14).

This foreshadowing serves as a focusing technique, enabling the reader to know what to look for in the narrative that follows.[28] (*c*) The child dies (2 Sam. 12:15b–19). (*a*) Absalom has his brother Amnon killed (2 Sam. 13:28–29, 32).

---

26. George E. Duckworth, *Foreshadowing and Suspense in the Epics of Homer, Apollonius, and Virgil* (New York: Haskill House, 1966).

27. Meir Sternberg, *The Poetics of Biblical Narrative* (Bloomington: Indiana University Press, 1987), 105, 285–308.

28. Ibid., 115.

Absalom is killed by Joab and his men (2 Sam. 18:14–15). Solomon has his brother and rival, Adonijah, killed (2 Kings 2:23–25). (*b*) Absalom goes in to his father's concubines in the sight of all Israel (2 Sam. 16:21–22). The foreshadowing allows the narrator to dispense with continual enactment of divine intervention that might overschematize the plot, and to benefit from the artistic gains of "omnipotence behind-the-scenes."[29]

This foreshadowing is much like the divine forecast of Acts 23:11: "Just as you have borne witness to my cause in Jerusalem, so you must also bear witness in Rome." What follows throughout the trials before authorities may seem like a secular narrative devoid of divine intervention, but the action is controlled by the foreshadowing of divine forecast. Following biblical models, it is a theological narrative with omnipotence behind the scenes.

2. Consider also the matter of foreshadowing through dreams or visions in the LXX. In Genesis 37:5–7, Joseph tells his brothers of his dream that they would bow down to him and that he would rule over them (v. 8). The well-known events of Joseph's sale into slavery in Egypt follow. Then because of famine the brothers are forced to come to Egypt to seek food. In 42:9, Joseph remembers the dream. Then when events take a turn for the worse with the brothers, in 43:23 they bow down before Joseph, in 43:28 they do obeisance before Joseph, and in 44:11 they fall to the ground before Joseph. Again the story is told in terms of divine omnipotence behind the scenes, much like Acts 27, in which Paul tells fellow travelers of the previous night's dream / vision that all would be saved (vv. 23–26). The apparently secular narrative that follows is very much a theological narrative.

Luke 8:22–25, together with its companion pieces in the large thought-unit (8:22–9:7), also functions as foreshadowing. In this case, it is not foreshadowing by prophecy but foreshadowing by demonstration. One hears both that Jesus' power controls the sea and that he has authority over demons, even in Gentile territory. Acts works out that foreshadowing both in terms of the Lord's protection of the Lord's servants on the sea (Acts 27) and in terms of authority over the demonic in Gentile territory (Acts 16:16–18; 19:13–20).

This usage resembles the LXX's use of foreshadowing by demonstration in the Elijah-Elisha cycles of 1 and 2 Kings. The first cycle dealing with Elijah tells stories of his accomplishments. Then the reader learns that Elisha is anointed as prophet in his stead (1 Kings 19:16), and that the Spirit of Elijah rests on Elisha (2 Kings 1:15). Following that, a series of events connected with Elisha depicts his deeds, which have similarities with deeds of Elijah. For example, Elisha parts the water (2 Kings 2:13–14) as Elijah had done (2 Kings 2:8); Elisha promises a gift of water (2 Kings 3:20) as Elijah had done (1 Kings 18:45); Elisha multiplies the oil (2 Kings 4:1–7) as Elijah had done (1 Kings 17:8–16); and Elisha raises a child (2 Kings 4:18–37) as Elijah had done (1 Kings 17:17–24). In these two cycles, the deeds of Elijah function as foreshadowing by demonstrating what will

---

29. The language is that of ibid., 106.

be accomplished by Elisha, who has the Spirit of Elijah's hero. Demonstrations of the Spirit in the Elijah cycle foreshadow events worked out in the Elisha cycle.

Whether it be foreshadowing by divine forecast, by dream, or by demonstration, Acts 27 and Luke 8:22–25 fit nicely into the overall Lukan literary and theological design.

Correspondence between Luke and Acts

Recognition of correspondences between persons and events in Luke and Acts has a long history. Given the evidence, such claims seem reasonable. Luke-Acts comes from a time and place in which Virgil could organize the *Aeneid* into two halves, Books 1–6 and Books 7–12, with each book of the second half balancing the corresponding book of the first.[30] Correspondence between Jesus' last journey to Jerusalem and Paul's final journey to Jerusalem is especially persuasive.[31] Examples include the following.

Luke 9:51–19:46 Jesus makes a final journey to Jerusalem (9:31, 51; 12:50; 13:33; 18:31–33) under divine necessity (13:33), involving disciples' lack of understanding (9:45; 18:34).	1.	*Acts 19:21–21:17* Paul makes a last journey to Jerusalem (20:3; 20:22–24, 37–38; 21:4, 10–11; 21:13) under divine necessity (20:22; 21:14), involving friends' lack of understanding (21:4, 12–13).
Luke 19:37 Jesus receives a good reception and the people praise God.	2.	*Acts 21:17–20* Paul receives a good reception and God is glorified.
Luke 19:45–48 Jesus goes into the Temple.	3.	*Acts 21:26* Paul goes into the Temple.
Luke 22:54 Jesus is seized.	4.	*Acts 21:30* Paul is seized.
Luke 22:26; 23:1; 23:8; 23:13 The four trials of Jesus (Sanhedrin, Pilate, Herod, Pilate).	5.	*Acts 23, 24, 25, 26* The four trials of Paul (Sanhedrin, Felix, Festus, Herod).
Luke 23:4, 14, 15, 22 Jesus is declared innocent.	6.	*Acts 23:9; 25:25; 26:31, 32* Paul is declared innocent.
Luke 24 Jesus is raised from the dead.	7.	*Acts 27:1–28:10* Paul is saved from death by God.

It is the last two sets of parallel events that concern us here. If Acts 23:12–26:32 functions as a declaration of Paul's innocence by human authorities, parallel to the declarations of Jesus' innocence by human authorities in Luke

---

30. George E. Duckworth, *Structural Patterns and Proportions in Virgil's "Aeneid"* (Ann Arbor: University of Michigan Press, 1962), 2–10.

31. C. H. Talbert, *Literary Patterns, Theological Themes, and the Genre of Luke-Acts* (Missoula, Mont.: Scholars Press, 1974), 15–23, gives a fuller discussion.

23:4, 14, 15, 22, can his deliverance from storm, shipwreck, and from snakebite be seen as a parallel to Jesus' resurrection?[32]

Jesus' death in Luke raises the question whether, from a human point of view, he is a guilty criminal and, from the divine perspective, is accursed. Declarations of his innocence by human authorities make it clear that his death is not the execution of the guilty but the innocent sufferings of a martyr. The vindication of his resurrection and exaltation reveals that he is not accursed of God but is Lord and Christ. Similarly, after Paul is taken into custody he is kept a prisoner, possibly indicating that, from a human vantage point, he is wicked. Moreover, he experiences shipwreck and snakebite, events that might convey that he was a wicked man receiving his just deserts from God. Declarations by human authorities of his innocence make it clear that he is no criminal, and the circumstances of his shipwreck and snakebite speak forcefully of his innocence and righteousness before God. Both Luke and Acts end with declarations of their respective heroes' innocence by both human and divine authority. In the Third Gospel, Jesus' vindication takes the form of his resurrection and exaltation; in Acts, Paul's vindication takes the form of deliverance from shipwreck and snakebite, and the fact that his prayers for healing were answered.[33]

•

The foregoing remarks have attempted to answer the two questions with which we began: (1) What theological content would the hearers of Luke-Acts have derived from sea-storm narratives in Luke 8:22–25 and Acts 27? and (2) How do these sea-storm narratives fit into the Lukan whole? At least a tentative answer can be given to both queries. Jesus possesses divine power over wind and storm, an authority he uses for the benefit of his "sent ones," both before and after Easter. That Paul was caught in a storm and shipwreck and was bitten by a serpent do not mean he was deemed guilty by God. The sea-storm narrative says the storm was due to natural causes, not divine justice. His deliverance was due to the divine plan, not Paul's own human prowess. The Malta narrative states that Paul is not a guilty man because he was bitten by a serpent. Rather he is a righteous man who is untouched by snakebite and whose prayers are answered by God. Acts 27:1–28:10 says, therefore, that Paul is deemed not guilty by God, but rather as righteous. God has pronounced Paul innocent in this thought-unit as human authorities did in 23:12–26:32. These conclusions, moreover, fit nicely into the larger Lukan literary and theological landscape.

---

32. M. D. Goulder, *Type and History in Acts* (London: SPCK, 1964), 61, describes the events of Acts 27 as Paul's "death" and those of Acts 28:1–10 as Paul's "resurrection," paralleling Jesus' death in Luke 23 and his resurrection in Luke 24.

33. This interpretation hardly qualifies as a candidate for Luke Johnson's scorned "allegorical" reading of Acts 27 in terms of Jesus' death and resurrection (*Acts,* 457).

Chapter 12

The Enigma of the Silent Closing
of Acts (28:16–31)

Daniel Marguerat

The way the Book of Acts ends is surprising, its enigmatic conclusion having resisted centuries of interrogation. At the end of his monumental work
(Luke-Acts), the evangelist Luke presents the activity of Paul, a prisoner, in
the capital of the empire. After the troubled voyage from Caesarea, Paul set-
tles into the company of a guard (28:16) and debates the Jewish delegation from
Rome (28:17–28); the book closes with the apostle evangelizing in the imperial
city (28:30–31). Considering the importance of the end of a literary work —
the force the last image may have on the reader or listener — Luke's choice is
perplexing.[1]

The foremost difficulty is not what the conclusion affirms, but *what it does not
say*. Why does Luke remain silent about the appeal to Caesar, which represents
the avowed motive for Paul's transfer to Rome (28:19)? The ending of Acts
comes after the interminable wait for the apostle's trial announced throughout
the book (23:11; 25:11–12; 26:32; 27:24), but which never occurs; it disappoints
the expectation of the reader. It is easy to understand that this expectation has
intrigued exegetes, and the early fathers[2] were no exceptions. Why did Luke
remain mute over the outcome of the trial, whether favorable (the release of the
apostle) or not (the death of Paul)? Has Luke kept silent intentionally, or did he
have the means to say more?

A second difficulty deals with the theological debate concerning what is essential in the conclusion (28:17–28): what is the verdict on *the relation between*

---

1. A first draft of this study has appeared as "The End of Acts (28:16–31) and the Rhetoric
of Silence," in *Rhetoric and the New Testament: Essays from the 1992 Heidelberg Conference*, ed. S. E.
Porter and T. H. Olbricht, JSNTSup 90 (Sheffield, 1993), 74–89. French version: " 'Et quand nous
sommes entrés dans Rome'. L'énigme de la fin du livre des Actes (28:16–31)," RHPR 73 (1993):
1–21. For this version I owe a lot to exchanges with colleagues in Greco-Roman literature, Claude
Calame (University of Lausanne) and Adalberto Giovannini (University of Geneva); their help was
both scholarly and friendly.

2. A survey of research can be found in H. J. Hauser's *Der Strukturen des Abschlusserzählung des
Apostelgeschichte (Apg 28:16–31)*, AnBib 86 (Rome, 1979), 1–3, and a more detailed survey in C. J.
Hemer, *The Book of Acts in the Setting of Hellenistic History*, WUNT 49 (Tübingen, 1989), 383–87.

Judaism and Christianity? A third difficulty concerns the final image (28:30–31): what signification should be given to this summary, which continues Paul's evangelizing preaching in Rome *as if suspended in time?*

These three questions guide my reflection. I will begin by (1) situating my entry into the problematic of the ending of Acts and then (2) identify the emergence in Greco-Roman writers of what I call a "rhetoric of silence," (3) paying particular attention to Hellenistic historiography. This will lead to (4) its outworking in Acts 27–28. The conclusions (5) will allow us to deal with the final statement concerning the relation between Judaism and Christianity, and with the final summary (6) of the book.

The Problematic of the Ending of Acts

The dissatisfaction felt at the ending of Acts has given birth to two types of hypotheses, one historical and the other theological.

Historical criticism assigns the premature conclusion of the work to a material cause. It was because of lack of papyrus, or an abandoned project of a third volume (Spitta, Zahn), or even that Luke had come to the end of his documentation (Cadbury, Harnack, Hemer).[3] In a more subtle manner, J. Roloff uses the mention in *1 Clement* 5 concerning "jealousy and treachery," which were the origins of persecutions against "the highest and straightest pillars" (Peter and Paul), to suppose that the martyrdom of Paul was linked with Christian intrigues that Luke does not allow himself to mention.[4] The common point of these historical hypotheses is that they all postulate the unintentional ending of Acts: the silence concerning the destiny of Paul is attributed to constraint, ignorance, or imposed muteness. The possibility that the author of Luke-Acts might have intended such a conclusion is rejected in the name of literary seemliness or by virtue of the reader's right to further historical information.

But a verification of the whole of Luke's work shows clearly that Acts 28:16–31 is hardly a precipitated ending.[5] On the one hand, Paul's apology before the

---

3. H. J. Cadbury hypothesizes that Luke's sources gave no detail on this point (*The Making of Luke-Acts* [London, 1958], 321). Harnack thought that Luke at the end of Acts had come up to his own time: *Neue Untersuchungen zur Apostelgeschichte und zur Abfassungszeit der synoptischen Evangelien*, Beiträge zur Einleitung in das Neue Testament 4 (Leipzig, 1911), 65–69; his position is unlikely considering the early date that it imposes on the editing of Acts, but has been taken up with slight modifications by Hemer (*Book of Acts*, 388–410).

4. "Die Paulus-Darstellung des Lukas," *EvT* 39 (1979): 510–31, esp. 522–24. See also P. W. Walaskay, *And So We Came to Rome: The Political Perspective of St Luke*, SNTSMS 49 (Cambridge, 1983), 18–22. The proposition of a Christian conspiracy against Paul goes back to O. Cullmann, *Saint Pierre, disciple, apôtre, martyr* (Neuchâtel, Switzerland, and Paris, 1952); it is based on a risky interpretation of ζῆλος καὶ ἔρις (*1 Clem.* 5:5), considered technical terms for a fratricidal fight on the basis of their proximity to Phil. 1:15.

5. In his work, which is now a classic, J. Dupont has shown this well: "La conclusion du livre des Actes et son rapport à l'ensemble de l'ouvrage de Luc," in *Nouvelles Études sur les Actes des Apôtres*, LD 118 (Paris, 1984), 457–511, esp. 483–511.

Jewish deputation in Rome (28:15–31) recapitulates the long history of judiciary conflict with the Jews which occupies the last section of the book (21:27; 26:32). On the other hand, Paul's dialogue with the Jews in Rome (28:17–28) takes up and hardens a scenario already set up in the inauguration of his ministry in the synagogue of Antioch of Pisidia (13:14–48): Paul begins by preaching to the Jews, but with their rejection, he announces the transfer of the word to the Gentiles.[6] Furthermore, by his choice of vocabulary, Luke has brought together the end and the beginning of Acts, as well as the beginning of his Gospel.[7] The frequent connections that the author weaves between the end and beginning of his work confirm the deliberate character of this ending.

Following Dibelius's works, *theological criticism* has measured the fullness of the literary and theological choices that are functions of Lukan historiography; the end of Acts is seen as the result of a theological strategy. One affirms that the program of the Resurrected One to make witnesses to the ends of the earth (1:8) has come about through Paul's arrival in Rome.[8] It is thought that Acts has been conceived by a theology of the word so that, for Peter (12:17) as for Paul, the biography of the witness disappears after the rise of Christian missions.[9] E. Haenchen popularized the apologetic vision of Luke, that it would have been prejudicial to the image of Rome to culminate the account with Paul's execution on the order of the emperor.[10] It is undeniable that the Lukan theology of the word and the apologetical aim played their roles. But we must note that (1) Rome did not coincide with the ἐσχάτον τῆς γῆς (the end of the earth)

---

6. In particular, Dupont shows that ἰδοὺ στρεφόμεθα εἰς τὰ ἔθνη (13:46b) forms an inclusio with τοῖς ἔθνεσιν ἀπεστάλη τοῦτο τὸ σωτήριον τοῦ Θεοῦ (28:28), with 18:6 as a relay point, ἀπὸ τοῦ νῦν εἰς τὰ ἔθνη πορεύσομαι. Announced twice, the decision to turn to the pagans receives added weight and an unquestionable determination at the end of Acts.

7. The expression βασιλεία τοῦ Θεοῦ, which summarizes Paul's preaching (28:23, 31), joins with the words of the Resurrected One at the beginning of Acts (1:3). The rare expression σωτήριον τοῦ Θεοῦ (28:28) forms an inclusio with the beginning of the evangelical story (Luke 2:30; 3:6), where it is already tied to the announcement of the division of Israel brought about by the revelation of universal salvation (Luke 2:34; 3:7–9). The inclusio of the end of Acts with the Simeon episode is theologically exploited by D. L. Tiede: "The ending of the narrative of Acts 28 is, therefore, not the end of the story, but it is a resumption of the themes sounded in Simeon's oracles" ("'Glory to Thy People Israel': Luke-Acts and the Jews," in *Luke-Acts and the Jewish People*, ed. J. B. Tyson [Minneapolis, 1988], 21–34, esp. 29).

8. Ph. H. Menoud, "Le plan des Actes des apôtres," in *Jésus-Christ et la Foi* (Neuchâtel, Switzerland, and Paris, 1975), 84–91, see p. 86. H. Conzelmann: "Der sowohl geographisch wie theologisch bedeutsamme 'Weg' des Apg fährt nach Rom als dem endgültigen Ziel" ("Der geschichtliche Ort der lukanischen Schriften im Urchristentum, in *Das Lukas-Evangelium*, ed. G. Braumann, Wege der Forschung 280 [Darmstadt, 1974], 224).

9. M. Dibelius defended the idea that Luke anticipates the account of Paul's martyrdom in the farewell discourse to the Ephesian elders (20:22–25), with a view to liberating the conclusion of his work for another theme: the perpetuity of the word. "Die Reden des Apostelgeschichte und die antike Geschichtsschreibung," *Aufsätze zur Apostelgeschichte*, 5th ed., FRLANT 60 (Göttingen, 1968), 131–36.

10. *Die Apostelgeschichte*, 6th ed., KEK (Göttingen, 1968), 654–55. To my knowledge, the proposal of a Lukan censure of the martyrdom of Paul (executed by order of Nero), with a view to insuring Christianity the favor of the Romans, was first formulated by K. Schrader, *Der Apostel Paulus*, vol. 5 (Leipzig, 1836), 573f.

of Acts 1:8[11] and the program of the resurrected Jesus was not accomplished in 28:31; (2) the end of Acts does not tell of the arrival of the word in Rome (it is already there: 28:15), but it tells of the apostle's arrival; and (3) if Luke had wanted to make the figure of the witness disappear behind the advancement of the mission, why is there such a focalization on the person of Paul from 15:36 on?

In my opinion, theological criticism stops too soon. It continues to think that the author of Acts ended his work *because he did not want to say more*, whether it be to obey a theological program or to spare the political power. Just like historical criticism, theological criticism cannot imagine the rhetorical function of an ending deliberately left open, an ending that intentionally plays on the silence. *Literary criticism* makes us attentive to the phenomenon of narrative conclusion, to its characteristics, its orchestrated abundance, and its programmed silence.[12]

Within the frame of the New Testament, the abrupt ending of the Gospel of Mark is instructive,[13] even if by contrast. The end of Mark is considered unfinished only when compared with Matthew 28 and Luke 24. On the contrary, the lack of fulfillment at the end of Acts appears to come from internal elements: Luke has Paul announce his death (20:35, 38), and repeats it in terms that harmonize it with the passion of Jesus (21:1; cf. Luke 18:32). The legal appearance before Caesar is demanded by the apostle (25:11), confirmed by Festus and Agrippa (25:12; 26:32), sealed by the Lord (27:24), and recalled by Paul as the goal of his voyage (28:19). In conclusion, from chapter 20 to 28, the author of Acts methodically constructs an expectation in the reader which he finally fails to satisfy. Is this inadvertent? Or is it because he forgets? Or is there a shift in strategy? The qualities of the writer are too clear to accredit the theory of a mistake. I rather think that Luke in chapters 27–28 organizes a concerted displacement of the reader's expectation which he has methodically built up to that point. In matters of narrative strategy, the author of Acts is no beginner.[14]

---

11. On this point, W. C. van Unnik seems to have said the essential: "Der Ausdruck 'ΕΩΣ ΕΣΧΑΤΟΥ ΤΗΣ ΓΗΣ' (Apostelgeschichte 1:8) und sein alttestamentlicher Hintergrund," in *Sparsa Collecta 1*, NovTSup 29 (Leiden, 1973), 386–401. Notwithstanding Ps. Sol. 8:16, Rome does not represent the end of the earth — at least from a Roman point of view — and Luke would surely not be insensitive to the fact that Rome qualified as the center of the world.

12. My theoretical references for a study of narrative closure in literature include F. Kermode, *The Sense of an Ending* (London, 1966; reprint, 1977); idem, *The Genesis of Secrecy: On the Interpretation of Narrative* (Cambridge, Mass., 1979); B. H. Smith, *Poetic Closure: A Study of How Poems End* (Chicago, 1968); R. Blau Du Plessis, *Writing beyond the Ending* (Bloomington, Ind., 1985); A. Kotin Mortimer, *La clôture narrative* (Paris, 1985): C. Cazale Berard, ed., *Fine della storia e storia senza fine*, Narrativa 4 (Paris, 1993); K. Stierle and R. Warning, *Das Ende: Figuren einer Denkform* (Munich, 1996).

13. I refer the reader first of all to the excellent book by J. L. Magness, *Sense and Absence: Structure and Suspension in the Ending of Mark's Gospel*, SBLSS (Atlanta, 1986), 83–85.

14. We can turn to the narrative "coup de force" represented in the drama of Ananias and Sapphira (5:1–11), which makes a breach in the original community (chaps. 2–6), or again the turning round in the conversion of Saul (chap. 9) after the negative presentation of the character in 7:57–8:3. But the clearest example of this process of deferred expectation that Luke imposes is Paul's constant return to the synagogue, despite his resolute decision to turn to the pagans (cf. 13:46 and 14:1, 18:6, and 18:19; concerning the succession of 28:28 and 28:30b, see below, "Ultimate

Surprisingly, we revisit an intuition concerning the text proposed by John Chrysostom in his *Homilies on Acts*. His commentary uses terms that a narratologist today would not disown:

> The author [Luke] conducts his narrative up to this point, and leaves the hearer thirsty so that he fills up the lack by himself through reflection. The outsiders [non-Christian writers] do also likewise; for knowing everything makes one slow and apathetic. But he does this, and does not tell what follows, deeming it superfluous inasmuch as for those who happen to read the scriptures, they only learn from there to add to the discourse. Consider indeed that what follows is absolutely identical with what comes before. (*Homily on Acts* 15; PG 60, 382)

According to Chrysostom, the incomplete ending of Acts (1) is the effect of a literary strategy well-attested in non-Christian literature; (2) aims at activating the reflection of the reader; and (3) requires that it be filled by extrapolation from what has preceded in the narrative.

The first assertion requires verification before one can commit to the others: by ending a literary work without telling his readers everything, does Luke conform to a pattern known in Greco-Roman literature? One may note that John the Evangelist has done this by resorting to the literary topos of unspeakable abundance ("Now Jesus did many other signs in the presence of his disciples, which are not written in this book," John 20:30).[15] What about the author of Acts? One should ask about the literary conventions that regulated the conclusion of a work in antiquity.

What Is a Rhetoric of Silence?

What rules in antiquity governed the conclusion of literary works? A brief glance at the research shows that the question has hardly been touched, while studies on the *prooemia* are abundant. The rhetoricians of old dealt much more with the beginning of a work than its ending.

The classic reference is found in Aristotle (*Poetics* 7.21–35): the end "is that which is inevitably or, as a rule, the natural result of something else but from which nothing else follows.... Well-constructed plots must not therefore begin and end at random, but embody the formulae we have started." In other words, by this double constraint the achievement results necessarily from the intrigue, and the intrigue leads necessarily to its accomplishment. Is this always the case? Clearly not!

Theological Disputation"). We have the feeling that far from a ploy of narrative skill, this strategy is taken into the service of an obvious theological intention.

15. This motif is found in Sir. 43:27; 1 Macc. 9:22; Justin, *Apol.* 1.31, 48.54; Lucian, *Dem.* 67; etc. Numerous examples are collected by W. Bauer, *Das Leben Jesu im Zeitalter der neutestamentlichen Apokryphen* (Tübingen, 1909), 364–65.

J. L. Magness has listed ancient works that violate the Aristotelian rule of narrative closure.[16] The *Iliad* and the *Odyssey* rank highest. Both Homeric works end, from the standpoint of the plot, by a quieting down: the *Iliad* closes on the gesture of Achilles giving Hector's corpse back to Priam and with the funeral laments of the Trojans (22.405–515);[17] the *Odyssey* terminates in Ulysses' triumph over the revolt in Ithaca and his return home (23.248–96). Tiresias predicts that Ulysses will have to leave Ithaca again on a new journey (11.119–37). Identifying this procedure of an open closure is paramount, since Homer in antiquity constitutes the source of all culture and the model for all literature. Not only do other authors adopt this pattern of narrative suspension (the most frequently cited example is Virgil's *Aeneid*),[18] but numerous works present themselves as a "sequel of Homer."[19]

With some exaggeration, Magness draws conclusions as to the frequency of narrative suspension in the ending of ancient works. His observations nevertheless uncover the rhetorical power of a non-narrated ending, of a rhetoric of silence which leads readers to supply the outcome of the story through their own reflection. Is it then legitimate to speak of a rhetoric of silence, whereas we have up to here limited ourselves to a few instances of narrative suspension? Independent of the attestations to come, the pertinence of the term seems established by the fact that ancient rhetoric is far from insensitive to the effect of silence. With this in mind, it is good to follow the reflections of two masters in rhetoric, Pseudo-Longinus and Quintilian.

In the *Treatise of the Sublime*, Pseudo-Longinus asserts that the first of the five sources of the sublime is the nobility of the mind (μεγαλοφροσύνη): "The sublime is the echo of the greatness of the soul" (IX, 2). Surprisingly, the example proposed is an instance of silence, namely the appearance in the Nekyia of Ajax, who refuses to answer the question of Ulysses. "Whence even without voice, the naked idea, of itself, sometimes wins the admiration by dint of the sole nobility of mind, just as in the Nekyia, the silence of Ajax is great and more sublime than any speech" (IX, 2). The silence of Ajax functions as a perceptible experience of μεγαλοφροσύνη; as such it expresses nothing, yet expresses the absolute.[20]

---

16. *Sense and Absence*, 55ff. Concerning the end of Acts, the hypothesis of a literary usage has been voiced by as subtle a precursor as Cadbury, *The Making of Luke-Acts*, 321–24.

17. The study of the ending of ancient works is made difficult by the frequent lack of knowledge regarding the primitive ending of the work; glossed endings abound. Concerning the *Iliad*, the termination at Book 22 is only a likely hypothesis (summary of the discussion in Magness, *Sense and Absence*, 28–30).

18. The *Aeneid* finishes with the murder of the Latin chief Turnus, whom Aeneas finishes off in a burst of anger. This ending is problematic, as underlined by the last verse of Virgil (12.952): *Vitaque cum gemitu fugit indignata sub umbra* ("And life with a groaning fled indignant under the shadows"). One encounters in the body of the narrative (12.808–40), under the guise of an agreement between Jupiter and Juno, a prediction of Aeneas's marriage with princess Lavinia; that union portends the peace concluded with the Latins and the founding of a new race, concretized by the founding of Rome.

19. See P. Salat, "La fin de l'Énéide," in *Le point final*, ed. A. Montandon, Faculté des Lettres et Sciences humaines de l'Université de Clermont-Ferrand II, n.s., 20 (Clermont-Ferrand, 1984), 11–18.

20. In his *Life of Apollonios of Tyana*, Philostratus is not far from Pseudo-Longinus when he

Quintilian encourages the rhetors to opt for a final summary (ἀνακεφαλαίω-σις) at the end of the speech (*Institutio oratoria* VI, 1), and Luke conforms to this at the end of his work. But Quintilian is not insensitive either to the rhetoric of the unsaid. In Book 2 of the *Institutio*, he elaborates on the virtue of not telling everything.

> In painting, what is attractive, it is the face as a whole; yet, if Apelle has shown an image of Antigonus in profile only, it was in order that the deformity of his gouged eye may be hidden. What then? Are there not in speech some details to be concealed, whether they must not be shown, or whether they cannot be expressed for the sake of dignity? Thus did Timanthes, a native of Cythnos, I believe, in the picture that made him win over Colotes of Teos. In the sacrifice of Iphegenia, he painted a sad Calchas, a yet sadder Ulysses and added to Maenalaus the maximum affliction that may be rendered by art; having exhausted all effects, not finding how to render the facial expression of the father fittingly, he veiled his [the father's] head and left it to everyone to figure out with his own mind (*et suo cuique animo dedit aestimandam*). (II, 13, 12–13)

Quintilian indicates a concerted recourse to the unsaid, with a view to soliciting the imagination of the reader.

The examples invoked thus far stem from the tragic poets and the Hellenistic novel. What about historiography, after which Luke-Acts is patterned first and foremost? Two ancient theoreticians of historiography may provide us with information at this point: Lucian of Samosata (c. 120–180) and Dionysius of Halicarnassus (end of the first century B.C.E.).

The Rhetoric of Silence in Hellenistic Historiography

In his treatise *How to Write History*, Lucian expatiates on how a historian ought to begin and construct his work, not on how he ought to finish it. Is this an indication of the freedom left to the author in concluding a work? Whatever the case, Lucian deals with silence in an apology of brevity, in which he defends the idea that "if you should skim over small and less necessary items, and speak abundantly on matters of importance, there are indeed many that one should even leave out" (56). These words plead for freedom and discernment on the part of the historian in the selection of recounted facts. It leads us to conclude that the scenario that Luke adopts to end Acts results from a deliberate choice. We can note therefore that the author of Acts chose to close his work by presenting the preaching of Paul in Rome (28:30–31) and that this short summary,

---

describes the pious respect with which the disciples of Pythagoras surround the transmission of the words of the master: "And all the revelations of Pythagoras were considered by his fellows as laws, and they honoured him as though he had been a messenger of Zeus, training themselves to the silence that is fitting before the deity; for they heard many divine and secret revelations, which it would have been difficult to keep to themselves if they had not begun by learning that silence is also word (καὶ τὸ σιωπᾶν λόγος)" (I, 1).

often considered insignificant by commentators, receives by its position *in fine* a strategic importance that has to be interpreted. But if Lucian's observations help us understand why Luke has chosen to say certain things, they do not indicate his reasons for *not saying* certain things.

The writings of Dionysius of Halicarnassus, especially his *On Thucydides* and his *Letter to Pompeius*, are more explicit.[21] According to Dionysius: "The first duty, and perhaps the most necessary one for all historians, is to choose a beautiful subject, pleasant to the readers" (*Ep. ad Pomp.* 3.767). The second duty is to determine "where to begin" and "how far one must go" (3.769). Herodotus is cited as a model because he begins by indicating the cause of the hostilities between Greeks and barbarians and "proceeds until he has shown the punishment and vengeance exercised upon the barbarians" (3.769). Dionysius privileges a reversion to the beginning in concluding the theme that constitutes "the beginning and the end" of history (καὶ ἀρχὴ καὶ τέλος ἐστὶ τῆς ἱστορίας, 3.767).

Thucydides, on the other hand, is a target for criticism. Not only does he fail to begin in the appropriate manner (*De Thuc.* 10.338), starting with the decline of the Greeks, but he does not conduct his work to a suitable end. Even though he has promised to "expose everything," Thucydides concludes by relating the battle of Cynossema in the twenty-first year of the war: "It would have been better, having related everything, to end History with the most admirable event and the one that must have been listened to with the most delight: the return of the fugitives from Phyle, which was for the city the beginning of the recovery of freedom" (*Ep. ad Pomp.* 3.771). Quite apart from the bad taste Dionysius embodies by presenting the Greeks in a position of weakness, one should retain his insistence on the thematic inclusion which the beginning and ending of the historiographical work must present.[22] As seen above,[23] the circularity between Acts 28 and Luke 2 / Acts 1 is not to be faulted on this point.

But what about the works which Dionysius criticizes? We know that Thucydides did not have time to finish the *Peloponnesian War* and botched up the ending; one can sense this from the absence of speeches, which Xenophon already felt as a deficiency.

The *Histories* of Herodotus conclude in Book 9 with a perfectly symbolic event: the defeat of Xerxes' troops at Sestos and the destruction of the bridges over the Hellespont, the same ones that had allowed Persian troops to invade

---

21. For a study of literary criticism in Dionysius of Halicarnassus, I have consulted the following: M. Egger, *Denys d'Halicarnasse: Essai sur la critique littéraire et rhétorique chez les Grecs au siècle d'Auguste* (Paris, 1902); W. Rhys Roberts, *Dionysius of Halicarnassus: The Three Literary Letters* (Cambridge, 1901); S. F. Bonner, *The Literary Treatises of Dionysius of Halicarnassus: A Study in the Development of Critical Method* (Amsterdam, 1969).

22. Dionysius reproaches: "Thucydides has not begun his history where one ought to, and he has not adapted to it the suitable end.... by no means the least part of a good arrangement is to begin where there should be nothing before, and to end where nothing is left to be desired" (*De Thuc.* 10.830). About Xenophon, on the contrary, he appreciates the fact that "everywhere, he has begun and ended in the most suitable and appropriate manner" (*Ep. ad Pomp.* 4.778).

23. See p. 286

Greece (9.114–20). After victory, in a gesture that seals the Persian defeat, the Athenians on their return home take away the cables of the bridge in order to consecrate them to their gods (9.121). The author concludes with a saying of Cyrus, who had once enjoined the Persians to withdraw into their territory and to renounce invaders in order to preserve their autonomy.[24] Dionysius of Halicarnassus is right: Herodotus closes on a theme which is fundamental to him, the theme of the limit; the ὕβρις of the Persians who started the war had consisted precisely in violating the limit in order to demand earth and water from the Greeks. But what Dionysius has not noticed is the lack of completion in this ending. Herodotus was announcing three woes to the Athenians: Darius, Xerxes, Artaxerxes.[25] His work ends under the reign of Xerxes; the prediction of the third woe remains like a shadow over the future, as an unfulfilled threat, with the overhanging saying of Cyrus, whose violation is denounced as insanity. The unsaid allows Herodotus to suspend the conflict between (Greek) culture and barbarism on a point of great fragility: the respect of a limit. The prediction of the three woes is a portent that the limit will not hold.

What shall we conclude? The attestation, both in Homer and in that master of historiography, Herodotus, of a narrative suspension in the ending has enough to impress when one knows the considerable role played by these works in ancient culture. The identification of this rhetoric of silence in poetry, theater, and the Hellenistic novel as well as in historiography leads to the conclusion that it existed as a literary convention which the Hebrew Bible did not ignore,[26] from which the author of Acts may have been able to draw inspiration.

The effect of this convention may be summed up in three points:

1. Narrative suspension is a literary device whereby the author, by failing to bring certain narrative data to their resolution, hinders the closure of the narrative world for the reader (thus Thucydides as read by Dionysius of Halicarnassus).

2. The closure effect must be achieved by the reader, who, in order to satisfy the need for completion, is tempted to finish the story in consonance with its plot (*Odyssey, Aeneid,* Herodotus).

3. The narrative, even without closure, may end with a scene (*Odyssey,*

---

24. The saying attributed to Cyrus is after all perfectly Greek: "In soft countries, he said, soft men are usually born; and it does not belong to the same soil to produce admirable fruit and men of good war. The Persians agreed; they withdrew after having surrendered to the opinion expressed by Cyrus; and they chose to be masters even though they lived in an infertile land, rather than being slaves to someone else while cultivating luxuriant plains" (9.122).

25. The earthquake that struck Delos is interpreted by Herodotus in these terms: "It seems to me that this wonder was sent by God as a portent of the evil to come among men. For in three generations, that of Darius, son of Hystaspses, that of Xerxes, son of Darius, and that of Artaxerxes, son of Xerxes, more woes will come on Greece than during the twenty generations which preceded Darius..." (VI.98).

26. P. Davies has made the observation that the second book of Kings ended with a narrative suspension through the symbolic scene of Jehoiachin's release (25:27–30); he has not been able to show that Luke has drawn direct inspiration from that ending in order to compose Acts 28 ("The Ending of Acts," *ExpTim* 94 [1982–83]: 334–35).

Aeneid) or a declaration (Herodotus) that functions as a metaphor or a synecdoche and induces the unspoken outcome of the narrative.[27]

Let us return to the Book of Acts. I have said that it contained two announcements for which the narrative offers no fulfillment: Paul's appeal to Caesar and the testimony to the Risen One "unto the ends of the earth" (1:8). According to what has just been said, one must ask: does the plot of the book contain indications allowing the reader to bring these announcements to their completion? I shall begin with the appeal to Caesar, reserving the second motif for the last section ("Paul the Exemplary Pastor").

Acts 27–28 and the Displacement of the Reader's Expectation

Paul, in order to escape the intrigue of his adversaries, uses the right that is his by Roman citizenship: he appeals to the imperial judicial court (25:11). This announcement lays out the end of the Book of Acts: it is predicted by God (23:11), communicated by Paul (25:11), sanctioned by the governor Festus (25:12, 25), recognized by King Agrippa (26:32), and confirmed by an angel during the storm (27:23). With all desired clarity, Luke prepared his readers for the appearance of the apostle before Caesar. But when the moment is about to be realized, the author of Acts consecrates fifty-nine verses to narrate the emotions of the trip to Rome, with abundant detail concerning the navigational maneuvers for which we hardly find parallels in Greek literature. Considering the strategic position of this episode (just a few lines from the end!), the voyage to Rome has a delaying effect which must have a specific function as to the reader's expectation. What is that function?

Since Ulysses and the *Odyssey*, the Hellenistic novel had made the sea voyage into the classic locus of the hero's identity quest; the symbolic quest operates there by way of a rescue from the powers of evil. Exegetes have pointed out how the ambivalence of the vocabulary of rescue (σῷζειν, διασῴζειν, σωτηρία)[28] makes the sea epic into a metaphor of salvation. It is also clear that the last two chapters of Acts are organized according to a two-part scheme: the tableau of Acts 27:1–28:10, devoted to the Gentiles, find its counterpart in the scene of Acts 28:11–31, devoted to the relation with Judaism. The narrative conclusion of 27:44 ("And so it was that all were brought safely [διασωθῆναι] to the land")

---

27. I borrow categories from Kermode, *Genesis of Secrecy,* 65. W. Iser speaks of the "gaps" of the text as an indispensable factor in the act of reading; meaning arises both from what is said and from the reader's projection on the unsaid, so that the silence of the text is not to be considered as an absence of meaning, but as an invitation to find the missing elements through projection ("Interaction between Text and Reader," in *The Reader in the Text,* ed. S. R. Suleiman and I. Crosman [Princeton, 1980], 106–19).

28. Acts 27:20, 31, 34, 43, 44; 28:1, 4. This is contrary to the opinion of A. George, who maintains the strictly profane character of σῴζειν/σωτηρία: "Le vocabulaire de salut," *Études sur l'oeuvre de Luc,* Sources bibliques (Paris, 1978), 297–320, esp. 308f.

must be read in that perspective: the rescue of the ship's passengers prefigures the salvation of all the nations of the earth, which already anticipates the quasi-eucharistic meal over which Paul presides aboard ship (27:33–37).[29]

Paul plays the leading role in that operation of salvation. Visited by God, inhabited by an unshakable confidence, equipped with an infallible foreknowledge concerning the future, the apostle to the Gentiles with his presence and wisdom dominates the unfurling tempest.[30] The divine visitation (27:23–24) interprets the rescue of the ship as a grace granted to Paul (κεχάρισταί σοι ὁ Θεός), making the apostle a mediator for the salvation of his 276 fellow passengers. The reader knows that Paul is not guilty of the crimes he is accused of by the Jews: Luke has made the statements of innocence into a leitmotiv (18:14–15; 20:26; 23:3, 9; 24:12–13; 25:18, 25; 26:31–32). But on the narrative plane, the pagans have yet to receive the certainty of it. For them the fantastic rescue in Acts 27 manifests the intervention of the God, who is Lord of the waters,[31] in favor of God's witness; for them providence attests the innocence of Paul.

G. B. Miles and G. Trompf have shown that, in Greek literature, protection from the peril of the waves is also a classic motif of the divine protection of the just.[32] Thus for the Jewish as well as for the Greek reader, the God of the ocean acquits the apostle in the eyes of the pagan world. It is tempting to conclude with these authors that since the apostle has been found guiltless by divine intervention, relating the appearance of Paul before a human court of justice, even

---

29. In her excellent article on the voyage to Rome, S. M. Praeder rightly maintains the eucharistic character of the meal, induced by the mimesis of the vocabulary from which Luke constructs the narrative of the Last Supper of Jesus (cf. Acts 27:35 and Luke 22:19); however, I think the absence of the distribution of bread is intentional. Luke avoids assimilating the crew of the ship with a Christian assembly. Praeder also notes the universalistic aims of the meal, concretized by the unusual abundance of categories of totality in this passage: 27:33, 35, 36, 37; cf. 27:24, 44 ("Sea Voyages in Ancient Literature and the Theology of Luke-Acts," *CBQ* 46 [1984]: 683–706, esp. 697–700; see also idem, "The Narrative Voyage: An Analysis and Interpretation of Acts 27–28," Ph.D. diss., Graduate Theological Union, 1980, 126–42).

30. Paul gives navigation advice (27:9–10); he comforts (27:21–26); he benefits from an angelic visitation (27:23–24); he foresees the flight of the sailors (27:31); he celebrates a quasi-eucharistic meal (27:35); his presence saves the life of the prisoners (27:43). Haenchen concludes the following from the Pauline episodes in Acts 27, which he views as redactional additions: "In this way Chapter 27 is fitted into the final section of the book, which again shows Paul the prisoner as the focal point of the action: he, the prisoner, saves them all!" (*The Acts of the Apostles: A Commentary* [Philadelphia, 1971], 709). On the victorious figure of the apostle in trial, see the study of J. Zumstein, "L'apôtre comme martyr dans les Actes de Luc," *RThPh* 112 (1980): 371–90, or *Miettes exégétiques*, Le Monde de la Bible 25 (Geneva, 1991), 183–205.

31. In addition to Old Testament tradition (mainly Jonah and the Psalms), see Luke 5:4–8; 8:22–25. Rabbinic literature also ties storms to the wrath of God, e.g., in the miraculous deliverance of Rabbi Gamaliel (*b. B. Meṣ.* 59b), or in relating the terror of Titus shaken by the waves on his return from Rome after the sack of Jerusalem (*Aboth Rabbi Nathan* 7).

32. G. B. Miles and G. Trompf, "Luke and Antiphon: The Theology of Acts 27–28 in the Light of Pagan Beliefs about Divine Retribution, Pollution, and Shipwreck," *HTR* 69 (1976): 259–67; G. Trompf, "On Why Luke Declined to Recount the Death of Paul: Acts 27–28 and Beyond," in *Luke-Acts: New Perspectives from the SBL Seminar*, ed. C. H. Talbert (New York, 1984), 225–39. Their thesis has been refined and expanded by D. Ladouceur, "Hellenistic Preconceptions of Shipwreck and Pollution as a Context for Acts 27–28," *HTR* 73 (1980): 435–49.

an imperial one, would become superfluous.[33] But two observations hinder me from adopting this conclusion.

First, the Malta episode (28:1–10) and the end of the voyage (28:11–16) present *a chain of arguments attesting the divine favor toward Paul.* (1) The apostle's immunity to the viper's bite leads the "barbarians" in Malta to abandon their idea that "Justice" (Δίκη) was pursuing a criminal (28:4); Paul is therefore innocent. (2) Even more, they regard him as a god (28:6b) — Luke does not care to correct that assessment (contrary to 14:14–18), for the barbarians are allowed to voice in an aberrant form a verdict which is substantially correct.[34] (3) The healing of "all the other" (οἱ λοιποί) inhabitants of the island leads to a profusion of honors showered upon Paul and his companions (28:10). (4) Through the ensign of the Dioscuri (28:11) under which the ship sails, Paul's arrival in Puteoli bears the signature of his innocence: the celestial twins are known not only as protectors of seafaring people, but as guardians of truth and the punishers of perjury.[35] To sum up: Paul's innocence crystallizes in a chain of signs adapted to the pagan world, but unfit for the dialogue with Judaism.

Second, Luke in Acts 28:17–28 does indeed set up a trial situation. But the roles are reversed. Let us look at the first interview (28:17–22). Paul is a prisoner, but he is the one who summons others to his own dwelling (28:17a). The Roman Jewish deputation, which on the narrative plane inherits the role of accuser, is installed as the judges before whom Paul pleads his innocence (28:17b–20); these judges — who are impartial since no rumor concerning Paul has reached them (28:21) — ratify Paul's innocence. At the second interview (28:23–28), Paul keeps the initiative, but the issue has changed: the debate is no longer about the apostle's innocence, but about the culpability of the Jews before the gospel (28:23). Paul interprets the audience's split reaction to his preaching by means of the word of judgment of Isa. 6:9–10 (28:25–27). The role reversal is then complete. The accusers, who first became judges, have become the ones judged. In accordance with the Holy Spirit (28:25), the accused wields the word of judgment: "For this people's heart has grown dull, and their ears are hard of hearing, and they have shut their eyes; so that they might not look with their eyes, and listen with their ears..." (28:27).

I spoke earlier of the reader's expectation being displaced by the author. This

---

33. Miles and Trompf, "Luke and Antiphon," 265: "Paul was put to the last test by forces and exigencies far more dreaded than the requirements of a human law court, and since he had been found guiltless, what need was there to recount the outcome of his appeal?" cf. also p. 267.

34. J. Roloff does not heed this narrative effect when he compares the Malta episode with the one in Lystra (chap. 14), and ascribes to a "naiv-unreflektierte Paulusverehrung" the lack of challenge to the Maltans' flawed theology, which regrettably assimilates the apostle with a god (*Die Apostelgeschichte*, NTD 5 [Göttingen, 1981], 366). But the narrator is more subtle. He leaves this judgment standing, which the reader knows to be wrong, but which testifies to a contextualized version of the recognition of the apostle's status. Luke is a master of the reconstitution of local color. R. I. Pervo (*Profit with Delight* [Philadelphia, 1987], 70ff.) has well grasped the Lukan taste for exotic coloring.

35. See M. Albert, *Le culte de Castor et Pollux en Italie* (Paris, 1883); Ladouceur, "Hellenistic Preconceptions," 443–48.

mechanism appears now more clearly. When Luke methodically constructs the
expectation of Paul's trial, this is not to censor it at the last moment for the sake
of political decency. Luke transforms the journey to Rome into a providential
manifestation of Paul's innocence in the eyes of the pagan world, and the Maltese are going to ratify it with their barbaric naïveté (28:1–10). The image of
the apostle arriving in Rome as a distinguished visitor, welcomed by a Christian
delegation (28:15), settled into the liberal status of the *custodia militaris* (28:16,
30),[36] receiving crowds of people at home (28:17, 23, 30) — this glowing image[37]
does not aim at sparing imperial justice, but rather at an exchange of roles. The
prisoner reaches the capital and stays there with the authority of one who shall
not be judged, but who shall be the bearer of judgment. The function of the
sequence in Acts 27:1–28:16 is to prepare for this reversal. This does not occur,
however, without a paradox: this man, bearer of a word of judgment, is in chains
(28:16b).

All this being said and done, why is there no mention of the outcome of the
trial? If the Lukan silence is neither ignorance nor political prudence, what is the
reason? My opinion is that Luke through the effect of judicial reversal reinterprets a fact that his readers will remember: the execution of the apostle in Rome,
perhaps at the close of his trial.[38] This subtle game with the reader's memory is
signaled by the limited length of the apostle's stay in Rome (v. 30: διετία), whose
result the reader does not have to learn. But Luke leans on this memory to reverse roles. It is not the apostle to the Gentiles, but the chosen people in Rome
who are judged. The reluctance of the author of Acts to recount the death of
witnesses also exercises its effect, which is more likely than an intended resemblance between the death of Paul and the resurrection of Jesus, as some have
suggested.[39] If the rhetoric of silence incites the reader to close the narrative
in accord with the plot, one understands the means that Luke has provided his
readers to guide them in the task of completion. Death is indeed announced
(20:35, 38; 21:11), but the account, which is suspended on the foundation of
the Pauline witness before the workings of Roman power (chaps. 21–26) and on

---

36. One should consult the study by H. W. Tajra, *The Trial of St. Paul*, WUNT 2:35 (Tübingen,
1989), 179–81.

37. Concerning the social image of Paul in Acts, in addition to the above-cited monograph by
Pervo, I would mention J. C. Lentz, *Luke's Portrait of Paul*, SNTSMS 77 (Cambridge, 1993).

38. The hypothesis of the death of Paul in Rome has sufficient support from literary and archae-
ological data (see G. Lüdemann, *Early Christianity according to the Traditions in Acts: A Commentary*
[London, 1989], 265–67).

39. While the tradition of the early church was content to tell of the martyrdom of Peter and
Paul, Acts lets both of them depart in the same manner, without relating their deaths. Beforehand,
both are the object of a miraculous deliverance (12:6–11; 28:31b). This silence concerning the death
of two witnesses has been seen in a typological perspective by M. D. Goulder, who discerns the recurrence of the death-resurrection cycle of Jesus (*Type and History in Acts* [London, 1964], 34–51,
esp. 36–39). Detailed analysis and approbation in W. Radl, *Paulus und Jesus im lukanischen Doppelwerk*, Europäische Hochschulschriften 23, 49 (Bern and Frankfurt, 1975), 222–51. This is to confuse
the shipwreck with the death of Paul and to forget the secondary position of the witness before the
master (cf. 27:24, 34–35; 28:23, 31); the absence of resurrection vocabulary in chaps. 12 and 27–28
does not support this interpretation either.

his confidence in the midst of the storm (chap. 27), bespeaks the witness who will face death without faltering.[40]

Positively, it is important for the author of Acts to hold on to the ending (28:30–31), in which the image of a preaching Paul remains; for it is upon this remembrance and activity that the world of the narration and the world of the reader are, in his view, articulated. We will also see that the second prediction left open in the Book of Acts, namely the testimony of the Risen One unto the ἐσχάτον τῆς γῆς (1:8), towers above this final summary, in which the reader sees the awaited accomplishment. I shall come to this, but only after paying attention to the theological dispute in 28:17–28.

The Ultimate Theological Disputation (28:17–28)

In accordance with the norm invoked by Quintilian and Dionysius of Halicar-nassus,[41] the conclusion of Acts resumes the fundamental theme of the work. It delivers the author's theological diagnosis of the relation between church and synagogue. It would be beyond the limits of this article to decide on the prickly question of the image of Judaism in Luke-Acts.[42] I limit my proposal to analyzing the narrative outcome of the conflict in which Luke brings Paul's ministry to an end. I have already noted the structure of reversal governing the passage; it is now necessary to observe the outcome of this reversal.

The *argumentative scenario* of this ultimate debate between Paul and his tra-dition of origin is remarkably constructed. Two interviews bring the prisoner apostle together with the Jewish deputation in Rome, probably composed of synagogue leaders. From the first (28:17–22) to the second interview (28:23–28), the author orchestrates a series of thematic shifts, moving to a culminating crescendo in the hard word of judgment of Isaiah 6. I have noted five shifts.

(1) The first shift passes from Paul's contestation (v. 19a) to the church's (22b: the same verb is used, ἀντιλέγεσθαι). (2) Paul transfers the debate of "this sect" (v. 22) to the proclamation of the kingdom (v. 23). (3) Paul passes from the proclamation of the kingdom (v. 24) to the history of salvation (vv. 25–27). (4) The Jewish deputation is invited to pass from knowledge concerning the contestation of the church (v. 22b) to another knowledge dealing with salvation to the pagans (v. 28a: the same term is used, γνωστόν). (5) Paul passes from a solidarity with Israel ("I have done nothing against the [NRSV: our] people or

---

40. This is essentially the image of the witness that, according to R. C. Tannehill, the reader is invited to carry from Acts 27 to the suspended ending of Acts 28 (*The Narrative Unity of Luke-Acts: A Literary Interpretation*, vol. 2 [Minneapolis, 1990], 355).

41. See above, p. 290ff.

42. I have touched on the question in "Juifs et chrétiens selon Luc-Actes," *Bib* 75 (1995): 126–46, found also in *Le déchirement: Juifs et chrétiens au premier siècle*, ed. D. Marguerat, Le Monde de la Bible 32 (Geneva, 1996), 151–78.

the customs of *the* [NRSV: *our*] *ancestors*," v. 17) to a distance ("The Holy Spirit was right in saying to *your ancestors* through the prophet Isaiah," v. 25).

These five shifts attest that the reorientation of salvation history (v. 28) is effected through Paul's destiny and the acceptance of his message. The first interview allows the apostle to present his apology. One scholar remarks that the modeling of Paul's martyrdom on the passion of Jesus is reinforced (vv. 17–18),[43] and that the speech points toward a validation of suffering in the name of the hope of Israel (v. 20). His exculpation by the Roman authorities shows the Jewish responsibility in his present destiny, but Paul defends himself against any hint of anti-Judaism in the clearest terms: it is because of *the hope of Israel* that he wears his chains (v. 20). This hope in the promises made to the ancestors, if it has as a primary objective the resurrection of the dead (26:6–7), finds its concretization in the intervention of God in Jesus (cf. Luke 2:37).[44] The Jewish deputation understands very well, since its answer (vv. 21–22) transfers the question from the person of Paul, who was not controversial in Rome, to "this sect," which is known to be "contested everywhere." The second interview (28:23–28) begins with Paul's testimony on the kingdom of God: his proclamation is christological (περὶ τοῦ Ἰησοῦ) and is argued from the scriptures (Moses and the prophets). According to a stereotype in Acts, present already in the Pentecost account (2:12–13), the hearers are divided in their reactions: certain are convinced and others "refused to believe" (v. 24). Thus Paul sees the actualization of the word of the Holy Spirit, written in Israel's past in the speech in Isa. 6:9–10, in the failure of his preaching. Consequently, the Jewish deputation is called to become aware that salvation, destined for the pagans, would from now on be addressed to them with success: "This salvation of God has been sent to the Gentiles; they will listen" (v. 28).

To what *theological result* does Paul's aborted dialogue with the Jews of Rome lead? In my view, Luke proceeds in an ambiguous manner, as he does often in the crucial passages of his work, and I will summarize his reading of the event in two terms, as an *opening* and as an *acknowledgment of failure*.

First, the most surprising observation is that in spite of the hard judgment of Isa. 6:9–10, neither Paul's discourse (according to Luke) nor the discourse of the narrator concludes by shutting out Judaism. Luke does not, as in other places, point to the Jewish group as a united front either in hostility (13:45) or in opposition (18:6). He notes a division in the audience between those "con-

---

43. S. M. Praeder notes the three points which differentiate Paul's apology in 28:18–20 from Acts 21:18–26, 32, bringing Paul's martyrdom closer to the trial of Jesus before Pilate, according to Luke 23. The three points are the giving into the hands of the Romans (Luke 18:32–33; 20:20; 23:1); the Roman desire to free him (Luke 23:16, 20, 22); and the Jewish opposition to this liberation (Luke 23:18, 21, 23). Paul's insistence on his innocence finds its parallel on the lips of Jesus in Luke 23:15 and 23:22 ("The Narrative Voyage," 161).

44. See Kl. Haacker, "Das Bekenntnis des Paulus zur Hoffnung Israels nach der Apostelgeschichte des Lukas," *NTS* 31 (1985): 437–51. Behind this apology, W. Stegemann assumes a Lukan response to the reproaches addressed by Judaism to Christianity: *Zwischen Synagoge und Obrigkeit: Zur historischen Situation der lukanischen Christen*, FRLANT 152 (Göttingen, 1991), 180–86.

vinced" (ἐπείθοντο) and the unbelievers (28:24); there is no reason to doubt that πείθομαι represents adherence to Paul's preaching.[45] The text does not underscore that the Jews could believe (the reader knows this already), but the fracturing split of the audience, its "a-symphony" (ἀσύμφωνοι, 28:25a). At this final moment, this separation takes on a symbolic value: unity through recognition of the kingdom of God in Jesus is not effected. It makes sense, therefore, to see in the inclusivity of Paul's hospitality (ἀπεδέχετο πάντας, v. 30) an invitation to include Jews (as individuals) among those to whom the Christian preaching is addressed. Paul's preaching mentioned in the end overcomes the opposition of the λαός/ἔθνη, which dominated verses 25–28, to recapitulate the universality of the addressees of the Christian mission.[46] To this sign of openness, one must add the rhetorical function of the word of judgment, as recalled by D. Moessner: "Isa. 6:9–10 does not foreclose the future by a condemnation, but forcefully exhorts to an ultimate repentance."[47] V. Fusco has also insisted that the accusation of hardening is a Deuteronomist theologoumenon that (1) is not to be confused with the decree of refusal; and that (2) leaves open the possibility of a future enlightenment by a salutary intervention of God.[48] It is then possible to follow F. Bovon when he sees in the καὶ ἰάσομαι αὐτούς of v. 27c, the hope of this divine sanctifying intervention for Israel;[49] the τοῦτο τὸ σωτήριον τοῦ Θεοῦ of v. 28 comes to confirm the salutary connotation of the end of the text of Isaiah. The signs of opening are then perceptible, but we must admit, they are hesitant.

Second, as a counterbalance to the sense of opening, the acknowledgment of failure is laid down with gravity. Over against the "a-symphony" of the chosen people, the triumphant agreement among Isaiah, Paul, and the Holy Spirit is set forth (28:25). The passing of salvation to the pagans, as prompted by Israel's refusal as announced in 13:46 and 18:6, is now sealed by the apostle's last word to Judaism (ῥῆμα ἕν, 28:25), which is at the same time the last word of Paul in Acts. Despite the desire the theologian might have, it is not reasonable to trivialize this final fact by inferring, as earlier in Acts, that Paul will proceed

---

45. The word pair of πείθομαι/ἀπιστέω (28:24) is the equivalent of πιστεύω/ἀπειθέω, which Luke uses in 14:1–2.

46. It is worth noting that the Jews' exit from the narrative, arranged by the Byzantine text (gloss of v. 29), was not precisely intended by the narrator. The gradation that he arranged between the three successive audiences (v. 17: τῶν Ἰουδαίων πρώτους; v. 23: πλείονες; v. 30: πάντας) culminates in universality. Luke did not "write off" Israel in his work. The formula of E. Haenchen — "Luke has written the Jews off" — does not apply to the received text: "The Book of Acts as Source Material for the History of Early Christianity," in *Studies of Luke-Acts: Essays Presented in Honour of P. Schubert*, 3d ed. (London, 1978), 258–78, esp. 278.

47. D. P. Moessner, "Paul in Acts: Preacher of Eschatological Repentance to Israel," *NTS* 34 (1988): 96–104.

48. V. Fusco, "Luke-Acts and the Future of Israel," *NovT* 38 (1996): 1–17, esp. 6–8.

49. F. Bovon, "Il a bien parlé à vos pères, le Saint-Esprit, par le prophète Ésaïe (Actes 28:25)," in *L'oeuvre de Luc*, LD 130 (Paris, 1987), 150. After the series of subjunctives following μήποτε, the passage to the indicative future may indicate an ulterior consequence (Blass-Debrunner-Rehkopf, §448, 28).

without changing his preaching to Israel despite the resistance he confronts.[50] The conclusive word of the apostle in v. 28 does not evoke only the eventuality of the Gentiles' hearing. It opposes this future hearing (ἀκούσονται) with the past non-hearing of Israel. The end of v. 28 insists on this opposition by the position of the καί, emphasizing the pronoun αὐτοί: "they" (the Gentiles) in contrast to "you" (Israel) will listen. From v. 25, the scope of the argument has changed from individuals (v. 24) to collective declarations such as λαός/ἔθνη; the destiny of Israel in its totality is opposed to the attitude of the pagans, with the intention to disqualify the chosen people. Even if the conversion of individuals within Judaism is envisaged and sought (v. 30, πάντες), the hope of unifying the Jewish people (v. 26, λαός)[51] around Jesus is lost.

Luke achieves this effect by placing the rupture between church and synagogue under the sign of historico-salvific continuity. But this rupture is no triumph. It consecrates the failure of apostolic preaching to convince Judaism that, in Jesus, the "hope of Israel" is manifested. This theological dimension of failure comes from a fact little noticed up to now: Luke is the only author of the New Testament who cites Isa. 6:9–10 by including the mandate given to the prophet: "Go to this people and say..." (28:26). Is Luke preoccupied with the exactness of the scripture?[52] I would rather say that the beginning of the quote is important to align Paul with the mandate given to the prophet. The motif of sending the prophet reminds the reader of the repeated mentions of Paul's vocation, cast in the language of prophetic vocations (22:21; 26:17; cf. 9:15).[53] Consequently, a similar failure of preaching establishes, under the pro-

---

50. R. L. Brawley postulates that for Luke, the preaching to Israel will proceed without change; he bases this on the resumption of the evangelization to the Jews, after Paul's resolution to turn to the Gentiles, in 13:46 and 18:6 ("Paul in Acts: Lucan Apology and Conciliation," in Talbert, *Luke-Acts*, 129–34, or *Luke-Acts and the Jews: Conflict, Apology, and Conciliation*, SBLMS 33 [Atlanta, 1987], 68–78). The same trivialization of the conclusive aspect of Acts 28 is found in R. C. Tannehill's *Narrative Unity*, 350f.; B. J. Koet's *Five Studies of Scripture in Luke-Acts*, Studiorum Novi Testamenti auxilia 14 (Louvain, 1989), 119–39; R. F. O'Toole, "Reflections on Luke's Treatment of Jews in Luke-Acts," *Bib* 74 (1993): 547–49 (with reference to Exod. 32:9; Isa. 63:10; 2 Chron. 36:16). Arguments against this reading: (1) the strategic choice of the conclusion refuses to be seen as the repetition of the scenario in 13:46 and 18:6; (2) there is a gradual process both geographical and chronological from Asia (13:46; στρεφόμεθα, indicating future) to Greece (18:6; πορεύσομαι, future), then to Rome (28:28; γνωστόν ἔστω ὑμῖν, present); (3) the author reserves for himself the citation of Isa. 6:9–10, which he shortens in 8:10 (cf. Mark 4:12), to make it appear *in extenso* in the narrative conclusion.

51. In the same direction, see now J. B. Tyson, *Images of Judaism in Luke-Acts* (New York, 1992), 174–78; idem, "Jews and Judaism in Luke-Acts: Reading as a Godfearer," *NTS* 41 (1995): 36–37. For a differing opinion, see H. van de Sandt, "Acts 28:28: No Salvation for the People of God?" *ETL* 70 (1994): 341–58, esp. 357–58.

52. T. Holz thinks it possible that Luke verified the citation by a codex of the LXX: *Untersuchungen über die alttestamentlichen Zitate bei Lukas*, TU 104 (Berlin, 1968), 33–37.

53. H. van de Sandt had identified, like me, this parallelism between sending the prophet and the mission of Paul, but he attributes it to the structure present in Ezek. 2:3–5; 3:4–7 ("Acts 28:28: No Salvation for the People of God?" *ETL* 70 [1994]: 341–58). See also D. P. Moessner, "Paul and the Pattern of the Prophet Like Moses in Acts," *SBLSP* 22 (1983): 203–12; idem, *Lord of the Banquet: The Literary and Theological Significance of the Lukan Travel Narrative* (Minneapolis, 1989), esp. 114–30, 296–307.

tection of the Spirit, a continuity between representatives of God. The apostle takes on and duplicates in the face of Israel the prophet's failure; he borrows the prophet's voice. Paul does not speak in vv. 26–27, but he makes *the prophet* speak in order to attest the continuity in the history of salvation.[54] This drama welds the past to the present and places the Christian preacher and the prophet side by side. Moreover, the call of Isaiah presents the refusal of Israel as the result of an act of God. It is finally to God that the mystery of the hardening of the people is returned.

Rather than ending on a tragic verdict, the Book of Acts — and this fact is of utmost importance theologically — closes on unresolved tension between the promised heritage for Israel and the historical turning that signifies its refusal.[55] How can one explain that in treating a theme so fundamental, Luke ends with an unclear position? We could, like V. Fusco, distrust the arguments *ex silentio* and collect indications throughout the Gospel attesting to the Lukan conviction concerning the future salvation of Israel.[56] But again, Luke is too good a narrator to have neglected the end of his work by forgetting to mention the future of Israel. In my opinion, the unresolved tension of Acts 28 signals that Luke does not have the definitive solution concerning the Israel question. There are only sketches of a solution. The narrator wanted the readers to have their own opinion by posing two correlates that he did not link systematically. On the one hand, the "salvation of God" is to be sought in the church, which recruits among Jews and Gentiles. On the other hand — the distant echo of Romans 9–11 may be felt here — the promises of the faithfulness of God to the people Israel are not annulled.

But the last word of the narrator is to be sought in the conclusive summary of vv. 30–31. We must now decipher the meaning of this epilogue — which has nothing to do with an appendix, theologically speaking — since it develops the idea of a universal opening achieved through prophecy (28:28, quoting Isa. 40:5).

---

54. F. Bovon was sensitive to this effect of "going back," which the process of the quotation organizes: "Il a bien parlé," 145–53, esp. 146 and 152f.

55. R. C. Tannehill discerningly concludes with the paradox Luke poses between the scriptural promises intended for Israel, and the historical experience of its refusal to see in the Christ the accomplishment of the hope of Israel: "The resulting tension, especially apparent in the tension between the promise in the Antioch sermon and the bitter words at the end of Acts, is not resolved in the narrative" ("Rejection by Jews and Turning to Gentiles: The Pattern of Paul's Mission in Acts," in *Luke-Acts and the Jewish People. Eight Critical Perspectives*, ed. J. B. Tyson [Minneapolis, 1988], 83–101, esp. 101). See also Tannehill, *Narrative Unity*, 352. Against this author ("Rejection by Jews," 93) we maintain that the final scene of Acts is not 28:17–28, but 28:30–31, and that consequently the work of Luke does not culminate in the tragic irony of the elected people denying the promise that is destined for them, but in the announcement of salvation open to the nations (see R. C. Tannehill, "Israel in Luke-Acts: A Tragic Story," *JBL* 104 [1985]: 69–85).

56. V. Fusco evokes the prophetic sayings of Luke 13:34–35; 19:41–44; and 21:24b (should we add Acts 3:21ff.?) concerning the future salvation of Israel and affirms that Acts 28:25–28 only mentions the "near future" ("Luke-Acts and the Future of Israel," esp. 9–15). But the weight given to the finale of Acts makes such a solution unlikely, which further highlights the new situation created by the repeated refusal of the Gospel as developed in the narrative of Acts.

Paul the Exemplary Pastor (28:30–31)

Among the typology of narrative closures delineated above,[57] the open-ended conclusion induces the unspoken outcome of the narrative through a scene functioning as metaphor or synecdoche. This is undeniably the case of the final summary presented in 28:30–31.

The redaction of this short summary shows how Luke can subtly use language. First, Paul's activity in Rome is chronologically limited: "He lived there two whole years" (v. 30a). The aorist ἐνέμεινεν and the temporal indication διετίαν ὅλην signal a period that is over, beyond which readers should use their own information and other narrative data. The summary has a biographical goal to close the activity of the hero of Acts. At the same time, the picture has a paradigmatic purpose. The syntactic construction, an imperfect indicative (ἀπεδέχετο, v. 30b) followed by a chain of participles (κηρύσσων, διδάσκων, v. 31), creates an effect of duration and idealism. That construction is typical of the summaries of Acts (2:42, 45–47; 5:16; 8:3; 12:25; 15:35; 18:11; 19:8–10; etc.), which describe the ideal state of the Christian community of mission.[58] The unlimited opening offered by Pauline evangelization is attested by the πάντας ("and welcomed all who come to him"), and Paul's three audiences are recapitulated: Jews, Gentiles, and Christians. The end of the book mentions all three of them (28:17, 23; 28:28; 28:15).

This summary confirms the traits that Luke, since chapter 9, has not ceased to ascribe to Paul as the ideal pastor and the model of the persecuted Christian. In the imperial capital where, like the apostle,[59] Christianity shall now find its "home,"[60] in that place where the Roman power organizes itself, there Paul preaches God's kingship.[61] His teaching holds together two entities that are no longer to be set apart: the βασιλεία τοῦ Θεοῦ[62] and the Lord Jesus Christ

---

57. See pp. 292–293.

58. "His theme of unstoppable growth and spread of God's Word no matter what the human opposition, plays itself out to the very end of his narrative" (W. S. Kevir, *Reading Luke-Acts* [Louisville, 1993], 109). V. Fusco has seen that the conclusion of Acts escapes an exclusively biographical interest as well as a strictly symbolic reading ("Progetto storiografico e progetto teologico nell'opera lucana," in *La storiografia nella Bibbia* [Bologna, 1986], 145–48).

59. Luke was certainly not insensitive either to the fact that the Hellenistic novels (as in the pattern of the *Odyssey*) frequently conclude with the hero's homecoming, or that coming to Rome represented a climax in the life of the great philosophers (see *The Life of Apollonios of Tyana* by Philostratus).

60. The work of Luke transfers the reader from Jerusalem to Rome, and from the Temple (Luke 1–2) to home (Acts 28). The symbolic connotation of Paul's "home" (28:16, 30) remains to be shown. V. K. Robbins sees an indication of the social context of the author, which he describes in "The Social Location of the Implied Author of Luke-Acts," in *The Social World of Luke-Acts*, ed. J. H. Neyrey (Peabody, Mass., 1991), 305–32, esp. 330: "Paul, like the Christian movement, has a rightful home within the Roman Empire." In the same volume, see J. H. Elliot's "Temple Versus Household in Luke-Acts: A Contrast in Social Institutions," 211–40.

61. R. J. Cassidy is (overly?) sensitive to implicit criticism of the Roman institution in the final summary: *Society and Politics in the Acts of Apostles* (Maryknoll, N.Y., 1987), 130–35 and 167–70.

62. Βασιλεία τοῦ Θεοῦ is a synthetic expression of the content of Paul's preaching (Acts 19:8; 20:25) and the message of Jesus (Luke 4:43; 8:1, etc.; Acts 1:3).

(v. 31). The apostle in chains testifies with a total freedom of speech (παρρησία), which is the effect of the Spirit, and without hindrance (ἀκωλύτως), which represents a promise for the future. The theological overtones of this description of the material condition of the apostle, prisoner but free, should not be underestimated;[63] in an ideal picture of the Pauline past, Luke draws up an agenda for the future.

But to whom does this agenda apply? Who must carry it out? For which category of readers is Paul set up as an exemplary pastor? The answer to these questions depends on a detail in the text which might appear trivial at first sight, which is why exegetes have not devoted a lot of attention to it. In Acts 28:16, Luke specifies that on "our" arrival in Rome, Paul was allowed to "stay at his own place (καθ' ἑαυτόν) with the soldier who was guarding him." A similar specification returns unexpectedly in the summary: Paul "lived there two whole years at his own expense (ἐν ἰδίῳ μισθώματι) ..." (28:30). Whatever the exact sense of the rare term μίσθωμα — payment and, by extension, rent, personal financial means[64] — this notation, in conjunction with the καθ' ἑαυτόν in v. 16, stresses the missionary's material autonomy. The portrait of the ideal pastor, which specified an audience (v. 30b) and the synthetic message (v. 31), is now completed by a technical datum on the external condition of missionary work.

In this miniature portrait of the missionary, in my view, Luke's interest in the perpetuation of the Pauline tradition of evangelism is manifest. One can go further. The noted interest in the Pauline mission makes it clear why this ending seems suspended in time. Around the 80s, when Luke was writing, the remembrance of the apostle is celebrated in pro-Pauline circles. The groups of evangelists, who will go on to conquer the empire, are recruited in these pro-Pauline circles. Luke, this great traveler and disciple of the apostle to the Gentiles, fascinated by the founding of the communities, was clearly close to the evangelists of the Pauline tendency. Maybe he, himself, was one. One indication could lead in this direction. Contrary to the movement of the apostolic mission in Acts, Paul in Rome remains sedentary; he does not go toward others, they come to his house (v. 30b). Maybe he was under constraint. Maybe this new sedentary mode of mission corresponds to the conditions of evangelization in Lukan Christianity. Whatever the case, Luke thinks of them — the carriers of the Pauline heritage — in writing this final summary in which the narrative world will meet the readers' world.[65] There was no question of ending with a

---

63. The semantic ambivalence of ἀκωλύτως, which is both juridical (the absence of physical restraint) and theological (sign of the unstoppable action of God), has been revealed by D. L. Mealand, "The Close of Acts and Its Hellenistic Greek Vocabulary," *NTS* 36 (1990): 583–97, esp. 589–95.

64. C. Spicq decides with hesitation for "rent" (*Lexique théologique du Nouveau Testament* [Fribourg, 1991], 1040–41). D. L. Mealand has clearly taken the position of the technical sense, "payment of rent" ("The Close of Acts," 583–87).

65. It is not unimportant that the third and last "we-sequence" in the Book of Acts ends precisely ... in Rome (27:1–28:16), indicating that the entry into the imperial capital was a collective entry of the apostle and his companions. Independent of the (hazardous) presence of a source, the end of this sequence favors my hypothesis of Lukan interest in the perpetuation of the Pauline mis-

celebration of the past, however glorious. The last image of Paul the evangelist, as Luke takes leave, requires recomposition in the life of readers.

Summary

The end of a literary work possesses a peculiar power. The end of the Book of Acts intrigues. But it has become clear that this enigmatic character does not result from the exegete's incapacity. A rhetorical procedure noted in Greco-Roman culture, "narrative suspension," allows the author of Acts consciously to use silence and ambivalence in editing the end of his monumental work. This astonishing narrative choice concretizes the theological challenge that the author of Acts has imposed on himself: to assign to Christianity a new place that the Pauline mission has gained — the Roman Empire — but at the same time to lead Christianity back to its Jewish roots. This intention fits into the conduct of the Pauline heritage. Luke wants to reinterpret the memory of the apostle's martyrdom by inverting the scheme of expected procedure (Acts 27–28), and to assure the perpetuation of his missionary work in the present.

For Luke, Paul's final theological debate with Judaism ends neither in the curse of Israel nor in a trivialization of its refusal.[66] By the apostle's arrival in Rome, a new step is taken in the history of salvation, which marks the failure of a hope in conversion for the entire Jewish people. But the account is voluntarily ambivalent, achieved by a theology which refuses to decide on the future of the relation between church and synagogue. The same disposition of openness characterizes the final scene of Paul evangelizing Rome (28:30–31). This portrayal of the ideal pastor points to the men and women, with Luke or those close to him, who by their missionary engagement perpetuate the memory of the apostle to the Gentiles. In this way, they were associated with the witness of the Risen One "to the ends of the earth" (1:8). The summary offers expectation and remains to be rewritten in the life of the reader at the moment he or she finishes reading the book.

---

sion. In the narrative, the "we" points to the existence of a group: are not the pro-Pauline evangelists called precisely to identify themselves with the historical group around the apostle? In this case, they are literally guided to Rome by the account.

66. The first position is held by J. T. Sanders, "The Jewish People in Luke-Acts," in Tyson, *Luke-Acts and the Jewish People*, 51–75 (the church breaks away from Judaism); the second is maintained by J. Jervell, *Luke and the People of God* (Minneapolis, 1972), 41–44 (the church is the continuation of Israel converted to Christ).

Driving to the Crux:
Luke's Gospel–Acts and the Story of Israel:
"Inasmuch as many ... it seemed good to me
also to write ... that you may have a firm
grasp of the true significance of the
traditions which you have been taught"
(Luke 1:1, 3 – 4)

Chapter 13

Israel's Future and the Delay of the Parousia, according to Luke

Michael Wolter

The State of Discussion

Of all the topics currently being discussed in Lukan research, the question of Israel's future doubtless counts among those least likely to generate consensus among scholars. Although scholars regularly understand the term "Israel" as referring to that part of the Jewish people that did not believe in Jesus, it is anything but certain that this actually corresponds to the Lukan understanding.[1] For the moment, however, I will leave this matter in abeyance and instead describe briefly the state of discussion itself.

On the one hand, some support the position that Luke considered Israel's rejection of the proclamation of Christ to have severed them forever from hope of salvation. E. Haenchen suggests that the citation of Isa. 6:9f. in Acts 28:26f. constitutes a rejection of Israel once and for all.[2] Similar statements have been made by J. Jervell ("the unbelieving portion of the people is rejected for all times"),[3] W. Eltester (with a degree of probability approaching certainty, Luke likely believed that the unrepentant part of the Jews had absolutely no hope of deliverance),[4] and H. Räisänen ("Jews who do not accept Jesus will be excluded

---

1. See P. G. Müller, "Die jüdische Entscheidung gegen Jesus nach der Apostelgeschichte," in *Les Actes des Apôtres*, ed. J. Kremer (Louvain, 1979), 523–31, esp. 524–26; F. Ó Fearghail, "Israel in Luke-Acts," *PIBA* 11 (1988): 23–43, esp. 24, 36ff.; and recently G. Harvey, *The True Israel* (Leiden, 1996), 238ff. For further treatment of this question, see below, p. 322.

2. E. Haenchen, "Judentum und Christentum in der Apostelgeschichte," *ZNW* 54 (1963): 155–87, esp. 185; cf. idem, *Die Apostelgeschichte*, 7th ed. (Göttingen, 1977), 112: "Unlike Paul, Luke no longer hopes for Israel's repentance"; 135: "For Luke, the Jews have been 'written off.'" See also English translation, *The Acts of the Apostles*, trans. Bernard Noble and Gerald Shinn (Philadelphia, 1971).

3. J. Jervell, *Luke and the People of God* (Minneapolis, 1972), 64; cf. idem, "Gottes Treue zum untreuen Volk," in *Der Treue Gottes Trauen: Festschrift Gerhard Schneider* (Freiburg, 1991), 15–27, here 25.

4. W. Eltester, "Israel im lukanischen Werk und die Nazarethperikope," in *Jesus in Nazareth*, ed. E. Grässer et al. (Berlin, 1972), 76–147, here 129.

from God's people and damned").[5] By contrast, other scholars insist that Luke did indeed believe that the nonbelieving part of Israel could hope to participate in eschatological salvation. In this sense, H. Merkel contests the finality of the charge of obduracy in Acts 28:26f. and suggests "this does not mean that Israel is to be written off. At the parousia, God will remove Israel's obduracy."[6] Others have expressed similar views, including A. W. Wainwright ("although he [Luke] believed that God had rejected Israel, he did not believe the rejection to be final"),[7] R. C. Tannehill ("hope for a happier outcome remains... for salvation through conversion"),[8] or D. L. Tiede ("the restoration, the consolation, the redemption... has only begun to be inaugurated in the present time of Luke's story").[9]

The difficulty in reaching a consensus in this question derives not only from the lack of interpretive consensus regarding the pertinent texts themselves, but also from the texts' inclination to point the interpreter in different directions. A few examples can illustrate this.

In Luke 13:35, Jesus announces that at his parousia,[10] inhabitants of Jerusalem who now reject him will greet him with the words of Ps. 117:26 (LXX): εὐλογημένος ὁ ἐρχόμενος ἐν ὀνόματι κυρίου. At first glance, this seems to indicate unambiguously that Luke expected Israel to venerate Jesus as its messianic king at his return from heaven (cf. Acts 1:11; 3:20). Not surprisingly, this text plays a central role among those who see an eschatological elimination of Israel's obduracy.[11]

---

5. H. Räisänen, "The Redemption of Israel," in Luke-Acts: Scandinavian Perspectives, ed. P. Luomanen (Helsinki and Göttingen, 1991), 94–114, here 106. See also J. Gnilka, Die Verstockung Israels (Munich, 1961), 153f.; S. G. Wilson, The Gentiles and the Gentile Mission in Luke-Acts (Cambridge, 1973); R. Maddox, The Purpose of Luke-Acts (Göttingen, 1982), 184f.; J. T. Sanders, "The Salvation of the Jews in Luke-Acts," in Luke-Acts: New Perspectives from the Society of Biblical Literature Seminar, ed. C. H. Talbert (New York, 1984), 104–28, esp. 115f.

6. H. Merkel, "Israel im lukanischen Werk," NTS 40 (1994): 371–98; here 397.

7. A. W. Wainwright, "Luke and the Restoration of the Kingdom to Israel," ExpTim 89 (1977/78): 76–79, here 79.

8. R. C. Tannehill, "Israel in Luke-Acts: A Tragic Story," JBL 104 (1985): 69–85, here 83, 85; cf. idem, The Narrative Unity of Luke-Acts, vol. 1: The Gospel according to Luke (Minneapolis, 1986), 163.

9. D. L. Tiede, "Glory to Thy People Israel," in Luke-Acts and the Jewish People, ed. J. B. Tyson (Minneapolis, 1988), 21–34, here 34. See also F. Mussner, "Die Idee der Apokatastasis in der Apostelgeschichte," in Praesentia Salutis (Düsseldorf, 1967), 223–34; Müller, "Entscheidung" (see above, n. 1), 527f.; F. Bovon, " 'Schön hat der heilige Geist durch den Propheten Jesaja zu euren Vätern gesprochen' (Act 28,25)," ZNW 75 (1984): 226–32, here 230; K. Haacker, "Das Bekenntnis des Paulus zur Hoffnung Israels nach der Apostelgeschichte des Lukas," NTS 31 (1985): 437–51, here 443ff.; Ó Fearghail, "Israel" (see above, n. 1), 35; J. B. Chance, Jerusalem, the Temple, and the New Age in Luke-Acts (Macon, Ga., 1988), 129ff.; L. R. Helyer, "Luke and the Restoration of Israel," JETS 36 (1993): 317–29; A. Buzzard, "Acts 1:6 and the Eclipse of the Biblical Kingdom," EvQ 66 (1994): 197–215; D. Ravens, Luke and the Restoration of Israel (Sheffield, 1995), 250ff.; V. Fusco, "Luke-Acts and the Future of Israel," NovT 38 (1996): 1–17.

10. See J. A. Fitzmyer, The Gospel according to Luke, vol. 2, AB 28A (New York, 1985), 1035; D. Zeller, "Entrückung zur Ankunft als Menschensohn (Lk 13,34f.; 11,29f.)," in A cause de l'Evangile: Festschrift Jacques Dupont (Paris, 1985), 513–30, here 515ff.; Fusco, "Luke-Acts" (see above, n. 9), 13.

11. See A. George, "Israël dans l'oeuvre de Luc," RB 75 (1968): 481–525, here 525; Mussner,

The interpretation, however, could be relativized effortlessly by pointing out that this proclamation says nothing about the fate of those who will greet Jesus with these words. T. W. Manson already spoke about being "too late,"[12] a view H. Räisänen has recently adopted with reference to Luke 13:25 (οὐκ οἶδα ὑμᾶς πόθεν ἐστέ).[13] The formulation of v. 35 does leave open the possibility that although the inhabitants of Jerusalem will indeed greet the "one who comes" as a messianic savior, he will nonetheless function as their judge (cf. Luke 19:27),[14] thereby excluding from participation in eschatological salvation members of Israel who have already refused to acknowledge the earthly Jesus as the Messiah. Support for this interpretation might also be drawn from Luke 13:23–30; 14:24; Acts 3:23.

Other texts, however, seem to stand in tension with this expectation. From the Lukan narrative perspective, the destruction of Jerusalem has already occurred and thus cannot be part of the events of the end time (cf. 21:20–24b);[15] Luke 19:41–44 understands this destruction as punishment that has already been visited upon Jerusalem *within history* for having rejected Jesus. According to Luke 21:24c, however, this punishment is temporary: ἄχρι οὗ πληρωθῶσιν καιροὶ ἐθνῶν. Whatever else this might mean,[16] together with 19:41–44 this prospect suggests that Luke did indeed reckon with the eschatological restoration of Jerusalem after its punishment was carried out. In this sense, J. B. Chance understood this reference as proof that according to Luke, Jerusalem would be restored after the conclusion of the καιροὶ ἐθνῶν in "its eschatological destiny as the city of salvation."[17] This interpretation receives additional support from

"Idee" (see above, n. 9), 233f.; Chance, *Jerusalem* (see above, n. 9), 130ff.; Helyer, "Luke" (see above, n. 9), 324f.; Merkel, "Israel" (see above, n. 6), 396f.; Fusco, "Luke-Acts" (see above, n. 9), 6ff.; see also W. Wiefel, *Das Evangelium nach Lukas* (Berlin, 1987), 266; C. A. Evans, "Prophecy and Polemic," in *Luke and Scripture*, ed. C. A. Evans and J. A. Sanders (Minneapolis, 1993), 171–211, here 178f.

12. T. W. Manson, *The Sayings of Jesus as Recorded in the Gospels according to St. Matthew and St. Luke* (London, 1949), 128.

13. Räisänen, "Redemption" (see above, n. 5), 105f.; see also Eltester, "Israel" (see above, n. 4), 130; Fitzmyer, *The Gospel according to Luke* (see above, n. 10), 1036; R. J. Shirock, "The Growth of the Kingdom in Light of Israel's Rejection of Jesus," *NovT* 35 (1993): 15–29, esp. 25.

14. See S. Schulz, *Q: Die Spruchquelle der Evangelisten* (Zurich, 1972), 358; Eltester, "Israel" (see above, n. 4), 130; Zeller, "Entrückung" (see above, n. 10), 518f.; J. D. Kingsbury, *Conflict in Luke* (Minneapolis, 1991), 57.

15. See H. Conzelmann, *Die Mitte der Zeit*, 6th ed. (Tübingen, 1977), 125f.; G. Braumann, "Die lukanische Interpretation der Zerstörung Jerusalems," *NovT* 6 (1963): 120–27.

16. Choices include the conclusion of the mission to the Gentiles (e.g., E. Grässer, *Das Problem der Parusieverzögerung in den synoptischen Evangelien und in der Apostelgeschichte*, 3d ed. [Berlin, 1977], 162; Fusco, "Luke-Acts" [see above, n. 9], 15) or the end of pagan foreign rule over Jerusalem as predetermined by God (e.g., E. Schweizer, *The Good News according to Luke*, trans. David E. Green [Atlanta, 1984], 317; G. Schneider, *Das Evangelium nach Lukas*, vol. 2: *Kapitel 11–24*, 2d ed. [Gütersloh/Würzburg, 1984], 424; Chance, *Jerusalem* [see above, n. 9], 135); the latter is more likely the case.

17. Chance, *Jerusalem* (see above, n. 9), 138; see also Wainwright, "Luke" (see above, n. 7), 77f.; Tannehill, "Israel" (see above, n. 8), 85; Fusco, "Luke-Acts" (see above, n. 9), 14f. Tannehill's association of 21:24c and 13:35 ("Israel" [see above, n. 8], 85: Jerusalem's oppression "will last only so long as it refuses to say 'Blessed is he who comes in the name of the Lord' ") is probably reading more from the text than is actually there. It is not the welcoming of Jesus as the messianic king

Luke 2:38, where the prophetess Hannah, as the so-called "reliable character" articulating the author's own views, identifies Jesus as the one from whom the deliverance of Jerusalem is to be expected.[18] Because this indirect proclamation has not yet been realized, this generates expectation in the reader, transcending not only the conclusion to the two-volume work itself, but also to Luke's own age.[19] Something similar applies to the expectations attaching to the special status of the Jewish people as expressed, for example, by Zechariah when he is filled by the Holy Spirit (1:67). In Luke 1:68–71, he announces the λύτρωσις of the people of God as "deliverance from our enemies and from the hand of all who hate us" (see also 1:54f., 74). In both Luke 24:21 and Acts 1:6, this hope in a special salvific expectation for Israel is reformulated without being rejected in substance.[20] Similarly, during Luke's own time the expectation has not yet been fulfilled, and from the Lukan point of view nothing militates against expecting it as part of that "universal restoration that God announced long ago through his holy prophets" (Acts 3:21).[21]

This particular perspective, which seems to entertain the special hope "of redemption for the Jewish people, for Israel qua Israel,"[22] stands in tension with yet another line of texts, one stretching through the entirety of the two-volume work from Jesus' inaugural sermon in Nazareth (Luke 4:16–30) to the concluding Pauline words at the end of Acts (Acts 28:26–28) and one that relativizes Israel's unique salvific-historical status over against the ἔθνη. First, the programmatic citation of Isa. 61:1–2 in Luke 4:18f. is stripped of its original orientation toward the juxtaposition of Israel and the Gentiles by omissions and the addition of Isa. 58:6.[23] Second, through the reference to Elijah and Elisha in Luke 4:25–27, Luke has Jesus make it clear that God's salvific initiative can also pass over Israel's own distress, and on balance, the Lukan understanding of the theme "kingdom of God" unmistakably revises the traditional understanding of the eschatological implementation of God's rule as a one-sided initiative against foreign rule on the

---

that will lead to restitution, but at most his actual coming itself. Accordingly, "the coming of the Messiah to the people of Jerusalem" also does not depend on their repentance (Tannehill, *Narrative Unity* [see above, n. 8], 1.156, on Acts 3:19–21; see also Mussner, "Idee" [see above, n. 9], 223f., and many others); rather, it is the repentance itself that will decide whether this coming will result in ἀναψύξεως or not (cf. analogous constructions with ὅπως ἄν in Gen. 18:19; Jer. 7:23).

18. Tannehill, *Narrative Unity* (see above, n. 8), 1.22; see also idem, "Israel" (see above, n. 8), 70.

19. This refutes H. Räisänen's objection to the earlier interpretation of Luke 21:24c: "Not a single word indicates that, after the sack of the city, Jerusalem would experience a reversal of its fortune with the Parousia" ("Redemption" [see above, n. 5], 98).

20. See, e.g., Mussner, "Idee" (see above, n. 9), 226f.; Wainwright, "Luke" (see above, n. 7), 76; D. L. Tiede, "The Exaltation of Jesus and the Restoration of Israel in Acts," *HTR* 79 (1986): 278–86, here 278; Tannehill, *Narrative Unity* (see above, n. 8), 1.11f.; Chance, *Jerusalem* (see above, n. 9), 133; Helyer, "Luke" (see above, n. 9), 326f.; Merkel, "Israel" (see above, n. 6), 397.

21. See Haacker, "Bekenntnis" (see above, n. 9), 442; Helyer, "Luke" (see above, n. 9), 328.

22. Räisänen, "Redemption" (see above, n. 5), 106.

23. See the detailed discussion in M. Albertz, "Die 'Antrittspredigt' Jesu im Lukasevangelium auf ihrem alttestamentlichen Hintergrund," *ZNW* 74 (1983): 182–206; M. Wolter, "Reich Gottes bei Lukas," *NTS* 41 (1995): 541–63, here 555f.

part of God for Israel.[24] Finally, in Acts 28:28 Luke has Paul disclose God's salvific plan to the Roman Jews, a plan designed to include the ἔθνη on an equal basis with the Jews from the outset; here Paul also establishes terminological inclusion to the beginning of the two-volume work itself (concerning ἀπεστάλη, cf. Luke 1:19, 26; 4:18, 43; concerning σωτήριον, cf. Luke 2:30; 3:6), making it clear that Luke is conceiving the universality of this salvific plan such that the only element left of Israel's own salvific-historical *exclusivity* is its chronological priority as the first addressee of the proclamation of Christ (cf. Acts 13:45).

As before, the understanding of Simeon's words concerning Jesus in Luke 2:34 is still disputed: οὗτος κεῖται εἰς πτῶσιν καὶ ἀνάστασιν πολλῶν ἐν Ἰσραήλ. On the one hand, these words are taken as a prediction of the schism that will occur in Israel itself concerning Jesus and the Christian proclamation, a schism Luke mentions repeatedly (the last time being Acts 28:24).[25] On the other hand, the earlier understanding has recently gained a small but growing number of adherents, namely, that with πτῶσις and ἀνάστασις Luke is referring to a sequence.[26] B. Koet recently devoted a thorough discussion to this view with reference to Isa. 51:17–23, finding that the "falling and rising, as in Isa. 51:17–23, represent two distinct stages within a *single* salvific-historical perspective; yet just as in Deutero-Isaiah the city of Jerusalem will rise again despite its destruction, so also does Luke believe that the one Israel, though fallen (as it has so often), can yet hope to be raised again based on the experience of salvation history."[27]

---

24. See H. Merklein, "Die Einzigkeit Gottes als die sachliche Grundlage der Botschaft Jesu," *JBTh* 2 (1987): 13–32, here 15ff.; J. J. Collins, "The Kingdom of God in the Apocrypha and Pseudepigrapha," in *The Kingdom of God in Twentieth-century Interpretation,* ed. W. Willis (Peabody, Mass., 1987), 81–97, here 95. See in general Maddox, *Purpose* (see above, n. 5), 42ff., 105ff.; Wolter, "Reich Gottes" (see above, n. 23).

25. So more recently G. Lohfink, *Die Sammlung Israels* (Munich, 1975), 30; Chance, *Jerusalem* (see above, n. 9), 55, 70; Tannehill, *Narrative Unity* (see above, n. 8), 1.30, 32; Ó Fearghail, "Israel" (see above, n. 1), 26; J. Nolland, *Luke 1–9:20* (Dallas, 1989), 121; F. Bovon, *Das Evangelium nach Lukas,* vol. 1: *Lk. 1,1–9,50* (Zurich and Neukirchen-Vluyn, 1989), 146f.; J. B. Tyson, *Images of Judaism in Luke-Acts* (New York, 1992), 50; R. E. Brown, *The Birth of the Messiah,* 2d ed. (New York, 1993), 461; M. L. Strauss, *The Davidic Messiah in Luke-Acts* (Sheffield, 1995), 119f.; Ravens, *Luke* (see above, n. 9), 174; J. O. York, *The Last Shall Be First* (Sheffield, 1991), 111ff.; Evans, *Prophecy* (see above, n. 11), 174. The latter two associate this proclamation with Luke 1:51–53 and understand it in connection with the characteristic Lukan "reversal" motif. The remark made by S. Farris, *The Hymns of Luke's Infancy Narratives* (Sheffield, 1985), 119, is noteworthy insofar as it reflects quite well the *status disputationis*: "While Luke 2:34–35 seems clearly to speak of a division within Israel, the hymns themselves look only on the more joyful side of salvation history," with the surprising aside: "There seems no reason to suppose that Luke had given up all hope for unrepentant Israel" (199).

26. Schweizer, *Luke* (see above, n. 16), 57; Tiede, "Glory" (see above, n. 9), 28; I. H. Marshall, *The Gospel of Luke* (Grand Rapids, Mich., 1978, 1992), 122; G. B. Caird, *The Gospel of St. Luke* (London, 1963), 64; M. Miyoshi, "Jesu Darstellung oder Reinigung im Tempel," *AJBL* 4 (1978): 85–111, here 98ff. Although W. Radl, *Der Ursprung Jesu* (Freiburg, 1996), also thinks these two terms are referring to a sequence applying to one and the same group, he allows the proclamation of the ἀνάστασις to be applied only "to that part of Israel that has come to believe in the Messiah Jesus" (227).

27. B. Koet, "Simeons Worte (Lk 2,29–32,34c–35) und Israels Geschick," in *The Four Gospels 1992: Festschrift Frans Neirynck* (Louvain, 1992), 2.1149–69, here 1157ff. (citation on 1163).

Something analogous can be observed with regard to the citation of Isa. 6:9–10 in Acts 28:26–27, simultaneously closing the circle I have taken in describing the state of discussion. Over against the interpretation of this text discussed at the outset,[28] an increasing number of scholars have recently begun understanding these two verses in a different sense, and have supported this position with cogent argumentation. For example, the referral of the statement about Israel's obduracy back to the Old Testament tradition[29] shows that the widespread tendency to equate obduracy and rejection has actually been read into the text,[30] whereas "within biblical tradition, hardening always implies the possibility of future enlightenment."[31]

Israel's Salvation and the Problem of Delay

This survey suggests that the current open-ended nature of the discussion of Luke's understanding of Israel's future derives especially from the obviously disparate nature of the pertinent texts themselves; the result has been that scholars tend to read these texts in a highly selective fashion. Responses in one direction or another come about when one series of texts is emphasized at the cost of another and then viewed as constituent for the Lukan position as a whole. No criteria, however, have yet been put forward that might justify one or the other decision and demonstrate the plausibility of that decision to the opposing view.

From an external perspective, a situation like this also represents an exegetical challenge insofar as it invites one to articulate the perspective that might take the debate beyond this inert point and integrate into a meaningful and coherent nexus the seemingly disparate statements about Israel's future found in Luke's two-volume work. I believe the historical experience of the delay of the parousia might offer such a perspective. The temporal distance separating Luke from the fundamental story of Christianity narrated in his two-volume work functions as the key to understanding his view of Israel's future.

Two considerations that previously had little to do with one another can be examined along with this thesis. The convergence of these two aspects in Luke 19:11–27 and Acts 1:6–8 shows that such a procedure is not imposing onto the

---

28. See above, p. 308.

29. See esp. H. van de Sandt, "Acts 28,28: No Salvation for the People of Israel?" *ETL* 70 (1994): 341–58, here 347ff.; Fusco, "Luke-Acts" (see above, n. 9), 7f. See also R. F. O'Toole, "Reflections on Luke's Treatment of Jews in Luke-Acts," *Bib* 74 (1993): 529–55, here 547ff.

30. See also C. A. Evans, *To See and Not Perceive* (Sheffield, 1989), 126: "The passage simply does not say this."

31. Fusco, "Luke-Acts" (see above, n. 9), 7; see also Chance, *Jerusalem* (see above, n. 9), 130; R. L. Brawley, *Luke-Acts and the Jews* (Atlanta, 1987), 76f.; Bovon, "'Schön'" (see above, n. 9), 230; D. W. Palmer, "Mission to Jews and Gentiles in the Last Episode of Acts," *RTR* 52 (1993): 62–73, here 66f., 71; Strauss, *Messiah* (see above, n. 25), 176; J. Zmijewski, *Die Apostelgeschichte* (Regensburg, 1994), 886.

two volumes a line of inquiry alien to the text itself.[32] These two texts share several common features:

Within the literary outline of the two-volume work, these two texts represent important *transition points*. Luke 19:11–27 concludes what is known as the journey narrative that from 9:51 onward portrays Jesus on his way to Jerusalem. After mentioning that goal three times (9:51; 13:22; 17:11; see also 13:33), Luke tells us in 19:11 that Jesus has almost reached Jerusalem (ἐγγὺς εἶναι Ἰερουσαλὴμ αὐτόν). An analogous situation obtains with regard to Acts 1:6–8. On the one hand, these verses are found in the account of the forty days between Easter and the ascension, linking the two parts of the two-volume work together, and on the other hand constitute in the larger sense the conclusion to the entire period extending from John the Baptist to the ascension, during which Jesus was together with his disciples (cf. Acts 1:21). In vv. 7–8, Luke also recounts the last words Jesus speaks before his ascension.

The two texts also exhibit an analogous *gradient* insofar as both correct an erroneous expectation. Luke 19:11 corrects the assumption that Jesus' spatial proximity to Jerusalem signals the temporal proximity of the revelation of divine rule;[33] Luke immediately has Jesus respond with the parable of the pretender to the throne (vv. 12–27). Acts 1:6 corrects the assumption that the outpouring of the Spirit promised in v. 5 will coincide with the restoration of the βασιλεία to Israel.[34] Luke has Jesus respond by referring to the unfathomable nature of the "times or periods that the Father has set" (v. 7) and to the notion of universal witness (v. 8).

In both texts, Jesus' dialogue partners erroneously anticipate that the revelation or reestablishment of the βασιλεία will come about within a *short temporal period* (cf. on the one hand παραχρῆμα in Luke 19:11, and the correspondence between ἐν τῷ χρόνῳ τούτῳ [Acts 1:6] and οὐ μετὰ πολλὰς ταύτας ἡμέρας [v. 5]).

Both texts correct this sense of near-expectation by *referring to distant places*. In Luke 19:12, the allegorization of Jesus' ascension as the journey of a throne pretender "to a *distant* country" rejects the assumption of the temporal nearness of the βασιλεία, just as in Acts 1:8 the sending of the apostles "to the ends of the earth" (ἕως ἐσχάτου τῆς γῆς)[35] shifts the date of the reestablishment of the

---

32. See also Tannehill, "Israel" (see above, n. 8), 84; idem, *Narrative Unity* (see above, n. 8), 1.258ff. ("the problem of eschatological delay is intertwined with the problem of Jewish rejection," 260); V. Fusco, " 'Point of View' and 'Implicit Reader' in Two Eschatological Texts, Lk 19,11–28, Acts 1,6–8," in *The Four Gospels 1992* (see above, n. 27), 1677–96, here 1690f., 1692.

33. See also Fusco, " 'Point of View' " (see above, n. 32), 1678.

34. Concerning ἀποκαθίστημι τὴν βασιλείαν τῷ Ἰσραήλ, see below, n. 38. See G. Schneider, *Die Apostelgeschichte*, vol. 1: *Einleitung: Kommentar zu Kap. 1,1–8,40* (Freiburg, 1982), 201.

35. This refers not to Rome as mentioned at the end of Acts, but rather, as W. C. van Unnik has persuasively shown, to the "ends, the most distant borders of the world" ("Der Ausdruck 'ΕΩΣ ΕΣΧΑΤΟΥ ΤΗΣ ΓΗΣ' [Apostelgeschichte I:8] und sein alttestamentlicher Hintergrund," in *Sparsa Collecta* [Leiden, 1973], 1.386–401, here 400).

βασιλεία for Israel, a date queried in v. 6, to the time after the attainment of this missionary goal.[36]

In both texts, Jesus' dialogue partners express a *salvific hope focused on Israel.* In Luke 19:11, it is the expectation expressed by Hannah that Jesus will liberate Jerusalem (2:38), the fulfillment of which seems to be near insofar as Jesus himself was now near Jerusalem. This hope is associated with the revelation of the βασιλεία τοῦ θεοῦ, whose ἀναφαίνεσθαι is being discussed here, insofar as it is quite unambiguously the liberation of Jerusalem itself from foreign rule that Israel expects from the eschatological reestablishment of divine rule.[37] In Acts 1:6, the apostles' expectation is focused on Israel's restoration to its share in God's universal dominion.[38]

In both texts, Jesus' response leaves this substantive aspect peculiarly *in abeyance.* In both instances, he neither unambiguously rejects nor expressly confirms the salvific expectations focused on Jerusalem in particular or on Israel in general. Rather, his response leaves both open.[39] Instead, discussion turns to the understanding of the *interim period* until the return (Luke 19:12) of the ἄνθρωπος εὐγενής after he receives his βασιλεία (v. 15), that is, until Jesus' own parousia or until the χρόνοι καὶ καιροί have been fulfilled as stipulated by the Father (Acts 1:7). In Luke 19:13ff., the disciples are commissioned in a juridical-parenetic fashion to "do business" and be successful during their master's absence with the gifts he has entrusted to them, and in Acts 1:8, Jesus commissions the apostles to witness in universality from Jerusalem to the ends of the earth.

Both texts exhibit an unmistakable tension between the *internal narrative point of view* (that of the actors) and the *external point of view* (that of the narrator and the implicit reader).[40] This tension prevents one from projecting directly onto the Lukan presentation the notion of near-expectation described in the exposition itself (Luke 19:11; Acts 1:6) and from presenting that notion as a position entertained during Luke's own period, that is, as one anticipating the imminent parousia.[41] In both instances, the expectation expressed by Jesus' dialogue part-

---

36. See E. Grässer, "Die Parusieerwartung in der Apostelgeschichte," in *Les Actes des Apôtres,* ed. J. Kremer (Louvain, 1979), 99–127, 112f.

37. See the arguments in this regard in Wolter, "Reich Gottes" (see above, n. 23), 547; see also Fusco, "'Point of View'" (see above, n. 32), 1690f.

38. In the sense of restoration to a position of rule, the expression ἀποκαθίστημι τινι τὴν βασιλείαν is attested in Dan. 4:36 (LXX); Josephus, *Ant.* 14.366; *Anthol. Graeca* 3.19; Apollodorus, *Bibl.* 1, 9, 28.

39. This open-ended nature is also reflected in the scholarship on Luke 19:11ff. Whereas J. Roloff writes that in Acts 1:6–8 this expectation is "corrected" (*Die Apostelgeschichte* [Göttingen, 1981], 23), Fusco finds that it "does not rule out the 'Jewish-centered' point of view, typical of Luke-Acts" ("'Point of View'" [see above, n. 32], 1679); see also Ravens, *Luke* (see above, n. 9), 34, on Luke 19:11ff.: "The implication is that the Kingdom will come when the man returns as King."

40. See in this regard in general E. Lämmert, *Bauformen des Erzählens,* 6th ed. (Stuttgart, 1975), 70ff.; F. K. Stanzel, *Theorie des Erzählens,* 5th ed. (Göttingen, 1991), 21ff. Fusco especially has drawn attention to the necessity of distinguishing between these two points of view in these texts ("'Point of View'" [see above, n. 32]).

41. At most, one might suggest that the issue was "the theological meaning of the *still* absent parousia" (K. Erlemann, *Naherwartung und Parusieverzögerung im Neuen Testament* [Tübingen, 1995],

ners is meaningful only within the *narrated* world belonging to the past rather than in the *discussed* world of the present, for the readers of the two-volume work already know, even without Jesus' response, that in neither case was this near-expectation justified. Neither did the βασιλεία τοῦ θεοῦ commence with Jesus' arrival in Jerusalem, nor did the outpouring of the Holy Spirit coincide with the restoration of the βασιλεία to Israel. Readers already know this from the course of history, and are thus in no need of enlightenment through Jesus. From the perspective of the Lukan present, then, Jesus' response explains only why the historically *past* "near-expectation" expressed by the characters of the narrative and focused on Israel's salvation was in fact unjustified; by contrast, the texts offer no answer to the question of how long *these readers themselves* might have to wait until the revelation of divine rule or until the reestablishment of the βασιλεία for Israel.[42]

Hence at two key transitional passages in his two-volume work, Luke brings into play the theme of delay with regard to the *near-expectation entertained by Jesus' own contemporaries* with regard to Israel's salvation. That these two elements are directly related in the Lukan view is also shown by the fact that Luke himself established this connection. Luke formulated the exposition (v. 11) of the parable drawn from Q concerning the entrusted money (Luke 19:12–27 // Matt. 25:14–30), thereby giving it its redactional orientation and meaning. Similarly, it was Luke who first inserted the theme of delay into the narrative by adding the element of the ἄνθρωπος εὐγενής having journeyed "to a distant country" (v. 12), an element not found in the Q version. The same applies to Acts 1:6–8, where probably only v. 7 comes from tradition,[43] while Luke again authors both the exposition (v. 6) as well as the promise of the Spirit and the commission for the apostles to witness "to the ends of the earth" (v. 8).

Luke operates quite analogously in Luke 24:21–26. Here he has the disciples in Emmaus discuss the disappointment of their original hope that the earthly Jesus might liberate Israel (v. 21), only so he can characterize this hope itself as part of an erroneous understanding of God's salvific plan (vv. 25f.). To the extent this hope was oriented toward the earthly Jesus, it had of course long since become anachronistic from the perspective of the readers. What is again noteworthy, however, is that here, too, Jesus' response leaves the substantive aspect of this hope (Israel's liberation) in abeyance.

168; my emphasis); see also W. Schenk, "Naherwartung und Parusieverzögerung," *ThV* 4 (1972): 47–69, here 50.

42. See in this regard Wolter, "Reich Gottes" (see above, n. 23), 561f. Yet another group of texts also demonstrates the openness of the Lukan position on this question. Luke 12:35–48 and 21:34–36 show that Luke is also able to explicate the unknown nature of the date of the parousia parenetically as the *possibility* of its immediate proximity, thereby correcting those who reckon with a longer period of waiting (see also 17:24–30). This also shows, however, that Luke by no means declares near-expectation as such to be "heretical" in any sense (G. Klein, "Eschatologie IV," *TRE* 10 [1982]: 270–99, here 294). In 17:23 and 21:8, Luke is warning merely against the false *basis* of near-expectation (see also Erlemann, *Naherwartung* [see above, n. 41], 165f., 168f.).

43. Perhaps also directly from Mark 13:32, a verse Luke passes over in his version of Jesus' eschatological discourse.

Luke 19:11–27 and Acts 1:6–8 (and implicitly also Luke 24:21–26) thus show that the association of the Israel question and the theme of delay derives from genuinely Lukan redactional considerations. For just this reason, however, it is all the more striking that in both instances there is obvious friction between the exposition (Luke 19:11; Acts 1:6) on the one hand, and Jesus' response on the other (Luke 19:12–27; Acts 1:7–8). Although both passages do indeed correct the erroneous notion of "near-expectation," from the readers' point of view this is actually quite superfluous. In both instances, the variously implied substantive issue remains in abeyance. Although in neither instance (nor in Luke 24:25f.) does Luke reject the content of this "near-expectation," he does end the parable in Luke 19:27 with a massive announcement of judgment,[44] and in Acts 1:8 gives the apostles a proclamatory commission taking them away from Jerusalem and far beyond Israel.

One can show, however, that the question of the date is indeed related to the issue of near-expectation, and that Luke — again from the point of view of his implied readers — takes as his point of departure for answering the question of Israel's future precisely the anachronistic "near-expectation" articulated in Luke 19:11 and Acts 1:6.

"Israel's Hope" as a Question of Temporal Perspective

When debates break down, it often helps to consider whether the question underlying the issue under dispute might be stated incorrectly or be based on false assumptions. In any case, the justification for examining anew the unspoken presuppositions in the present debate derives from the fact that it is not a Lukan question being discussed, but a Pauline one. That is, Paul, not Luke, asks whether God has rejected the people (Rom. 11:1), or whether unbelieving Israel's currently bleak salvific status will continue forever (11:11). As is well-known, Paul answered both questions with a resounding "no," expressing his own certainty that God will indeed one day rescue God's people (11:25–27), because "the gifts and the calling of God are irrevocable" (11:28b, 29). God's own election of Israel cannot be suspended because of the latter's refusal to believe the gospel (see also Rom. 3:1, 6).

The debate surrounding the Lukan view of Israel's future is characterized on both sides more or less explicitly along this line of inquiry. The Pauline exposition assumes a controlling function especially among authors who think that Luke indeed is counting on Israel enjoying a salvific future.[45] This can already

---

44. See in this regard Räisänen's drastic description (contra R. C. Tannehill), "Redemption" (see above, n. 5), 98: "Instead of a 'lingering hope' for the restoration of Israel, Luke confronts us with eschatological genocide."

45. Though see also Haenchen, "Judentum" (see above, n. 2); Eltester, "Israel" (see above, n. 4), 118f.; Maddox, *Purpose* (see above, n. 5), 43; Roloff, *Apostelgeschichte* (see above, n. 39), 375;

be observed in A. von Harnack,[46] and more recently the Pauline announcement of the savior coming from Zion at the end of days — that is, the parousia-Christ appointed for Israel — has been applied especially to Acts 3:20f., where Luke has Peter associate the return of the χριστὸς Ἰησοῦς with the eschatological realization of the prophetic promises.[47] In support of this view, H. Merkel also points out that Luke was probably familiar with Paul's Letter to the Romans.[48]

Like Paul, Luke picks up the motif of obduracy on the part of the people of God to explain Israel's "utterly incomprehensible"[49] historical refusal to believe, and in this respect he and Paul do indeed have something in common. This does not by a long shot mean, however, that the two rhetorical questions in Rom. 11:1, 11, concerning Israel's present status before God and its future can be imputed to Luke as well; for a qualitative distinction obtains between Luke and Paul, making such a transference utterly anachronistic — namely, the distance of more than thirty years between Paul's Letter to the Romans and Luke's two-volume work in the light of the absent parousia. Hence it was nothing other than the delay of the parousia itself that made it impossible for Luke to speak about "Israel" in the same way Paul did. Indeed, Luke cannot even *ask* about "Israel" and its future in the same way as Paul because, as a result of history, Luke occupies a completely different position and must begin with completely different presuppositions.

In his Letter to the Romans, Paul still anticipated that the present generation of Christians would experience the parousia (cf. 13:11f.), and the same naturally also applied to the present generation of Israel. This also means, however, that members of the people of God who, because of their obduracy (11:7, 25), have failed to respond to the preaching of Christ are the same ones whom Paul believes the savior from Zion will liberate from the ἀσέβειαι and ἁμαρτίαι (11:26f.).[50] Israel's obdurate generation, the current generation, and the parousia generation were the same for Paul in Romans 11, and given his

---

A. Weiser, *Die Apostelgeschichte*, vol. 2: *Kapitel 13–28* (Gütersloh and Würzburg, 1985), 683; Jervell, "Treue" (see above, n. 3), 23.

46. A. v. Harnack, *Die Apostelgeschichte* (Leipzig, 1908), 214: "A notion such as that in Rom. 11:25ff. cannot have been that alien to Luke"; see also George, "Israël" (see above, n. 11), 525; Wiefel, *Das Evangelium nach Lukas* (see above, n. 11), 266; Haacker, "Bekenntnis" (see above, n. 9), 446f.; Chance, *Jerusalem* (see above, n. 9), 132; Ravens, *Luke* (see above, n. 9), 205ff.; Fusco, "Luke-Acts" (see above, n. 9), 6ff., 1 n. 1).

47. F. Mussner (*Traktat über die Juden* [Munich, 1979], 52–67, here 64–67) discusses Acts 1:6–8; 3:19–21 in this sense from the perspective of Rom. 11:26; see also Müller, "Entscheidung" (see above, n. 1), 527; Merkel, "Israel" (see above, n. 6), 397f.

48. Merkel, "Israel" (see above, n. 6), 397.

49. Ibid., 396.

50. This does not mean, of course, that Paul is expecting this deliverance such that it "passes Jesus by" (U. Kellermann, "Jesus — das Licht der Völker," *KuI* 7 [1992], 10–27, here 24). What Paul means is perhaps best expressed by O. Hofius: "'All Israel' will thus attain salvation differently than will the Gentile Christians and the 'remnant' who already believe in Christ, namely, not on the basis of the missionary preaching of the church, but directly through the kyrios himself. But precisely thus, it does not attain salvation without Christ or without the gospel or without faith in Christ. But if Israel, through its direct encounter with Christ himself, does hear the gospel, and does recognize Christ as the kyrios, and does come to saving faith in him, this means that Israel is coming to faith in

"near-expectation" of the parousia itself, he had no reason to think beyond his own present.

All is completely different for Luke. From his own temporal perspective of the failure of the parousia's arrival, the identification of the generation of Israel living in Paul's own day — a generation that had largely rejected the apostolic preaching of Christ — with the generation living in Luke's as the "parousia generation" was sundered. Because Luke cannot say anything definitive about the proximity or remoteness of Jesus' return, neither does he know whether the generation living in his own age is identical with the "parousia generation."[51] This is of no consequence for the present discussion, however, and can thus be set aside.

It is of crucial significance, however, that from his own vantage point in history, Luke is, unlike Paul, *looking back* at the generation that was addressed by the apostolic mission, a generation that largely rejected that preaching and whose rejection Paul explained with reference to Isa. 6:9–10 (Acts 28:26–27). From the Lukan perspective, that generation, like the apostolic age itself, thus belongs to a distant, irretrievable past. And because that generation has in the meantime died out, its rejection of the preaching of Christ is also definitive and unalterable, as is the judgment of obduracy as well. Those in that generation who rejected the apostolic preaching of Christ no longer have the chance to repent, a chance that might have allowed them to revise their own behavior in the way made possible in Luke's own day for the inhabitants of Jerusalem (cf. Acts 2:38; 3:17–19; 5:30f.).[52]

That this portrayal corresponds to the Lukan view can be seen especially in Acts 13:46, according to which the Jews in Pisidian Antioch demonstrate by rejecting the λόγος τοῦ θεοῦ that they judge themselves "to be unworthy of eternal life," thereby of their own volition excluding themselves from salvation.[53] Of course, this statement applies quite specifically only to the Jews in Pisidian

---

the same way as Paul himself" ("Das Evangelium und Israel," *Paulusstudien*, 2d ed. [Tübingen, 1994], 175–202, here 197–98).

51. See above, p. 315 and n. 42.

52. The Jerusalem Jews could have this second chance because in the Lukan understanding their rejection of the earthly Jesus was based on ignorance (see Luke 23:34; Acts 3:17; 13:27). The post-Easter preaching of Christ by the witnesses eliminates this ignorance such that there is no longer any excuse for renewed rejection.

53. This statement plays a remarkably meager role in scholarship on this topic. For example, neither Müller, "Entscheidung" (see above, n. 1); Wainwright, "Luke" (see above, n. 7); Haacker, "Bekenntnis" (see above, n. 9); nor O'Toole, "Reflections" (see above, n. 29) discuss it at all. On balance, it usually stands in the shadow of the ensuing announcement that Paul and Barnabas would turn their attention to the ἔθνη living in Antioch (e.g., Ó Fearghail, "Israel" [see above, n. 1], 32f.; Räisänen, "Redemption" [see above, n. 5], 104f.; Helyer, "Luke" [see above, n. 9], 323; Ravens, *Luke* [see above, n. 9], 236; Fusco, "Luke-Acts" [see above, n. 9], 4f.; Tannehill, *Narrative Unity*, 2.172f.; Chance, *Jerusalem* [see above, n. 9], 130; Strauss, *Messiah* [see above, n. 25], 175ff.). H. Merkel tries to lessen the statement's significance by attributing its motivation to "the blasphemy of the spirit present in the post-Easter period" ("Israel" [see above, n. 6], 395). The text, however, says nothing about the Holy Spirit; moreover, it parallels the statement about the rejection of eternal life expressly with the rejection (ἀπωθεῖσθαι) of God's word. The same interest guides D. L. Tiede's assertion that the statement is "a part of the rhetorical baggage of the tradition" and need not be taken that literally (*Prophecy and History in Luke-Acts* [Philadelphia, 1980], 121).

Antioch who reject the Christ message, and may not be expanded — as one broad line of interpretation has done — to "the Jews"[54] or "the Jewish people" as a whole.[55] A similar scene takes place shortly thereafter in Corinth; there the Lukan Paul symbolically shakes the dust from his clothes,[56] thereby ending his relationship with the city's Jews who resist his preaching of Christ, leaving them to "be covered" with their own guilt ("your blood be on your own heads!" 18:6).[57] Finally, 28:26–27 speaks the last, hyperbolic operative word concerning this generation of the λαός: It has remained obdurate and has died obdurate, and from the Lukan perspective it is thus to be written off with regard to participation in the καιροὶ ἀναψύξεως that will come with the parousia of the χριστὸς Ἰησοῦς. At the eschatological resurrection of the righteous and unrighteous (Acts 24:15), they will doubtless be counted among the latter. Their fate will be that described by the Lukan Peter in Acts 3:23 with reference to both Deut. 18:19 and Lev. 23:19: "And it will be that every ψυχή who does not listen to that prophet will be utterly rooted out of the λαός."[58]

This assessment of the obdurate generation of the apostolic period does not allow the conclusion that Luke considers the Jews *as a whole* to be obdurate and moving toward the same fate. Such insinuation fails to take seriously the retrospective point of view of Luke the historian; indeed, his own portrayal of the πρῶτοι among the Roman Jews in Acts 28:17–22 seems to mark something of a new beginning in the history of the preaching of Christ to the Jews.[59] Compared with the Jerusalemite πρῶτοι τοῦ λαοῦ or τῶν Ἰουδαίων (Luke 19:47; Acts 25:2), Luke portrays them as quite unprejudiced and interested in the proclamation concerning the Christ (cf. 28:22 with 24:5). Luke thus seems to envision a new epoch of the Christian mission beginning in Rome, and not a word suggests that this mission will not reach Jews as well.[60]

---

54. M. Dibelius, *Aufsätze zur Apostelgeschichte*, ed. H. Greeven (Göttingen, 1951), 168 n. 1.

55. Haenchen, *Apostelgeschichte* (see above, n. 2), 135; also 402: "The Jews in Antioch who come to envy the Christians are at the same time the Jews in the larger sense." See also Tyson, *Images* (see above, n. 25), 140; Wilson, *Gentiles* (see above, n. 5), 223; concerning the criticism of this generalization, see also Brawley, *Luke-Acts* (see above, n. 31), 72f.

56. Concerning this act, see H. J. Cadbury, "Dust and Garments," in *The Beginnings of Christianity*, ed. F. J. Foakes Jackson and K. Lake (London, 1933), 5.269–77, here 274f.

57. The only real parallel here is 2 Sam. 1:16 (with qualification also Ezek. 33:9); only this passage mentions that the "blood" of the dead person is upon his own "head," that is, that he himself bears the blood-guilt provoked by the murder.

58. This also confirms the sense of Luke 2:34 (see above, p. 311): Because their rejection of the Christ proclamation is irrevocable, there is no possibility of turning the πτῶσις into ἀνάστασις for this part of Israel.

59. This is suggested especially by v. 21. See also Ó Fearghail, "Israel" (see above, n. 1), 34: "Unlike the situation in Antioch and Corinth no Jewish opposition follows." The most likely interpretation of the last words of Acts is that of W. Stegemann, *Zwischen Synagoge und Obrigkeit* (Göttingen, 1991), 133, and Ravens, *Luke* (see above, n. 9), 241: With ἀκωλύτως, Luke is characterizing not the behavior of the state authorities, but that of the Roman Jews.

60. See the formulation ἀπεδέχετο πάντας τοὺς εἰσπορευομένους πρὸς αὐτόν in 28:30 and the interpretation in Merkel, "Israel" (see above, n. 6), 396; Weiser, *Die Apostelgeschichte* (see above, n. 45), 2.683f. (with bibliography).

How does Luke envision the further development of Israel's reaction to the preaching of Christ? He does not say, as H. Merkel, whose remarks are representative of what scholarship now generally asserts, suggests: "Conversions of individual Jews are ... possible now as before."[61] Although this is doubtless true,[62] it is not difficult to extrapolate facts from the pertinent texts. Luke does not know when the parousia will come; he mentions only a *terminus ante quem non* (which he also cannot fix chronologically), namely, the Christian mission's attainment of the ἔσχατον τῆς γῆς (Acts 1:8). That is, the parousia will not occur until all people (including, of course, the Jews) have been reached by the Christian mission and given the opportunity to react positively or negatively to it. Among those belonging to Israel, this preaching of Christ will continue to provoke schism, even among the relatively open πρῶτοι of the Roman Jews (28:24). Those who resist the message of Christ will receive virtually the same verdict as those in Antioch and Corinth: Their resistance shows that they consider themselves unworthy of eternal life (13:46) and will bring about their own ruin (18:6). Hence, as soon as their rejection of the preaching of Christ has become irrevocable, either through their deaths or through the commencement of the parousia itself, they will share the fate of the obdurate generation of the apostolic age.

God's Unbelievable Work (Acts 13:41)

We have found that Luke presents Jesus' dialogue partners in Luke 19:11 and Acts 1:6 in a light similar to that in which he presents the disciples at Emmaus in Luke 24:21, namely, as representatives of Israel's hope; in so doing, he views them together with Mary, Zechariah, and Hannah.[63] The difference is that unlike the latter, the former articulate their expectation that the fulfillment of their hopes is imminent. Luke then has Jesus himself correct that expectation. Viewed from the perspective of the Lukan present, however, the moment on which this "near-expectation" is focused already belongs to the past, and this difference between the two points of view is decisive for understanding the issue at hand.

An additional difference is that the unidentified αὐτοί in Luke 19:11 and the apostles in Acts 1:6 know nothing yet about the parousia being delayed, which is why Jesus must instruct them accordingly, whereas Luke can assume his readers already know about the delay. The parousia delay thereby makes obsolete the "near-expectation" articulated in Luke 19:11 and Acts 1:6. Acts 1:8 shows with particular clarity that although the apostles expected the βασιλεία to be reestablished for Israel in the imminent future, its failure to materialize did not empty the interim period of history of all meaning. Rather this delay has been

---

61. Merkel, "Israel" (see above, n. 6), 396.

62. See also the accurate remark of E. Richard, "The Divine Purpose," in *New Perspectives* (see above, n. 6), 188–209, here 199: "The ears of God's people are closed and their eyes are blind, but as long as they have Moses and the prophets the mission remains possible."

63. See above p. 310.

made to serve a salvific-historical goal, namely, to provide space for the history of the preaching of Christ that begins in Jerusalem and that is carried "to the ends of the earth." In Acts, Luke portrays the course of this history up to Rome, and his portrayal also explains why the "near-expectation" formulated in 1:6 (and in Luke 19:11) needed to be corrected: because the history of proclamation inaugurated by the delay of the parousia itself[64] proved to be not only a history of the expansion of God's word (cf. Acts 6:7; 12:24; 13:49; 19:10, 20), but also a history of its rejection by large parts of Israel — rejection through the passage of time that has now become irrevocable. It is *this* knowledge that bestows content on the differences between the two points of view described above, since the corrective to the notion of "near-expectation" expands to include both the presuppositions and object of that "near-expectation."[65] Luke wants to make this connection between date and content transparent; the key device he employs is the anachronism[66] of "near-expectation" expressed in Luke 19:11 and Acts 1:6. In retrospect, this "near-expectation" proves to be substantively deficient as well, since it does not take account of the subsequent course of history. The universal mission enacted through God's own plan precipitated a schism in Israel itself such that large parts of the people of God had lost all hope of salvation. Hence this "near-expectation" is obsolete not only for *temporal* reasons, but also because of its moribund content: (1) The obsolete soteriological paradigms upon which it is based do not take into account the universalization of God's salvific plan for the people of God, which includes the requisite time and space for its realization. (2) The eschatological apportionment of salvation and condemnation is decided exclusively according to one's attitude toward Jesus of Nazareth as the proclaimed Messiah, an assertion discontinuous with Israel's traditional messianic expectations. Because traditional Jewish messianic expectation does not take into account Israel's crisis, Luke portrays that expectation as rendered obsolete by the delay of the parousia. Consequently, the delayed parousia is part of the solution to the problem rather than constitutive of it.

Luke addresses this topic at two central junctures in his two-volume work, probably because of the problems of identity and legitimacy with which his congregations had to deal.[67] In communities with both Jewish and Christian populations during the Lukan period, the Christian churches were especially pressed by whether these largely Gentile Christian congregations could consider themselves part of the chosen people of God addressed by the salvific promises of scripture, or whether the Jewish people had greater right to claim these promises for themselves. In the face of this problem, Luke is concerned with assuring

---

64. See G. Schneider, *Parusiegleichnisse im Lukas-Evangelium* (Stuttgart, 1975), 88f.; R. Pesch, *Die Apostelgeschichte*, vol. 1: *Apg 1–12* (Zurich and Neukirchen-Vluyn, 1986), 68; W. Radl, *Das Lukas-Evangelium* (Darmstadt, 1988), 135.

65. See above, p. 314.

66. See above, p. 314.

67. See in this regard the presentation by E. Plümacher, "Acta-Forschung 1974–1982," *TRu*, n.s., 48 (1983): 1–56, esp. 45ff.; see also chap. 10 in this volume.

these Christian communities of their own unbroken continuity with the salvific promises applying to Israel.[68] By the same token, for those members of Israel who do not believe in Christ, everything depends on whether they accept the Christ proclamation; if they do not, they remain outside and are cast out of the βασιλεία (Luke 13:25, 28) or are excluded from the people of God (Acts 3:23). The Lukan view is that nonbelieving Jews can claim membership in Israel only as long as the Christ proclamation has not yet reached them and been irrevocably rejected.[69] The continuing "absence" of the parousia has already brought about precisely this condition for "many in Israel" (Luke 2:34).

All this has semantic consequences for Luke's concept of Israel. Nowhere, of course, does Luke refer to the Christian church as "Israel" or, especially, identify it as the "true Israel" while relegating the nonbelieving part of the λαός to "Judaism."[70] Nothing of this sort can be found anywhere in Luke's two-volume work. On the other hand, Christian congregations do enter unmistakably into the history of the fulfillment of promises originally made to Israel, and Luke is now able to apply to the Gentile Christians the concept of λαός[71] in this salvific and historically qualified sense (Acts 15:14; see also 18:10).

We can perhaps make the disparate source findings more transparent by shifting the inquiry from the level of the *denotative* meaning of the Lukan concept of "Israel" — the level at which this problem has always been discussed — to that of its *significative* or *connotative* meaning.[72] The question is thus not which group Luke was denoting as "Israel," but rather what understanding he had of "Israel." The Stephen speech (Acts 7:1–53) and especially the Pauline missionary discourse in Pisidian Antioch (Acts 13:16–41) provide sufficient material in this regard. According to this view, "Israel's" identity is constituted by the special quality of its history, determined and shaped only by God's actions. It was initiated by God's election of the patriarchs of the λαός (13:17; see also 7:2–3) and acquired its continuity through the uninterrupted guidance, preservation,

---

68. It is for this reason that in several places Luke has Paul emphasize that his own Christ proclamation stands in continuity with Israel's eschatological expectation and that, paradoxically, Paul is accused and imprisoned — namely, because he proclaims the message of Jesus' resurrection as the fulfillment of God's promise and Israel's hope (see Acts 13:32f.; 23:6; 24:25, 21; 26:6–8; 28:20).

69. See also Lohfink, *Sammlung* (see above, n. 25), 61.

70. Thus with differing accentuation, e.g., Conzelmann, *Mitte* (see above, n. 15), 135; Haenchen, *Apostelgeschichte* (see above, n. 2), 208; Eltester, "Israel" (see above, n. 4), 121; Lohfink, *Sammlung* (see above, n. 25), 55 et passim. In the following discussion, I am modifying my own position as formulated in "Reich Gottes" (see above, n. 23), 563 n. 89.

71. See H. Frankemölle, "λαός," *Exegetical Dictionary of the New Testament* (Grand Rapids, Mich., 1991), 2.339–44 (with bibliography).

72. A fine explanation of this distinction can be found in the *Kleines Wörterbuch sprachwissenschaftlicher Fachausdrücke,* ed. R. Conrad (Hanau, 1984), 49: "The significative meaning encompasses conceptual contents as representations of reality (notions, concepts), while the denotative meaning of a linguistic unit refers to the actual object itself in reality. A conceptual representation constituting the significative meaning of a symbolic entity is called its *designate . . . ,* the object in reality to which the symbol refers is called its *denotative. . . .*" As an example, the predication ὁ χριστὸς τοῦ θεοῦ in Luke 9:20 has as its *denotative* the person Jesus of Nazareth (namely, as the "object in reality"), whereas its *designate,* that is, the object of its significative meaning, are the messianic notions (namely, "conceptual contents") associated with the Christ predication.

and deliverance God granted to the people in fulfillment of promises (7:4–5, 9–10, 17; 13:17–19). This history also included the sending and appointment of the "ruler and liberator" Moses (7:25, 31–36, 38; citation in v. 35), the judges, and the kings Saul and David (13:20–22). In 13:23, Paul then has Jesus follow immediately upon David, asserting that Jesus came from David's line and that God brought him to Israel κατ᾽ ἐπαγγελίαν.[73] Here it becomes clear that for Luke, all those for whom this Jesus has become σωτήρ stand in continuity with Israel's history.[74]

If from this perspective one seeks the referent of the term "Israel," one cannot simply say that Luke is referring thereby to the Christian church; for Luke, Israel always remains a diachronic salvation-historical entity.[75] At the same time, according to the Lukan understanding, Israel's history is carried forward in the Gentiles and Jews who believe in Christ, and the church is without doubt an integral part of Israel. As such, it, too, can view itself as a legitimate heir to the promises given the people of God.

This also explains how in the infancy narratives Luke is able to articulate these eschatological expectations — expectations regarding Israel's own salvation but, at least in Luke's present, as yet unfulfilled — without having to correct them as in Luke 19:11, 24:21, and Acts 1:6. The hopes expressed by Zechariah (1:68–75), Simeon (2:29–32), and Hannah (2:38) can thus be understood as representing the author's own implicit position because as unfulfilled hopes they point beyond the Lukan present and not to some point before Luke's writing.[76] This leaves such hopes open to the delayed parousia and for the crisis and remodeling of Israel which accompany them. In substance, the expectations expressed by Jesus' dialogue partners in Luke 19:11; 24:21; Acts 1:6 also remain in effect; that is, Luke anticipates without a doubt that at his parousia, the Messiah Jesus will fulfill the prophetic promises in preparing for Israel καιροὶ ἀναψύξεως (Acts 3:20f.); that he will liberate both Israel and Jerusalem (Luke 1:68ff.; 2:38; 19:11; 24:21; probably also 21:24); that he will restore the βασιλεία for Israel (Acts 1:6); and that he will reign forever on the throne of David over the house of Jacob (Luke 1:32–33). The difference now is that Israel will include completely different people, and the apportionment of salvation and condemnation will be decided by completely different criteria than implied by the "near-expectation" in Luke 19:11 and Acts 1:6.[77] The previous failure of the parousia to take place has already fixed this result, for those who be-

---

73. See of course also Luke 1:32–33, 54–55, 68–75; 2:11, 25–32; see in this regard Ó Fearghail, "Israel" (see above, n. 1), 25–26.

74. See Acts 2:40, 47; 4:9–10, 12; 5:31; 11:14; 13:26, 38–39; 11:11; 16:17, 30–31.

75. See also Harvey, *Israel* (see above, n. 1), 242: "The unity of the group named 'Israel' is its history"; see also 244: "'Israel' is seen as a group with a history of involvement with a God whose typical activities are to be seen as operating through Jesus and his followers."

76. See also U. Busse, "Das 'Evangelium' des Lukas: Die Funktion der Vorgeschichte im lukanischen Doppelwerk," in *Der Treue Gottes Trauen* (see above, n. 3), 161–79; here 172ff.

77. Ó Fearghail, "Israel" (see above, n. 1), 36, points out succinctly that "in continuity there is discontinuity."

longed to the past generations, in the Lukan present. When in these texts Luke nonetheless still articulates what for his own age was an anachronistic notion of "near-expectation" — doing so precisely so that he can then immediately correct it — this can only be because he is thereby preparing for the change in the traditional understanding of Israel already anticipated by the Emmaus disciples (Luke 24:21).

Hence the words from Hab. 1:5 that Paul cites at the conclusion of his own inaugural address in Pisidian Antioch acquire a programmatic character, because they openly articulate the explosive nature of this problem, a problem whose solution Luke is seeking in his work. The words can thus also stand as a superscription over the entire two-volume enterprise, insofar as they qualify the included πράγματα as a work performed by God "that you will never believe, even if someone should explain it to you" (Acts 13:41b).

Chapter 14

The Story of Israel within the Lukan Narrative

Robert C. Tannehill

Introduction

One of the richest ways of reading Luke and Acts is as the story of God's promise to Israel — a promise given to Abraham and made more specific to David — concerning the salvation of Israel through a Messiah who will also be the savior of all nations. This is a rich way of reading because it enables us to interpret the significance of much material emphasized in Luke-Acts. This approach also enables us to link Luke with Acts as two parts of a long and complex story, with enriching cross-references.[1]

When we focus on human characters, it is not obvious that Luke-Acts is a unified narrative, for the person central to Luke (Jesus) disappears from the stage in much of Acts. Nor does Acts have a single human protagonist. Yet even a narrative that focuses on a number of characters in turn and is partly episodic may reward reading it as a unified narrative if we can discern a central purpose. This central purpose will enable us to understand some episodes as progress toward the goal, other episodes as encounters with resistance. The episodes take on meaning as they relate to the underlying purpose that someone is striving to realize.

In Luke-Acts no single character remains on the human stage, but there is an overarching purpose, the purpose of God. "The purpose of God" (ἡ βουλὴ τοῦ θεοῦ) is an important theological phrase in Luke-Acts, appearing in Luke

---

1. Mikeal Parsons and Richard Pervo have questioned the unity of Luke-Acts and, in particular, have raised questions about my way of interpreting the narrative unity of Luke-Acts. See *Rethinking the Unity of Luke and Acts* (Minneapolis: Fortress, 1993). Parsons and Pervo say that the narrative unity about which I write "is almost exclusively at the level of story and does not reckon adequately with the disunity at the discourse level" (83). The distinction between story and discourse has limited value, in my opinion. (It can sharpen our sense of the particular way the story is told — the discourse — by asking us to imagine other ways in which the same basic series of events — the story — might have been told.) Contrary to the quotation from Parsons and Pervo, I am interested in story as discoursed, i.e., in the way that literary techniques are used to present a series of events in a particular light, which may include presenting them as parts of a larger whole. In any case, the points made in this essay will, I think, withstand Parsons and Pervo's skepticism.

7:30; Acts 2:23; 4:28; 13:36; 20:27 (cf. 5:38–39). The narrator and key characters share an awareness that the purpose of God is the dominant reality behind
events. At the beginning of Luke this purpose is indicated by references to what
God "spoke" to Abraham and David (Luke 1:55, 69–70), namely, promises of
salvation that are now coming to fulfillment for Israel and the Gentiles (1:68–
71; 2:30–32; 3:6). The Lukan infancy narrative is crucially important because
it establishes the theological context for the whole of the following narrative. It
introduces the narrative as the story of God fulfilling promises of salvation for
Israel and the nations. This introduction invites the reader to read the rest of
the story in this light.

Narrative analysis can be a subtler way of studying what redaction critics call
the "theology" of Luke-Acts. Narrative has special ways of projecting what is
sometimes called an "ideological point of view."[2] A story is likely to include a
number of ideological points of view, expressed by different characters, but one
of these may be dominant. The hierarchy of points of view depends on the authority of the voices expressing them. The point of view of the implied author —
which we may infer from the norms and values that dominate the story — appears through statements of a reliable narrator and through statements attributed
to those characters with highest authority. These are reliable characters; that is,
they reliably express the implied author's viewpoint.[3] In the narrative world of
Luke-Acts, God is the figure of highest authority. The perspective of God is
expressed by highlighted scripture references and through designated spokespersons, first by the one whom God designates "my Son" (Luke 3:22), and then by
others presented as inspired prophets. These persons are granted authority by the
narrative. Thus they become the means by which a dominant point of view is expressed. Some of them are also commissioned by God to share in fulfilling God's
purpose. Thus commission statements can also be a clue to how God's purpose
is understood. In addition, the narrative provides an interpretive overview by
offering previews and reviews of events at certain points. Previews and reviews,
highlighted scripture references, commission statements, and interpretive statements by reliable characters provide our best clues to understanding the purpose
of God from the Lukan perspective.[4] Looking at events from the perspective of
the purpose of God, we can understand how they fit together to create a unified
story in two volumes.

God's goal of bringing salvation to both Jews and Gentiles is also the goal of
the narrative. This goal defines what is required for a happy or successful outcome. There is resistance to God's purpose, however, which introduces tension.
In particular, developing opposition makes it doubtful whether Israel will par-

---

2. See Boris Uspensky, *A Poetics of Composition* (Berkeley: University of California Press, 1973),
8–16.

3. See Wayne Booth, *The Rhetoric of Fiction*, 2d ed. (Chicago: University of Chicago Press,
1983), 18.

4. See Robert Tannehill, *The Narrative Unity of Luke-Acts: A Literary Interpretation*, 2 vols.
(Philadelphia and Minneapolis: Fortress, 1986, 1990), 1.21–22.

ticipate in the salvation being offered. This problem is highlighted, rather than resolved, at the end of Acts. Thus Luke-Acts is anything but a simple success story. The importance of Jewish resistance within the plot of Luke-Acts led me elsewhere to interpret the story of Israel as a tragic story.[5] I do not mean that the whole of Luke-Acts is tragic but that there is a tragic aspect to the very important story of Israel within Luke-Acts. The narrative makes use of literary resources to emphasize this tragedy.

The tension between the divine promise of salvation for Israel and resistance by Jewish leaders and some of the people is a major theme that enables us to trace an unfolding plotline encompassing many of the characteristic scenes of Luke-Acts. I will discuss some of the highlights of this plotline in what follows.

Three Promise Traditions as Specifications of the Purpose of God

The Lukan infancy narrative is an extended celebration of the fulfillment of God's promises of salvation to Israel. The infancy narrative also discloses that these promises will include the Gentiles. This disclosure comes, however, only after the strongest affirmations of God's merciful help for Israel. These affirmations are found in the statements of angels (God's messengers) and inspired prophets, figures of high authority in the Lukan narrative world. I will concentrate on three scriptural promises that are important in Luke 1–2 and also in Acts. They are the promise to Abraham, the promise to David, and promises in Isaiah concerning salvation and light. The Lukan understanding of these promises cited in the infancy narrative will be clarified and developed in Acts.

First, the *promise to Abraham.* In 1:54–55 Mary attributes the help that Israel is now receiving from God, through the coming birth of the Messiah, to God's fulfillment of what God "spoke to our fathers," first of all "to Abraham." The reference to the Abraham promise is picked up and developed by Zechariah in 1:72–75,[6] where it is described as God's "oath" to free the people of Israel from their "enemies," so they can engage in the cultic service of God without fear. An expanded version of this promise is found in Stephen's speech (Acts 7:5–7), where it is connected with possession of the promised land. In Mary's and Zechariah's hymns it is made clear that God is acting for Israel in fulfillment of the promise to Abraham. The promise to Abraham also has a prominent place at the end of Peter's Temple speech in Acts 3. Peter refers to his audience as "sons of the prophets and the covenant" and then describes the covenant with Abraham. At that point a significant expansion takes place, for the content of the Abraham covenant is described in these terms: "In your seed all the families

---

5. See Robert Tannehill, "Israel in Luke-Acts: A Tragic Story," *JBL* 104 (1985): 69–85.
6. On thematic connections among the angelic announcements and prophetic hymns of Luke 1–2, see Tannehill, *Narrative Unity,* 1.42–43.

of the earth will be blessed" (Acts 3:25). The oath or covenant that brings salvation to Israel also brings blessing to the other peoples. Inclusion of Gentiles does not mean Israel's exclusion, for in 3:26 Peter speaks of blessing for his Jewish audience as well. The Abraham promise is a promise of blessing for Israel that will also bring blessing to the Gentiles.

Second, we must consider the *promise to David*. Gabriel's announcement to Mary in Luke 1:32–33 plays upon God's promise to David of a successor to David's throne, who would be acknowledged as God's son, leading to a Davidic kingship that will last "forever" (cf. 2 Sam. 7:12–16). Zechariah's hymn combines this promise to David with the Abraham promise (see 1:69–75). Zechariah describes the promised successor to David as a "horn of salvation" (1:69). Later an angel will confirm to the shepherds that the Davidic Messiah who has just been born is a "savior" (2:11). In the first proclamation of the risen Jesus, Peter returns to this promise to David, stating that it has been fulfilled through the resurrection of Jesus as Messiah (Acts 2:30–31). The fulfillment of the promise to David is also the central theme of Paul's synagogue sermon in Antioch of Pisidia (13:22–23, 32–35). As in the infancy narrative, Jesus, the promised offspring of David, is described as "savior" for Israel (Acts 13:23). The promise to David is similar to the promise to Abraham. It is found in Jewish scripture and benefits first of all the Jewish people. But the enthronement of the Davidic Messiah, which takes place through Jesus' exaltation to God's right hand, will also benefit the Gentiles. This point is made in Acts 15:16–17 through a quotation of Amos 9:11–12 that resembles the LXX. The restoration of the ruined dwelling of David will result in "all the Gentiles" seeking the Lord. Once again, the fulfillment of a central promise of Jewish scripture is understood to bring saving benefits to both Jews and Gentiles. Jewish messianism is not understood as a support for ethnic exclusion. Quite the contrary. Neither is this messianism so torn from its Jewish roots as to lose its special relevance for Jews.[7]

The location of references to the Abraham and David promises within the narrative — at the beginning of both volumes and in the most important and extensive theological statements of the beginning chapters — underscores their importance. At the beginning of Luke, the annunciation to Mary centers on fulfillment of the promise to David, the Magnificat ends with fulfillment of the promise to Abraham, and the Benedictus refers to both promises. Similarly, Peter's initial mission speeches in Acts (the Pentecost speech and the Temple speech in Acts 2 and 3) refer first to the promise to David and then to the promise to Abraham. The beginning of Luke sets a theological context for understanding the rest of the story. In particular, it leads the audience to understand the story of Jesus in light of these scriptural promises. Then the audience is reminded of the same promises at the beginning of Acts.

---

7. The interpretation of scriptural promises in Luke-Acts involves a revisionary process that is discussed by Robert Brawley in "The Blessing of All the Families of the Earth: Jesus and Covenant Traditions in Luke-Acts," *SBLSP* (1994): 252–68.

But we must also consider a *third promise tradition, which stems from Isaiah.* Rather than attempting to discuss the numerous references to Isaiah in Luke-Acts, I will concentrate on references to a "light of the Gentiles" (φῶς ἐθνῶν) and to salvation, using σωτήριον, a rare word in the New Testament.[8] Here we can see again how a particular promise tradition is introduced in the Lukan infancy narrative and then is expanded and interpreted in Acts. Both the "light" and "salvation" language appear in Simeon's hymn (see Luke 2:30–32), as he declares to God that he has seen "your salvation" (τὸ σωτήριόν σου) and then describes this salvation as a "light for revelation of Gentiles" (φῶς εἰς ἀποκάλυψιν ἐθνῶν). The reference to light for the Gentiles comes from two similar texts, Isa. 42:6 and 49:6. The use of σωτήριον probably reflects Isa. 40:5 (LXX), since this verse is quoted a little later in Luke 3:6. This verse is the result of a Lukan extension of a quotation found in Matt. 3:3 and Mark 1:3. The primary purpose of the Lukan extension is probably to include the sentence "and all flesh will see the salvation (τὸ σωτήριον) of God," a promise of inclusive salvation that fits the Lukan perspective. Simeon's words are the first mention of the Messiah's significance for the Gentiles. Previously it has been said repeatedly that Jesus Messiah means salvation for the Jews. The introduction of Gentiles in 2:32 does not mean that they are replacing the Jews, for the one who is "light" for the Gentiles is also "glory of your people Israel." The careful inclusion of both Jews and Gentiles is important. It is typical of Luke-Acts. Paul's commission will be described in a similar way: he is sent to both Jews and Gentiles (see Acts 9:15; 20:21; 22:15; 26:16–17).

When we follow this promise tradition into Acts, we find that it is influential at key places in the narrative. The commission of the apostles to be witnesses "to the end of the earth" in Acts 1:8 picks up a phrase from the rest of Isa. 49:6 (LXX), which reads, "I have set you for a covenant of the people, for a light of the Gentiles, so that you may be for salvation to the end of the earth." That Isa. 49:6 is indeed the source of the phrase in Acts 1:8 is shown by a fuller quotation of Isaiah in Acts 13:47. "The end of the earth" is the final destination of a mission that begins in Jerusalem and Judea, that is, with Jews. Acts 1:8 might lead one to believe that the Jewish phase of the mission will close early, leaving only a Gentile mission from that point on. The narrative contradicts such an interpretation. When Paul leaves Jerusalem and Judea, he still preaches to Jews as well as Gentiles, regularly beginning his mission in a Jewish synagogue. Indeed, the Jews deserve to hear about Jesus first, since he is their Messiah. (According to 3:26 and 13:46, the preachers had to speak "to you [the Jews] first.") This priority is seen not only in Jesus' requirement that his witnesses begin in Jerusalem but also in Paul's mission, which regularly begins in the local synagogue.

The quotation of Isa. 49:6 in Acts 13:47 justifies Paul's turning to the Gentiles. He does so, however, only when Jewish opposition makes further work

---

8. This word is found only in Luke 2:30; 3:6; Acts 28:28; Eph. 6:17.

among the Jews impossible. Until then, he is under obligation to preach to the Jews. ("It was necessary that the word of God be spoken first to you," Acts 13:46.) The pattern of Paul's mission contradicts the supposition that Isa. 49:6 is being read as warrant for an exclusively Gentile mission. Paul provides a retrospective summary of his mission in Acts 26:12–23. His statement comes to a climax by another appropriation of the light imagery from Isaiah: the risen Messiah "is going to proclaim light both to the people [i.e., the Jewish people] and to the Gentiles." In Jesus' name, Paul has been delivering this twofold proclamation. We could also say that Simeon was already proclaiming light to Jews and Gentiles in Luke 2:30–32. The reading of Isa. 49:6 is consistent from Luke 2 through Acts 26. This text proclaims God's will that the saving revelation be taken to the Gentiles, but this is to happen as part of a double mission that includes the Jews.

Of course, one may ask whether Paul's concluding statement in Acts 28:25–28 marks the end of the Jewish mission. This statement is linked to the passages we have been discussing, for v. 28 refers to "this salvation (σωτήριον) of God," which has now been sent to the Gentiles. This term σωτήριον, probably borrowed from Isa. 40:5 (LXX), has not been used since the salvation proclamations of Luke 2:30 and 3:6, where it was tied to references to saving light for both Gentiles and Israel, and to the proclamation of salvation for "all flesh."[9] That this term returns at the end of Acts shows its thematic importance in Luke-Acts, and the thematic importance of the Isaiah passages which it brings to summary expression. But in Acts 28:25–28 Paul says to the Roman Jews that they have been blind and deaf; therefore "this salvation of God" has been sent to the Gentiles. Does this mark a change in the previous pattern of mission? From now on will this salvation be offered to Gentiles only? I think not. However, this announcement does highlight a tragic turn in the narrative, for the hopes for the Jewish people in the infancy narrative are not coming to fulfillment. (For further discussion of the end of Acts, see below.)

We have now discussed three promise traditions taken from Jewish scripture that have an important place in the infancy narrative of Luke and also link Luke with Acts, where these promise traditions are further developed and interpreted. These three promise traditions make important contributions to the Lukan understanding of God's purpose in the world, which is the underlying project that turns the many episodes of the story into a unified, developing plot.

We have been studying some important indications of the unity of Luke-Acts, both a theological unity and a unity of narrative plot. Now we must consider more carefully the place of Israel in this story, starting with a few comments about the resistance Jesus faces.

---

9. Jacques Dupont recognized the significance of this link between the end of Acts and the beginning of Luke. See *The Salvation of the Gentiles: Essays on the Acts of the Apostles* (New York: Paulist, 1979), 16.

Resistance to Jesus in Luke

The resistance that Jesus will face within Israel is indicated already in Simeon's oracle to Jesus' parents (Luke 2:34–35), and in the first scene of Jesus' public ministry, the rejection in Nazareth (4:16–30). This rejection could be understood as a purely local event of limited significance. Yet the people of Nazareth are especially inflamed by Jesus' reference to prophets sent to help Gentiles (4:25–28), which seems to be an early signal of a later problem. Paul, like Jesus, preaches in a synagogue, which leads to conflict when Jews become jealous of the outsiders who are attracted (see Acts 13:44–45). As portrayed in the narrative, there are Jews who don't want to hear about salvation for all flesh because they believe the benefits belong to them. Inevitably, the mission will come into conflict with these people.

There are also conflicts over other issues, especially with the scribes and Pharisees. The Pharisees are regularly presented as Jesus' opponents in the Gospel. They have a rhetorical function: they represent the view that Jesus wishes to correct, thus making Jesus' view stand out more sharply. Therefore, it is easy to read them as negative stereotypes. There are, however, some scenes in Luke in which the narrative allows us to view Pharisees as round characters, capable of favorable development, not as negative stereotypes. Simon the Pharisee in Luke 7:36–50 can be viewed as a round character, if we wish.[10] This observation indicates the need for caution about the more thoroughly negative view of Pharisees that some interpreters attribute to Luke.[11]

Some developments are discernible in the relation between Jesus and the religious authorities in Luke, and the record of Jesus' relation to the Jewish people or crowds shows shifts in emphasis: on the one hand, there is strong support for Jesus; on the other hand, Jesus delivers strong warnings because of an inadequate response. However, I cannot pause here to discuss the developing relations between Jesus and the religious authorities or between Jesus and the people.[12]

Something must be said, however, about the major crisis in the relation of Jesus to Israel that increasingly dominates the narrative as Jesus approaches Jerusalem. Jesus comes to claim his place as messianic king, but he is rejected by the Jewish leaders in Jerusalem, and even the people, who support Jesus strongly while he is teaching in the Temple (19:47–48; 20:19; 21:37–38), cry for his death before Pilate (23:13–24). Later the attitude of the people again changes.

---

10. See Robert Tannehill, "Should We Love Simon the Pharisee? Hermeneutical Reflections on the Pharisees in Luke," *CurTM* 21 (1994): 424–33.

11. See Jack Dean Kingsbury, *Conflict in Luke* (Minneapolis: Fortress, 1991), 21–28; idem, "The Pharisees in Luke-Acts," in *The Four Gospels 1992: Festschrift Frans Neirynck,* ed. F. van Segbroeck et al. (Louvain: Louvain University Press, 1992), 2.1497–1512; John Darr, *On Character Building: The Reader and the Rhetoric of Characterization in Luke-Acts* (Louisville: Westminster/John Knox, 1992), 85–126.

12. On Jesus and the authorities, see Tannehill, *Narrative Unity,* 1.167–99. On Jesus and the people, see 1.141–66.

By the time of Jesus' death the people are showing signs of remorse (23:48), and when Peter calls them to repentance, many will respond (Acts 2:38–41; 4:4). Nevertheless, when Jesus is rejected by the Jewish authorities in Jerusalem, they are rejecting "the things that lead to peace" (19:42), according to Luke, with fateful consequences for Jerusalem and the Jewish people. The four passages that address Jerusalem and prophesy its fate have an important role in the plot (see 13:33–35; 19:41–44; 21:20–24; 23:27–31).

It is important to catch the dominant tone of these passages. Jesus speaks words of anguished longing and lament (13:34; 19:42). He is depicted as weeping (19:41), although Luke, in comparison to Mark, tends to avoid references to Jesus' emotions.[13] There is a strong sense of pathos, and the last scene (23:27–31) adds to it by presenting women weeping for Jesus, who are then told that they must weep for themselves and their children. The suffering of innocents clearly increases the pathos. These four scenes, which build up to the crucifixion and help to set the tone for it, constitute one major reason for interpreting the story of Israel in Luke-Acts as tragic. The tragic aspect is even clearer when we realize that Jesus in 19:42–44 is using key terms previously used by Zechariah in celebrating God's salvation for Israel (1:68–79).[14] The same key terms are being used but now in a lament, because what was promised is being lost. The contrasting use of the key terms indicates the tragic turn in the plot.

We are encouraged to read Luke and Acts as a continuous narrative not only by the reference in the preface to Acts (1:1–2) to the previous book, but also by the commission statement at the end of Luke (24:47–49), which summarizes key themes that anticipate the narrative in Acts.[15] Following these literary clues, and reading Luke and Acts in continuity, has consequences for our understanding of Luke. It is more than the story of Jesus. It is part of a larger story concerning the fulfillment of God's purpose of salvation for "all flesh" (Luke 3:6). More specifically, the larger story relates the fulfillment of the divine promises discussed earlier in this essay. These promises are in process of fulfillment, but the process is not complete. Indeed, there seems to be a major obstacle to this fulfillment. Jesus was rejected in Jerusalem. With him Jerusalem rejected the messianic "peace" being offered (19:42). The divine purpose of salvation for Jerusalem, the symbolic center of the Jewish people, appears to be blocked.

If we take account of the specific promises to Israel highlighted in the infancy narrative, the end of Luke does not provide a satisfactory resolution. The narrative makes us aware of this lack of resolution through comments of disciples that remind us of promises in the infancy narrative. These comments also provide a connecting thread between Luke and Acts. The Emmaus disci-

---

13. See Joseph Fitzmyer, *The Gospel according to Luke*, AB (Garden City, N.Y.: Doubleday, 1981), 95.

14. See the references to "peace," "enemies," "visitation," and "knowledge." Note also the connection between 19:38 and 2:14. For discussion, see Tannehill, *Narrative Unity*, 1.159–60.

15. Ibid., 1.295.

ples express their disappointed hope: "We were hoping that he was the one who was going to redeem Israel" (Luke 24:21). The phrase "redeem Israel" (using λυτροῦσθαι) takes us back to the infancy narrative, for this stem has not been used since Zechariah proclaimed that God "has visited and redeemed (ἐποίησεν λύτρωσιν) his people" (1:68) and Anna spoke of the "redemption (λύτρωσιν) of Jerusalem" (2:38). This redemption, however, has not happened, as the disciples' sad comment reminds the reader. The theme continues in Acts 1:6. Jesus has been raised from the dead and has appeared to the disciples. But the disciples' question in Acts 1:6 reminds us that there is still something outstanding in the biblical promises. They ask when the kingdom will be restored to Israel. In reply, Jesus rejects their desire to specify a time, but his response need not be understood as a rejection of the basic hope of a restored kingdom for Israel. Indeed, the angel Gabriel promised that the Messiah would "rule over the house of Jacob forever, and of his kingdom there will be no end" (Luke 1:33). Thus the infancy narrative's anticipations of salvation for Israel as a nation, which include rescue from oppressor nations (cf. 1:71, 74), reappear in the narrative as unfulfilled hopes as we make the transition from the end of Luke to the beginning of Acts.

Paul and Israel

The rejection of Jesus in Jerusalem is not the last word. Peter's speeches at Pentecost and in the Temple call the residents of Jerusalem to repentance for their share in Jesus' death, offering them forgiveness (Acts 2:37–40; 3:19–20, 26). The first two mission speeches in Acts are basically repentance speeches directed to a particular audience — the residents of Jerusalem at the time of Jesus' death — in light of their rejection of Jesus. Thus they are responses to a problem that has surfaced in the plot.[16] These speeches have a powerful effect (2:37, 41; 4:4). The tide appears to be turning. But the Temple authorities intervene, the opposition increases, Stephen is killed, and the Jerusalem disciples are scattered by a "great persecution" (8:1). Thus the bitter opposition that caused Jesus' death reappears in Acts.

Opposition continues as Acts turns to Paul as the principal figure. There are repeated references to Jewish opponents as Paul moves from place to place. The drama of the Jewish people and its Messiah continues to be played out through the story of Paul. Two aspects of this story deserve special attention: (1) The scenes in which Paul announces that he is turning to the Gentiles in the face of Jewish opposition. (2) The series of interrogation and trial scenes in which Paul responds to Jewish accusers after his arrest in Jerusalem.

---

16. On the narrative significance of Peter's mission speeches, see further Robert Tannehill, "The Functions of Peter's Mission Speeches in the Narrative of Acts," *NTS* 37 (1991): 400–414.

Paul's Announcements of Turning to the Gentiles

The first of the scenes in which Paul announces a turn to the Gentiles is set in Antioch of Pisidia.[17] This is also the setting of a major speech in a synagogue, which provides the fullest account of Paul's missionary preaching to Jews. In order to provide a balanced interpretation, it is important to pay attention to the speech in 13:16–41 as well as to the later announcement in 13:46–47. In the speech Paul affirms the election of Israel by God (13:17) and announces the fulfillment of the promise of a Messiah for Israel, a fulfillment that has taken place through the resurrection of Jesus (13:22–23, 32–33). Paul emphasizes that his message is a word of salvation for his audience of Jews and God-fearers (13:26). Thus the Paul of Acts is aligned with the promise traditions — which are first of all promises to Israel — that first appear in the Lukan infancy narrative and that reappear in Acts. But on the following sabbath, when "nearly the whole city" gathers to hear Paul, Jews become jealous and oppose Paul, who then announces that "we are turning to the Gentiles" (13:46). This announcement is justified by a citation of Isa. 49:6, which reintroduces the "light of the Gentiles" tradition.

In the narrative context Paul's announcement cannot mean that he will never again preach to Jews, for he immediately does so in the next city (14:1). The announcement of turning to the Gentiles must be taken with the rest of 13:46, where the statement of Paul and Barnabas begins, "To you [the Jews] it was necessary that the word of God be spoken first." Turning to the Gentiles is a special event because Paul and the other missionaries are under obligation to speak to the Jews first. When bitter opposition makes it impossible to continue, Paul is released from this obligation and can begin a mission that no longer centers in the synagogue. That a turning to the Gentiles takes place at a special time is a result of the priority of the Jews as God's special people, to whom the promises first of all apply. (Peter's preaching agrees with this perspective, for he says that God's servant was sent "to you first," you who are "the sons of the prophets and the covenant" [Acts 3:25–26]). Paul's preaching in Antioch of Pisidia is a major scene that highlights the tension between God's saving purpose for Israel, now being fulfilled, and rejection of that fulfillment by many Jews. The mission is able to move forward by turning to the Gentiles, but God's saving purpose will be incomplete so long as the covenant people do not accept God's salvation.

Brief episodes similar to the scene in Antioch of Pisidia are placed in Corinth and Ephesus (18:5–6; 19:8–10). When Paul announces that he is turning to the Gentiles in 18:6, he also says, "I am clean" (or "innocent"), indicating that he has been under an obligation which, if previously abandoned, would have rendered him guilty. The major scene that we must consider, however, is the

---

17. On this scene see further Robert Tannehill, "Rejection by Jews and Turning to Gentiles: The Pattern of Paul's Mission in Acts," in *Luke-Acts and the Jewish People: Eight Critical Perspectives*, ed. Joseph Tyson (Minneapolis: Augsburg, 1988), 83–89; idem, *Narrative Unity*, 2.164–75.

final one of Acts, Paul's encounter with the Roman Jews (28:17–28).[18] That the last major scene of Acts presents Paul in conversation with Jews indicates the importance of the issues raised by Jewish resistance.

Paul's discussion with the Roman Jews is actually a double scene (28:17–22, 23–28), for Paul makes statements on two different days. The first statement is a summary of Paul's arrest and the defense scenes that follow (21:27–26:32). Paul insists strongly that he has done nothing against the Jewish people or their customs. He is a loyal Jew. The very chain he wears is a sign of his loyalty; he wears it "for the sake of the hope of Israel" (28:20; the hope of Israel is an important theme of the defense scenes discussed below). Thus Paul denies that either he or his mission is anti-Jewish. This statement is further response to accusations raised against Paul in 21:20–21, 28, accusations that hover behind much of the narrative that follows.

The Roman Jews are not presented as hardened opponents. They are willing to hear Paul's message (28:22). Furthermore, their response is not wholly nega- tive. "Some were being persuaded," even though others were not (28:24). It may be surprising, then, that Paul responds with what seems like a scathing denun- ciation. In evaluating Paul's response, we must note several things: (1) Paul was evidently seeking a communal response — recognition by the Jewish community in Rome that Jesus is the fulfillment of God's promises. The division among the Roman Jews is sufficient indication that there will not be a favorable communal response, and Paul reacts to this situation. (2) The quotation from Isa. 6:9–10 includes the instruction to the prophet, "Go to this people and say..." This is a reminder that Paul's way of speaking has biblical precedent, that he is, in fact, assuming the prophetic role previously assigned to Isaiah. Seen in biblical per- spective, Paul is not being anti-Jewish (the charge he denied in 28:17). (3) The words from Isaiah are deeply ironic. They speak of ears, eyes, and heart, organs of perception and understanding, that contradict their own purpose. The ex- treme rhetoric is an attempt to get the Roman Jews to hear their deafness and see their blindness. (4) The announcement of turning to the Gentiles in 28:28 has a similar purpose. It is not primarily an attempt to justify a Gentile mission. The rights of the Gentiles are well established by Acts 15. That is not the issue here. The statement that the Gentiles will hear contrasts with the Roman Jews' failure to hear and is part of Paul's rebuke.

This strong rebuke does not mean an end to the Jewish mission. To be sure, that Acts ends on this note gives the scene extra weight. If we were to consider this scene in isolation from Acts as a whole, we could only say that Paul is rebuk- ing the Roman Jews. However, there have been other scenes of Jewish rejection, leading to a turning to the Gentiles. Although there have also been positive responses from Jews, a pattern has developed. When the narrative ends with

---

18. On this scene see further Tannehill, "Rejection by Jews," 92–101; idem, *Narrative Unity,* 2.344–57.

Paul's rebuke of a Jewish community, the conflict with Jews assumes a certain permanence. There is no more narrative that might end this conflict.

Perhaps the scene suggests a change from the conditions of Paul's mission. This change is not the end of a Jewish mission but the end of the possibility of preaching to Jewish assemblies, as Paul has done. Witnessing to individual Jews is still possible. This possibility is suggested by the concluding summary of Paul's two years in Rome. The statement in v. 24 that some of the Jews were being persuaded provides a motive for visits to Paul by some of these Jews. They were already favorably impressed and would want to discuss Paul's message further. Then the remark in v. 30 that Paul was welcoming "all" who were coming to him would indicate that he is continuing his mission to both Jews and Gentiles, within the limits possible as a prisoner. In doing so, Paul is being faithful to his commission, which was a charge to carry the word to both Jews and Gentiles (9:15; 20:21; 22:15; 26:16–17).

Paul's commission comes from the Lord Jesus, who speaks with the authority of God, according to the norms of the implied author. This commission gives Paul an important role in the realization of God's purpose of salvation for "all flesh" (cf. Luke 2:30–32; 3:6). The negative trend in the narrative, represented by repeated scenes of Jewish rejection, is a frustration of the divine will for Israel. It is contrary to the divine purpose announced in Luke 1–2, which remains the underlying purpose behind the whole narrative. Thus Acts ends on a negative note for which the prediction of success among the Gentiles does not adequately compensate. The story of Israel, so far as the narrator could tell it, is tragic. The beginning of the narrative aroused great hopes for Israel, but these hopes are not being realized. The resulting tragedy is highlighted in the words of Jesus when he weeps over Jerusalem, and in the words of Paul when he speaks of the tragic irony of ears that refuse to hear. Emphasis on these scenes does not mean that the narrator has no hope for change. Indeed, faith in God and belief in the scriptural promises requires such hope. But the narrative does not point to any concrete signs of change in the response of Jews. It can only point to Paul as a model of faithful witness in difficult times (28:30–31).

Paul's Defense Scenes

Some hope of success in a Jewish mission may be found in the scenes of Paul's defense that dominate 21:17–26:32. In this major section of Acts, Paul is primarily defending himself against accusations that he has betrayed the Jewish people and their faith. Devoting so much space to this issue shows its importance to the implied author. The issue is important because the implied author regards the Jewish people as important and believes the divine promises made to them.

This long section of Acts begins by highlighting two sets of charges against Paul.[19] Paul responds throughout the series of defense scenes (and even in 28:17–

19. On the scenes of Paul's defense, see further Robert Tannehill, "The Narrator's Strategy in

20, when he is in Rome). The sum of these charges is that Paul has betrayed the Jewish people, for his mission is an attack on Judaism. The first of these charges comes from Christian Jews who believe that Paul is teaching Diaspora Jews "apostasy from Moses, saying that they should not circumcise their children nor walk by the customs" (21:21). The Christian opponents of Paul drop out of the narrative, but their charge merges with the charge of the Jews who mob Paul in the Temple, shouting "this is the fellow who is teaching everyone everywhere against the people and the law and this place [the Temple]" (21:28). The opponents are referring to three marks of Jewish identity: they are a people chosen by God, governed by God's law, with a divinely established Temple in Jerusalem. The opponents believe that Paul is attacking Judaism in his teaching by rejecting all three of these identity markers.

The defense scenes are framed by two major speeches by Paul (22:1–21; 26:1–23). In the first Paul is defending himself before the mob of Jewish attackers; he emphasizes, in an autobiographical statement, his Jewish roots and the Jewish roots of his mission. This emphasis will continue in later scenes, but there are also important developments. In 23:6 Paul makes a short statement to the Sanhedrin: "I am a Pharisee, a son of Pharisees. I am on trial concerning hope and resurrection of the dead." This statement is more than a tactical move to cause dissension between Pharisees and Sadducees in the Sanhedrin, for it is the first expression of a theme that will be developed in following chapters of Acts. We can only understand its importance by tracing its development in the narrative. As a defense strategy, we can say that Paul is trying to change the main issue in his coming trial, but I believe that there is a second motive behind this statement, a missionary motive that will become apparent in Acts 26. For the moment, we should note that Paul makes no reference to the resurrection of Jesus in his statement to the Sanhedrin. He speaks only of a resurrection hope shared with other Pharisees. This reticence, not characteristic of Paul previously, continues into the following scenes. In 24:14–15, in the trial before Felix, Paul again insists that he shares with other Jews the hope in resurrection, and the speech ends by referring back to Paul's statement about resurrection to the Sanhedrin (24:21). It is also remarkable that christological argument from scripture, important in previous speeches, is largely absent from Paul's defense speeches. (There is a general reference to scripture in 26:22.) If, as many believe, the purpose of these scenes is to assure Christian believers that their faith is firmly linked to Jewish roots and Jewish scripture, a major source of argument is being ignored. Nor can these scenes be explained as apologetic directed to the Roman world. Romans would find much of the argument irrelevant but would probably be impressed by one detrimental fact highlighted by the narrative: the claim of many Christians to Judaism is sharply contested by Jewish authorities acknowledged by Rome. A different explanation of these scenes is necessary. Paul is being

---

the Scenes of Paul's Defense," *Foundations and Facets Forum* 8 (1992): 255–69; idem, *Narrative Unity,* 2.268–329.

defended; he is also being presented as a model of a resourceful missionary who seeks and finds common ground with suspicious and antagonistic Jews.[20] Because of the antagonism, Paul develops a circuitous witness that builds on a base acknowledged by many Jews. This second purpose appears in the climactic defense scene before King Agrippa (Acts 26).

In 25:19 Festus indicates that the previous talk of resurrection included Paul's claim that Jesus had been resurrected. This remark anticipates the end of Paul's speech to King Agrippa (26:23) but does not preempt its climactic impact, since the remark is relegated to a report by Festus. The speech of Paul in Acts 26 has multiple functions. For the reader it is a review and summary of Paul's role in the unfolding purpose of God. Thus it has great importance in understanding the Lukan view of Paul. In the immediate context, it is a defense speech that, at the end, turns into a missionary appeal. There is a literary signal of this shift in function. In v. 2 Paul refers to making his defense and in v. 6 he says, "I stand being judged" (or "on trial," ἕστηκα κρινόμενος), but in vv. 22–23 he says, "I stand bearing witness" (ἕστηκα μαρτυρόμενος) and gives his witness to the risen Messiah. Agrippa recognizes the shift to an evangelistic appeal, as the following dialogue shows (vv. 25–29).

The theme of resurrection hope has an important role in this evangelistic appeal. This theme is inserted into Paul's autobiographical narrative when Paul refers to himself as a Pharisee (see vv. 6–8). In a short digression, Paul declares that he is being accused concerning the very hope and promise that the Jews eagerly hope to attain. This is ironic. Indeed, it is tragic irony, for it means that Jews are rejecting what they deeply desire and what rightly belongs to them. The hope in question is hope in resurrection of the dead, as v. 8 indicates. It may seem strange that hope in resurrection is viewed as the central hope of Judaism. However, more than individual life after death is at stake. In the Lukan perspective, the Jewish hope in resurrection is tied to the Jewish hope for a messianic kingdom. Resurrection life is an aspect of the Messiah's kingdom, which has consistently been presented as central to Jewish hope. Already in the first chapter of Luke, the angel Gabriel said that the Messiah Jesus would "reign over the house of Jacob forever, and of his kingdom there will be no end" (Luke 1:33). The Messiah's kingdom is eternal because the resurrected Jesus does not die. This point was emphasized by Paul in Acts 13:34–35. The speech of which these verses are a part proclaims that the promise of the Davidic Messiah for Israel has been fulfilled through the resurrection of Jesus (13:32–33). The promise of the messianic kingdom to which Paul refers in this, his first major speech, includes the promise of resurrection life to which he refers in his last major speech. A peculiar phraseology provides evidence for this connection. In 13:32 Paul refers to "the promise made to the fathers" (τὴν πρὸς τοὺς πατέρας ἐπαγγελίαν γενομένην); in 26:6 the phrase is repeated, including the word order (τῆς εἰς τοὺς πατέρας ἡμῶν

---

20. Paul's speech to the Ephesian elders (20:18–35) makes clear that Paul is presented, in part, as a model for later church leaders.

ἐπαγγελίας γενομένης). The promise of a messianic kingdom and the promise of resurrection life flow together in Lukan thought, for the Messiah is "first of the resurrection of the dead" (26:23). He is the first of many. More than his own resurrection is at stake, for through him comes resurrection life for others (cf. Acts 3:15; 4:2). Thus Paul in the trial scenes is able to move from hope in a general resurrection to hope in a messianic kingdom for Israel established by a resurrected Messiah.

Conclusion

Luke and Acts are a unified narrative because the different events reported relate to a single underlying purpose, God's purpose of bringing salvation to all flesh. This purpose remains constant and is presented consistently through use of three promise traditions that appear in the infancy narrative and reappear in Acts. Each of these promise traditions is used to indicate that Gentiles are included in God's salvation, but the implied author does not lose sight of the fact that these are first of all promises to Israel. The Pauline portion of Acts does not show a loss of interest in Jews and Judaism. Indeed, the issue of Paul and Judaism dominates Acts 21:17–28:31. The point of the lengthy defense scenes is not to prepare for a final rejection of Judaism but to defend Paul against the view that he has betrayed Judaism and to provide through him an example of how a resourceful missionary might appeal to Jews, in spite of growing antagonism. The ending of Acts does not imply that the Jews have finally lost their chance. The negative response of many Jews is a major theological problem for the implied author, for God has promised salvation to the Jews. This problem is not solved at the end of the narrative. Much of the narrative will be misunderstood if we do not recognize that the fate of the Jewish people remains a central concern throughout Luke-Acts.

The persistent concern with Jewish rejection in Luke-Acts shows that the implied author is not content with salvation for a remnant. God's promises are understood to apply to Israel as a people, not to a remnant. These promises are being fulfilled through Jesus Messiah, the implied author believes, but many Jews refuse to recognize Jesus as their Messiah. The acceptance of Jesus by a Jewish minority is not a satisfactory solution. The anguish of Paul as he speaks his final words to the Roman Jews reflects the anguish of the implied author, who cannot accept this situation as a satisfactory fulfillment of God's promises to Israel.

Whether there should be a Christian mission to the Jews is a subject of debate among Christians today. In my view, concern for the Jewish people and belief in the scriptural promises would have led the author of Luke-Acts to continue mission to the Jews. Today, however, Christians must consider whether almost two millennia of history lead to a different conclusion: that God has a continuing purpose for Jews as a separate people. This conclusion permits respectful dialogue that need not lead to conversion.

Chapter 15

"Israel" and the Story of Salvation

One Theme in Two Parts

I. Howard Marshall

Introduction: Looking at Luke-Acts as a Whole and as Two Parts

The useful term "Luke-Acts" owes its popularity, if not its origin, to a trend-setting work by H. J. Cadbury in 1927.[1] The term probably did not gain widespread usage until the development of redaction criticism after the Second World War with its emphasis on Luke as an author who worked creatively and independently on his sources. The term expresses that in some sense the Gospel of Luke and the Acts of the Apostles constitute a united work.

Within recent years the apparent self-evidentiality of this unity of the Gospel and Acts as two parts of a single account has been called in question by M. C. Parsons and R. I. Pervo, who have rightly challenged scholars to examine the basis for what was in danger of becoming an unquestioned and unexamined assumption.[2] Nevertheless, it is safe to say that their challenge has probably led to a stronger, because better defended, case for the unity of Luke-Acts. That case has been made largely on *literary* grounds. The question is not, of course, one of common authorship, which would be answered by looking at the language, style, and theology of the two books and discussing whether these show that they were written by the same person; the vast majority of modern critics answer the question affirmatively. Rather it is the question whether the two books, as we now have them, are deliberately intended to be read as two parts of the one story. It is the difference between arguing that *Marlborough* and *The Second World War* are both written by the same author (W. S. Churchill) and arguing that the several volumes of the latter work are indeed parts of one continuous narrative conceived as a whole.

---

1. H. J. Cadbury, *The Making of Luke-Acts* (London: Macmillan, 1927; reprint, London: SPCK, 1958).

2. M. C. Parsons and R. I. Pervo, *Rethinking the Unity of Luke and Acts* (Minneapolis: Fortress, 1993). An earlier form of the proposal was M. C. Parsons, "The Unity of the Lukan Writings: Rethinking the *Opinio Communis*," in *With Steadfast Purpose: Essays on Acts in Honor of Henry Jackson Flanders, Jr.*, ed. N. H. Keathley (Waco, Tex.: Baylor University Press, 1990), 29–53.

In the case of Luke, it is possible that he wrote the Gospel first as a work on its own, and then at a later date conceived the idea of a sequel, so that the two books belong closely together, with the possibility that the first was edited at the time of composition of the second so as to make them fit together better. It is also possible, and in my view more likely, that he conceived of the two books right from the beginning as complementary parts of one, unified work. I have argued elsewhere for this view, and the argument was essentially a literary one, based on the evidence of the prologues to the Gospel and Acts, the interrelations of some details in the two books, and the way in which the Gospel ends.[3] Other writers have drawn particular attention to structural elements which bind the two books closely together. The argument against the hypothesis based on the difference in genre of the two books is one that can be answered. We may, then, assume that we are dealing with a single work, written in two parts, whatever the manner of its composition.

What now needs further discussion is the question of the *theological* relationship of the two books.[4] It would seem self-evident that if Luke-Acts is a single work by one author, then it is possible to write a theology of Luke-Acts as a whole, and it would also seem self-evident that one can write theologies of the Gospel and of Acts respectively, just as there exist books both on the theology of Paul and also on the theologies of his individual writings. The parallel is not, to be sure, an exact one, since Paul's letters were not written as parts of one single, united corpus. In another place I have discussed the legitimacy of writing a theology of Acts and the kind of approach that should be taken.[5] This discussion is necessary because the whole enterprise has been questioned as a dubious procedure methodologically. That the task has been successfully carried out is sufficient defense.[6] Equally, one can write a theology of the Gospel.[7] But, just as it would be difficult to write on one Pauline letter without putting it into the context of the corpus as a whole, so obviously one cannot write about the Gospel without taking Acts into account and vice versa.[8]

Scholars are generally better at taking into account the preceding context of a work rather than the following context, meaning, for the present case, reading Acts in the light of having already read the Gospel. Scholars are not as good at the inverse procedure, reading the Gospel in the light of what follows. My instinct used to be to question the approach of exegetes who argued that a pas-

---

3. I. H. Marshall, "Acts and the 'Former Treatise," in *The Book of Acts in Its Ancient Literary Setting,* ed. B. W. Winter and A. D. Clarke (Grand Rapids, Mich.: Eerdmans, 1993), 163–82.

4. This point was, of course, addressed by Parsons and Pervo (see above, n. 2).

5. See the introductory essay to Winter and Clarke, *Book of Acts,* 6 (see above, n. 3).

6. J. C. O'Neill, *The Theology of Acts* (London: SPCK, 1961; reprint, 1970); H. C. Kee, *Good News to the Ends of the Earth: The Theology of Acts* (London: SCM Press, 1990); J. Jervell, *The Theology of Acts* (Cambridge: Cambridge University Press, 1996).

7. J. B. Green, *The Theology of the Gospel of Luke* (Cambridge: Cambridge University Press, 1995).

8. To be sure, there is not a lot of theological reference to Acts in Green's work.

sage should be read in the light of what follows for echoes and allusions,[9] but the idea that one reads with a mind empty of what may lie ahead has been crit- icized, and it has been argued cogently that people read books — and especially scripture — many times so that there can be connections made both forward and backward.[10] Literary studies of the NT adopt this assumption and look for literary links. Perhaps, therefore, I should be less skeptical about this method of interpretation.

The problem that I am tackling, in the light of this consideration, is twofold. I am concerned with (1) the way in which Luke tells a story that develops over two volumes, and (2) the consequent manner in which the following material should influence our reading and understanding of the Gospel. It is easy enough to read Acts as a sequel to the Gospel. But with C. K. Barrett we should be asking whether we should read the Third Gospel as, inter alia (as he is careful to point out), a preface to Acts.[11] Barrett's argument is largely concerned with points of detail which prepare for or point forward to Acts. However, behind his discussion lies a concern with the theological issue; Barrett agrees with van Unnik that Acts is the confirmation of the Gospel, but also asks whether Luke is the preparation for Acts. He thinks that both propositions are true, and draws the significant conclusion that Luke-Acts is "the first New Testament." The spe- cific question of the theological relation of the Gospel to Acts, however, is not treated in detail.

In a previous study related to this question I outlined some points that seemed significant. The topic was the purpose of the Gospel, and I argued that the pur- pose could be understood only in light of the fact that Luke wrote a sequel. His purpose was to present salvation to his readers, with Acts offering "the confir- mation of the gospel,"[12] helping the church to cope with the problem of the rejection of the gospel by "the Jews," and showing how the new people of God is brought together. He produced a story with various threads tying it together.[13]

This approach firmly places the Gospel of Luke alongside Acts and makes the

---

9. For example, I would question the interpretation of John 2:1 which interpreted the "third day" when the wedding was held at Cana in relation to the "third day" of the resurrection, or even more so, relating the time of day in John 4:6 to the time when Pilate was judging and condemning Jesus in 19:14 (R. H. Lightfoot, *St John's Gospel: A Commentary* [Oxford: Oxford University Press, 1956], 105, 122).

10. See the unpublished paper by I. du Plessis, "Integrating Historical and Literary Study: Luke as Case Study," presented at the Luke-Acts Seminar of the SNTS meeting, Prague, 1995.

11. "The Third Gospel as a Preface to Acts: Some Reflections," in *The Four Gospels 1992: Festschrift Frans Neirynck* ed. F. van Segbroeck et al. (Louvain: Louvain University Press, 1992), 2.1451–66. Earlier the same point had been made by C. H. Talbert, *Literary Patterns, Theological Themes, and the Genre of Luke-Acts* (Missoula, Mont.: Scholars Press, 1974), 30 n. 3. Talbert's earlier suggestion (in *Jesus and Man's Hope*, vol. 1, ed. D. G. Miller [Pittsburgh: Perspective, 1970], 202) that Acts has logical priority in Luke's plan may be true, but is based on the dubious argument that Luke's purpose in writing was to combat heresy.

12. W. C. van Unnik, "The Book of Acts: The Confirmation of the Gospel," *NovT* 4 (1960): 26–59.

13. "Luke and his 'Gospel,'" in *The Gospel and the Gospels*, ed. P. Stuhlmacher (Grand Rapids, Mich.: Eerdmans, 1991), 272–92.

relationship between the two the proper context for the interpretation of each part. A powerful opponent of this approach is B. S. Childs, who adopts the view that the prologue (Luke 1:1–4) is concerned purely with the Gospel and that the Gospel stands within the canonical context of the Four Gospels.[14] Nevertheless, Childs has to admit that Acts is the continuation of the Gospel and that Luke wrote a two-volume work which has been divided as a result of canonization, so that the two volumes have different canonical functions. The weakness of his position throws considerable doubt on the whole idea of "canonical context" as the proper context for interpretation. It would be wiser to assign a double function to the Gospel, both as part of the fourfold Gospel and as part of the two-volume work "Luke-Acts." In any case, we are concerned with the author's intention rather than with the consequences for the subsequent interpretation of the Gospel that may arise from its grouping with the other Gospels, and its separation from Acts.

The way in which the topic has been framed has centered generally on Acts. Why did Luke think it necessary to write a sequel to the Gospel and what exactly does Acts do? That is to say, the oddity of what Luke did has been seen in the composition of a second volume that somehow disturbs the tidy pattern of the "Gospel" genre. Again, to recapitulate points made elsewhere, we do well to remember that Luke's enterprise may not have been so revolutionary as we sometimes suppose. The thesis that it was revolutionary depends on the assumption that there was one fixed way of dealing with Christian beginnings, and that Luke had the genius to be a nonconformist. But the major premise that there was a fixed form, namely that of the Gospel pure and simple, falls apart when we remember that the real revolution lay in writing the first Gospel — a literary genre whose novelty continues to puzzle critics — and that one can hardly speak of a fixed form when there are scarcely any examples of the genre.[15] There was, in other words, no constraint tying Luke to a single volume about Jesus at a time when the Gospel genre was still an experiment, and there was room for further experimenting.

The significant point is that Luke saw that writing just a life of Jesus was inadequate as a means of supplying the Christian church with its roots. The Gospel is an unfinished story, and the question of what happened afterwards is crucial. The Gospel does not explain how the preaching of the gospel and the formation of the church took place. Within the limits of a Gospel, in the sense of the story of the earthly life of Jesus, authors cannot go beyond Jesus' commands or prophecies about what must happen after he has gone, or teaching that represents the guidance of the Paraclete, so that Jesus to some extent speaks out of the post-Easter perspective. But descriptions of events which happened

---

14. *The New Testament as Canon: An Introduction* (London: SCM Press, 1984), 96–116.

15. Or, at least, scarcely any that have survived. Admittedly, Luke refers to the many before him who attempted to draw up an account of what had happened, but the "many" is generally held to be somewhat conventional.

subsequently could scarcely have been included without expanding the medium of *vaticinium ex eventu* to ridiculous proportions.

Why, then, did Luke's predecessors and colleagues not do what he did? If Luke found it necessary to tell the stories both of Jesus and of his followers, why did the other evangelists not do so? We have no evidence that any did so and wrote books that have not survived, or intended to do so but failed to achieve their purpose. All we do have is the interesting fact that the scribe responsible for the longer ending of Mark thought it necessary to conclude with the statement that "they went out and preached everywhere, the Lord working with them and confirming the word through the signs that accompanied it" (16:20; cf. Heb. 2:4). Here is the Book of Acts in summary, in a comment perhaps inspired by it.

This lack of works like Luke's may well suggest that the purposes of the other evangelists were different. They were asking questions about Jesus and his mission, whereas Luke was more concerned with the roots of the people of God. However, I see no grounds whatever for the statement by W. Marxsen that "by contrast with Luke the standpoint of both Mark and Matthew make any kind of continuation unthinkable."[16]

But we must not be diverted along this fascinating track. The aim of the present study is primarily to understand the Gospel better in the light of the sequel, rather than simply to frame a theology which will fit Luke-Acts.

What effects should knowing that the Gospel is part of Luke-Acts have on our reading of the Gospel? Suppose that all trace of Acts had been lost: would our reading of the Gospel then be different? Do we in fact read the Gospel differently because it has a sequel? Or have interpreters not sufficiently taken into account, in reading the Gospel, that it has a sequel? Does the sequel open our minds to points that we might have otherwise missed or help us recognize emphases that did not stand out previously?

Two kinds of material may be distinguished. First, there are prophetic passages whose fulfillment lies in Acts, passages whose "historical referent," so to speak, is future, and that future is in Acts. All the Gospels contain passages which are prophetic, whether "apocalyptic" material dealing with events that lay beyond Luke's horizon in Acts or more "historical" material dealing with the period after Jesus.[17] We should then ask whether the prophetic materials in Luke are framed to anticipate the story in Acts. One outstanding example of what I have in mind is the way in which Peter's affirmation in Luke 22:33 differs from the wording in the other Gospels, referring to his readiness not only to die but also *to go to prison* with Jesus, words that doubtless point forward to Acts 12.

The second kind of material consists of passages which take on fuller or different meaning in the light of the sequel. Thus, in the absence of indications to

---

16. *Introduction to the New Testament* (Oxford: Blackwell, 1968), 155f. He continues: "Of course Matthew (and — with certain reservations — also Mark) could have written a Church history; however, this would not have been a continuation of their original works, but a history of the continuing influence of these works, which is something quite different."

17. This is admittedly a very rough-and-ready distinction.

the contrary, the language used in Mary's song in Luke 1 might be understood in apocalyptic terms of the future consummation of the kingdom of God, or even taken politically, addressing the hopes of downtrodden Jews. Placed within its context in the Gospel it is arguable that the imagery should be understood in terms of what actually happened in the ministry of Jesus, rather than in more narrowly political terms.[18] M. Korn would go even further and claim that Luke 1–2 as a whole prefigures the entire story of Luke-Acts.[19] Again, Luke makes six references to the apostles, in contrast to one each in the other three Gospels. Within the context of Luke-Acts, we may conclude that this heightened emphasis on the apostles is due to the important role that they are to play subsequently.

I shall make some trial probes to see whether this general hypothesis is justified. It is, of course, possible that we shall find that the fact of the sequel makes no difference, or that some of the links and effects detected by scholars are illusory.[20]

The Closure and Commencement of the Gospel

I begin by looking at the ending of the Gospel. It would seem probable that, if the Gospel has a sequel, the end should lead readers to expect more. In the other Gospels the ending will function more as a closure, and nothing more.

The functions of the final scene in the Gospel of Luke have been discussed in great detail by M. C. Parsons, who has shown that the story of the ascension serves as a narrative ending in the Gospel but as a narrative beginning in Acts.[21] The ascension story in the Gospel functions as closure.

I agree with this statement of what should surely have been obvious. But the question arises whether this neat distinction between closing and opening functions, and assigning them to the Gospel and Acts, respectively, is correct. I would argue that the ending of the Gospel also functions to prepare the reader for a sequel. Parsons is aware of this:

---

18. I. H. Marshall, "The Interpretation of the Magnificat: Luke 1:46–55," in *Der Treue Gottes Trauen: Beiträge zum Werk des Lukas (Für Gerhard Schneider)*, ed. C. Bussmann and W. Radl (Freiburg: Herder, 1991), 181–96.

19. M. Korn, *Die Geschichte Jesu in veränderter Zeit: Studien zur bleibenden Bedeutung Jesu im lukanischen Doppelwerk* (Tübingen: Mohr, 1993). See the discerning review of the significance of this work by D. P. Moessner (*JBL* 114 [1995]: 336–38). Korn's book covers much of the same ground as the present essay, and I would find it hard to detail the points at which he has influenced my presentation.

20. One obvious example of the latter is H. Conzelmann's conclusion regarding Luke's understanding of time. The conjunction of Gospel and Acts is said to make the Gospel a part of "salvation history" and to place the coming of Jesus not at the end of history but rather in the middle of time. This view requires considerable qualification, but I do not propose to retread familiar ground. See I. H. Marshall, *Luke: Historian and Theologian*, 3d ed. (Exeter: Paternoster Press, 1988), 76–88.

21. M. C. Parsons, *The Departure of Jesus in Luke-Acts: The Ascension Narratives in Context* (Sheffield: Sheffield Academic Press, 1987). His book is in effect a full-scale expansion of remarks by C. K. Barrett, *Luke the Historian in Recent Study* (London: Epworth, 1961), 55–58.

While the readers are being ushered out the Temple gate where they first entered the story, they glance over their shoulders and the image of disciples praising their God, despite the absence of their Lord, is indelibly imprinted upon their hearts and minds. At that moment, the narrator/guide at their elbows whispers in their ears a command "Go thou and do likewise!" and an invitation "And please come again!"[22]

It is that note of invitation which is significant. It needs much more emphasis than Parsons gives it.

The presence of invitation is probable in view of the context of Luke's readers. At least thirty years had passed since the death of Jesus, and the continuing existence of the church was obviously familiar. What had happened since bore some relationship to Jesus. The other Gospel writers make the point in their own ways. In each Gospel, Jesus issues instructions which are not fulfilled within the limits of the books; programs for the future are implied. Luke follows this pattern in developing a program for the future in the closing scene of the Gospel. The crucial passage is Luke 24:47–49, which is comparable in position and significance with the "Great Commission" in Matt. 28:16–20. But Luke writes a second part which is of roughly equal length to the Gospel and which continues the story. The significant fact for our purpose is that the closure of the Gospel is composed to lead the reader to what is to follow. The end of the Gospel acts both as closure and as an invitation to continue reading.

The ending is also important for tying closely the story of the suffering and resurrection of Christ with the preaching to nations, by clamping them together in a single sentence and by establishing both as divinely necessitated and grounded in scriptural prophecy. That Luke is telling one story could not be stressed more vigorously or clearly.

The disciples are thus given explicit marching orders for the immediate future, together with a promise that is not fulfilled within the story. So the story is left unfinished with people praising God in the Temple; the reader knows that this scene must change.

I recognize the possible objection that much the same things might be said about the endings of the other Gospels. The readers of Mark know that the Gospel must be preached, and will be preached everywhere (Mark 13:10; 14:9); they also know that Jesus will "go before" the disciples into Galilee (14:28), where they will meet him (16:8). Whatever that prophecy or command means, it is left unfulfilled. Equally, the enigmatic present ending of Mark's Gospel in 16:8 cries out for continuation, which I believe was originally part of the Gospel.[23] But here we have to resist speculation since we have no idea what such a narrative might have contained. All we can say is that the Gospel of Mark, as it has come to us,

---

22. Parsons, Departure of Jesus, 113.
23. For the fullest exposition of the case see R. H. Gundry, Mark: A Commentary on His Apology for the Cross (Grand Rapids, Mich.: Eerdmans, 1993), 1009–21.

does nothing at the end to lure us to the story of the church, but merely excites intense curiosity regarding the outcome of the women's flight from the tomb.

Matthew, of course, concludes with a meeting in Galilee, where the great commission is delivered, which might lead us to expect a sequel relating how it was obeyed. But the passage has a sense of climax, and somehow we are left looking back and up to Jesus. The ending does not make us ask how the eleven disciples fulfilled their commission, but rather makes us feel — I grant that this is a subjective impression that other readers may not share — that the commission is directed to us. The scene's function is to round off and complete what Jesus had to say to his disciples.

Where Matthew has a commission to be obeyed, Luke gives a prophecy of what will take place according to the purpose of God, and a command concerning the place of the disciples. The command to the Eleven is in effect a condition to be fulfilled if they are to be clothed with power from on high. The last verse of the Gospel has them obeying this condition, and rouses the expectation of fulfillment of the promise.[24]

From the ending of the Gospel I turn briefly to the preface. Scholarly opinion is divided whether the preface intends to introduce the Gospel or Luke-Acts as a whole. The case for the latter view has been strengthened by Barrett, who holds that the preface covers both books, thus explaining some of its obscurities.[25] The division of opinion suggests that it is difficult to use the preface as evidence for the unity of Luke-Acts, but that it can certainly be read as an introduction to both volumes.[26] This approach surely makes better sense of the reference to the πράγματα (events) "which have taken place," an odd phrase to refer simply to the life of Jesus and that invites a wider interpretation. Similarly, the use of "among us" makes better sense if the author refers to the experience of readers.

The Controlling Theme — The Proclaimer and the Proclaimed

In the following I argue that we may see the Gospel differently in the light of its sequel from the way we would see it if there was no sequel. The first

---

24. But again, is this different from Mark 16:7?

25. "The Third Gospel," 1463–64. This view is also shared by F. Bovon, *Das Evangelium nach Lukas* (Zurich: Benziger; Neukirchen: Neukirchener, 1989), 1.42; C. A. Evans, *Luke* (Peabody, Mass.: Hendrickson, 1990), 17; R. H. Stein, *Luke* (Nashville: Broadman, 1992), 62 (both say that the preface refers primarily to the Gospel); C. F. Evans, *Saint Luke* (London: SCM, 1990), 120f.; D. L. Bock, *Luke 1:1–9:50* (Grand Rapids, Mich.: Baker Books, 1994), 56. For a restriction of the preface to the Gospel see J. Nolland, *Luke 1–9:20* (Waco, Tex.: Word, 1989), 11. In the most detailed discussion of the preface, L. C. A. Alexander allows it as "a possibility (at least as far as preface-convention is concerned) that Luke did not have the narrative of Acts immediately in mind when he wrote Luke 1.1–4" (*The Preface to Luke's Gospel: Literary Convention and Social Context in Luke 1.1–4 and Acts 1.1* [Cambridge: Cambridge University Press, 1993], 146).

26. See now the work of M. Korn for further defense of this view.

.iestion concerns the theme of Luke-Acts. Luke's statement is that he writes to Theophilus to give him an account of the things which have been taking place among them, and which now constitute the content of "the word." He is therefore writing about events which have become the subject of Christian proclamation, and the account can take the form of a narrative. When we turn to Acts, we find that the "former treatise" was concerned with what Jesus began to do and to teach. But, as is well-known, there is no balancing clause indicating the content of the second treatise. The implication is that the narrative is going to be continued, and that Acts is the same narrative. The first volume is couched as a narrative about Jesus and his activities, including his teaching. It shares the broad literary characteristics of the other Gospels, and thus it is not a "sermon," like the speeches in Acts, nor an epistle, nor a collection of sayings of Jesus. In that Luke presents an account of the life of Jesus from birth to death (and resurrection), it is correct to call it a biography with a religious purpose or motivation.[27]

This very obvious point needs to be made in order to establish what is going on and what is the book's center of attention. A Gospel is a narrative about Jesus. It is a book in which Jesus has already become the proclaimed: the Gospel is an act of proclamation about Jesus. The force of this point is evident when we contrast the Synoptic Gospels with the Gospel of Thomas, in which the embryonic narrative structure cannot conceal that it is essentially a repetition of the teachings of Jesus, in which the proclaimer continues to proclaim.

When we come to the second volume, the thrust has become very plain. We have the account of the spread of the "word" told according to what its chief proclaimers did. Because a word is something to be proclaimed, it was entrusted to specific witnesses. This shift from Jesus to the word is significant.

The shift means that we now go back to the Gospel and discover that Jesus himself is also a servant of the word; his significance lies in his activity, and who he is, in carrying out this role. He is in familiar terms both the Proclaimer and the Proclaimed, with the effect that the distinction between these two terms to some extent collapses. He is primarily the Proclaimer in Luke and the Proclaimed in Acts, but he is also the Proclaimed in Luke and the Proclaimer in Acts.

In what ways is he the Proclaimed in Luke? As noted, the form of a Gospel means that the Proclaimer is Proclaimed. But there is more to it. Jesus does talk about himself and his mission, and this is part of his message. He announces who he is in 4:18f., where the Proclaimer and his proclamation can hardly be separated. The demonic cries concern him and not his message (4:41f.). He talks about himself in 4:43. The word about *him* spreads (5:15). The question of his identity is important (5:21). People are called to follow him (5:27). His behavior is discussed (5:30–32) and even questions about the behavior of the disciples become questions about him. He talks about his own status as Son of Man (6:5).

---

27. R. A. Burridge, *What Are the Gospels? A Comparison with Graeco-Roman Biography* (Cambridge: Cambridge University Press, 1992).

Even the Sermon on the Plain directs attention to the preacher (6:22, 46–49). This point could be followed further. In short, Jesus becomes the object of his own activity.[28] The suggestion that he focused on the kingdom of God and kept himself in the background is not true. It is inconceivable that the Gospel writers and their sources were misinformed on this point or tendentiously altered the tradition.

This focus becomes all the sharper in Acts where the preaching centers on him, at least in the mission statements to Jews. Thus the shift from the kingdom to the Messiah in Acts is by no means the big step that it is sometimes thought to be.

I suggest, then, that the existence of Acts alerts us that Jesus is both the Proclaimer and the Proclaimed in the Gospel, and examination of the Gospel confirms this hypothesis. We might want to ask if, in the Gospel, Jesus is both active and passive, to what extent this is the case in Acts. Specifically, is he active as well as the object of proclamation in Acts? To what extent does Acts continue what he began to do and teach?[29]

Apostleship and Witness

This question provides the link to a second point in which the Gospel and Acts may be interrelated. It is the question of the relationship between Jesus and his agents.

In the Gospel the *shaliach* (sending) principle provides the means of extension of Jesus' work, in that those whom he sends are equivalent to Jesus in authority (Luke 10:16). This applies both to the Twelve and the Seventy-two, both of whom are "sent" by Jesus. Luke makes much more of the sending/apostle motif in his Gospel than the other evangelists. The language of "sending" is not particularly prominent in Acts (22:21; 26:17), although the apostles are at the center of the proclamation to Jews. In place of "sending" we find the concept of witness.

Witness terminology is sparse in the Gospel.[30] Of the references only 24:48 refers to the activity of disciples, and it refers to their post-Easter role. But the word-group is common in Acts. The activity of witness commences only after events have taken place to which witness is borne. Apostles are thus transformed into witnesses. But this suggests that, to some extent, the apostles are to be

---

28. This is an observation of some significance for the study of Jesus himself. The constant refrain that he did not teach about himself, except indirectly, or that he made no claims about himself, simply does not stand.

29. I have disputed previously the idea that Jesus in Acts is in heaven, absent and inactive (Marshall, *Luke: Historian and Theologian*, 179–82). But the point may be taken further by considering to what extent, if any, Jesus is active in and through his agents.

30. The uses are μαρτυρέω, to witness, 4:22; μαρτυρία, witness, 22:71; μαρτύριον, witness, 5:14 (cf. Mark 1:44); 9:5 (cf. Mark 6:11); 21:13 (cf. Mark 13:9); and μάρτυς, witnessing person, 11:48; 24:48.

understood as witnesses in the Gospel, despite the lack of witness terminology. From Acts it emerges that the apostles were those who had been with Jesus in his active ministry, from the baptism by John to the ascension; therefore, their activity in the Gospel is implicitly that of seeing and hearing the things of which they would later speak. It would seem that Acts 1:21f. functions as the equivalent of the little phrase in Mark 3:14, "so that they might be with him," which Luke curiously omits. It would be valuable to see whether and how far Luke emphasizes this element of "being with Jesus" in the Gospel. We may draw the conclusion that the Gospel is integrated into the theme of witness in that it depicts Part One of the process, namely seeing and hearing what Jesus did and said. Acts then depicts Part Two of the process, the proclamation of what had been experienced in Part One. Without Part One the apostles would not seem to have the necessary qualification for witnessing.

A second question concerns the place of Luke's second group of missionaries. Granted that the Twelve are brought back to original strength after the loss of Judas and continue to operate in Acts, what happens to the Seventy-two? They fade from sight after returning to Jesus. The Mission of the Seventy-two is unnecessary to the story if it does not point forward. The common view, which there is no reason to dispute, is that the *mission* of the Seventy-two is intended to foreshadow the mission to the Gentiles. (The number seventy-two is a reference to the nations of the world.) Luke could not record a mission to Gentiles in the Gospel, since there was no historical basis, but he could include an incident which is symbolic of the mission. In the same way, the crowd at Pentecost is Jewish, but the language of the list of peoples in Acts 2:9–11 foreshadows the spread of the gospel among the Gentiles.

The similarities between the instructions to the Twelve and the Seventy-two, and what happens in the mission in Acts, have been observed by commentators.[31] Preaching and healing, acceptance and rejection — with the response of wiping off dust — traveling and being dependent on the people evangelized are common features.

Can the symbolism be extended? Do *the Seventy-two themselves* have symbolic significance? In Luke 10:1 is the peculiar statement that they were to go "to every town and place where he himself intended to go." But it seems unlikely, if not impossible, that one person could follow up visits made by thirty-six pairs in a short period. It seems necessary to understand that Jesus was simply going to go in and through them. This is confirmed by 10:16, which applies the *shaliach* principle to the mission of the Seventy-two. The impossibility of a literal understanding of 10:1 suggests that the Seventy-two symbolize those who will take part in the Gentile mission. Their mission is historical but is also symbolic of what is to come.

The Seventy-two are a larger group with a wider ministry than that of the

---

31. R. C. Tannehill, *The Narrative Unity of Luke-Acts: A Literary Interpretation* (Philadelphia: Fortress, 1986), 1.232–37.

Twelve. I suggest that we should distinguish between the Twelve as messengers to Israel, who continue that mission in Acts, and the Seventy-Two, who symbolize Paul and others as missionaries to Gentiles. If the number had been seventy rather than seventy-two, I would have more confidence seeing the group as parallel to the Seven in Acts 6. This equation, however, will not work as it stands. It is easier to see a parallel between forty years and forty days than between seventy disciples in pairs and seven serving tables; in any case, the number of disciples is almost certainly seventy-two. In addition, the Seven of Acts are associated not with Gentiles but with Hellenists who are Jews. The parallel, therefore, is nonexistent.

We should be careful of oversimplification. Even though the Twelve are missionaries and witnesses to Israel, Peter goes to Gentiles and Paul goes to Jews. Luke is never simple!

A further point is that the tasks of the Twelve and the Seventy-two are identical apart from literary variation. So, in principle, the task of witness is not confined to the Twelve. Similarly, we note (1) that the tasks undertaken by the Seven are similar to those of the Twelve, despite the fact that they were appointed to look after tables; and (2) that the tasks of Paul and his companions parallel those of Peter and his companions in what appears to be a fairly deliberate pattern.[32]

The Message — The Kingdom and the Messiah

Luke's frequent use of εὐαγγελίζομαι (to preach good news) as a term to describe the activity of Jesus and his followers and to characterize its content is well-known.[33] He emphasizes that their task was one of spoken proclamation, and that the message was intended to bring joy and gladness (Luke 2:10; 8:13; Acts 8:8). The verb creates continuity between the Gospel and Acts. Its Lukan significance is more conspicuous because the word is not found in Matthew and Mark (except Matthew 11 [Q]). The curious feature is the absence of the noun εὐαγγέλιον (gospel), which appears only in Acts 15:7 and 20:24.[34]

Luke agrees with the other Synoptic Gospels that the theme of this good news

---

32. Note the thesis of Peter Bolt, who confines witness proper in Acts to the Twelve and Paul, of whom alone the noun "witness" is used ("Mission and Witness," in *Witness to the Gospel: The Theology of Acts*, ed. I. H. Marshall and D. Peterson [Grand Rapids, Mich.: Eerdmans, 1998], 191–214). But the description of Stephen (Acts 22:20) has then to be explained away.

33. Marshall, *Luke: Historian and Theologian*, 159–61.

34. Mark 1:1 is not used by Luke. Mark 1:14 // Matt. 4:23 (cf. Matt. 9:35) and 1:15 disappear in the reformulation of Luke's story. Mark 8:35 and 10:29 are both edited by Luke (9:24; 18:29), but in both cases Matthew (16:25; 19:29) also differs from Mark, and one might wonder whether these "minor agreements" point to a version of Mark which lacked the slightly cumbersome phrase. Mark 13:10 is adapted in Matt. 24:14 but completely reworded in Luke 21:13; Mark 14:9 is preserved in Matt. 26:13, but the story is omitted by Luke. Can we see a tendency here, or is it just a matter of chance? (In any case, the lack of the noun unites Luke and Acts.)

was the kingdom of God. There is continuity with Acts, which makes clear that the message of the apostles is also *formally* about the kingdom of God. That the kingdom of God is said to be the theme of postresurrection instruction by Jesus (Acts 1:3) implies that the disciples were to be concerned with the kingdom in their own thought and teaching. Of the eight references in Acts, five refer to the kingdom of God as the content of teaching and preaching (8:12; 19:8; 20:25; 28:23, 31). Only once is the term used in actual teaching (14:22). With respect to the *content* of the teaching, however, three of the references identify teaching about the kingdom of God with teaching about Jesus (8:12; 28:23, 31). There is one significant reference to the preaching of "another king, namely Jesus" (17:7). When we look at the actual teaching and preaching in Acts, it is clear that the subject is Jesus rather than the kingdom of God. The preaching is intended to communicate that Jesus is the exalted Lord and Christ (Acts 2:36; 5:43; 9:22; 17:3; 18:5).[35] For Acts, then, to preach about the kingdom of God is to preach about Jesus.

If we turn back to the Gospel, other points stand out. First is that, as non-Jewish readers, we may fail to realize how closely the concepts of the Messiah and the kingdom of God belong together. The Messiah is the agent of God who rules on God's behalf in the kingdom. He is the son of David, the king. Consequently Jewish readers of the Gospel would link the kingdom of God to the Messiah more readily than we might. The role of Jesus in announcing the coming and nature of the kingdom of God would raise questions as to his relationship with the kingdom. Speaking of him as Messiah would imply that he was the ruler of the kingdom of God.

Second, the announcement of the birth of Jesus at the outset is related to "his kingdom," to the throne of David and rule over the house of Jacob (1:33). If we translate the crucial phrase as "his rule," there can be no doubt that the Messiah rules over the kingdom of God; he is the agent in setting up a kingdom which can be called the kingdom of God or the kingdom of the Messiah. The idea of Jesus as king is transparent in the parable in 19:12, 15, and the theme is addressed directly in 22:29f. and 23:42. Thus for Luke the kingdom of God and the kingdom of the Messiah are the same thing, and to speak of the kingdom of God is to speak of the kingship of Jesus.

Hence there is a smooth transition from Jesus' proclamation of the kingdom of God, which is implicitly a self-proclamation, to the apostles' proclamation of the Messiah in Acts, which is equally a proclamation of the kingdom of God.

What is interesting is that this equation is especially prominent in Luke as compared with Matthew and Mark where, by the same reasoning, it is implicit (Matt. 13:41; 16:28; 20:21; Mark 10:37). But, in any case, all three Gospels clearly identify Jesus as the king and son of David, especially in the crucifixion scene.

---

35. Whatever we make of the mysterious passage about the Twelve (Eleven) ruling with Jesus, in Acts their function is to witness to the rule of Jesus (cf. Acts 1:6–8).

We can conclude that, in light of Acts, there is a case for seeing the Gospel's references to the kingdom of God much more in terms of the coming of the Messiah, Jesus, whose rule is announced in 1:33. The tendency to argue that the Gospels, and more particularly Jesus himself, are concerned with the kingdom of God and not with the Messiah is contrary to Luke's understanding.[36]

Discipleship and Community

If I am right so far, the theme of Luke-Acts is the kingdom of God and the Messiah. Elsewhere I have argued that the theme is to be understood in terms of salvation; that is, the Messiah functions as savior and the kingdom of God as the powerful action of God to save people and establish a community of the saved. We must therefore consider the theme of the community in Luke-Acts.

A word of great significance here is the term μαθητής (disciple). Three points can be made about the usage.[37]

First, it is the most common term in all four Gospels for people who responded positively to the mission of Jesus. Each of the evangelists uses it with frequency.[38] The word is also applied to disciples of Moses, John the Baptist, and the Pharisees; nevertheless, in a Christian context it is used absolutely and self-evidently to refer to disciples of Jesus.[39]

Second, in all four Gospels the word is surprisingly rare on the lips of Jesus.[40] How did Jesus use the term and why did it become so common in the Gospels?

Third, the word is not found outside the Gospels except in Acts, where it is used of former disciples and of new believers, both Jews and Gentiles — and

---

36. The use of the term κύριος ("lord") in Luke may enhance this conclusion. The facts are that in Mark the term is scarcely used for Jesus (vocative, Mark 7:28; ambiguous in 11:3 [request for colt]; used of "Messiah" in 12:37); in Matthew are the same third-person usages, plus 24:42 in a parabolic context / application, but there are also a far greater number of vocative uses. In Luke we have again the vocative uses, but also a significant number of narrative uses referring to Jesus. It is probable that Luke anticipates the later status of Jesus, but significantly the term appears in editorial comments (whether from Luke himself, or from a source), and not anachronistically on the mouths of actors in the story. Luke reminds readers that Jesus speaks and acts with the authority of one who will later be attested by God through the apostolic witnesses as "Messiah and Lord." See my brief discussion in The Gospel of Luke, 285.

37. See R. N. Longenecker, ed., Patterns of Discipleship in the New Testament (Grand Rapids, Mich.: Eerdmans, 1996).

38. Note the comment of K. H. Rengstorf that Luke deliberately avoids using the word in the passion story after the Last Supper and Gethsemane (TDNT 4.442f.).

39. The word "disciples" tends to be qualified by "his" in the Gospels, although this is not rigidly true. In Acts the term, except in 9:1, is used absolutely. It has become self-evident whose disciples are meant. Consequently, "disciple" probably remains a relational term that brings out the link between Christians and the Lord.

40. The references are Matt. 10:24f. // Luke 6:40; Mark 14:14 // Matt. 26:18 // Luke 22:11; Luke 14:26f., 33; John 8:31; 13:35; 15:8. Other people use the term (Mark 2:18 // Matt. 9:14; Mark 7:5 // Matt. 15:2; Mark 9:18 // Matt. 17:16 // Luke 9:40; Luke 19:39; John 7:3; 9:27f.; 18:17, 25), and also angels (Mark 16:7 // Matt. 28:7).

implicitly of the whole group of disciples. This usage is found from Acts 6:1 to 21:16, and is applied to people in Jerusalem and the Judean area generally, Damascus, Antioch, and the places evangelized by Paul.[41] Whereas the disciples tend to be passive in the Gospel, in Acts they develop into actors in their own right.[42]

These facts put Luke's usage into perspective. The term brings out the continuity between the followers of Jesus and the church after Easter. But "disciple" is not attested as a self-designation of believers outside Acts, although I can see no reason why the term applied to followers of the earthly Jesus should not be used after Easter. There is no reason in principle why the usage should not be historical.[43]

In the Gospel the word "disciple" and teaching are associated, so that one has an idea of what a disciple is or ought to be. In Acts, however, "disciple" is simply a label with no developed significance.[44]

The significance of this usage is that discipleship ties the followers of the earthly Jesus and believers in the risen Lord as one group. We need therefore to ask whether the use of the term in Acts affects its understanding in the Gospel. Does the use of the word "disciple" in Luke imply that a community is beginning, whose history will continue? There is, after all, little sign of a community beyond the group of immediate helpers. The broad group called "disciples" develops naturally without apparent effort.

Another indicator of continuity lies in the verb "to believe." In Acts, what makes a person a Christian is expressed by the verb πιστεύω (to believe). It is a beginning action, but also a continuing attitude. The object of faith can be Jesus or the Christian message and so on, or the phrase may be used absolutely. The verb is less prominent in Luke (used nine times) than in Mark (ten times) — the number of occurrences of "Christian" is also small — but the noun is more frequent. In 8:12f. the verb is introduced redactionally into the explanation of the parable of the sower, in what has been thought to be a piece of "Christian" vocabulary. This is a formulation not readily intelligible without presupposing the Christian usage.[45] The connection of faith and salvation is thus underlined. The comparative frequency of "repentance" in the Gospel is likewise to be noted. Luke appears to be emphasizing continuity between the response to Jesus' message in the Gospel and response to the preaching in Acts.

---

41. Although "disciple" is not found elsewhere in the NT, it is found in later sources (Ignatius; M Poly.; Diognetus 11.1; Abercius inscr.). In some of these passages it applies specifically to martyrs.

42. Green, Theology, 102.

43. So H. Weder, ABD 2.207–10, who speaks of a "pre-Lukan linguistic use" which may have been dropped because it caused confusion with adherents of schools of philosophy.

44. I see no evidence that Luke views the disciples in the Gospel as other than a historical group of followers of Jesus who combine imperfection and faithfulness; they have no symbolic value. The elaborate theories with regard to their role in Mark have little or no basis in Luke.

45. The noun πίστις (faith) is more common in Luke, where it occurs eleven times — four times from Mark; two times from Q; plus 7:50; 17:5 (Q or Q^R); 17:19; 18:8; 22:32. The formula "your faith has saved you" is repeated three times.

Salvation and Israel

Against this background we are now in a position to consider another central issue. In the Gospel the term "savior" is used once of God (Luke 1:47) and once of Jesus (Luke 2:11). It is not surprising that pious Israelites in the period before the Messiah should refer to God as their savior. It may, however, be surprising that the birth of a savior needs to be announced to Israelites, unless it is assumed that shepherds are apostates. Why should the people of God need a savior apart from God? But from the beginning the "Messiah" is described as a savior for Israelites, and his coming is seen as the means by which God brings salvation. The Messiah is to be seen as God's agent, doing for God's people what they cannot do for themselves; therefore, it is natural that God's own title of "savior" should be applied to him. From the beginning salvation is linked not just to deliverance from enemies but also to forgiveness of sins. The far-reaching implication is that there is a way of forgiveness independent of the sacrificial system, corresponding to the direct action of God found in the Old Testament. The Gospel of Luke shows Israel that, although it is the people of God, it needs salvation, and that the Messiah whom God sends functions as savior as well as ruler in the kingdom of God. The bringing of salvation is described in the account of Zacchaeus, depicted as dishonest and grasping, but who then undergoes a change of heart which turns him into a generous giver. Elsewhere in the Gospel salvation is linked to faith, whether the "healing" be physical or spiritual. Twice the verb "to save" is used for what one might call "Christian" salvation (8:12; 13:23).

Against this sketch we must place the evidence of Acts. Again we note that when the title of savior is applied to Jesus it concerns his role in relation to Israel (Acts 5:31; 13:23). The apostles proclaim salvation to the Jews and to the Gentiles; there is no indication that Jews do not need to be saved. The new feature is that salvation is *also* for the Gentiles. A verdict passed on Jews in general as a crooked generation rests on the rulers' rejection of Jesus the Messiah, supreme agent of God.

The contours of salvation are the same throughout Luke-Acts. Does this affect the reading of the Gospel? In Acts it becomes clearer that Jews who do not accept Jesus as Messiah are guilty in the sight of God and need forgiveness, paradoxically offered in the name of the one whom they were in danger of rejecting. But we did not need Acts to tell us this fact in view of the portrayal of Jesus in the Gospel as the divine agent. What emerges, therefore, is that for Christian readers Luke-Acts is one story in two stages. Readers can use material in the Gospel in the same way as material in Acts when confronted by the coming of the Messiah and Lord. That is, the tendency to read the Gospel merely as a record of history is corrected by reading Acts. Repetition in Acts demonstrates that Luke also portrays the coming of a savior, the human need which he meets, and the divisive effects of his coming as people respond positively or negatively to him.

We must now relate these findings to the concept of Israel. The term "Israel" is comparatively frequent in Luke-Acts. It is used to refer to the Jews as the people of Israel. He is their God (Luke 1:16), they are his people (Luke 2:32), and therefore he cares for them (Luke 1:54). But to be a member of Israel — like being "saved" — does not mean that people are all that they should be. Greater faith is displayed by some outside Israel (Luke 7:9). Many of the sons of Israel need to be turned to God by the son promised to Zechariah and Elizabeth (Luke 1:16), and even godly people look forward to the day when God will bring comfort to God's people (Luke 2:25). The birth story implies that the coming of Jesus is the manifestation of this "comfort." The disciples' disappointed comment that they thought that Jesus would redeem Israel (Luke 24:21) is shown true in a way that they had not envisaged. All this is confirmed by the proclamation of Jesus: the denial of comfort to the rich in Luke 6:24 confirms that the promise of the kingdom to the poor in 6:20 is, in effect, a promise of such comfort. The message is double-edged even for members of Israel: some will rise and some will fall (Luke 2:34). The Twelve will "rule" Israel as the consummation of God's rule (Luke 22:30).

These points are confirmed and developed in Acts. The term "Israel" continues to be used for the Jewish people of Old Testament times (Acts 7:23, 37, 42) and their descendants to whom the teaching of the apostles is addressed (Acts 2:36; 4:10; 5:21; 9:15; 10:36); "this people Israel" encompasses past and present members (Acts 13:17), and it is to them that John the Baptist and Jesus brought messages (Acts 13:23f.). They have a hope for the future which, for Paul, involves the activity of Jesus (Acts 28:20).

Acts gives greater significance to the little phrase in Luke 2:31f., in which God's salvation is linked to "all peoples," and specifically to the Gentiles. Simeon's prayer places the Gentiles before Israel, and the worldwide scope of mission is fleetingly adumbrated. The temptation to play down his wider reference would be strong if Acts did not exist to confirm the truth of the statement. The comments of Jesus in Luke 4:25–27 on the prophets' message to those outside Israel likewise gain force from Acts. They show that God's purpose is not confined to Israel as the Jewish people. Certainly Luke's diction does not expand the term "Israel" to include believing Gentiles. In Luke the term "people" is used consistently for the "crowd" (of Israelites) or the Jewish people collectively, and only in 2:31 is the plural used of Gentile nations. Similarly, in Acts the term is used for Israel or the crowd, and only rarely is used otherwise. Acts 4:25 quotes an OT reference (Ps. 2:1) to peoples of the world; Acts 15:14 describes how God is to take a people from the Gentiles (cf. 18:10). Luke does not redefine "Israel" to refer either to the Jewish people who responded to the gospel (as a "new" Israel), or to the combination of believing Jews and Gentiles as a new people of God. One almost gains the impression of two parallel operations, one addressed to Jews and the other to Gentiles. In fact, the churches consist ideally of both Jews and Gentiles sharing in table fellowship, an ideal generally but not always realized. For Luke the proper term for this is "church," and it would appear that he uses this term for the new people of God composed of Jews and Gentiles (Acts 20:28).

The kingdom is not to be restored to Israel — at least not for the time being; the disciples are to be witnesses to the whole world. The question is whether, for Luke, the story of Israel has come to an end, except insofar as its members accept the Messiah and come into his church. Has the term "Israel" become contaminated by the unbelief of many present members, and by an exclusivism that precludes its use as the name for a new people of God? Yet the name is retained for the people whom God chose and for whom he has salvation, comfort, and hope. There is a place for it in the future, if the Twelve are to be its judges and if the kingdom is to be restored to it, but these sayings appear marginal to the main thrust of Luke-Acts.[46] At least for the foreseeable future, the focus is on the church.

Conclusion

I have established that Luke and Acts belong together. Five aspects of thematic continuity include Jesus as Proclaimer and Proclaimed — the central figure in both books; the sending of apostles and witnesses; the prominence of the kingdom and Messiah; discipleship as the response to the Gospel throughout; and salvation offered to all people. Jesus is presented as savior to both Jews and Gentiles, uniting believers from Israel and the nations in the new community, the church of God.

When we read the Gospel in light of Acts, the latter helps in understanding the kingdom of God, the Messiah, and salvation as universal themes. Discipleship is spelled out more fully. We see these motifs in a broader perspective than we might have otherwise. Acts shows that events in the Gospel are of a piece with what happens after Easter.

The means of conveying the message in both the Gospel and Acts is narrative with embedded teaching. This is important in directing attention to a significant common element in the genres of the two parts. The differences are already apparent and spring from the fact that the Gospel is a narrative about Jesus, and Acts is a narrative about his followers — and we should perhaps look no further for an explanation of differences between the two works than this shift in subject(s).

There is thus a wholeness about the composition; the two parts help to explain one another. The theological unity of the Gospel and Acts has become more apparent than any disparity in subject. The Gospel leads naturally and inevitably into Acts, which places the life of Jesus in the broader context of "the things that have been fulfilled among us."

---

46. The temptation is to set aside these two very difficult texts (Luke 22:29f.; Acts 1:6–8) and to press on with the simpler task of integrating the rest of Luke's teaching, but this would be dangerous. The presence of such texts warns against oversimplification of the evidence.

Conclusion

"And some were persuaded..."

David P. Moessner and David L. Tiede

This volume marks a sea change in the interpretation of Luke's two volumes. *Jesus and the Heritage of Israel* invites the reader to regard the two books of Luke and Acts together as narrative crafted to persuade. Although remarkably different from one another in source material and generic "feel," these two books were crafted into a two-volume whole to make an argument or case. From the beginning in which Theophilus is assured of a new narrative proposal (Luke 1:1–4) to Paul's final efforts to "persuade them about Jesus from the law of Moses and from the prophets" (Acts 28:23–31), Luke-Acts presses the point that Jesus is the fulfillment of the heritage of Israel. Though far from unanimous on many points, the diverse group of contributors to this volume charts a new landscape in which the breathtaking array of characters and plots of Luke's persuasive project are etched in crisp relief.

But Luke's case was far from simple. The scholarship of this volume demonstrates the complex craft of the narrative argument. The birth stories in the Gospel (1:5–2:52) announce the themes often overheard in the words and deeds of Jesus, and replayed in the actions and speeches of the disciples in Acts. From the first appearance of the angel to Zechariah in the Temple to Paul's preaching in Rome, the truth to which the narrative testifies meets with both disbelief and faith (Luke 1:20, 63–64; Acts 28:24–25). Luke's argument, therefore, can only be grasped in depth through careful attention to its narrative, rhetorical, historical, and intertextual integrity.

The authors in this volume also make their cases, each with a particular theme, expertise, and interdisciplinary approach. Each has wrestled with the "unity" of Luke's enterprise, the significance of Israel, and Jesus as Israel's heritage. Without rehearsing the details of each contribution, the reader's attention is drawn to the following points in each essay.

Part I: The Prologues as "Claimers" of the Heritage

The four contributors to Part One all agree that the two prologues express narrative continuity by linking *two* volumes to produce *one* larger story of Israel's

358

heritage. Yet they diverge regarding the rhetorical means by which the prologues effect this continuity, and regarding the resulting character of the whole.

The Formal Functions of the Prologues in Their Greco-Roman Literary Setting

For L. C. A. Alexander, the Gospel prologue is essentially "an address label" of an author at home in the world of technical, scientific prose, whose rational, sober discourse assures the reader of a careful handling of the tradition. The unusually personal tone of Luke 1:1–4 also lends confidence that the author has followed the tradition reliably, and writes it accurately. The secondary prologue of Acts, on the other hand, alerts the reader that "the narrative of Acts presupposes the narrative of the Gospel and is a continuation of it." Still, it is only through a "retrospective rereading" of the whole narrative, from back to front, that the clues in both *prooemia* can be detected. These clues encourage reading Luke-Acts *intertextually* "within the grand narrative of Israel's history." Luke 1:1–4 signals Luke's decision to write a "comfortingly humanistic affair" of modest purpose. Alexander writes that Luke presents no startling new information, nothing strange or shocking, and no bombastic claims to be revealing 'the truth.' The 'sense of security' . . . is precisely what Luke's prefaces provide for the reader in tune with ancient preface convention."

Daryl Schmidt, on the other hand, argues squarely against the rhetoric of technical, scientific "school" prose, marshaling evidence that the Gospel prologue is replete with the "rhetoric of Hellenistic historiography." References in Luke 1:1–4 to a beginning for the events described, eyewitness evidence, orderly narrative logic, assurances of truth-telling from an unbiased point of view, and claims of the version's convincing qualities are all integral to the aims of Hellenistic historiographical *prooemia* and evoke clear and unequivocal expectations that a historiographical narrative follows. To be sure, Luke-Acts should not be compared with the historiography of an earlier period, for example, to Herodotus or Thucydides. Nevertheless, when Luke follows his *prooemium* with the language and motifs familiar to the Septuagintal stories of ancient Israel (Luke 1:5ff.), or closes Acts with Paul's conversion, "directly reminiscent of the commissionings of Jeremiah and Ezekiel," the informed reader will soon recognize this narrative resembles the biblical narrative, depicting "events of momentous significance" to characters who are composites of biblical heroes.

The Material Claims of the Prologues and Ancient Greek Poetics

Vernon Robbins draws out the implications of what Alexander refers to as profession-oriented, middlebrow Greek by utilizing exercises from introductions to essays and speeches in the *Progymnasmata* of Theon and of Hermogenes. Geared for students completing a secondary level of education and specializing in the "re-performance" of well-known traditions into a persuasive argument, these rhetorical conventions effect continuity between Luke's two volumes such that "the words and deeds of Jesus' followers in Acts 'grow out' of the words and deeds of Jesus in the Gospel." The "chreiai" of Acts 1:1–14, for instance, weave speech and action of the main characters to continue the story of Israel through Jesus' disciples. "Jesus' response reconfigures [the disciples'] perception of the kingdom of Israel by introducing a program whereby the words and deeds of Jesus will be taken to the end of the earth." These words are "authorized by Jesus himself, the founder and validator of the Christian movement." Whereas, for Schmidt, historiographical rhetoric provides the hermeneutical key to relating the events of one volume to the other, Robbins finds that key in the rhetorical power of the chreiai, which articulate and intertwine the dialogical modes of discourse to be elaborated in the ensuing narrative.

David Moessner, parting company with the three previous analyses, places greater stock in the "literary location" of Luke's enterprise as divulged in Luke 1:1–4 and echoed later in Papias's comments (cited in Eusebius's *Ecclesiastical History* [III.39.14–16]) on the deficiencies of Mark's Gospel. Rather than signal a specific genre (Schmidt) or appeal to a particular intellectual tradition (Alexander) or social location (Robbins), Luke, Moessner argues, legitimates his narrative in the context of other competitors, and therefore draws upon the terms of debate in Hellenistic *poetics*. Moessner finds the following chain telling — the author's credentials (παρηκολουθηκότι), the resulting improvement in narrative arrangement (καθεξῆς), together with the superior benefit to the reader (ἡ ἀσφάλεια). This catena of topoi is common within *prooemia* in a wide range of Hellenistic genres, and in a variety of socio-literary contexts. Such clustering renders paramount Luke's claim to re-constellate a common tradition in a superior fashion: what the church would later call a "Gospel" — a narrative in one volume — Luke writes in two volumes. Luke's plan to rewrite the "events brought to fruition," announced in the Gospel prologue, is revitalized in the preface to Acts as a "carefully crafted plot of the overarching plan of God consummated in Jesus, Messiah of Israel." This means that Acts does not witness *to* the Gospel but is at the heart of the witness *of* the Gospel.

•

The interpretive sea change is marked in all these essays both by extensive research into the Hellenistic rhetorical conventions upon which Luke draws, and by awareness that it is Luke's claim on Israel's tradition that is being advanced. All four authors view the Gospel prologue as an introduction to the larger story, in two volumes, of Jesus of Nazareth as Israel's heritage. The material relation of Luke 1:1–4 to the narrative itself, however, is perceived differently, and can be represented by a continuum. Alexander, for whom Luke 1:1–4 falls "deliberately outside" the narrative, with hints to the story of Israel, is at one end. Moessner, for whom the Gospel prologue is an interactive frontispiece announcing seminal themes while intimating a strategy for their plotting in the larger narrative, is at the continuum's opposite.

Although the four essayists focus on a very small portion of Luke and Acts, their own renditions of the prologues provide overtures to the whole. Questions, however, still remain. What rhetorical score is Luke himself playing and for whom is he performing? Do the prologues "re-sound" in the narrative and, if so, how more precisely? To what extent do the prologues invite readers to read the two volumes *intertextually* as well as *intratextually*, within the larger repertoire of Israel's traditions?

Part II: The Narrative Claims (of) the Heritage

The second part investigates Luke's larger literary project to tell and re-tell the traditions of Israel, which reach their pinnacle in Jesus of Nazareth. Whether in refiguring previous Jesus traditions or in configuring the continuing Jesus traditions of Acts, the methods of these authors attend to the rich and manifold ways Luke makes his claims.

In an introduction, Richard Pervo challenges the alleged continuity of Luke and Acts and all other (post)modern attempts to join what the pre-modern church never joined. Why, Pervo asks, do contemporary scholars insist on Luke and Acts as "one flesh," when the earliest, not to mention the consistent, witness of the church relates the volumes as "parent to child"? " 'Luke-Acts' is a modern construct, not yet seventy-five years old.... [T]he work belongs to a twentieth-century genre." Acts is a sequel in an ongoing story; it does not constitute the main action. Though Luke has come perilously close to creating two stories — "one book portraying the culmination of a 'religion' and another describing the birth of a new cult" — the "second" story is a logical outcome of the first, which often foreshadows and anticipates it.

Pervo's insights throw out the gauntlet to the rest of Luke's interpreters who "read" with some version of "Luke-Acts." Does Luke's treatment of Jesus' life and his followers constitute one action, one greater story centered on God's relation to Israel? Pervo's analysis provokes new understanding of the public consequences of Luke's project. In light of Luke's effort to legitimate the "new" cult in Acts, together with the rejection by most Jews of this book's exclusive claims, is Luke really the "interpreter of Israel"?

Reminting the Coin of Hellenistic Jewish Narratives: *"Events that have come to fruition" (Luke 1:1)*

All three contributors in this section discover in Hellenistic Jewish narratives parallels shedding new light on the shape and purpose of Luke's two volumes.

William Kurz surveys Josephus and the Hellenistic deuterocanonical 1 and 2 Maccabees, Tobit, and Judith. He finds a common understanding — developed in varying ways, to various degrees — of providence or of a "plan" representing a shared legacy from the Jewish scriptures. To be sure, the narrative device of promise, or prophecy, and fulfillment is neither deployed nor developed to the same extent in these works as in Luke and Acts, yet "such a widespread and deep-seated biblical worldview provides confirming evidence for the narrative linkage between the Lukan Gospel and Acts." Not only do Luke and Acts "fulfill" biblical prophecies and promises, but Acts also fulfills prophecies and anticipations from the first volume. Together the two volumes pass on the biblical heritage promised to Israel in Jesus Messiah, include Gentiles as "Israel's glory," and warn disbelieving Jews not to let themselves be cut off from the one fulfilled people.

Carl Holladay discovers fundamental agreement between Hellenistic Jewish historians — he discusses Demetrius, Artapanus, Eupolemus, and Pseudo-Eupolemus — and Luke in recounting the biblical story. Like the historians, Luke writes to provide unified apologetic to a wider, if not sympathetic audience, as well as to make their history intelligible to themselves. While Holladay stresses the partial, provisional nature of the comparisons, due to the fragmentary and sometimes distorted evidence that survives these historians, he nevertheless is confident of the "common features of their literary horizons." Similar to Artapanus, for example, Luke enthusiastically promotes the traditions he represents, including what Jesus continued to do and to teach his followers, most notably Peter and Paul, the latter of whom is portrayed as "the transmitter of Israel's traditions to the nations." Like Eupolemus, Luke attempts to understand the biblical story as a whole and to update it to his own time, such that Luke's second volume, although exhibiting its own narrative integrity, becomes part of "a 'preconceived plan' of history that culminates in Christ." Though none of these four historians develops anything approaching Luke's scheme of promise and fulfillment, they have already begun to "conceptualize the biblical story in ways that the Bible itself does not."

Gregory Sterling echoes many of the sentiments of the previous two contributors, discovering in Stephen's speech (Acts 7) a model of narrative which retold the story of Israel. The story was retold through LXX stories of heroes of the faith, who were associated with the origins of particular Diaspora communities. Luke draws upon this body of exegetical traditions among Greek-speaking Jews, according to Sterling, to introduce Stephen's speech at a critical moment in Luke-Acts — "on the cusp where Jewish Christianity and Gentile Christianity meet." Sterling compares Luke's treatment of Abraham, Joseph, and Moses traditions in Acts 7 to three Hellenistic Jewish historians cited by Polyhistor — Cleodemus Malchus, Pseudo-Eupolemus, and Artapanus. Luke is also compared with Demetrius, Ezekiel (the tragedian), the author of the *Assumption of Moses*, Philo, and Josephus. Luke demonstrates, Sterling writes, "that the [Christian] mission was in harmony with God's dealings with the ancestors." Similar to the ways Diaspora Jews had retold stories to legitimate their existence and to become integrated in foreign lands, so Luke, whom Sterling believes was probably also a Diaspora Jew, found in these ancestral traditions a "biblical warrant for the early Christian mission beyond Jerusalem."

All three scholars agree that Hellenistic Diaspora Judaism is the primary soil which has nourished the Hellenistic author Luke, and that in a variety of ways Luke "remints" the coin of Hellenistic Jewish narrative. Luke's interpretive context, apparently shared with the implied reader, is thoroughly Hellenistic; Luke's point to be scored is profoundly a Christian interpretation of the faith of Israel. Luke's knowledge of the LXX and of similar renderings in Diaspora literature now forces interpreters to drop the stereotype "Luke the Gentile, evangelist for the Gentiles" to consider "Luke the Hellenist, evangelist for Jews and Gentiles."

Engaged in a Public Enterprise in the Context of Greco-Roman Prototypes: "Events that have come to fruition... of all that Jesus began to do and to teach" (Luke 1:1–Acts 1:1)

The five authors and four essays grouped under this rubric examine the two volumes in light of Hellenistic narrative-rhetorical conventions regarding speeches, sea voyages, and narrative closings.

Speeches

David Balch offers a critique of the types and purposes of speeches in Hellenistic historiography in arguing that Luke aims to rewrite "events that have come to fruition" in a more complete form than his predecessors. Luke accomplishes this goal primarily by constructing speeches "that indicate the causes and consequences of the events of salvation history," including especially Jewish Christians' acceptance of foreigners as integral to the fulfillment of God's design. This "fuller" account is already signaled in Luke 1:1–4 by ἀκριβῶς (v. 3) and squares particularly with Dionysius of Halicarnassus's use of this adverb. Dionysius uses the word to help stress the importance of speeches in proper historiographical portrayals of cause and effect. Moreover, Luke's full account can be appreciated in the continuity of the two volumes themselves, accomplished in large measure by such speeches. Most notable are the unique inaugural addresses of Jesus in Nazareth (Luke 4) and Peter at Pentecost (Acts 2), which announce God's intention to take Israel's salvation to the nations. Such accounts not only persuade Luke's audience to accept foreigners into their salvation communities, but also reflect contemporary debates among Jews concerning relations to Gentiles — evidenced in the Hellenistic Jewish writings of 2 Maccabees, Eupolemus, the Greek additions to Esther, and the *Letter of Aristeas*.

Eckhard Plümacher observes that Luke's use of mission speeches in Acts — in particular, those of Peter to Cornelius's household (Acts 10) and of Paul to the synagogue of Pisidian Antioch (Acts 13) — is strikingly similar to Dionysius's view of the function of speeches in a larger historiographical work. Speeches, in Dionysius's view, must not be withheld since they are both catalyst and cause of decisive moments. The impact of Luke's mission speeches on the church's development makes it clear that one of Luke's overarching concerns is to demonstrate how the mission of the church had itself become a powerful legitimation for the essentially Gentile church it had created. When the church was facing a crisis of legitimation and identity as it was being severed from its origins, and could no longer claim visible continuity with the founding believers of Israel, Luke carefully crafted a two-volume history, showing how events involving Jesus in the Gospel dovetail into the history of the people of God in Acts. The scheme of promise and fulfillment within Israel's salvation history is authenticated by eyewitnesses of the "Jesus kerygma" in the first volume for the developing church of the sequel volume: "The Jesus-witness which comes to expression in the mission speeches led to the Gentile mission; as such, it also was able to legitimate the results of that mission, namely, the Gentile church." The importance of the speeches shows that Luke-Acts "belongs not in the context of biography, and certainly not in the context of the novel, but rather in the sphere of the writing of history."

Sea Voyages

Charles Talbert and J. H. Hayes present a comprehensive, nuanced taxonomy of sea-voyage passages in Greco-Roman literature in their investigation of Paul's sea voyage (Acts 27) and Jesus' calming of the sea (Luke 8). Taking into consideration expressed and unexpressed cultural assumptions, they delineate four types of sea voyages based on causality and outcome, and classify both Acts 27 and Luke 8:22–25 as storms due to other than a divine cause with an outcome due to gods or God. To be sure, God does not judge Paul by inflicting a storm or serpent bite, but the Mediterranean listener would have heard in Luke 8 "a claim for Jesus' divine authority.... [T]hat Paul is delivered from storm and shipwreck in Acts 27 is due to the divine power of the Lord, a power demonstrated in Luke 8:22–25." For Talbert and Hayes, Jesus' actions in the storm foreshadow Acts 27. Luke shares with Mediterranean antiquity not only the belief that a divine will or necessity governs events, but also that this divine will is often disclosed to humans through divine forecast in oracles, prophecies, dreams, visions, demonstrations, and so on. Much of the theological unity of Luke-Acts, therefore, derives from the manifold ways — especially reflective of the LXX — in which Luke shows how God's plan is carried out, consummated through storm and shipwreck and Paul preaching the gospel before Caesar in Rome.

Narrative Closings

Daniel Marguerat addresses the unresolved ending of Acts by reviewing the ancient literary convention of narrative conclusion — "its characteristics, its orchestrated abundance, and its programmed silence." Similar to narrative suspensions in Homer and Herodotus, to which Marguerat refers, Luke refrains from bringing to fulfillment Paul's appeal to Caesar (Acts 25:11) and Christ's mandate to be a witness to the end of the earth (1:8); closure must be effected by the reader according to the plot and/or from clues such as a metaphor or synecdoche, which suggest the unspoken outcome. Citing John Chrysostom's comments on the close of Acts, Marguerat concludes that Luke follows a well-attested literary strategy by organizing a "concerted displacement of the reader's expectation which he has methodically built up to that point." Instead of Paul's accusers putting him to death, Luke inverts the anticipated outcome by making Paul the accuser of Israel, placing the people on trial by citing the prophetic words of Isaiah. Luke thus reinterprets the memory of Paul's witness by leaving an unresolved tension between the future of Israel and its heritage of salvation in Messiah Jesus. The epilogue in Acts 28:30–31 functions as synecdoche, portraying Paul as the ideal pastor-evangelist, proclaiming openly to all and still debating openly with Judaism. By suspending Paul in an open-ended conclusion, Luke prods readers to fill in the ending with two convictions that Luke himself has yet fully to unite: first, "the 'salvation of God' is to be sought in the church recruited among Jews and Gentiles," and second, "the promises of the faithfulness of God to Israel are not annulled."

The five investigators of Luke's two-volume narrative again demonstrate that to view Luke as an interpreter of Israel is by no means to underestimate the Hellenistic environment of his project. The volumes are redolent with the tropes and topoi of Hellenism and the Hellenistic Judaism of the Mediterranean basin. The two volumes together forge an unbreakable connection between "all that Jesus began to do and to teach" and the carrying of this name "before Gentiles and kings and the people of Israel."

Driving to the Crux: Luke's Gospel–Acts and the Story of Israel: "Inasmuch as many... it seemed good to me also to write... that you may have a firm grasp of the true significance of the traditions which you have been taught" (Luke 1:1, 3–4)

Three essays conclude *Jesus and the Heritage of Israel* with similar concerns, but with significant differences in methods of argumentation, modes of presentation, and conclusions. All three authors attend to the story of Luke-Acts as a whole. From varying perspectives, all see a comprehensive narrative strategy as the author's primary means for communicating meaning.

Michael Wolter engages a theme cultivated over a century of German historical and theological scholarship — the delay of the parousia — but sees the topic in a new historical and literary light. According to Wolter, Luke is not preoccupied with apologizing for the delay (cf. 2 Pet. 3:4). Furthermore, Paul's concerns for the way God will keep the promises to Israel belonged to an earlier time. In Luke's era, the anticipated "redemption of Jerusalem" (Luke 2:38) had evidently not occurred. This distinctive historical setting provides "the key to understanding [Luke's] view of Israel's future." Wolter's literary analysis identifies the unresolved questions of Luke 19:11–27 and Acts 1:6–8 as critical to the purposes of the narrative. Memories of the hopes of Jesus' early followers for the redemption of Jerusalem and restoration of the kingdom to Israel (see also Luke 24:21) provide occasions for reinterpreting present realities and for directing the reader's attention to the larger world of Christian mission. The "universal mission" to Gentiles as well as Jews has produced both a schism in Israel and redefinition of the fulfillment of the promises and the people to whom they are made. "[A]ccording to the Lukan understanding," Wolter writes, "Israel's history is carried forward in the Gentiles and Jews who believe in Christ." As Wolter reads Luke-Acts, historic or empirical Israel has been both fulfilled and displaced in God's economy by Jews and Gentiles who believed in Jesus when they heard his messiahship proclaimed; the parousia has been delayed to provide time for this continuing proclamation and the redefinition of Israel. "The difference now is that Israel will include completely different people, and the apportionment of salvation and condemnation will be decided by completely different criteria than implied by the 'near-expectation' in Luke 19:11 and Acts 1:6."

Robert Tannehill makes few direct historical arguments, but keeps his interpretation close to the narrative unity of Luke-Acts. In a carefully nuanced elaboration of his earlier studies of the tragic quality of Luke's story, Tannehill rejects theories that Israel has been displaced or superseded in God's saving purposes. From the beginning of Luke's narrative and at its resumption in the beginning of Acts, the audience is led to understand the story of Jesus in light of scriptural promises. Tannehill highlights three promise traditions which focalize "the Lukan understanding of God's purpose in the world, which is the underlying project that turns the many episodes of the story into a unified, developing plot." In elucidating the speeches in Acts, Tannehill argues that, according to Luke, Israel's hope for a messianic kingdom is established by a resurrected Messiah. The final defense speeches of Paul and his parting words in Acts 21:17–28:31, rather than foreclosing on future salvation to resistant Jews, shows that Paul has not betrayed Judaism and provide "an example of how a resourceful missionary might appeal to Jews, in spite of growing antagonism." Thus the tragic pathos of the story is no simple verdict on Israel, because God, the most "reliable" character, is also profoundly moved and frustrated. That many Jews rejected the Messiah is a major theological problem. And this problem is not solved at the end. "The mission is able to move forward by turning to the Gentiles, but God's saving purpose will be incomplete so long as the covenant people do not accept God's salvation."

Howard Marshall invites a rereading of the Gospel of Luke in the light of Acts as its sequel and asks, "Do we in fact read the Gospel differently because it has a sequel?" He draws particular attention to "prophetic passages whose fulfillment lies in Acts" and "passages which take on fuller or different meaning in the light of the sequel." His inventive approach offers perspective on several critical aspects of the sea change in the interpretation of Luke-Acts. The oft-cited shift, moving Jesus from the active subject of the Gospel to the passive object of the word *about* Jesus in Acts, becomes in the context of Marshall's controlling question a distinction which to some extent collapses as Jesus assumes active and passive roles in both volumes. This unity of "the Proclaimer and the Proclaimed" constitutes for Marshall the controlling theme that makes Luke and Acts two volumes of *one* narrative story. The response Jesus demands in the Gospel is of a piece with the response demanded by witnesses and proclaimers in Acts, such that in both volumes Jesus as Messiah is the core of the kingdom of God and God's new act of salvation. Hence, Marshall writes, "[T]he tendency to read the Gospel merely as a record of history is corrected by reading Acts." Israel remains the term for the ancient covenant people and their descendants, who, by the end of Acts, have largely rejected their Messiah. But Luke's emphasis is on the "new people of God," the church, comprised of both Jews and Gentiles. "There is place for [Israel] in the future, if the Twelve are to be its judges and if the kingdom is to be restored to it, but these sayings appear marginal to the main thrust of Luke-Acts. At least for the foreseeable future, the focus is on the church."

Readers acquainted with the previous work of these three scholars will observe the accommodations — as well as the contributions — each has made to the sea change in Lukan interpretation to which this volume attests. While all place different emphasis on Israel at the end of Acts and describe its refusal to believe in Messiah Jesus differently, they still regard God's promises to Israel as the script or tradition to which Luke's narrative lays claim. All three focus on the conviction in Luke-Acts that, in the midst of the conflicts he provokes, Jesus puts Israel to the test, contends for its soul, and fulfills their scriptures — in short, he is the Messiah promised to Israel. Researchers and students scanning for challenges and consequences for interpretation will glimpse a promising future.

"And some were persuaded, while others doubted!"

Good research stimulates further thought and scholarship, and the work of the Luke-Acts Seminars of the Society of Biblical Literature and the Society for New Testament Studies over the past decade already has demonstrated the capacity to provoke fruitful questions and important disagreements. The audiences that first heard these essays signaled a lively interest, and the publication of *Jesus and the Heritage of Israel* will give still wider exposure to these deliberations. Creative scholarly minds and interested communities will see unanticipated avenues of research and inquiry.

Following publication of *Jesus and the Heritage of Israel*, several kinds of scholarly research hold promise.

1. Further studies of *Luke's persuasive project* are needed to explore comparable literary and oral rhetorical conventions within and beyond the New Testament. Studies of narrative conventions and speeches will prove whether the larger shape of Luke's argument has been more clearly defined in this sea change of scholarship. Which traditions of persuasion are decisive? Luke clearly lived at the nexus of several cultures in the Hellenistic era, aspiring to the educated prose of the Greek historians

and poets while remaining deeply at home in the vernacular of the Greek Bible. Can further scholarship provide clearer pictures of the traditions available? These literary comparisons will make Luke's choices more interesting and evident.

2. Explorations of *Luke's hermeneutical project* have received a significant new challenge in *Jesus and the Heritage of Israel*. Emerging studies in "comparative midrash" have only begun to suggest the varied readings of Israel's scriptures existing when Luke-Acts was written. Luke does not read the scriptures like Paul or the author of Hebrews, and not in the mode of the sectarians of Qumran or the Platonists of Alexandria. But if Luke-Acts is rightly understood as a persuasive narrative and Jesus' place in Israel's heritage is the crucial issue, then the scriptural interpretation in this work must be thoroughly explored in comparison with contemporaries.

3. Older historical questions about *Luke's audience* also gain renewed currency. If Luke's project was formulated to persuade, the argument had to be plausible to someone. These concerns raise sociohistorical questions which cannot be resolved solely from reading the narrative. The "implied" or "intended" or "likely" reader will finally remain elusive. But the quest matters, if for no other reason than the enduring need to understand who was Jewish and who was Christian in the late first century C.E. What was the relationship among Jews who did not follow Jesus and those who did? What was the relationship of Jews and non-Jewish messianists? If Luke's argument were only plausible to Gentile Christians, it becomes more hostile, less imbued with the spirit of Israel's prophets so frequently cited.

The answers to these literary, hermeneutical, and historical inquiries matter differently to communities of interpretation at the dawn of the third millennium. The scholars who pursue the research are themselves located in varied institutional and faith contexts. Luke-Acts is still a sacred text in Christian communities, a heretical commentary for Judaism, and for many others a powerful historical artifact of the Western tradition. If the currents of the sea change in interpretation continue to reach religious communities, then Christians will need to see that earlier anti-Semitic readings are profoundly wrong on rhetorical and historical grounds, as well as on moral grounds. Jews will be pressed to recognize that debates in Israel depicted in Luke-Acts were no more intense than those among other Jewish parties such as between Pharisees and Zealots or between Sadducees and Qumranites. The public consequences are so evident that no interpretation dare feign disinterest. On the contrary, all readings of this foundational Christian narrative must be accountable within *and* beyond confessional and secular contexts.

Finally, all of these methods of academic inquiry and communities of reading point to Luke's convictions about God. This God is "the reliable character" in the narrative. Moreover, as Luke's own investment in the "events brought to fruition" makes clear (Luke 1:1–4), this God is also the God of Israel's scriptures, before whom Jesus was "a prophet mighty in deed and word . . . the Christ" (Luke 24:19, 26). And in Luke's vision of the larger public domain, this is "the God who made the world and everything in it . . . the Lord of heaven and earth" (Acts 17:24). Amid a sea change of interpretation, the quest for the theology of Luke-Acts becomes again a vital narrative, rhetorical, hermeneutical, and historical enterprise.

Index of Ancient Sources

NEW TESTAMENT

GRECO-ROMAN SOURCES

Index of Modern Authors